P9-EDY-732

DOCUMENTS OF THE

CHRISTIAN
CHURCH

Chris Maunder is Senior Lecturer in Theology and Religious Studies at
York St John, and a Trustee for Marian Studies Roehampton.

DOCUMENTS OF THE

CHRISTIAN CHURCH

Fourth Edition

ORIGINAL EDITIONS SELECTED AND EDITED BY
HENRY BETTENSON

THIRD AND FOURTH EDITIONS EDITED BY
CHRIS MAUNDER

OXFORD
UNIVERSITY PRESS

OXFORD
UNIVERSITY PRESS

PREFACE TO THE FOURTH EDITION

Henry Bettenson published the first two editions of *Documents of the Christian Church* in 1943 and 1963, respectively. The selections were so well chosen that the *Documents* became a standard text book which many theologians and church historians will remember from their undergraduate days. In the 1990s, with so many new developments in the churches, it became clear that a revised edition was needed. Since the second edition, events and movements such as the Second Vatican Council; black, liberation and feminist theology; moral dilemmas created by changing social attitudes to sexuality; church strategy in the crisis of AIDS; Christian participation in major political changes like the fall of communism in East Europe—all needed to be recorded to take their place in the long and unfolding story of the Christian churches documented here. Henry Bettenson had died in 1979, so the task of preparing a third edition fell to me, and it was published in 1999. However, the world of the early twenty-first century has seen new challenges; the rapid rate of change necessitates this new fourth edition in 2011. At the same time, the original selections made by Bettenson remain; they are still regarded, nearly fifty years after the second edition, as providing a well informed and instructive overview of Christian history. Because of its size, *Documents* has gaps that Bettenson himself acknowledged; nevertheless, the volume has not been equalled by any other in its popularity and accessibility.

In the preface to the third edition, I wrote, commenting on the changes between 1963 and 1999, 'Theology, it could be argued, tends less to the establishment-centred and ecclesiastical, more to the marginal and prophetic; it is also confronted more than ever with the creative challenge of pluralism and religious change. An increasing number of scientific and technological advances bring with them complex ethical dilemmas, as the churches seek to interpret the contemporary world with the long-standing Christian means of scripture, tradition, and reason.' Eleven years later, these words could be used again to contrast the context of the current edition with the theological world in which Bettenson prepared his original material. Foremost among the challenges of pluralism is the crisis over the Middle East that deepened with the 9/11 attack on New York; it has been difficult for church leaders and politicians alike to prevent this becoming a wholesale confrontation between the global cultures of Christianity and Islam. The need for an initiative of reconciliation and mutual understanding is an important task for the churches today. Unfortunately, at a popular level, too many Christians regard Islam—which they misunderstand and generalize—as a dangerous rival in the battle for hearts and minds. For the sake of a faithful record, I have included an excerpt from a book with which I disagree strongly, Patrick Sookhdeo's *The Challenge of Islam to the Church and its Mission*. I hope by doing this that I demonstrate that the primary aim of *Documents of the Christian Church* is to register a range of positions across the Christian debate and not to pretend that views opposite to those of the editor do not exist. The fiercest arguments in Christianity today continue to be between those whom we could loosely term 'conservative' and 'liberal', and this occurs in most denominations. The subsections on mission and the Anglican Communion exemplify this. At the same time, progress towards inter-denominational ecumenism has seen many positive moves in the 2000s, to which the subsection on Christian unity testifies.

Much of the new material represents debate on issues with origins in the twentieth century but which, in the new century, has reached heightened levels of urgency and concern. The third edition covered global poverty; the environment; new genetic technologies. These areas are continued into the new edition. The beginning of the twenty-first century saw the *Jubilee* campaign, which argued for an eradication of global debt based on biblical principles. World poverty also creates the phenomena of migration and asylum seeking, and the churches have been pastorally involved in the challenges and injustices that these create. Also unavoidable in recent history is the global recession of 2008, which has spread the problems of debt, both personal and national, and which will have repercussions for years to come. The environmental focus has moved from pollution to 'global warming' and then 'climate change'; this is reflected in Christian theological approaches. Genetic mapping and engineering has developed to the point where there are very serious ethical questions with which the churches have to engage.

A pastoral theological approach to disabilities is not new, but a great deal more emphasis on access and participation in many societies in the 2000s has led to a growing literature on disability theology. This issue does raise the question concerning the extent to which the churches take a lead on, or (sometimes belatedly) respond to, social change in the modern age. Probably the most tragic example of churches not keeping pace with the more enlightened aspects of modern social and moral progress is in the areas of domestic violence and child abuse, where some churches have a poor record of monitoring and intervention. No area has weakened more critically the mission of the Christian churches in Europe and the USA than the many instances of unchallenged child abuse among the clergy.

On a more positive side, the work of Philip Jenkins has charted the development of a buoyant Christianity in the southern countries of the globe, and hence there is a new subsection on the global growth of Christianity. European Christians are coming to terms with the fact that the locus of the Christian world is shifting quite rapidly. Assuming that the current economic imbalance between 'north' and 'south' remains in place, this may intensify the development of radical theologies which remind the churches of the substantial amount of biblical text that calls for social justice. In Europe and the USA, the debate between Christians and humanists or atheists appears to have taken on a greater urgency with the arguments of anti-religious writers such as Richard Dawkins being answered from within the churches. The churches' mission in a 'secular' and 'multi-faith' society is covered in two new subsections of material in the new edition. There is also the argument that Christianity may become more true to itself in what is referred to as 'Post-Christendom', a society which does not take the Christian gospel for granted, and in which Christian faith is not 'respectable'. In this context, the non-established churches may have more in the way of experiences and resources upon which to draw.

I would like to remember the people who were acknowledged for their help in preparing the third edition: the late Professor Adrian Hastings; Kevin Kelly; Brother Pim of the Taizé Community; Austin Flannery; Lesley Verity; Liz Gillings; Colin Davey; Ed Pinsent; Noel Davies; Anne Hosking; various churches and publishers.

For the fourth edition, I am once again indebted to York St John University (formerly the College of Ripon and York St John when I edited the third edition), which has provided the context and support in which I was able to undertake the work. The Head of Theology & Religious Studies, Richard Noake, encouraged my endeavours and suggested the excerpt on faith schools. Natalie Laybourne, currently an undergraduate student in Theology & Religious Studies, helped me to ensure that the text of each excerpt was accurate. My warm thanks should also be recorded for the very helpful advice from the churches which came from: Malcolm Brown (Church of England); Thomas Bruch (Lutheran Council of Great Britain); Theodore Gill (World Council of Churches); Jane Shuyler and Phil Tanis (Reformed Church in America);

Vicki Wallace (United Methodist Church); Philip Wood (Anabaptists); the church members who made up the group of readers provided by Oxford University Press. Finally, I would like to thank Elizabeth Robottom of Oxford University Press, who was always responsive and helpful when dealing with my enquiries.

The additions that the fourth edition makes to the third are mainly in Section XVIII, on the first decade of the twenty-first century. Sections I–XIII of the third edition are unchanged, and Sections XIV to XVII have had seven new subsections added in the light of advice given by church representatives and readers, gratefully received.

Chris Maunder

York St John University
13 December 2010

PREFACE TO THE FIRST EDITION

In the selection of these documents the aim has been to provide illustrations of the development of the Church and of her doctrines for the benefit of the general reader and the general student: a volume of this size, covering so long a stretch of time and on so wide a subject, could not pretend to include anything that was not familiar to the specialist. But it is hoped that a large part of the documents referred to in books of general interest and elementary scope have been here included in one volume. There are, as there must be, many large and obvious gaps. Perhaps the most glaring is the entire omission of any reference to Eastern Christendom between the Great Schism and the year 1922. But since many things had to be left out, and since it cannot be denied, though it may well be regretted, that in this country the study of the Eastern Church since the schism, even to an elementary degree, is almost confined to specialists, it seemed best to make no attempt to illustrate an important subject which could be treated neither adequately nor profitably in a book of such a size and with such an aim.

In general it has been thought of more value to give a few documents at some length rather than a multitude of scraps, and to prefer, at the cost of some disproportion, groups of connected documents to an impartial sprinkling of discontinuous material; and similarly, in respect of annotations and introductions, not to attempt equality of treatment but to employ, on certain of the more important topics or on points where the general reader might be expected to welcome some elucidation, a fullness which could not be extended to every case.

It is unlikely that any two persons could be found who should agree on what should be included in such a book and what omitted; nor would agreement more easily be found on the arrangement to be imposed on the material once selected. This book is divided into two unequal portions. The first part deals with the early Church, to the time when the Fourth Oecumenical Council issued the last of the series of definitions and decrees to which all the historic churches refer as the expressions of the consent of the Church Universal in antiquity. The first section treats of the external relation of the Church and its development as an organization first unrecognized, then persecuted by the state, then tolerated and later patronized within the state, until it becomes the partner of Empire, able in some relations to assert its mastery over the secular power. The remaining sections, save the last, deal with the doctrinal developments of this period, the gradual shaping of the instruments of Christian faith and worship; and these sections close with the classic formulation of the touchstone of orthodoxy in the Canon of Vincent. As a kind of pendant to these records of high and often bitter controversy a short section on Christian inscriptions, mainly from the Catacombs, illustrates the popular Christianity of the first centuries; it is but a feeble and partial light that we derive from this source on this most interesting subject, but it is all that we have, except a few fragments of papyri, and they tell us little.

In the second and larger part such an arrangement under doctrinal topics did not seem possible, and the selections are given generally in chronological order; with the exception that those relating to the English Church are given in separate sections. And here may be announced what an inspection of these sections will make manifest, that this book is compiled from an Anglican standpoint, and that the Church of England receives a proportion of illustrations which is only in perspective from that point of view. Even if this be taken into account it might be argued that too many legal documents, of considerable length, belonging to the reigns of Henry VIII and Elizabeth, have been included at the expense of things of wider importance. But the position and character of the Church of England cannot be understood without reference to the documents which display the way in which her independence of the Roman See was asserted, and her relation to the state explicitly or implicitly defined, or left without a right definition.

A list in the Bibliography shows the sources from which these selections are derived. The editor has to acknowledge his chief indebtedness to the collections of Kidd, Denzinger, Mirbt, and Gee and Hardy. A separate note acknowledges the copyright passages printed by permission.

For the annotations and introductions the editor claims no originality, except for any errors of ineptitudes they may contain. Those in Part I owe most to Bethune-Baker's *Introduction to the History of Early Christian Doctrine*; for Part II the editor is deeply indebted to those two masterpieces of compressed erudition *The History of the Medieval Church* by Miss M. Deanesley, and *The History of the Modern Church* by Dr J. W. C. Wand (Bishop of London 1945-55).

The editor is responsible for the translations except where another source is named; but in most cases these versions have been with the former translations diligently compared and revised, and the authorities who have been so consulted are those given in the List of Books.

In the sections on the English Church references to Gee and Hardy are given where abridgements have been made of documents of which they print the whole.

H.B.

September 1942

SUPPLEMENTARY NOTE

THE editor is deeply indebted to those who have pointed out errors and suggested improvements; and especially to Dr Ernest Evans, Canon of Bradford, for his valuable help.

H.B.

February 1946

CONTENTS

Part I

THE EARLY CHURCH (TO THE COUNCIL OF CHALCEDON, 451)

Section I The Church and the World

Part II
FROM THE COUNCIL OF CHALCEDON TO THE PRESENT

Section XIII The Roman Catholic Church at the Second Vatican Council

Section XIV The Twentieth-Century World Churches: Justice, Peace, and the Environment

Contents   xxiii

PART I
The Early Church
(to the Council of Chalcedon, 451)

SECTION I
The Church and the World

I. REFERENCES TO CHRISTIANITY IN CLASSICAL AUTHORS

a. Tacitus (*c.*60–*c.*120)

The Trial of Pomponia Graecina, AD 57   Tacitus, *Annales,* xiii. 32

Pomponia Graecina, a woman of high rank (the wife of Aulus Plautius,[1] who, as I have mentioned, was granted an ovation for his British campaign), was accused of foreign superstition and handed over to her husband for trial. He followed ancient precedent in hearing a case which involved his wife's legal status and her honour in the presence of members of the family, and pronounced her innocent. Pomponia's long life was passed in unbroken sadness; for after the death of Julia,[2] Drusus's daughter, she lived forty years in the dress of mourning with only sorrow in her heart. This escaped punishment in Claudius's reign, and thereafter was turned to her glory.

[The surmise that the 'foreign superstition' was Christianity is supported by third-century Christian inscriptions commemorating members of the *gens Pomponia*. And 'the retirement and sobriety of a Christian might well appear a kind of perpetual mourning to the dissolute society of the Neronian period' (Furneaux, *Tac. Ann.* ad loc.).]

The Neronian Persecution, 64   Tacitus, *Annales,* xv. 44

But all the endeavours of men, all the emperor's largesse and the propitations of the gods, did not suffice to allay the scandal or banish the belief that the fire[3] had been ordered. And so, to get rid of this

---

[1] Conquered the southern part of Britain AD 43–7.

[2] Great-granddaughter of Pomponia, d. of Atticus, probably a relation. Put to death AD 43 (Dio).   [3] The great fire of Rome, summer AD 64.

rumour, Nero set up[1] as the culprits and punished with the utmost refinement of cruelty a class hated for their abominations,[2] who are commonly called Christians. Christus, from whom their name is derived, was executed at the hands of the procurator Pontius Pilate in the reign of Tiberius. Checked for the moment, this pernicious superstition again broke out, not only in Judaea, the source of the evil, but even in Rome, that receptacle for everything that is sordid and degrading from every quarter of the globe, which there finds a following. Accordingly, arrest was first made of those who confessed [sc. *to being Christians*]; then, on their evidence, an immense multitude was convicted, not so much on the charge of arson as because of hatred of the human race. Besides being put to death they were made to serve as objects of amusement; they were clad in the hides of beasts and torn to death by dogs; others were crucified, others set on fire to serve to illuminate the night when daylight failed. Nero had thrown open his grounds for the display, and was putting on a show in the circus, where he mingled with the people in the dress of a charioteer or drove about in his chariot. All this gave rise to a feeling of pity, even towards men whose guilt merited the most exemplary punishment; for it was felt that they were being destroyed not for the public good but to gratify the cruelty of an individual.

b. Suetonius (*c*.75–160)

*The Expulsion of the Jews from Rome, c.*52   Suet. *Vita Claudii*, xxv. 4
(cf. Acts 18: 2)

... Since the Jews were continually making disturbances at the instigation of Chrestus, he [Claudius] expelled them from Rome. ...

[This probably refers to quarrels between Jews and Christian teachers.]

The Neronian Persecution, 64   Suet. *Vita Neronis*, xvi

In his reign many abuses were severely punished and repressed, and as many new laws were instituted; a limit was set to expenditure; the public banquets were reduced to gifts of food; the sale of cooked food in taverns was forbidden, except for pulses and greens, whereas formerly every kind of delicacy was offered; punishment was inflicted

---

[1] *Subdidit*; used of fraudulent substitution, or false suggestion. Tac. does not believe in their guilt.
[2] Infanticide, cannibalism, incest, etc., were alleged against them. 'Three things are alleged against us; atheism, Thyestean feasts, Oedipodean intercourse.'—Athenagoras, *Legatio pro Christianis*, iii, cf. p. 13.

on the Christians, a set of men adhering to a novel and mischievous superstition; he put a stop to the pranks of the charioteers, who from long immunity had assumed the right of ranging at large and cheating and robbing for amusement; the pantomimes and their companies were banished.

c. Pliny (the Younger) (62–*c*.113)

*Christians in Bithynia, c.*112   Plin. *Epp.* X (*ad Traj.*), xcvi

It is my rule, Sire, to refer to you in matters where I am uncertain. For who can better direct my hesitation or instruct my ignorance? I was never present at any trial of Christians; therefore I do not know what are the customary penalties or investigations, and what limits are observed. [2] I have hesitated a great deal on the question whether there should be any distinction of ages; whether the weak should have the same treatment as the more robust; whether those who recant should be pardoned, or whether a man who has ever been a Christian should gain nothing by ceasing to be such; whether the name itself, even if innocent of crime, should be punished, or only the crimes attaching to that name.[1]

Meanwhile, this is the course that I have adopted in the case of those brought before me as Christians. [3] I ask them if they are Christians. If they admit it I repeat the question a second and a third time, threatening capital punishment; if they persist I sentence them to death. For I do not doubt that, whatever kind of crime it may be to which they have confessed, their pertinacity and inflexible obstinacy should certainly be punished. [4] There were others who displayed a like madness and whom I reserved to be sent to Rome, since they were Roman citizens.

Thereupon the usual result followed; the very fact of my dealing with the question led to a wider spread of the charge, and a great variety of cases were brought before me. [5] An anonymous pamphlet was issued, containing many names. All who denied that they were or had been Christians I considered should be discharged, because they called upon the gods at my dictation and did reverence, with incense and wine, to your image which I had ordered to be brought forward for this purpose, together with the statues of the deities; and especially because they cursed Christ, a thing which, it is said, genuine Christians cannot be induced to do. [6] Others named by the informer first said that they were Christians and then denied it;

---

[1] See previous note, p. 2.

declaring that they had been but were so no longer, some having recanted three years or more before and one or two as long ago as twenty years. They all worshipped your image and the statues of the gods and cursed Christ. [7] But they declared that the sum of their guilt or error had amounted only to this, that on an appointed day they had been accustomed to meet before daybreak, and to recite a hymn antiphonally[1] to Christ, as to a god, and to bind themselves by an oath,[2] not for the commission of any crime but to abstain from theft, robbery, adultery and breach of faith, and not to deny a deposit when it was claimed. After the conclusion of this ceremony it was their custom to depart and meet again to take food; but it was ordinary and harmless food, and they had ceased this practice after my edict in which, in accordance with your orders, I had forbidden secret societies. [8] I thought it the more necessary, therefore, to find out what truth there was in this by applying torture to two maidservants, who were called deaconesses.[3] But I found nothing but a depraved and extravagant superstition, and I therefore postponed my examination and had recourse to you for consultation.

[9] The matter seemed to me to justify my consulting you, especially on account of the number of those imperilled; for many persons of all ages and classes and of both sexes are being put in peril by accusation, and this will go on. The contagion of this superstition has spread not only in the cities, but in the villages and rural districts as well; yet it seems capable of being checked and set right. [10] There is no shadow of doubt that the temples, which have been almost deserted, are beginning to be frequented once more, that the sacred rites which have been long neglected are being renewed, and that sacrificial victims are for sale everywhere, whereas, till recently, a buyer was rarely to be found. From this it is easy to imagine what a host of men could be set right, were they given a chance of recantation.

---

[1] 'carmen...dicere secum invicem'—'carmen,' generally translated 'hymn', may mean any set form of words; here perhaps a responsorial or antiphonal psalm, or some kind of litany.
[2] 'sacramentum'—the word chosen by the Christians—might suggest to Romans a conspiracy. The Catilinarian conspirators took a 'sacramentum' (Sall. *Cat.* xxii.).
[3] 'ministrae' probably represents the Greek διάκονοι. If so, this is the last reference to 'deaconesses' till the fourth century, when they attained some importance in the East. They seem to have been unknown in the West until the recent establishment of the office in the Anglican Church.

Trajan's Policy towards Christians   *Trajan to Pliny* (Plin. *Epp.* x. xcvii)

You have taken the right line, my dear Pliny, in examining the cases of those denounced to you as Christians, for no hard and fast rule can be laid down, of universal application. [2] They are not to be sought out; if they are informed against, and the charge is proved, they are to be punished, with this reservation—that if any one denies that he is a Christian, and actually proves it, that is by worshipping our gods, he shall be pardoned as a result of his recantation, however suspect he may have been with respect to the past. Pamphlets published anonymously should carry no weight in any charge whatsoever. They constitute a very bad precedent, and are also out of keeping with this age.

II. CHRISTIANITY AND ANCIENT LEARNING

a. The 'Liberal' View—'The Light that lighteth every man'

Justin, *Apology* (*c*.150), I. xlvi. 1–4

But lest any, to turn men from our teaching, should attack us with the unreasonable argument that we say that Christ was born one hundred and fifty years ago in the time of Cyrenius, and that he taught what we affirm he taught thereafter in the time of Pontius Pilate, if, I say, they should find fault with us for treating as irresponsible all men born before him, let us solve this difficulty by anticipation. [2] We are taught that Christ is the first-born of God, and we have shown above that He is the reason (Word) of whom the whole human race partake, [4] and those who live according to reason are Christians, even though they are accounted atheists. Such were Socrates and Heraclitus among the Greeks, and those like them. ...

Apol. II. xiii

For myself, when I learned of the wicked disguise which through false report was cast over the divine teaching of Christians by the evil demons in order to turn away others, I laughed at this disguise and at the opinions of the multitude; [2] and I declare that I prayed and strove with all my might to be found a Christian, not because the teachings of Plato are contrary to those of Christ, but because they are not in all respects like them; as is the case with the doctrines of the others, Stoics, poets and prose-authors. [3] For each discoursed rightly, seeing that which was kin to Christianity[1] through a share in the seminal divine reason (Word); but they that have uttered contrary

---

[1] τὸσυγγενές—perhaps 'what was suited to him', cf. § 6, 'according to a man's capacity'.

opinions seem not to have had the invisible knowledge and the irrefutable wisdom. [4] Whatever has been uttered aright by any men in any place belongs to us Christians; for, next to God, we worship and love the reason (Word) which is from the unbegotten and ineffable God; since on our account He has been made man, that, being made partaker of our sufferings, he may also bring us healing. [5] For all the authors were able to see the truth darkly, through the implanted seed of reason (the Word) dwelling in them. [6] For the seed and imitation of a thing, given according to a man's capacity is one thing; far differing is the thing itself, the sharing of which and its representation is given according to his grace.

b. The Negative View—'The Wisdom of This World'

Tertullian (*c*.160–240), *De praescriptione haereticorum* (*c*.200), vii

It is this philosophy which is the subject-matter of this world's wisdom, that rash interpreter of the divine nature and order. In fact, heresies are themselves prompted by philosophy. It is the source of 'aeons,' and I know not what infinite 'forms' and the 'trinity of man' in the system of Valentinus.[1] He was a Platonist. It is the source of Marcion's[2] 'better God,' 'better,' because of his tranquillity. Marcion came from the Stoics. Again, when it is said that the soul perishes, that opinion is taken from the Epicureans. The denial of the restoration of the flesh is taken over from the universal teaching of the philosophers; the equation of matter with God is the doctrine of Zeno; and when any assertion is made about a God of fire, then Heraclitus comes in. Heretics and philosophers handle the same subject-matter; both treat of the same topics—Whence came evil? And why? Whence came man? And how? And a question lately posed by Valentinus— Whence came God? Answer: 'From *enthymesis* and *ectroma*'![3] Wretched Aristotle! who taught them dialectic, that art of building up and demolishing, so protean in statement, so far-fetched in conjecture, so unyielding in controversy, so productive of disputes; self-stultifying, since it is ever handling questions but never settling anything. ... What is there in common between Athens and Jerusalem? What between the Academy and the Church? What between heretics and

---

[1] See p. 33.   [2] See p. 39.
[3] ἐνθύμησις, 'conception' (or, perhaps, 'mental activity'), plays an important but not easily explicable part in the complicated cosmogony and theogony of Valentinus. ἔκτρωμα, 'abortion', was a term applied to the chaotic material world, before its organization and endowment with an intellectual soul.

Christians? ... Away with all projects for a 'Stoic,' a 'Platonic' or a 'dialectic' Christianity! After Christ Jesus we desire no subtle theories, no acute enquiries after the gospel. ...

c. Another 'Liberal' Clement of Alexandria (*c.*200), *Stromateis*, I. v. 28

Thus philosophy was necessary to the Greeks for righteousness, until the coming of the Lord. And now it assists towards true religion as a kind of preparatory training for those who arrive at faith by way of demonstration. For 'Thy foot shall not stumble' if thou attribute to Providence all good, whether it belong to the Greeks or to us. For God is the source of all good things; of some primarily, as of the old and new Testaments; of others by consequence, as of philosophy. But it may be, indeed, that philosophy was given to the Greeks immediately and primarily, until the Lord should call the Greeks. For philosophy was a 'schoolmaster' to bring the Greek mind to Christ, as the Law brought the Hebrews. Thus philosophy was a preparation, paving the way towards perfection in Christ.

III. CHURCH AND STATE

[For the policy of Nero and Trajan, see above, pp. 2 ff.]

a. The Rescript of Hadrian to Caius Minucius Fundanus, Proconsul of Asia, *c.*152

From the original given by Tyranius Ruginus (345–?410) in his translation of Euseb. H.E. IV. ix (Justin, Apol. I. lxix, gives a Greek translation)

I received the letter written to me by your predecessor, the most illustrious Serenius Granianus, and it is not my pleasure to pass by without enquiry the matter referred to me, lest the inoffensive should be disturbed, while slanderous informers are afforded an opportunity of practising their vile trade. [2] Now, if our subjects of the provinces are able to sustain by evidence their charges against the Christians, so as to answer before a court of justice, I have no objection to their taking this course. But I do not allow them to have recourse to mere clamorous demands and outcries to this end. For it is much more equitable, if any one wishes to accuse them, for you to take cognizance of the matters laid to their charge. [3] If therefore any one accuses and proves that the aforesaid men do anything contrary to the laws, you will pass sentences corresponding to their offences. On the other hand, I emphatically insist on this, that if any one demand a writ of summons against any of these Christians, merely as a slanderous accusation, you proceed against that man with heavier penalties, in proportion to the gravity of his offence.

b. Tertullian on Persecution   Tert. *Apology* (197), ii

If it is certain that we are the most guilty of men, why do you treat us differently from our fellows, that is, from other criminals? Since it is only fair that the same guilt should meet with the same treatment. When others are accused on the charges which are brought against us they employ their own tongues and hired advocacy to plead their innocence. They have full opportunity of reply and cross-examination; for it is not permitted to condemn men undefended and unheard. Christians alone are not allowed to say anything to clear themselves, to defend truth, to save a judge from injustice. That alone is looked for, which the public hate requires—the confession of the name, not the investigation of the charge. ...

c. Christian Loyalty to the Emperor   *Apol.* xxix–xxxii

xxix. ... We sin, then, against the imperial majesty in this, that we do not make him subject to his own possessions (sc. *the idols of the gods*); that we do not perform a mockery by offering a service for his safety, when we do not suppose that safety to rest in hands soldered with lead. But you, to be sure, are religious in seeking it where it is not, in asking it from those who have it not to give, passing by him in whose power it lies. Moreover, you persecute those who know where to seek it, who, because they know, are also able to obtain it.

xxx. For we call upon God for the safety of the Emperor, upon God the eternal, God the true, God the living, whose favour, beyond all others, the Emperor desires. ...

xxxi. But, you say, we merely flatter the Emperor; and we feign the prayers we utter, to evade persecution. ... Examine God's words, our scriptures, which we do not conceal, and which many accidents put into the hands of those without [the Church]. Know from them that a superfluity of benevolence is enjoined on us, even so far as to pray God for our enemies and to entreat blessings for our persecutors.[1] Who are greater enemies and persecutors of Christians than those with treason against whom we are charged? But the Scripture says expressly and clearly, 'Pray for kings, and princes, and powers, that all may be peace for you.'[2] For when the empire is disturbed, then we,

---

[1] Matt. 5: 44.   [2] 1 Tim. 2: 2.

remote though we be from the disorders, find ourselves sharing in the calamity, in the disturbance of the other members.

xxxii. There is another and a greater need for us to pray for the Emperor, and, indeed, for the whole estate of the empire, and the interests of Rome. For we know that the great upheaval which hangs over the whole earth, and the very end of all things, threatening terrible woes, is only delayed by the respite granted to the Roman empire.[1] Because we would not experience these things, we favour Rome's long continuance when we pray that they be delayed. ... In the Emperor we reverence the judgement of God, who has set him over the nations. ...

d. The Neronian Persecution

The Martyrdom of SS. Peter and Paul   Clement of Rome, *Ep. to Corinthians* (c.95), v

Let us come to the heroes nearest to our times. ... Let us set before our eyes the good apostles; Peter, who by reason of unrighteous jealousy endured not one or two but many labours, and having thus borne his witness went to his due place of glory. Paul, by reason of jealousy and strife, pointed out the prize of endurance. ... When he had preached in the East and in the West he received the noble renown of his faith. Having taught righteousness to the whole world, even reaching the bounds of the West, and having borne witness before rulers, he thus left the world and went to the holy place, becoming the greatest pattern of endurance.

e. The Martyrdom of Polycarp, Bishop of Smyrna, 155

From *Martyrium Polycarpi* [A letter from the Church of Smyrna. The first Martyrology]

I. II. [At the festival of Caesar a number of Christians were set to fight the wild beasts.]

III. ... All the crowd, astonished at the noble conduct of the God-beloved and God-fearing race of Christians, cried out, 'Away with the atheists;[2] let search be made for Polycarp.'

V. But the most admirable Polycarp when first he heard of this was not dismayed, but wished to remain in the city. The majority, however, prevailed on him to withdraw. And he withdrew to a small

---

[1] Cf. 2. Thess. 2: 6, 'that which restraineth', generally interpreted in the early Church as the power of Rome.

[2] An epithet commonly applied to Christians because they refused to worship heathen idols and had no images or shrines of their own.

estate not far from the city. There he passed the time with a few
companions, wholly occupied night and day in prayer for all men and
for the churches throughout the world; as, indeed, was his habit.
And while at prayer he fell into a trance three days before his arrest
and saw his pillow set on fire. And he turned and said to his companions,
'I must needs be burned alive.'

VI. Now since they that sought him were persistent he departed
to another estate. Then straightway they were upon him, and when
they did not find him they apprehended two young servants. Of whom
one confessed under torture; for it was impossible for him to escape,
since they that betrayed him were of his own household. Then the
sheriff,[1] who bore by God's appointment the same name (sc. as our
Lord's judge), being called Herod, hastened to bring him into the stadium, that he might fulfil his own appointed lot by becoming a partner of
Christ, and that his betrayers might undergo the punishment of Judas
himself.

VII. So, on the day of the preparation, mounted police with their
usual arms set out about supper-time, taking with them the servant,
hurrying 'as against a thief.' And at a late hour they came up to the
place and found him in a cottage, lying in an upper room. He could
have gone away to another farm, but he would not, saying 'The will of
God be done.' So, hearing their arrival, he came down and talked
with them, while all that were present marvelled at his age and constancy,
and that there was so much ado about the arrest of such an old man.
Then he ordered that something should be served for them to eat and
drink, at that late hour, as much as they wanted. And he besought
them that they should grant him an hour that he might pray freely.
They gave him leave, and he stood and prayed, being so filled with the
grace of God that for two hours he could not hold his peace, while they
that heard were amazed, and the men repented that they had come
after so venerable an old man.

VIII. When he had brought to an end his prayer, in which he
made mention of all, small and great, high and low, with whom
he had had dealings, and of the whole Catholic Church throughout the
world, the time had come for him to depart. And they set him on an
ass and led him into the city. Now it was a high Sabbath. And there met
him the sheriff Herod, and his father Nicetes, who removed him into
their carriage, and tried to persuade him, sitting by his side and saying,

---

[1] εἰρήναρχος—'officer of the peace', 'chief constable'. Frequently mentioned in
inscriptions.

'Now what harm is there is saying "Lord Caesar," and in offering incense, and so on, and thus saving thyself?' He at first made no reply, but since they persisted he said, 'I do not intend to do what you advise.' Then, failing to persuade him, they began to use threatening words; and they pulled him down hastily, so that he grazed his shin as he descended from the carriage. Without turning back, as if he had suffered no hurt, he went on with all speed, and was led to the stadium, wherein the tumult was so great that no one could be heard.

IX. Now, as he was entering the stadium, there came to Polycarp a voice from heaven, 'Be strong, Polycarp, and play the man.' And no one saw the speaker, but the voice was heard by those of our people who were there. Thereupon he was led forth, and great was the uproar of them that heard that Polycarp had been seized. Accordingly, he was led before the Proconsul, who asked him if he were the man himself. And when he confessed the Proconsul tried to persuade him, saying, 'Have respect to thine age,' and so forth, according to their customary form; 'Swear by the genius[1] of Caesar,' 'Repent,' 'Say, "Away with the atheists!"' Then Polycarp looked with a severe countenance on the mob of lawless heathen in the stadium, and he waved his hand at them, and looking up to heaven he groaned and said, 'Away with the atheists.' But the Proconsul urged him and said, 'Swear, and I will release thee; curse the Christ.' And Polycarp said, 'Eighty and six years have I served him, and he hath done me no wrong; how then can I blaspheme my king who saved me?'

X. But the Proconsul again persisted and said, 'Swear by the genius of Caesar'; and he answered, 'If thou dost vainly imagine that I would swear by the genius of Caesar, as thou sayest, pretending not to know what I am, hear plainly that I am a Christian. And if thou art willing to learn the doctrine of Christianity, grant me a day and hearken to me.' Then said the Proconsul, 'Persuade the people.' Polycarp replied, 'Thee I had deemed worthy of discourse, for we are taught to render to authorities and the powers ordained of God honour as is fitting. But I deem not this mob worthy that I should defend myself before them.'

XI. Then said the Proconsul, 'I have wild beasts; if thou repent not, I will throw thee to them.' But he said, 'Send for them. For repentance from better to worse is not a change permitted to us; but to change from cruelty to righteousness is a noble thing.' Then said the

---

[1] *Genius (fortuna, numen) Caesaris.* An oath invented under Julius Caesar (Dio Cassius, xliv. 6). Under Augustus certain days were set apart for worship of the Emperor's genius; and the practice grew under later Emperors.

Proconsul again, 'If thou dost despise the wild beasts I will make thee to be consumed by fire, if thou repent not.' And Polycarp answered, 'Thou threatenest the fire that burns for an hour and in a little while is quenched; for thou knowest not of the fire of the judgement to come, and the fire of the eternal punishment, reserved for the ungodly. But why delayest thou? Bring what thou wilt.'

XII. As he spake these words and many more, he was filled with courage and joy; and his countenance was full of grace, so that no only did it fall not in dismay at what was being said to him, but on the contrary the Proconsul was astonished, and sent his herald to proclaim thrice in the midst of the stadium, 'Polycarp hath confessed himself to be a Christian.' When this was proclaimed by the herald the whole multitude of Gentiles and Jews who dwelt in Smyrna cried out with ungovernable rage and in a loud voice, 'This is the teacher of Asia, the father of the Christians, the destroyer of our gods, that teacheth many not to sacrifice nor worship.' They kept shouting this, asking Philip, the Asiarch,[1] to loose a lion at Polycarp. But he said that it was not lawful for him, since he had finished the sports. Then they decided to shout with one accord that he should be burned alive. For the matter of his vision of the pillow must needs be fulfilled, when he saw it burning while he was at prayer, and turned and said prophetically to his companions, 'I must needs be burned alive.'

XIII. And now things happened with such speed, in less time than it takes to tell; for the mob straitway brought together timber and faggots from the workshops and baths, the Jews giving themselves zealously to the work, as they were like to do. ... They were about to nail him to the stake, when he said, 'Let me be as I am. He that granted me to endure the fire will grant me also to remain at the pyre unmoved, without being secured with nails.'

XV. When he had ended his prayer the firemen lighted the fire. And a great flame flashed forth: and we, to whom it was given to see, beheld a marvel. ... The fire took the shape of a vault, like a ship's sail bellying in the wind, and it made a wall round the martyr's body; and there was the body in the midst, like a loaf being baked or like gold and silver being tried in the furnace. ...

XVI. So at length the lawless ones, seeing that his body could not be consumed by the fire, bade an executioner approach him to drive in a dagger. And when he had done this there came out [a dove and]

---

[1] The head of the confederation of chief cities in the province of Asia (the *Commune Asiae*). He presided at games as 'chief priest' of Asia.

abundance of blood so that it quenched the fire, and all the multitude marvelled at the great difference between the unbelievers and the elect.
...

f. **Persecution at Lyons and Vienne**, *177*   The Epistle of the Gallican Churches: ap. Eusebius, H.E. v. i

The servants of Christ who sojourn in Vienna and Lugdunum of Gaul to the brethren throughout Asia and Phrygia who hold the same faith and hope as we do of redemption; peace, grace and glory from God the Father and Christ Jesus our Lord.

We are not competent to describe the magnitude of the tribulation here, the extent of the rage of the Gentiles against the saints and the sufferings of the blessed martyrs. ... Not only were we excluded from public buildings, baths and markets, but even the mere appearance of any one of us was forbidden, in any place whatsoever. ...

First, they nobly endured all that came upon them at the hands of the jostling mob and rabble; they were hooted at, struck, dragged about, plundered, stoned, hemmed in; and all other indignities they suffered which an inflamed rabble is wont to inflict on its enemies and foes. At length, being brought into the forum by the chiliarch[1] and the chief men of the city, they were examined before the mob, and having confessed were put into prison until the arrival of the governor. ...

They apprehended also certain heathen slaves of ours, for the governor ordered that we should all be examined in public. And they, through a lying in wait of Satan, fearing the tortures they saw the saints suffering, falsely accused us, when the soldiers so urged them, of Thyestean feasts and Oedipodean intercourse,[2] and of things of which it is not lawful either to speak or think, nor even to believe that any such things were ever done among them. And when these statements were noised abroad all were inflamed against us, so that even such as were before moderate towards us through kinship were now greatly angered, and raged against us. Then was fulfilled that saying of our Lord, 'The time shall come wherein he that killeth you will think that he doeth God service.' ...

Now the blessed Pothinus, who had been entrusted with the ministry of the bishopric of Lugdunum, and was more than ninety years of age

---

[1] Literally 'commander of a thousand men'. A regular term for a commander of a garrison of any size.

[2] See above, p. 2. Thyestes in ignorance ate the flesh of his two sons; Oedipus in ignorance married his own mother.

and quite feeble in body ... was brought to the judgement seat, escorted by the city magistrates and all the rabble, with all kinds of hooting. And being asked by the governor who was the God of the Christians, he said, 'If thou be worthy, thou shalt know.' Whereupon he was pulled about without pity, those nearest maltreating him in every way with hands and feet, while those at a distance hurled at him whatever came to hand, every one thinking it a great neglect and impiety if any wantonness was left untried; for so they thought to avenge their gods. ...

g. Persecution under Decius, 249–251

A *libellus* (certificate of sacrifice) discovered at Fayoum (Egypt), 1893; Milligan, *Greek Papyri*, 48

[The Edict of Decius, 250, commanded provincial governors and magistrates, assisted where necessary by local notables, to superintend the sacrifices to the gods and to the genius of the Emperor, to be performed by all on a fixed day. Many recanted; others bought certificates or had them procured by pagan friends. There seems to have been wholesale connivance by the officials.]

TO THE COMMISSIONERS FOR SACRIFICES IN THE VILLAGE OF ALEXANDER'S ISLAND, FROM AURELIUS DIOGENES, SON OF SATABUS, OF THE VILLAGE OF ALEXANDER'S ISLAND, AGED 72; SCAR ON RIGHT EYEBROW.

I have always sacrificed to the gods, and now in your presence, in accordance with the terms of the edict, I have done sacrifice and poured libations and tasted the sacrifices, and I request you to certify to this effect. Farewell.

PRESENTED BY ME, AURELIUS DIOGENES.

I CERTIFY THAT I WITNESSED HIS SACRIFICE, AURELIUS SYRUS.

Dated this first year of the Emperor Caesar Gaius Messius Quintus Trajanus Decius, Pius, Felix, Augustus, the 2nd of Epiph. (26 June 250).

h. Persecution under Valerian, 253–260   Cyprian, *Ep.* lxxx. 1

[Valerian seems to have favoured Christianity at the beginning of his reign, and there were many Christians in his palace, 'Caesariani' being mentioned in the Rescript (v. Dionysius of Alexandria ap. Euseb. VII. x. 3 ff.). The following extract gives the drift of his second Rescript. The first had ordered sacrifices to be made by bishops and priests and had forbidden Christians to assemble, or to use their cemeteries, on pain of death.]

... There are many various and unauthenticated rumours going about, but the truth is as follows; Valerian sent a Rescript to the Senate ordering that bishops, priests and deacons should forthwith be punished; that senators, men of rank and Roman knights should be degraded and lose their property, and if, having been deprived of their possessions, they should still remain Christians, then they should also lose their heads; that matrons should be deprived of their property and banished; and that any members of Caesar's household who had confessed before, or should now confess, should lose their property and be sent in chains to forced labour on Caesar's farms.

i. The Rescript of Gallienus, 261   Euseb. *H.E.* vii. xiii. 2

[By an edict, the text of which is lost, in 260, the basilicas were restored, the cemeteries reopened and freedom of worship granted. Christianity became a *religio licita*.]

The Emperor Caesar Publius Licinius Gallienus, Pius, Felix, Augustus, to Dionysius, Pinnas, Demetrius and the other bishops. I have enjoined that the benefit of my bounty be put into execution throughout the world, that they may keep away from places of worship. And therefore you may act upon the order contained in my Rescript, so that no one shall molest you. And this which you are now lawfully permitted to accomplish has already for a long time been conceded by me. Therefore Aulus Cyrenius, the chief administrator, will observe this order which I have given.

j. Persecution under Diocletian, 303–305

[Diocletian seems to have been favourable at first. His wife and daughter were catechumens, and Eusebius tells of the great increase of the Church in the early part of his reign (*H.E.* vii. i.). The change in his attitude was due (according to Lactantius, *De mortibus persecutorum*, xi) to the influence of Galerius. Gallienus's edict was repealed, Valerian's laws re-enacted.]

Euseb. *H.E.*
IX. x. 8. ... It was enacted by their majesties Diocletian and Maximian that the meetings of Christians should be abolished. ...

VII. ii. 4. March 303. ... Imperial edicts were published everywhere ordering that the churches be razed to the ground, that the Scriptures be destroyed by fire, that those holding office be deposed and they of the household be deprived of freedom, if they persisted in the profession of Christianity. 5. This was the first edict against us. But not long after other decrees were issued, which enjoined that the rulers of the churches in every place be first imprisoned, and thereafter every means be used to compel them to sacrifice.

Euseb. *De martyribus Palaestinae*, iii. 2
April 304. ... Imperial edicts were issued, in which, by a general decree, it was ordered that all the people without exception should sacrifice in the several cities and offer libations to the idols.

k. The Attempt to Restore Paganism under Maximin, 308–311

308. Euseb. *De m. P.* ix. 2

Therefore a host of letters from Maximin was issued everywhere throughout every province. The governors, and also the military commander, by edicts, letters and public ordinances pressed the magistrates, generals and notaries to implement the imperial decree which ordered that the idols' ruins be rebuilt with all speed; that all without exception—men, women, slaves and children, even infants in arms—should sacrifice and offer oblations. ...

311. Euseb. viii. xiv. 9

Maximin ... ordered temples to be erected in every city, and the sacred groves to be speedily restored, which had fallen into ruin through lapse of time. He set idol-priests in every place and city, and over them he appointed in each province a high priest, one of the officials who had specially distinguished himself in all kinds of service, giving him a body of troops and a personal guard. ...

l. Edict of Toleration, 311   Lactantius, *De mort. pers.* xxxiv

[Issued by Galerius on his death-bed, after years of strenuous persecution, and bearing the names also of his colleagues Constantine and Licinius. The other colleague, Maximin Daza, ruler of Egypt and Syria, refused to sign.]

Among our other regulations to promote the lasting good of the community we have hitherto endeavoured to restore a universal conformity to the ancient institutions and public order of the Romans; and in particular it has been our aim to bring back to a right disposition the Christians who had abandoned the religion of their fathers. ... 3. After the publication of our edict ordering the Christians to conform to the ancient institutions, many of them were brought to order through fear, while many were exposed to danger. 4. Nevertheless, since many still persist in their opinions, and since we have observed that they now neither show due reverence to the gods nor worship their own God, we therefore, with our wonted clemency in extending pardon to all, are pleased to grant indulgence to these men, allowing Christians the right to exist again and to set up their places of worship; provided always that they do not offend against public order. 5. We will in a further instruction explain to the magistrates how they should conduct themselves in this matter. In return for this indulgence of ours it will be the duty of Christians to pray to God for our recovery, for the public weal and for their own; that the state may be preserved from danger on every side, and that they themselves may dwell safely in their homes.

m. The 'Edict of Milan', March(?) 313   Lact. *De mort. pers.* XLVIII

2. When we, Constantine and Licinius, Emperors, met at Milan in conference concerning the welfare and security of the realm, we decided that of the things that are of profit to all mankind, the worship of God ought rightly to be our first and chiefest care, and that it was right that Christians and all others should have freedom to follow the kind of religion they favoured; so that the God who dwells in heaven might be propitious to us and to all under our rule. 4. We therefore announce that, notwithstanding any provisions concerning the Christians in our former instructions, all who choose that religion are to be permitted to continue therein, without any let or hindrance, and are not to be in any way troubled or molested. 6. Note that at the same time all others are to be allowed the free and unrestricted practice of their religions; for it accords with the good order of the realm and the peacefulness of our times that each should have freedom to worship God after his own choice; and we do not intend to detract from the honour due to any religion or its followers. 7. Moreover, concerning the Christians, we before gave orders with respect to the places set apart for their worship. It is now our pleasure that all who have bought such places should restore them to the Christians, without any demand for payment. ...

[8.9. Churches received by gift and any other places formerly belonging to Christians to be restored. Owners may apply for compensation.]

10. You are to use your utmost diligence in carrying out these orders on behalf of the Christians, that our command may be promptly obeyed, for the fulfilment of our gracious purpose in establishing public tranquillity. 11. So shall that divine favour which we have already enjoyed, in affairs of the greatest moment, continue to grant us success, and thus secure the happiness of the realm.

n. Constantine's Support of the Church

Restitution of Church Property   Constantine to Anulinus, Proconsul of
   Africa, 313: Euseb. *H.E.* x. v. 15–17

Greeting, our most esteemed Anulinus. It is the custom of our Benevolence to will that those things which rightly belong to another not only be left undisturbed, but also be restored. 16. Whence it is our wish that when you receive this letter, if any of these things belonged to the Catholic Church of the Christians, in any city or in other places, you shall cause them to be restored immediately to their churches. For we have decided that what these same churches before possessed be restored to their rightful owners. 17. Therefore, as your Fidelity perceives this our injunction and command to be most emphatic, make haste to have restored to them with all speed all things before belonging to them by right, whether gardens or buildings or whatever they may be, that we may learn that you have responded to this our injunction with your most careful obedience. Farewell, our most esteemed and beloved Anulinus.

A Grant to the Clergy   Constantine to Caecilian, Bishop of Carthage, 313: Euseb. *H.E.* x. vi

Since we have been pleased that in all the provinces of Africa, Numidia and Mauretania some subsidy towards their expenses should be granted to certain specified ministers of the legitimate and most holy Catholic religion, I have given instructions to Ursus, the illustrious *catholicus* [finance controller], to take measures for the payment of 3000 *folles*[1] to your Firmness. 2. Therefore, when you have received the above sum, command that it be distributed to all the aforesaid, according to the brief sent to you by Hosius.[2] 3. But if you should find that anything is wanting towards the fulfilment of my purpose in regard to all these, you shall demand whatever you may find to be needful from Heracleides, our treasurer, without fear of question. For when he was present I commanded him that if your Firmness should ask him for any money, he should provide for payment without delay. 4. And since I have learned that some men of unstable mind wish to turn the people from the most holy and Catholic Church by shameful and corrupt courses, know that I have given commands to Anulinus, the Proconsul, and also to Patricius, Vicar of the Prefects, in their presence, that they should give their special attention to this among other matters and that they should not tolerate this if it happened. 5. Therefore if you should see any such men continue in their madness, approach the above-mentioned judges without delay and report it, so that they may correct them as I commanded them in their presence. The Divinity of the great God preserve you for many years.

Exemptions for the Clergy   Constantine to Anulinus, 313: Euseb. *H.E.* x. vii

Since it is plain that when that religion is set at nought, in which is preserved the crowning reverence for the most holy celestial Being, great dangers are brought upon public affairs; but that, when legally adopted

---

[1] A sum of money of uncertain amount.   [2] See p. 20.

and safeguarded, it affords to the Roman name the greatest prosperity, and exceptional felicity to the affairs of all mankind, which is the gift of the divine beneficence—it has seemed good that those men who, with due sanctity and attendance to this law, proffer their personal services to the ministry of the divine religion should receive the reward of their toils, most esteemed Anulinus. 2. Wherefore it is my wish that those within the province entrusted to you, in the Catholic Church, over which Caecilian presides, who proffer their services to this holy religion, who are usually called clerics, be completely exempt from public duties, that they be not drawn away from the service due to the Divinity by any error or sacrilegious falling away, but may rather fulfil the service of their own law without any hindrance. For it seems that, when they render the greatest homage to the Divinity, then the greatest benefits befall the commonweal.

Constantine and Church Discipline   The Case of Caecilian and the
     Donatists, 316: Augustine, *c. Cresconium*, iii. 82 (*Op.* ix. 476 ff.)

[Caecilian had fallen foul of much popular sentiment in his diocese of Carthage by his efforts to restrain the excessive adulation of martyrs and confessors which was undermining ecclesiastical authority. Hence arose the Donatist schism. (For the points at issue, see below, p. 85). The Donatists appealed to Constantine, who called a council at Rome, Oct. 313, and in 314 convened the Synod of Arles. The Donatists appealed to the Emperor in person against the adverse decision.]

At the investigation I clearly perceived that Caecilian was completely blameless; a man who observed the customary duties of his religion, and devoted himself to it as was incumbent on him. It was plain that no fault could be found in him, such as had been, by the inventions of his enemies, alleged against him in his absence.

o. Constantine's Legislation in Favour of the Church

Suppression of Soothsayers, 319   *Cod. Theod.* ix. xvi. 1 (*Nullus haruspex*)

The Emperor Constantine Augustus to Maximus.

No soothsayer may approach his neighbour's threshold, even for any other purpose. Friendship with men of this profession must be put away, even if it be of long standing. A soothsayer who approaches his neighbour's house is to be burnt; anyone inviting him, whether by persuasion or by money reward, is to be deprived of his goods and banished to an island. Those wishing to follow their own superstition will be allowed to practise its peculiar rites in public.

Anyone who brings an accusation of this offence is, in our judgement, no informer; on the contrary, he merits a reward.

Given at Rome, the 1st of February in the consulate of Constantine Augustus (his fifth) and Licinius Caesar.

State Recognition of Sunday, 321   Cod. Justinianus, III. xii. 3 (*Corp. Jur. Civ.* ii. 127)

Constantine to Elpidius. All judges, city-people and craftsmen shall rest on the venerable day of the Sun. But countrymen may without hindrance attend to agriculture, since it often happens that this is the most suitable day for sowing grain or planting vines, so that the opportunity afforded by divine providence may not be lost, for the right season is of short duration. 7 March 321.

Cod. Theod. II. viii. 1

The Emperor Constantine Augustus to Elpidius. Just as we thought it most unfitting that the day of the Sun, with its venerable rites, should be given over to the swearing and counter-swearing of litigants and their unseemly brawls, so it is a pleasant and joyful thing to fulfil petitions of special urgency on that day. Therefore on that festal day let all be allowed to perform manumission and emancipation; and let nothing that concerns this be forbidden. 3 July 321.

p. A Letter from Hosius, Bishop of Cordova (296–357), to Constantius   Athanasius, *Hist. Ar.* 44

[Hosius had been the ecclesiastical adviser of Constantine; suggested and took a leading part in the Nicene Council, a vigorous champion of Athanasius. Constantius, now sole Emperor, a fanatical Arian, was trying by threats to get Hosius' support (and succeeded, by violence, in obtaining his signature to the 'Blasphemy of Sirmium' in 357). Constantius secured the condemnation of Athanasius, at Milan, 355, where he showed his conception of his relation to the Church by the famous saying, 'Let my will be deemed a canon among you, as it is among the Syrian bishops (Arians).' Ath. *Hist. Ar.* 33.]

... Cease, I implore you, from these proceedings. Remember that you are but mortal; and be fearful of the day of judgement and keep yourself pure with that day in view. Do not interfere in matters ecclesiastical, nor give us orders on such questions, but learn about them from us. For into your hands God has put the kingdom; the affairs of his Church he has committed to us. If any man stole the Empire from you, he would be resisting the ordinance of God: in the same way you on your part should be afraid lest, in taking upon yourself the government of the Church, you incur the guilt of a grave offence. 'Render unto Caesar the things that are

Caesar's and unto God the things that are God's.' We are not permitted to exercise an earthly rule; and you Sire, are not authorized to burn incense. I write thus to you out of concern for your salvation. As for the contents of your letter; I am determined not to write to the Arians. I anathematize their heresy. And I will not subscribe to the indictment of Athanasius; for both we, and the Church of Rome, and the whole synod, acquitted him.

q. Julian the Apostate (361–363) on Toleration
Julian, *Ep.* lii. (to the people of Bostra, 362)

I had imagined that the prelates of the Galilaeans were under greater obligations to me than to my predecessor. For in his reign many of them were banished, persecuted and imprisoned; and many of the so-called heretics were executed. ... All this has been reversed in my reign; the banished are allowed to return, and confiscated goods have all been restored to the owners. But such is their folly and madness that, just because they can no longer be despots, or carry out their designs first against their brethren and then against us, the worshippers of the gods, they are inflamed with fury and stop at nothing in their unprincipled attempts to alarm and enrage the people. They are irreverent to the gods and disobedient to our edicts, lenient as they are. For we allow none of them to be dragged to the altars unwillingly; and we announce publicly that any of them who wish to share in our lustrations and libations must first offer expiatory sacrifices and pray to the gods, the averters of evil. So far are we from wishing to admit any of the impious to our sacred rites before they have cleansed their souls by prayers to the gods and their bodies by the prescribed ablutions. ...

It is therefore my pleasure to announce and publish to all the people by this edict, that they must not abet the seditions of the clergy. ... They may hold their meetings, if they wish, and offer prayers according to their established use. ... And for the future let the people live in harmony. Let no one be at variance, or do wrong to another; neither you that are in error to those who worship the gods, as is right and proper, in the manner handed down from earliest antiquity; nor let the worshippers of the gods destroy or plunder the house of those who are misled by ignorance rather than deliberate choice. Men should be taught and won over by reason, not by blows, insults and corporal punishments. I therefore most earnestly admonish the adherents of the true religion not to injure or insult the Galilaeans in any way, either by physical attack or by reproaches. Those who are in the wrong in matters of supreme importance are objects of pity rather than of hate. ...

r. Julian on Christianity. The Worship of Jesus and the Martyrs

Julian *contra Christianos*, apud Cyril Alex. *contra Julianum*, x (Op. ix. 326 ff.)

But you, unfortunately, do not abide by the tradition of the apostles, which in the hands of their successors deteriorated into greater blasphemy. Neither Paul, nor Matthew, nor Luke, nor Mark had the audacity to say that Jesus is God. But the worthy John, realizing that by that time a vast number of people in many of the Greek and Italian cities were infected with the disease, and hearing, I fancy, that the tombs of Peter and Paul were being worshipped (privately, no doubt, but still worshipped), John, I say, was the first to have the audacity to make this assertion.

This evil was inaugurated by John. But who can find a fitting denunciation of this additional innovation of yours, the introduction of many recent dead bodies [as objects of worship], besides that original dead body? You have filled all places with tombs and monuments. ... You think that not even the words of Jesus are to be listened to on this question. ... Jesus says (Matt. xxii. 27) that sepulchres are full of uncleanness. How is it then that you invoke God upon them?

s. Gratian (375–383) on the Trial of Bishops. Jurisdiction of the Roman See

[For the decisions of the Council of Sardica, 343, on this matter see p. 84.]

A Petition from the Roman Synod, 382, to Valentinian II and Gratian: Migne, *P.L.* xiii. 581

[Text of this extract given also in Puller, *Primitive Saints and the See of Rome*, 145 ff.]

(9) ... We request your Clemency, that your Piety would think fit to order that if any shall have been condemned by the judgement either of Damasus [Bishop of Rome, 366–384] or of ourselves, who are Catholics, and shall unjustly wish to retain his church, or shall through contumacy refuse to attend when summoned by a synod of bishops, that he be brought to Rome either by those illustrious men, the Praetorian Prefects of your Italy or by the Vicar (of the city); or, if a question of this kind arise in more distant parts, that the examination be committed by the local courts to the Metropolitan; or, if the Metropolitan be himself the accused, that he should be ordered to go without delay to Rome, or to such judges as the Bishop of Rome may appoint. ... If there should be any suspicion of favour or unfairness on the part of the Metropolitan or of any other bishop, then let him have the right of appeal to the Bishop of Rome, or to a synod of at least fifteen bishops of his neighbourhood.

Gratian's Reply: *P.L.* xiii. 586 (*C.S.E.L.* xxxv. i. 57: Puller, op. cit. 145 ff.)
(6) We will that whosoever has been condemned by the judgement of Damasus,[1] which he has given with the advice of five or seven bishops,[1] or who has been condemned by the judgement and advice of those bishops who are Catholics, ...

[Granting the points of the petition except that contumacious bishops from the nearer parts are either to be remitted to the episcopal tribunal, or to be summoned to Rome. The alternatives presumably refer to different classes, the first to those condemned by a synod, the second to those condemned by the pope, i.e. in each case the recalcitrant bishop is to appear before the original court.]

t. Gratian's Ruling on Ecclesiastical and Civil or Criminal Cases,
376   *Qui mos est* (*Cod. Theod.* xvi. ii. 23)

In ecclesiastical matters the same custom is to be followed as in secular cases: namely, that if any questions arise out of disagreements or minor offences, pertaining to religious observance, these are to be tried locally, by the diocesan synods; with the exception of such cases as involve some civil or criminal offence which requires their being heard by the ordinary or extraordinary judges, or by officials of high rank.

u. Theodosius I (379-395) on Catholic and Heretic
Cunctos populos, 380 (*Cod. Theod.* xvi. i. 2)

It is our desire that all the various nations which are subject to our Clemency and Moderation, should continue in the profession of that religion which was delivered to the Romans by the divine Apostle Peter, as it hath been preserved by faithful tradition; and which is now professed by the Pontiff Damasus and by Peter, Bishop of Alexandria, a man of apostolic holiness. According to the apostolic teaching and the doctrine of the Gospel, let us believe the one deity of the Father, the Son and the Holy Spirit, in equally majesty and in a holy Trinity. We authorize the followers of this law to assume the title of Catholic Christians; but as for the others, since, in our judgement, they are foolish madmen, we decree that they shall be branded with the ignominious name of heretics, and shall not presume to give to their conventicles the name of churches. They will suffer in the first place the chastisement of the divine condemnation, and in the second the punishment which our authority, in accordance with the will of Heaven, shall decide to inflict.

---

[1] It is uncertain whether this is a proviso or a statement of fact.

Nullus haereticus, 381 (*Cod. Theod.* XVI. v. 6)

... Let them be entirely excluded even from the thresholds of churches, since we permit no heretics to hold their unlawful assemblies in the towns. If they attempt any disturbance, we decree that their fury shall be suppressed and that they shall be expelled outside the walls of the cities, so that the Catholic churches throughout the world may be restored to the orthodox bishops who hold the faith of Nicaea.

v. The Edict of Valentinian III, 445. The Primacy of the Pope

Constitutio Valentiniani III, Leo, *Ep.* xi: *P.L.* liv. 636 ff.

We are convinced that the only defence for us and for our Empire is in the favour of the God of heaven: and in order to deserve this favour it is our first care to support the Christian faith and its venerable religion. Therefore, inasmuch as the pre-eminence of the Apostolic See is assured by the merit of S. Peter, the first of the bishops, by the leading position of the city of Rome and also by the authority of the holy Synod, let not presumption strive to attempt anything contrary to the authority of that See. For the peace of the churches will only then be everywhere preserved when the whole body acknowledge its ruler. Hitherto this has been observed without violation; but Hilary, Bishop of Arles,[1] as we have learnt from the report of that venerable man Leo, the pope of Rome, has with contumacious presumption ventured upon certain unlawful proceedings; and thus an abominable confusion has invaded the church beyond the Alps. ... By such presumptuous acts confidence in the Empire, and respect for our rule is destroyed. Therefore in the first place we put down so great a crime: and, beyond that, in order that no disturbance, however slight, may arise among the churches, and the discipline of religion may not appear to be impaired in any case whatever, we decree, by a perpetual edict, that nothing shall be attempted by the Gallican bishops, or by those of any other province, contrary to the ancient custom, without the authority of the venerable people of the Eternal City. But whatsoever the authority of the Apostolic See has enacted, or shall enact, let that be held as law for all. So that if any bishop summoned before the pope of Rome shall neglect to attend, let him be compelled to appear by the governor of the province. ...

---

[1] Hilary had presided at a synod which deposed Chelidonius, Bishop of Besançon. C. refused to resign, was excommunicated, went to Rome and appealed to Leo, who admitted him to communion. Hilary went to Rome to protest. But Leo acquitted C., ordered his reinstatement and deprived H. of the primacy he had exercised in the Gallican church.

SECTION II
Creeds

I. THE APOSTLES' CREED

a. 'The Old Roman Creed'

[From Epiphanius, lxxii. 3 (*P.G.* xliii. 385 D). The creed of Marcellus, Bishop of Ancyra, delivered to Julius, Bishop of Rome, *c*.340. Marcellus had been exiled from his diocese through Arian influence and spent nearly two years at Rome. On departing he left this statement of his belief.

Rufinus, priest of Aquileia, *Expositio in Symbolum,* *c*.400 (*P.L.* xxi. 335 B), compares the creed of Aquileia with the Roman creed which he believed to be the rule of faith composed by the Apostles at Jerusalem, which had been retained as the baptismal creed in the Roman Church. This creed differs from that of Marcellus only in small details.]

1. I believe in God almighty [*Ruf.* the Father almighty]
2. And in Christ Jesus, his only son, our Lord
3. Who was born of the Holy Spirit and the Virgin Mary
4. Who was crucified under Pontius Pilate and was buried
5. And the third day rose from the dead
6. Who ascended into heaven
7. And sitteth on the right hand of the Father
8. Whence he cometh to judge the living and the dead
9. And in the Holy Ghost
10. The holy church
11. The remission of sins
12. The resurrection of the flesh
13. The life everlasting. [*Ruf. omits.*]

b. A Gallican Creed of the Sixth Century

[Extracted from a sermon (pseudo-Augustinus, 244) of Caesarius, Bishop of Arles, 503–543.]

(1) I believe in God the Father almighty
(2) I also believe in Jesus Christ his only son, our Lord,
(3) conceived of the Holy Spirit, born of the Virgin Mary,
(4) suffered under Pontius Pilate, crucified, dead and buried; he descended into hell,
(5) rose again the third day,
(6) ascended into heaven,
(7) sat down at the right hand of the Father,

(8) thence he is to come to judge the living and the dead.
(9) I believe in the Holy Ghost,
(10) the Holy Catholic Church, the communion of saints,
(11) the remission of sins,
(12) the resurrection of the flesh and life eternal.

[The complete 'Apostles' Creed,' as we know it, is found first in *Dicta Abbatis Pirminii de singulis libris canonicis scarapsus* (i.q. *excarpsus*, excerpt), *c*. 750.]

II. THE NICENE CREED

(a) The Creed of Caesarea   Epist. *Euseb. apud* Socrates, *H.E.* i. 8

[At the council of Nicaea (325) Eusebius of Caesarea, the historian, suggested the adoption of the creed of his own church. It ran thus:]

We believe in one God, the Father All-sovereign, the maker of things visible and invisible;

And in one Lord Jesus Christ, the Word of God, God of God, Light of Light, Life of Life, Son only-begotten, Firstborn of all creation, begotten of the Father before all the ages, through whom also all things were made; who was made flesh for our salvation and lived among men, and suffered, and rose again on the third day, and ascended to the Father, and shall come again in glory to judge the living and dead;

We believe also in one Holy Spirit.

(b) The Creed of Nicaea

[Eusebius' creed was orthodox, but it did not deal explicitly with the Arian position. It was taken as a base, and put forward by the council in this revised form (additions and alterations in italic type):]

We believe in one God the Father All-sovereign, maker of all things visible and invisible;

And in one Lord Jesus Christ, the Son of God, *begotten of the Father*, only-begotten, *that is, of the substance*[1] *of the Father*, God of God, Light of Light, *true God of true God*, begotten not made, of one substance[2] *with the Father*, through whom all things were made, *things in heaven and things on the earth*; who for us men and for our salvation *came down* and

---

[1] ἐκ τῆς οὐσίας τοῦ πατρός, 'from the inmost being of the Father', inseparably one. (See note on p. 35).

[2] ὁμοούσιον τῷπατρί, sharing one being with the Father, and therefore distinct in existence though essentially one.

was made flesh, *and became man*,[1] suffered, and rose on the third day, ascended into the heavens, is coming to judge living and dead.

And in the Holy Spirit.

And those that say 'There was when he was not,'

and, 'Before he was begotten he was not,'

and that, 'He came into being from what-is-not,'[2]

or those that allege, that the son of God is

'Of another substance or essence'

or 'created,'

or 'changeable'[3]

or 'alterable,'[4]

these the Catholic and Apostolic Church anathematizes.

(c) The 'Nicene' Creed

[Found in Epiphanius, *Ancoratus*, 118, c. AD 374, and extracted by scholars, almost word for word, from the Catechetical Lectures of S. Cyril of Jerusalem; read and approved at Chalcedon, 451, as the creed of '(the 318 fathers who met at Nicaea and that of) the 150 who met at a later time' (i.e. at Constantinople, 381). Hence often called the Constantinopolitan or Nicaeno-Constantinopolitan creed, and thought by many to be a revision of the creed of Jerusalem held by Cyril. See, for discussions, Hort, *Two Dissertations* (1876), Burn, *Introduction to the Creeds* (1899), and Kelly, *Early Christian Creeds* (1950).]

We believe in one God the Father All-sovereign, maker of heaven and earth, and of all things visible and invisible;

And in one Lord Jesus Christ, the only-begotten Son of God, Begotten of the Father before all the ages, Light of Light, true God of true God, begotten not made, of one substance[5] with the Father, through whom all things were made; who for us men and for our salvation came down from the heavens, and was made flesh of the Holy Spirit and the Virgin Mary,

---

[1] ἐνανθρωπήσαντα, taking on himself all that makes man man, expanding σαρκωθέντα, 'was made flesh'; or perhaps, 'lived as man among man,' expanding and safeguarding the Caesarean 'lived among men,' ἐν ἀνθρώποις πολιτευσάμενον. But this seems less likely.

[2] ἐξ οὐκ ὄντων, 'from nothingness.'

[3] i.e. *morally* changeable.

[4] The additions, 'God of God' (from the creed of Nicaea) and '(from the Father) and the Son', occur first in the 'Creed of Constantinople' as recited at the third Council of Toledo, 589. The latter phrase, the '*filioque* clause,' had already been used at an earlier council of Toledo, 447: it gained popularity in the West and was inserted in most versions of the creed, except that of the Roman Church, where Leo III in 809 refused to insert it. But in 867 Nicholas I was excommunicated by Photius, Bishop of Constantinople, for having corrupted the creed by this addition.

[5] See note (2) on the Creed of Nicaea, p. 26.

and became man, and was crucified for us under Pontius Pilate, and suffered and was buried, and rose again on the third day according to the Scriptures, and ascended into the heavens, and sitteth on the right hand of the Father, and cometh again with glory to judge living and dead, of whose kingdom there shall be no end:

And in the Holy Spirit, the Lord and the Life-giver, that proceedeth from the Father,[1] who with Father and Son is worshipped together and glorified together, who spake through the prophets:

In one holy Catholic and Apostolic Church:

We acknowledge one baptism unto remission of sins. We look for a resurrection of the dead, and the life of the age to come.

SECTION III

The Earliest Testimony to the Gospels

I. THE TRADITION OF THE ELDERS

Papias, Bishop of Hierapolis (*c.*130), *Expositions of the Oracles of the Lord*, in Euseb. *H.E.* iii. 39

Five books of Papias are extant, bearing the title *Expositions of the Oracles of the Lord*. Irenaeus relates that this is his only work, and says, 'Papias, the hearer of John and companion of Polycarp, a man of an earlier generation, testifies to these things in his fourth book. His work is in five volumes.' Such is the evidence of Irenaeus. Now Papias himself in the introduction to his writings makes no claim to be a hearer and eyewitness of the holy Apostles, but to have received the contents of the faith from those that were known to them. He tells us this in his own words: 'I shall not hesitate to set down for you, along with my interpretations, all things which I learnt from the elders with care and recorded with care, being well assured of their truth. For, unlike most men, I took pleasure not in those that had much to say but in those that teach the truth; not in those who record strange precepts, but in those who relate such precepts as were given to the Faith from the Lord and are derived from the Truth itself. Besides, if ever any man came who had been a follower of the elders, I would enquire about the sayings of the

---

[1] See note (4) on previous page.

elders; what Andrew said, or Peter, or Philip, or Thomas, or James, or John, or Matthew, or any other of the Lord's disciples; and what Aristion says, and John the Elder, who are disciples of the Lord. For I did not consider that I got so much profit from the contents of books as from the utterances of a living and abiding voice.'

[Eusebius goes on to speak with scorn of some of the stories handed down by Papias, and in particular of his millenarian exegesis of certain of our Lord's parables. 'Clearly,' he says, 'he was very weak of intellect,' although in a former passage (III. 36, 2), according to many MSS, he pays a tribute to his erudition.]

14. Now in his own writings he transmits other narratives of the words of the Lord which come from the afore-mentioned Aristion, and also traditions derived from John the Elder. To these I will refer the curious, merely adding to the above quotations from his works the tradition he preserves concerning Mark, the writer of the gospel. He says: 'The Elder used to say this also: Mark became the interpreter of Peter and he wrote down accurately, but not in order, as much as he remembered[1] of the sayings and doings of Christ. For he was not a hearer or a follower of the Lord, but afterwards, as I said, of Peter, who adapted his teachings to the needs of the moment and did not make an ordered exposition of the sayings of the Lord. And so Mark made no mistake when he thus wrote down some things as he remembered[1] them; for he made it his especial care to omit nothing of what he heard, and to make no false statement therein.' This is what Papias relates concerning Mark.

Now concerning Matthew it is stated: 'So then Matthew recorded the oracles[2] in the Hebrew tongue, and each interpreted them to the best of his ability.'

Papias also makes use of testimonies from the former epistle of John, and likewise from the epistle of Peter.

II. THE EVANGELISTS AND THEIR SOURCES
Irenaeus, Bishop of Lyons, end of second century: *Adversus haereses*, III. 1. i
(in Euseb. *H.E.* v. 8)

Matthew published his gospel among the Hebrews in their own tongue, when Peter and Paul were preaching the Gospel in Rome and founding the church there. After their departure Mark, the disciple and interpreter of Peter, himself handed down to us in writing the substance of Peter's

---

[1] Or, perhaps, 'he (Peter) related'. The Greek ἐμνημόνευσευ, ἀπεμνημόνευσευ, could bear either meaning.

[2] τὰ λόγια, 'prophetic discourses'. This *may* be the document known as Q.

preaching. Luke, the follower of Paul, set down in a book the gospel preached by his teacher. Then John, the disciple of the Lord, who also leaned on his breast, himself produced his gospel, while he was living at Ephesus in Asia.

III. THE MURATORIAN CANON
Text in Westcott, *Canon of N.T.*, App. C.

[Written in barbarous Latin, by a careless and ignorant scribe, probably in the eighth century. The Greek original probably dated from the end of the second century.]

... at which he [? S. Mark] was present and thus set them down.

The third book of the Gospel is that according to Luke. Luke, the physician, when, after the Ascension of Christ, Paul had taken him to himself as one studious of right [*or, probably*, as travelling companion] wrote in his own name what he had been told [*or* in order], although he had not himself seen the Lord in the flesh. He set down the events as far as he could ascertain them, and began his story with the birth of John.

The fourth gospel is that of John, one of the disciples. ... When his fellow-disciples and bishops exhorted him he said, 'Fast with me for three days from to-day, and then let us relate to each other whatever may be revealed to each of us.' On the same night it was revealed to Andrew, one of the Apostles, that John should narrate all things in his own name as they remembered them. ...

Moreover the Acts of all the Apostles are included in one book. Luke addressed them to the most excellent Theophilus, because the several events took place when he was present; and he makes this plain by the omission of the passion of Peter and of the journey of Paul when he left Rome for Spain.

For the Epistles of Paul ... he wrote to not more than seven churches, in this order: the first to the Corinthians, the second to the Ephesians, the third to the Philippians, the fourth to the Colossians, the fifth to the Galatians, the sixth to the Thessalonians, the seventh to the Romans. ... He wrote besides these one to Philemon, one to Titus, and two to Timothy. These were written in personal affection; but they have been hallowed by being held in honour by the Catholic Church for the regulation of church discipline. There are extant also a letter to the Laodiceans and another to the Alexandrians, forged under Paul's name to further the heresy of Marcion. And there are many others which cannot be received into the Catholic Church. For it is not fitting for gall to be mixed with honey.

The Epistle of Jude indeed, and two bearing the name of John, are accepted in the Catholic Church; also Wisdom, written by the friends of Solomon in his honour. We receive also the Apocalypse of John and [1]that of Peter, which[1] some of us refuse to have read in the Church. But the *Shepherd* was written very recently in our time by Hermas, in the city of Rome, when his brother, Bishop Pius, was sitting in the Chair of the Church of Rome. Therefore it ought also to be read; but it cannot be publicly read in the Church to the people, either among the Prophets, since their number is complete [?], or among the Apostles, to the end of time.
. . .

SECTION IV
The Person and Work of Christ

I. IGNATIUS, BISHOP OF ANTIOCH, C.112

The Incarnation   *Ad Eph.* vii. 2

There is one physician, fleshly and spiritual, begotten and unbegotten,[2] God in man, true life in death, both of Mary and of God, first passible then impassible,[2] Jesus Christ our Lord.

II. IRENAEUS

a. The 'Recapitulation' in Christ   *Adv. haer.* iii. xviii

Now it has been clearly demonstrated that the Word which exists from the beginning with God, by whom all things were made, who was also present with the race of men at all times, this Word has in these last times, according to the time appointed by the Father, been united to his own workmanship and has been made passible man. Therefore we can set aside the objection of them that say, 'If he was born at that time it follows that Christ did not exist before then.' For we have shown that the Son of God did not then begin to exist since he existed with the Father always; but when he was incarnate and made man, he recapitulated [*or* summed up] in himself the long line of the human race, procuring

---

[1]–[1] A probable emendation reads, 'and one epistle only of Peter; a second is extant, which, etc.'
[2]–[2] Contrast *Ad Magn.* vi. 1: ' ... Jesus Christ who was with the Father before the ages and appeared in the fullness of time.'

for us salvation thus summarily, so that what we had lost in Adam, that is, the being in the image and likeness of God, that we should regain in Christ Jesus.

Adv. haer. v. xxi. 1

... This is why the Lord declares himself to be the Son of Man, because he recapitulates [sums up] in himself the original man who was the source from which sprang the race fashioned after woman; that as through the conquest of man our race went down to death, so through the victory of man we might ascend to life.

b. The Sanctification of each Stage of Life   *Adv. haer.* ii. xxii. 4

... He came to save all through himself; all, that is, who through him are born into God, infants, children, boys, young men and old. Therefore he passed through every stage of life: he was made an infant for infants, sanctifying infancy; a child among children, sanctifying those of this age, an example also to them of filial affection, righteousness and obedience; a young man amongst young men, an example to them, and sanctifying them to the Lord. So also amongst the older men; that he might be a perfect master for all, not solely in regard to the revelation of the truth, but also in respect of each stage of life. And then he came even unto death that he might be 'the firstborn from the dead, holding the pre-eminence among all' (Col. 1: 18), the Prince of Life, before all and preceding all.

c. The Redemption from the Power of Satan

[An early statement of the ransom theory of the Atonement]

Adv. haer. v. i. 1

... The powerful Word, and true man, redeeming [ransoming] us by his own blood in a reasonable way, gave himself as a ransom for those who have been led into captivity. And since the Apostasy [i.e. the rebellious spirit, Satan] unjustly held sway over us, and though we were by nature [the possession] of Almighty God, estranged us against nature, making us his own disciples; therefore the Word of God, mighty in all things and not lacking in his own justice, acted justly even in the encounter with the Apostasy itself, ransoming from it that which was his own, not by force, in the way in which it secured the sway over us at the beginning, snatching insatiably what was not its own; but by persuasion, as it became God to receive what he wished; by persuasion, not by the use of force, that the principles of justice might not be infringed, and, at the same time, that God's original creation might not perish.

2. By his own blood then the Lord redeemed us, and gave his life for our life, his flesh for our flesh; and he poured out the Spirit of the Father to bring about the union and communion of God and man, bringing down God to men through the Spirit while raising man to God through his incarnation, and in his advent [*or* by his presence] surely and truly giving us incorruption through the communion which we have with God. ...

III. TERTULLIAN

The Incarnation of the Logos   Apol. xxi

[The same teaching is given in more technical language in the treatise *Adversus Praxean*.]

... God made this universe by his word and reason and power. Your philosophers also are agreed that the artificer of the universe seems to be Logos—that is, word and reason ... [e.g. Zeno and Cleanthes]. ... We also lay it down that the word and reason and virtue, by which we have said that God made all things, have spirit as their substance. ... This Word, we have learnt, was produced [*prolatum*] from God, and was generated by being produced, and therefore is called the Son of God, and God, from unity of substance with God. For God too is spirit. When a ray is projected from the sun it is a portion of the whole sun; but the sun will be in the ray because it is a ray of the sun; the substance is not separated but extended. So from spirit comes spirit, and God from God, as light is kindled from light. ... This ray of God ... glided down into a virgin, in her womb was fashioned as flesh, is born as man mixed with God.[1] The flesh was built up by the spirit, was nourished, grew up, spoke, taught, worked, and was Christ.

IV. DIONYSIUS, BISHOP OF ROME (259–268), ON THE TRINITY AND THE INCARNATION

Ap. Athanasius, *De decretis*, 26

[Giving an extract from a letter to Dionysius of Alexandria (247–65), censuring certain of his expressions. The correspondence between the Dionysii illustrates two points of importance in the history of theology: (i) The straitness of the orthodox way, in many places, between the Scylla and Charybdis of opposite heresies—Dionysius of A. approached tritheism in combating Sabellianism;

---

[1] In *Adv. Prax.* xxvii, T. repudiates the notion that the 'mixture' made a 'tertium quid', and safeguards the distinction of 'substances'. 'We see the double status, the two not confused but conjoined in one person.... The spirit in him went about its own business, that is, the deeds of virtue, the works and signs, while the flesh underwent its own sufferings, hungering ... thirsting, weeping ... and in the end it died.'

(ii) The necessity of an agreed technical vocabulary. See note at the end of this extract.]

In this connexion I may naturally proceed to attack those who divide and cut up and destroy that most revered doctrine of the Church of God, the Monarchy, reducing it to three powers and separated substances (ὑποστάσεις) and three deities. For I learn that there are some of you, among the catechists and teachers of the Divine Word, who inculcate this opinion, who are, one might say, diametrically opposed to the views of Sabellius; he blasphemously says that the Son is the Father and the Father the Son, while they in a manner preach three Gods, dividing the sacred Monad into three substances foreign to each other and utterly separate. For the Divine Word must of necessity be united to the God of the Universe, and the Holy Spirit must have his habitation and abode in God; thus it is absolutely necessary that the Divine Triad be summed up and gathered into a unity, brought as it were to an apex, and by that Unity I mean the all sovereign God of the Universe. ... Equally to be censured are they who hold that the Son is a work,[1] and think that the Lord came into being,[1] whereas the Divine Oracles testify to a generation fitting and becoming to him, but not to any fashioning or making. ... For if he came to be a Son, there was when he was not[1]; but he was always, if, that is, he is in the Father, as he himself says, and if the Christ is Word and Wisdom and Power, as, you know, the Divine Scriptures say he is, and if these are attributes of God. For if the Son came into being there was when these attributes were not; therefore there was a time when God was without them; which is most absurd. ... Neither then must we divide into three deities the wonderful and divine Monad: nor hinder the dignity and exceeding majesty of the Lord by describing him as a 'work.' But we must believe in God the Father all sovereign, and in Jesus Christ his Son and in the Holy Spirit, and hold that the Word is united to the God of the universe. For 'I,' says he, 'and the Father are one,' and 'I in the Father and the Father in me.' For thus both the Holy Triad and the holy preaching of the Monarchy will be preserved.

[Note on the terms ὑπόστασις and οὐσία. Primary meaning, that which underlies a thing, which makes it what it is, its essence.
    Used in two senses: (i) General: the essence shared by many particulars, as men, e.g., share a common ὑπόστασις of 'man-ness' in virtue of which they are men; (ii) Particular: the essence of the individual, in virtue of which it is itself;

---

[1] As the Arians held. See pp. 41 ff.

almost='person'. John Smith is John Smith because of an ὑπόστασις, 'John Smithness'.

D. of A. uses ὑπ in sense (ii). D. of R. thinks of sense (i), and certainly many might be led to heresy by misunderstanding the significance of the term as used by D. of A.

There is precisely the same ambiguity in the term οὐσία, which up to the fourth century is used as a synonym (e.g. in the creed of Nicaea and in Athanasius).

The Cappadocian fathers (Basil and the two Gregorys) were largely responsible for the distinction, which gradually became standard, between οὐσία confined to sense (i), and ὑπόστασις confined to sense (ii), 'person or character' (approximately).

Note (*a*) that the Latin for both οὐσία and ὑπόστασις is *substantia*, the exact translation of ὑπόστασις; *essentia*, the equivalent of οὐσία, never gained currency. Hence a further difficulty between D. of A. thinking in Greek and D. of R. thinking in Latin, and in general between East and West; (*b*) that the Greek theologians tended to avoid the use of πρόσωπον to express sense (ii), since the Sabellians had made use of it to describe a mere temporary rôle (see p. 42). Hence the choice of ὑπόστασις to express what the Latins were free to express by the more natural *persona*, the exact equivalent of πρόσωπον (see Bethune-Baker, *Early Hist. of Christian Doctrine*, 116 f., 231–8).]

V. ATHANASIUS ON THE ATONEMENT

Athanasius, 296–373, *De incarnatione* (*c*.318)

a. Salvation by Restoration

VI. [God's goodness could not acquiesce in the ruin of his handiwork.]

VII. But though this is unavoidable, there is on the other side the honour of God's character, so that God may appear consistent in his decree about the death. ... What then ought God to do about this matter? Demand repentance ... ? But this would not safeguard the honour of God's character; for he would remain inconsistent if death did not hold sway over men. ... What else was needed [to restore man from corruption] but the Word of God, who in the beginning made everything from nothing?

For it was his task to restore the corruptible to uncorruption, and to maintain the honour of the Father before all. For being the Word of the Father and above all, it followed that he alone was also able to re-create everything and to be ambassador for all men with the Father.

VIII. ... And thus, taking a body like to ours, because all men were liable to the corruption of death he surrendered it to death instead of all, and offered it to the Father; ... that by all dying in him the law touching the corruption of mankind might be abolished (inasmuch as its power was fulfilled in the Lord's body, and no longer has capacity against men who are like him), and that he might turn back to incorruption men who had reverted to corruption, and quicken them from death by the appropriation of his body and by the grace of his resurrection. ...

IX. ... The Word takes on a body capable of death, in order that, by partaking in the Word that is above all, it might be worthy to die instead of all, and might remain incorruptible through the indwelling Word, and that for the future corruption should cease from all by the grace of his resurrection. ... Hence he did away with death for all who are like him by the offering of a substitute [equivalent]. For it was reasonable that the Word, who is above all, in offering his own temple and bodily instrument as a substitute-life for all, fulfilled the liability in his death, and thus the incorruptible Son of God, being associated with all mankind by likeness to them, naturally clothed all with incorruption in the promise concerning the resurrection.

b. Salvation by Revelation

XI–XIII. [Man had lost the knowledge of God and the image of God in which he was made. How could he be restored? Only by God's Word.]

XIV. ... Therefore, wishing to help men, he [the Word] naturally dwells with men as man, taking to himself a body like other men. And from things of sense, that is by the works of his body, [he teaches them] so that they who were unwilling to know him from his universal providence and guidance may through the works of his body recognize the Word of God in the body and through him come to the knowledge of the Father.

XV. ... For this reason was he born, appeared as man, and died and rose again ... that, whithersoever men have been lured away, he may recall them from thence, and reveal to them his own true Father; as he himself says, 'I came to seek and to save that which was lost.'

VI.   THE ATONEMENT: THE TRANSACTION WITH THE DEVIL
Rufinus of Aquileia, *c.*400, *Comm. in Symb. Apost.* 14 ff.

[This theory of the atonement, by which the deceiver is deceived, is first hinted at in Ignatius, *Ad Eph.* 19, 'The ruler of this age was deceived by the virginity of Mary, her child-bearing, and the death of the Lord,' a passage which appealed to the imagination of many of the fathers. The full story of the ransom and the bait is due to Gregory of Nyssa, *Oratio Catechetica*, xxi–xxvi, reproduced by Rufinus. The ransom idea was repudiated by Gregory of Nazianzus (*Orat.* xlv. 22. 'Was it paid to the evil one? Monstrous thought! The devil receives a ransom not only *from* God but *of* God. ... To the Father? But we were not in bondage to him. ... And could the Father delight in the death of his Son?'). But it seized the imagination and was employed, either as an explanation or as a vivid 'popular' illustration, by Leo, Gregory the Great, Augustine (using the simile of the 'mousetrap'), and many others in the West, until the theory of Anselm took possession of the field.]

The purpose of the incarnation … was that the divine virtue of the Son of God might be as it were a hook hidden beneath the form of human flesh … to lure on the prince of this age to a contest; that the Son might offer him his flesh as a bait and that then the divinity which lay beneath might catch him and hold him fast with its hook. … Then, as a fish when it seizes a baited hook not only fails to drag off the bait but is itself dragged out of the water to serve as food for others; so he that had the power of death seized the body of Jesus in death, unaware of the hook of divinity concealed therein. Having swallowed it, he was caught straightway; the bars of hell were burst, and he was, as it were, drawn up from the pit, to become food for others. …

VII. HERESIES CONCERNING THE PERSON OF CHRIST

a. Docetism

[The assertion that Christ's human body was a phantasm, and that his sufferings and death were mere appearance. 'If he suffered he was not God; if he was God he did not suffer.']

Ignatius, *Ad Trall*, ix, x

Turn a deaf ear therefore when any one speaks to you apart from Jesus Christ, who was of the family of David, the child of Mary, who was truly born, who ate and drank, who was truly persecuted under Pontius Pilate, was truly crucified and truly died. … But if, as some godless men, that is, unbelievers, say, he suffered in mere appearance (being themselves mere appearances), why am I in bonds?

b. Gnosticism

[The attempt to interpret Christ in terms of heathen philosophy, or 'theosophy'.]

1. *The Syrian Type*—Saturninus (or Saturnilus), *c.*120 Irenaeus, *Adv. haer.* 1. xxiv. 1, 2

Saturninus was of Antioch. … Like Menander, he taught that there is one Father, utterly unknown, who made Angels, Archangels, Virtues, Powers; and that the world, and all things therein, was made by certain angels, seven in number. …

The Saviour he declared to be unborn, incorporeal and without form, asserting that he was seen as a man in appearance only. The God of the Jews, he affirms, was one of the Angels; and because all the Princes wished to destroy his Father, Christ came to destroy the God of the

Jews, and to save them that believed on him, and these are they who have a spark of his life. He was the first to say that two kinds of men were fashioned by the Angels, one bad, the other good. And because the demons aid the worst, the Saviour came to destroy the bad men and the Demons and to save the good. But to marry and procreate they say is of Satan. ...

2. *The Egyptian Type*—Basilides, *c*.130   Irenaeus, *Adv. haer.* 1. xxiv. 3–5

[The main tenets of Basilides were reproduced in a more poetical and popular form by Valentinus, *c*.140, the most influential of Gnostic teachers.]

Basilides, that he may seem to have found out something higher and more plausible, vastly extends the range of his teaching, declaring that Mind was first born of the Unborn Father, then Reason from Mind, from Reason, Prudence, from Prudence, Wisdom and Power, and from Wisdom and Power the Virtues, Princes and Angels, whom he also calls 'the First.' By them the First Heaven was made; afterwards others were made, derived from these, and they made another Heaven like to the former, and in like manner others ... [in all, 365 Heavens].

4. Those Angels who hold sway over the later Heaven, which is seen by us, ordered all things that are in the world, and divided among them the earth and the nations upon the earth. And their chief is he who is held to be the God of the Jews. He wished to subdue the other nations beneath his own people, the Jews, and therefore all the other Princes resisted him and took measures against him. ... Then the Unborn and Unnamed Father ... sent his First-begotten Mind (and this is he they call Christ), for the freeing of them that believe in him from those who made the world. And he appeared to the nations of them as a man on the earth, and performed deeds of virtue. Wherefore he suffered not, but a certain Simon, a Cyrenian, was impressed to bear his cross for him; and Simon was crucified in ignorance and error, having been transfigured by him, that men should suppose him to be Jesus, while Jesus himself took on the appearance of Simon and stood by and mocked them. ... If any therefore acknowledge the crucified, he is still a slave and subject to the power of them that made our bodies; but he that denies him is freed from them, and recognises the ordering of the Unborn Father.

5. Again, he holds that salvation concerns only the soul, the body being by nature corruptible. That the Prophecies themselves were from the Princes who made the world, and the Law in particular from their Prince who brought the people out of the land of Egypt. Again, he bids men despise and take no account of things offered to idols, but to use

them without fearfulness, and to treat as a matter of indifference the indulgence in other practices and in lust of all kinds. ...

3. *The Judaizing Type*—Cerinthus and the Ebionites, late first century
Irenaeus, *Adv. haer.* i. xxvi. 1, 2

[The Ebionites are classed with Gnostics because of their connection with Cerinthus.]

A certain Cerinthus[1] also in Asia taught that the world was not made by the first God, but by a certain Virtue far separated and removed from the Principality which is above all things, a Virtue which knows not the God over all. He added that Jesus was not born of a virgin but was the son of Joseph and Mary, like other men, but superior to all others in justice, prudence and wisdom. And that after his baptism Christ descended upon him in the form of a dove, from that Principality which is above all things; and that then he revealed the Unknown Father and performed deeds of virtue, but that in the end Christ flew back, leaving Jesus, and Jesus suffered and rose again, but Christ remained impassible, being by nature spiritual.

2. Those who are called Ebionites ... use only the Gospel according to Matthew; they reject the Apostle Paul, calling him an apostate from the law. The prophetic writings they strive to expound with especial exactness; they are circumcised, and persevere in the customs according to the Law, and in the Jewish mode of life, even to the extent of worshipping Jerusalem, as if it were the abode of God.

4. *The Pontic Type*—Marcion, *c.*160   Irenaeus, *Adv. haer.* i. xxvii. 2–3

Marcion of Pontus took his [Cerdon's] place and amplified his teaching, impudently blaspheming him who is declared to be God by the Law and the Prophets; calling him a worker of evils, delighting in wars, inconstant in judgement and self-contradictory. While he alleges that Jesus came from the Father who is above the God that made the world; that he came to Judaea in the time of Pontius Pilate the governor, who was the procurator of Tiberius Caesar, and was manifest in the form of a man to all that were in Judaea, destroying the prophets and the Law and all the works of that God who made the world, whom he calls also the Ruler of the Universe. Moreover he mutilated the Gospel according to Luke, removing all the narratives of the Lord's birth, and also removing much of the teaching of the discourses of the Lord wherein he is most

---

[1] For the story of S. John and Cerinthus, see p. 74.

manifestly described as acknowledging the maker of this universe to be his father. Thus he persuaded his disciples that he himself was more trustworthy than the apostles, who handed down the Gospel; though he gave to them not a Gospel but a fragment of a Gospel. He mutilated the Epistles of the Apostle Paul in the same manner, removing whatever is manifestly spoken by the Apostle concerning the God who made the world, where he says that he is the father of our Lord Jesus Christ, and setting aside all the Apostle's teaching drawn from the Prophetic writings which predict the advent of the Lord.

2. And then he says that salvation will be of our souls only, of those souls which have learned his teaching; the body, because forsooth it is taken from the earth, cannot partake in salvation.

c. **Monarchianism**
[The emphasis on the unity of God]

1. *Patripassianism*
[The Son identified with the Father]

Tertullian, *Adv. Praxean*, 1

The devil has striven against the truth in manifold ways. He has sometimes endeavoured to destroy it by defending it. He champions the unity of God, the omnipotent creator of the world, only to make out of that unity a heresy. He says that the Father himself descended into the virgin, was himself born of her, himself suffered; in fact that he himself was Jesus Christ. ... It was Praxeas who first brought this kind of perversity from Asia to Rome ... he put the Paraclete to flight and crucified the Father.

2. *Sabellianism*
[One God in three temporary manifestations]

Epiphanius, Bishop of Salamis, *c*.375, *Adv. haereses*, lxii. 1

Not long ago, indeed quite recently, a certain Sabellius came to the fore, and from him the Sabellians get their name. His opinions, with some insignificant exceptions, coincide with those of the Noetians. Most of his followers are to be found in Mesopotamia and at Rome; and it was foolishness that brought them to that state.

Their doctrine is, that Father, Son and Holy Spirit are one and the same being, in the sense that three names are attached to one substance. A close analogy may be found in the body, soul and spirit of man. The body is as it were the Father; the soul is the Son; while the Spirit is to the Godhead as his spirit is to a man. Or take the sun; it is one substance, but it has three manifestations,[1] light, heat, and the orb itself. The heat ... is (analogous to) the Spirit; the light to the Son; while the Father himself is represented by the actual substance. The Son was at one time emitted, like a ray of light; he accomplished in the world all that pertained to the dispensation of the Gospel and man's salvation, and was then taken back into heaven, as a ray is emitted by the sun and then withdrawn again into the sun. The Holy Spirit is still being sent forth into the world and into the successive individuals who are worthy to receive it. ...

[Patripassianism and Sabellianism are now usually called Modal Monarchianism. 'Dynamic' or 'Adoptianist' Monarchianism, associated chiefly with Theodotus of Byzantium, took over the doctrine of the Ebionites (see p. 39) and held the Son to be a mere man endued with Divine power.]

d. Arianism

1. *The Letter of Arius to Eusebius, Bishop of Nicomedia, c.321*
   Theodoret, Bishop of Cyrus, 423–58, *H.E.* I. v

To his dearest lord, the man of God, the faithful and orthodox Eusebius, Arius, unjustly persecuted by Pope Alexander on account of that all-conquering truth which you also champion, sends greeting in the Lord.

Since my father Ammonius is going into Nicomedia, I thought it my duty to salute you by him, and at the same time to advise that naturally charitable disposition of yours, which you display towards the brethren for the sake of God and his Christ, how grievously the bishop attacks and persecutes us, and comes full tilt against us, so that he drives us from the city as atheists because we do not concur with him when he publicly preaches, 'God always, the Son always; at the same time the Father, at the same time the Son; the Son co-exists with God, unbegotten; he is ever-begotten, he is not born-by-begetting; neither by thought nor by any moment of time does God precede the Son; God always, Son always, the Son exists from God himself'.

Eusebius, your brother, Bishop of Caesarea, Theodotus, Paulinus, Athanasius, Gregory, Aetius, and all the other bishops of the East, have been condemned for saying that God existed, without beginning, before the Son; except Philogonius, Hellanicus and Macarius, men who are heretics and unlearned in the faith; some of whom say that the Son is an effluence, others a projection, others that he is co-unbegotten.

To these impieties we cannot even listen, even though the heretics threaten us with a thousand deaths. But what we say and think we both

---

[1] πρόσωπα.

have taught and continue to teach; that the Son is not unbegotten, nor part of the unbegotten in any way, nor is he derived from any substance; but that by his own will and counsel he existed before times and ages fully God, only-begotten, unchangeable.

And before he was begotten or created or appointed or established, he did not exist; for he was not unbegotten. We are persecuted because we say that the Son has a beginning, but God is without beginning. For that reason we are persecuted, and because we say that he is from what is not. And this we say because he is neither part of God nor derived from any substance. For this we are persecuted; the rest you know.

I trust that you are strong in the Lord, mindful of our afflictions, a true fellow-disciple of Lucian, Eusebius.

2. 'The Arian Syllogism'   Socrates (c.440), H.E. i. v

After Peter, Bishop of Alexandria, who was martyred under Diocletian, Achillas succeeded to the see, and after Achillas Alexander succeeded in the above-mentioned period of peace. He, by his fearless conduct of affairs, welded the church together. On one occasion, at a gathering of his presbyters and the rest of the clergy, he essayed a rather ambitious theological disquisition on the Holy Trinity, a metaphysical explanation of the Unity in Trinity. But one of the presbyters of his diocese, Arius by name, a man not lacking in dialectic, thinking that the bishop was expounding the doctrine of Sabellius the Libyan, from love of controversy espoused a view diametrically opposed to the teaching of the Libyan, and attacked the statements of the bishop with energy. 'If,' said he, 'the Father begat the Son, he that was begotten had a beginning of existence; hence it is clear that there was [a time] when[1] the Son was not. It follows then of necessity that he had his existence from the non-existent.'

3. The Letter of the Synod of Nicaea, 325:   Condemnation of Arius
Socrates, H.E. i. ix

To the Church of the Alexandrians, holy, by the grace of God, and great, and to the beloved brethren throughout Egypt, Libya and Pentapolis, the bishops assembled at Nicaea, who constitute the great and holy Synod, send greeting in the Lord.

---

[1] ἦν ὅτε οὐκ ἦν—Arius was careful to avoid saying 'There was a *time* when the Son was not', since he was begotten 'before time'. English idiom cannot render his phrase literally.

2. Since by the grace of God, and at the summons of our most God-beloved sovereign Constantine, a great and holy Synod has been constituted at Nicaea out of various cities and provinces, it appeared to us necessary, on all considerations, to send a letter to you from the sacred Synod, in order that you may be able to know what was discussed and examined, and what was decided and decreed.

3. In the first place, examination was made into the impiety and lawlessness of Arius and his followers, in the presence of our most God-beloved sovereign Constantine; and it was unanimously decided that his impious opinion should be anathematized, together with all the blasphemous sayings and expressions which he has uttered in his blasphemies, affirming that 'the Son of God is from what is not' and 'there was [a time] when he was not'; saying also that the Son of God, in virtue of his free-will, is capable of evil and good, and calling him a creature and a work. All these utterances the holy Synod anathematized, not enduring the hearing of so impious, or rather of so demented, an opinion, and such blasphemous sayings. ...

[For the Creed of Nicaea see Section II, pp. 26 ff.]

e. Attempts to Overthrow the Nicene Formulas

[The decisions of Nicaea were really the work of a minority, and they were misunderstood and disliked by many who were not adherents of Arius. In particular the terms ἐκ τῆς οὐσίας and ὁμοούσιος aroused opposition, on the grounds that they were unscriptual, novel, tending to Sabellianism (taking οὐσία in the sense of particular reality—see note on pp. 34–5) and erroneous metaphysically. Athanasius was twice exiled, and when ninety bishops assembled at Antioch for the dedication of Constantine's 'Golden Church' a council was held and a 'Creed of the Dedication' put forward as a substitute for that of Nicaea, in spite of, or perhaps because of, a letter from Pope Julius urging Athanasius' restoration.]

1. *The Dedication Creed, 341*   Ath. *De synodis*, 23 (*P.G.* xxvi. 721)

In accordance with the tradition of the Gospel and of the Apostles[1] we believe in one God, Father all sovereign, framer, maker and providential ruler of the universe, from whom all things come into being.

And in one Lord Jesus Christ his son, God only-begotten, through whom are all things, who was begotten from the Father before all the ages, God from God, whole from whole,[2] sole from sole, complete from

---

[1] Note the appeal to tradition and Scripture (see note above).

[2] A metaphysical objection to the Nicene terms was that they implied a partition of the deity (οὐσία being taken as meaning ὕλη, material substance), as if Father and Son were (or possessed) portions of one whole.

complete, king from king, lord from lord, living Word, living wisdom, true light, way, truth, resurrection, shepherd, door, unchangeable and immutable; invariable image of the deity,[1] essence, purpose, power and glory of the Father, first-born before every creature [*or* of all creation[2]], who was in the beginning with God, God the Word, according to the statement of the Gospel, 'And the Word was God'; through whom all things were made and in whom all things consist; who in the last days came down from above, and was begotten of a virgin, according to the Scriptures, and was made man, mediator between God and man, Apostle of our faith and Captain of life, as he says: 'I came down from heaven not to do my own will but the will of him that sent me.'[3] Who suffered for us and rose again on the third day, and ascended into heaven, and sat down on the right hand of the Father, and is coming again with glory and power to judge living and dead.

And in the Holy Spirit, who is given to them that believe for comfort, hallowing and perfecting, as also our Lord Jesus Christ commissioned his disciples, saying, 'Go ye forth and make disciples of all the nations, baptizing them into the name of the Father and of the Son and of the Holy Spirit'; namely, of a Father who is truly Father, a Son who is truly Son and a Holy Spirit who is truly Holy Spirit, the titles not being given in a vague or meaningless way[4] but accurately denoting the particular existence[5] [or personality] and rank and glory of each that is so named, so that they are three in existence [personality] but one in agreement.

This is the faith that we hold, from beginning to end, and before God and Christ. Therefore we anathematize every heretical false opinion. If any teaches, contrary to the sound and right faith of the Scriptures, that there was a time or season or age before the begetting of the Son of God, let him be anathema.

If any one says that the Son is a creature as one of the creatures, or an offspring as one of the offspring, a work as one of the works[6] ... let him be anathema.

---

[1] εἰκων . . τῆς οὐσίας . . τοῦ πατρός, susceptible of a Nicene or of an Arian interpretation.

[2] Arians could interpret the words in the latter sense.

[3] A text very congenial to the Arians.

[4] As the Sabellians interpreted the titles they might be called temporary nicknames of the Deity. Sabellianism is regarded as the real foe by the framers of this creed.

[5] ὑπόστασις, see note pp. 34–5.

[6] No real condemnation of Arianism, though the phrasing is meant to convey that impression. Arius avoided saying that there was a *time* when the Son was not; ἦν ὅτε οὐκ ἦν was his phrase. Similarly, he did not teach that the Son was a creature, etc., *as one of the creatures*, etc. The Arian withers were unwrung.

[A shorter version of this creed was made soon afterwards, and this became the basis of Arian confessions in the East. The Western bishops at the Council of Sardica, 343, upheld Athanasius and the Creed of Nicaea, denouncing all attempts to supplant it.

In 344/5 another Synod of Antioch brought out a fresh edition, with elaborate explanations, designed to conciliate the West, which earned for it the title of the 'Macrostich'—'The Long-winded Creed.' It is more 'Nicene' in tone than the earlier editions, but at least susceptible of semi-Arian interpretation, especially in the use of the phrase 'like the Father' (ὅμοιος τῷ Πατρί).]

2. The Blasphemy of Sirmium, 357   Soc. H.E. II. 30

[Athanasius retired into exile in 356, and in the next year a council at Sirmium agreed to a creed of thoroughgoing Arianism to which Hilary of Poitiers ('the Athanasius of the West') gave the name which has clung to it (Hil. *De synodis*, 11).]

Since there seemed to be some dispute concerning the faith, all the matters were carefully examined and discussed at Sirmium in the presence of Valens, Ursacius, Germinius and the rest.

It is agreed that there is one God, the Father all-sovereign, as is universally believed, and his only Son, Jesus Christ our Lord and saviour, begotten from him before ages. But that two Gods must not be spoken of, since the Lord himself says, 'I go to my Father and your Father and my God and your God' (Jn. xx. 17). ...

But many are disturbed by questions about 'substance,' or in Greek *ousia*, that is, to make it more clearly understood, about the term *homoiousion* [of the same substance], or the phrase *homoiousion* [of like substance]. Therefore no mention ought to be made of these, nor any exposition of them in the church; for this reason, that they are not contained in the divine Scriptures and because they are beyond the understanding of man. Also because no one can explain the birth of the Son, of whom it is written 'Who shall explain [declare] his generation' (Is. liii. 8). ... There is no doubt that the Father is greater ... than the Son in honour, renown and deity and in the very name of Father, for the Son himself testifies 'He that sent me is greater than I' (Jn. xiv. 28). And every one knows that this is catholic doctrine, that there are two persons of the Father and the Son; and that the Father is greater, the Son subject together with all the things that the Father has subjected to himself. That the Father has not a beginning, is invisible, immortal and impassible; that the Son has been born from the Father, God from God, light from light ... that from the Virgin Mary he ... the Son of God our Lord and God ... took man, by means of which he shared in suffering.

3. *An Attempted Compromise. The 'Dated Creed',* 359   Soc. H.E. ii. 37;
   Ath. *De syn.* 8

[The 'moderates' ('Acacians'—after Acacius, Bishop of Caesarea—'semi-Arians',
'Homoeans') met at Sirmium to draw up a creed to be accepted by an Oecumenical Council. It derived its nickname from the preface, 'The Catholic Faith was
published ... on May 22.' The Athanasians saw something ludicrous in the
ascription of such a date, or of any precise date, to the Catholic Faith (Ath. *De
Syn.* 8).]

We believe in one God, the only and the true God, the Father all-
sovereign, creator and artificer of all things;

And in one only-begotten Son of God, who, before all ages, and before
all beginning and before conceivable time and before all comprehensible
being [substance], was begotten impassibly from God; and through him
the ages were set in order and all things came into being; begotten as
only-begotten, only from the only Father, God from God, like to the
Father that begat him, according to the Scriptures. No one knows his
begetting save the Father that begat him. We know that he, the only-
begotten Son of God, at the Father's bidding came from the heavens
for the putting away of sin, was born of the Virgin Mary, went about
with the disciples, fulfilled all his stewardship [economy] according to
the Father's will, was crucified, died, and descended to the lower
regions, and set in order all things there, and the gate-keepers of
Hades were affrighted when they saw him (Job xxxviii. 17, LXX); and
he rose from the dead the third day and had converse with the
disciples, and fulfilled all his stewardship; and when thirty days were
accomplished he ascended into the heavens, and sits at the right hand
of the Father, and is to come at the last day in his Father's glory, giving
to each according to his works. ...

But the term 'essence' (οὐσία) has been taken up by the Fathers
rather unwisely, and gives offence because it is not understood by the
people. It is also not contained in the Scriptures. For these reasons we
have decided to do away with it, and that no use at all shall be made of it
for the future in connexion with God, because the divine Scriptures
nowhere use it of the Father and the Son. But we say that the Son is
like the Father in all things, as the holy Scriptures say and teach.

[This compromise was accepted by E. and W., meeting separately. In the W. 'in
all things' was omitted after 'like the Father,' and in this form the creed was issued
as the catholic faith in 360, after a council at Constantinople. 'The world groaned
and marvelled at finding itself Arian' (Jerome, *Dial. adv. Lucif.* 19). But Hilary and
Athanasius (restored 362) gradually converted the 'moderates' and the Nicene
faith and formula were vindicated at the council of Constantinople, 381.

Basil of Ancyra, a member of the conference at Sirmium, was at pains to point out that 'like to the Father in all things' must include likeness in οὐσία and was therefore enough to exclude difference (Epiph., *Haer.* lxxiii. 12–22); and Athanasius and Cyril make use of the term. This was the position taken at the council of Ancyra, 358, called under the presidency of Basil to protest against the 'Blasphemy.' But it was clearly designed as a bridge for at least the semi-Arians. And the omission of 'in all things' made the formula 'like the Father' intolerable to the 'Nicene' party.]

SECTION V

The Problem of the Relation of the Divinity and the Humanity in Christ

[By the end of the Arian controversy the true divinity and true humanity of Christ had been established as Catholic doctrine. Theological speculation was in the next century chiefly concerned with the problem of the mode of the union of deity and manhood. Three important heresies led to the Definition of Chalcedon.]

I. APOLLINARIANISM

[Apollinarius, Bishop of Laodicea (d. 392), was a vigorous opponent of Arianism, and thus his teaching on the union of the two natures in Christ emphasized the divinity of our Lord at the expense of his full manhood. He held that in Christ the logos took the place of the human soul (i.e. the *rational* soul, or mind).

The opinions of A. have come down to us largely in fragments preserved by his critics, and in their representations.]

An Examination of Apollinarianism   Gregory of Nazianzus, Archbishop of Constantinople, 380/1, *Ep.* ci.

Do not let men deceive themselves and others by saying that the 'Man of the Lord,' which is the title they give to him who is rather 'Our Lord and God,' is without a human mind. We do not separate the Man from the Deity, no, we assert the dogma of the unity and identity of the Person, who aforetime was not man but God, the only Son before all ages, who in these last days has assumed manhood also for our salvation; in his flesh passible, in his Deity impassible; in the body circumscribed, uncircumscribed in the Spirit; at once earthly and heavenly, tangible and intangible, comprehensible and incomprehensible; that by one and the same person, perfect man and perfect God, the whole humanity, fallen through sin, might be created anew.

If any one does not believe that holy Mary is the mother of God, he is cut off from the Deity. ... If any assert that the manhood was fashioned and afterwards endued with the Deity, he also is to be condemned. ... If any bring in the idea of two sons, one of God the Father, the other of the mother, may he lose his share in the adoption. ... For the Godhead and the manhood are two natures, as are soul and body, but there are not two Sons or two Gods. ... For both natures are one by the combination, the Godhead made man or the manhood deified, or whatever be the right expression. ...

If any should say that the Deity worked in him by grace ... but was not and is not united with him in essence ... If any assert that he was ... accounted worthy of sonship by adoption ... If any say that his flesh came down from heaven and is not from hence, but is above us, not of us ... (let him be anathema).

If any one has put his trust in him as a man without a human mind, he is himself devoid of mind and unworthy of salvation. For what he has not assumed he has not healed; it is what is united to his Deity that is saved. ... Let them not grudge us our entire salvation, or endue the saviour only with the bones and nerves and appearance of humanity.

But, he urges, he could not contain two complete natures. Certainly not, if you are thinking of him physically. A bushel measure will not hold two bushels. ... But if you will consider the mental and the incorporeal, bear in mind that in my one personality I can contain soul, reason, mind, and Holy Spirit. ... If they rely on the text 'The Word was made flesh' ... they do not realize that such expressions are used by *synecdoche*, whereby the part stands for the whole.

[Apollinarianism was condemned at a synod at Alexandria, 362, by synods at Rome under Damasus, and at Constantinople, 381.]

II. NESTORIANISM

[Nestorius, Bishop of Constantinople, 428–431, represents the extreme of the 'Antiochene' type of thought on this question. The theologians at Antioch tended to stress the reality of the manhood of Christ, in contrast with the more 'mystical' school of Alexandria, whose chief concern was to emphasize his full divinity. Nestorius seems to have learnt his doctrine from his master, Theodore of Mopsuestia, who illustrated the union (or conjunction, συνάφεια, and this word represents more precisely the Nestorian view, and shows its unacceptability) by the union of husband and wife, who become 'one flesh' while remaining two separate natures and persons.]

a. The Anathemas of Cyril of Alexandria   Cyril, Bishop of Alexandria, 412–444, *Ep.* xvii

[The controversy began in 428 with Nestorius' objection to the ascription to the Virgin of the title Θεοτόκος ('God-bearer', not so startling as the English 'Mother of God', the Greek stressing the Deity of the Son rather than the privilege of the mother). The title had been commonly used, at least since Origen, and the 'Alexandrians' were quick to see the implications of his contention. Cyril secured the condemnation of Nestorius by a synod at Rome, Aug. 430; ratified the sentence at a synod at Alexandria, and sent to Constantinople a long letter expounding his doctrine and ending with the twelve anathemas.]

1. If any one does not acknowledge that Emmanuel is in truth God, and that the holy Virgin is, in consequence, 'Theotokos,' for she brought forth after the flesh the Word of God who has become flesh, let him be anathema.

2. If any one does not acknowledge that the Word which is from God the Father was personally [καθ' ὑπόστασιν] united with flesh, and with his own flesh is one Christ, that is, one and the same God and man together, let him be anathema.

3. If any one in the one Christ divides the persons [ὑποστάσεις] after their union, conjoining them with a mere conjunction in accordance with worth, or a conjunction effected by authority or power, instead of a combination according to a union of natures [καθ' νωσιν φυσίκην], let him be anathema.

4. If any one distributes between two characters [πρόσωπα] or persons [ὑποστάσεις] the expressions used about Christ in the gospels, etc. … applying some to the man, conceived of separately, apart from the Word, … others exclusively to the Word … , let him be anathema.

5. If any one presumes to call Christ a 'God-bearing man' [Θεοφόρον νθρωπον] … , let him be anathema.

6. If any one presumes to call the Word the God or Lord of Christ … , let him be anathema.

7. If any one says that Jesus as man was operated [νηργῆσθαι] by God the Word, and that the 'glory of the only-begotten' was attached to him, as something existing apart from himself … , let him be anathema.

8. If anyone presumes to say that 'the man who was assumed is to be worshipped together with the Divine Word' … , let him be anathema.

9. If any one says that the one Lord Jesus Christ was glorified by the Spirit, as if he exercised a power alien to himself which came to him through the Spirit … , let him be anathema.

12. If any one does not confess that the Word of God suffered in the flesh and was crucified in the flesh ... , let him be anathema.

[This letter, with the anathemas, was approved at the Council of Ephesus in 431.]

b. Cyril's Exposition   Cyril, *Ep.* iv
[This 'Dogmatic Letter' (the 'Second letter to Nestorius'), Feb. 430, was read and approved at Ephesus and later at Chalcedon. The later letter with the anathemas (above) was not formally sanctioned at Chalcedon.]

... We do not [in saying that the Word 'was incarnate,' etc.] assert that there was any change in the nature of the Word when it became flesh, or that it was transformed into an entire man, consisting of soul and body; but we say that the Word, in a manner indescribable and inconceivable, united personally [καθ' ὑπόστασιν] to himself flesh animated with a reasonable soul, and thus became man and was called the Son of man. And this was not by a mere act of will or favour, nor simply adopting a rôle [πρόσωπον, *or* taking to himself a person]. The natures which were brought together to form a true unity were different; but out of both is one Christ and one son. We do not mean that the difference of the natures is annihilated by reason of this union; but rather that the Deity and Manhood, by their inexpressible and inexplicable concurrence into unity, have produced for us the one Lord and Son Jesus Christ. It is in this sense that he is said to have been born also of a woman after the flesh, though he existed and was begotten from the Father before all ages. ... It was not that an ordinary man was first born of the holy Virgin, and that afterwards the Word descended upon him. He was united with the flesh in the womb itself, and thus is said to have undergone a birth after the flesh, inasmuch as he made his own the birth of his own flesh.

In the same way we say that he 'suffered and rose again.' We do not mean that God the Word suffered in his Deity ... for the Deity is impassible because it is incorporeal. But the body which had become his own body suffered these things, and therefore he himself is said to have suffered them for us. The impassible was in the body which suffered.

In the same way do we speak of his death. ...

Thus it is one Christ and Lord that we acknowledge, and as one and the same we worship him, not as a man with the addition of the Word ... because the body of the Lord is not alien from the Lord; and it is with this body that he sits at the Father's right hand. ...

We must not then separate the one Lord Christ into two Sons. Some who do this make a show of acknowledging a union of persons; but this does not avail to restore their doctrine to soundness. For Scripture does not say 'the Word united to himself the person of a man,' but 'the Word was made flesh.' And that means precisely this, that he became partaker of flesh and blood, just as we do, and made our body his own. He was born of a woman; but he did not cast aside his being God and his having been begotten of God the Father. He assumed our flesh; but he continued to be what he was. ...

III. EUTYCHIANISM

[In 433 a creed of union was drawn up to reconcile the Alexandrine and Antiocheme views, 'Theotokos' was admitted, and 'union' used instead of 'conjunction'. But neither party was really satisfied, and the Alexandrians, who were troubled at what seemed to them an excessive insistence on the distinction of the two natures, were ready, after the death of Cyril, to support the extreme 'Alexandrianism' of Eutyches, an elderly monk of Constantinople, whose anti-Nestorian zeal far outran his imperceptible theological discretion. In November 448 he was summoned to attend a synod at Constantinople to answer charges of heresy.]

a. **The Admissions of Eutyches**   Conc. Const. Sessio vii. (Mansi, vi. 744)

Flavian (Archbp. of Const.). Do you acknowledge Christ to be of two natures?

Eutyches. I have never yet presumed to speculate about the nature of my God, the Lord of heaven and earth; I admit that I have never said that he is consubstantial with us. ... I confess that the holy Virgin is consubstantial with us, and that of her our God was incarnate. ...

Florentius. Since the mother is consubstantial with us, then surely the Son is also?

E. Please observe that I have not said that the body of a man became the body of God, but the body was human, and the Lord was incarnate of the Virgin. If you wish me to add that his body is consubstantial with ours, I will do so; but I take the word consubstantial in such a way as not to deny that he is the Son of God. Hitherto I have altogether avoided the phrase 'consubstantial after the flesh.' But I will use it now, since your Holiness demands it. ...

Florentius. Do you or do you not admit that our Lord who is of the Virgin is consubstantial [with us] and of two natures after the incarnation?

E. ... I admit that our Lord was of two natures before the union, but after the union one nature. ... I follow the doctrine of the blessed Cyril and the holy fathers and the holy Athanasius. They speak of two natures before the union, but after the union and incarnation they speak of one nature not two.

[Eutyches was condemned, and appealed to Leo, Bishop of Rome, who upheld Flavian. But the Emperor Theodosius II called a Council at Ephesus under the presidency of Dioscorus, successor to Cyril in the see of Alexandria and heir to all that was worst in Cyril's character and methods of theological controversy, and at the 'Robber Council,' 449 ('Latrocinium'—Leo, *Ep.* 45), Eutyches was upheld and Flavian deposed. But Theodosius died in 450 and in the next year the Council of Chalcedon approved the 'Tome of Leo' and formulated the 'Chalcedonian Definition.']

b. The Tome of Leo   Leo, Bishop of Rome, 440–461, *Ep.* xxviii (to Flavian), 13 June 449

['Peter has spoken through Leo. This is the teaching of Cyril. Anathema to him that believes otherwise' (the bishops at Chalcedon).]

I. [Eutyches' foolishness and misunderstanding of Scripture.]

II. He did not realize what he ought to hold concerning the Incarnation of the Word of God, and he had not the will to seek out the light of understanding by diligent study in the wide range of Holy Scripture. But he might at least have received with careful hearing that common and universal confession, in which the whole body of the faithful acknowledge their belief in GOD THE FATHER ALMIGHTY AND IN JESUS CHRIST HIS ONLY SON OUR LORD WHO WAS BORN OF THE HOLY GHOST AND THE VIRGIN MARY. For by these three statements the devices of almost all heretics are overthrown. God is believed to be both Almighty and Father; it follows that the Son is shown to be co-eternal with him, differing in no respect from the Father. For he was born God of God, Almighty of Almighty, co-eternal of eternal; not later in time, not inferior in power, not dissimilar in glory, not divided in essence. The same only-begotten, eternal Son of the eternal Father was born of the Holy Ghost and the Virgin Mary. But this birth in time has taken nothing from, and added nothing to, that divine eternal nativity, but has bestowed itself wholly on the restoration of man, who had been deceived: that it might overcome death and by its own virtue overthrow the devil who had the power of death. For we could not overcome the author of sin and death, unless he had taken our nature and made it his own, whom sin could not defile nor death retain, since he was conceived of the Holy Spirit, in the womb of his Virgin Mother, whose virginity remained entire in his birth as in his conception. ... That birth, uniquely marvellous and marvellously unique, ought not to be understood in such a way as to preclude the distinctive properties of the kind [i.e. of humanity] through the new mode of creation. For it is true that the Holy Spirit gave fruitfulness to the Virgin, but the reality of his body was received from her body. ...

III. Thus the properties of each nature and substance were preserved entire, and came together to form one person. Humility was assumed by majesty, weakness by strength, mortality by eternity; and to pay the debt that we had incurred, an inviolable nature was united to a nature that can suffer. And so, to fulfil the conditions of our healing, the man Jesus Christ, one and the same mediator between God and man, was able to die in respect of the one, unable to die in respect of the other.

Thus there was born true God in the entire and perfect nature of true man, complete in his own properties, complete in ours [*totus in suis, totus in nostris*]. By 'ours' I mean those which the Creator formed in us at the beginning, which he assumed in order to restore; for in the Saviour there was no trace of the properties which the deceiver brought in, and which man, being deceived, allowed to enter. He did not become partaker of our sins because he entered into fellowship with human infirmities. He assumed the form of a servant without the stain of sin, making the human properties greater, but not detracting from the divine. For that 'emptying of himself,' whereby the invisible rendered himself visible, and the Creator and Lord of all willed to be a mortal, was a condescension of compassion, not a failure of power. Accordingly, he who made man, while he remained in the form of God, was himself made man in the form of a servant. Each nature preserves its own characteristics without diminution, so that the form of a servant does not detract from the form of God.

The devil boasted that man, deceived by his guile, had been deprived of the divine gifts and, stripped of the dower of immortality, had incurred the stern sentence of death; that he himself had found some consolation in his plight from having a companion in sin. He boasted too that God, because justice required it, had changed his purpose in respect of man whom he had created in such honour, therefore there was need of a dispensation for God to carry out his hidden plan, that the unchangeable God, whose will cannot be deprived of its own mercy, might accomplish the first design of his affection towards us by a more secret mystery; and that man, driven into sin by the devil's wicked craftiness, should not perish contrary to the purpose of God.

IV. The son of God therefore came down from his throne in heaven without withdrawing from his Father's glory, and entered this lower world, born after a new order, by a new mode of birth. After a new order, inasmuch as he is invisible in his own nature, and he became visible in ours; he is incomprehensible[1] and he willed to be comprehended;

---

[1] 'Not spatially circumscribed.'

continuing to be before time, he began to exist in time. ... By a new
mode of birth, inasmuch as virginity inviolate which knew not the desire
of the flesh supplied the material of flesh. From his mother the Lord took
nature, not sin. Jesus Christ was born from a virgin's womb, by a
miraculous birth. And yet his nature is not on that account unlike to
ours, for he that is true God is also true man. There is no unreality in this
unity since the humility of the manhood and the majesty of the deity are
alternated [*invicem sunt, or* 'exist in reciprocity']. For just as the God
[deity] is not changed by his compassion, so the man [manhood] is not
swallowed up by the dignity [of the Godhead]. Each nature [form, *sc.* of
God and of servant] performs its proper functions in communion with
the other; the Word performs what pertains to the Word, the flesh what
pertains to the flesh. The one is resplendent with miracles, the other
submits to insults. The Word withdraws not from his equality with the
Father's glory; the flesh does not desert the nature of our kind. ... And
so it does not belong to the same nature to say 'I and the Father are one'
and 'The Father is greater than I.'[1] For although in the Lord Jesus Christ
there is one person of God and man, yet the source of the contumely
which both share is distinct from the source of the glory which they also
share. ...

c. **The Definition of Chalcedon**, 451   Council of Chalcedon, Actio V.
Mansi, vii. 116 f.

Therefore, following the holy Fathers, we all with one accord teach men
to acknowledge one and the same Son, our Lord Jesus Christ, at once
complete in Godhead and complete in manhood, truly God and truly
man, consisting also of a reasonable soul and body; of one substance
[ὁμοούσιος] with the Father as regards his Godhead, and at the same
time of one substance with us as regards his manhood; like us in all
respects, apart from sin; as regards his Godhead, begotten of the Father
before the ages, but yet as regards his manhood begotten, for us men and
for our salvation, of Mary the Virgin, the God-bearer [Θεοτόκος]; one
and the same Christ, Son, Lord, Only-begotten, recognized IN TWO
NATURES, WITHOUT CONFUSION, WITHOUT CHANGE, WITHOUT DIVISION,
WITHOUT SEPARATION;[2] the distinction of natures being in no way
annulled by the union, but rather the characteristics of each nature
being preserved and coming together to form one person and subsistence
[ὑπόστασις], not as parted or separated into two persons, but one and

---

[1] Jn. x. 30, xiv. 28. Contrast the 4th Anathema of Cyril, p. 49.
[2] ἐν δύο φύσεσιν, ἀσυγχύτως ἀτρέπτως, ἀδιαιρέτως ἀχωρίστως.

the same Son and Only-begotten God the Word, Lord Jesus Christ; even as the prophets from earliest times spoke of him, and our Lord Jesus Christ himself taught us, and the creed of the Fathers has handed down to us.

SECTION VI
Pelagianism. Human Nature, Sin, and Grace

I. THE TEACHING OF PELAGIUS

[Pelagius was a British monk, probably of Irish origin. He came to Rome in 400 and was distressed at the low state of conduct there. Feeling that there was need of more moral effort, he was shocked by the prayer in S. Augustine's *Confessions*, 'Give what thou commandest and command what thou wilt.' His teaching seems to have aroused no stir until he went to Carthage after the sack of Rome in 410.]

a. Letter to Demetrias   *Ep. ad Demetriadem*, 16, *ad fin.*, *P.L.* xxxiii. 1110

... Instead of regarding the commands of our illustrious King as a privilege ... we cry out at God, in the scornful sloth of our hearts, and say, 'This is too hard and difficult. We cannot do it. We are only human, and hindered by the weakness of the flesh.' Blind folly and presumptuous blasphemy! We ascribe to the God of knowledge the guilt of twofold ignorance; ignorance of his own creation and of his own commands. As if, forgetting the weakness of men, his own creation, he had laid upon men commands which they were unable to bear. And at the same time (God forgive us!) we ascribe to the Just One unrighteousness and cruelty to the Holy One; the first, by complaining that he has commanded the impossible, the second, by imagining that a man will be condemned by him for what he could not help; so that (the blasphemy of it!) God is thought of as seeking our punishment rather than our salvation. ... No one knows the extent of our strength better than he who gave us that strength. ... He has not willed to command anything impossible, for he is righteous; and he will not condemn a man for what he could not help, for he is holy.

b. Pelagius on Human Freedom   Pelagius, *Pro libero arbitrio, ap.*
Augustine, *De gratia Christi* (418)

We distinguish three things and arrange them in a definite order. We put
in the first place '*posse*' [ability, possibility]; in the second, '*velle*' [voli-
tion]; in the third, '*esse*' [existence, actuality]. The *posse* we assign to
nature, the *velle* to will, the *esse* to actual realization. The first of these,
posse, is properly ascribed to God, who conferred it on his creatures;
while the other two, *velle* and *esse*, are to be referred to the human agent,
since they have their source in his will. Therefore man's praise lies in his
willing and doing a good work; or rather this praise belongs both to man
and to God who has granted the possibility of willing and working, and
who by the help of his grace ever assists this very possibility. That a man
has this possibility of willing and effecting any good work is due to God
alone. ... Therefore (and this must be often repeated because of your
calumnies), when we say that it is possible for a man to be without sin, we
are even then praising God by acknowledging the gift of possibility which
we have received. He it is that bestowed this *posse* on us, and there is no
occasion for praising the human agent when we are treating of God
alone; for the question is not about *velle* or *esse*, but solely about the
possible.

c. Pelagius Denies Original Sin   *Pro lib. arb., ap.* Aug. *De peccato
originali,* 14

Everything good and everything evil, in respect of which we are either
worthy of praise or of blame, is *done by us,* not *born with us.* We are not
born in our full development, but with a capacity for good and evil;
we are begotten as well without virtue as without vice, and before the
activity of our own personal will there is nothing in man but what God
has stored in him.

II.   TEACHING ASCRIBED TO PELAGIUS AND COELESTIUS
Aug. De gestis Pelagii, 23

[Coelestius, a disciple of Pelagius, was accused at a synod of Carthage, 412, and
condemned. Pelagius was opposed in Palestine by Jerome, but his teaching was
approved after two synods in 415. Aug. *d. g. P.* deals with the second of these
synods.]

Then follow statements alleged against Pelagius, which are said to be
found in the teaching of Coelestius, his disciple;

   i. Adam was created mortal, and he would have died, whether he
sinned or not.

ii. Adam's sin injured himself alone, not the human race.

iii. The Law, as well as the Gospel, leads to the Kingdom.

iv. There were men without sin before Christ's coming.

v. New-born infants are in the same condition as Adam before the Fall.

vi. It is not through the death or the fall of Adam that the whole human race dies, nor through the resurrection of Christ that the whole human race rises again.

Certain other points were raised against him, put forward on the mention of my name ... ;

That a man can be without sin, if he choose.

That infants, even if unbaptized, have eternal life.

That rich men who have been baptized are not credited with any good that they may seem to have done, unless they give up all they have; nor otherwise can they enter the Kingdom of God.

III. THE DOCTRINE OF AUGUSTINE

a. The Saying which Troubled Pelagius   Augustine, Bishop of Hippo, 396–430, *Confessions* (400), x. 40

I have no hope at all but in thy great mercy. Grant what thou commandest and command what thou wilt. Thou dost enjoin on us continence, 'And when I knew,' saith one, 'that none could be continent, except God gave it, this also was itself a part of wisdom, to know whose gift it was' (Wisdom viii. 21, Vulgate). Truly by continence are we bound together and brought back into that unity from which we were dissipated into a plurality. For he loves thee too little who loves anything together with thee, which he loves not for thy sake. O love that ever burnest and art never quenched! O Charity, my God, enkindle me! Thou commandest continence. Grant what thou commandest and command what thou wilt.

b. Augustine on Grace   *De spiritu et littera* (412), 5

We for our part assert that the human will is so divinely aided towards the doing of righteousness that, besides being created with the free choice of his will, and besides the teaching which instructs him how he ought to live, he receives also the Holy Spirit, through which there arises in his heart a delight in and a love of that supreme and unchangeable Good which is God; and this arises even now, while he still walks by faith and not by sight. That by this earnest, as it were, of the free gift he may burn to cleave to his Maker, and be on fire to approach to a share in the true light; that from him from whom he has his being he may also derive his blessedness. A man's free choice avails only to lead him to sin, if the way of truth be hidden from him. And when it is plain to him what he should do and to what he should aspire, even then, unless he feel delight and live therein, he does not perform his duty, nor undertake it, nor attain to the good life. But to the end that we may feel this affection 'the love of God is shed abroad in our hearts' not 'through the free choice which springs from ourselves,' but 'through the Holy Spirit which has been given to us' (Romans iv. 5).

Prevenient Grace   Aug. *Ep.* ccxvii (427) (to Vitalis)

[Against the 'semi-Pelagian' denial of prevenient grace. The main argument is that if the first movement towards God must come of man's free choice, how can we pray to God to effect the conversion of the heathen?]

30. ... If, as I prefer to think in your case, you agree with us in supposing that we are doing our duty in praying to God, as our custom is, for them that refuse to believe, that they may be willing to believe, and for those who resist and oppose his law and doctrine that they may believe and follow it. If you agree with us in thinking that we are doing our duty in giving thanks to God, as is our custom, for such people when they have been converted ... then you are surely bound to admit that the wills of men are *prevented*[1] by the grace of God, and that it is God who makes them to will the good which they refused; for it is God whom we ask so to do, and we know that it is meet and right to give thanks to him for so doing. ...

Irresistible Grace   Aug. *De correptione et gratia* (427), 34-8

34. Now two kinds of assistance are to be distinguished. There is the assistance without which a state of affairs does not come about [*adjutorium sine quo non fit*], and there is the assistance by which it does come about [*quo fit*]. For example, we cannot live without food, but the fact that food is available will not keep a man alive if he desires to die. ... But in the case of blessedness, when it is bestowed on a man who is without it, he becomes perpetually blessed. ... Thus this is an assistance both *sine quo non* and *quo*. ... Now the first man was created upright, in a state of

---

[1] *Voluntates hominum Dei gratia praeveniri* 'are started,' 'set going,' hence 'prevenient' grace. Cf. BCP collect for Easter 'by thy special grace preventing us thou dost put into our minds good desires ... ' and Trinity xvii 'that thy grace may always prevent and follow us ... ' and in the Communion Service 'Prevent us ... and further us.'

We pray for 'prevenient' grace, to be followed by 'co-operating' grace.

good; he was given the possibility of sinlessness [*posse non peccare*], the possibility of immortality [*posse non mori*], the possibility of not losing that state of good: and in addition he was given the aid of perseverance, not so that by this assistance it might come about that he should in fact persevere [i.e. not the *a. quo fit*], but because without it he could not persevere of his free choice [i.e. the *a. sine quo non*]. To the saints, on the other hand, who are predestinated to the kingdom of God by the grace of God, the aid of perseverance which is given is not that granted to the first man, but that kind which brings the gift of actual perseverance [i.e. it is *quo fit*, not merely *sine quo non*] ... by means of which they cannot but persevere.

38. ... Since they will not in fact persevere unless they both *can* and *will* ... their will is so kindled by the Holy Spirit that they *can*, just because they *will*, and they *will* just because *God works in them so to will*. For if, in the great weakness of this mortal life (a weakness, remember, that had to be, in order that, to exclude boasting, 'strength might be made perfect in weakness'), if in this weakness their own will should be left unaided, so that, *if they willed*, they might continue in the help of God, without which they could not persevere, and if God should not work in them so to will in the midst of so many and so great infirmities, then their will itself would fail and they would not be able to persevere. They would either fail to will, through infirmity, or their will would be too weak to secure its own fulfilment.

Therefore assistance was bestowed on the weakness of man's will, that it might be unalterably and irresistibly influenced by divine grace; and that, weak as it was, it might still not fail nor be overcome by any adversity. So it came about that man's will, when weak and powerless, and as yet in a lowly state of good, still persevered, by God's strength, in that good; while the will of the first man, though strong and healthy, possessed of the power of free choice, and in a state of greater good, did not persevere in that good; and the reason was that though God's assistance was not lacking, it was the assistance without which it could not persevere even if it so willed, and not assistance of that kind by which God might work in man so to will. Doubtless to the strongest he vouchsafed to do what he willed; but for them that were weak he reserved his own gift whereby they should most irresistibly will what is good, and most irresistibly refuse to forsake it.

c. Augustine's Teaching on Predestination   De dono perseverantiae (428), 35

Will any man presume to say that God did not foreknow those to whom he would grant belief? And if he foreknew this, then he certainly foreknew his own kindness, with which he vouchsafes to deliver us. This, and nothing but this, is the predestination of saints; namely, the foreknowledge and planning of God's kindnesses, by which they are most surely delivered, whoever are delivered. As for the rest, where are they left by God's righteous judgement save in the mass of perdition where they of Tyre and Sidon were left? And they, moreover, would have believed, had they seen the wondrous miracles of Christ. But it was not granted to them to believe, and therefore the means of believing was denied them. From this it is clear that some have in their minds a gift of understanding naturally divine, by which they may be moved to faith, if they hear the words or see the signs which are adapted to their intelligences. And yet if they are not, in the higher judgement of God, separated from the mass of perdition by the predestination of grace, then neither those words nor those deeds are applied to them. ... The Jews, on the other hand, were left in the same mass of ruin because they could not believe the ... mighty works which were done before their eyes. ... 'He hath blinded their eyes and hardened their heart, that they should not see with their eyes and understand with their heart, and be converted, and I should heal them' (Isaiah vi. 10, John xii. 40). Now the eyes of the men of Tyre and Sidon were not so blinded, nor their heart so hardened, for they would have believed, had they seen the mighty works such as the Jews saw. But their capacity for belief availed them nothing, because they were not so predestinated by him whose 'judgements are inscrutable and whose ways past finding out'. ... (Rom. xi. 33).

d. Augustine's Conception of Freedom

'Whose service is perfect freedom' (BCP Collect for Peace)

De civitate Dei, x. 30

[For Augustine freedom means not the freedom of responsible choice but the freedom of unimpeded activity. He speaks of *liberum arbitrium* but he thinks of *libera voluntas*.]

... [describing the eternal felicity of the City of God] ...

It does not follow that they will not have free choice because sins will have no power to attract them. Nay rather, it will be more truly free, when set free from the delight of sinning, to enjoy the steadfast delight of not sinning. For the first freedom of choice, which was given to man when he was created upright, gave the ability not to sin, but also the ability to sin. This new freedom will be the more powerful just because it will not have power to sin; and this, not by its unaided natural ability, but by the gift of God. ... God is unable to sin; he who partakes of God has received from him the inability to sin. ... The first immortality, which Adam lost by sinning, was the ability not to die [*posse non mori*], the new immortality will be the inability to die [*non posse mori*]. In the same way, the first freedom of choice conferred the ability not to sin [*posse non peccare*]; the new freedom will confer the inability to sin [*non posse peccare*]. ... It surely cannot be said that God himself has not freedom of choice, because he is unable to sin?

e. **Freedom and Grace**   Aug. *Ep.* clvii (to Hilarius)

[Augustine's doctrine of grace and predestination is religious rather than philosophical; it springs, that is, from his personal experience of conversion, and from his sense of his own helplessness and dependence on God. The moral objections of Pelagius are of less account to him. Thus a more personal statement like this seems more just to him and more persuasive to us than the elaborations and rhetoric of his treatises.]

5. Freedom of choice then avails for the performance of good works if it receive divine assistance; and this comes about by praying and acting with humility. But, if a man is deprived of divine assistance, then, be he never so excellent in knowledge of the Law, he will in no wise be firm and solid in righteousness, but blown up with the deadly swelling of an irreverent pride. The Lord's prayer itself teaches this. For it were vain for us to pray to God and say 'Lead us not into temptation' if this had been put in our power, so that we could fulfil our petition with no aid from him. ...

8. Now this free will [*libera voluntas*] will be the more free the more it is healthy; and it will be the more healthy the more it is subject to the divine mercy and grace. For of itself the will prays and says, 'Direct my steps according to thy word, and no unrighteousness shall have domination over me' (Ps. cxix. 133). How can a will be free if it is under the domination of unrighteousness? And observe who it is that is invoked, in order to escape that domination. It says, not, 'Direct my steps according to free choice, etc.,' but, 'according to thy word, etc.' It is a prayer, not a promise, a confession, not a profession; a desire for the fullness of liberty, not a boast of personal ability. ...

10. This freedom of will [*voluntas*] is not therefore removed because it is assisted; it is assisted just because it is not removed. For he that says to God 'be thou my helper' confesses that he wills to fulfil what he has

commanded, but that he asks the aid of him who commanded that he may have power to fulfil it. So that man 'when he knew that none could be continent except God granted it (Wisdom viii. 21, Vulg.) approached God and prayed.' Assuredly he approached willingly, he prayed willingly. He would not have prayed, if he had not had the will. But, if he had not prayed, what power would his will have had? Although he may have the power before he make his prayer, what does it avail him, unless he render thanks, as a result of that power, to him from whom he has to ask the power which he as yet has not? ...

Grace will assist us if we are not presumptuous about our own virtues, and 'mind not high things but are of one mind with the humble' (Romans xii. 16, Vulg. *humilibus consentientes*); if we give thanks for what we already have power to do, while for those things for which we have not yet power to entreat God in supplication with yearning desire [will—*voluntas*]; if we support our prayer with fruitful works of kindness, by giving, that it may be given to us, by forgiving, that we may be forgiven. ...

IV. THE COUNCIL OF CARTHAGE, 417.
CANONS ON SIN AND GRACE
Mansi, iii. 811

[The African Church refused to accept the decision of Palestine (see p. 56). Two synods in 416 renewed the condemnation of Coelestius, and this was approved by Pope Innocent I. But Innocent died in that year and his successor Zosimus supported Pelagius and Coelestius. But the Council of Carthage pronounced decisively against the Pelagian views, Imperial edicts were issued against the heretics, and Zosimus accepted the African views. Many bishops subscribed unwillingly and eighteen were deposed.]

1. If any one says that Adam, the first man, was created mortal, so that, whether he sinned or not, he would have died from natural causes, and not as the wages of sin, let him be anathema.

2. If any one says that new-born children need not be baptized, or that they are baptized for the remission of sins, but that no original sin is derived from Adam to be washed away in the laver of regeneration, so that in their case the baptismal formula 'for the remission of sins' is to be taken in a fictitious and not in its true sense, let him, etc.

3. That there is in the Kingdom of Heaven, or in any other place, any middle place, where children who depart this life unbaptized live in bliss.
...

4. That the grace of God, by which man is justified through Jesus Christ our Lord, avails only for the remission of sins already committed, and not for assistance to prevent the commission of sins. ...

5. That this grace ... only helps us to avoid sin in this way; that by it we are given by revelation an understanding of God's commands that we may learn what we ought to strive for and what we ought to avoid, but that it does not give us also the delight in doing, and the power to do, what we have recognized as being good. ...

6. That the grace of justification is given to us that we may more easily perform by means of grace that which we are bidden to do by means of our free choice; as if we could fulfil those commands even without the gift of grace, though not so easily. ...

7. That the words of the Apostle S. John, 'If we say that we have no sin, etc.' (1 Jn. i. 8), are to be taken as meaning that we should say that we have sin not because it is true but out of humility. ...

8. That in the Lord's prayer the saints say 'Forgive us our trespasses' not for themselves, because for them this prayer is unnecessary, but for others among their people who are sinners. ...

9. That the saints say these words out of humility and not because they are true. ...

V. THE SYNOD OF ARLES, C.473. 'SEMI-PELAGIANISM'[1]

Faustus of Rhegium, *Ep. ad Lucidum* (473), *P.L.* liii. 683. Mansi, vii. 1010

[The decisions of Carthage were not popular throughout the Church, and the full Augustinian doctrine did not win wide acceptance. Pelagius, many thought then, as many think now, was in the main right in what he affirmed (i.e. human responsibility, the need for co-operation with grace, that there is meaning in calling God just, etc.), but generally wrong in what he denied (the inherited disposition to sin, the need for infant baptism, and the actual sinfulness of mankind). In Gaul John Cassian and Faustus of Rhegium tried to avoid the extremes on both sides, and under the influence of their teaching the Synod of Arles condemned these propositions:]

That the labour of human obedience is not to be joined with the grace of God.

That after the fall of the first man free choice [*arbitrium voluntatis*] was utterly extinguished.

---

[1] Note that the label 'semi-Pelagianism', with the suggestion 'half-heretical', is inaccurate when applied to views of this kind. It is often to this day ignorantly employed as a term of reproach against similar views. 'Semi-Augustinianism would be at least as accurate and less question-begging' (Bethune-Baker, *Early Hist. of Christian Doctrine*, 321).

That Christ has not undergone death for the salvation of all men.

That the foreknowledge of God impels man violently towards death, or that those who perish perish in accordance with the will [*voluntas*] of God.

That any man who has sinned after baptism lawfully received dies 'in Adam' [i.e. through original sin].

That from Adam up to Christ none from among the Gentiles were saved against the coming of Christ [*in adventum Christi*] by the first grace of God [i.e. through the law of nature], and that they lost their freedom of choice in their first parent.

That the patriarchs and prophets or all the greatest saints lived in paradise even before the times of redemption.

[The following assertion was made:]

Man's effort and endeavour is to be united with God's grace; man's freedom of will [*libertatem voluntatis*] is not extinct but attenuated and weakened, he that is saved is in danger, and he that has perished could have been saved.

VI. THE COUNCIL OF ORANGE, 529. REACTION FROM 'SEMI-PELAGIANISM'
Mansi, viii. 712 ff.

[Twenty-five canons were passed, accepting most of the Augustinian teaching, very largely in A.'s own words. But predestination to evil (which A. did not explicitly teach, though it seems implicit in much of his doctrine and was emphasized by many of his followers) was anathematized. These propositions were condemned:]

Canon 1. That by the offence of the disobedience of Adam it was not the whole man [i.e. in respect of body and soul] that was changed for the worse, but that the freedom of his soul remained unimpaired, and only his body was subject to corruption ... (Ezek. xviii. 20; Rom. vi. 16; 2 Peter ii. 19).

2. That Adam's disobedience injured himself alone and not his offspring, or that only the death of the body, the wages of sin, was transmitted through one man to the whole human race, and not sin also, the death of the soul ... (Rom. v. 12).

3. That God's grace can be bestowed in response to human invocation, but that it is not that very grace that brings it about that it is invoked by us ... (Rom. x. 20; Is. lxv. 1).

4. That in order that we may be purged from sin our will [*voluntas*] anticipates God; and that it is not through the infusion of the Holy Spirit and his operation in us that we wish to be purged ... (Prov. viii. 35, 'The will is prepared by the Lord,' LXX; Phil. ii. 13).

5. That the beginning, as well as the increase of faith and the very desire of believing ... is not through the gift of grace ... but is in us by nature ... (Phil. i. 6, 29; Eph. ii. 8).

6. That to us who, without the grace of God, believe, will, desire, etc. ... mercy is divinely bestowed, and not that it is through the action of the Holy Spirit that we believe, etc., as we ought ... (1 Cor. iv. 7).

7. That by the force of nature we can rightly think or choose anything that is good ... without the Holy Spirit's illumination. ... (Jn. xv. 5; 2 Cor. iii. 5).

8. That some can come to the grace of baptism by mercy, but others through free choice (which is certainly corrupted in all born since the fall) ... (Jn. vi. 4; Matt. xvi. 17; 1 Cor. xii. 13).

... [A series of less formal articles.] ...

12. God loves us as being such as we are about to become by his gift, not as we are by our own merit.

. . . .

25. Truly the gift of God is to love God. He has given it that he may be loved, he who loves when he is not loved. We were loved when we pleased him not, that there might spring up in us that which should please him (Rom. v. 5).

[These affirmations are appended:]

That through the sin of the first man, free choice was so warped and weakened that thereafter no one is able to love God as he ought, or believe in God, or do anything for God that is good, except the grace of God's mercy prevent [*praeveniret*, see note on p. 60] him (Phil. i. 6, 29; Eph. ii. 8; 1 Cor. iv. 7, vii. 25; James i. 17; Jn. iii. 27).

We also believe this according to the Catholic Faith, that after grace has been received through baptism all the baptized, with the aid and co-operation of Christ, have the power and the duty to perform all things that pertain to the soul's salvation, if they will labour faithfully.

But not only do we not believe that some have been predestinated to evil by the divine power, but also, if there be any who will believe so evil a thing, we say to them, with all detestation, anathema. ...

[The synods of Arles and Orange have been included in this section for convenience. For the final decision of the Roman Church on this doctrine, at Trent, see pp. 264 ff.]

[In all these documents on grace and free will the term *liberum arbitrium* has been translated 'freedom of choice' or 'free choice' to distinguish it from *voluntas*, which has a more emotional and less judicial connotation. It is not suggested that our authors always felt or observed this distinction; in fact it is suggested on p. 60 that the failure to do so is a source of confusion in the thought of Augustine. But that is all the more reason for distinguishing the terms.]

SECTION VII

The Church, the Ministry, and the Sacraments

I. THE CHRISTIAN MINISTRY AT THE
END OF THE FIRST CENTURY
Clement of Rome (*c*.95), *Epistle to the Corinthians*, xl ff.

xl. Since all this is clear, and we have gazed into the depths of Divine knowledge, we are bound to perform in due order all that the master bade us accomplish at their proper seasons. He ordered that the offerings and services should be performed at their appointed times and seasons, not at random and without order; and also by his own supreme will he himself appointed the place and the ministers of their performance, that all might be done according to his good pleasure and so be acceptable to his will. Therefore they that make their offerings at the appointed seasons are acceptable and blessed, for in following the ordinances of the master they do not err. To the high priest are given his special ministrations, a special place is reserved for the priests, and special duties are imposed upon the levites, while the layman is bound by the ordinances concerning the laity.

xli. Let each of you, brethren, in his own order give thanks to God with a good conscience, not transgressing the appointed rule of his service, in reverence. For it is not in every place, brethren, that the perpetual sacrifices are offered, or the freewill offerings, the sin offerings and the guilt offerings, but in Jerusalem only; and even there the offering is made not in every place, but before the sanctuary at the altar, when the offering has been inspected by the high priest and ministers aforesaid.

Therefore all who act contrary to the due performance of his will incur the penalty of death. You see, brethren, that, as we have been accounted worthy of a fuller knowledge, so we are exposed to a greater peril.

xlii. The Apostles for our sakes received the gospel from the Lord Jesus Christ; Jesus Christ was sent from God. Christ then is from God, and the Apostles from Christ. Both therefore came in due order from the will of God. Having therefore received his instructions and being fully assured through the Resurrection of our Lord Jesus Christ, they went forth with confidence in the word of God and with full assurance of the Holy Spirit, preaching the gospel that the Kingdom of God was about to come. And so, as they preached in the country and in the towns, they appointed their firstfruits (having proved them by the Spirit) to be bishops and deacons [overseers and ministers] of them that should believe. And this was no novelty, for of old it had been written concerning bishops and deacons; for the Scripture says in one place, 'I will set up their bishops in righteousness, and their deacons in faith' (Is. lx. 17).[1]

xliv. Our Apostles knew also, through our Lord Jesus Christ, that there would be strife over the dignity of the bishop's office. For this reason therefore, having received complete foreknowledge, they appointed the aforesaid, and after a time made provision that on their death other approved men should succeed to their ministry. . . .

II. THE MINISTRY AND SACRAMENTS
Ignatius (*c*.112), *Epistle to the Smyrnaeans*, c. viii

Avoid divisions as the beginning of evils. All of you follow the bishop as Jesus Christ followed the Father, and follow the presbytery as the Apostles; and respect the deacons as the commandment of God. Let no man perform anything pertaining to the church without the bishop. Let that be considered a valid Eucharist over which the bishop presides, or one to whom he commits it. Wherever the bishop appears, there let the people be, just as, wheresoever Christ Jesus is, there is the Catholic Church. It is not permitted either to baptize or hold a love-feast apart from the bishop. But whatever he may approve, that is well-pleasing to God, that everything which you do may be sound and valid.

---

[1] Not LXX, which has 'princes' and 'overseers': Hebrew, 'officers' and 'taskmasters'.

III. A CHURCH ORDER OF THE SECOND CENTURY

The Didache, or Teaching of the Twelve Apostles

[Discovered at Constantinople, 1875. Date uncertain; authorship unknown; prov-
enance and importance disputed. The work is in three parts: Chapters I–V being
a manual of conduct (the 'Two Ways'), VI–X a manual of instruction on worship,
XI–XVI regulations about the ministry.]

VII. Concerning baptism, baptize in this way. Having first rehearsed all
these things, baptize in the name of the Father and of the Son and of the
Holy Ghost, in living water. But if you have not living water, baptize into
other water; and, if thou canst not in cold, in warm. If you have neither,
pour water thrice on the head in the name, etc. ... Before the baptism let
the baptizer and the baptized fast, and others if they can. And order the
baptized to fast one or two days before. ...

IX. Concerning the Eucharist, give thanks in this way. First for the
cup; 'We give thanks to thee, our Father, for the holy vine of David thy
servant, which thou madest known to us through thy servant Jesus. To
thee be the glory for ever.' And for the broken bread; 'We give thanks to
thee, our Father, for the life and knowledge, which thou madest known
to us through thy servant Jesus. To thee be the glory for ever. As this
broken bread was scattered upon the hills, and was gathered together and
made one, so let thy Church be gathered together into thy kingdom from
the ends of the earth; for thine is the glory and the power through Christ
Jesus for ever.'

Let none eat or drink of your Eucharist, save such as are baptized into
the name of the Lord. For concerning this the Lord hath said; 'Give not
that which is holy to the dogs.'

X. And after ye are filled, give thanks thus: 'We give thee thanks, Holy
Father, for thy holy name, which thou hast made to tabernacle in our
hearts, and for the knowledge, faith and immortality which thou hast
made known to us through thy servant [*or* Son] Jesus. To thee be the
glory for ever. Thou, Lord Almighty, didst create all things for thy name's
sake, and gavest food and drink to men for their enjoyment, that they
might give thee thanks; and to us thou didst grant spiritual food and
drink and life eternal, through thy servant [*or* Son]. Above all we thank
thee that thou art mighty. To thee be glory for ever. Remember, Lord, thy
Church, to deliver her from all evil and to make her perfect in thy love,
and to gather from the four winds her that is sanctified into thy kingdom
which thou didst prepare for her; for thine is the power and the glory for
ever. Let grace come, and let this world pass away. Hosanna to the God of

David. If any is holy, let him come: if any is not holy, let him repent. Maranatha. Amen.'

But allow the prophets to give thanks as much as they will.

XI. Whoever then shall come and teach you all the aforesaid, receive him. But if the teacher himself turn and teach another doctrine to destroy this, do not listen to him; but if it be to the increase of righteousness and of the knowledge of the Lord, receive him as the Lord. Now, as concerning the apostles and prophets, according to the teaching of the gospel, so do ye; and let every apostle that cometh to you be received as the Lord; and he shall stay but one day, and, if need be, the next day also; but if he stay three days he is a false prophet. When the apostle goeth forth, let him take nothing but bread, [to suffice] till he reach his lodging: if he ask money he is a false prophet. Ye shall not try or judge any prophet speaking in spirit. For 'Every sin shall be forgiven, but this sin shall not be forgiven.' But not every one that speaketh in spirit is a prophet, but only if he have the ways of the Lord. Therefore by their ways shall be known the false prophet and the prophet. Every prophet that appointeth a table in spirit eats not thereof; otherwise he is a false prophet. Every prophet that teacheth the truth, if he doeth not the things that he teacheth, is a false prophet. Every prophet, approved as true, that doeth something for the worldly mystery of the Church, but teacheth not to do what he himself doeth, shall not be judged of you; for he hath his judgement with God. For even so did also the prophets of old. But whosoever shall say in spirit, 'Give me money, or other things,' ye shall not listen to him; but if he bid you give for others that are in need, let no man judge him.

XII. Let every one that 'cometh in the name of the Lord' be received: then, when ye have proved him, ye shall know, for ye can know the right hand from the left. If he that cometh be a passer-by, give him all the help ye can; but he shall not stay, except, if there be need, two or three days. If he wish to abide with you, being a craftsman, let him work and eat. If he have no craft, use your common sense to provide that he may live with you as a Christian, without idleness. If he be unwilling so to do, he is a 'Christmonger.' Beware of such.

XIII. But every true prophet that willeth to abide with you is 'worthy of his food.' In like manner a true teacher is also, like the labourer, 'worthy of his food.' Therefore thou shalt take and give to the prophets every firstfruit of the produce of the winepress and the threshing floor, of oxen and sheep. For the prophets are your high-priests. If ye have no prophet, give them to the poor. If thou art making a batch of bread, take the firstfruit and give according to the commandment. In like manner when thou openest a jar of wine or oil, take the firstfruit and give it to the prophets. And of money and raiment and any other possession take the firstfruit, as may seem good to thee, and give it according to the commandment.

XIV. On the Lord's day assemble and break bread and give thanks, having first confessed your sins, that your sacrifice may be pure. If any have a dispute with his fellow, let him not come to the assembly till they be reconciled, that your sacrifice be not polluted. For this is the sacrifice spoken of by the Lord; 'In every place and at every time offer to me a pure sacrifice; for I am a great king, said the Lord, and my name is wonderful among the Gentiles; (Mal. i. 11, 14).

XV. Elect therefore for yourselves bishops and deacons worthy of the Lord, men that are gentle and not covetous, true men and approved; for they also minister to you the ministry of the prophets and teachers. Therefore despise them not; for these are they that are honoured of you with the prophets and teachers. ...

IV. CHRISTIAN WORSHIP IN THE SECOND CENTURY
Justin (*c*.150), *Apology*, i. lxv–lxvii

lxv. After thus washing him who has been persuaded and has given his assent, we bring him to those that are called the brethren, where they are assembled, to offer prayers in common, both for ourselves and for him who has been illuminated and for all men everywhere, with all our hearts, that as we have learned the truth so we may also be counted worthy to be found good citizens and guardians of the commandments, that we may be saved with an eternal salvation.

We salute one another with a kiss when we have ended the prayers. Then is brought to the president of the brethren bread and a cup of water and wine. And he takes them and offers up praise and glory to the Father of all things, through the name of his Son and of the Holy Ghost, and gives thanks at length that we are deemed worthy of these things at his hand. When he has completed the prayers and thanks-giving all the people present assent by saying *Amen*. *Amen* in the Hebrew tongue signifies 'so be it.' When the president has given thanks and all the people have assented, those who are called deacons with us give to those present a portion of the Eucharistic bread and wine and water, and carry it away to those that are absent.

lxvi. This food is called with us the Eucharist, and of it none is allowed to partake but he that believes that our teachings are true, and has been washed with the washing for the remission of sins and unto regeneration, and who so lives as Christ directed. For we do not receive them as ordinary food or ordinary drink; but as by the word of God, Jesus Christ our Saviour took flesh and blood for our salvation, so also, we are taught, the food blessed by the prayer of the word which we received from him, by which, through its transformation, our blood and flesh is nourished, this food is the flesh and blood of Jesus who was made flesh. For the Apostles in the memoirs made by them, which are called gospels, have thus narrated that the command was given; that Jesus took bread, gave thanks, and said, 'This do ye in remembrance of me; this is my body.' And he took the cup likewise and said, 'This is my blood,' and gave it to them alone. This very thing the evil demons imitated in the mysteries of Mithras, and commanded to be done. For, as you know, or can discover, bread and a cup of water are set out in the rites of initiations with the repetition of certain words.

lxvii. Now we always thereafter remind one another of these things; and those that have the means assist them that are in need; and we visit one another continually. And at all our meals we bless the maker of all things through his son Jesus Christ and through the Holy Ghost. And on the day which is called the day of the sun there is an assembly of all who live in the towns or in the country; and the memoirs of the Apostles or the writings of the prophets are read, as long as time permits. Then the reader ceases, and the president speaks, admonishing us and exhorting us to imitate these excellent examples. Then we arise all together and offer prayers; and, as we said before, when we have concluded our prayer, bread is brought, and wine and water, and the president in like manner offers up prayers and thanksgivings with all his might; and the people assent with *Amen*; and there is the distribution and partaking by all of the Eucharistic elements; and to them that are not present they are sent by the hand of the deacons. And they that are prosperous and wish to do so give what they will, each after his choice. What is collected is deposited with the president, who gives aid to the orphans and widows and such as are in want by reason of sickness or other cause; and to those also that are in prison, and to strangers from abroad, in fact to all that are in need he is a protector.

We hold our common assembly on the day of the sun, because it is the first day, on which God put to flight darkness and chaos [*lit.* matter] and made the world, and on the same day Jesus Christ our saviour rose from the dead; for on the day before that of Saturn they crucified him; and on the day after Saturn's day, the day of the sun, he appeared to his Apostles and disciples and taught them these things, which we have also handed on to you for your consideration.

V.   APOSTOLICAL SUCCESSION

a. The First Extant Use of the Technical Term   Hegesippus (*c*.175) in
  Euseb., *H.E.* iv. xxii, 2

The Church of Corinth remained in the right doctrine down to the
episcopate of Primus at Corinth. I had converse with them on my voyage
to Rome, and we took comfort together in the right doctrine. After
arriving in Rome I made a succession down to Anicetus, whose deacon
was Eleutherus. To Anicetus succeeded Soter, who was followed by
Eleutherus. In every succession and in every City things are ordered
according to the preaching of the Law, the Prophets and the Lord.

b. Irenaeus on Tradition and Succession   *Adv. haereses,* iii

ii. 1. When they [*sc.* the heretics] are refuted out of the Scriptures they
betake them to accusing the Scriptures themselves as if there were
something amiss with them and they carried not authority, because the
Scriptures, they say, contain diverse utterances, and because the truth
cannot be found in them by those that know not the tradition. For that,
they say, has been handed down not by means of writings but by means
of the living voice; wherefore also Paul said: 'Howbeit we speak wisdom
among the perfect: yet a wisdom not of this world.' And this wisdom
each one of them claims to be that which he has found by himself, that is,
a thing invented. ...

  2. Yet when we appeal again to that tradition which is derived from the
Apostles, and which is safeguarded in the churches through the successions of presbyters, they then are adversaries of tradition, claiming to be
wiser not only than the presbyters but even than the Apostles, and to
have discovered the truth undefiled. ... Thus it comes about that they
now agree neither with the Scriptures nor with tradition. ... Such,
beloved, are our adversaries in this conflict, men after the fashion of
slippery snakes, seeking to escape every way. ...

  iii. 1. Those that wish to discern the truth may observe the apostolic
tradition made manifest in every church throughout the world. We can
enumerate those who were appointed bishops in the churches by the
Apostles, and their successors [*or* successions] down to our own day,
who never taught, and never knew, absurdities such as these men
produce. For if the Apostles had known hidden mysteries which they
taught the perfect in private and in secret, they would rather have
committed them to those to whom they entrusted the churches. For
they wished those men to be perfect and unblameable whom they left as

their successors and to whom they handed over their own office of authority. But as it would be very tedious, in a book of this sort, to enumerate the successions in all the churches, we confound all those who in any way, whether for self-pleasing, or vainglory, or blindness, or evilmindedness, hold unauthorized meetings. This we do by pointing to the apostolic tradition and the faith that is preached to men, which has come down to us through the successions of bishops; the tradition and creed of the greatest, the most ancient church, the church known to all men, which was founded and set up at Rome by the two most glorious Apostles, Peter and Paul. For with this church, because of its position of leadership and authority, must needs agree every church, that is, the faithful everywhere; for in her the apostolic tradition has always been preserved by the faithful from all parts.

2. The blessed Apostles, after founding and building up the church, handed over to Linus the office of bishop. Paul mentions this Linus in his epistles to Timothy (2 Tim. iv. 21). He was succeeded by Anacletus, after whom, in the third place after the Apostles, Clement was appointed to the bishopric. He not only saw the blessed Apostles but also conferred with them, and had their preaching ringing in his ears and their tradition before his eyes. In this he was not alone; for many still survived who had been taught by the Apostles. Now while Clement was bishop there arose no small dissension among the brethren in Corinth, and the church in Rome sent a most weighty letter to the Corinthians urging them to reconciliation, renewing their faith and telling them again of the tradition which he had lately received from the Apostles. ...

3. Euarestus succeeded this Clement, Alexander followed Euarestus; then Sixtus was appointed, the sixth after the Apostles. After him came Telesphorus, who had a glorious martyrdom. Then Hyginus, Pius, Anicetus and Soter; and now, in the twelfth place from the Apostles, Eleutherus occupies the see. In the same order and succession the apostolic tradition in the Church and the preaching of the truth has come down to our time. ...

4. And then Polycarp, besides being instructed by the Apostles and acquainted with many who had seen the Lord, was also appointed by the Apostles for Asia as bishop of the church in Smyrna. Even I saw him in my early youth; for he remained with us a long time, and at a great age suffered a martyrdom full of glory and renown and departed this life, having taught always the things which he had learnt from the Apostles, which the Church hands down, which alone are true. There testify to these things all the churches throughout Asia, and the successors of Polycarp down to this day, testimonies to the truth far more trustworthy

and reliable than Valentinus and Marcion and the other misguided persons.

Polycarp, when staying in Rome in the time of Anicetus, converted many of the before-mentioned heretics to the Church of God, declaring that he had received this one and only truth from the Apostles, the truth which has been handed down by the Church. There are also some who heard him relate that John, the disciple of our Lord, went to the baths at Ephesus; and seeing Cerinthus inside he rushed out without taking a bath, saying, 'Let us flee, before the baths fall in, for Cerinthus the enemy of the truth is inside.' ...

iv. 1. Since therefore there are so many proofs, there is now no need to seek among others the truth which we can easily obtain from the Church. For the Apostles have lodged all that there is of the truth with her, as with a rich bank, holding back nothing. And so anyone that wishes can draw from her the draught of life. This is the gateway of life; all the rest are thieves and robbers. ...

Adv. haer., iv. xxvi. 2

Therefore we ought to obey only those presbyters who are in the Church, who have their succession from the Apostles, as we have shown; who with their succession in the episcopate have received the sure gift of the truth according to the pleasure of the Father. The rest, who stand aloof from the primitive succession, and assemble in any place whatever, we must regard with suspicion, either as heretics and evil-minded; or as schismatics, puffed up and complacent; or again as hypocrites, acting thus for the sake of gain and vainglory. All these have fallen from the truth.

c. **Tertullian on Tradition and Succession** *De praescriptione haereticorum,* xx, xxi

xx. ... The Apostles first bore witness to the faith of Christ Jesus throughout Judaea; they founded churches there, and then went out into the world and preached to the nations the same doctrine of the same faith. They likewise founded churches in every city, from which the other churches thereafter derived the shoot of faith and the seeds of doctrine—yea, and are still deriving them, in order to become churches. It is through this that these churches are themselves apostolic, in that they are the offspring of apostolic churches. Every kind of thing must needs be classed in accordance with its origin. And so the churches, many and great as they may be, are really the one Primitive Church issuing from the Apostles, which is their source. So all are primitive and all Apostolic, while all are one. And this unity is proved by the peace they share, by their title of brotherhood, by their contract of hospitality; for these privileges have but one ground, the one tradition of the same revelation [*sacramentum*].

xxi. It is therefore on this ground that we put forward our ruling [*praescriptio*], namely that if Jesus Christ sent out the Apostles to preach, no others are to be accepted as preachers but those whom Christ appointed, since 'No other knoweth the Father save the Son and he to whom the Son hath revealed him.' And the Son seems not to have revealed him to any but the Apostles whom he sent to preach—assuredly to preach what he revealed to them. But what they preached, that is, what Christ revealed to them, this, on my ruling, ought to be established solely through those same churches which the Apostles themselves founded by preaching to them as well by the living voice, as the phrase is, as by their Epistles afterwards. If this is so, it follows straightway that all doctrine which accords with those apostolic churches, the sources and originals of the Faith, must be reckoned as the truth, since it preserves without doubt what the churches received from the Apostles, the Apostles from Christ, and Christ from God. ... We are in communion with the apostolic churches; there is no difference of doctrine; this is the testimony of the truth.

Ibid. xxxii

But if any of these [heresies] are bold enough to insert themselves into the Apostolic age, in order to seem to have been handed down from the Apostles because they existed under the Apostles, we can say: Let them then produce the origins of their churches; let them unroll the list of their bishops, an unbroken succession from the beginning so that that first bishop had as his precursor and the source of his authority one of the Apostles or one of the apostolic men who, though not an Apostle, continued with the Apostles. This is how the apostolic churches report their origins; thus the church of the Smyrnaeans relates that Polycarp was appointed by John, the church of Rome that Clement was ordained by Peter. ...

d. Tertullian on the Priesthood of the Laity *De Exhortatione Castitatis, 7*

... Are not we laymen priests also? It is written: 'He hath also made us a kingdom and priests to God and his Father.' The difference between the Order and the people is due to the authority of the church and the consecration of their rank by the reservation of a special bench for the order. Thus where there is no bench of clergy you offer and baptize and are your own sole priest. For where there are three, there is a church, though they be laymen. Therefore if you have the rights of a priest in your own person when necessity arises, you ought likewise to have the discipline of a priest, where it is necessary to exercise his rights. ...

[On this oft-quoted passage it is to be observed: (i) That T. is writing as a Montanist, against second marriages, as unlawful equally for laity and clergy, and he himself, in his orthodox days, reproached heretics because 'they endue even the laity with the functions of the priesthood' (*De praescr.* 41); (ii) that, even so, he is speaking of cases of necessity.]

e. **Cyprian on the Unity of the Church**   Cyprian, Bishop of Carthage, 248–258, *De catholicae ecclesiae unitate*, 4–6

[The words in square brackets are found in certain MSS but not in the earliest. Some MSS give two versions, one with and one without the interpolations. The words in italics are omitted in the interpolated MSS. Many scholars see the hand of a forger bolstering up Roman claims. Others, including Chapman, Harnack, and Batiffol, think that Cyprian wrote a second edition, having in view (according to Chapman) the Novatian schism at Rome.]

If any one consider and examine this, there is no need of lengthy treatment and argument. It can easily be proved to the mind of faith by a brief statement of the truth. The Lord says to Peter, 'I say unto thee that thou art Peter, etc.' (Matt. xvi. 18, 19). [And again after his resurrection he says to him, 'Feed my sheep.'] He builds his church upon [him] *one man*; [and to him he gives his sheep to be fed;] and though he gives to all the Apostles an equal power and says, 'As my Father sent me, etc.' (Jn. xx. 21–23), yet he has [appointed the one chair[1] and] ordained by his authority the source [and system] of unity *beginning from one man* [Certainly the other Apostles were what Peter was, but primacy is given to Peter that it may be shewn that the Church is one and the chair[1] one. And all are pastors, but one flock is indicated which is fed by all the Apostles with unanimous consent.] *that he might manifest the unity.* Certainly the other Apostles were what Peter was, *endued with an equal fellowship both of honour and power*; but the beginning is made from unity, that the Church of Christ may be shewn to be one. To this one Church the Holy Spirit points in the Song of Songs, in the person of our Lord, saying, 'My dove, my spotless one, is but one; she is the only one of her mother, elect of her that bare her' (Cant. vi. 9). He that holds not this unity of the Church, does he think that he holds the faith? He that strives against and resists the church, [he that deserts the chair of

---

[1] *Cathedra.*

Peter upon whom that Church was founded,] is he confident that he is in the Church? For the blessed apostle Paul also teaches this same thing and sets forth the sacrament of unity, saying, 'there is one body, etc.' (Eph. iv. 4, 5).

5. This unity we ought to hold and preserve, especially we who preside in the Church as bishops, that we may prove the episcopate itself to be one and undivided. Let no one deceive the brotherhood with falsehood; no one corrupt our faith in the truth by faithless transgression. The episcopate is one; the individual members have each a part, and the parts make up the whole. The Church is a unity; yet by her fruitful increase she is extended far and wide to form a plurality; even as the sun has many rays, but one light; and a tree many boughs but one trunk, whose foundation is the deep-seated root; and as when many streams flow down from one source, though a multitude seems to be poured out from the abundance of the copious supply, yet in the source itself unity is preserved. Cut off a ray from the sun's orb; the unity of light refuses division: break a branch from the tree; the broken member cannot bud; sever the stream from its fount; once severed it is dried up. So also the Church, flooded with the light of the Lord, extends her rays over all the globe: yet it is one light which is diffused everywhere and the unity of the body is not broken up. She stretches forth her branches over the whole earth in rich abundance; she spreads far and wide the bounty of her onward flowing streams; yet there is but one head, one source, one mother, abounding in the increase of her fruitfulness. Of her womb are we born, by her milk are we nourished, and we are quickened from her breath.

6. The spouse of Christ cannot be made an adulteress; she is undefiled and chaste. She knows but one home, and guards with virtuous chastity the sanctity of one chamber. She it is who preserves us for God, who enrols into the Kingdom the sons she has borne. Whoso stands aloof from the Church and is joined to an adulteress is cut off from the promises given to the Church; and he that leaves the Church of Christ attains not to Christ's rewards. He is an alien, an outcast, an enemy. He cannot have God for his father who has not the Church for his mother. If any one was able to escape outside of Noah's ark, then he also escapes who is outside the doors of the Church. ...

7. This sacrament of unity, this bond of peace inseparable and indivisible, is indicated when in the Gospel the robe of the Lord Jesus Christ was not divided at all or rent but they cast lots for the raiment of Christ, who should put on Christ for clothing, and so the raiment was received whole and the robe was taken unspoilt and undivided. Divine scripture

speaks, and says, 'But as for the robe, since it was seamless from the part above, woven throughout, they said among themselves: "Let us not rend it, but cast lots for it, whose it shall be."' That garment betokened the unity which comes 'from the part above,' that is, from heaven and from the Father, a unity which could not be rent at all by him that received it and had it in possession, but he took it indivisibly in its unbreakable entirety. He that rends and divides the Church of Christ cannot possess the clothing of Christ. ...

f. Cyprian on the Episcopate   *Epistle* xxxiii. 1

Our Lord, whose precepts and admonitions we are bound to observe, ordered the high office of bishop and the system of his Church when he speaks in the Gospel and says to Peter, 'Thou art Peter, etc.' (Matt. xvi. 18, 19). ... Thence age has followed age and bishop has followed bishop in succession, and the office of the episcopate and the system of the Church has been handed down, so that the Church is founded on the bishops and every act of the Church is directed by these same presiding officers. Since this has been established by divine ordinance, I am astonished that certain persons have been rash and bold enough to choose to write to me in such a manner as to send their letter in the Church's name, when the Church consists of the bishop, the clergy and all the faithful. ...

Ep. lxvi. 7

In this place (Jn. vi. 67–69, 'Lord, to whom shall we go? etc.') Peter, upon whom the Church had to be built, speaks as representing the Church, for our instruction. For although the proud and arrogant multitude of them that refuse to obey may take themselves off, still the Church never departs from Christ, and the Church is made up of the people united to their priest and the flock that cleaves to its shepherd. Hence you should know that the bishop is in the Church and the Church in the bishop, and that if any one be not with the bishop he is not in the Church; and that they vainly beguile themselves who, not being at peace with the priests of God, approach by stealth and trust by underhand means to enter into communion with certain persons; whereas the Church is one and may not be rent or sundered, but should assuredly be bound together and united by the glue of the priests who are in harmony one with another.

[*Sacerdos*, 'priest,' normally means 'bishop' in Cyprian.]

VI. EUCHARISTIC DOCTRINE

a. Ignatius   Ign. *Ep. ad Smyrn. 6*

They [the Docetics] abstain from the Eucharist and prayer because they do not admit that the Eucharist is the flesh of our saviour Jesus Christ, which suffered for our sins, which the Father in his goodness raised up.

Ad Eph. *xx. 2*

... breaking one bread, which is the medicine of immortality, the antidote against death which gives eternal life in Jesus Christ.

b. Irenaeus   *Adv. haer.* iv. xviii. 4–6

Inasmuch therefore as the Church offers in simplicity of heart, her gift is rightly considered a pure sacrifice with God. ... For we are bound to make our oblation to God and in all things to be found grateful to God the creator, with a pure mind and faith without hypocrisy, with fervent love offering the firstfruits of his own creatures. And this oblation the Church alone offers pure to the creator, presenting to him with thanksgiving from his creation. The Jews offer it not for their hands are full of blood: for they did not receive the Word [? through] which [? it] is offered to God. Nor do any of the synagogues of the heretics. For some of them say that there is another Father besides the creator, and so, in offering to him, they shew him to be desirous and covetous of another's goods. But they that say that the things pertaining to us were made through decay, and ignorance and passion, sin against their own Father, in offering to him the fruits of ignorance, passion and decay; rather insulting him than rendering thanks.

How will they allow that the bread over which thanksgiving has been said is the body of their Lord, and that the chalice is the chalice of his blood, if they say that he is not the son of the creator of the world; that is to say, his Word through whom the tree bears fruit and the fountains flow and the earth yields first the blade, then the ear, then the full corn in the ear?

5. How, again, do they say that the flesh which is nourished by the body and blood of the Lord passes into corruption and attains not unto life? Either, then, let them change their opinion or let them abstain from offering the aforesaid things. But our belief is in accord with the

Eucharist, while the Eucharist confirms our opinion. For we offer to him the things that are his, proclaiming harmoniously the unity of flesh and spirit. For as the bread of the earth, receiving the invocation of God, is no longer common bread but Eucharist, consisting of two things, an earthly and a heavenly; so also our bodies, partaking of the Eucharist, are no longer corruptible, having the hope of eternal resurrection.

c. **An Early Eucharistic Canon (c.225)**   From *The Apostolic Tradition* of Hippolytus (*The So-called Egyptian Church Order*, ed. Connolly, *Texts and Studies*, viii. 4)

[Probably part compilation, part composition; the source of the Church Orders of the East, the *Didascalia, Apostolic Constitutions*, etc.]

The Bishop: The Lord be with you.
People: And with thy spirit.
B.: Lift up your hearts.
P.: We lift them up unto the Lord.
B.: Let us give thanks unto the Lord.
P.: It is meet and right.
B.: We give thee thanks, O God, through thy beloved son [? servant] Jesus Christ, whom thou didst send to us in the last times to be a saviour and redeemer and the messenger of thy will; who is thy inseparable Word, through whom thou madest all things, and in whom thou wast well pleased. Thou didst send him from Heaven into the Virgin's womb; he was conceived and was incarnate, and was shown to be thy Son, born of the Holy Spirit and the Virgin; Who, fulfilling thy will and preparing for thee a holy people, stretched out his hands in suffering, that he might free from suffering them that believed on thee.

Who when he was being betrayed to his voluntary suffering, that he might destroy death, break the chains of the devil, tread Hell underfoot, bring forth the righteous [therefrom] and set a bound [to it], and that he might manifest his Resurrection, took bread and gave thanks to thee and said: TAKE, EAT: THIS IS MY BODY WHICH IS BROKEN FOR YOU. Likewise also the cup, saying: THIS IS MY BLOOD WHICH IS SHED FOR YOU. AS OFT AS YE DO THIS YE SHALL DO IT IN REMEMBRANCE OF ME.

Wherefore we, being mindful of his death and resurrection, do offer unto thee this bread and this cup, giving thanks unto thee for that thou hast deemed us worthy to stand before thee and minister as thy priest. And we beseech thee that thou wouldst send thy Holy Spirit upon the oblation of thy Holy Church;[1] and that thou wouldst grant it to all the saints who partake, making them one, for fulfilment of the Holy Spirit and for the confirmation of their faith in truth; that we may praise and glorify thee through thy Son [servant] Jesus Christ, through whom be glory and honour to thee, to the Father and to the Son with the Holy Spirit in thy Holy Church, both now and for ever. Amen.

d. Tertullian on the Eucharist *De corona*, 3

The sacrament of the Eucharist, which was instituted by the Lord at a meal-time and enjoined upon all, we take in assemblies before daybreak, and only from the hands of the presidents.

Reservation of the Sacrament Tert. *Ad uxorem*, ii. 5
[Speaking of the dangers of having even a 'tolerant' heathen husband.]

Will not your husband know what it is that you taste in secret before any food? And if he knows that it is bread, he is not likely to believe it to be what it is said to be. And will every husband, not knowing about these things, merely put up with the practice? Will he not grumble? Will he not have suspicions, whether it be bread or poison?

Cf. *De oratione*, 14. ... the body of the Lord having been received and reserved. ...

e. Cyprian on the Eucharist *Epistle* lxiii. 14

If Christ Jesus our Lord and God is himself the high priest of God the Father and first offered himself as a sacrifice to the Father, and commanded this to be done in remembrance of himself, then assuredly the priest acts truly in Christ's room, when he imitates what Christ did, and he offers then a true and complete sacrifice to God the Father, if he so begin to offer as he sees Christ himself has offered.

VII. TWO HERESIES ON THE NATURE OF THE CHURCH AND THE MINISTRY

a. Montanism Euseb. *H.E.* v. xvi. 7

... In a certain village in that part of Mysia over against Phrygia, Montanus, they say, first exposed himself to the assaults of the adversary through his unbounded lust for leadership. He was one of the recent

---

[1] This is the clause technically known as the *Epiclesis* (Invocation) of the Holy Spirit.

converts, and he became possessed of a spirit, and suddenly began to rave in a kind of ecstatic trance, and to babble in a jargon, prophesying in a manner contrary to the custom of the Church which had been handed down by tradition from the earliest times.

8. Some of them that heard his bastard utterances rebuked him as one possessed of a devil ... remembering the Lord's warning to guard vigilantly against the coming of false prophets. But others were carried away and not a little elated, thinking themselves possessed of the Holy Spirit and of the gift of prophecy. 9. ... And he also stirred up two women and filled them with the bastard spirit so that they uttered demented, absurd and irresponsible sayings. ... And these people blasphemed the whole Catholic Church under heaven, under the influence of their presumptuous spirit, because the Church granted to the spirit of false prophecy neither honour nor admission. 10. For the faithful in Asia met often and in many places throughout Asia upon this matter ... and rejected the heresy, and thus people were expelled from the Church and debarred from communion.

Hippolytus, *Refutatio omnium haeresium,* viii. 19

... They have been deceived by two females, Priscilla and Maximilla by name, whom they hold to be prophetesses, asserting that into them the Paraclete spirit entered. ... They magnify these females above the Apostles and every gift of Grace, so that some of them go so far as to say that there is in them something more than Christ. These people agree with the Church in acknowledging the Father of the universe to be God and Creator of all things, and they also acknowledge all that the Gospel testifies of Christ. But they introduce novelties in the form of fasts and feasts, abstinences and diets of radishes, giving these females as their authority. ...

Tertullian, *De anima,* ix. *c*.210

[After he had become a Montanist.]

... We have among us now a sister who has been granted gifts of revelations, which she experiences in church during the Sunday services through ecstatic vision in the Spirit. ... And after the people have been dismissed at the end of the service it is her custom to relate to us what she has seen. ... 'Among other things,' says she, 'there was shown to me a soul in bodily form, and it appeared like a spirit; but it was no mere something, void of qualities, but rather a thing which could be grasped, soft and translucent and of etherial colour, in form at all points human.'

b. Donatism   Augustine, *De baptismo,* iv. 16, 18

[In origin (*supra*, p. 19) a schism rather than a heresy, Donatism raised the question whether the validity of the sacraments, as distinct from their effectiveness, depended on the worthiness of minister or recipient. S. Augustine gives the classic statement of the objectivity of the sacraments.]

... Therefore, since it is possible that Christ's sacrament may be holy, even among those on the devil's side ... and even if they are such in heart when they received the sacrament ... the sacrament is not to be re-administered ... ; to my mind it is abundantly clear that in the matter of baptism we have to consider not who he is that gives it, but what it is that he gives; not who he is that receives, but what it is that he receives. ...

18. ... wherefore, any one who is on the devil's side cannot defile the sacrament, which is of Christ. ... When baptism is administered in the words of the gospel, however great be the perverseness of either minister or recipient, the sacrament itself is holy on his account whose sacrament it is. In the case of one who receives baptism from a misguided man, if he receive not the perverseness of the minister but the holiness of the mystery, being united to the Church in good faith and hope and charity, he receives the remission of his sins. ... But if the recipient be himself misguided, then that which is administered does not avail for his salvation while he remains in his error; on the other hand, that which he receives remains holy in the recipient, and is not renewed to him if he be brought into the right way.

[This view, the 'Roman' view of Stephen as opposed to that of Cyprian, was sanctioned in the West by the councils of Arles (314)[1] and Nicaea. It was only partially accepted in the East. Cyril of Jerusalem insists on the rebaptism of heretics (*Procat.* 7), and Athanasius (*Or. c. Ar.* ii. 42, 43) on the necessity of 'right intention,' and rules out Arian baptism. The practice of rebaptizing heretics remained, and remains, the general custom in the East.]

---

[1] *Council of Arles, Canon* 8. ... If anyone come to the Church from a heresy let them ask him the Creed [*sc.* used at his baptism], and if it shall appear certain that he was baptized in the Father and the Son and the Holy Spirit, let him receive only the laying on of hands, that he may receive the Holy Spirit. But if, when he is asked, his reply does not contain this Trinity, let him be baptized.

SECTION VIII

The Authority of the Holy See

I. THE CLAIMS OF ROME, 341

Julius, Bishop of Rome, 337–52: *ap.* Ath. *Apol. c. Ar.* 35

[A letter to the council of Antioch, 341 (see p. 43), urging the restoration of Athanasius and Marcellus.]

... Dearly beloved, the judgements of the Church are no longer according to the Gospel, but tend only to banishment and death. Now suppose, as you allege, that there was some guilt attached to these men, the trial ought to have been conducted according to the Canon of the Church and not in this manner. Letters ought to have been written to us all, that in this way all might contribute to a just decision. For the men in question were bishops, and the churches concerned were no ordinary churches, but those which the Apostles themselves had governed in person.

And why were we not written to about the church of Alexandria in particular? Do you not realize that it has been the custom for word to be sent to us first, that in this way just decisions may be arrived at from this place? If therefore any suspicion was directed against the bishop there, word ought to have been sent to the bishop of this place. But they neglected to inform us, and proceeded at their own pleasure and on their own authority; and now they wish to obtain our approval of their decisions, though we never condemned him [Athanasius]. This is not in accordance with the constitutions of Paul or the directions of the traditions of the Fathers. I am informing you of the tradition handed down from the blessed Apostle Peter.

II. APPEALS TO THE ROMAN SEE

Council of Sardica, 343. Text (of the Canons on Roman authority) in Denzinger, *Enchiridion*, 3004 ff.

Canon III. Bishop Hosius[1] said: This also must be added, that no bishop pass from his province into another province in which there are bishops; unless he happen to have been invited by his brethren lest we should seem to shut the doors of friendship [charity].

Again, it must be provided, that if, in any province, any bishop have a case against his brother and fellow-bishop neither of them shall call in bishops from another province as arbitrators. But if any bishop have had

---

[1] See p. 18.

his case judged, and considers that he has sound and good cause for a re-trial of the case, then, if you are so good as to agree, let us honour the memory of the Apostle Peter and provide that letters be sent to Julius, Bishop of Rome, by those who tried the case, so that, if need be, the trial may be renewed by means of the neighbouring bishops, and let him appoint arbitrators. But if he is unable to agree that the matter is in need of re-trial, then the first decision shall hold good.

Is this agreed?

The synod; Agreed.

Canon V. Bishop Hosius said: Resolved, that if a bishop has been accused and the assembled bishops of that region have deposed him, and he has appealed and had recourse to the most blessed bishop of the Roman church, and is desirous that he should hear his case; then if he should think it just that his case should be reopened, let him think fit to write to the appellant's fellow-bishops of the adjacent provinces, that they may make careful and exact enquiry into the details, and give sentence according to what they believe to be the truth. But if anyone who claims a fresh trial should by his entreaty move the Roman bishop to send one of the presbyters of his personal suite, then it shall be in the power of the bishop [of Rome] if he so decide, to send representatives to sit in judgement with the bishops; such representatives to have the authority of him from whom they were sent. If he think the bishops competent to judge the matter and to decide on the bishop's case, then he shall act as it seems best to his most wise counsel.

III. JEROME ON THE ROMAN SEE
Ep. xv (to Pope Damasus, 376), 1, 2

[The letter appeals for an authoritative pronouncement on the expression τρεῖς ὑποστάσεις, now coming into currency through the influence of the Cappadocian Fathers (see pp. 34–5). Jerome, taking ὑπόστασις in the sense of 'essence' (=οὐσία), was alarmed.]

Since the East, rent asunder by feuds of long standing, is tearing to shreds the seamless robe of the Lord ... I think it my duty to consult the chair of Peter ...

2. I am terrified by your eminence, yet your benevolence attracts me. From the priest I claim the preservation of the victim, from the shepherd the due protection of the sheep. Away with all trace of pride; let Roman majesty withdraw. It is to the successor of the fisherman that I address myself, to the disciple of the cross.

As I follow no leader save Christ, so I communicate with none save your Beatitude, that is, with the chair of Peter. For this, I know, is the

Rock on which the Church is built. This is Noah's ark, and he who is not found in it shall perish when the flood overwhelms all. ...

IV. INNOCENT I, 401–417. ON THE PAPAL AUTHORITY
Ep. xxix, Jan. 417; *P.L.* xx. 582

[To the African bishops, approving their appeal to him to support the condemnation of Pelagianism (see p. 62).]

1. ... [We approve your action in following the principle of the Fathers] that nothing which was done even in the most remote and distant provinces should be taken as finally settled unless it came to the notice of this See, that any just pronouncement might be confirmed by all the authority of this See, and that the other churches might from thence gather what they should teach. ...

V. PAPAL AUTHORITY DEFIED BY THE AFRICAN BISHOPS
Prosper, *Contra collatorem,* v. 3 (*P.L.* li. 227)

[Pope Zosimus (417–418) received confessions of faith from Pelagius and Coelestius, and declared them orthodox. He then wrote to the African bishops reproving them for their hasty action. They replied (appealing 'from Pope ill-informed ... '):]

We decree that the judgement against Pelagius and Coelestius issued by the venerable Bishop Innocent from the see of the most blessed Peter shall hold good until they both distinctly and explicitly acknowledge that the grace of God is needed in every act, both for the perception and for the performance of what is right. ...

VI. THE AFRICAN BISHOPS ON APPEALS TO ROME
Synod of Carthage, 424. Mansi, iii. 839 ff.

[Apiarius, an African priest, was deposed by his bishop and appealed to Zosimus, who ordered his reinstatement, alleging as authority for his intervention a 'canon of Nicaea,' meaning the canons of Sardica (see p. 84). The Africans refused, saying that they could not find this canon. The two following Popes, Boniface and Coelestine, were unable to assert their authority, and it was to the latter that this letter (often referred to as *Optaremus,* from its opening word) was addressed. (The Eastern and African bishops were not present at the Council of Sardica, and its canons were only known in the West; they appear not to have won general acceptance, even in the West, till the sixth century.)]

To our dearly beloved lord and honoured brother. Coelestine,—We could wish that in sending you this letter concerning Apiarius' clearing of himself we could feel a like pleasure to that expressed in your letter. ... Faustinus [bishop of Potentia, the pope's delegate] ... violently opposed the whole synod, greatly insulting us on the pretext of asserting the privileges of the Roman church, demanding the restoration of Apiarius to communion on the ground that your Holiness ... has restored him. ... [Apiarius saved trouble by confessing to the charges]. ...

Therefore, with all respect, we earnestly entreat you for the future not to be ready to admit to a hearing persons that come from this region, nor to be willing to receive into communion those that have been excommunicated by us. Your Reverence will readily observe that this has been forbidden by the Nicene canons. ... [1] For the Nicene canons have most clearly committed not only the inferior clergy but also the bishops themselves to the judgement of their own metropolitan. For with singular wisdom and justice they enacted that all causes should be concluded in the places where they arose. And they did not think that the grace of the Holy Spirit would be wanting in any province for the bishops of Christ to judge and firmly to maintain the right, especially since any one who considers himself wronged by any decision has the right to appeal to the synod of his province or to a General Council. Unless it be supposed that God can inspire one individual with justice and withhold it from a multitude of bishops in council. And how can we place confidence in an overseas tribunal, since it will not be possible to send the required witnesses? ... And we can find no sanction from any council of the Fathers for your sending delegates. ... If any should desire you to send delegates, do not comply; lest we should seem to be introducing the murky pride of the world into the Church of Christ, which shows to them that desire to see God the light of simplicity and the radiance of humility. ...

VII.   ROME AND CONSTANTINOPLE

a. The Council of Constantinople, 381. Proximate Honour   Canon 3.
Mansi, iii. 560 C; Bright, *Canons of the First Four General Councils*, xxii

The Bishop of Constantinople to have the primacy of honour next after the Bishop of Rome, because Constantinople is New Rome.

b. The Council of Chalcedon, 451. Parallel Jurisdiction   Canons 9, 28.
Mansi, vii. 361; Bright, *Canons*, xli, xlvii

[These canons were denounced by Leo and never accepted in the West.]

9. Any cleric having a suit against another cleric may not leave his own bishop nor have recourse to the secular courts. Let him first try the case

---

[1] Nicaea, Canon V.

before his own bishop, or, with the consent of the bishop, before arbiters agreed on by both parties. ... But if a cleric have a case against his own or any other bishop, let it be judged by the synod of his own province. But if any bishop or cleric have a suit against the metropolitan, let him have recourse to the Exarch of the diocese [i.e. the superior metropolitan of a group of provinces] or to the chair of the Imperial city of Constantinople, and plead his cause before him.

28. Following the judgement of the holy Fathers in all things, and acknowledging the canon of the 150 most religious bishops [i.e. the Council of Const. 381] which has just been read, we also determine and decree the same things with regard to the privileges of the most holy city of Constantinople, New Rome. For to the throne of Old Rome, the Fathers gave privileges with good reason, because it was the imperial city. And the 150 bishops, with the same consideration in view, gave equal privileges to the most holy throne of New Rome; judging with good reason that the city honoured by the monarchy and the senate, and enjoying equal privileges with the old imperial Rome, should likewise receive equal rank in matters ecclesiastical, holding the second place after her.

We likewise decree that the metropolitans, but only the metropolitans, of the dioceses of Pontus, Asia and Thrace (together with the bishops of those dioceses who are among the barbarians) shall be ordained by the said most holy chair of the most holy church of Constantinople. But that each metropolitan of these dioceses shall ordain the bishops of his province, as has been laid down by the divine canons. ...

[At this time the unit of ecclesiastical, as of imperial, organization was the *province*, and a *diocese* was a group of provinces. These terms were later reversed, taking the meanings which they retain to this day.]

[For Edicts of Gratian and Valentian III see above, pp. 22–4.]

SECTION IX

Doctrine and Development. The Vincentian Canon

Vincent of Lerins, *Commonitorium* (434) (ed. Moxon, *Cambridge Patristic Texts*)

II. (1) I have therefore continually given the greatest pains and diligence to enquiring, from the greatest possible number of men outstanding in holiness and in doctrine, how I can secure a kind of fixed and, as it were, general and guiding principle for distinguishing the true Catholic Faith from the degraded falsehoods of heresy. And the answer that I receive is always to this effect; that if I wish, or indeed if any one wishes, to detect the deceits of heretics that arise and to avoid their snares and to keep healthy and sound in a healthy faith, we ought, with the Lord's help, to fortify our faith in a twofold manner, firstly, that is, by the authority of God's Law, then by the tradition of the Catholic Church.

(2) Here, it may be, some one will ask, Since the canon of Scripture is complete, and is in itself abundantly sufficient, what need is there to join to it the interpretation of the Church? The answer is that because of the very depth of Scripture all men do not place one identical interpretation upon it. The statements of the same writer are explained by different men in different ways, so much so that it seems almost possible to extract from it as many opinions as there are men. Novatian[1] expounds in one way, Sabellius[2] in another, Donatus[3] in another, Arius,[4] Eunomius[5] and Macedonius[6] in another, Photinus,[7] Apollinaris[8] and Priscillian[9] in another, Jovinian,[10] Pelagius[11] and Caelestius[11] in another, and latterly Nestorius[12] in another. Therefore, because of the intricacies of error, which is so multiform, there is great need for the laying down of a rule for the exposition of Prophets and Apostles in accordance with the standard of the interpretation of the Church Catholic.

(3) Now in the Catholic Church itself we take the greatest care to hold THAT WHICH HAS BEEN BELIEVED EVERYWHERE, ALWAYS, AND BY ALL.

That is truly and properly 'Catholic,' as is shown by the very force and meaning of the word, which comprehends everything almost universally. We shall hold to this rule if we follow universality [i.e. œcumenicity], antiquity, and consent. We shall follow universality if we acknowledge

---

[1] A rigorist on the question of the re-admission to the Church of those who had lapsed under persecution. Seceded in 251, becoming the first anti-pope.

[2] See p. 40.

[3] See p. 83.

[4] See pp. 41–3.

[5] A radical Arian, holding that the Son is *unlike* (ἀνόμοιος) the Father and *of a different substance* (ἑτεροούσιος).

[6] Bishop of Constantinople, 342. Denied the divinity of the Holy Spirit; deposed 360.

[7] Bishop of Sirmium, second half of fourth century. An 'Adoptianist Monarchian' (see p. 41).

[8] See pp. 47 ff.

[9] Bishop of Abila in Spain. Taught a kind of Manichean Gnosticism (see pp. 37 ff.). Executed *c*.385, the first to be executed for heresy (but on the ground that his teaching led to immorality).

[10] *c*.385. Jerome wrote a polemic against his depreciation of virginity and asceticism.

[11–11] See pp. 56 ff.

[12] See p. 48.

that one Faith to be true which the whole Church throughout the world confesses; antiquity, if we in no wise depart from those interpretations which it is clear that our ancestors and fathers proclaimed; consent, if in antiquity itself we keep following the definitions and opinions of all, or certainly nearly all, bishops and doctors alike.

III. (4) What then will the Catholic Christian do, if a small part of the Church has cut itself off from the communion of the universal Faith? The answer is sure. He will prefer the healthiness of the whole body to the morbid and corrupt limb.

But what if some novel contagion try to infect the whole Church, and not merely a tiny part of it? Then he will take care to cleave to antiquity, which cannot now be led astray by any deceit of novelty.

What if in antiquity itself two or three men, or it may be a city, or even a whole province be detected in error? Then he will take the greatest care to prefer the decrees of the ancient General Councils, if there are such, to the irresponsible ignorance of a few men.

But what if some error arises regarding which nothing of this sort is to be found? Then he must do his best to compare the opinions of the Fathers and enquire their meaning, provided always that, though they belonged to diverse times and places, they yet continued in the faith and communion of the one Catholic Church; and let them be teachers approved and outstanding. And whatever he shall find to have been held, approved and taught, not by one or two only but by all equally and with one consent, openly, frequently and persistently, let him take this as to be held by him without the slightest hesitation.

[Vincent proceeds to illustrate the test of universality with reference to Donatism, antiquity by the case of Arianism, consent by the case of Nestorius.]

SECTION X

Christian Inscriptions Illustrating the Popular Christianity of the Third and Fourth Centuries

[Text of these in Nunn, *Christian Inscriptions* (Texts for Students SPCK, 11), to which the numbers refer.]

From the Cemetery of Priscilla (first to third century)

Stafilius, peace be with thee in God. Hail and farewell.(12)

Tertius my [our] brother be of good courage; no one is immortal.(14)
O Father of all, take into they keeping Irene, Zoe and Marcellus whom
thou didst make; thine be the glory in Christ.[1]   (15)

From Various Sources (third and fourth centuries)

Little Hermas, light, may thou live in God the Lourd Chreist. Aged ten
yares sevun munths.   *Lateran.* (24)

[An illiterate inscription, in Greek letters but partly in Latin words.]

To dear Cyriacus, our sweetest son. Mayest thou live in the Holy Spirit.
                                        Cemetery of Callixtus. (26)
Septimus Praetextatus Caecilianus,[2] the servant of God, after a worthy
life.[3] I do not repent that I have served thee thus and I give thanks unto
thy name. He gave up his soul to God, aged thirty-three years six months.
                                        Cemetery of Callixtus. (39)
Florentius set up this inscription for his well-deserving son Appro-
nianus, who lived one year, nine months and five days. Since he was truly
beloved by his grandmother and she saw that he was destined for death,
she asked of the church that he should depart from this life a believer.
                                                    Lateran. (40)

[Evidence for infant baptism in the early Church.]

Pray for thy parents, Matronata Matrona. She lived 1 yr. 52 d.
                                                    Lateran. (36)
Atticus, sleep in peace, secure in thy safety, and pray anxiously for our
sins.   *Found near S. Sabina.* (37)

[An echo of Cyprian, *De mortalitate*, xxvi: 'There are a great number of dear ones
awaits us: a thronging crowd of parents, brethren, sons eagerly expects us, secure
in their own safety and still anxious concerning ours' (Nunn).]

I, Petronia, wife of a Levite [i.e. deacon], of modest countenance, here lay
down my bones and place them in their resting place. Cease from
weeping, my husband and sweet children, and believe that it is not
right to mourn one that lives in God.   *Source unknown.* (41)

[In elegiac couplets.]

---

[1] This monogram (XP, the first letters of Christ in Greek) is frequent in these
inscriptions.
[2] Inscription found near the tomb of S. Cecilia. Evidently a connexion or a slave of her
family.
[3] Perhaps 'the slave, after a life worthy of God'.

A Third-Century Epitaph from Autun

[Found in fragments in the cemetery of S. Pierre l'Estrier, Autun, in 1839. Now in the museum of Autun. Greek elegiacs. Some conjectural restorations, but the general sense is clear.]

Divine offspring of the heavenly Fish,[1] preserve a reverent heart when thou takest the drink of immortality that is given among mortals. Comfort thy soul, beloved, with the ineffable fountains, in the never-failing waters of Wisdom, giver of riches. Take the honey-sweet food of the Saviour of saints and eat it with hunger, holding the Fish in thy hands. Fill me with the Fish, I pray thee, Lord Saviour.

May my mother sleep well, I pray thee, Light of the dead.

Aschandius my father, dearly beloved of my heart, with my sweet mother and my brethren, remember thy Pectorius in the peace of the Fish.   (42)

---

[1] The Fish is a frequent title of our Lord in inscriptions of the early Church; the Greek for 'fish' being formed acrostically by the Greek for 'Jesus Christ, the Son of God, Saviour', thus:

Ιησοῦς
Χριστός
Θεοῦ
Υιός
Σωτήρ

The initial letters of this inscription are an acrostic ἰχθύς.

PART II

From the Council of Chalcedon to the Present

From Chalcedon to the Breach between East and West

I. THE EASTERN AND WESTERN CHURCHES

a. The Henotikon of Zeno, 482   Zeno (Emperor, 474–91) *apud* Evagrius, *H.E.* iii. 14

[After Chalcedon, Nestorianism, which had flourished in the most easterly part of the Roman Empire, with its centre at Edessa, was propagated in Persia by Barsumas, and thus arose the schismatic Persian (Assyrian) Church. The Monophysites remained strong in Syria and Egypt. Zeno was forced into exile for two years, his rival being supported by the Monophysites, and the Henotikon (Edict of Reunion) sought to end the schism, which was a political danger. But the suggestion of the edict that the Council of Chalcedon might have erred aroused indignation in the West, and Pope Simplicius excommunicated the Patriarchs of Alexandria and Constantinople and the Emperor himself. Hence arose a schism which lasted until the accession of the Justin, 518, who reaffirmed the definition of Chalcedon.]

The Emperor Zeno Caesar, pious, victorious, supreme, everworshipful Augustus, to the very reverend bishops and clergy, and the monks and people throughout Alexandria, Egypt, Libya and Pentapolis.

WE are convinced that the source and stay of our sovereignty, its strength and impregnable safeguard, is that only genuine and true faith which, by the inspiration of God, was published by the 318 holy Fathers assembled at Nicaea, and confirmed by the 150 holy Fathers who, in like manner, met in council at Constantinople. We therefore endeavour night and day by every means, by prayer, by strenuous exertions, by legislation, to promote in every part the increase of the holy Catholic and Apostolic Church, the undefiled and immortal mother of our realm; that the pious laity, remaining in peace and harmony to Godward, may, with the bishops, the dearly beloved of God, the most pious clergy, the archimandrites and monks, offer up acceptably their sacrifice on behalf of our sovereignty. So long as our great God and Saviour Jesus Christ, who was incarnate and born of Mary, the Holy Virgin and God-bearer, approves and readily accepts our harmonious worship and service, so long will the power of our enemies be overwhelmed and dispersed, and the blessings of peace, of favourable weather and abundant crops, and all that is to man's benefit, will be freely bestowed upon us.

Wherefore, since this irreproachable faith is the safeguard of ourselves and of the Roman commonwealth, we have received petitions from pious archimandrites and hermits, beseeching us with tears that the churches should be restored to unity, that the members should be joined together, which the enemy of all good has from of old striven earnestly to rend asunder, knowing that he will meet with defeat if ever he attacks the body when it is entire. For of the countless generations which time has borne away from this life in the course of so many years it has happened that some have passed away deprived of the laver of regeneration, while others have been carried off without having partaken in the divine Communion; and murders innumerable have been committed, and not the earth only but the very air has been polluted by the abundance of bloodshed. Who would not pray for the transformation of this state of things into good?

Therefore we were eager that you should be informed that we and the churches throughout the world neither have held nor do we hold nor shall we hold, nor do we know of any that hold, any other symbol or teaching or definition of faith or creed other than the aforementioned holy symbol of the 318 holy Fathers, which the aforesaid 150 holy Fathers confirmed, and if any hold such, we count him an alien. For we are assured that this symbol alone is the safeguard of our sovereignty, as we said, and all who desire the saving illumination are baptized on their acceptance of this alone. This is the symbol followed by all the holy Fathers in council at Ephesus, when they proceeded to pass sentence of deposition on Nestorius and those who followed him in his opinions; which Nestorius we also anathematize, together with Eutyches, and all such as hold opinions contrary to the above-mentioned. At the same time we accept the twelve chapters of Cyril, of blessed memory, late Archbishop of the holy Catholic church of the Alexandrians.

Moreover we confess that the Only-begotten Son of God, himself God, who truly took upon himself manhood, our Lord Jesus Christ, who in respect of his Godhead is consubstantial with the Father, and consubstantial with us in respect of his manhood; we confess that he, having come down and been made incarnate of the Holy Spirit and the Virgin Mary, the God-bearer, is one, not two; for we assert that both his miracles and also the sufferings which he, of his own will, endured in the flesh, belong to one single person; we in no wise admit them that make a division or confusion, or bring in a phantom; seeing that his truly sinless incarnation from the God-bearer did not bring about the addition of a Son, for the Holy Trinity existed as a Trinity even when one member, God the Word, became incarnate.

Knowing then that neither the holy orthodox churches in all parts nor the priests who are at their head, the dearly beloved of God, nor our own sovereignty, have admitted, or do admit, any symbol or definition of faith other than the holy teaching aforesaid, we have without hesitation joined ourselves to it. And we write this to you for your assurance, not as producing a new form of faith. And we anathematize any one who has held or holds any other opinion, either now or at any other time, whether at Chalcedon or at any synod whatsoever; and in particular do we anathematize the before-mentioned Nestorius and Eutyches and all who upheld their teachings.

Join yourselves therefore to the Church, your spiritual mother, and in her enjoy the same communion with us, in accordance with the aforesaid one and only definition of the faith, that of the 318 holy Fathers. For your all-holy mother, the Church, waits to embrace you as her true children, and longs to hear your voice that she loves so well which has been so long withheld. Hasten then; for by so doing you will secure for yourselves the favour of our Lord and Saviour and God, Jesus Christ, as well as the approval of our sovereignty.

b. The 'Three Chapters'

The Canons of the Second Council of Constantinople, 553 Mansi, ix. 375, D ff.

[The works of three Nestorian or semi-Nestorian theologians, Theodore of Mopsuestia (see p. 48), Theodoret of Cyrus, and Ibas of Edessa had been summarized as the 'Three Chapters' and approved at Chalcedon. But the Monophysites prevailed upon the Emperor Justinian, through the influence of his wife, Theodora, to condemn the 'Three Chapters' by an edict of 543. Pope Vigilius was persuaded or intimidated into confirming this condemnation, but the opposition aroused in the West led him to demand an Oecumenical Council; this met at Const. and condemned the 'Chapters.' Thus 'the East was conciliated at the expense of the West' (M. Deanesley, *History of the Medieval Church*, p. 11).]

1. If any one does not acknowledge the one nature or substance (οὐσία) of the Father, Son and Holy Spirit, their one virtue and power, a consubstantial Trinity, one Godhead worshipped in three persons (ὑποστάσεις) or characters (πρόσωπα), let him be anathema. For

there is one God and Father, from whom are all things, and one Lord Jesus Christ, through whom are all things, and one Holy Spirit, in whom are all things.

2. If any one does not confess that there are two begettings of God the Word, one before ages, from the Father, timelessly and incorporeally, the other in the last days, the begetting of the same person, who came down from heaven and was made flesh of the Holy and Glorious God-bearer and ever-virgin Mary, and was born of her, let him be anathema.

3. If any one says that there was one God the Word who did miracles, and another Christ who suffered, or that God the Word was with Christ when he was born of a woman, or was in him, as one person in another, and not that there was one and the same Lord Jesus Christ, incarnate and made man, and that the miracles and the sufferings which he endured voluntarily in the flesh pertained to the same person, let him be anathema.

4. If any one says that the union of God the Word to a man was effected in respect of grace, or working, or equality of honour, or authority, or was relative, or temporary, or 'dynamic';[1] or that it was according to the good pleasure (of the Word), God the Word being pleased with the man ...

5. If any one takes the one personality (ὑπόστασις) of our Lord Jesus Christ in a sense which allows it to stand for several personalities, and by this means attempts to introduce two personalities or two characters in the mystery of Christ, and says that of those two characters introduced by him there is one personality in respect of worth and honour and adoration, as Theodore and Nestorius have written in their madness; and slanders the holy Council of Chalcedon by alleging that the phrase 'one personality' was there used with this impious intention; and does not confess that the Word of God was united to flesh in respect of personality (καθ᾽ ὑπόστασιν) ...

6. If any one applies the title 'God-bearer' (θεοτόκος) to the glorious and ever-virgin Mary in an unreal and not in a true sense, as if a mere man was born, and not God the Word made flesh and born of her, while the birth is to be 'referred' to God the Word, as they say inasmuch as he was with the man that was born ...

---

[1] [κατά] ἀναφοράν, ἤ σχέσιν, ἤ δύναμιν, perhaps 'effected by promotion, or possession, or power'.

10. If any one does not confess that he who was crucified in the flesh, our Lord Jesus Christ, is the true God and Lord of glory, and one of the Holy Trinity, let him be anathema.

[The remaining four canons deal with the opinions of the three theologians in more detail.]

c. The Monothelite Controversy

The Third Council (*in Trullo*) of Constantinople, 681   Mansi, xi. 635 C ff.

[Chalcedon left the Eastern Monophysites in schism, and the Monophysite tendency of the Second Council of Const. had not repealed the Chalcedonian definition. Meanwhile the threat to the Eastern Empire from the Persians and the Arabs made the schism politically dangerous. Cyrus, patriarch of Alexandria, encouraged by the Emperor, suggested to Pope Honorius that the schismatics might be reconciled by a formula (which had been put forward by Sergius of Const.) which admitted the two natures but only one 'divine-human operation or will' (ἐνέργεια ἢ θέλημα). Honorius, who seems to have thought the terminology a matter of indifference, on the ground that the sinless human will of Christ could not be in conflict with his divine will, and that two wills acting in unison are indistinguishable from one will, agreed with this 'monothelite' formula, which was published by Heraclius in the *Ecthesis*, 638. But the successors of Honorius saw in it the thin end of a Monophysite wedge, and Martin in 649 condemned the *Ecthesis*. There followed a schism which lasted till 681, when the Arab conquest of Egypt and Syria left no reason for conciliating the monophysites at the expense of antagonizing the West. The Emperor deposed the patriarch, asked Pope Agatho for guidance, and a council reckoned as the Sixth Oecumenical met in the *Trullus* (domed chamber) of the palace. The Monothelites, including Honorius, were condemned, and the schism was ended.]

[After rehearsing the Chalcedonian doctrine of the person of Christ the definition proceeds:]

We also preach two natural wills in him and two natural operations [ἐνέργειαι], without division, without change, without separation, without partition, without confusion. This we preach in accordance with the teaching of the holy Fathers. And two natural wills, not contrary (God forbid), as the impious heretics assert, but his human will following his divine and omnipotent will, not resisting it nor striving against it, but rather subject to it. For the will of the flesh had to be moved, but to be subjected to the divine will, according to the all-wise Athanasius. For as his flesh is said to be, and is, the flesh of God the Word so the natural will of the flesh is said to belong to God the Word, and does so belong; as he himself says, 'I came down from Heaven not to do mine own will, but the will of the Father that sent me' (John vi. 38), calling his own that will of the flesh, since the flesh also was made his own.

For as his all-holy and immaculate ensouled flesh was not destroyed by being deified, but persisted in its own state and sphere; so also his human will was not destroyed by being deified, but was rather preserved, as Gregory the theologian says: 'For the willing that we understand to be an act of the Saviour's will is not contrary to God but is wholly deified.'

d. The Iconoclastic Controversy   Definition of the Second Council of Nicaea, 787: Actio VII. Mansi, xiii. 378 D ff.

[The controversy began with the Iconoclastic edict of Leo III (the Isaurian) in 726. His motives included the desire to purify the debased Christianity of much of the East, and especially the Balkans, where the continual raids of Slavs, Bulgars, Saracens, etc., had demoralized the population and almost destroyed learning. Christianity here was fast becoming a degraded superstition, inferior, intellectually and morally, to Arab monotheism. The edict gave rise to rioting, Pope Gregory II denounced it, and the imperial cities of Italy rebelled. In 730 Leo deposed the patriarch of Constantinople, seized part of the papal lands, and placed the dioceses of S. Italy and Sicily under Constantinople; but incessant wars against the Arabs prevented him from enforcing his decision in the W.

The Second Council of Nicaea, held under the influence of the Empress Irene, when the emperor was a boy, was followed by a temporary healing of the breach between E. and W., but it broke out again in 815. This breach, since it left the papacy without protection against the Lombards, was one of the causes of the founding of the Frankish Empire; though Charlemagne took the side of the iconoclasts, repudiated Nicaea II,[1] and asked the Pope to excommunicate the Emperor; a request which Hadrian I refused.]

... Proceeding as it were on the royal road and following the divinely inspired teaching of our holy Fathers, and the tradition of the Catholic Church (for we know that this tradition is of the Holy Spirit which dwells in the Church), we define, with all care and exactitude, that the venerable and holy images are set up in just the same way as the figure of the precious and life-giving cross; painted images, and those in mosaic and those of other suitable material, in the holy churches of God, on holy vessels and vestments, on walls and in pictures, in houses and by the roadsides; images of our Lord and God and Saviour Jesus Christ and of our undefiled Lady, the holy God-bearer, and of the honourable angels, and of all saintly and holy men. For the more continually these are observed by means of such representations, so much the more will the beholders be aroused to recollect the originals and to long after them, and to pay to the images the tribute of an embrace and a reverence of

---

[1] At a Council at Frankfurt, 794, where Nicaea was misrepresented as enjoining the payment to images of *servitium* and *adoratio* as to the Holy Trinity.

honour,[1] not to pay to them the actual worship[2] which is according our faith, and which is proper only to the divine nature: but as to the figure of the venerable and life-giving cross, and to the holy Gospels and the other sacred monuments, so to those images to accord the honour of incense and oblation of lights, as it has been the pious custom of antiquity. For the honour paid to the image passes to its original, and he that adores an image adores in it the person depicted thereby. ...

e. Nicholas I on the Apostolic See From the letter *Preposueramus quidem*, 865, to the Emperor Michael: *Ep.* 8. Mansi, xv. 196 D ff.

[During much of the ninth century the papacy was under the domination of the Franks, who exacted this price for their protection of the papal patrimony against the Saracens. But during the pontificate of Nicholas I (858–867) the Frankish empire under Louis II was weakened by the attacks of the Norsemen and Nicholas was able to assert the independence of the Pope, and even to intervene in the Empire, and successfully to defy Louis in the matter of the divorce of Lothar of Lorraine. In the West the papal position was immensely strengthened by his acceptance of the Pseudo-Isidorian Decretals (the 'Forged Decretals'), and in the East he rebuked the Emperor for deposing Ignatius (see p. 101) without consulting the Roman See.]

... The judge shall be judged neither by Augustus, nor by any cleric, nor by the people. ... The First See shall not be judged by any. ... Where have you read that the emperors your predecessors intervened in synodal assemblies, unless it may be, in those which were concerned with the faith, which is universal, and the business of all, and which is of importance not to the clergy only, but also to the laity and to the whole body of Christians? ... The higher the authority of the courts against whose judgements a complaint is laid, the greater must be the eminence of that court whose decision is sought, until by stages that See is reached whose decision is either amended by itself, the deserts of the case so compelling, or is reversed for the judgement of God alone, without further question.

Furthermore, if you do not listen to us, it remains that you be held by us as our Lord Jesus Christ enjoins us to hold those who refuse to hear the Church of God; especially since the privileges of the Roman Church, confirmed in S. Peter by the words of Christ, ordained in the Church itself, observed from of old, proclaimed by the holy universal synods and ever venerated by the whole Church, can by no means be diminished, infringed or altered, since no effort of man has power to remove a

---

[1] τιμητικὴ προσκύνησις.   [2] ἀληθινὴ λατρεία.

foundation which God has laid, and what God has established stands firm and unshakeable. ... These privileges, then, were bestowed on this holy Church by Christ: they were not bestowed by the Synods, but were merely proclaimed and held in veneration by them. ...

Wherefore since according to the Canons the judgments of lesser tribunals must be referred to a tribunal having greater authority, that is, for their reversal or confirmation; it is immediately clear that the judgements of the Apostolic See, than which there is no greater authority, cannot be handled by any other tribunal, nor is it permissible for any to sit in judgement upon its decision. Appeals are to be made to that See from any part of the world. Such is the meaning of the canons. But no appeal is allowed from that See. ... We do not say that the decision of the said See cannot be amended; some of the facts may have been withheld, or the See may have made a decree of a dispensatory nature in view of the circumstances of the time or of some serious and compelling reasons. ...

But, we beg you, do not make any claim to the prejudice of God's Church; for that Church does nothing to the prejudice of your dominion, since it rather offers supplication to the eternal Godhead for the stability of your Empire and with constant devotion prays for your safety and your eternal salvation. Do not usurp the things that are her own; do not seek to take from her the things which have been entrusted to her alone, knowing that every one that has the administration of the affairs of this world ought to be kept away from sacred matters, to just the same extent as it is fitting that no member of the ranks of the clergy and the warriors of God should be immersed in any secular business. In fact we are utterly at a loss to understand how those who have been given the right to preside only over human, and not over divine, affairs, may presume to sit in judgement on those through whom divine affairs are administered. Before the coming of Christ it was the case that there existed, in a type, men who were at once kings and priests: sacred history tells us that the holy Melchisedech was one of these. The devil, as one who ever strives, with his tyrannical spirit, to claim for himself what belongs to the worship of God, has imitated this example in his own members, so that pagan emperors might be spoken of as being at the same time the chief pontiffs. But when he was found who was in truth both king and pontiff, thereafter the emperor did not lay hands on the rights of the pontificate, nor did the pontiff usurp the name of emperor. For that one and the same 'mediator between God and man, the man Christ Jesus'

(1 Tim. ii. 5), so separated the functions of the two authorities, giving each its own proper activities and distinct honours (desiring that these properties should be exalted by the medicine of humility and not brought down again to the depths by man's arrogance), that Christian emperors should have need of the pontiffs with regard to eternal life, while the pontiffs should make use of the emperor's laws with regard to the course of temporal affairs, and these alone: so that the activity of the spirit might be set free from carnal interruptions.

II. THE BREACH BETWEEN EAST AND WEST, 1054
From the letter *In terra pax hominibus* from the Roman Church
to Michael Cerularius, Sept. 1053. Mansi, xix. 638 B ff.

[The breach caused by the Iconoclastic controversy was scarcely healed when the 'Photian schism' separated the E. from the W. Ignatius, patriarch of Const., had been deposed by the court and replaced by a certain Photius. Nicholas I demanded compensation for his violated rights. After some negotiation P. defied the Pope and in 867 attacked the introduction of Latin rites and the 'double procession' (see p. 27) into the Church of Bulgaria, and in the same year a Council at Constantinople declared the Roman Church heretical on certain points, condemned her interference in the E., and excommunicated Nicholas. An Oecumenical Council (Constantinople IV) in 870 failed to compose the quarrel, which was only patched up in 920.

The 1054 schism was the result of the clash of two powerful personalities, of Pope Leo IX and Michael Cerularius. In 1024 the Emperor had asked John XIX for the recognition of the independence of the Church of Const, in her own sphere. This was refused. In 1053 Cerularius, fearing an alliance between Emperor and Pope which might result in the transfer of the Greek province in S. Italy from his jurisdiction, and perhaps in other infringements of his authority, decided upon schism. He ordered the closing of all churches of the Latin rite in Const. In 1054, in spite of the Emperor's efforts at mediation, the Roman legates at Constantinople excommunicated the patriarch. Cerularius anathematized them in reply and the schism was complete.]

5. ... You are said to have publicly condemned the Apostolic and Latin Church, without either a hearing or a conviction. And the chief reason for this condemnation, which displays an unexampled presumption and an unbelievable effrontery, is that the Latin Church dares to celebrate the commemoration of the Lord's passion with unleavened bread. What an unguarded accusation is this of yours, what an evil piece of arrogance! You 'place your mouth in heaven, while your tongue, going through the world',[1] strives with human arguments and conjectures to undermine and subvert the ancient faith. ...

---

[1] Cf. Ps. 73: 9.

11. ... In prejudging the case of the highest See, the see on which no judgement may be passed by any man, you have received the anathema from all the Fathers of all the venerable Councils.

32. As a hinge, remaining unmoved, opens and shuts a door, so Peter and his successors have an unfettered jurisdiction over the whole Church, since no one ought to interfere with their position, because the highest See is judged by none. ...

SECTION II
The Empire and the Papacy

I. CHARLEMAGNE AND EDUCATION, 789
From Admonitio generalis, cap. 72

... Let the ministers of the altar of God adorn their ministry by good behaviour, and likewise the other orders who observe a rule, and the congregations of monks. We implore them to lead such a life as befits their profession as God himself commanded in the gospel. 'Let your light so shine before men, that they may see your good works, and glorify your Father which is in heaven,' so that by our example many may be led to serve God. Let them join and associate to themselves not only children of servile condition, but also sons of freemen. And let schools be established in which boys may learn to read. Correct carefully the Psalms, the signs in writing, the songs, the calendar, the grammar, in each monastery or bishopric, and the Catholic books; because often men desire to pray to God properly, but they pray badly because of incorrect books. And do not permit mere boys to corrupt them in reading or writing. If the Gospel, Psalter, and Missal have to be copied let men of mature age do the copying, with the greatest care.

II. 'THE DONATION OF CONSTANTINE', EIGHTH CENTURY
Haller, *Quellen zur Geschichte der Enstebung des Kirchenstaates*, 1907, p. 241.
(Translation based on Laffan, *Select Documents,* I.) Mirbt, *Quellen,* 228.

[This document, which purports to be a deed of gift from Constantine to Pope Sylvester, was included in the 'Forged Decretals,' and it played a great part in subsequent controversies. Its authority was unquestioned till the fifteenth century, when its authenticity was impugned by many eminent churchmen and its falsity finally proved by Lorenzo Valla. It is now completely discredited.]

In the name of the holy and undivided Trinity, the Father, the Son and the Holy Spirit. The Emperor Caesar Flavius Constantinus in Christ Jesus (one of the same Holy Trinity our Saviour, Lord and God) faithful, merciful, mighty, beneficent, Alamannicus, Gothicus, Sarmaticus, Germanicus, Brittanicus, Hunicus, pious, fortunate, victorious, triumphant, ever August; to the most holy and blessed father of fathers, Silvester, Bishop of the Roman city and Pope; and to all his successors, the pontiffs, who shall sit in the chair of blessed Peter to the end of time; as also to all the most reverend and God-beloved Catholic bishops, by this our imperial constitution subjected throughout the world to this same Roman church, whether they be appointed now or at any future time—Grace, peace, love, joy, long-suffering, mercy from God the Father almighty and Jesus Christ His Son and the Holy Spirit be with you all. ... For we wish you to know ... that we have forsaken the worship of idols ... and have come to the pure Christian faith, the true light and everlasting life. ...

For when a horrible and filthy leprosy invaded all the flesh of my body and I was treated by many assembled doctors but could not thereby attain to health, there came to me the priests of the Capitol, who said I ought to erect a font on the Capitol and fill it with the blood of innocent children and that by bathing in it while it was warm I could be healed. According to their advice many innocent children were assembled; but, when the sacrilegious priests of the pagans wished them to be slaughtered and the font filled with their blood, our serenity perceived the tears of their mothers and I thereupon abhorred the project; and, pitying them, we ordered their sons to be restored to them, gave them vehicles and gifts and sent them back rejoicing to their homes. And when the day had passed, and the silence of night had descended upon us and the time of sleep had come, the apostles SS. Peter and Paul appeared to me saying, 'Since thou hast put an end to thy sins and hast shrunk from shedding the blood of the innocent, we are sent by Christ, our Lord God, to impart to thee a plan for the recovery of thy health. Hear therefore our advice and do whatever we bid thee. Silvester, bishop of the city of Rome, flying from thy persecutions, is in hiding with his clergy in the caverns of the rocks on Mount Serapte. When thou hast called him to thee, he will show thee the pool of piety; and, when he has thrice immersed thee therein, all the strength of this leprosy will leave thee. When that is done, make this return to thy Saviour, that by thy command all the churches throughout the world be restored; and purify thyself in this way, by abandoning all the superstition of idols and adoring and worshipping the living and true God, who alone is true, and devote thyself to His will. ... '

Therefore I rose from sleep and followed the advice of the holy apostle. ... The Blessed Silvester ... imposed on me a period of penance ... then the font was blessed and I was purified by a triple immersion. And when I was at the bottom of the font I saw a hand from heaven touching me. And I rose from the water cleansed ... from the filthiness of leprosy. ...

And so the first day after my reception of the mystery of Holy Baptism and the cure of my body from the filthiness of leprosy I understood that there is no other God than the Father, the Son and the Holy Spirit, whom most blessed Silvester, the Pope, preaches, a Trinity in unity and Unity in trinity. For all the gods of the nations, whom I have hitherto worshiped, are shown to be demons, the works of men's hands. And the same venerable father told us clearly how great power in heaven and earth our Saviour gave to His Apostle, blessed Peter, when in answer to questioning He found him faithful and said: 'Thou art Peter, and upon this rock I will build My Church; and the gates of hell shall not prevail against it.' Attend, ye mighty, and incline the ear of your heart to what the good Lord and Master gave in addition to His disciple when He said: 'I will give unto thee the keys of the kingdom of heaven, and whatsoever thou shalt bind on earth shall be bound in heaven, and whatsoever thou shalt loose on earth shall be loosed in heaven.' And when I learned these things at the mouth of the blessed Silvester, and found that I was wholly restored to health by the beneficence of blessed Peter himself, we— together with all our satraps and the whole senate, and the magnates and all the Roman people, which is subject to the glory of our rule— considered that, since he is seen to have been set up as the vicar of God's Son on earth, the pontiffs who act on behalf of that prince of the apostles should receive from us and our empire a greater power of government than the earthly clemency of our imperial serenity is seen to have conceded to them; for we choose the same prince of the apostles and his vicars to be our constant witnesses before God. And inasmuch as our imperial power is earthly, we have decreed that it shall venerate and honour his most holy Roman Church and that the sacred see of blessed Peter shall be gloriously exalted above our empire and earthly throne. We attribute to him the power and glorious dignity and strength and honour of the Empire, and we ordain and decree that he shall have rule as well over the four principal sees, Antioch, Alexandria, Constantinople, and Jerusalem, as also over all the churches of God in all the world. And the pontiff who for the time being presides over that most holy Roman Church shall be the highest and chief of all priests in the whole world, and according to his decision shall all matters be settled which shall be taken in hand for the service of God or the confirmation of the faith of

Christians. For it is right that the sacred law should have the centre of its power there where the Founder of the sacred laws, our Saviour, commanded blessed Peter to have the chair of his apostolate, and where, bearing the suffering of the cross, he accepted the cup of a blessed death and showed himself an imitator of his Lord and Master; and that there the nations should bow their necks in confession of Christ's name, where their teacher, blessed Paul, the apostle, offered his neck for Christ and was crowned with martyrdom. There for ever let them seek a teacher, where lies the holy body of that teacher; and there, prone in humility, let them perform the service of the heavenly King, God, our Saviour, Jesus Christ, where proudly they used to serve the empire of an earthly king. ...

To the holy apostles, my lords the most blessed Peter and Paul, and through them also to blessed Silvester, our father, supreme pontiff and universal pope of the city of Rome, and to the pontiffs, his successors, who to the end of the world shall sit in the seat of blessed Peter, we grant and by this present we convey our imperial Lateran palace, which is superior to and excels all palaces in the whole world; and further the diadem, which is the crown of our head; and the mitre; as also the super-humeral, that is, the stole which usually surrounds our imperial neck; and the purple cloak and the scarlet tunic and all the imperial robes; also the rank of commanders of the imperial cavalry. ...

And we decree that those most reverend men, the clergy of various orders serving the same most holy Roman Church, shall have that eminence, distinction, power and precedence, with which our illustrious senate is gloriously adorned; that is, they shall be made patricians and consuls. And we ordain that they shall also be adorned with other imperial dignities. Also we decree that the clergy of the sacred Roman Church shall be adorned as are the imperial officers. ...

Wherefore that the pontifical crown should not be made of less repute, but rather that the dignity of a more than earthly office and the might of its glory should be yet further adorned—lo, we convey to the oft-mentioned and most blessed Silvester, universal pope, both our palace, as preferment, and likewise all provinces, palaces and districts of the city of Rome and Italy and of the regions of the West; and, bequeathing them to the power and sway of him and the pontiffs, his successors, we do (by means of fixed imperial decision through this our divine, sacred and authoritative sanction) determine and decree that the same be placed at his disposal, and do lawfully grant it as a permanent possession to the holy Roman Church.

Wherefore we have perceived that our empire and the power of our government should be transferred and removed to the regions of the East and that a city should be built in our name in the best place in the province of Byzantium and our empire there established; for it is not right that an earthly emperor should have authority there, where the rule of priests and the head of the Christian religion have been established by the Emperor of heaven. ...

Given at Rome, March 30th, when our lord Flavius Constantinus Augustus, for the fourth time, and Galliganus, most illustrious men, were consuls.

III. CHURCH AND STATE

a. Decree on Papal Elections, 1059[1]　　Doeberl, *Monumenta*, iii. Mirbt, 272

[The eleventh century saw the reform of monasticism and the inauguration of a line of worthy Popes by Henry III. And the Lateran Council of 1059, under Nicholas II, struck at an evil which was the cause of much that was wrong with the Church—the control of appointments by laymen.]

... We [Pope Nicholas II] decree and establish (3) that, on the death of the pontiff of this Roman universal church, the cardinal bishops shall first confer with most diligent consideration and then shall summon the cardinal clergy to join them; and afterwards the rest of the clergy and people shall give their assent to the new election. (4) That, lest the disease of venality creep in by any means, godly men shall take the chief part in the election of the pontiff, and the others shall follow their lead. This method of election is regular and in accordance with the rules and decrees of the Fathers ... especially with the words of St. Leo; 'No argument,' he says, 'will permit them to be considered bishops who have not been elected by the clergy, nor demanded by the people, nor consecrated by the bishops of the province with the approval of the metropolitan.' But since the Apolistic See is raised above all churches in the world and therefore can have no metropolitan over it, the cardinal bishops without doubt perform the function of a metropolitan, when they raise the elected pontiff to the apostolic eminence. (5) They shall elect someone from out of this [Roman] church, if a suitable candidate be found; if not, he shall be chosen from another church. (6) Saving the honour and reverence due to our beloved son Henry, who at present is acknowledged King and, it is hoped, will be Emperor, by God's grace; as

---

[1] The translation of this and the three following extracts is based on that of Laffan, op. cit.

we have granted to him and to such of his successors as obtain this right in person from the apostolic see. (7) But, if the perversity of evil and wicked men shall make it impossible to hold a pure, fair and free election in the city, the cardinal bishops with the godly clergy and catholic laymen, even though they be few, shall have the right and power to elect the pontiff of the Apostolic See in any place which they shall consider most convenient. (8) After an election has been clearly made, if the fierceness of war or the malignant endeavours of any man shall prevent him who is elected from being enthroned on the apostolic chair according to custom, the elected shall nevertheless have authority as Pope to rule the holy Roman church and to dispose of its resources, as we know that blessed Gregory did before his consecration. ...

b. **Letter of the Synod of Worms to Gregory VII, January 1076**

Bernheim, *Quellen zur Geschichte des Investiturstreits*, 1907, i. 68

[Gregory annoyed Henry IV by suspending certain German bishops. Henry retorted by nominating bishops to Italian sees. The Pope threatened excommunication, and Henry then made common cause with the disaffected German bishops and at the Synod of Worms this manifesto was drawn up.]

Siegfried, Archbishop of Mainz, Udo of Trier, William of Utrecht, Hermann of Metz, Henry of Liége, Ricbert of Verden, Bibo of Toul, Hozemann of Speyer, Burckhard of Halberstadt, Werner of Strassburg, Burchard of Basel, Otto of Constance, Adalbero of Wurzburg, Rodbert of Bamberg, Otto of Regensburg, Ellinard of Freising, Udalric of Eichstadt, Frederick of Munster, Eilbert of Minden, Hezil of Hildesheim, Benno of Osnabrück, Eppo of Naumburg, Imadus of Paderborn, Tiedo of Brandenburg, Burchard of Lausanne, Bruno of Verona—to brother Hildebrand.

Although, when thou didst first seize the control of the church, it was clear to us how unlawful and wicked a thing thou hadst presumed to do contrary to right and justice with thy well-known arrogance; nevertheless we thought fit to draw a veil of indulgent silence over the evil beginnings of thine inauguration, hoping that these iniquitous preliminaries would be amended and cancelled by the integrity and diligence of the rest of thy reign. But now, as the lamentable condition of the whole church sadly proclaims, thou art consistently and pertinaciously faithful to thine evil beginnings, in the increasing iniquity of thine actions and decrees. ... The flame of discord, which thou didst arouse with baneful factions in the Roman church, thou hast spread with senseless fury throughout all the churches of Italy, Germany, Gaul and Spain. For to the utmost of thy power thou hast deprived the bishops of all the power, known to have been divinely given to them by the grace of the Holy Spirit, Who operates above in all ordinations. Thou hast given all oversight over ecclesiastical matters to the passions of the mob. None is now acknowledged a bishop or a priest, unless by unworthy subservience he has obtained his office from thy magnificence. Thou hast thrown into wretched confusion all the vigour of the apostolic institution and that perfect mutuality of the members of Christ, which the teacher of the gentiles so often commends and inculcates. Thus, because of thine ambitious decrees—with tears it must be said—the name of Christ has all but perished. Who is not astounded by thine unworthy conduct in arrogating to thyself a new and unlawful power in order to destroy the due rights of the whole brotherhood? For thou dost assert that, if the mere rumour of a sin committed by a member of our flocks reaches thee, none of us has henceforth any power to bind or loose him, but thou only or he whom thou shalt specially delegate for the purpose. Who, that is learned in the sacred scriptures, does not see that this decree exceeds all madness? Wherefore ... we have decided, by common consent, to make known to thee that on which we have hitherto kept silence, namely why thou canst not now, nor ever couldst preside over the apostolic see. Thou didst bind thyself with a corporal oath in the time of Emperor Henry of blessed memory that never in the Emperor's lifetime, nor in that of his son, our present reigning and glorious King, wouldst thou thyself accept the papacy, or, as far as in thee lay, wouldst thou suffer another to accept it, without the consent and approval of the father, while he was alive, or of the son while he lived. And there are to-day many bishops who witnessed that oath; who saw it with their eyes and heard it with their ears. Remember too how, when ambition to be pope moved several of the cardinals, to remove all rivalry on that occasion, thou didst bind thyself with an oath, on condition that they did the same, never to hold the papacy. See how faithfully thou hast kept these oaths!

Further, when a synod was held in the time of Pope Nicholas, whereat 125 bishops assisted, it was established and decreed under pain of anathema that none should ever be made Pope except by the election of the cardinals, the approbation of the people and the consent and authorization of the king. And of that decision and decree thou thyself wast the author, sponsor and signatory.

Also thou hast, as it were, filled the whole church with the stench of a grave scandal by living more intimately than is necessary with a woman not of thy kin. This is a matter of propriety rather than of morality; and yet this general complaint is everywhere made, that at the apostolic see all judgements and all decrees are the work of a woman, and that the whole church is governed by this new senate of a woman. ...

Wherefore henceforth we renounce, now and for the future, all obedience unto thee—which indeed we never promised to thee. And since, as thou didst publicly proclaim, none of us has been to thee a bishop, so thou henceforth wilt be Pope to none of us.

c. Deposition of Henry IV by Gregory VII, February 1076
Doeberl, op. cit. iii. 26. Mirbt, 147

Blessed Peter, chief of the apostles, incline thine holy ears to us, I pray, and hear me, thy servant, whom from infancy thou hast nourished and till this day hast delivered from the hand of the wicked, who have hated and do hate me for my faithfulness to thee. ... Especially to me, as thy representative, has been committed, and to me by thy grace has been given by God the power of binding and loosing in heaven and on earth. Relying, then, on this belief, for the honour and defence of thy church and in the name of God Almighty, the Father, the Son and the Holy Ghost, through thy power and authority, I withdraw the government of the whole kingdom of the Germans and of Italy from Henry the King, son of Henry the Emperor. For he has risen up against thy Church with unheard of arrogance. And I absolve all Christians from the bond of the oath which they have made to him or shall make. And I forbid anyone to serve him as King. For it is right that he who attempts to diminish the honour of thy church, shall himself lose the honour which he seems to have. And since he has scorned to show Christian obedience, and has not returned to the Lord whom he has deserted—holding intercourse with the excommunicate; committing many iniquities; despising my warnings, which, as thou art my witness, I have sent to him for his salvation, separating himself from thy church and trying to divide it—on thy behalf I bind him with the bond of anathema. Trusting in thee I thus bind him that the peoples may know and acknowledge that thou art Peter and that on thy rock the Son of the living God has built his church and that the gates of hell shall not prevail against it.

d. Gregory VII's Letter to the Bishop of Metz, 1081   Doeberl, op. cit. iii.
40 ff. Mirbt, 297

[The struggle with Henry IV was going against Gregory at this time. His deposition of Henry had provoked sympathy for the Emperor, and at councils at Mainz and Brixen, called by Henry, the Pope was declared deposed. This letter to Bishop Hermann is the fullest exposition of the papalist point of view.]

Bishop Gregory, servant of the servants of God, to his beloved brother in Christ, Hermann bishop of Metz, greeting and apostolic benediction. It is doubtless owing to a dispensation of God that, as we learn, thou art ready to endure trials and dangers in defence of the truth. For such is His ineffable grace and wonderful mercy that He never allows His chosen ones completely to go astray—never permits them utterly to fall or to be cast down. For, after they have been afflicted by a period of persecution—a useful term of probation as it were,—He makes them, even if they have been for a time fainthearted, stronger than before. Since, moreover, manly courage impels one strong man to act more bravely than another and to press forward more boldly—even as among cowards fear induces one to flee more disgracefully than another,—we wish, beloved, with the voice of exhortation, to impress this upon thee: thou shouldst the more delight to stand in the army of the Christian faith among the first, the more thou art convinced that the conquerors are the most worthy and the nearest to God. Thy request, indeed, to be aided, as it were, by our writings and fortified against the madness of those who babble forth with impious tongue that the authority of the holy and apostolic see had no authority to excommunicate Henry—a man who despises the Christian law; a destroyer of the churches and of the empire; a patron and companion of heretics—or to absolve any one from the oath of fealty to him, seems to us to be hardly necessary when so many and such absolutely decisive warrants are to be found in the pages of Holy Scripture. Nor do we believe, indeed, that those who (heaping up for themselves damnation) impudently detract from the truth and contradict it have added these assertions to the audacity of their defence so much from ignorance as from a certain madness.

For, to cite a few passages from among many, who does not know the words of our Lord and Saviour Jesus Christ who says in the gospel: 'Thou art Peter and upon this rock will I build my church, and the gates of hell shall not prevail against it; and I will give unto thee the keys of the kingdom of Heaven; and whatsoever thou shalt bind upon earth shall be bound also in Heaven, and whatsoever thou shalt loose upon earth shall be loosed also in Heaven'? [Matthew xvi, 18, 19.] Are kings excepted here? Or are they not included among the sheep which the Son of God committed to St Peter? Who, I ask, in view of this universal concession of the power of binding and loosing, can think that he is withdrawn from the authority of St Peter, unless, perhaps, that unhappy man who is unwilling to bear the yoke of the Lord and subjects himself to the burden of the devil, refusing to be among the number of Christ's sheep? It will help him little to his wretched liberty that he shake from his proud neck the divinely granted power of Peter. For the more any one, through pride, refuses to bear it, the more heavily shall it press upon him unto damnation at the judgement.

The holy fathers, as well in general councils as in their writings and doings, have called the Holy Roman Church the universal mother, accepting and serving with great veneration this institution founded by the divine will, this pledge of a dispensation to the church, this privilege entrusted in the beginning and confirmed to St Peter the chief of the apostles. And even as they accepted its statements in confirmation of their faith and of the doctrines of holy religion, so also they received its judgements—consenting in this, and agreeing as it were with one spirit and one voice: that all greater matters and exceptional cases, and judgements over all churches, ought to be referred to it as to a mother and a head; that from it there was no appeal; that no one should or could retract or reverse its decisions. ...

... Shall not an authority founded by laymen—even by those who do not know God,—be subject to that authority which the providence of God Almighty has for His own honour established and in his mercy given to the world? For His Son, even as He is undoubtingly believed to be God and man, so is He considered the highest priest, the head of all priests, sitting on the right hand of the Father and always interceding for us. Yet He despised a secular kingdom, which makes the sons of this world swell with pride, and came of His own will to the priesthood of the cross. Who does not know that kings and leaders are sprung from men who were ignorant of God, who by pride, robbery, perfidy, murders—in a word, by almost every crime at the prompting of the devil, who is the prince of this world—have striven with blind cupidity and intolerable presumption to dominate over their equals, that is, over mankind? To whom, indeed, can we better compare them, when they seek to make the priests of God bend to their feet, than to him who is head over all the sons of pride[1] and who, tempting the Highest Pontiff Himself, the Head of priests, the Son of the Most High, and promising to Him all the kingdoms of the world, said: 'All these I will give unto Thee if Thou wilt fall down and worship me'?[2] Who can doubt but that the priests of Christ are to be considered the fathers and masters of kings and princes and of all the faithful? Is it not clearly pitiful madness for a son to attempt to subject to himself his father, a pupil his master; and for one to bring into his power and bind with iniquitous bonds him by whom he believes

---

[1] Job 41: 34.   [2] Matt. 4: 9.

that he himself can be bound and loosed not only on earth but also in Heaven? This the emperor Constantine the Great, lord of all the kings and princes of nearly the whole world, plainly understood—as the blessed Gregory reminds us in a letter to the emperor Maurice, when, sitting last after all the bishops in the holy council of Nicaea, he presumed to give no sentence of judgement over them, but addressed them as gods and decreed that they should not be subject to his judgement but that he should be dependent upon their will. ...

... Many pontiffs have excommunicated kings or emperors. For, if particular examples of such princes is needed, the blessed pope Innocent excommunicated the emperor Arcadius for consenting that St John Chrysostom should be expelled from his see. Likewise another Roman pontiff, Zacchary, deposed a king of the Franks, not so much for his iniquities as because he was not fitted to exercise so great power. And in his stead he set up Pepin, father of the emperor Charles the Great, in his place—releasing all the Franks from the oath of fealty which they had sworn him. As, indeed, the holy church frequently does by its authority when it absolves servitors from the fetters of an oath sworn to such bishops as, by apostolic sentence, are deposed from their pontifical rank. And the blessed Ambrose—who, although a saint, was still not bishop over the whole church—excommunicated and excluded from the church the emperor Theodosius the Great for a fault[1] which, by other priests, was not regarded as very grave. He shows, too, in his writings that gold does not so much excel lead in value as the priestly dignity transcends the royal power; speaking thus towards the beginning of his pastoral letter: 'The honour and sublimity of bishops, brethren, is beyond all comparison. If one should compare them to resplendent kings and diademed princes it would be far less worthy than if one compared the base metal lead to gleaming gold. For, indeed, one can see how the necks of kings and princes are bowed before the knees of priests; and how, having kissed their right hands, they believe themselves strengthened by their prayers.' And a little later: 'Ye should know, brethren, that we have mentioned all this to show that nothing can be found in this world more lofty than priests or more sublime than bishops.'

Furthermore every Christian king, when he comes to die, seeks as a pitiful suppliant the aid of a priest, that he may escape hell's prison, may pass from the darkness into the light, and at the judgement of God may appear absolved from the bondage of his sins. Who, in his last hour

---

[1] A savage massacre in Thessalonica, 390, as a reprisal for a riot.

(what layman, not to speak of priests), has ever implored the aid of an earthly king for the salvation of his soul? And what king or emperor is able, by reason of the office he holds, to rescue a Christian from the power of the devil through holy baptism, to number him among the sons of God, and to fortify him with the divine unction? Who of them can by his own words make the body and blood of our Lord,—the greatest act in the Christian religion? Or who of them possesses the power of binding and loosing in heaven and on earth? From all of these considerations it is clear how greatly the priestly office excels in power.

Who of them can ordain a single clerk in the holy Church, much less depose him for any fault? For in the orders of the Church a greater power is needed to depose than to ordain. Bishops may ordain other bishops, but can by no means depose them without the authority of the apostolic see. Who, therefore, of even moderate understanding, can hesitate to give priests the precedence over kings? Then, if kings are to be judged by priests for their sins, by whom can they be judged with better right than by the Roman pontiff?

In short, any good Christians may far more properly be considered kings than may bad princes. For the former, seeking the glory of God, strictly govern themselves, whereas the latter, seeking the things which are their own and not the things of God, are enemies to themselves and tyrannical oppressors of others. Faithful Christians are the body of the true king, Christ; evil rulers, that of the devil. The former rule themselves in the hope that they will eternally reign with the Supreme Emperor, but the sway of the latter ends in their destruction and eternal damnation with the prince of darkness, who is king over all the sons of pride.

It is certainly not strange that wicked bishops are of one mind with a bad king, whom they love and fear for the honours which they have wrongfully obtained from him. Such men simoniacally ordain whom they please and sell God even for a paltry sum. As even the elect are indissolubly united with their Head, so also the wicked are inescapably leagued with him who is the head of evil, their chief purpose being to resist the good. But surely we ought not so much to denounce them as to mourn for them with tears and lamentations, beseeching God Almighty to snatch them from the snares of Satan in which they are held captive, and after their peril to bring them at last to a knowledge of the truth.

We refer to those kings and emperors who, too much puffed up by worldly glory, rule not for God but for themselves. Now, since it belongs to our office to admonish and encourage every one according to the rank or dignity which he enjoys, we endeavour, by God's grace, to arm emperors and kings and other princes with the weapon of humility,

that they may be able to allay the waves of the sea[1] and the floods of
pride. For we know that earthly glory and the cares of this world usually
tempt men to pride, especially those in authority. So that they neglect
humility and seek their own glory, desiring to lord it over their brethren.
Therefore it is of especial advantage for emperors and kings, when their
minds tend to be puffed up and to delight in their own glory, to discover
a way of humbling themselves, and to realize that what causes their
complacency is the thing which should be feared above all else. Let
them, therefore, diligently consider how perilous and how much to be
feared is the royal or imperial dignity. For very few are saved of those
who enjoy it; and those who, through the mercy of God, do come to
salvation are not so glorified in the Holy Church by the judgement of the
Holy Spirit as are many poor people. For, from the beginning of the
world until our own times, in the whole of authentic history we do not
find seven emperors or kings whose lives were as distinguished for
religion and so adorned by miracles of power as those of an innumerable
multitude who despised the world—although we believe many of them to
have found mercy in the presence of God Almighty. For what emperor or
king was ever so distinguished by miracles as were St Martin, St Antony
and St Benedict—not to mention the apostles and martyrs? And what
emperor or king raised the dead, cleansed lepers, or healed the blind? See
how the Holy Church praises and venerates the Emperor Constantine of
blessed memory, Theodosius and Honorius, Charles and Louis as lovers
of justice, promoters of the Christian religion, defenders of the churches:
it does not, however, declare them to have been resplendent with such
glorious miracles. Moreover, to how many kings or emperors has the
holy church ordered chapels or altars to be dedicated, or masses to be
celebrated in their honour? Let kings and other princes fear lest the more
they rejoice at being placed over other men in this life, the more they will
be subjected to eternal fires. For of them is written: 'The powerful shall
powerfully suffer torments.'[2] And they are about to render account to
God for as many men as they have had subjects under their dominion.
But if it be no little task for any private religious man to guard his own
soul: how much labour will there be for those who are rulers over many
thousands of souls? Moreover, if the judgement of the Holy Church
severely punishes a sinner for the slaying of one man, what will become
of those who, for the sake of worldly glory, hand over many thousands to
death? And such persons, although after having slain many they often

---

[1] Psalm 93: 4.
[2] Wisdom 6: 6. Greek, 'Mighty men shall be searched out mightily.'

say with their lips 'I have sinned,' nevertheless rejoice in their hearts at the extension of their (so-called) fame. They do not regret what they have done. Nor are they grieved at having sent their brethren down to Tartarus. As long as they do not repent with their whole heart, nor agree to give up what they have acquired or kept through bloodshed, their repentance remains without the true fruit of penitence before God.

Therefore they should greatly fear and often call to mind what we have said above, that out of the innumerable host of kings in all countries from the beginning of the world, very few are found to have been holy; whereas in one single see—the Roman—of the successive bishops from the time of blessed Peter the Apostle, nearly one hundred are counted amongst the most holy. And why is this, unless because kings and princes, enticed by vain glory, prefer, as has been said, their own things to things spiritual, whereas the bishops of the Church, despising vain glory, prefer God's will to earthly things? The former are quick to punish offences against themselves, but lightly tolerate those who sin against God. The latter readily pardon those who sin against themselves, but do not readily forgive offenders against God. The former, too bent on earthly achievements, think little of spiritual ones; the latter, earnestly meditating on heavenly things, despise the things of earth. ...

Therefore let those whom Holy Church, of its own will and after proper counsel, not for transitory glory but for the salvation of many, calls to have rule or dominion, humbly obey. And let them always beware in that point as to which St Gregory in that same pastoral book[1] bears witness: 'Indeed, when a man disdains to be like to men, he is made like to an apostate angel. Thus Saul, after having possessed the merit of humility, came to be swollen with pride when at the summit of power. Through humility, indeed, he was advanced; through pride, rejected—God being witness who said: "When thou wast small in thine own eyes, did I not make thee head over the tribes of Israel?"[2]' And a little further on: 'Moreover, strange to say, when he was small in his own eyes he was great in the eyes of God; but when he seemed great in his own eyes he was small in the eyes of God.' Let them also carefully retain what God says in the gospel: 'I seek not my own glory'; and, 'He who will be the first among you shall be the servant of all.'[3] Let them always prefer the honour of God to their own; let them cherish and guard justice by observing the rights of everyman; let them not walk in the counsel of the ungodly but, with an assenting heart, always consort with good men. Let them not

---

[1] *Reg. Past.* II. vi.   [2] I Sam. 15: 17.   [3] Jn. 8: 50, Matt. 20: 27.

seek to subject to themselves or to subjugate the Holy Church as a handmaid; but above all let them strive, by recognizing the teachers and fathers, to render due honour to the eyes of the Church—the priests of God. For if we are ordered to honour our fathers and mothers after the flesh—how much more our spiritual ones! And if he who has cursed his father or mother after the flesh is to be punished with death—what does he merit who curses his spiritual father or mother? Let them not, led astray by worldly love, strive to place one of their own sons over the flock for which Christ poured forth His blood, if they can find some one who is better and more useful than he: lest, loving their son more than God, they inflict the greatest damage on the Holy Church. For he who neglects to provide to the best of his ability for such a want—and, one might say, necessity—of Holy Mother Church is openly convicted of not loving God and his neighbour as a Christian should.

For if this virtue, love, has been neglected, no matter what good any one does he shall be without any fruit of salvation. And so by humbly doing these things, and by observing the love of God and of their neighbour as they ought, they may hope for the mercy of Him who said: 'Learn of Me, for I am meek and lowly of heart.'[1] If they have humbly imitated Him they shall pass from this servile and transitory kingdom to a true kingdom of liberty and eternity.

IV. THE END OF THE STRUGGLE OVER INVESTITURE

a. **The Concordat of Worms, September 1122**   Doeberl, op. cit. iii. 59 ff. Mirbt, 305

[Concessions were made on both sides; but the papacy had the best of it, for Henry V agreed to surrender existing practice.]

1. Agreement of Pope Calixtus II

I, Calixtus, Bishop, servant of the servants of God, do grant to thee, beloved son, Henry—by the grace of God Emperor of the Romans, Augustus—that the elections of bishops and abbots of the German kingdom, who belong to that kingdom, shall take place in thy presence, without simony or any violence; so that if any dispute shall arise between the parties concerned, thou, with the counsel or judgement of the metropolitan and the co-provincial bishops, shalt give consent and aid to the party which has the more right. The one elected shall receive the

----

[1] Matt. 11: 29.

regalia from thee by the sceptre and shall perform his lawful duties to thee on that account. But he who is consecrated in the other parts of thy empire [i.e. Burgundy and Italy] shall, within six months, and without any exaction, receive the regalia from thee by the sceptre, and shall perform his lawful duties to thee on that account (saving all rights which are known to belong to the Roman church). Concerning matters in which thou shalt make complaint to me, and ask aid—I, according to the duty of my office, will furnish aid to thee. I give unto thee true peace, and to all who are or have been of thy party in this conflict.

2. Edict of the Emperor Henry V

In the name of the holy and indivisible Trinity I, Henry, by the grace of God Emperor of the Romans, Augustus, for the love of God and of the holy Roman church and of our lord Pope Calixtus, and for the salvation of my soul, do surrender to God, and to the holy apostles of God, Peter and Paul, and to the Holy Catholic Church, all investiture through ring and staff; and do grant that in all the churches that are in my kingdom or empire there may be canonical election and free consecration. All the possessions and regalia of St Peter which, from the beginning of this discord unto this day, whether in the time of my father or in mine have been seized, and which I hold, I restore to that same Holy Roman Church. And I will faithfully aid in the restoration of those things which I do not hold. The possessions also of all other churches and princes, and of all other persons lay and clerical which have been lost in that war: according to the counsel of the princes, or according to justice, I will restore, as far as I hold them; and I will faithfully aid in the restoration of those things which I do not hold. And I grant true peace to our lord Pope Calixtus, and to the Holy Roman Church, and to all those who are or have been on its side. And in matters where the Holy Roman Church shall ask aid I will grant it; and in matters concerning which it shall make complaint to me I will duly grant to it justice. All these things have been done by the consent and counsel of the princes. Whose names are here adjoined: Adalbert archbishop of Mainz; F. archbishop of Cologne; H. bishop of Ratisbon; O. bishop of Bamberg; B. bishop of Spires; H. of Augsburg; G. of Utrecht; Ou. of Constance; E. abbot of Fulda; Henry, duke; Frederick duke; S. duke; Pertolf, duke; Margrave Teipold; Margrave Engelbert; Godfrey, count Palatine; Otto, count Palatine; Berengar, count.

I, Frederick, archbishop of Cologne and arch-chancellor, have ratified this.

b. Innocent III on Empire and Papacy

'The Moon and the Sun' *Sicut universitatis conditor. Ep.* i. 401, October 1198 P.L. ccxiv. 377. Mirbt, 326

The Creator of the universe set up two great luminaries in the firmament of heaven; the greater light to rule the day, the lesser light to rule the night. In the same way for the firmament of the universal Church, which is spoken of as heaven, he appointed two great dignities; the greater to bear rule over souls (these being, as it were, days), the lesser to bear rule over bodies (those being, as it were, nights). These dignities are the pontifical authority and the royal power. Furthermore, the moon derives her light from the sun, and is in truth inferior to the sun in both size and quality, in position as well as effect. In the same way the royal power derives its dignity from the pontifical authority: and the more closely it cleaves to the sphere of that authority the less is the light with which it is adorned; the further it is removed, the more it increases in splendour.

V. THE POPE AND IMPERIAL ELECTIONS

The Statement of the Papal Claim by Innocent III

Decretal *Venerabilem*, March 1202. *Corpus Iuris Canonici* (Friedberg) ii. 80. Mirbt, 323

[A letter from Innocent to the Duke of Zähringen justifying his intervention in a disputed election to the kingship of the Romans.]

... We acknowledge, as we are bound, that the right and authority to elect a king (later to be elevated to the Imperial throne) belongs to those princes to whom it is known to belong by right and ancient custom; especially as this right and authority came to them from the Apostolic See, which transferred the Empire from the Greeks to the Germans in the person of Charles the Great. But the princes should recognize, and assuredly do recognize, that the right and authority to examine the person so elected king (to be elevated to the Empire) belongs to us who anoint, consecrate and crown him. For it is a generally observed rule that the examination of a person belongs to him who has the duty of the laying-on of hands. For suppose that the princes elected a sacrilegious man or an excommunicate, a tyrant or an imbecile, a heretic or a pagan; and that not just by a majority, but unanimously, are we bound to anoint, consecrate and crown such a person? Of course not. ...

And it is evident from law and custom that when in an election the votes of the princes are divided we may, after due warning and a fitting interval, favour one of the parties. ... For if after such due notice the princes cannot or will not agree, will not the Apostolic See be without an advocate and defender, and thus be punished for their fault?

VI. THE BULL 'CLERICIS LAICOS', 1296
Corpus Iuris Canonici, ii. 1062. Mirbt, 369

[The object of this bull was to prevent the taxing of the clergy to provide money for the waging of wars. It was bitterly resented by Edward I, who was trying to extract large sums from both clergy and laity. He replied by outlawing the clergy; to which the Pope retorted by claiming Scotland as a papal fief and forbidding Edward to invade it. Edward countered by securing from a parliament at Lincoln an Act forbidding him to answer to the Pope for his temporal rights.]

Boniface Bishop, servant of the servants of God, for the perpetual record of the matter. That laymen have been very hostile to the clergy antiquity relates; and it is clearly proved by the experiences of the present time. For not content with what is their own the laity strive for what is forbidden and loose the reins for things unlawful. Nor do they prudently realize that power over clerks or ecclesiastical persons or goods is forbidden them: they impose heavy burdens on the prelates of the churches and ecclesiastical persons regular and secular, and tax them, and impose collections: they exact and demand from the same the half, tithe, or twentieth, or any other portion or proportion of their revenues or goods; and in many ways they try to bring them into slavery, and subject them to their authority. And, we regret to say, some prelates of the churches and ecclesiastical persons, fearing where there should be no fear, seeking a temporary peace, fearing more to offend the temporal majesty than the eternal, acquiesce in such abuses, not so much rashly as improvidently, without obtaining authority or licence from the Apostolic See. We therefore, desirous of preventing such wicked actions, decree, with apostolic authority and on the advice of our brethren, that any prelates and ecclesiastical persons, religious or secular, of whatsoever orders, condition or standing, who shall pay or promise or agree to pay to lay persons collections or taxes for the tithe, twentieth, or hundredth of their own rents, or goods, or those of the churches, or any other portion, proportion, or quantity of the same rents, or goods, at their own estimate or at the actual value, under the name of aid, loan relief, subsidy, or gift, or by any other title, manner, or pretext demanded, without the authority of the same see:

And also whatsoever emperors, kings, or princes, dukes, earls, or barons, powers, captains, or officials, or rectors, by whatsoever names they are called, of cities, castles, or any places whatsoever, wheresoever situate, and all others of whatsoever rank, eminence or state, who shall impose, exact, or receive the things aforesaid, or arrest, seize, or presume to take possession of things anywhere deposited in holy buildings, or to command them to be arrested, seized, or taken, or receive them when taken, seized, or arrested, and also all who knowingly give aid, counsel, or support, openly or secretly, in the things aforesaid, by this same should incur sentence of excommunication. Universities, too, which may have been to blame in these matters, we subject to ecclesiastical interdict.

The prelates and ecclesiastical persons above mentioned we strictly command, in virtue of their obedience, and on pain of deposition, that they in no wise acquiesce in such things without express leave of the said see, and that they pay nothing under pretext of any obligation, promise, and acknowledgment whatsoever, made in the past, or in existence before this time, and before such constitution, prohibition, or order come to their notice, and that the seculars aforesaid do not in any wise receive it; and if the clergy do pay, or the laymen receive, let them fall under sentence of excommunication by the very deed.

Moreover, let no one be absolved from the aforesaid sentences of excommunications and interdict, save at the moment of death, without authority and special leave of the Apostolic See, since it is part of our intention that such a terrible abuse of secular powers should not be carried on under any pretence whatever, any privileges whatsoever notwithstanding, in whatsoever tenors, forms or modes, or arrangement of words, conceded to emperors, kings and the others aforesaid; and we will that aid be given by no one, and by no persons in any respect in contravention of these provisions.

Let it then be lawful to none at all to infringe this page of our constitution, prohibition, or order, or to gainsay it by any rash attempt; and if any one presume to attempt this, let him know that he will incur the indignation of Almighty God, and of his blessed apostles Peter and Paul.

Given at Rome in St Peter's on the 25th of February in the second year of our Pontificate.

VII. THE BULL 'UNAM SANCTAM', 1302
Corpus Iuris Canonici ii. 1245 Mirbt, 372

[Boniface, by *Clericis laicos*, offended not only Edward but also Philip IV of France, whose reply took the form of the prohibition of the export of money from France, thus cutting off French contributions to Rome. *Unam Sanctam* defined the papal claims. Philip was exasperated and sent an agent to seize Boniface at Anagni. The papal palace was plundered, the Pope's life was threatened, and he was imprisoned for some days. He died within a few weeks of the outrage.]

We are obliged by the faith to believe and hold—and we do firmly believe and sincerely confess—that there is one Holy Catholic and Apostolic Church, and that outside this Church there is neither salvation nor remission of sins. ... In which Church there is 'one Lord, one faith, one baptism.'[1] At the time of the flood there was one ark of Noah, symbolizing the one Church; this was completed in one cubit[2] and had one, namely Noah, as helmsman and captain; outside which all things on earth, we read, were destroyed. ... Of this one and only Church there is one body and one head—not two heads, like a monster—namely Christ, and Christ's vicar is Peter, and Peter's successor, for the Lord said to Peter himself, 'Feed My sheep.'[3] 'My sheep' He said in general, not these or those sheep; wherefore He is understood to have committed them all to him. Therefore, if the Greeks or others say that they were not committed to Peter and his successors, they necessarily confess that they are not of Christ's sheep, for the Lord says in John, 'There is one fold and one shepherd.'[4]

And we learn from the words of the Gospel that in this Church and in her power are two swords, the spiritual and the temporal. For when the apostles said, 'Behold, here' (that is, in the Church, since it was the apostles who spoke) 'are two swords'—the Lord did not reply, 'It is too much,' but 'It is enough.'[5] Truly he who denies that the temporal sword is in the power of Peter, misunderstands the words of the Lord, 'Put up thy sword into the sheath.'[6] Both are in the power of the Church, the spiritual sword and the material. But the latter is to be used for the Church, the former by her; the former by the priest, the latter by kings and captains but at the will and by the permission of the priest. The one sword, then, should be under the other, and temporal authority subject to spiritual. For when the apostle says 'there is no power but of God, and the powers

---

[1] Eph. 4: 5.   [2] Gen. 6: 16.   [3] John 21: 17.
[4] John 10: 16. 'Fold' translates the Vulgate 'ovile'; the Greek is ποίμνη, 'flock'.
[5] Luke 22: 38.   [6] John 18: 11.

that be are ordained of God'[1] they would not be so ordained were not one sword made subject to the other. ...

Thus, concerning the Church and her power, is the prophecy of Jeremiah fulfilled, 'See, I have this day set thee over the nations and over the kingdoms,' etc.[2] If, therefore, the earthly power err, it shall be judged by the spiritual power; and if a lesser power err, it shall be judged by a greater. But if the supreme power err, it can only be judged by God, not by man; for the testimony of the apostle is 'The spiritual man judgeth all things, yet he himself is judged of no man.'[3] For this authority, although given to a man and exercised by a man, is not human, but rather divine, given at God's mouth to Peter and established on a rock for him and his successors in Him whom he confessed, the Lord saying to Peter himself, 'Whatsoever thou shalt bind,' etc.[4] Whoever therefore resists this power thus ordained of God, resists the ordinance of God. ... Furthermore we declare, state, define and pronounce that it is altogether necessary to salvation for every human creature to be subject to the Roman pontiff.

SECTION III

Monasticism and the Friars

I. THE RULE OF S. BENEDICT
Migne, *P.L.* lxvi. 215 ff. Mirbt, 194–200

[Benedict of Nursia was born at Rome at the close of the fifth century. He renounced the world at the age of fourteen, and finally settled at Monte Cassino, where he founded his monastery. He died in 543. By the ninth century his Rule had superseded all others; and it formed the basis of the new orders, such as the Cluniacs and Cistercians.]

I. Of the Kinds of Monks.

II. Of the Character of the Abbot.

III. *Of calling the Brethren to Counsel.*—Whenever matters of importance have to be dealt with in the monastery, let the abbot summon the whole congregation and himself put forward the question that has arisen. Then, after hearing the advice of the brethren let him think it over by himself and do what he shall judge most advantageous. Now we have said that all should be summoned to take counsel for this reason, that it is

---

[1] Romans 10: I.   [2] Jer. 1: 10.   [3] I Cor. 2: 15.   [4] Matt 16: 19.

often to the younger that the Lord reveals what is best. But let the brethren give advice with all subjection of humility, so as not to presume obstinately to defend their own opinions; rather let the matter depend on the abbot's judgement, so that all should submit to whatever he decide to be best. Yet, just as it becomes the disciples to obey their master, so it behoves him to order all things with prudence and justice. And in all things let all follow the Rule as their guide: and let no one diverge from it without good reason. Let no one in the monastery follow his own inclinations, and let no one boldly presume to dispute with his abbot, whether within or without the monastery. If anyone so presume, let him be subject to the discipline of the Rule. The abbot, for his part, should do everything in the fear of the Lord and in observance of the Rule; knowing that he will surely have to give account to God for all his decisions, as to a most impartial judge. If it happen that matters of less moment have to be dealt with, let him avail himself of the advice of the seniors only; as it is written: 'Do all things with counsel, and thou shalt not thereafter repent' [Ecclus. xxxii. 19.]

VIII. *Of the Divine Office at Night.*—In the winter time, that is from the First of November until Easter, according to what is reasonable, they must rise at the eighth hour of the night, so that they rest a little more than half the night, and rise when they have had their full sleep. But let the time that remains after vigils be spent in study by those brothers who have still to learn any part of the psalter or lessons. From Easter, moreover, until the aforesaid First of November, let the hour of keeping vigils be so arranged that, after a short interval, in which the brethren may go out for the necessities of nature, lauds, which are always to be said at break of day, may follow immediately.

XVI. *How Divine Office shall be said in the Daytime.*—As the prophet says: 'Seven times in the day do I praise Thee.' This sacred number seven will thus be fulfilled by us if, at lauds, at the first, third, sixth, ninth hours, at vesper time and at 'completorium' we perform the duties of our service; for it is of these hours of the day that he said: 'Seven times in the day do I praise Thee' [Ps. cxix. 164]. For, concerning the night hours, the same prophet says: 'At midnight I arose to confess unto thee' [*ibid*. 62]. Therefore, at these times, let us give thanks to our Creator concerning the judgements of his rightousness; that is, at matins, etc. ... and at night we will rise and confess to him. ...

XX. *Of Reverence in Prayer.*—When we make application to men in high positions we do not presume to do so without reverence and humility; how much more, then, are we bound to entreat God, the Lord of all, with all humility and devout purity of heart. And we must recognize that we are heard not for our much speaking, but for our purity of heart and tears of contrition. Therefore our prayer must be brief and pure—unless it chance to be prolonged with the inspiration of God's grace. When we assemble together, let the prayer be quite brief; and let us all rise together, when the Prior gives the signal.

XXI. *Of the Deans of the Monastery.*—If the congregation be a larger one, let there be chosen from it brothers of good reputation and of godly life; and let them be made deans. And they shall be watchful over their deaneries in all things, according to the commands of God and the precepts of their abbot. And the deans elected shall be such that the abbot may with confidence share his burdens with them. And they shall not be elected according to seniority, but according to the merit of their life and their learning and wisdom. And, should any one of these deans be found to be blameworthy, being puffed up by pride; and if, after being admonished once and again and a third time, he be unwilling to amend—let him be deposed; and let another, who is worthy, be chosen in his place.

XXII. *How the Monks are to sleep.*—Let them sleep in separate beds, and let their beds be suitable to their manner of life, as the Abbot shall appoint. If possible, let them all sleep in one room. But if there be too many for this, let them take their rest in groups of 10 or 20, with seniors in charge of each group. Let a candle be kept burning in the cell until morning. Let them sleep clothed, girdled with belts or cords—but without knives at their sides, lest they injure themselves in sleep. And thus let the monks be always ready; and, when the signal is given, let them rise without delay and rival one another in their haste to the service of God, yet with all reverence and modesty.

Let not the younger brothers have beds by themselves, but dispersed among the seniors. And when they rise for the service of God let them gently encourage one another, because the sleepy ones are apt to make excuses.

XXIII. *Of Excommunication for Faults.*—If a brother be found contumacious or disobedient, proud or a grumbler, or in any way acting contrary to the holy Rule and despising the orders of his seniors, let him, according to the Lord's commandment, be privately admonished once and twice by his seniors. If he do not then amend, let him be publicly rebuked before all. But if even then he do not correct himself, let him be subjected to excommunication, if he understands the gravity of this penalty. If, however, he is incorrigible, let him undergo corporal chastisement.

XXIV. *Of the Extent of Excommunication.*—The extent of the excommunication or discipline is to be regulated according to the gravity of the fault; and this is to be decided by the abbot's discretion. If a brother be found guilty of a lighter fault, he shall be excluded from the common table; he shall also intone neither psalm nor antiphon in the oratory, or read a lesson, until he has atoned. He shall take his meals alone, after those of the brethren; if, for example, the brothers have their meal at the sixth hour, he shall have his at the ninth. ...

XXV. *Of Grave Faults.*—The brother who is held guilty of a graver fault shall be suspended both from table and from the oratory. None of the brothers may in any way consort with him, or have speech with him. He shall be alone at the labour enjoined upon him, and continue in the sorrow of penitence; knowing that terrible sentence of the Apostle who said that such a man was given over to the destruction of the flesh in order that his soul might be saved at the day of the Lord [1 Cor. v. 5]. His portion of food he shall take alone, in the measure and at the time that the abbot shall appoint as suitable for him. Nor shall he be blessed by any one who passes by, nor the food that is given him.

XXVI. *Of those who, without being ordered by the Abbot, consort with the Excommunicated.*—If any brother presume, without an order of the abbot, in any way to associate with an excommunicated brother, or to speak with him, or to give an order to him: he shall suffer the same penalty of excommunication.

XXVII. *What care the abbot should exercise with regard to the Excommunicated.*—The abbot shall show the utmost solicitude and care towards brothers that offend: 'They that be whole need not a physician, but they that are sick [Matt. ix. 12]. And therefore he ought to use every means, as a wise physician; to send 'playmates,' i.e. older and wiser brothers, who, as it were secretly, shall console the wavering brother and lead him to the atonement of humility. And they shall comfort him lest he be overwhelmed by excess of sorrow. But rather, as the same apostle says [2 Cor. ii. 8], charity shall be confirmed in him, and he shall be prayed for by all. For the abbot should employ the utmost solicitude, and take care with all prudence and diligence, lest he lose any of the sheep entrusted to him. For he should know that he has undertaken the care of weak souls, not the tyranny over the strong. And he shall fear the threat of the prophet through whom the Lord says: 'Ye did take that which ye saw to be strong, and that which was weak ye did cast out' [? cf. Ezek. xxxiv]. And let him imitate the pious example of the good Shepherd, who, leaving the ninety and nine sheep upon the mountains, went out to seek the one sheep that had gone astray: and He had such compassion upon its infirmity, that He deigned to place it upon His sacred shoulders, and thus to carry it back to the flock.

XXVIII. *Of those who, being often rebuked, do not amend.*—If any brother, having frequently been rebuked for any fault, do not amend even after he has been excommunicated, a more severe chastisement shall fall upon him; that is, the punishment of the lash shall be inflicted upon him. But if he do not even then amend; or, if perchance (which God forbid) puffed up with pride he try even to defend his deeds: then the abbot shall act as a wise physician. If he have applied the fomentations, the ointments of exhortation, the medicaments of the Divine Scriptures; if he have proceeded to the last cauterization of excommunication, or flogging, and if he see that his efforts avail nothing: let him also (what is more powerful) call in the prayer of himself and all the brothers for him: that God who can do all things may work a cure upon a sick brother. But if he be not healed, even in this way, then at last the abbot may use the surgeon's knife, as the apostle says: 'Remove evil from you' [I Cor. v. 13], lest one diseased sheep contaminate the whole flock.

XXIX. *Whether Brothers who leave the Monastery ought again to be received.*—A brother who goes out, or is cast out, of the monastery for his own fault, if he wish to return, shall first promise every amends for the fault on account of which he departed; and thus he shall be received into the lowest degree—so that thereby his humility may be proved. But if he again depart, up to the third time he shall be received. Knowing that after this every opportunity of return is denied to him.

XXX. *Concerning Boys under Age, how they shall be corrected.*—Every age or intelligence ought to have its proper bounds. Therefore as often as boys or youths, or those who are less able to understand how great is the punishment of excommunication; as often as such persons offend, they shall either be punished with extra fasts, or coerced with severe blows, that they may be healed.

XXXIII. *Whether the Monks should have anything of their own.*— More than any thing else is this vice of property to be cut off root and branch from the monastery. Let no one presume to give or receive anything without the leave of the abbot, or to retain anything as his own. He should have nothing at all: neither a book, nor tablets, nor a pen—nothing at all. For indeed it is not allowed to the monks to have bodies or wills in their own power. But for all things necessary they must look to the Father of the monastery; nor is it allowable to have anything which the abbot has not given or permitted. All things shall be common to all, as it is written: 'Let not any man presume or call anything his own' [Acts iv. 32]. But if any one is found delighting in this most evil vice:

being warned once and again, if he do not amend, let him be subjected to punishment.

XXXIV. *Whether all ought to receive Necessaries equally.*—As it is written: 'It was divided among them singly, according as each had need' [Acts iv. 35]: whereby we do not say—far from it—that there should be respect of persons, but a consideration for infirmities. Wherefore he who needs less, let him thank God and not be grieved; but he who needs more, let him be humiliated on account of his weakness, and not made proud on account of the indulgence that is shown him. And thus all members will be in peace. Above all, let not the evil of grumbling appear, on any account, by the least word or sign whatever. But, if such a grumbler is discovered, he shall be subjected to stricter discipline.

XXXV. *Of the Weekly Officers of the Kitchen.*—The brothers shall wait on each other in turn that no one shall be excused from the kitchen-work, unless he be prevented by sickness, or by preoccupation with some matter of great necessity whereby is gained a greater reward and increase of charity. ... An hour before each meal the weekly servers are to receive a cup of drink and a piece of bread over and above their ration, so that they may wait on their brethren without grumbling or undue fatigue. But on solemn days they shall fast till after Mass. ...

XXXVI. *Of the Sick Brethren.*—Before all things, and above all things, care must be taken of the sick; so that the brethren shall minister to them as they would to Christ himself; for he said: 'I was sick and ye visited me' [Matt. xxv. 36], and 'Inasmuch as, etc.' [ibid. 40]. But let the sick, on their part, remember that they are being cared for to the honour of God; and let them not by their abundance offend the brothers who serve them: which (offences) nevertheless are patiently to be borne, for, from such, a greater reward is acquired. Wherefore let the abbot take the greatest care that they suffer no neglect. And for these infirm brothers a cell shall be set apart, and a servitor, God-fearing, and diligent and careful. The use of baths shall be offered to the sick as often as is necessary: to the healthy, and especially to youths, more rarely. The eating of meat also shall be allowed to the sick, and to the delicate, to assist their recovery. But when they have grown better, they shall all, in the usual manner, abstain from flesh. The abbot, moreover, shall take the greatest care that the sick be not neglected by the cellarer or by the servitors: for whatever fault is committed by the disciples recoils upon him.

XXXVII. *Of the Old and Young.*—Although human nature itself is prone to have consideration of these ages—that is, old age and infancy,—nevertheless the authority of the Rule also should provide for them. Their weakness shall always be taken into account, and in the matter of food, the strict tenor of the Rule shall by no means be observed, as far as they are concerned; but they shall be treated with kind consideration, and may anticipate the regular (canonical) hours [*sc.* of meals].

XXXVIII. *Of the Weekly Reader.*—At the meal times of the brothers there should always be reading; no one may dare to take up the book at random and begin to read there; but he who is about to read for the whole week shall begin his duties on Sunday. And, entering upon his office after Mass and Communion, he shall ask all to pray for him, that God may avert from him the spirit of elation. And this verse shall be said in the oratory three times by all, he however beginning it: 'O Lord, open Thou my lips, and my mouth shall show forth Thy praise.' And thus, having received the benediction, he shall enter upon his duties as reader. And there shall be the greatest silence at table, so that no whispering or any voice save the reader's may be heard. And whatever is needed, in the way of food, the brethren should pass to each other in turn, so that no one need ask for anything. But if anything should be wanted let them ask for it by means of a sign rather than by speech. ...

XXXXIX. *Of the Amount of Food.*—We think it sufficient for the daily meal, either at the sixth or the ninth hour, that there be, at all seasons, two cooked dishes. And this because of the weaknesses of different people, so that he who happens not to be able to eat of one may make his meal of the other. Let two dishes, then, suffice for the brethren: or if fruits or fresh vegetables are obtainable, a third may be added. Let one pound of bread suffice for a day, whether there be one principal meal, or both dinner and supper. If there is to be supper, the cellarer must keep back a third of the pound, to be given out at supper. But if unusually heavy work has been done it shall be in the discretion and power of the abbot to make some addition, avoiding excess, above all things, that no monk be overtaken by indigestion. ... All must abstain from the flesh of four-footed beasts, except the delicate and the sick.

XL. *Of the Amount of Drink.*—Each one has his own gift from God, the one in this way, the other in that [1 Cor. ix. 17]. Therefore it is with some hesitation that the amount of daily sustenance for others is fixed by us. Nevertheless, in view of the weakness of the infirm we believe that one pint of wine a day is enough for each one. Let those to whom God gives the ability to endure abstinence know that they will have their reward. But the prior shall judge if either the nature of the locality or labour, or the heat of summer, requires more; taking care in all things lest satiety or drunkenness creep in. Indeed we read that wine is not suitable for monks at all. But because, in our day, it is not possible to persuade the monks of this, let us agree at least as to the fact that we should not drink to excess, but sparingly. For wine can make even the wise to go astray. Where, moreover, owing to local conditions, the amount aforesaid cannot be provided,—but much less or nothing at all—those who live there shall bless God and shall not grumble. And we admonish them as to this above all: that they be without grumbling.

XLI. *At what Hours the Brothers ought to take their Refection.*—From the holy Easter time until Pentecost the brothers shall have their refection at the sixth hour; and at evening they shall sup. From Pentecost, moreover, through the whole summer—unless the monks have hard labour in the fields, or the extreme heat of the summer oppress them—they shall fast on Wednesday and Friday until the ninth hour: but on the other days they shall have their meal at the sixth hour. Which sixth hour, if they have ordinary work in the fields, or if the heat of summer is not great, shall be kept to for the meal; and it shall be for the abbot to decide. And he shall so arrange all things, that their souls may be saved on the one hand; and that, on the other, what the brothers do they shall do without any justifiable grumbling. Moreover, from the 13th of September to the beginning of Lent they shall have their meal at the ninth hour. But during Lent they shall have the meal in the evening, at such time as enables them to finish in daylight. ...

XLII. *Of Silence after Compline.*—Monks should practise silence at all times, but especially in the hours of night. Therefore on all days, whether fasting days or otherwise, let them sit together as soon as they have risen from supper (if it be not a fast day) and let one of them read the 'Collations' ['Selections'] or 'Lives of the Fathers,' or something else which may edify the hearers. But not the Heptateuch, or 'Kings'; for it will not profit weak intellects to listen to that part of Scripture at that hour; but they may be read at other times. ... At the end of the reading ... let them say Compline [*Completorium*] and when that is over, let no one be allowed to speak to anyone. If anyone be found breaking this law of silence he shall undergo severe punishments. Unless the presence of guests should require speech, or the abbot should chance to issue some order. But, even so, let it be done with the utmost gravity and moderation.

XLVIII. *Of the daily Manual Labour.*—Idleness is enemy of the soul. And therefore, at fixed times, the brothers ought to be occupied in manual labour; and again, at fixed times, in sacred reading. Therefore we believe that both these ought to be arranged thus: from Easter until the 1st of October, on coming out of Prime they shall do what labour may be necessary until the fourth hour. From the fourth hour until about the sixth, they shall apply themselves to reading. After the meal of the sixth hour, moreover, rising from table, they shall rest in their beds in complete silence; or, perchance, he that wishes to read may read to himself in such a way as not to disturb any other. And None shall be said rather before the time, about the middle of the eighth hour; and again they shall work at their tasks until evening. But, if the needs of the place or poverty demand that they labour at the harvest, they shall not grieve at this: for then they are truly monks if they live by the labours of their hands; as did also our fathers and the apostles. Let all things be done with moderation, however, on account of the fainthearted. From the 1st of October, moreover, until the beginning of Lent they shall be free for reading until the end of the second hour. At the second hour Terce shall be said, and all shall labour at the task which is enjoined upon them until the ninth. The first signal of None having been given, they shall each one leave off his work; and be ready when the second signal strikes. After the meal they shall be free for their readings or for psalms. But in the days of Lent, from dawn until the end of the third hour, they shall be free for their readings; and, until the end of the tenth hour, they shall do the labour that is enjoined on them. In which days of Lent they shall each receive a book from the library; which they shall read entirely through in order. These books are to be given out on the first day of Lent. Above all there shall certainly be appointed one or two elders, who shall go round the monastery at the hours in which the brothers are engaged in reading, and see to it that no troublesome brother chance to be found who is engaged in idleness or gossip instead of reading. ... On Sunday all shall be occupied in reading, except those who are assigned to various duties. But if any is so negligent or slothful that he lacks the will or the ability to read, let some task within his capacity be given him, that he be not idle. For the weak or delicate brethren some work or craft must be found to keep them from idleness while not overwhelming them with such heavy labour as to drive them away. The abbot is to take their infirmity into consideration.

XLIX. *Of the Observance of Lent.*—The life of a monk should be always as if Lent were being kept. But few have virtue enough for this, and so we urge that during Lent he shall utterly purify his life, and wipe out, in that holy season, the negligence of other times. This is duly performed if we abstain from vices and devote ourselves to prayer with weeping, to study and heartfelt contrition and to abstinence. And so, in those days, let us of ourselves make some addition to our service—special prayers, and special abstinence in food and drink; so that each of us shall offer, over and above his appointed portion, a freewill offering to God, with the joy of the Holy Spirit. Let him discipline his body in respect of food, drink, sleep, chatter, and mirth; and let him look forward to holy Easter with the joy of spiritual longing. And let each announce his offering to the abbot that it may be done with his prayers and with his approval. For whatever is done without the leave of the spiritual father is to be set down to presumption and pride, and not to the credit of a monk.

L. *Of those who work away from the Monastery, or those on a Journey.* [They must observe the Hours.]

LI. *Of those who go on Short Journeys.* [They must not eat outside, without leave of the abbot.]

LIII. *Of the Reception of Guests.*—All guests are to be received as Christ himself; for He Himself said: 'I was a stranger and ye took Me in' [Mt. xxv. 35]. And to all, fitting honour shall be shown; but, most of all, to servants of the faith and to pilgrims. When, therefore, a guest is announced, the prior or the brothers shall run to meet him, with every service of love. And first they shall pray together; and thus they shall be joined together in peace. Which kiss of peace shall not first be offered, unless a prayer have preceded, on account of the wiles of the devil. In the salutation itself, moreover, all humility shall be shown. In the case of all guests arriving or departing: with inclined head, or with prostrating of the whole body upon the ground, Christ, who is also received in them, shall be adored. The guests moreover, having been received, shall be conducted to prayer; and afterwards the prior, or one whom he himself orders, shall sit with them. The law of God shall be read before the guest that he may be edified; and, after this, every kindness shall be shown. A fast may be broken by the prior on account of a guest; unless, perchance, it be a special day of fast which cannot be violated. The brothers, moreover shall continue their customary fasts. The abbot shall give water into the hands of his guests; and the abbot as well as the whole congregation shall wash the feet of all guests. This being done, they shall say this verse: 'We have received, O Lord, Thy loving-kindness in the midst of Thy temple' [Ps. xlvii. 8, Vulgate=xlviii. 9, E.V.]. Chiefly in the reception of the poor and of pilgrims shall care be most anxiously shown: for them Christ is received the more. For the very fear of the rich exacts honour for them. The kitchen of the abbot and the guests shall be by itself; so that guests coming at uncertain hours, as is always happening in a monastery, may not disturb the brothers. Into the control of this kitchen, two brothers, who can well fulfil that duty, shall enter yearly; and to them, according as they shall need it, help shall be administered; so that they may serve without grumbling. And again, when they are less occupied they shall go out where they are commanded to, and labour. ...

LIV. *Whether a Brother may receive Letters or Gifts.* [No; except by leave of the abbot.]

LV. *Of Clothing.*—Clothing shall be given to the brothers according to the nature of the places where they dwell, or the climate. For in cold regions more is required; but in warm, less. This is a matter for the abbot to decide. We nevertheless consider that for temperate places a cowl and tunic apiece shall suffice—the cowl in winter hairy, in summer fine or worn—and a scapular for work. And for the feet, shoes and stockings. Concerning the colour and size of all which things the monks shall not talk; but they shall be such as can be found in the province where they are or as can be bought the most cheaply. The abbot, moreover, shall provide, as to the measure, that those vestments be not short for those using them; but of suitable length. And, when new ones are received, they shall always straightway return the old ones, to be kept in the wardrobe for the benefit of the poor. It is enough, moreover, for a monk to have two tunics and two cowls; a spare one for nights, and to permit them to wash the things themselves. Everything, then, that is over this is superfluous, and ought to be removed. And the shoes, and whatever is old, they shall return when they receive something new. And those who are sent on a journey shall receive cloths for the loins from the wardrobe; which on their return they shall restore, having washed them. And there shall be cowls and tunics somewhat better than those which they have ordinarily: which, when they start on a journey, they shall receive from the wardrobe, and, on returning, shall restore. For bedding, a mattress, a woollen blanket, a woollen under-blanket, and a pillow shall suffice. And these beds are frequently to be searched by the abbot for private property. And, if anything is found belonging to any one which he did not receive from the abbot, he shall be subjected to the most severe discipline. And, in order that this vice of property may be cut off at the roots, all things which are necessary shall be given by the abbot: that is, a cowl, a tunic, shoes, stockings, girdle, a knife, a pen, a needle, a handkerchief, tablets: so that all excuse of necessity shall be removed.

LVIII. *Concerning the Manner of receiving Brothers.*—When any new comer applies for admission, an easy entrance shall not be granted him: but, as the Apostle says, 'Try the spirits if they be of God' [I John iv. I]. Therefore, if he who comes perseveres in knocking, and is seen after four or five days to endure with patience the insults inflicted upon him, and the difficulty of entrance, and to persist in his demand, entrance shall be allowed him, and he shall remain for a few days in the cell of the guests. After this he shall be in the cell of the novices, where he shall meditate and eat and sleep. And an elder brother shall be appointed for him who shall be capable of saving souls, who shall watch him with the closest scrutiny, and make it his care to see if he reverently seek God, if he be zealous in the service of God, in obedience, in suffering shame. And all the harshness and roughness of the means through which God is approached shall be told him in advance. If he promise perseverance in his steadfastness, after the lapse of two months this Rule shall be read to him in order, and it shall be said to him: 'Behold the law under which thou dost wish to serve; if thou canst observe it, enter; but if thou canst not, depart freely.' If he have stood firm thus far, then he shall be taken into the aforesaid cell of the novices; and again he shall be tried with every kind of endurance. And, after the lapse of six months, the Rule shall be read to him; that he may know upon what he is entering. And, if he stands firm thus far, after four months the same Rule shall again be re-read to him. And if, having deliberated with himself, he shall promise to keep everything, and to obey all the commands that are laid upon him: then he shall be received in the congregation; knowing that it is decreed, by the law of the Rule, that from that day he shall not be allowed to depart from the monastery, nor to free his neck from the yoke of the Rule, which, after such long deliberation, he was at liberty either to refuse or receive. He who is to be received, moreover, shall, in the oratory, in the presence of all, make promise concerning his steadfastness and the change in his manner of life and his obedience to God and to His saints; so that if, at any time, he act contrary, he shall know that he shall be condemned by Him whom he mocks. ...

LXIV. *Of the Appointing of an Abbot.*—In appointing an abbot this principle shall always be observed: that such a one shall be put into office as the whole congregation, according to the fear of God, with one heart—or even a part, however small, of the congregation with more prudent counsel—shall have chosen. He who is to be ordained, moreover, shall be elected for merit of life and learnedness in wisdom; even though he be the lowest in rank in the congregation. But even if the whole congregation with one consent shall have elected a person willing to connive at their vices (which God forbid), and those vices shall in any way come clearly to the knowledge of the bishop to whose diocese that place pertains, or to the neighbouring abbots or Christians: the latter shall not allow the consent of the wicked to prevail, but shall set up a worthy steward of the house of God; knowing that they will receive a good reward for this, if they do it in pureness of heart and with zeal for God. Just so they shall know, on the contrary, that they have sinned if they neglect it. The abbot who is ordained, moreover, shall reflect always what burden he is undertaking, and to whom he is to render account of his stewardship.

He shall know that he ought rather to be of help than to command. He ought, therefore, to be learned in the divine law, that he may know how to bring forth both the new and the old; chaste, sober, merciful. He shall always exalt mercy over judgement, that he may obtain the same. He shall hate vice, he shall love the brethren. In his blame itself he shall act prudently and do nothing excessive; lest, while he is too desirous of removing the rust, the vessel be broken. And he shall always suspect his own frailty; and shall remember that bruised reed is not to be crushed. By which we do not say that he shall permit vice to be nourished; but prudently, and with charity, he shall remove it, according as he finds it to be expedient in the case of each one, as we have already said. And he shall strive rather to be loved than feared. He shall not be troubled and anxious; he also shall not be too obstinate; he shall not be jealous and too suspicious; for then he will have no rest. In his commands he shall be prudent, and shall consider whether they be of God or of the world. He shall use discernment and moderation with regard to the labours which he enjoins, thinking of the discretion of holy Jacob who said: 'if I overdrive my flocks they will die all in one day.' [Gen. xxxiii. 13]. Accepting therefore this and other testimony of discretion the mother of the virtues, he shall so temper all things that there may be both what the strong desire, and the weak do no shrink from. And, especially, he shall keep the present Rule in all things; ...

LXV. *Of the Provost.*—[Not to consider himself a 'second abbot.']

LXVI. *Concerning the Doorkeepers of the Monastery.*—At the door of the monastery shall be placed a wise old man who shall know how to receive a reply and to return one; whose ripeness of age will not permit him to gossip. The doorkeeper ought to have a cell next to the door; so that those arriving may always find one present from whom they may receive a reply. And straightway, when any one has knocked, or a poor man has called out, he shall answer, 'Thanks be to God!' or shall give the blessing; and with all the gentleness of the fear of God he shall quickly give a reply with the fervour of charity. And if this doorkeeper need assistance he may receive a younger brother.

A monastery should, if possible, be so arranged that everything necessary—that is, water, a mill, a garden, a bakery—may be available, and different trades be carried on, within the monastery; so that there shall be no need for the monks to wander about outside. For this is not at all good for their souls. We wish, moreover, that this Rule be read very often in the congregation; lest any of the brothers excuse himself on account of ignorance.

LXVIII. *If Impossibilities are enjoined.*—If it happen that any over-whelming or impossible task is set him, a brother should receive the command of one in authority with all meekness and obedience. But if he sees that the weight of the burden is utterly beyond his strength, let him, with patience and at the convenient time, suggest to his superior what makes it impossible—without presumption or obstinacy or answering back. If, after this suggestion, the command of the superior stand as it was first given, the subordinate shall realize that thus it is expedient for him: and he shall obey, with all charity, and will trust in God's help.

LXIX. *No one shall take it on himself to take another's part.*

LXX. *No one shall take it on himself to strike another without orders.*

LXXI. *Monks shall obey each other.*

LXXII. *Of the Good Zeal which the Monks should have.*—[A zeal mingled with charity, patience, and tolerance for others.]

LXXIII. *Concerning the Fact that not every Righteous Observance is decreed in this Rule.*—We have written out this Rule that we may show those observing it in the monasteries how to have some honesty of character, or the beginning of conversion. But for those who hasten to the perfection of living, there are the teachings of the holy Fathers; the observance of which leads a man to the heights of perfection. For what page, or what discourse, of Divine authority in the Old or the New Testament does not contain a most perfect rule for human life? Or what book of the holy Catholic Fathers does not tell us with the voice of a trumpet how by the right path we may come to our Creator? And the reading aloud of the Fathers, and their decrees, and their lives; also the Rule of our holy Father Basil—what else are they except instruments of virtue for well-living and obedient monks? We blush with shame for the idle, and the evil-living and the negligent. Thou that hastenest to the heavenly country, perform with Christ's aid this Rule which is written down as the least of beginnings: and then at length, under God's protection, thou wilt come to the greater things that we have mentioned; to the heights of learning and virtue.

II. THE RULE OF S. FRANCIS, 1223
Bullarium Romanum (editio Taurinensis), iii. 394 ff.

[The original Rule of S. Francis consisted of a few precepts from the gospels. But the rapid expansion of the Order brought the need of more detailed regulations. This Rule was approved by Pope Honorius III in 1223.]

1. This is the Rule and way of life of the brothers minor; to observe the holy Gospel of our Lord Jesus Christ, living in obedience, without

personal possessions, and in chastity. Brother Francis promises obedience and reverence to our Lord Pope Honorius, and to his canonical successors, and to the Roman Church. And the other brothers shall be bound to obey brother Francis and his successors.

2. If any wish to adopt this way of life, and shall come to our brothers, they shall send them to their provincial ministers; to whom alone, and to no others, permission is given to receive brothers. And the ministers shall carefully examine them in the Catholic faith and the sacraments of the Church. And if they believe all these, and will confess them faithfully and observe them steadfastly to the end; and if they have no wives, or if they have them and the wives have already entered a convent, or if with permission of the diocesan bishop they shall have given them permission to do so—they themselves having already taken a vow of continence, and their wives being of such age that no suspicion can arise in connection with them: the ministers shall tell them, in the words of the holy Gospel, to go and sell all that they have and carefully give it to the poor. But if they shall not be able to do this, their good will is enough. And the brothers and their ministers shall be careful not to concern themselves about their temporal goods; so that they may freely do with those goods exactly as God inspires them. But if advice is required, the ministers shall be allowed to send them to some God-fearing men by whose counsel they shall dispense their goods to the poor. After that they shall be given the garments of probation: namely two gowns without cowls and a belt, and hose and a cape down to the belt: unless to these same ministers something else may at some time seem to be preferable in the sight of God. And, when the year of probation is over, they shall be received into obedience; promising always to observe this way of life and Rule. And, according to the mandate of the lord pope, they shall never be allowed to break these bonds. For according to the holy Gospel, no one putting his hand to the plough and looking back is fit for the kingdom of God. And those who have now promised obedience shall have one gown with a cowl, and another, if they wish it, without a cowl. And those who really need them may wear shoes. And all the brothers shall wear humble garments, and may repair them with sack cloth and other remnants, with God's blessing. And I warn and exhort them lest they despise or judge men whom they shall see clad in soft garments and in colours, enjoying delicate food and drink; but each one shall rather judge and despise himself.

3. The clerical brothers shall perform the divine service according to the order of the holy Roman Church; excepting the psalter, of which they may have extracts. But the lay brothers shall say twenty-four

Paternosters at matins, five at lauds, seven each at Prime, Terce, Sext and None, twelve at Vespers, seven at the Completorium; and they shall pray for the dead. And they shall fast from the feast of All Saints to the Nativity of the Lord; but as to the holy season of Lent, which begins after the Epiphany of the Lord and continues forty days, a season the Lord consecrated by his holy fast—those who fast during this time shall be blessed of the Lord, and those who do not wish to fast shall not be bound to do so; but otherwise they shall fast until the Resurrection of the Lord. At other times the brothers shall not be bound to fast save on the sixth day (Friday); but when there is a compelling reason the brothers shall not be bound to observe a physical fast. But I advise, warn and exhort my brothers in the Lord Jesus Christ, that, when they go into the world, they shall not quarrel, nor contend with words, nor judge others. But let them be gentle, peaceable, modest, merciful and humble, with honourable conversation towards all, as is fitting. They ought not to ride, save when necessity or infirmity clearly compels them so to do. Into whatsoever house they enter let them first say, 'Peace be to this house.' And according to the holy Gospel it is lawful for them to partake of all dishes placed before them.

4. I strictly command all the brothers never to receive coin or money either directly or through an intermediary. The ministers and guardians alone shall make provision, through spiritual friends, for the needs of the infirm and for other brothers who need clothing, according to the locality, season or cold climate, at their discretion. ...

5. Those brothers, to whom God has given the ability to work shall work faithfully and devotedly and in such a way that, avoiding idleness, the enemy of the soul, they do not quench the spirit of holy prayer and devotion, to which other and temporal activities should be subordinate. As the wage of their labour they may receive corporal necessities for themselves and their brothers but not coin nor money, and this with humility, as is fitting for servants of God, and followers of holy poverty.

6. The brothers shall possess nothing, neither a house, nor a place, nor anything. But, as pilgrims and strangers in this world, serving God in poverty and humility, they shall confidently seek alms, and not be ashamed, for the Lord made Himself poor in this world for us. This is the highest degree of that sublime poverty, which has made you, my dearly beloved brethren, heirs and kings of the Kingdom of Heaven; which has made you poor in goods but exalted in virtues. Let this be 'your portion,' which leads you to 'the land of the living' [Ps. cxlii. 5]. If you cleave wholly to this, beloved, you will wish to have for ever in Heaven nothing save the name of Our Lord Jesus Christ. Wherever the brethren are, and

shall meet together, they shall shew themselves as members of one family; each shall with confidence unfold his needs to his brother. A mother loves and cherishes her son in the flesh; how much more eagerly should a man love and cherish his brother in the Spirit? And if any of them fall sick the other brothers are bound to minister to him as they themselves would wish to be ministered to.

7. But if any of the brethren shall commit mortal sin at the prompting of the adversary: in the case of those sins concerning which it has been laid down that recourse must be had to the provincial ministers, the aforesaid brethren must have recourse to them without delay. Those ministers, if they are priests, shall with mercy enjoin penance: if they are not priests they shall cause it to be enjoined through others, who are priests of the order, as it seems to them most expedient in the sight of God. They must beware lest they become angry and disturbed on account of the sin of any brother; for anger and indignation hinder love in ourselves and others.

8. All the brothers shall be bound always to have one of the brothers of the order as minister general and servant of the whole brotherhood, and shall be strictly bound to obey him. On his death the election of a successor shall be made by the provincial ministers and guardians in the chapter at Pentecost, at which the provincial ministers shall always be bound to assemble, wherever the minister general provides; and this once in three years or at a greater or less interval, according as is ordered by the aforesaid minister. And if at any time it shall be clear to the whole body of provincial ministers and guardians that the said minister does not suffice for the service and common advantage of the brethren, it shall be the duty of the said brethren who have the right of election to elect another as their guardian, in the name of God. But after the chapter held at Pentecost the ministers and guardians may (if they so wish and it seem expedient) call together their brethren, in their several districts, to a chapter, once in that same year.

9. The brothers shall not preach in the diocese of any bishop who has forbidden them to do so. And none of the brothers shall dare to preach at all to the people unless he has been examined and approved by the minister general of this brotherhood and the privilege of preaching has been granted him. I also exhort these same brothers that in all their preaching their language shall be pure and careful, to the advantage and edification of the people; preaching to them of vices and virtues, punishment and glory; and let their discourse be brief; for the words which the Lord spoke upon earth were brief.

10. The brothers who are the ministers and servants of the other brothers shall visit and admonish their brothers and humbly and lovingly correct them; not teaching them anything which is against their conscience and our Rule. But the brothers who are subjected to them shall remember that, before God, they have discarded their own wills. Wherefore I strictly charge them that they obey their ministers in all things which they have promised God to observe, and which are not contrary to their conscience and to our Rule. And wherever there are brothers who are conscious of their inability to observe the Rule in the spirit, they may and should have recourse to their ministers. But the ministers shall receive them lovingly and kindly, and shall exercise such familiarity towards them, that they may speak and act towards them as masters to their servants; for so it ought to be, that the ministers should be the servants of all the brothers. I warn and exhort, moreover, in Christ Jesus the Lord, that the brothers be on their guard against all pride, vainglory, envy, avarice, care and worldly anxiety, detraction and murmuring. And they shall not be concerned to teach those who are ignorant of letters, but shall take care that they desire to have the spirit of God and its holy workings; that they pray always to God with a pure heart; that they have humility, patience, in persecution and infirmity; and that they love those who persecute, revile and attack us. For the Lord saith: 'Love your enemies, and pray for those that persecute you and speak evil against you. Blessed are they that suffer persecution for righteousness sake, for theirs is the kingdom of Heaven. He that is steadfast unto the end shall be saved.'[1]

11. I strictly charge all the brethren not to hold conversation with women so as to arouse suspicion, nor to take counsel with them. And, with the exception of those to whom special permission has been given by the Apostolic Chair, let them not enter nunneries. Neither may they become fellow god-parents with men or women, lest from this cause a scandel may arise among the brethren or concerning brethren.

12. Whoever of the brothers by divine inspiration may wish to go among the Saracens and other infidels, shall seek permission to do so from their provincial ministers. But to none shall the ministers give permission to go, save to those whom they shall see to be fit for the mission.

[1] Matt. 5: 44, 10, 10: 22.

Furthermore, I charge the ministers on their obedience that they demand from the lord pope one of the cardinals of the holy Roman Church, who shall be the governor, corrector and protector of the fraternity, so that, always submissive and lying at the feet of that same Holy Church, steadfast in the Catholic faith, we may observe poverty and humility, and the holy Gospel of our Lord Jesus Christ; as we have firmly promised.

SECTION IV

The Church and Heresy

I. THE EPISCOPAL INQUISITION AND THE SECULAR ARM

From the Decrees of the Fourth Lateran Council, 1215: Mansi, xxii. 982 ff.

[The Church of the twelfth century was disturbed by various heresies, the most dangerous of which were those of the Albigensians and Waldensians. The former were Manichean in theory and rigorously ascetic in practice, though their opponents accused them of antinomian excesses; the latter began by trying to recapture what they conceived to have been the simplicity of the Apostolic Church; but they, like many other groups who started with this aim, tended towards an intransigent sectarianism. The Third Lateran Council in 1179, under Alexander III, invoked the aid of secular power; 'Although the discipline of the Church does not carry out bloody retributions, being content with priestly judgement: still it is aided by the regulations of catholic princes, so that men often seek a salutary remedy for fear of incurring corporal punishment. Therefore … we decree that [the Albigensians] and their supporters and abettors lie under an anathema, and we prohibit, under pain of anathema, anyone to dare to keep them in his house or on his land, or to support them or to have dealings with them' (cap. 27, Mansi xxii. 231; Denzinger, No. 401). In 1208 Innocent III started the Albigensian Crusade; but this failed to extirpate the heretics, and in 1220 a papal inquisition was entrusted to the friars and superimposed on the bishops' courts.]

3. … Convicted heretics shall be handed over for due punishment to their secular superiors, or the latter's agents. If they are clerks, they shall first be degraded. The goods of the laymen thus convicted shall be confiscated: those of the clergy shall be applied to the churches from which they drew their stipends.

… If a temporal Lord neglects to fulfil the demand of the Church that he shall purge his land of this contamination of heresy, he shall be excommunicated by the metropolitan and other bishops of the province.

If he fails to make amends within a year, it shall be reported to the Supreme Pontiff, who shall pronounce his vassals absolved from fealty to him and offer his land to Catholics. The latter shall exterminate the heretics, possess the land without dispute and preserve it in the true faith. ...

Catholics who assume the cross and devote themselves to the extermination of heretics shall enjoy the same indulgence and privilege as those who go to the Holy Land. ...

7. Further we add that every archbishop and bishop, in person or by his archdeacon or other suitable and trustworthy persons, shall visit each of his parishes, in which there are said to be heretics, twice or at least once a year. And he shall compel three or more men of good reputation, or even, if need be, the whole neighbourhood, to swear that, if any of them knows of any heretics or of any who frequent secret conventicles or who practise manners and customs different from those common amongst Christians, he will report them to the bishop. The bishop shall summon those accused to appear before him; and, unless they clear themselves of the accusation, or if they relapse into their former mischief, they shall receive canonical punishment. ...

II. THE JUSTIFICATION OF THE INQUISITION

S. Thomas Aquinas (1225–74), *Summa Theologica*, ii. Q. xi

Article III. *Whether heretics should be tolerated*
[In favour of toleration: (1) 2 Tim. 2: 24, (2) 1 Cor. 11: 19, (3) Matt. 8: 30. On the other hand: Tit. 3: 10, 11.]

I reply that, with regard to heretics, two considerations are to be kept in mind: (1) on their side, (2) on the side of the Church.

(1) There is the sin, whereby they deserve not only to be separated from the Church by excommunication, but also to be shut off from the world by death. For it is a much more serious matter to corrupt faith, through which comes the soul's life, than to forge money, through which temporal life is supported. Hence if forgers of money or other malefactors are straightway justly put to death by secular princes, with much more justice can heretics, immediately upon conviction, be not only excommunicated but also put to death.

(2) But on the side of the Church there is mercy, with a view to the conversion of them that are in error; and therefore the Church does not straightway condemn, but *after a first and a second admonition*, as the

Apostle teaches (Tit. iii. 10]. After that, if he be found still stubborn, the Church gives up hope of his conversion and takes thought for the safety of others, by separating him from the Church by sentence of excommunication; and, further, leaves him to the secular court, to be exterminated from the world by death. ...

Article IV. *Whether those who return from heresy are to be taken back by the Church*

... *I reply that* the Church, agreeably with the Lord's institution, extends her charity to all, not only to friends but also to foes who persecute her [Matt. v. 44]. Now an essential part of charity is to will the good of one's neighbour and to work for that end. But good is two-fold: there is the spiritual good, the soul's salvation, which is the principal object of charity; for this is what a man ought, out of charity, to will for another. Hence, as far as this good is concerned, heretics who return, however often they have relapsed, are received by the Church to Penance by means of which the way of salvation is opened to them.

Now the other good is that which is a secondary object of charity, namely, temporal good; such as the life of the body, worldly property, a good reputation, ecclesiastical or secular position. This good we are not bound out of charity to will for others, except in order to the external salvation both of them and of others. Hence if the existence of any of such goods in an individual might be able to hinder eternal salvation in many, we are not bound in charity to will that good for that individual; rather should we wish him to be without it; for eternal salvation is to be preferred to temporal good; and, besides, the good of many is to be preferred to the good of one. Now if heretics who return were always taken back, so that they were kept in possession of life and other temporal goods, this might possibly be prejudicial to the salvation of others; for they would infect others, if they relapsed, and also if they escaped punishment others would feel more secure in lapsing into heresy. ... Therefore, in the case of those who return for the first time, the Church not only receives them to Penance, but preserves their lives, and sometimes by dispensation restores them to their former ecclesiastical position, if they seem to be genuinely converted. ... But when, after being taken back, they again relapse ... they are admitted to Penance, if they return, but not so as to be delivered from sentence of death. ...

SECTION V
The Conciliar Movement

I. THE DECREE OF THE COUNCIL OF CONSTANCE, 'SACROSANCTA' (APRIL 1415)
Hardt, *Rerum magni Conc. Const.* (1700) iv. 98. Mirbt, 392

[The movements inspired by Wycliffe in England, Hus in Bohemia, Groot in the Netherlands, whatever the extravagances of some of their followers, bore witness to a widespread feeling of discontent with the state of the Church; while the schism in the papacy—with one pope at Avignon and an anti-pope in Rome—was intolerable to the devout Christian. A group of moderate reformers, the chief of whom was Gerson, chancellor of Paris University, suggested the holding of a general council, since the *plenitudo potestatis* of the Church resided, they held, in the whole body of the faithful, represented by an oecumenical council. A council at Pisa in 1409 tried to heal the schism, but failed. The next council met at Constance in 1414, healed the schism, condemned Wycliffe and Hus, but failed to reform the Church. The new Pope elected by the council, Martin V, asserted that councils were subordinate to the Pope, and that any reform must be left to him. This was in defiance of the council to which he owed his election, which had passed the following decree.]

This holy Council of Constance ... declares, first that it is lawfully assembled in the Holy Spirit, that it constitutes a General Council, representing the Catholic Church, and that therefore it has its authority immediately from Christ; and that all men, of every rank and condition, including the Pope himself, is bound to obey it in matters concerning the Faith, the abolition of the schism, and the reformation of the Church of God in its head and its members. Secondly it declares that any one, of any rank and condition, who shall contumaciously refuse to obey the orders, decrees, statutes or instructions, made or to be made by this holy Council, or by an other lawfully assembled general council ... shall, unless he comes to a right frame of mind, be subjected to fitting penance and punished appropriately: and, if need be, recourse shall be had to the other sanctions of the law. ...

II. THE BULL 'EXECRABILIS' OF PIUS II (JANUARY 1460)
Bullarium Romanum, v. 149. Mirbt, 406

[The Council of Basle, 1431–38, met with an impressive programme: the reform of the Church, the healing of the schism with the East, and the final settlement of the Hussite heresy. This last was accomplished by means of concessions, and a military victory over the extremists. The negotiation with the Greeks failed, and the reforms suggested were in many respects too clearly prompted by partisan jealousy of papal prerogatives to command acceptance. In 1438 a council was held

at Florence to continue negotiations with the Greeks, while a kind of 'rump' of
the Basle council continued to sit, and made itself ridiculous by electing an anti-
pope. The Council of Florence sat until 1458, but failed to secure its main object,
and in 1460 Pope Pius II (who had reconciled Frederick III to the papacy and so
deprived the councils of the support of the temporal power in any anti-papal
attempts) struck the final blow at the attempt at constitutional reform.]

There has sprung up in our time an execrable abuse, unheard of in
earlier ages, namely that some men, imbued with the spirit of rebellion,
presume to appeal to a future council from the Roman Pontiff, the
vicar of Jesus Christ, to whom in the person of blessed Peter it was
said, 'Feed my sheep' and 'Whatsoever thou shalt bind on earth shall be
bound in heaven'; and that not from a desire for a sounder judgement
but to escape the penalties of their misdeeds. Any one who is not wholly
ignorant of the laws can see how this contravenes the sacred canons and
how detrimental it is to Christendom. And is it not plainly absurd to
appeal to what does not now exist and the date of whose future existence
is unknown? Wishing therefore to cast out from the Church of God this
pestilent poison and to take measures for the safety of the sheep committed to our care, and to ward off from the sheep-fold of our Saviour all
that may offend ... we condemn appeals of this kind and denounce
them as erroneous and detestable. ...

[Though the Council of Basle failed to carry out its reforming programme,
England, France, and the Empire secured the points in which they were most
interested in their struggle against papal encroachments. Provisors and Praemunire remained in the English statute book. The French clergy accepted the
Pragmatic Sanction of Bourges and in 1439 a German diet drew up the Pragmatic
Sanction of Mainz, with similar provisions. Contributions to Rome were
restricted; papal provisions forbidden, and the machinery of provincial and
diocesan synods was continued. These Concordats incorporated many of the
suggestions of Basle, and by them Martin V saved his face and the situation.]

SECTION VI

Scholasticism

I. S. ANSELM'S 'ONTOLOGICAL PROOF' OF GOD'S EXISTENCE

Anselm (1033–1109), *Proslogion*, iii and iv

[Anselm was the ablest and most influential of the theologians of the eleventh
century (among whom were Lanfranc, Roscelin of Compiègne, and Fulbert of
Chartres) who applied the logic of the schools to theological controversy and

speculation. The argument of the existence of God in the *Proslogion* is perhaps the most brilliant of all attempts to prove God's existence *a priori*.]

III. *That the non-existence of God is inconceivable*

This proposition is indeed so true that its negation is inconceivable. For it is quite conceivable that there is something whose non-existence is inconceivable, and this must be greater than that whose non-existence is conceivable. Wherefore, if that thing than which no greater thing is conceivable can be conceived as non-existent; then, that very thing than which a greater is inconceivable is not that than which a greater is inconceivable; which is a contradiction.

So true is it that there exists something than which a greater is inconceivable, that its non-existence is inconceivable: and this thing art Thou, O Lord our God!

So truly therefore dost Thou exist, O Lord my God, that Thy nonexistence is inconceivable; and with good reason; for if a man's mind could conceive aught better than Thou, the creature would rise above the Creator and judge Him; which is utterly absurd. And in truth whatever else there be beside Thee, may be conceived as non-existent. Thou alone, therefore, most truly of all, and therefore most of all, hast existence: because whatever else there is, is not so truly existent, and therefore has less the prerogative of existence.

[Anselm's argument was answered by a monk named Gaunilo in *Liber pro Insipiente* (*A Plea for the Fool*—who 'said in his heart, There is no God,' a text with which Anselm makes play in the *Proslogion*). He objected that the existence of an *idea* in the mind does not entail the existence of a corresponding *reality* outside the mind. Anselm retorted with a distinction between *perfection in its own kind and absolute perfection*. It is only to the latter that we must ascribe necessary existence.]

From the *Responsio Anselmi*

But, you say, this is the same as if one were to conceive the idea of an island, surpassing all lands in fertility, named (from the difficulty or rather impossibility of finding what is non-existent) 'the lost island,' and to say, it must indubitably exist in *reality*, because a man easily conceives the *idea* of it when described in words. I answer with confidence; if a man will find anything existing either in fact or in thought only, so excellent that nothing more excellent is conceivable, and if he be able to apply to it my train of argument, then will I discover and present to him his 'lost island,' to be lost no more.

II. S. ANSELM ON THE ATONEMENT

Anselm, *Cur deus homo?*

[The 'Ransom Theory' of the Atonement (see pp. 32, 36) held the field in Christian theology from the days of Gregory the Great till Anselm. The 'Satisfaction Theory' of Anselm is expounded in one of the few books that can be truly called epoch-making. 'It has affected, though in different degrees, and by way now of attraction, now of repulsion, all soterio-logical thought since his time' (Mozley, *Doctrine of the Atonement*). The following abstract is taken from Norris, *Rudiments of Theology*, 1878, appendix III, pp. 305 ff.]

Book I

xi. The problem is, how can God forgive man's sin? To clear our thoughts let us first consider what sin is, and what satisfaction for sin is. ... *To sin* is to fail to render to God His due. What is due to God? Righteousness, or rectitude of will. He who fails to render this honour to God, robs God of that which belongs to Him, and dishonours God. This is *sin*. ... And what is satisfaction? It is not enough simply to restore what has been taken away; but, in consideration of the insult offered, more than what was taken away must be rendered back.

xii. Let us consider whether God could properly remit sin by mercy alone without satisfaction. So to remit sin would be simply to abstain from punishing it. And since the only possible way of correcting sin, for which no satisfaction has been made, is to punish it; not to punish it, is to remit it uncorrected. But God cannot properly leave anything uncorrected in His kingdom. Moreover, so to remit sin unpunished, would be treating the sinful and the sinless alike, which would be incongruous to God's nature. And incongruity is injustice.

xiii. It is necessary, therefore, that either the honour taken away should be repaid, or punishment should be inflicted. Otherwise one of two things follows—either God is not just to Himself, or He is powerless to do what He ought to do. A blasphemous supposition.

xx. The satisfaction ought to be in proportion to the sin. ...

xxi. And thou has not yet duly estimated the gravity of sin. Suppose that thou wast standing in God's presence, and some one said to thee—'Look yonder.' And God said. 'I am altogether unwilling that thou shouldest look.' Ask thyself whether there be aught in the whole universe for the sake of which thou oughtest to indulge that one look against the will of God. Not to preserve the whole creation from perishing oughtest thou to act against the will of God. And shouldest thou so act, what canst thou pay for this sin? Thou canst not make satisfaction for it, unless thou payest something greater than the whole creation. All that is created, that is, all that is not God, cannot compensate the sin.

Book II

iv. It is necessary that God should fulfil His purpose respecting human nature. And this cannot be except there be a complete satisfaction made for sin; and this no sinner can make.

vi. Satisfaction cannot be made unless there be some One able to pay to God for man's sin something greater than all that is beside God. ... Now nothing is greater than all that is not God, except God Himself. None therefore can make this satisfaction except God. And none ought to make it except man. ... If, then, it be necessary that the kingdom of heaven be completed by man's admission, and if man cannot be admitted unless the aforesaid satisfaction for sin be first made, and if God only *can*, and man only *ought* to make this satisfaction, then necessarily One must make it who is both God and man.

xi. He must have something to offer greater than all that is below God, and something that He can give to God voluntarily, and not as in duty bound. Mere obedience would not be a gift of this kind; for every rational creature owes this obedience as a duty to God. But *death* Christ was in no way bound to suffer, having never sinned. So death was an offering that He could make as of free will, and not of debt. ...

xix. Now One who could freely offer so great a gift to God, clearly ought not to be without reward. ... But what reward could be given to One who needed nothing—One who craved neither gift nor pardon? ... If the Son chose to make over the claim He had on God to man, could the Father justly forbid Him doing so, or refuse to man what the Son willed to give him?

xx. What greater mercy can be conceived than that God the Father should say to the sinner—condemned to eternal torment, and unable to redeem himself—'Receive my only Son, and offer Him for thyself,' while the Son Himself said—'Take me, and redeem thyself'?

And what greater justice than that One who receives a payment for exceeding the amount due, should, if it be paid with a right intention, remit all that is due?'

III. S. THOMAS AQUINAS, 1225–74

[Scholasticism reached its height in the writings of the Dominican friar, Thomas of Aquino, 'The Angelic Doctor'. His systematic exposition of the Catholic Faith in terms of Aristotelian philosophy produced a revolution in Christian thought, for Augustine and Anselm, and Christian thinkers in general before Aquinas, had regarded Platonism as the specifically Christian philosophy. In the thirteenth century the works of Aristotle became known through the writings of the Arabian philosophers, Avicenna and Averrhöes, and the Jew Maimonides, and the translations and commentaries of such men as Albert of Cologne and Robert Grosseteste, Bishop of Lincoln. At first the students of Aristotle were suspected of 'Averrhoist' heresy (the chief error of which was the reduction of God to a mere First Cause, latent in the uncreated and eternal universe), but the modified Aristotelianism which was the foundation of the monumental *Summa Theologica* of Aquinas soon won acceptance, and the teaching of Aquinas was set up by Leo XIII as the classical exposition of Catholic Doctrine.]

a. Aquinas on Belief   *De veritate*, Q. xiv. art. 1

... Our understanding, existing in potentiality, is moved to activity by one of two things; either by its proper object, which is an intelligible form ... or by the will. ... So then our understanding, in potentiality, is variously situated with respect to the members of a contradiction.[1] For sometimes it is not inclined more to one member than to the other, either because of lack of evidence or because of the apparent equality of the evidence for both sides; and this is the state of *doubt*, when a man wavers between two contradictory opinions. But sometimes the understanding is inclined more to one side than to the other, yet the evidence which so inclines it is not of sufficient weight to determine the complete acceptance of that side, and hence a man accepts one conclusion, but without fully excluding the contradictory; and this is the state of *opinion*. ... Sometimes, however, the understanding, in potentiality, is determined to the extent of complete adhesion to one side; and it is thus determined sometimes by the intelligible object, sometimes by the will. It may be determined by the object either mediately or immediately: immediately, when the truth of intelligible propositions appears at once and without doubt from consideration of the intelligible object; and this is the state of *the man who understands* the axioms [*principia*], which are at once recognized as true when their terms are known ...; it is determined mediately when the understanding, upon recognition of the definitions of the terms, is determined to one side of a contradiction

---

[1] A contradiction in the technical sense; a pair of propositions one of which must, and both of which cannot, be true—e.g. 'All men are liars.' 'Some men are not liars.'

in virtue of these fundamental axioms; and this is the state of *knowledge*. But sometimes the understanding cannot be determined to one side of a contradiction either at once, through the very definitions of the terms, as in the case of axioms, or in virtue of the axioms, as in the case of demonstrable conclusions; but it is determined through the agency of the *will*, which chooses to assent to one side, definitely and positively, through some influence which is sufficient to move the will but not the intellect, namely the fact that it seems good or fitting to assent to this side; this is the state of *belief*, as when a man believes in the words of someone because to believe seems becoming or advantageous; and thus we are moved to believe in certain sayings inasmuch as eternal life is promised to us as a reward for belief, and by this reward our will is moved to assent to what is said, although our understanding is not so moved by any evidence presented to it. ...

The state of *understanding* involves assent ... but it does not involve reasoning (*cogitatio*). ... While the state of *knowledge* involves both reasoning and assent; but the reasoning is the cause of the assent and the assent brings reasoning to a close. For as a result of the application of axioms to conclusions assent is given to conclusions by resolving them into axioms, and at that point the movement of reason is stayed and brought to rest ... and thus assent and reason are not in this case involved on, as it were, equal terms; but reasoning induces assent, and assent brings the process to rest. In the case of belief, however, assent and reasoning are on, as it were, equal terms. For here assent, as has been said, is not caused by reasoning but by the will. But since the understanding is not in this way brought to its one proper termination, viz. to the vision of the intelligible object, hence it is that its motion is not brought to rest but is still employed in reasoning and enquiry on the objects of faith, however firmly it assents to them. ... And hence the understanding of the believer is said to be taken captive (2 Cor. x. 5), because it is determined by external considerations, not by its own proper processes. Hence, too, it comes that in a believer motions may surge up contrary to that which he most firmly holds, a thing which does not happen in a man who understands, or in one who knows. ...

b. Aquinas on the Incarnation   *Summa Theologica*, iii. Q. i. art. i–iii

[A great subject of debate among the schoolmen was the question: Would the Incarnation have taken place if Adam had not sinned? Traditional theology had the support of Athanasius and Augustine for the view that the Incarnation depended on the Fall, and the Church in her missal proclaimed the paradox of Adam's transgression and its blessed consequence: *O felix culpa!*—'O happy fault, which deserved to have so great and glorious a redeemer!' But in the twelfth century Rupert of Deutz argued that the Incarnation was the predetermined purpose of God when he created the world; and Alexander of Hales (thirteenth century) held the same view, on the ground that it is of the essence of the *summum bonum* to have *summa diffusio*; and for the same reason Duns Scotus refused to believe that the appearance of the Son was a contingent event. Aquinas and Bonaventure allow the force of this contention to the extent of admitting the fittingness of the Incarnation, but both decide, on Scriptural grounds, that it was contingent on the Fall.]

Article I. *Whether it was fitting that God should be made flesh*

... I *reply* that what is fitting to any given thing is that which belongs to it in accordance with the principle of its own nature; thus it befits man to reason inasmuch as man is rational by nature. Now the nature of God is the essence of goodness ... and hence whatever pertains to the principle of the good befits God. It pertains to the principle of the good that it should communicate itself to others. ... Hence it pertains to the principle of the highest good that it should communicate itself to creation in the highest way; and this communication reaches its highest when 'he so joins created nature to himself that one person comes into being from three constituents, the Word, the Spirit, and the flesh' (Augustine, *De Trinitate*, xiii. 17). Hence it is manifest that it was fitting that God should be made flesh. ...

Article II.[1] *Whether it was necessary for the restoration of the human race that the Word of God should be made flesh*

We thus proceed to the second article:

1. It might seem that it was not necessary. For the Word of God being perfect God ... gained no accession of virtue by the assumption of flesh. If, therefore, the incarnate Word of God repaired human nature, then that restoration could have been wrought by him even without the assumption of flesh.

2. Furthermore, for the restoration of human nature, which had fallen through sin, nothing might seem to be required but that man should make satisfaction for his sin. But man, as it seems, could have made satisfaction for sin, for God ought not to require from man more than he is able to give; and since he is more prone to pity than to punish, as he

---

[1] This article is given in full partly because of its intrinsic interest, but also to illustrate S. Thomas's method; the question is proposed, objections stated, followed by an authoritative statement on the other side (*sed contra*); then Aquinas replies in a concise essay on the subject, and the debate (as it may be called, since the form is modelled on academic disputations) is concluded with the answers to the objections.

reckons the act of sin punishable, so he ought to reckon the contrary act as meritorious. Therefore it was not necessary, etc.

3. Furthermore, it is of especial importance for man's salvation that he should reverence God. ... But men reverence God the more from the very fact that they consider him as raised up above all things and removed from the sense of men. ... Therefore it might seem not to be profitable for man's salvation that God should become like to us by the assumption of flesh.

But on the other hand, that through which the human race is liberated from perdition is needful for man's salvation. But the mystery of the divine Incarnation is of this sort, according to that saying, God so loved the world that he gave his only-begotten son; that everyone who believes on him should not perish but have eternal life (John iii. 16). Therefore it was necessary, etc.

I reply that there are two senses in which a thing is said to be necessary for the fulfilment of a purpose. In one sense a thing is said to be necessary because without it the purpose cannot be attained; as food is necessary for the preservation of human life. In another sense it signifies a means to the more satisfactory attainment of the end in view; thus a horse is necessary for a journey. The Incarnation was not necessary in the first sense for the restoration of human nature. For God, through his omnipotent power, could have restored human nature in many other ways. But it was necessary in the second sense. Hence Augustine says (*De Trinitate*, xiii. 10), 'But we have to demonstrate not that there was no other way possible for God, for all things lie equally under his power; but that there was no other way more fitting by which our misery might be healed.' And this point may be examined with respect to the promotion of man towards good. In the first place, with respect to faith, which is made more sure in that it believes in the utterances of God himself; hence Augustine says (*De civit. Dei*, xi, 2), 'In order that man should walk towards faith with more assurance, truth itself, the Son of God, taking manhood on himself, founded and established the faith.' Secondly, with respect to hope, which is thereby raised to the highest degree; hence Augustine says (*De Trin.* xiii. 10), 'Nothing was so necessary for the raising of our hope, than that it should be proved to us how much God loved us. And what testimony could be more manifest than that the Son of God deigned to enter into fellowship with us?' Thirdly, with respect to charity, which is thereby aroused in the highest degree; hence Augustine says (*De catechizandis rudibus*, iv), 'What greater reason is there for the Lord's advent, than to the end that God might display his love towards us?', adding later, 'So that, if it was irksome for us to love God, it may not now be irksome at least to return his love.' Fourthly, in respect of right conduct, in which he offered himself as an example to us; hence

Augustine says (*Sermon* xxii, *De nativitate Domini*), 'We were not to follow man, who could be seen; we were to follow God, who could not be seen. Wherefore, that man might be shewn one whom he might both see and follow, God was made man.' Fifthly, in respect of the full participation in divinity, which is man's true blessedness and the end of human life; and this is conferred on us by the humanity of Christ; for Augustine says (*Sermon* xiii, *De nat. Dom.*), 'God became man, that man might become God.' In the same way this was also useful for the removal of evil. For in the first place man is thereby taught not to take the devil for his superior, nor to honour him who is the origin of evil; hence Augustine says (*De Trin.* xiii. 17), 'Since human nature could be so conjoined to God as to make one person, let not those malignant spirits in their arrogance dare to place themselves above mankind on the ground that they are not of flesh.' Secondly, we are thereby taught how great is the dignity of human nature, that we may not pollute it by sinning; hence Augustine says (*De vera religione*, xvi), 'God has showed us how high is the place of human nature in creation, in that he appeared to men in true manhood.' And Pope Leo says (*Serm. De nativitate*, i), 'Christian man, recognize your dignity; and, having been made a colleague of the divine nature, do not, through unworthy behaviour, return to the old low estate.' Thirdly, as Augustine says (*De Trin.* xii. 17), for the removal of man's presumption, 'that the grace of God, with no previous merits on our part, may be commended in the manhood of Christ.' Fourthly, because (ibid.) 'the pride of man, which is the greatest hindrance to his adherence in God, can be reproved and remedied by that great humility of God.' Fifthly, for the freeing of man from enslavement to sin; as Augustine says (*De Trin.* xiii. 13), 'It was right that the devil should be overcome by the righteousness of the man Jesus Christ; and this was done by Christ making satisfaction for us.' Now a mere man could not have made satisfaction for the whole human race; while it was not right for God to make satisfaction; hence it was needful that Jesus Christ should be both God and man. Hence also Pope Leo says (*Serm. De nativ.* loc. cit.), 'Weakness is assumed by strength, lowliness by majesty, mortality by eternity; that, as was fitting for our healing, one and the same mediator between God and man might be able to die as a result of the one nature, and rise again as a result of the other. For were he not true God he would not bring us healing, were he not true man he would not present us an example.' And many other advantages are given thereby which are beyond the apprehension of man's intelligence.

Therefore, *in reply to the first point*, that line of reasoning takes 'necessary' in the first sense, describing that without which a given purpose cannot be attained.

In reply to the second, a satisfaction can be said to be sufficient in two senses. In one sense it means completely sufficient, when the satisfaction is of such worth as to make an adequate recompense for the sin committed. The satisfaction of a mere man could not in this way be sufficient for sin. For the whole of human nature was corrupted by sin, and the good of an individual, or of many individuals, could not make an equivalent recompense for the harm done to all human nature. Then again, a sin against God has a kind of infinity arising from the infinity of the divine majesty—for an offence is the greater in proportion to the greatness of him against whom it is committed. And hence for a worthy satisfaction the act of satisfaction must needs have an infinite efficacy, that is to say, it must needs be an act of God and man. In another sense the satisfaction of man can be called sufficient incompletely, that is, dependent on the acceptance of him who is content with it, although it has not adequate worth. In this way the satisfaction of a mere man is sufficient. And because everything incomplete presupposes something complete, which is its support, it follows that any satisfaction of a mere man has efficacy from the satisfaction of Christ.[1]

In reply to the third, God did not diminish his majesty by assuming flesh, consequently the ground of reverence towards him is not diminished; for reverence is increased by the increase of the knowledge of God. And because he wishes to come nearer to us through the assumption of flesh, he has drawn us the more to the knowledge of himself.

Article III. *Whether God would have been made flesh if man had not sinned*

... *I reply that* there are divers opinions on this point. Some say that even if man had not sinned, God would have been made flesh. Others assert the contrary; and it seems that we ought to agree with their assertion. For those things which issue solely from the will of God, beyond anything that is due to the creature, can only become known to us as far as they are handed down in sacred Scripture, through which

---

[1] Duns Scotus maintained, against the view of Anselm and Aquinas: i. That the sin of finite man cannot be infinite. ii. That Christ's merit belonged to his human nature and was therefore finite (*In IV libros sententiarum*, iii. 19).

Every created oblation has the value assigned to it by God in his acceptance of it' (op. cit. iii. 20). The redemption of Christ was efficacious because God chose to accept it. But He might have accepted another satisfaction, had He so willed.

the divine will is made known to us. And hence, since the ground of the Incarnation is everywhere in sacred Scripture put down as a result of the sin of the first man, it is more fittingly said that the work of the Incarnation was ordained by God as a remedy for sin; and therefore that without sin there would have been no Incarnation. Although the power of God is not limited to this; for God could have been made flesh, even had there been no sin. ...

c. Aquinas on the Atonement   *S.T.* iii. Q. xlviii. art. i–iv.

Article I. *Whether the passion of Christ effected our salvation by way of merit*

... *I reply that* ... grace was given to Christ not only as to an individual but in so much that he is the head of the Church, that is, in order that it might from him redound to the members; therefore the works of Christ have the same effect, with respect both to himself and to his members, as have the works of another man, established in grace, with respect to that man. Now it is clear that any man, established in grace, who suffers for righteousness' sake, merits salvation for himself by that very suffering (Matt. v. 10). ... Hence Christ through his passion merited salvation not only for himself but for all his members.

Article II. *Whether the passion of Christ effected our salvation by way of satisfaction*

We thus proceed to the second article:

1. It seems that the passion of Christ did not effect our salvation by way of satisfaction. For it seems that to make satisfaction is the part of the sinner. ...

2. Furthermore, satisfaction can never be made by means of a greater offence. But the greatest offence was perpetrated in the passion of Christ, since his slayers committed the most grievous of sins. ...

3. Further, satisfaction implies a certain equality with the fault, since it is an act of justice. But Christ's passion does not seem to be equal to all the sins of the human race, since Christ suffered according to the flesh, not according to the godhead (1 Peter iv. 1). ...

I reply that he makes a proper satisfaction who offers to the person offended something which gives him a delight greater than his hatred of the offence. Now Christ by suffering as a result of love and obedience offered to God something greater than what might be exacted in compensation for the whole offence of humanity; firstly, because of the greatness of the love, as a result of which he suffered; secondly, because of the worth of the life which he laid down for a satisfaction, which was the life of God and man; thirdly, because of the comprehensiveness of his passion and the greatness of the sorrow which he took upon himself. ... And therefore the passion of Christ was not only sufficient but a superabundant satisfaction for the sins of the human race (1 John ii. 2). ...

Therefore, *in reply to the first point*, the head and the members are as it were one mystical person; and thus the satisfaction of Christ belongs to all the faithful as to his members. ...

In reply to the second, the love of Christ in his suffering outweighed the malice of them that crucified him. ...

In reply to the third, the worth of Christ's flesh is to be reckoned, not according to the nature of flesh, but according to the person who assumed it, inasmuch as it was the flesh of God, from whom it gained an infinite worth.

Article III.　*Whether Christ's passion wrought salvation by way of sacrifice*

... I reply that a thing is properly called a sacrifice when it is done to pay the homage properly due to God, to propitiate him. Hence, as Augustine says (*De Civ. Dei*, x. 6), 'A true sacrifice is every work which is performed in order that we may inhere in God in holy fellowship, a work, that is, directed to that end of good in which we can attain true blessedness.' Now Christ, he goes on to say, 'offered himself for us in his passion'; and it was this voluntary undergoing of the passion which, above all, rendered it acceptable to God.[1] Hence it is manifest that the passion of Christ was a true sacrifice. ...

Article IV.　*Whether Christ's passion wrought our salvation by way of redemption*

... I reply that man was bound, through sin, in two respects; first, in servitude to sin. ... The devil, by inducing man to sin, had overcome him and therefore man was assigned to the devil as a slave. Secondly, in respect to the incurring of a penalty ... according to the justice of God. ... Therefore, since the passion of Christ was sufficient and superabundant for the sin of the human race and the penalty incurred, his passion was a kind of ransom, by which we were freed from both these obligations. ...

---

[1] Cf. the famous saying of S. Bernard: *Non mors Deo, sed voluntas placuit sponte morientis*—'It was not the death that was pleasing to God, but the will of him who died of his own accord.'

d. Aquinas on the Eucharist. The Doctrine of Transubstantiation

[*A Note on the Development of Eucharistic Doctrine, ninth to twelfth centuries.*
The doctrine of the Eucharist was not a subject of controversy in the first
centuries, and therefore the need for precise formulation did not arise. The
tendency to advance from the assertion of the real presence of Christ's flesh
and blood to a precise theory of the mode of this presence in the elements was
more marked in the East than in the West, and most distinct in the *De Fide
Orthodoxa* of John of Damascus, *c.*750. In the West the influence of Augustine, of
whom, 'obscure though his view of the Eucharist undoubtedly is, it is at any rate
certain that he did not believe in transubstantiation' (Gore, *Dissertations*, 232),
was for many centuries predominant, and during that period the Western writers
are on the whole content to speak of the consecrated elements as signs.

In the ninth century Paschasius Radbertus published a treatise, *On the Body
and Blood of the Lord*, in which he pushed to extremes the language of John
Damascene, ' ... though the body and blood of Christ remain in the figure of
bread and wine, yet we must believe them to be simply a figure and that, after
consecration, they are nothing else than the body and blood of Christ ... and
that I may speak more marvellously, to be clearly the very flesh which was born of
Mary, and suffered on the cross and rose from the tomb ... ' (op. cit. i. 2). This
view was opposed by Rabanus Maurus, who strongly attacked the notion that the
'body' of the Eucharist was the same as the 'flesh' of the incarnate Lord. And
Ratramnus, a monk of the abbey of which Radbert was abbot, went so far in
combating the doctrine of his superior as sometimes to appear to hold the
'virtualist' position—viz. that through consecration the Eucharistic elements are
made spiritually efficacious for the faithful recipient without any 'real' or 'objective' change. But the teaching of Paschasius had won its way to general acceptance by the middle of the eleventh century, and when Berengar of Tours in 1050
proclaimed his adherence to the 'teaching of John the Scot' (*sc.* Scotus Erigena, to
whom Ratramnus' work seems to have been ascribed) he was opposed by
Lanfranc and condemned at Rome. In 1059 he was induced to assent to a most
materialistic statement of the 'faith delivered by Pope Nicholas II and the Roman
synod': 'that the bread and wine placed on the altar are after consecration not
only a sacrament but also the true body and blood of our Lord Jesus Christ and
that these are sensibly handled and broken by the hands of priests and crushed by
the teeth of the faithful, not only sacramentally but in reality ... ' (Mansi, xix.
900). In 1079, after he had persisted in teaching his former doctrine, Berengar was
again forced to profess his orthodoxy, this time under Gregory VII, who had
formerly been sympathetic and now required merely an assertion of belief in the
'substantial' change of the elements into 'the real flesh of Christ which was born
of the Virgin, etc. ... ' (Mansi, xx. 524).

Peter Lombard, the most influential theologian of the twelfth century, maintained the 'substantial' presence of Christ's body under the accidents of the
elements, but recognized the philosophical difficulties entailed in any precise
statement of 'transubstantiation'. He repudiated the assertion (contained in
Berengar's confession of 1059, and in many anti-Berengarian writers) of the
breaking of Christ's body in the fraction of the bread.

The term transubstantiation seems to have been adopted in the twelfth
century; but it is impossible to say at what time it came to have a technical

meaning, that is, to convey more than the assertion that the elements after consecration are 'really' the body and blood. So that when in 1215 the 4th Lateran Council decreed that 'the body and blood are truly contained in the sacrament of the altar under the species of bread and wine; the bread being transubstantiated into the body and the wine into the blood by the power of God ...' (Mansi, xxii. 982), it is impossible to assert with confidence that this statement anticipates the authorization by the Council of Trent of the kind of doctrine elaborated by S. Thomas.

In its technical sense transubstantiation denotes a doctrine which is based on the Aristotelian philosophy as taught by the schoolmen, according to which a physical object consists of 'accidents,' the properties perceptible by the senses, and an underlying 'substance' in which the accidents inhere, and which gives to the object its essential nature. According to the doctrine of transubstantiation the accidents of bread and wine remain after consecration, but their substance is changed into that of the body and blood of Christ.]

Summa Theologica, iii. Q. lxxv

Article II. *Whether the substance of bread and wine remain in this sacrament after consecration*

... *I reply* that it has been held that the substance of bread and wine remain in this sacrament after consecration. But this is an untenable position, for in the first place it destroys the reality of this sacrament, which demands that in the sacrament there should be the true body of Christ, which was not there before consecration. Now a thing cannot be in a place where it was not before except either by change of position, or by the conversion of some other thing into it; as a fire begins to be in a house either because it is carried there or because it is kindled. But it is clear that the body of Christ does not begin to be in the sacrament through change of position. ... Therefore it remains that the body of Christ can only come to be in the sacrament by means of the conversion of the substance of bread into his body; and that which is converted into anything does not remain after the conversion. ... This position is therefore to be avoided as heretical.

Article III. *Whether the substance of bread or wine is annihilated after the consecration of this sacrament*

... *I reply* that, since the substance of bread or wine does not remain in the sacrament, some have thought it impossible that their substance should be converted into that of the body or blood of Christ, and therefore have maintained that through the consecration the substance of bread or wine is either resolved into underlying matter [*sc.* the four elements] or annihilated. ... But this is impossible, because it is impossible to suppose the manner in which the true body of Christ begins to be in the sacrament, unless by conversion of the substance of bread; and this conversion is ruled out by the supposition of the annihilation of the substance of bread, or its resolution into underlying matter. ...

Article IV. *Whether bread can be converted into the body of Christ*

... *I reply* that this conversion is not like natural conversions but is wholly supernatural, effected solely by the power of God. ... All conversion which takes place according to the laws of nature is formal. ... But God ... can produce not only a formal conversion, that is, the supersession of one form by another in the same subject, but the conversion of the whole being, that is, the conversion of the whole substance of A into the whole substance of B. And this is done in this sacrament by the power of God, for the whole substance of bread is converted into the whole substance of Christ's body. ... Hence this conversion is properly called transubstantiation.

Article V. *Whether in this sacrament the accidents of bread and wine remain after the conversion*

... *I reply* that it is apparent to sense that after consecration all the accidents of bread and wine remain. And this indeed happens with reason, by divine providence. First, because it is not customary but abhorrent for men to eat man's flesh and to drink man's blood. Therefore Christ's flesh and blood are set before us to be taken under the appearances of those things which are of frequent use, namely bread and wine. Secondly, lest this sacrament should be mocked at by the infidels, if we ate our Lord under his proper appearance. Thirdly, in order that, while we take the Lord's body and blood invisibly, this fact may avail towards the merit of faith. ...

Ibid. Q. lxxvi

Article VI. *Whether the body of Christ is in this sacrament as in a place*

... *I reply* that ... the body of Christ is not in this sacrament according to the proper mode of spatial dimension [*quantitas dimensiva*], but rather according to the mode of substance. Now any body has a position in space according to the mode of spatial dimension, inasmuch as its extension is measured thereby. Hence Christ's body is not in this sacrament as in a place, but in the mode of substance, i.e. in the way in which a substance is contained by dimensions; for the substance of Christ's body takes the place of the substance of bread. Hence, as the substance of bread was not subject to its own dimensions locally, but in the mode of substance, neither is Christ's body. But the substance of Christ's body is not the subject of these dimensions, as was the substance of bread, and therefore the substance of bread was locally there by reason of its dimensions, because its position was fixed by means of its proper dimensions; whereas the substance of Christ's body has its position fixed by means of dimensions not its own, in such a way that, conversely, the proper dimensions of Christ's body have their position fixed by means of substance, and this is contrary to the principle of a body having position. Wherefore Christ's body is in no way locally in this sacrament. …

Ibid. Q. lxxvii

Article I. *Whether the accidents remain without a subject in this sacrament*

… *I reply* that the accidents which are observed by sense to remain after consecration are not in the substance of bread and wine as in a subject, for that does not remain … , nor in the substantial form, for that does not remain, and if it did remain, could not be a subject. … It is also clear that accidents of this kind are not in the substance of Christ's body and blood as in a subject, for the substance of the human body can in no way be qualified by these accidents; nor is it possible that the body of Christ, being glorious and impassible, should be changed so as to take on itself qualities of this kind. … Therefore it remains that the accidents in this sacrament remain without a subject, and this can indeed be brought about by the power of God. For since the effect depends more on the first cause than on the second, God, who is the first cause of substance and accident, is able, through his infinite power, to keep the accident in being, even after the removal of the substance through which it was kept in being, as through its proper cause. …

Article II. *Whether in this sacrament the spatial dimension [quantitas dimensiva] of bread or wine is the subject of other accidents*

We thus proceed to the second article:

1. It might seem that it is not. … For the subject of an accident is not an accident. … But spatial dimension is a kind of accident. Therefore it cannot be the subject of other accidents.

.   .   .   .

Therefore, *in reply to the first point*, an accident cannot in itself (*per se*) be the subject of another accident, for it has no existence in itself. But, as having existence in another thing, one accident is said to be the subject of another, inasmuch as one accident is received in the subject through the mediation of another; as surface is said to be the subject of colour. Hence, when an accident is divinely given the power to exist in itself, it is acdlso able to be in itself the subject of another accident. …

SECTION VII

The Church in England until the Reformation

I. GREGORY THE GREAT AND THE CHURCH
OF ENGLAND

a. Letter of Gregory to Eulogius, Patriarch of Alexandria, 598

Greg. Ep. vii. 30

[When Gregory became Pope the Anglo-Saxons had driven British Christianity into Brittany, Cornwall, and Wales. Gregory planned to buy Anglian slave-boys to be put into monasteries and afterwards to be sent as missionaries to England. In 596 he sent off a band of forty monks under Augustine, prior of a Roman monastery. In 597 they arrived in Thanet, and in the same year Ethelbert of Kent was baptized at Canterbury and Augustine was consecrated bishop by Virgilius of Arles, Metropolitan and Papal Vicar of Gaul. At Canterbury Augustine set up his Cathedral and founded there an episcopal 'familia'—a kind of domestic combination of public school and theological seminary—and later established nearby a Benedictine monastery.]

Gregory to Eulogius, bishop of Alexandria. ... Since your good deeds bear fruit in which you rejoice as well as others, I am making you a return for benefits received by sending news of the same kind. And this is that whilst the people of the English, placed in a corner of the world, still remained without faith, worshipping stocks and stones, I resolved, aided in this by your prayers, that I ought with God's assistance to send to this people a monk from my monastery to preach. He, by licence given from me, was made bishop by the bishops of the Germanies and with their encouragement was brought on his way to the people aforesaid in the ends of the world; and already letters have reached us telling of his safety and of his work, that both he and they who were sent with him are radiant with such great miracles amongst this people, that they seem to reproduce the powers of the apostles in the signs that they display. Indeed, on the solemn feast of the Lord's Nativity now past, more than ten thousand Angles, according to our information, were baptized by the same our brother and fellow-bishop. I have told you this that you may know not only what you do among the people of Alexandria by speaking, but also what you accomplish in the ends of the world by prayer. For your prayers are in that place where you are not, whilst your holy deeds are exhibited in that place where you are.

b. Gregory's Advice to Augustine on Liturgical Provision for England, 601

Bede, *H.E.* i. 27. Greg. *Ep.* xi. 64

[In 598 Augustine sent to Gregory for direction on certain points of organization and discipline.]

Augustine's Second Question: Whereas the faith is one and the same, are there different customs in different Churches? and is one custom of masses observed in the Holy Roman Church, and another in that of the Gauls?

Pope Gregory answers: You know, my brother, the custom of the Roman Church, in which you remember you were brought up. But my advice is that you should make a careful selection of anything that you have found either in the Roman [Church] or [that] of the Gauls, or any other Church, which may be more acceptable to Almighty God, and diligently teach the Church of the English, which as yet is new in the faith, whatsoever you can gather from the several Churches. For things are not to be loved for the sake of places, but places for the sake of good things. Choose, therefore, from each Church those things that are pious, religious, and seemly, and when you have, as it were, incorporated them, let the minds of the English be accustomed thereto.

c. Gregory's Scheme of Organization for the English Church, 601

Bede, *H.E.* i. 29: Greg. *Ep.* xi. 65. [Translation, Gee and Hardy, *Documents Illustrative of English Church History* (hereafter 'G. and H.'), 1896, iv.]

To the most reverend and holy brother and fellow-bishop, Augustine, Gregory, servant of the servants of God. Although it is certain that the unspeakable rewards of the eternal kingdom are kept for those who labour for God Almighty, it is, however, necessary for us to render to them the benefits of honours, that from this recompense they may be able to labour more abundantly in the zeal of their spiritual work. And because the new Church of the English is brought to the grace of almighty God by the bounty of the same Lord, and by your toil, we grant to you the use of the pall in the same to perform the solemnities of masses only, so that in several places you ordain twelve [several] bishops to be under your authority so far as that the bishop of the City of London ought always hereafter to be consecrated by his own synod and receive the pall of honour from this holy and Apostolic See which, by God's authority, I serve. Moreover we will that you send a bishop to York, whom you shall have seen fit to ordain—yet only so that if the same city shall receive the word of God along with the neighbouring places, he himself also ordain twelve bishops, and enjoy the honour of metropolitan, because if our life last we intend, with the Lord's favour, to give him also the pall. But we will that he be subject to your authority, my brother, and that after your decease he should preside over the bishops he has ordained, but without being in any wise subject to the Bishop of London. Moreover, for the future, let there be this distinction of honour between the bishops of the City of London and of York, that he himself take the precedence who has been first ordained. But whatever things are for the zeal of Christ must be done by common counsel and harmonious action: let them arrange these concordantly, let them take right views and give effect to their views without any mutual misunderstanding. But you, my brother, shall have subject to you not only the bishops you ordain, and not solely those ordained by the Bishop of York, but as well all the priests of Britain, by the authority of our Lord Jesus Christ, so that from the lips and life of your holiness they may receive the form both of correct belief and of holy life, and fulfilling their office in faith and morals, may, when the Lord wills, attain the kingdom of heaven. May God keep you safe, most reverend brother. Dated the 22nd of June in the 19th year of the reign of Mauritius Tiberius, the most pious Augustus, in the 18th year after the consulship of the same lord, in the 4th indiction.

II. THE FIRST NATIONAL SYNOD OF ENGLISH CLERGY

The Council of Hertford, 673   Bede, *H.E.* iv. 5. [Translation, G. and H. v]

[In 669 the Pope sent Theodore, a Greek monk, to England to be archbishop. The English Church had already (at the Council of Whitby in 664) agreed to fall in with the customs of the Western Church and to surrender the special characteristics of the Celtic Christianity which had been spread by Celtic missionaries in Northumbria and which had its centre at Lindisfarne. This subjection of the Celtic North to Canterbury was largely the work of Wilfrid. Theodore carried on the work of organization.]

In the name of our Lord God and Saviour Jesus Christ, in the perpetual reign and government of our Lord Jesus Christ. It seemed good that we should come together according to the prescription of the venerable canons, to treat of the necessary affairs of the Church. We are met together on this 24th day of September, the first indication, in a place called Hertford, I, Theodore, bishop of the Church of Canterbury, appointed thereto, unworthy as I am, by the Apostolic See, and our most reverend brother Bisi, bishop of the East Angles, together with our brother and fellow-bishop Wilfrid, bishop of the nation of the Northumbrians, who was present by his proper legates, as also our brethren and fellow-bishops, Putta, bishop of the Castle of the Kentish-men, called Rochester, Leutherius, bishop of the West Saxons, and Winfrid, bishop of the province of the Mercians, were present; and when we were assembled and had taken our proper places, I said: I beseech you, beloved brethren, for the fear and love of our Redeemer, that we may faithfully enter into a common treaty for the sincere observance of whatsoever has been decreed and determined by the holy and approved fathers. I enlarged upon these and many other things tending unto charity, and the preservation of the unity of the Church. And when I had finished my speech I asked them singly and in order whether they consented to observe all things which had been of old canonically decreed by the fathers? To which all our fellow-priests answered: we are all well agreed readily and cheerfully to keep whatever the canons of the holy fathers have prescribed. Whereupon I presently produced the book of canons, and pointed out ten particulars, which I had marked as being in a more special manner known by me to be necessary for us, and proposed that all would undertake diligently to observe them, namely:

1. That we shall jointly keep Easter Day on the Lord's Day after the fourteenth day of the moon in the first month.

2. That no bishop invade the diocese [*parochia*] of another, but be content with the government of the people committed to him.

3. That no bishop be allowed to offer any molestation to monasteries consecrated to God, nor to take away by violence anything that belongs to them.

4. That the monks themselves go not from place to place, that is from one monastery to another, without the leave of their own abbot, but continue in that obedience which they promised at the time of their conversion.

5. That no clerk, leaving his own bishop, go up and down at his own pleasure, nor be received wherever he comes without the commendatory letters of his bishop; but if he be once received and refuse to return when he is desired so to do, both the receiver and the received shall be laid under an excommunication.

6. That strange bishops and clerks be content with the hospitality that is freely offered them, and let not any of them exercise any priestly function without permission of the bishop in whose diocese he is known to be.

7. That a synod be assembled twice in the year. But because many occasions may hinder this, it was jointly agreed by all that once

in the year it be assembled on the first of August at the place called Cloveshoo.

8. That no bishop put himself before another out of an affectation of precedence, but that every one observe the time and order of his consecration.

9. We had a conference together concerning increasing the number of bishops in proportion to the number of the faithful, but we determine nothing as to this point at present.

10. As to matrimony: that none be allowed to any but what is lawful. Let none commit incest. Let no one relinquish his own wife, but for fornication, as the Gospel teaches. But if any shall have dismissed a wife to whom he has been lawfully married, let him not be coupled to another if he wish to be a true Christian, but remain as he is, or be reconciled to his wife. ...

III. WILLIAM THE CONQUEROR AND THE CHURCH

a. **Refusal of Fealty to the Pope**   *Letter to Gregory VII (c.1075)*: Giles, *Patres Eccl. Angl.*: Lanfranc, i. 32, Letter x

William, by the grace of God the renowned king of the English and duke of the Normans, sends greetings of friendship to Gregory, the most noble Shepherd of the Holy Church.

Your legate Hubert came to me as your representative, Holy Father, and ordered me to do fealty to you and to your successors, and to think better of my decision about the money[1] which my predecessors were accustomed to send to the Roman Church: I agreed to one of these requests, but not to the other. I refused to do fealty, and I will not do it; for I did not promise it, nor do I find that my predecessors did fealty to yours. As to the money, it has been carelessly collected for almost three years, during the time that I was in Gaul. Now that I have returned to my kingdom, by the mercy of God, what has been collected is being sent by the aforesaid legate, and the remainder will be dispatched, when opportunity is offered, by the legate of Lanfranc, our trusty Archbishop.

Pray for us, and for the well-being of our realm, for we have loved your predecessors and wish to love you with all our heart and to hear you obediently, above all things.

---

[1] i.e. 'Peter's Pence'.

b. The Royal Supremacy   Three Canons from Eadmer, *Hist. Nov.* i. 6

I will set down some of the new regulations which [William] instituted: ...

1. He would not allow any inhabitant of any part of his dominion to acknowledge as apostolic the pontiff of the city of Rome, except at his own order, or to receive from him any communication whatsoever, unless it were first shewn to himself.

2. When the primate of his realm (that is, the Archbishop of Canterbury or Dorobernia) presided over a general Council of bishops, he did not allow him to make any order or prohibition unless it had first been ordered by him in accordance with his own will.

3. He would not permit any one, not even any of his bishops, to summon for trial, to excommunicate, or to constrain by any sanction of ecclesiastical punishment, any of his barons or ministers accused of incest, adultery, or any capital crime, except at his own bidding.

IV.   HENRY AND ANSELM

a. The Constitutional Position of the Archbishop   *Henry's Letter to Anselm*, 1100. Anselm, *Epp.* iii. xli. (Migne, *P.L.* clix 75). Stubbs, *S.C.*[9] 120

[Henry had been crowned in the absence of Anselm. This letter explains the reason.]

Henry, by the grace of God king of the English, to his most excellent spiritual father Anselm, bishop of Canterbury, greetings and tokens of all amity. Dearest father, know that my brother King William is dead, and I, having been, by God's will, elected by the clergy and people of England, and already consecrated king (though against my will, because of your absence), I, with all the people of England, ask you, as our father, to come with all speed to take care of me, your son, and of the said people, whose souls have been committed to your care.

To your counsel, and to theirs who with you ought to take counsel for me, I commend my own self and the people of the whole realm of England: and I pray you not to be displeased with my having received the royal blessing without you; had it been possible, I would have received it more willingly from you than from any other. But since enemies were ready to rise against me and the people which I have to govern, there was such necessity that my barons and the said people did not wish it to be longer postponed. And this was the reason why I received my consecration from your representatives.

I would, indeed, have sent you some from my personal suite, and by them I might have dispatched money to you; but owing to my brother's death the whole world is in so disturbed a state all round this realm of England that it would have been utterly impossible for them to reach you in safety. I therefore advise and enjoin you to come by way of Witsand, and not through Normandy, and I will have my barons at Dover to meet you, and money for your journey, and you will find means, by God's help, to repay any debts you have incurred.

Therefore hasten, good father, to come, lest our mother, the Church of Canterbury, so long storm-tossed and desolate,[1] should suffer any further loss of souls because of your absence.

Witness, Girard, bishop, William, bishop-elect of Winchester, William Warelwast, Earl Henry, Robert FitzHaimon, Haimon, my steward, and others, both bishops and barons. Farewell.

b. The Settlement of Bec, 1107   Eadmer, *Hist. Nov.* iv. 91. [Translation G. and H. xx]

[After much negotiation and much correspondence with the Pope a compromise was arranged between Henry and Anselm at Bec.]

On the first of August an assembly of bishops, abbots, and nobles of the realm was held at London in the king's palace. And for three successive days, in Anselm's absence, the matter was thoroughly discussed between king and bishops concerning church investitures, some arguing for this, that the king should perform them after the manner of his father and brother, not according to the injunction and obedience of the pope. For the pope in the sentence which had been then published, standing firm, had conceded homage, which Pope Urban had forbidden, as well as investiture, and in this way had won over the king about investiture, as may be gathered from the letter we have quoted above. Afterwards, in the presence of Anselm and a large concourse, the king agreed had ordained that henceforward no one should be invested with bishopric or abbacy in England by the giving of a pastoral staff or the ring, by the king or any lay hand; Anselm also agreeing that no one elected to a prelacy should be deprived of consecration to the office undertaken on the ground

---

[1] Anselm had been appointed by William II in 1093 (after the see had been vacant for four years, while William enjoyed the revenues). Continual friction with the king over his oppression of the Church made it impossible for Anselm to perform the duties of his office. At length Anselm went to Rome in 1099 to fetch his pall, and was present at a synod which condemned lay investiture. William died in 1100, but Anselm could not give way on this point. Hence his absence at the coronation.

of homage, which he should make to the king. After this decision, by the advice of Anselm and the nobles of the realm, fathers were instituted by the king, without any investiture of pastoral staff or ring, to nearly all the churches of England which had been so long widowed of their shepherds.

V. THE CONSTITUTIONS OF CLARENDON, 1164
Text in Stubbs, *S.C.*[9] 163 ff.

[The codification of Canon Law culminated in the *Decretum* of Gratian in 1148. Secular law was still largely uncodified and governed by unwritten customs. Thus there was a wide borderland between cases which belonged to church jurisdiction and those to which the secular courts could demonstrate their claim. This was one chief cause of the struggle between Becket and Henry II over the trial of criminous clerks. The other was the spread of education which gave to many men who had no intention of taking orders the standard of literacy which was the test of clerkship. Henry was eager to assert the competence of the royal law-courts. Becket was a keen supporter of canonical justice. In 1163, at the Council of Westminster, both sides stated their cases. Henry demanded that criminous clerks, convicted by church courts, should be handed over to his courts for punishment. Becket claimed that this was uncanonical and also inequitable as involving two trials. The Constitutions put forward in the next year in a Council at Clarendon restricted church privileges and jurisdiction.]

In the year 1164 from our Lord's Incarnation, the fourth of the pontificate of Alexander, the tenth of Henry II, most illustrious king of the English, in the presence of the same king, was made this record or report of a certain part of the customs, liberties, and dignities of his ancestors, that is of King Henry his grandfather, and of others, which ought to be observed and held in the realm. And owing to strifes and dissensions which had arisen between the clergy and Justices of the lord the king and the barons of the realm, in respect of customs and dignities of the realm, this report was made before the archbishops and bishops and clergy, and the earls and barons and nobles of the realm. And these same customs, recorded by the archbishops and bishops, and earls and barons, and by those of high rank and age in the realm, Thomas Archbishop of Canterbury, and Roger Archbishop of York, and Gilbert Bishop of London, and Henry Bishop of Winchester, and Nigel Bishop of Ely, and William Bishop of Norwich, and Robert Bishop of Lincoln, and Hilary Bishop of Chichester, and Jocelyn Bishop of Salisbury, and Richard Bishop of Chester, and Bartholomew Bishop of Exeter, and Robert Bishop of Hereford, and David Bishop of St David's, and Roger elect of Worcester, conceded, and by word of mouth steadfastly promised on the word of truth, to the lord the king and his heirs, should be kept and observed in good faith and without evil intent, these being present: Robert Earl of Leicester, Reginald Earl of Cornwall, Conan Earl of Brittany, John Earl of Eu, Roger Earl of Clare, Earl Geoffrey de Mandeville, Hugh Earl of Chester, William Earl of Arundel, Earl Patrick, William Earl of Ferrers, Richard de Luci, Reginald de St Valery, Roger Bigot, Reginald de Warenne, Richer de Aquila, William de Braose, Richard de Camville, Nigel de Mowbray, Simon de Beauchamp, Humphry de Bohun, Matthew de Hereford, Walter de Mayenne, Manser Biset the steward, William Malet, William de Courcy, Robert de Dunstanville, Jocelin de Balliol, William de Lanvallei, William de Caisnet, Geoffrey de Vere, William de Hastings, Hugh de Moreville, Alan de Neville, Simon son of Peter, William Maudit the chamberlain, John Maudit, John Marshall, Peter de Mara, and many other lords and nobles of the realm, as well clerical as lay.

Now of the recorded customs and dignities of the realm a certain part is contained in the present document of which part these are the chapters:

1. If controversy shall arise between laymen, or clergy and laymen, or clergy, regarding advowson and presentation to churches, let it be treated or concluded in the court of the lord the king.

2. Churches belonging to the fee of the lord the king cannot be granted in perpetuity without his own assent and grant.

3. Clerks cited and accused of any matter shall, when summoned by the king's Justiciar, come into the king's own court to answer there concerning what it shall seem to the king's court should be answered there, and in the church court for what it shall seem should be answered there; yet so that the king's justice shall send into the court of holy Church to see in what way the matter shall be there treated.[1] And if the clerk be convicted, or shall confess, the Church must not any longer protect him.

4. Archbishops, bishops, and persons of the realm[2] are not allowed to depart from the kingdom without leave of the lord the king; and if they do depart, they shall, if the king so please, give security that neither in going nor in staying, nor in returning, will they seek the ill or damage of the lord the king or realm.

5. Excommunicate persons are not to give pledge for the future, nor to take oath, but only to give security and pledge of abiding by the Church's judgement that they may be absolved.

---

[1] A very uncanonical provision.   [2] Beneficed clergy.

*6. Laymen are not to be accused save by appointed and legal accusers and witnesses in the presence of the bishop, so that the archdeacon do not lose his right nor anything due to him therein. And if the accused be such that no one wills or dares to accuse them, the sheriff, when requested by the bishop, shall cause twelve lawful men from the neighbourhood [*de visineto*] or the town to swear before the bishop that they will show the truth in the matter according to their conscience.

†7. No one who holds of the king in chief, and none of his demesne officers are to be excommunicated, nor the lands of any one of them to be put under an interdict unless first the lord the king, if he be in the country, or his Justiciar if he be outside the kingdom, be applied to, in order that he may do right for him; and so that what shall appertain to the royal court be concluded there, and that what shall belong to the church court be sent to the same to be treated there.

8. In regard to appeals, if they shall arise, they must proceed from the archdeacon to the bishop, and from the bishop to the archbishop. And if the archbishop fail in showing justice, they must come at last to the lord the king, that by his command the dispute be concluded in the archbishop's court, so that it must not go further[1] without the assent of the lord the king.

9. If a claim shall arise between a clerk and a layman, or between a layman and a clerk, in respect of any tenement which the clerk wishes to bring to frank-almoign,[2] but the layman to a lay fee, it shall be concluded by the consideration of the king's chief Justiciar on the report of twelve lawful men, whether the tenement belong to frank-almoign or the lay fee, before the king's Justiciar himself. And if the report be that it belongs to frank-almoign, it shall be decided in the church court, but if to the lay fee, unless both claim under the same bishop or baron, it shall be decided in the king's court. But if both appeal concerning this fee to the same bishop or baron, it shall be pleaded in his own court; so that for making the award he who was first seised, lose not his seisin until the matter be settled by the decision.

10. If any one of a city, or castle, or borough, or a demesne manor of the lord the king, be cited by archdeacon or bishop for any offence for which he ought to answer to them, and refuse to give satisfaction at their citations, it is well lawful to place him under interdict; but he must not be

---

* These provisions were allowed by the papacy.
† This was disallowed, but enforced.
[1] i.e. to Rome.
[2] Held by Church without feudal obligations.

excommunicated before the chief officer of the lord the king of that town be applied to, in order that he may adjudge him to come for satisfaction. And if the king's officer fail in this, he shall be at the king's mercy, and thereafter the bishop shall be able to coerce the accused be ecclesiastical justice.

*11. Archbishops, bishops, and all persons of the realm[1] who hold of the king in chief, have their possessions from the lord the king as barony, and are answerable therefore to the king's Justices and ministers, and follow and do all royal rights and customs, and like all other barons, have to be present at the trials of the court of the lord the king with the barons until cases arise involving loss of limbs or death.

12. When an archbishopric or bishopric is vacant, or any abbey or priory of the king's demesne, it must be in his own hand, and from it he shall receive all revenues and rents as demesne. And when they come to provide for the church, the lord the king must cite the chief persons of the church, and the election must take place in the chapel of the lord the king himself, with the assent of the lord the king, and the advice of the persons of the realm whom he shall have summoned to do this. And the person elected shall there do homage and fealty to the lord the king as to his liege lord for his life and limbs and earthly honour, saving his order, before he be consecrated.

*13. If any of the nobles of the realm withhold from the archbishop or bishop or archdeacon his right of doing justice in regard of himself or his people, the lord the king must bring them to justice. And if perchance any one should withhold from the lord the king his right the archbishops and bishops and archdeacons must judge him, so that he gives satisfaction to the lord the king.

*14. The goods of those who are under forfeit of the king, no church or cemetery is to detain against the king's justice, because they belong to the king himself, whether they be found inside churches or outside.

15. Decisions concerning debts due under pledge of faith or without pledge of faith are to be in the king's justice.

*16. Sons of villeins [*rusticorum*] ought not to be ordained without the assent of the lord on whose land they are known to have been born.

Now the record of the aforesaid royal customs and dignities was made by the said archbishops and bishops, and earls and barons, and the nobles and elders of the realm, at Clarendon, on the fourth day before the

---

[1] Beneficed clergy.
* These provisions were allowed by the papacy.

Purification of the Blessed Mary, ever Virgin, the lord Henry the king's son, with his father the lord the king being present there. There are moreover many other great customs and dignities of holy Mother Church and the lord the king and the barons of the realm, which are not contained in this document. And let them be safe for holy Church and the lord the king and his heirs and the barons of the realm, and be inviolably observed for ever.

[Becket would not consent to the Clarendon Constitutions. The Council of Northampton supported the king, but Becket refused to accept its findings in a spiritual matter—as he held it to be—and appealed to Rome. Peace was arranged and Becket returned in 1170, only to exasperate the king by excommunicating the bishops who had infringed the rights of Canterbury in assisting the Archbishop of York in the coronation of the king's son. His action provoked the king's hasty exclamation and the too literal interpretation of it by the four knights. After the murder the king had to abjure the uncanonical provisions of the Constitutions as the price of the Pope's absolution. He abandoned the claim to punish criminous clerks; sanctioned the unrestricted right of appeal to Rome in ecclesiastical cases. But the king kept the jurisdiction in cases of advowson and over church lands except those held in frank-almoign; and the method of election of bishops remained in force till 1214.[1]]

VI.   THE POPE'S INTERDICT ON ENGLAND, 1208
Wilkins, *Concilia*, i. 526 [Translation G. and H. xxiv]

[John fell foul of Innocent III over his practice of keeping bishoprics vacant and appropriating their revenues. Matters came to a head over a disputed election to the see of Canterbury in 1205. Appeal was made to the Pope, who summoned the monks of Canterbury to Rome, and induced them to elect a cardinal, Stephen Langton. John refused to accept him, and Innocent placed England under an interdict. The following instructions as to its observance were given in reply to the bishops of London, Ely, and Worcester.]

Innocent the bishop [*episcopus*], etc., to the Bishops of London, Ely, and Worcester, greeting and apostolic blessing. We reply to your inquiries, that whereas by reason of the interdict new chrism cannot be consecrated on Maundy Thursday, old must be used in the baptism of infants, and, if necessity demand, oil must be mixed by hand of the bishop, or else priest, with the chrism, that it fail not. And although the viaticum seem to be meet on the repentance of the dying, yet, if it cannot be had, we who read it believe that the principle holds good in this case, 'believe and thou has eaten,' when actual need, and not contempt of religion, excludes the

---

[1] The foregoing account is derived mainly from M. Deanesley, *History of the Medieval Church*, 140 ff.

sacrament, and the actual need is expected soon to cease. Let neither gospel nor church hours be observed in the accustomed place, nor any other, though the people assemble in the same. Let religious men, whose monasteries people have been wont to visit for the sake of prayer, admit pilgrims inside the church for prayer, not by the greater door, but by more secret place. Let church doors remain shut save at the chief festival of the church, when the parishioners and others may be admitted for prayer into the church with open doors. Let baptism be celebrated in the usual manner with old chrism and oil inside the church with shut doors, no lay person being admitted save the godparents; and if need demand, new oil must be mixed. Penance is to be inflicted as well on the whole as the sick; for in the midst of life we are in death. Those who have confessed in a suit, or have been convicted of some crime, are to be sent to the bishop or his penitentiary, and, if need be, are to be forced to this by church censure. Priests may say their own hours and prayers in private. Priests may on Sunday bless water in the churchyard and sprinkle it; and can make and distribute the bread when blessed, and announce feasts and fasts and preach a sermon to the people. A woman after childbirth may come to church, and perform her purification outside the church walls. Priests shall visit the sick, and hear confessions, and let them perform the commendation of souls in the accustomed manner, but they shall not follow the corpses of the dead, because they will not have church burial. Priests shall, on the day of the Passion, place the cross outside the church, without ceremony, so that the parishioners may adore it with the customary devotion.

VII. JOHN'S CONCESSION OF THE KINGDOM TO THE POPE, 1213
Stubbs, S.C.⁹ 279

[In 1209 Innocent excommunicated John. When this failed of the desired effect he declared John deposed in 1212 and invited the French king to invade the country. Thereupon John submitted and made this declaration to the papal legate Pandulf, at Dover, 15 May 1213; the act of surrender was renewed at London before Nicholas, Bishop of Tusculum, where the homage was performed. It is unknown whether the surrender was suggested from Rome, or offered by John.]

John, by the grace of God king of England, lord of Ireland, duke of Normandy and Aquitaine, earl of Anjou, to all the faithful in Christ who shall inspect this present charter, greeting. We will it to be known by all of you by this our charter, confirmed by our seal, that we, having offended God and our mother the holy Church in many things, and being on that account known to need the Divine mercy, and unable to make any worthy offering for the performance of due satisfaction to God and the Church, unless we humble ourselves and our realms—we, willing to humble ourselves for Him who humbled Himself for us even to death, by the inspiration of the Holy Spirit's grace, under no compulsion of force or of fear, but of our good and free will, and by the unanimous advice of our barons, offer and freely grant to God and His holy apostles Peter and Paul, and the holy Roman Church, our mother, and to our lord the Pope Innocent and his catholic successors, the whole realm of England and the whole realm of Ireland, with all their rights and appurtenances, for the remission of our sins and those of all our race, as well quick as dead; and from now receiving back and holding these, as a feudal dependant, from God and the Roman Church, in the presence of the prudent man Pandulf, subdeacon and one of the household of the lord the pope, do and swear fealty for them to the aforesaid our lord the Pope Innocent and his catholic successors and the Roman Church, according to the form written below, and will do liege homage to the same lord the Pope in his presence if we shall be able to be present before him; binding our successors and heirs by our wife, for ever, that in like manner to the supreme pontiff for the time being, and to the Roman Church, they should pay fealty and acknowledge homage without contradiction. Moreover, in proof of this our perpetual obligation and concession, we will and establish that from the proper and special revenues of our realms aforesaid, for all service and custom that we should render for ourselves, saving in all respects the penny of blessed Peter, the Roman Church receive 1000 marks sterling each year, to wit at the feast of St Michael 500 marks, and at Easter 500 marks; 700 to wit for the realm of England, and 300 for the realm of Ireland; saving to us and our heirs, our rights, liberties, and royalties. All which, as aforesaid, we willing them to be ratified and confirmed in perpetuity bind ourselves and our successors not to contravene. And if we or any of our successors shall presume to attempt this, whoever he be, unless he come to his senses after due admonition, let him forfeit right to the kingdom, and let this charter of obligation and concession on our part remain in force for ever.

The Oath of Fealty

I, John, by the grace of God king of England and lord of Ireland, from this hour forward will be faithful to God and the blessed Peter and the Roman Church, and my lord the Pope Innocent and his successors who succeed in catholic manner: I will not be party in deed, word, consent, or counsel, to their losing life or limb or being unjustly imprisoned. If I am aware of anything to their hurt I will prevent it and will have it removed if I can; or else, as soon as I can, I will signify it, or will tell such persons as I shall believe will surely tell them. Any counsel they entrust to me, whether personally or by their messengers or their letter, I will keep secret, and will consciously disclose to no one to their hurt. The patrimony of blessed Peter, and specially the realm of England and the realm of Ireland, I will aid to hold and defend against all men to my ability. So help me God and these holy gospels. Witness myself at the house of the Knights of the Temple near Dover, in the presence of the lord H. Archbishop of Dublin; the lord J. Bishop of Norwich; G. FitzPeter, Earl of Essex, our justiciar; W. Earl of Salisbury, our brother; W. Marshall, Earl of Pembroke; R. Count of Boulogne; W. Earl of Warenne; S. Earl of Winchester; W. Earl of Arundel; W. Earl of Ferrers; W. Brewer; Peter, son of Herbert; Warren, son of Gerald. The 15th day of May in the 14th year of our reign.

VIII.   JOHN'S ECCLESIASTICAL CHARTER, 1214
Stubbs, *S.C.*[9] 283

[John's concession of his kingdom to the Pope secured the relaxation of the interdict, but the enlistment of the papal authority on the side of the royal tyranny aroused the barons, who had refrained from taking advantage of John's difficulties with the Church. The following charter seems to have been designed to secure the aid of the Church against the demands of the barons; but it failed in this attempt.]

John, by the grace of God king of England, lord of Ireland, duke of Normandy and Aquitaine, earl of Anjou, to the archbishops, the bishops, earls, barons, knights, bailiffs, and to all who shall see or hear these letters, greeting. Since by the grace of God, of the uninfluenced and free will of both parties, there is full agreement concerning damages and losses in the time of the interdict, between us and our venerable fathers Stephen, archbishop of Canterbury, primate of all England, and cardinal of the Holy Roman Church, and Bishops William of London, Eustace of Ely, Giles of Hereford, Joscelin of Bath and Glastonbury, and Hugh of Lincoln—we wish not only to make satisfaction to them, as far as in God we can, but also to make sound and beneficial provision for all the Church of England for ever; and so whatsoever custom has been hitherto observed in the English Church, in our own times and those of our predecessors, and whatsoever right we have claimed for ourselves hitherto in the elections of any prelates, we have at their own petition, for the salvation of our soul and the souls of our predecessors and successors kings of England, freely of our uninfluenced and spontaneous will, with the common consent of our barons, granted and ordained, and by this our present charter have confirmed: that henceforth in all and singular the churches and monasteries, cathedral and conventual, of all our kingdom of England, the elections of all prelates whatsoever, greater or less, be free for ever, saving to ourselves and our heirs the custody of vacant churches and monasteries which belong to us. We promise also that we will neither hinder nor suffer nor procure to be hindered by our ministers that in all and singular the churches and monasteries mentioned, after the prelacies are vacant, the electors should, whenever they will, freely set a pastor over them, provided that leave to elect be first asked of us and our heirs, which we will not deny nor defer. And if by chance, which God forbid, we should deny or defer, let the electors, none the less, proceed to make canonical election; and likewise, after the election is held, let our assent be demanded, which in like manner we will not deny, unless we put forth some reasonable excuse and lawfully prove it, by reason of which we should not consent. Wherefore we will and firmly enjoin that when churches or monasteries are vacant, no one in anything proceed or presume to proceed in opposition to this our concession and ordinance. But if any do ever at any time proceed in opposition to this, let him incur the malediction of Almighty God and of us.

Witnesses: Peter, bishop of Winchester ... [12 barons]. ...

Given by the hand of Master Richard de Marisos, our Chancellor, at the New Temple in London, the 21st day of November, in the 16th year of our reign.

IX. THE CHURCH CLAUSES OF MAGNA CARTA, 1215
Stubbs, *S.C.*[9] 292, 302

[The grievances of churchmen had been redressed in 1214. The first and last clauses of Magna Carta merely confirm the liberties then granted.]

1. [We] have in the first place granted to God, and confirmed by this our present charter, for us and our heirs for ever, that the Church of England be free, and have her rights intact, and her liberties unimpaired; and so we will it to be observed, which appears from the fact that freedom of elections which is considered to be most important and more necessary for the Church of England, we have by our uninfluenced and spontaneous will, before discord had arisen between us and our barons, granted and confirmed by our charter, and have secured its confirmation by the lord Pope Innocent III, which we shall observe and also will that it be

observed in good faith by our heirs for ever. We have also granted to all
free men of our realm for us and our heirs for ever, all the liberties
mentioned below, to have and to hold for them and their heirs of us and
our heirs.

63. Wherefore we will and firmly command that the English Church
be free, and that the men in our realm have and hold all the aforesaid
liberties, rights, and grants, well and in peace, freely and quietly, fully and
wholly, to themselves and their heirs of us and our heirs in all things and
places for ever, as is aforesaid. Moreover an oath has been taken, as well
on our side as on that of the barons, that all these things aforesaid shall be
observed with good faith and without evil disposition. The aforesaid and
many others being witness. Given by our hand in the meadow which is
called Runnymede between Windsor and Staines, on the fifteenth day of
June in the seventeenth year of our reign.

X.   STATUTES OF PROVISORS AND PRAEMUNIRE
13 Richard II. stat. 2. 16 Richard II. cap. 5
Statutes of the Realm, ii. 69 and 84
[G. and H. xxxix, xl. Translation slightly altered]

[The papal right to provide to English benefices had long been a grievance, but it
was particularly resented when the papal residence at Avignon, which brought
the Pope under French influence, coincided with the Hundred Years War. In 1351
this practice was forbidden by the first Statute of Provisors, and this was supple-
mented in 1353 by the Statute of Praemunire, forbidding appeals to Rome, and
especially designed to prevent appeals to Avignon on the part of aliens who had
been 'provided'. These measures were later repeated, with additional safeguards, in
1390 and 1393 respectively. These are the measures given below.]

a. Provisors

Whereas the noble King Edward, grandfather of our present lord the
king, at his Parliament holden at Westminster on the Octave of the
Purification of our Lady, the five-and-twentieth year of his reign, caused
to be rehearsed the statute made at Carlisle[1] in the time of King Edward,
son of King Henry, touching the estate of the Holy Church of England;
the said grandfather of the present king, by the assent of the great men of
his realm, in the same Parliament, holden the said five-and-twentieth
year, to the honour of God and of Holy Church, and of all his realm, did
ordain and establish, that the free elections to archbishoprics, bishoprics,
and all other elective dignities and benefices in England, should hold

---

[1] In 1307. Directed against abuses of papal patronage and forbidding religious houses in
England to send to alien superiors money or goods.

from thenceforth in the manner as they were granted by his progenitors, and by the ancestors of other lords, the founders; and that all prelates and other people of Holy Church, which had advowsons of any benefices by the gift of the king, or of his progenitors, or of other lords and donors, should freely have their right of collation and presentation; and in addition a certain punishment was ordained in the same statute on those who accept any benefice or dignity contrary to the said statute made at Westminster the said twenty-fifth year, as aforesaid; which statute our lord the king has caused to be recited in this present Parliament at the request of his Commons in the same Parliament, the tenor whereof is as follows:

Whereas of late in the Parliament of Edward of good memory, king of England, grandfather of our present lord the king, in the twenty-fifth year of his reign, holden at Carlisle, the petition heard, put before the said grandfather and his council in the said Parliament by the commons of the said realm, containing: That whereas the Holy Church of England was established, within the realm of England, by the aforesaid grandfather and his ancestors, and by the earls, barons and other nobles of the realm and their ancestors, on the estate of bishops, who should teach the law of God to them and to their people, and should perform works of hospitality, of alms, and other works of charity, in the places where the churches were established, for the benefit of the souls of their founders, their heirs, and all Christian people; and certain properties, in fees, lands, rents and also in advowsons, whose total value is very great, were assigned by the said founders [*foundors*] to bishops and to other people of the Holy Church of the said realm to have charge of the same and especially of the possessions which were assigned to archbishops, bishops, abbots, priors, religious, and all other people of Holy Church, by the kings of the said realm, earls, barons, and other great men of his realm; the said kings, earls, barons, and other nobles, as lord and advowees, have had and ought to have the custody of such vacancies, and the right of presentation and the collation to the benefices belonging to such prelacies.

And the said kings in times past, for the safeguard of the realm, when they had need, were wont to have the greatest part of their council of such prelates and clerks so advanced; the pope of Rome, accroaching to him the overlordship of such possessions and benefices, does give and grant the same benefices to aliens, who never dwelt in England, and to cardinals, who could not dwell here, and to others as well aliens as denizens, as if he had been patron or advowee of the aid dignities and benefices, as he was not of right by the law of England; in this way, if these should be suffered, there would scarcely be any benefice within a short time in the said realm which would not be in the hands of aliens and denizens by virtue of such provisions, contrary to the good will and disposition of the founders of the same benefices; and so the elections of archbishops, bishops, and other religious would cease, and the alms, works of hospitality, and other works of charity, which should be done in the said places, would be discontinued, the said grandfather, and other lay-patrons, in the time of such vacancies, would lose their right of presentation, the said council would perish, and goods without limit would be carried out of the realm; thus making void the estate of the Holy Church of England, and annulling the will of the said grandfather, and the earls, barons, and other nobles of the said realm, and obstructing and bringing to naught the laws and rights of his realm, and doing great damage to his people, and subverting all the estate of all his said realm, against the good disposition and will of the first founders, by the assent of the earls, barons, and other nobles, and of all the said commons, at their instant request, the damage and grievances aforesaid being considered in the said full Parliament, it was provided, ordained, and established, that the said oppressions, grievances, and damages in the same realm from henceforth should not be suffered in any manner.

And now it is shown to our lord the king in this present Parliament holden at Westminster, on the Octave of the Purification of Our Lady, the five-and-twentieth year of his reign of England, and the twelfth of France, by the grievous complaint of all the commons of his realm, that the grievances and mischiefs aforesaid do daily abound, to the greater damage and destruction of all the realm of England, more than ever were before, viz. that now anew our holy father the pope, by procurement of clerks and otherwise, has reserved, and does daily reserve to his collation generally and especially, as well archbishoprics, bishoprics, abbeys, and priories, as all other dignities and other benefices of England, which are in the advowson of people of Holy Church, and gives the same as well to aliens as to denizens, and takes of all such benefices the first-fruits, and many other profits, and a great part of the treasure of the said realm is carried away and spent out of the realm, by the purchasers of such graces aforesaid; and also by such private reservations, many clerks, advanced in this realm by their true patrons, which have peaceably holden their preferments for a long time, are suddenly ejected; whereupon the said Commons have prayed our said lord the king, that since the right of the crown of England, and the law of the said realm is such, that if mischiefs and damages happen to his realm, he ought, and is bound by his oath, with the accord of his people in his Parliament to this end, to remedy this, and to enact laws for the removal of the mischiefs and damages thus arising.

Our lord the king ... with the assent of all the great men and the commons of the said realm, to the honour of God, and profit of the said Church of England, and of all his realm, has ordered and established: that the free elections of archbishops, bishops, and all other dignities and benefices elective in England, shall continue from henceforth in the manner as they were granted by the king's progenitors, and the ancestors of other lords, founders.

And that all prelates and other people of Holy Church, which have advowsons of any benefices by the king's gift, or of any of his progenitors, or of other lords and donors, to do divine service, and other charges thereof ordained, shall have their right of collation and presentation freely to the same, in the manner as they were enfeoffed by their donors. And in case reservation, collation, or provision be made by the court of Rome, to any archbishopric, bishopric, dignity, or other benefice, in disturbance of the free elections, collations, or presentations aforenamed, that, at the same time of the vacancy, as such reservations, collations, and provisions ought to take effect, our lord the king and his heirs shall have and enjoy, for the same time, the collations to the archbishoprics, bishoprics, and other dignities elective, which be of his advowson, such as his progenitors had before that free election was granted; seeing that the election was first granted by the king's progenitors upon a certain condition, namely that they should ask leave of the king to choose, and after the election should receive his royal assent, and not in other manner. Which conditions not being kept, the thing ought by reason to resort to its first nature. ...

[Similarly, in cases of provision to religious houses, or to benefices.]

Saving to them [the holders of advowsons] the right of their advowsons and their presentation, when no collation or provision by the court of Rome is made thereof, or where that the said people of Holy Church shall or will, to the same benefices, present or make collation; and that their presentees may enjoy the effect of their collations or presentation. And in the same manner every other lord, of what condition he be, shall have the right of collation or presentation to the houses of religion which are in his advowson, and other benefices of Holy Church which pertain to the same houses. And if such advowees do not present to such benefices within the half-year after such vacancy, nor the bishop of the place give the same by lapse of time within a month after half a year, that then the king shall have thereof the right of presentation and collation, as he has of others in his own advowson demesne.

And in case that the presentees of the king—or the presentees of other patrons of Holy Church, or of their advowees, or they to whom the king, or such patrons or advowees aforesaid, have given benefices pertaining to their presentments or collation—be disturbed by such provisors, so that they may not have possession of such benefices by virtue of the presentation or collation to them made, or that they which are in possession of such benefices be impeached upon their said possessions by such provisors, then the said provisors, their agents, executors, and attornies, shall be attached by their bodies, and brought in to answer; and if they be convicted, they shall abide in prison without being let to mainprize or bail, or otherwise delivered, till they have made fine and random to the king at his will, and satisfaction to the party that shall feel himself injured. And nevertheless before that they be delivered, they shall make full renunciation, and find sufficient surety that they will not attempt such things in time to come, nor sue any process by themselves, nor by others, against any man in the said court of Rome, nor in any part elsewhere, for any such imprisonments or renunciations, nor any other thing depending of them. And in case that such provisors, agents, executors, or attornies be not found, that the exigent shall run against them by due process, and that writs shall go forth to take their bodies wherever they be found, as well at the king's suit, as at the suit of the party.

And that in the meantime the king shall have the profits of such benefices so occupied by such provisors, except abbeys, priories, and other houses, which have colleges or convents, and in such houses the colleges or convents shall have the profits; saving always to our lord the king, and to all other lords, their old right.

... And if any do accept a benefice of Holy Church contrary to this statute, and the fact be duly proved, if he be beyond the sea, he shall abide exiled and banished out of the realm for ever, and his lands and tenements, goods and chattels shall be forfeited to the king; if he be within the realm, he shall be also exiled and banished, as is aforesaid, and shall incur the same forfeiture, and take his way, so that he be out of the realm within six weeks next after acceptance. And if any receive any such person banished coming from beyond the sea, or remaining within the realm after the said six weeks, having knowledge thereof, he shall be also exiled and banished, and incur such forfeiture as is aforesaid. ...

Provided nevertheless, that all they for whom the pope, or his predecessors, have provided any archbishopric, bishopric, or other dignity, or other benefices of Holy Church, of the patronage of people of Holy Church, in respect of any voidance before the said twenty-ninth day of January, and thereof were in actual possession before the same twenty-ninth day, shall have and enjoy the said archbishoprics, bishoprics, dignities, and other benefices peaceably for their lives, notwithstanding the statutes and ordinances aforesaid. And if the king send by letter, or in other manner, to the court of Rome, at the entreaty of any person, or if any other send or sue to the same court, whereby anything is done contrary to this statute, touching any archbishopric, bishopric, dignity, or other benefice of Holy Church within the said realm, if he that makes such motion or suit be a prelate of Holy Church, he shall pay to the king the value of his temporalties for one year; and if he be a temporal lord, he shall pay to the king the value of his lands and possessions not moveable for one year; and if he be another person of a more mean estate, he shall pay to the king the value of the benefice for which suit is made, and shall be imprisoned for one year. ...

b. Praemunire

Whereas the Commons of the realm in this present Parliament have showed to our redoubtable lord the king, grievously complaining, that whereas the said our lord the king, and all his liege people, ought of right, and of old time were wont, to sue in the king's court, to recover their presentation to churches, prebends, and other benefices of Holy Church, to the which they had right to be present, the cognizance of this plea pertains only to the king's court by the old right of his crown, used and approved in the time of all his progenitors kings of England; and when judgement shall be given in the same court upon such a plea, the archbishops, bishops, and other spiritual persons which have institution to such benefice within their jurisdiction, are bound to make, and have made, execution of such judgements at the king's commandment during all the time aforesaid without interruption (for a lay person cannot make such execution), and also are bound of right to make execution of many other of the king's commandments, of which right the crown of England has been peaceably seized, as well in the time of our said lord the present king, as in the time of all his progenitors to this day:

But now of late divers processes are made by the holy father the pope, and censures of excommunication upon certain bishops of England, because they have made execution of such commandments, to the open disinheritance of the said crown and to the detriment of our said lord the king, his law, and all his realm, if remedy be not provided.

And also it is said, and a common clamour is made, that the said holy father the pope has ordained and purposed to translate some prelates of the same realm, some out of the realm, and some from one bishopric to another within the same realm, without the king's assent and knowledge, and without the assent of the prelates, which are to be translated, which prelates be very profitable and necessary to our said lord the king, and to all his realm; by which translations, if they should be allowed, the statutes of the realm would be defeated and made void; and his said liege sages of his council, without his assent, and against his will, carried away and gotten out of his realm, and the substance and treasure of the realm shall be carried away, and so the realm be destitute as well of council as of substance, to the final destruction of the same realm; and so the crown of England, which has been so free at all times, that it has been in no earthly subjection, but immediately subject to God in all things touching the royalty of the same crown, and to none other, should be submitted to the pope, and the laws and statutes of the realm by him defeated and made void at his will, to the perpetual destruction of the sovereignty of our lord the king, his crown, and his royalty, and of all his realm, which God defend.

And moreover, the Commons aforesaid say, that the said things so attempted are clearly against the king's crown and his royalty, used and approved from the time of all his progenitors; wherefore they and all the liege commons of the same realm will support our said lord the king, and his said crown and his royalty, in the cases aforesaid, and in all other cases attempted against him, his crown, and his royalty in all points, to live and to die.

And moreover they pray the king, and require him by way of justice, that he would examine all the lords in the Parliament, as well spiritual as temporal, severally, and all the estates of the Parliament, how they think of the cases aforesaid, which be so openly against the king's crown, and in derogation of his royalty, and how they will stand in the same cases with our lord the king, in upholding the rights of the said crown and royalty.

Whereupon the Lords temporal so demanded, have answered every one by himself, that the cases aforesaid are clearly in derogation of the king's crown, and of his royalty, as it is well known, and has been for a long time known, and that they will support the same crown and royalty in these cases, and in all other cases which shall be attempted against the same crown and royalty in all points with all their power.

And moreover it was demanded of the Lords spiritual there being, and the proxies of others being absent, their advice and will in all these cases; which lords, that is to say, the archbishops, bishops, and other prelates—being in the said Parliament severally examined, making protestations that it is not their mind to deny nor affirm that our holy father the pope may not excommunicate bishops, nor that he may make translation of prelates after the law of Holy Church—answered and said, that if any executions of processes made in the king's court, as before were made, by any, and censures of excommunications be made against any bishops of England, or any other of the king's liege people, for that they have made execution of such commandments; and that if any executions of such translations be made of any prelates of the same realm, which prelates be very profitable and necessary to our said lord the king, and to his said realm, or that the sage people of his council, without his assent, and against his will, be removed and carried out of the realm, so that the substance and treasure of the realm may be consumed—that the same is against the king and his crown, as it is contained in the petition before named.

And likewise the same proxies, every one by himself examined upon the said matters, have answered and said in the name of and for their lords, as the said bishops have said and answered, and that the said Lords spiritual will and ought to be with the king in these cases in lawfully maintaining his crown, and in all other cases touching his crown and his royalty, as they are bound by their allegiance.

Whereupon our said lord the king, by the assent aforesaid, and at the request of his said Commons, has ordained and established, that if any purchase or pursue, or cause to be purchased or pursued, in the court of Rome, or elsewhere, any such translations, processes, and sentences of excommunication, bulls, instruments, or any other things whatsoever, which touch our lord the king, against him, his crown, and his royalty, or his realm, as is aforesaid, and they which bring [the same] within the realm, or receive them, or make thereof notification, or any other execution whatsoever within the same realm or without, that they, their attorneys, agents, maintainers, abettors, supporters, and advisers, shall be put out of the king's protection, and their lands and tenements, goods and chattels, forfeited to our lord the king; and that they be attached by their bodies, if they may be found, and brought before the king and his council, there to answer to the cases aforesaid, or that process be made against them by *Praemunire facias*,[1] in manner as it is ordained in other statutes concerning provisors, and others who sue, in any other court, in derogation of the royalty of our lord the king.

---

[1] A corruption of *praemoneri facias*, the opening words of the writ to the sheriff 'Cause A. B. to be forwarned,' *sc.* to appear to answer the charge.

XI. WYCLIFFE AND THE LOLLARDS

a. **Propositions of Wycliffe condemned at London, 1382, and at the Council of Constance, 1415**   *Fasciculi Zizaniorum*, 227–82 (Rolls Series) Mansi, xxvii. 1207 E ff.

[John Wycliffe (1324–84) was the leading scholar of the University of Oxford, where he spent most of his life—for he seems to have done very little in his parish of Lutterworth. He was a protégé of John of Gaunt, and so had political importance when his teaching gained a following through the work of the 'poor preachers' whom he sent out. The most notable points in his teaching were: the theory of 'dominion by grace'—lordship, spiritual or temporal, derived directly from God as opposed to the feudal conception of derivation through intermediaries, which was paralleled by the conception of grace derived through the Pope and the hierarchy, and which influenced much of Catholic theology; his acceptance of the Bible as the sole rule of faith, interpreted without any historical perspective; and his teaching about the sacraments, and especially the Mass. His teaching had a great influence on John Hus, the Bohemian reformer, who also was condemned at Constance. The Lollards pushed academic theories to their practical conclusions and became more a party of political revolutionaries than of Church reformers—'the Levellers of the Middle Ages' (Wakeman).]

1. [1] That the material substance of bread and the material substance of wine remain in the Sacrament of the altar.

2. That the accidents of bread do not remain without a subject (substance) in the said Sacrament.

3. That Christ is not in the Sacrament essentially and really, in his own corporeal presence.

4. That if a bishop or priest be in mortal sin he does not ordain, consecrate or baptize.

5. That it is not laid down in the Gospel that Christ ordained the Mass.

6. That God ought to obey the devil.[2]

7. That if a man be duly penitent any outward confession is superfluous and useless.

10. That it is contrary to Holy Scripture that ecclesiastics should have possessions.

14. That any deacon or priest may preach the word of God apart from the authority of the Apostolic See or a Catholic bishop.

15. That no one is civil lord, or prelate, or bishop, while he is in mortal sin.

---

[1] The propositions are numbered as at Constance. *Fasc. Ziz.* give a different order.
[2] i.e. 'Dominion by grace' cannot be put into operation in the world as it is.

16. That temporal lords can at their will take away temporal goods from the church, when those who hold them are sinful (habitually sinful, not sinning in one act only).

17. That the people can at their own will correct sinful lords.

18. That tithes are mere alms, and that parishioners can withdraw them at their will because of the misdeeds of their curates.

20. That he who gives alms to friars is by that fact excommunicate.

21. That any one who enters a private religion [i.e. religious house], either of those having property or of menidicants, is rendered more inapt and unfit for the performance of the commands of God.

22. That holy men have sinned in founding private religions.

23. That the religious who live in private religions are not of the Christian religion.

24. That friars are bound to gain their livelihood by the labour of their hands, and not by begging.

[The above are common to the proceedings at London and at Constance. Many other propositions, of which a few are given below, were condemned at Constance. They are more extreme in tone and are probably to be attributed more to the Lollards than to Wycliffe himself.]

28. That the confirmation of young men, the ordination of clerics, the consecration of places are reserved for the Pope and bishops on account of the desire for temporal gain and honour.

30. That the excommunication of the Pope or of any prelate is not to be feared, because it is the censure of antichrist.

34. That all of the order of mendicants are heretics.

35. That the Roman Church is the synagogue of Satan, and the Pope is not the next and immediate vicar of Christ and the Apostles.

42. That it is fatuous to believe in the indulgences of the Pope and the bishops.

43. That all oaths made to corroborate human contracts and civil business are unlawful.

b. The Lollard Conclusions, 1394 *Fasciculi Zizaniorum*, 360–9 (Rolls Series) [Translation G. and H. xli]

1. That when the Church of England began to go mad after temporalities, like its great step-mother the Roman Church, and churches were authorized by appropriation in divers places, faith, hope, and charity began to flee from our Church, because pride, with its doleful progeny of moral sins, claimed this under title of truth. This conclusion is general,

and proved by experience, custom, and manner or fashion, as you shall afterwards hear.

2. That our usual priesthood which began in Rome, pretended to be of power more lofty than the angels, is not the priesthood which Christ ordained for His apostles. This conclusion is proved because the Roman priesthood is bestowed with signs, rites, and pontifical blessings, of small virtue, nowhere exemplified in Holy Scripture, because the bishop's ordinal and the New Testament scarcely agree, and we cannot see that the Holy Spirit, by reason of any such signs, confers the gift, for He and all His excellent gifts cannot consist in any one with mortal sin. A corollary to this is that it is a grievous play for wise men to see bishops trifle with the Holy Spirit in the bestowal for orders, because they give the tonsure in outward appearance in the place of white hearts;[1] and this is the unrestrained introduction of antichrist into the Church to give colour to idleness.

3. That the law of continence enjoined on priests, which was first ordained to the prejudice of women, brings sodomy into all the Holy Church, but we excuse ourselves by the Bible because the decree says that we should not mention it, though suspected. Reason and experience prove this conclusion: reason, because the good living of ecclesiastics must have a natural outlet or worse; experience, because the secret proof of such men is that they find delight in women, and when thou hast proved such a man mark him well, because he is one of them. A corollary to this is that private religions and the originators or beginning of this sin would be specially worthy of being checked, but God of His power with regard to secret sin sends open vengeance in His Church.

4. That the pretended miracle of the sacrament of bread drives all men, but a few, to idolatry, because they think that the Body of Christ which is never away from heaven could by power of the priest's word be enclosed essentially in a little bread which they show the people; but God grant that they might be willing to believe what the evangelical doctor[2] says in his Trialogus (iv. 7), that the bread of the altar is habitually the Body of Christ, for we take it that in this way any faithful man and woman can by God's law perform the sacrament of that bread without any such miracle. A final corollary is that although the Body of Christ has been granted eternal joy, the service of Corpus Christi, instituted by Brother Thomas [Aquinas], is not true but is fictitious and full of false

---

[1] *Alborum cervorum* = 'white harts'!

[2] i.e. Wycliffe, who in the *Trialogus* ('Three-cornered Discussion'—between Truth, Falsehood, and Prudence) expounded his views on the Eucharist.

miracles. It is no wonder; because Brother Thomas, at that time holding with the pope, would have been willing to perform a miracle with a hen's egg; and we know well that any falsehood openly preached turns to the disgrace of Him who is always true and without any defect.

5. That exorcisms and blessings performed over wine, bread, water and oil, salt, wax, and incense, the stones of the altar, and church walls, over clothing, mitre cross, and pilgrims' staves, are the genuine performance of necromancy rather than of sacred theology. This conclusion is proved as follows, because by such exorcisms creatures are honoured as being of higher virtue than they are in their own nature, and we do not see any change in any creature which is so exorcized, save by false faith which is the principal characteristic of the Devil's art. A corollary: that if the book of exorcizing holy water, read in church, were entirely trustworthy we think truly that the holy water used in church would be the best medicine for all kinds of illnesses—sores, for instance; whereas we experience the contrary day by day.

6. That king and bishop in one person, prelate and judge in temporal causes, curate and officer in secular office, puts any kingdom beyond good rule. This conclusion is clearly proved because the temporal and spiritual are two halves of the entire Holy Church. And so he who has applied himself to one should not meddle with the other, for no one can serve two masters. It seems that hermaphrodite or ambidexter would be good names for such men of double estate. A corollary is that we, the procurators of God in this behalf, do petition before Parliament that all curates, as well superior as inferior, be fully excused and should occupy themselves with their own charge and no other.

7. That special prayers for the souls of the dead offered in our Church, preferring one before another in name, are a false foundation of alms, and for that reason all houses of alms in England have been wrongly founded. This conclusion is proved by two reasons: the one is that meritorious prayer, and of any effect, ought to be a work proceeding from deep charity, and perfect charity leaves out no one, for 'Thou shalt love thy neighbour as thyself.' And so it is clear to us that the gift of temporal good bestowed on the priesthood and houses of alms is a special incentive to private prayer which is not far from simony. For another reason is that special prayer made for men condemned is very displeasing to God. And although it be doubtful, it is probable to faithful Christian people that founders of a house of alms have for their poisonous endowment passed over for the most part to the broad road. The corollary is: effectual prayer springing from perfect love would in general embrace all whom God would have saved, and would do away with that

well-worn way or merchandise in special prayers made for the posses-
sionary mendicants and other hired priests, who are a people of great
burden to the whole realm, kept in idleness: for it has been proved in one
book, which the king had, that a hundred houses of alms would suffice
in all the realm, and from this would rather accrue possible profit to the
temporal estate.

8. That pilgrimages, prayers, and offerings made to blind crosses or
roods, and to deaf images of wood or stone, are pretty well akin to
idolatry and far from alms, and although these be forbidden and imagi-
nary, a book of error to the lay folk, still the customary image of the
Trinity is specially abominable. This conclusion God clearly proves,
bidding alms to be done to the needy man because they are the image
of God, and more like than wood or stone; for God did not say, 'let us
make wood or stone in our likeness and image,' but man; because
the supreme honour which clerks call *latria* appertains to the Godhead
only; and the lower honour which clerks call *dulia* appertains to man and
angel and to no inferior creature. A corollary is that the service of the
cross, performed twice in any year in our church, is full of idolatry, for if
that should, so might the nails and lance be so highly honoured; then
would the lips of Judas be relics indeed if any were able to possess them.
But we ask you, pilgrim, to tell us when you offer to the bones of saints
placed in a shrine in any spot, whether you relieve the saint who is in joy,
or that almshouse which is so well endowed and for which men have
been canonized, God knows how. And to speak more plainly, a faithful
Christian supposes that the wounds of that noble man, whom men call St
Thomas, were not a case of martyrdom.

9. That auricular confession which is said to be so necessary to the
salvation of a man, with its pretended power of absolution, exalts the
arrogance of priests and gives them opportunity of other secret collo-
quies which we will not speak of; for both lords and ladies attest that, for
fear of their confessors, they dare not speak the truth. And at the time of
confession there is a ready occasion or assignation, that is for 'wooing,'
and other secret understandings leading to mortal sins. They themselves
say that they are God's representatives to judge of every sin, to pardon
and cleanse whomsoever they please. They say that they have the keys of
heaven and of hell, and can excommunicate and bless, bind and loose, at
their will, so much so that for a drink, or twelve pence, they will sell the
blessing of heaven with charter and close warrant sealed with the common seal. This conclusion is so notorious that it needs not any proof. It is
a corollary that the pope of Rome, who has given himself out as treasurer
of the whole Church, having in charge that worthy jewel of Christ's

passion together with the merits of all saints in heaven, whereby he grants pretended indulgence from penalty and guilt, is a treasurer almost devoid of charity, in that he can set free all that are prisoners in hell at his will, and cause that they should never come to that place. But in this any Christian can well see there is much secret falsehood hidden away in our Church.

10. That manslaughter in war, or by pretended law of justice for a temporal cause, without spiritual revelation, is expressly contrary to the New Testament, which indeed is the law of grace and full of mercies. This conclusion is openly proved by the examples of Christ's preaching here on earth, for he specially taught a man to love his enemies, and to show them pity, and not to slay them. The reason is this, that for the most part, when men fight, after the first blow, charity is broken. And whoever dies without charity goes the straight road to hell. And beyond this we know well that no clergyman can by Scripture or lawful reason remit the punishment of death for one mortal sin and not for another; but the law of mercy, which is the New Testament, prohibits all manner of manslaughter, for in the Gospel: 'It was said unto them of old time, Thou shalt not kill.' The corollary is that it is indeed robbery of poor folk when lords get indulgences from punishment and guilt for those who aid their army to kill a Christian people in distant lands for temporal gain, just as we too have seen soldiers who run into heathendom to get them a name for the slaughter of men; much more do they deserve ill thanks from the King of Peace, for by our humility and patience was the faith multiplied, and Christ Jesus hates and threatens men who fight and kill, when He says: 'He who smites with the sword shall perish by the sword.'

11. That the vow of continence made in our Church by women who are frail and imperfect in nature, is the cause of bringing in the gravest horrible sins possible to human nature, because, although the killing of abortive children before they are baptized and the destruction of nature by drugs are vile sins, yet connexion with themselves or brute beasts of any creature not having life surpasses them in foulness to such an extent as that they should be punished with the pains of hell. The corollary is that, widows and such as take the veil and the ring, being delicately fed, we could wish that they were given in marriage, because we cannot excuse them from secret sins.

12. That the abundance of unnecessary arts practised in our realm nourishes much sin in waste, profusion, and disguise. This, experience and reason prove in some measure, because nature is sufficient for a man's necessity with few arts. The corollary is that since St Paul says: 'having food and raiment, let us be therewith content,' it seems to us that

goldsmiths and armourers and all kinds of arts not necessary for a man, according to the apostle, should be destroyed for the increase of virtue; because although these two said arts were exceedingly necessary in the old law, the New Testament abolishes them and many others.

This is our embassy, which Christ has bidden us fulfil, very necessary for this time for several reasons. And although these matters are briefly noted here they are however set forth at large in another book, and many others besides, at length in our own language, and we wish that these were accessible to all Christian people. We ask God then of His supreme goodness to reform our Church, as being entirely out of joint, to the perfectness of its first beginning.

[Foxe's translation of some contemporary verses added to the foregoing document]

The English nation doth lament of these vile men their sin,
Which Paul doth plainly dignify by idols to begin.
But Gehazites full ingrate from sinful Simon sprung,
This to defend, though priests in name, make bulwarks great and
    strong.
Ye princes, therefore, whom to rule the people God hath placed
    With justice' sword, why see ye not this evil great defaced?

c. ***De Haeretico Comburendo*, 1401**   2 Henry IV. cap. 15: *Statutes of the Realm*, ii. 125 [Translation from G. and H. xlii]

[This Act was the first step taken by Parliament against the Lollards though Letters Patent had been issued against them, and its marks the beginning of official persecution of heresy in England. The Inquisition never functioned in England, except for the trial of the Templars, and the suppression of heresy was left to the bishops. The Act was expanded under Henry V, repealed under Henry VIII, revived under Mary, and again repealed under Elizabeth.]

Whereas it is showed to our sovereign lord the king on behalf of the prelates and clergy of his realm of England in this present Parliament, that although the Catholic faith, founded upon Christ, and by His apostles and the Holy Church sufficiently determined, declared, and approved, has been hitherto by good and holy and most noble progenitors of our sovereign lord the king in the said realm, amongst all the realms of the world, most devoutly observed, and the English Church by his said most noble progenitors and ancestors, to the honour of God and of the whole realm aforesaid, laudably endowed, and in her rights and liberties sustained, without that the same faith or the said Church was hurt or grievously oppressed, or else disturbed by any perverse doctrine or wicked, heretical, or erroneous opinions:

Yet nevertheless divers false and perverse people of a certain new sect, damnably thinking of the faith of the sacraments of the Church and the authority of the same, and, against the law of God and of the Church, usurping the office of preaching, do perversely and maliciously, in divers places within the said realm, under the colour of dissembled holiness, preach and teach in these days, openly and privily, divers new doctrines and wicked, heretical, and erroneous opinions, contrary to the same faith and blessed determinations of the Holy Church.

And of such sect and wicked doctrine and opinions, they make unlawful conventicles and confederacies, they hold and exercise schools, they make and write books, they do wickedly instruct and inform people, and, as much as they may, excite and stir them to sedition and insurrection, and make great strife and division among the people, and do daily perpetrate and commit other enormities horrible to be heard, in subversion of the said Catholic faith and doctrine of the Holy Church, in diminution of God's honour, and also in destruction of the estate, rights, and liberties of the said English Church; by which sect and wicked and false preachings, doctrines, and opinions of the said false and perverse people, not only the greatest peril of souls, but also many more other hurts, slanders, and perils, which God forbid, might come to this realm, unless it be the more plentifully and speedily helped by the king's majesty in this behalf, namely:

Whereas the diocesans of the said realm cannot by their jurisdiction spiritual, without aid of the said royal majesty, sufficiently correct the said false and perverse people, nor refrain their malice, because the said false and perverse people go from diocese to diocese, and will not appear before the said diocesans, but the same diocesans and their jurisdiction spiritual, and the keys of the church, with the censures of the same, do utterly disregard and despise, and so they continue and exercise their wicked preachings and doctrines, from day to day, to the utter destruction of all order and rule of right and reason.

Upon which novelties and excesses above rehearsed, the prelates and clergy aforesaid, and also the Commons of the said realm being in the same Parliament, have prayed our sovereign lord the King, that his royal highness would vouchsafe in the said Parliament to provide a convenient remedy: the same our sovereign lord the king—graciously considering the premises, and also the laudable steps of his said most noble progenitors and ancestors, for the conservation of the said Catholic faith, and sustentation of God's honour, and also the safeguard of the estate, rights, and liberties of the said English Church, to the praise of God, and merit of our said sovereign lord the king, and prosperity and honour of all his said realm, and for the eschewing of such dissensions, divisions, hurts, slanders, and perils, in time to come, and that this wicked sect, preachings, doctrines, and opinions should from henceforth cease and be utterly destroyed—by the assent of the estates and other discreet men of the realm, being in the said Parliament, has granted, stablished, and ordained from henceforth firmly to be observed: That none within the said realm, or any other dominions, subject to his royal majesty, presume to preach, openly or privily, without the licence of the diocesan of the same place first required and obtained—curates in their own churches, and persons hitherto privileged, and others of the canon law granted, only except. And that none, from henceforth, preach, hold, teach, or instruct anything, openly or privily, or make or write any book contrary to the Catholic faith or determination of the Holy Church, nor that any of such sect and wicked doctrines and opinions shall make any conventicles, or in any wise hold or exercise schools. And also that none from henceforth in any wise favour such preacher, or maker of any such and the like conventicles, or holding or exercising schools, or making or writing such books, or so teaching, informing, or exciting the people, nor them, nor any of them, maintain or in any wise sustain.

And that all and singular having such books or any writings of such wicked doctrine and opinions, shall really, with effect, deliver, or cause to be delivered, all such books and writings to the diocesan of the same place within forty days from the time of the proclamation of this ordinance and statute. And if any person or persons, of whatsoever kind, estate, or condition he or they be, from henceforth do or attempt against the royal ordinance and statute aforesaid, in the premises or in any of them, or such books, in form aforesaid, do not deliver, then the diocesan of the same place, in his diocese, such person or persons, in this behalf defamed or evidently suspected, and every of them, may, by the authority of the said ordinance and statute, cause to be arrested, and under safe custody in his prisons to be detained, till he or they, of the articles laid to him or them in this behalf, canonically purge him or themselves, or else such wicked sect, preachings, doctrines, and heretical and erroneous opinions abjure, according as the laws of the Church do require; so that the said diocesan, by himself or his commissaries, do openly and judicially proceed against such persons so arrested and remaining under his safe custody to all effect of the law, and determine that same business, according to the canonical decrees, within three months after the said arrest, any lawful impediment ceasing.

And if any person, in any case above expressed, be, before the diocesan of the place, or his commissaries, canonically convicted, then the same diocesan may cause to be kept in his prison the said person so convicted according to the manner of his default, and after the quality of the offence, according and as long as to his discretion shall seem expedient, and moreover put the same person to pay a pecuniary fine to the lord the king, except in cases where he, according to the canonical decree, ought to be left to the secular court, according as the same fine shall seem competent to the diocesan, for the manner and quality of the offence, in which case the same diocesan shall be bound to certify the king of the same fine in his exchequer by his letters patent sealed with his seal to the effect that such fine, by the king's authority, may be required and levied to his use of the goods of the same person so convicted.

And if any person within the said realm and dominions, upon the said wicked preachings, doctrines, opinions, schools, and heretical and erroneous informations, or any of them, be, before the diocesan of the same place, or his commissaries, convicted by sentence, and the same wicked sect, preachings, doctrines and opinions, schools and informations, do refuse duly to abjure, or by the diocesan of the same place, or his commissaries, after abjuration made by the same person, be pronounced relapsed, so that according to the holy canons he ought to be left to the secular court, whereupon credence shall be given to the diocesan of the same place, or to his commissaries in this behalf—then the sheriff of the county of the same place, and the mayor and sheriff or sheriffs, or mayor and bailiffs of the city, town, or borough of the same county nearest to the same diocesan or the said commissaries, shall be personally present in preferring of such sentences, when they, by the same diocesan or his commissaries, shall be required: and they shall receive the same persons and every of them, after such sentence promulgated, and them, before the people, in a high place [*eminenti*] cause to be burnt, that such punishment may strike fear to the minds of others, whereby no such wicked doctrine and heretical and erroneous opinions, nor their authors and favourers in the said realm and dominions, against the Catholic faith, Christian law, and determination of the Holy Church be sustained (which God forbid), or in any wise suffered. In which all and singular the premises concerning the said ordinance and statute, the sheriffs, mayors, and bailiffs of the said counties, cities, boroughs, and towns shall be attending, aiding, and supporting, to the said diocesan and his commissaries.

SECTION VIII

The Reformation on the Continent

I. THE LUTHERAN REFORMATION

a. The Bull Unigenitus of Clement VI, 1343 *Corpus Iuris Canonici* (Friedberg), ii. 1304. Kidd, *Documents of the Continental Reformation*, 1

[The practical abuse which aroused Luther was the sale of indulgences by the Dominican John Tetzel to finance the building of S. Peter's at Rome. The theory on which such indulgences were based is authoritatively defined in this bull, which set the seal on doctrines which had been developed by the Schoolmen.]

The Only-begotten Son of God deigned to come down from his Father's bosom into the womb of his mother, in whom and from whom by an ineffable union he joined the substance of our mortal nature to his godhead, in unity of Person; uniting what was permanent with what was transitory, which he assumed in order that he might be able to redeem fallen man and for him make satisfaction to God the Father. For when the fullness of time came, God sent his own Son, made under the law, born of a woman, that he might redeem them that were under the law, that they might receive the adoption of sons. For he himself having been made for us by God, wisdom, righteousness, sanctification, and redemption [1 Cor. i. 30], not through the blood of goats or calves, but through his own blood entered once for all into the holy place, having obtained eternal redemption [Heb. ix. 12]. For not with corruptible things, with silver and gold, did he redeem us, but with the precious blood of himself, a lamb without spot or blemish (1 Pet. i. 18 f.], the precious blood which he is known to have shed as an innocent victim on the altar of the cross, not a mere drop of blood (although, because of its union with the Word, that would have sufficed for the redemption of the whole human race), but as it were a copious flood, so that from the sole of the foot to the crown of the head there was found no soundness in him [Is. i. 6]. Wherefore therefrom (so that the pitifulness of such an effusion be not rendered idle, useless or superfluous) how great a treasure did the holy Father acquire for the Church Militant, wishing to enrich his sons with treasure, that so men might have an infinite treasure, and those who avail themselves thereof are made partakers of God's friendship. Now this treasure is not hidden in a napkin nor buried in a field, but he entrusted it to be healthfully dispensed—through blessed Peter, bearer of heaven's keys, and his successors as vicars on earth—to the faithful, for fitting and reasonable causes, now for total, now for partial remission of punishment due for temporal sins [or of temporal punishment for sins], as well generally as specially (as they should understand it to be expedient with God), and to be applied in mercy to them that are truly penitent and have confessed. And to this heap of treasure the merits of the blessed Mother of God and of all the elect, from the first just man to the last, are known to have supplied their increment: and no diminution or washing away of this treasure is in any wise to be feared, as well because of the infinite merits of Christ (as aforesaid) as because the more men are drawn to righteousness as a result of its application by so much the more does the heap of merits increase. ...

b. The Machinery of Indulgences
Instructions issued by Albert of Mainz   Gerdesii, *Introductio in Historiam Evangelii saeculo XVI renovati*, 1. Suppl. 90 ff. Extracts in Kidd, 6

... The first grace is the complete remission of all sins; and nothing greater than this can be named, since sinful man, deprived of the grace of God, obtains complete remission by these means and once more enjoys God's grace; moreover, through this remission of sins the punishment which one is obliged to undergo in purgatory on account of the affront to the Divine Majesty is all remitted, and the pains of purgatory completely blotted out. And although nothing is precious enough to be given in exchange for such a grace—since it is a free gift of God and grace is beyond price—yet in order that Christian believers may be the more easily induced to procure the same, we establish the following rules, to wit:

In the first place, every one who is contrite in heart, and has made oral confession, shall visit at least the seven churches indicated for this purpose, to wit, those in which the papal arms are displayed, and in each church shall say five Paternosters and five Ave Marias in honour of the five wounds of our Lord Jesus Christ, whereby our salvation is won, or one Miserere, which psalm is particularly well adapted for obtaining forgiveness of sins. ...

The method of contributing to the chest, for the construction of the said fabric of the Chief of the Apostles.

Firstly the penitentiaries and confessors, after they have explained to those making confession the greatness of this kind of plenary remission and of these privileges, shall ask them for how large a contribution, in money or in other temporal goods, they would wish, in good conscience, to be spared this method of full remission and privileges; and this is to be done that they may be more easily induced to contribute. And because

the conditions of men, and their occupations, are so various and manifold, and we cannot consider and assess them individually, we have
therefore decided that the rates can be determined thus, according to
recognized classifications. ...

[Then follows a graded schedule of rates: kings and their families, bishops, etc.,
25 Rhenish gold guilders; abbots, counts, barons, etc., 10; lesser nobles and
ecclesiastics and others with incomes of 500, 6 guilders; citizens with their
own income, 1 guilder; those with less, 1/2. Those with nothing shall supply
their contribution with prayer and fasting, 'for the kingdom of heaven should
be open to the poor as much as the rich.]

The second principal grace is a 'confessional' [confessional letter] replete
with the greatest, most important and hitherto unheard of privileges. ...

Firstly, the privilege of choosing a suitable confessor, even a regular of
the mendicant orders. ...

[The other privileges include the power given to this confessor to
absolve in cases normally 'reserved' for the Apostolic See.]

The third important grace is the participation in all the benefits of the
Church universal; which consists in this, that contributors toward the
said building, together with their deceased parents, who have departed
this world in a state of grace, shall now and for eternity be partakers in all
petitions, intercessions, alms, fastings, prayers, in each and every pilgrimage, even those to the Holy Land; furthermore, in the stations at
Rome, in masses, canonical hours, mortifications, and all other spiritual
benefits which have been, or shall be, brought forth by the universal,
most holy Church militant or by and of its members. Believers who
purchase confessional letters may also become participants in all these
things. Preachers and confessors must insist with great perseverance
upon these advantages, and persuade believers not to neglect to acquire
these benefits along with their confessional letter.

We also declare that in order to obtain these two most important
graces, it is not necessary to make confession, or to visit the churches and
altars, but merely to procure the confessional letter. ...

The fourth important grace is for those souls which are in purgatory,
and is the complete remission of all sins, which remission the pope
brings to pass through this intercession, to the advantage of said souls,
in this wise: that the same contribution shall be placed in the chest by a
living person as one would make for himself. It is our wish, however, that
our subcommissioners should modify the regulations regarding contributions of this kind which are given for the dead, and that they should

use their judgement in all other cases where, in their opinion, modifications are desirable.

It is, furthermore, not necessary that the persons who place their contributions in the chest for the dead should be contrite in heart and have orally confessed, since this grace is based simply on the state of grace in which the dead departed, and on the contribution of the living, as is evident from the text of the bull. Moreover preachers shall exert themselves to make this grace more widely known, since through the same, help will surely come to departed souls, and the construction of the church of St. Peter will be abundantly promoted at the same time. ...

c. **The Ninety-Five Theses, 1517** Loescher, *Reformationsacta*, i. 438 ff. Kidd, 11

[The theses were posted on the door of the Castle Church in Wittenberg on 31 October 1517. This was the usual procedure for giving notice of such disputations, which were a regular feature of University life, and there was nothing dramatic in the action. Luther was confident that he would have papal support when he had exposed the evils of the traffic in indulgences.]

A disputation of Master Martin Luther, Theologian, for the elucidation of the virtue of Indulgences.

From a zealous desire to bring to light the truth, the following theses will be maintained at Wittenberg, under the presidency of the Rvd. Fr. Martin Luther, Master of Arts, Master of Sacred Theology and official Reader therein. He therefore asks that all who are unable to be present and dispute with him verbally will do so in writing. In the name of our Lord Jesus Christ. Amen.

1. Our Lord and Master Jesus Christ, in saying 'Repent ye, etc.,' meant the whole life of the faithful to be an act of repentance.

2. This saying cannot be understood of the sacrament of penance (i.e. of confession and absolution) which is administered by the priesthood.

3. Yet he does not mean interior repentance only; nay, interior repentance is void if it does not externally produce different kinds of mortifications of the flesh.

4. And so penance remains while self-hate remains (i.e. true interior penitence); namely right up to entrance into the kingdom of heaven.

5. The pope has neither the wish nor the power to remit any penalties save those which he has imposed at his own will or according to the will of the canons.

6. The pope has no power to remit guilt, save by declaring and confirming that it has been remitted by God; or, to be sure, by remitting

the cases reserved to himself. If he neglected to observe these limitations the guilt would remain.

7. God does not remit the guilt of any without subjecting him to be humbled in all respects before the priest, God's vicar.

8. The canons of penance are imposed only on the living, and nothing ought to be imposed on the dying in accordance with them.

9. Hence the Holy Spirit does well for us through the pope, by always making exception in his decrees, in the case of the article of death and of necessity.

10. Those priests who, in the case of dying, reserve canonical penances for purgatory, act ignorantly and unrightly.

11. That tares concerning the changing of canonical penance into penance in purgatory seem surely to have been sown when the bishops were asleep.

12. Canonical penances were of old imposed not after absolution but before, as evidence of true contrition.

13. The dying pay all their dues by their death and are already dead to the laws of the canons, having relaxation from their jurisdiction.

14. Any deficiency in spiritual health or in charity on the part of a dying man must needs bring with it fear, and the greater the deficiency the greater the fear.

15. This fear and dread is enough of itself (to pass over all else) to effect the penance of purgatory, since it is but little removed from the dread of despair.

16. In fact, the difference between Hell, Purgatory, and Heaven seems to be the same as that between despair, almost despair and confidence.

17. It seems certain that for souls in purgatory charity is increased in proportion as dread is diminished.

18. It does not seem to be proved, either by any arguments or from Scripture, that such souls are debarred from earning merit or from increasing in charity.

19. Nor does this seem to be proved; that they are sure and confident of their own blessedness; or, at least that all are so, though we may be quite sure of it.

20. The pope by his plenary remission of all penalties does not understand the remission of all penalties absolutely, but only of those imposed by himself.

21. Therefore those preachers of indulgences are in error who allege that through the indulgences of the pope a man is freed from every penalty.

22. For he remits to souls in purgatory no penalty which they had been bound, according to the canons, to pay in this life.

23. If any complete remission of penalties can be given to any one it is sure that it can be given only to the most perfect; that is, to very few:

24. And therefore it follows that the greater part of the people is deceived by this indiscriminate and liberal promising of freedom from penalty.

25. The same power over purgatory which the pope has in general, is possessed by every bishop and curate in his particular diocese and parish.

26. The pope does well in giving remission to souls, not by the power of the keys (he has no such power) but through intercession.

27. Those who assert that a soul straightway flies out (of purgatory) as a coin tinkles in the collection-box, are preaching an invention of man (*hominem praedicant*).

28. It is sure that when a coin tinkles greed and avarice are increased; but the intercession (*suffragium*) of the church is in the will of God alone.

29. Who knows whether all souls in purgatory wish to be redeemed? (Remember the story told of S. Severinus and S. Paschal.)

30. No one is sure of the truth of his contrition, much less about the consequence of plenary remission.

31. A man who truly buys his indulgences is as rare as a true penitent, that is, very rare.

32. Those who think themselves sure of salvation through their letters of pardon will be damned for ever along with their teachers.

33. We must especially beware of those who say that those pardons of the pope are that inestimable gift of God by which man is reconciled to God.

34. For these gifts of pardon apply only to the penances of sacramental satisfaction which have been established by man.

35. Those who teach that contrition is not needed to procure redemption or indulgence are preaching doctrines inconsistent with Christianity.

36. Every Christian who is truly contrite has plenary remission both of penance and of guilt as his due, even without a letter of pardon.

37. Any true Christian, living or dead, partakes of all the benefits of Christ and the Church, which is the gift of God, even without letters of pardon.

38. Still the pope's distribution and pardon is not to be despised, since it is, as I have said, a declaration of divine remission.

39. It is very difficult, even for the most learned theologians, to emphasize, in their public preaching, the bounty of indulgences and, at the same time, the need for true contrition.

40. True contrition asks for penance and accepts it with love; but the bounty of indulgences relaxes the penalty and induces hatred of it. Such at least is its tendency.

41. Apostolic pardons are to be preached with caution lest the people should suppose that they are more important than other works of charity.

42. Christians must be taught that it is not the intention of the pope that the buying of pardons is to be regarded as comparable with works of mercy.

43. Christians are to be taught that to give to the poor or to lend to the needy is a better work than the purchase of pardons.

44. And that because through a work of charity charity is increased and man advances in goodness; whereas through pardons there is no advance in goodness but merely an increased freedom from penalty.

45. Christians are to be taught that a man who sees a brother in need and passes him by to give his money for the purchase of pardon wins for himself not the indulgences of the pope but the indignation of God.

46. Christians are to be taught that unless they have an abundant superfluity of means they are bound to keep back what is needful for their own households and in no wise to squander their substance on the purchase of pardons.

47. Christians are to be taught that the purchase of pardons is a matter of free choice, not of commandment.

48. Christians are to be taught that in dispensing pardons the pope has more desire (as he has more need) for devout prayer on his behalf than of ready money.

49. Christians are to be taught that the pope's pardons are useful if they do not put their trust in them, but most harmful if through them they lose the fear of God.

50. Christians must be taught that if the pope knew the exaction of the preachers of indulgences he would rather have S. Peter's basilica reduced to ashes than built with the skin, flesh and bones of his sheep.

51. Christians are to be taught that the pope (as in his duty) would desire to give of his own substance to those poor men from many of whom certain sellers of pardons are extracting money; that to this end he would even, if need be, sell the basilica of Saint Peter.

52. Confidence in salvation through letters of indulgence is vain; and that even if the commissary, nay, even if the pope himself, should pledge his soul as a guarantee.

53. They are the enemies of Christ and of the people who, on account of the preaching of indulgences, bid the word of God be silent in other churches.

54. A wrong is done to the word of God when in the same sermon an equal or a longer time is devoted to indulgences than to God's word.

55. This must needs be the intention of the pope; that if the granting of pardons, which is an affair of little importance, is celebrated with a single bell, with single processions and ceremonies, then the Gospel, which is the most important thing, should be preached with the accompaniment of a hundred bells, a hundred processions, a hundred ceremonies.

56. The treasures of the church, whence the pope gives indulgences, are neither sufficiently designated nor known among the people of Christ.

57. It is at least clear that they are not temporal treasures, for they are not scattered abroad but only collected by these numerous sellers of indulgences.

58. Nor are they the merits of Christ and the saints, for these, without the pope's aid, work the grace of the inner man and the crucifixion, death and descent to hell of the outer man.

59. Saint Lawrence said that the poor were the treasures of the Church, but in speaking thus he was using the language of his own time.

60. Without rashness we say that the keys of the Church, given by the merit of Christ, are that treasure.

61. For it is clear that for the remission of penalties and the absolution of (special) cases the power of the pope alone suffices.

62. The true measure of the Church is the sacrosanct Gospel of the glory and grace of God.

63. But this is deservedly most hated, since it makes the first last.

64. Whereas the treasure of indulgences is deservedly most popular, since it makes the last first.

65. Thus the Gospel treasures are nets, with which of old they fished for men of riches.

66. The treasures of indulgences are nets, with which they now fish for the riches of men.

67. Indulgences, according to the declarations of those who preach them, are the greatest graces; but 'greatest' is to be understood to refer to them as producers of revenue.

68. They are in fact of little account as compared with the grace of God and the piety of the cross.

69. Bishops and curates are bound to admit the commissaries of the apostolic pardons with all reverence.

70. But still more are they bound to apply their eyes and ears to the task of making sure that they do not preach the figments of their own imagination instead of the pope's commission.

71. If any one speaks against the truth of the apostolic pardons, let him be anathema and accursed.

72. But blessed be he that strives against the wanton and disorderly preaching of the sellers of pardons.

73. As the pope justly inveighs against those who by any device contrive the detriment of the business of pardons.

74. So much the more he intends to inveigh against those who use the pretext of pardons to contrive the detriment of holy charity and truth.

75. To hold that papal pardons are of such power that they could absolve even a man who (to assume the impossible) had violated the mother of God is to rave like a lunatic.

76. We say, on the contrary, that papal pardons cannot take away the least of venial sins, as regards guilt.

77. To say that not even if Saint Peter were pope could he give greater graces, is a blasphemy against Saint Peter and the pope.

78. We say, as against this, that any pope, even Saint Peter, has greater graces than these, to wit, the Gospel, virtues, graces of administrations [or of healings], etc. as in 1 Cor. xii.

79. It is blasphemy to say that the cross adorned with the papal arms is as effectual as the cross of Christ.

80. Bishops, curates and theologians who allow such teaching to be preached to the people will have to render an account.

81. This wanton preaching of pardons makes it hard even for learned men to defend the honour of the pope against calumny, or at least against the shrewd questions of the laity.

82. They ask: Why does not the pope empty purgatory on account of most holy charity and the great need of souls, the most righteous of causes, seeing that he redeems an infinite number of souls on account of sordid money, given for the erection of a basilica, which is a most trivial cause?

83. Why do requiems and anniversaries of the departed continue, and why does he not return the benefactions offered on their behalf, or suffer them to be taken back, since it is now wrong to pray for the redeemed?

84. What is this piety of God and the pope, in allowing the impious and hostile to secure, on payment of money, a pious soul, in friendship with God, while they do not redeem of free charity a soul that is of itself pious and beloved, on account of its need?

85. The penitential canons have long been repealed and are dead in effect and by disuse. Why then are dispensations from them still conceded by indulgences, for payment, as if they were still in full force?

86. The pope's riches at this day far exceed the wealth of the richest millionaires (*cuius opes sunt opulentissimis Crassis crassiores*), cannot he therefore build one single basilica of S. Peter out of his own money, rather than out of the money of the faithful poor?

87. What does the pope remit or dispense to those who through perfect contrition have the right to plenary remission and dispensation?

88. What greater good would be gained by the Church if the pope were to do a hundred times a day what he does once a day; i.e. distribute these remissions and dispensations to any of the faithful?

89. If the pope by means of his pardons now seeks the salvation of souls rather than payment, why does he suspend letters and pardons formerly granted, since they are equally efficacious?

90. To suppress these careful arguments of the laity merely by papal authority, instead of clearing them up by a reasoned reply, is to expose the Church and the pope to the ridicule of the enemy and to render Christians unhappy.

91. Now if pardons were preached according to the spirit and mind of the pope all these questions would easily be disposed of; nay, they would not arise.

92. And so let all those prophets depart who say to Christ's people 'Peace, peace' and there is no peace.

93. And farewell to all those prophets who say to Christ's people 'the cross, the cross' and there is no cross.

94. Christians are to be exhorted to endeavour to follow Christ, their head, through pains, deaths, and hells.

95. And so let them trust to enter heaven rather through many tribulations than through the false confidence of peace.

d. The Leipzig Disputation, 1519   Luther, *Opera Latina*, iii. 476–7. From Eck's account of the debate

[In his interview with the legate Cajetan Luther refused to retract, and in a letter to Leo X appealed 'from pope ill-informed and his pretended commission . . . to our holy lord Leo X, by divine providence, pope, to be better informed'. Then he appealed to 'a future General Council'. The mediation of Charles von Miltiz was more successful and Luther wrote his submission to the Pope. But von Miltiz had conceded too much, and Luther's admissions in the debate at Leipzig between Eck, Professor of Theology at Ingoldstadt, and Carlstadt, Professor at Wittenberg, a follower of Luther, showed how far Luther was prepared to depart from the old opinions. The debate is still carried on in the academic spirit in which it had started with the Wittenberg theses; but Luther admitted the fallibility of a General Council and showed his willingness to question the decisions of the Pope. The Reformation had begun.]

Luther denies that Peter was the chief of the apostles; he declares that ecclesiastical obedience is not based on divine right, but that it was introduced by the ordinance of men or of the emperor. He denies that the Church was built upon Peter: 'Upon this rock,' etc. And though I quoted to him Augustine, Jerome, Ambrose, Gregory, Cyprian, Chrysostom, Leo and Bernard, with Theophilus, he contradicted them all without a blush; and said that he would stand alone against a thousand, though supported by no other, because Christ only is the foundation of the Church, for other foundation can no man lay. I demolished that by quoting Revelation xii, about the twelve foundations, whereupon he defended the Greeks and schismatics, saying that even if they are not under obedience to the pope, still they are saved.

Concerning the tenets of the Bohemians, he said that some of their teachings condemned in the council of Constance are most Christian and evangelical; by which rash error he frightened away many who before were his supporters.

Among other things, when I pressed upon him, 'If the power of the pope is only of human right and by the consent of believers, whence comes your monk's costume that you wear? Whence have you the licence to preach and to hear the confessions of your parishioners?' etc., he replied that he wished there were no order of mendicants, and said many other scandalous and absurd things: that a council, because it consists of men, can err; that it is not proved from sacred Scripture that there is a purgatory, etc.,—all this you will see by reading our disputation, since it was written down by most trustworthy reporters. ...

e. Two Treatises of 1520

1. *The Appeal to the German Nobility* *Luther's Werke* (Weimar), xi. 405–15. [Translation based on Wace and Buchheim, *Luther's Primary Works*. Extracts in Kidd, 35.]

[Charles V had been elected Emperor in 1519. He was of German blood and reputed to be favourable to reform. In this, his great political effort, Luther appealed in German to the national feeling of Germany.]

Dr Martin Luther, to his Most Serene and Mighty Imperial Majesty, and to the Christian Nobility of the German Nation:

The grace and strength of God be with you, Most Serene Majesty! And you, most gracious and well-beloved lords!

It is not out of mere arrogance and perversity that I, an individual, poor and insignificant, have taken it upon me to address your lordships. The distress and misery which oppress all ranks of Christendom, especially in Germany, have moved not me alone, but everybody, to cry aloud for help; this it is that now compels me to cry out and call upon God to send down his Spirit upon some one who shall reach out a hand to this wretched people. Councils have often put about some remedy, which has always been promptly frustrated by the cunning of certain men, so that the evils have only grown worse; which malice and wickedness I now intend, God helping me, to expose, so that, being known, they may cease to effect such scandal and injury. God has given us a young[1] and noble sovereign for our leader, thereby stirring up fresh hope in our hearts; our duty is to do our best to help him and to avail ourselves to the full of this opportunity and his gracious favour.

The Romanists have, with great adroitness, drawn three walls round themselves, with which they have hitherto protected themselves, so that no one could reform them, whereby all Christendom has suffered terribly.

First, if pressed by the temporal power, they have affirmed and maintained that the temporal power has no jurisdiction over them, but, on the contrary, that the spiritual power is above the temporal.

Secondly, if it were proposed to admonish them with the Scriptures, they objected that no one may interpret the Scriptures but the Pope.

Thirdly, if they are threatened with a council, they invented the notion that no one may call a council but the Pope.

Thus they have privily stolen from us our three sticks, so that they may not be beaten. And they have dug themselves in securely behind their three walls, so that they can carry on all the knavish tricks which we now observe. ...

Now may God help us, and give us one of those trumpets that overthrew the walls of Jericho, so that we may blow down these walls of straw and paper, and that we may have a chance to use Christian rods for the chastisement of sin, and expose the craft and deceit of the devil; thus we may amend ourselves by punishment and again obtain God's favour.

Let us, in the first place, attack the first wall.

---

[1] Charles V was 19 at this time.

There has been a fiction by which the Pope, bishops, priests, and monks are called the 'spiritual estate'; princes, lords, artisans, and peasants are the 'temporal estate.' This is an artful lie and hypocritical invention, but let no one be made afraid by it, and that for this reason: that all Christians are truly of the spiritual estate, and there is no difference among them, save of office. As St Paul says (1 Cor. xii), we are all one body, though each member does its own work so as to serve the others. This is because we have one baptism, one Gospel, one faith, and are all Christians alike; for baptism, Gospel, and faith, these alone make spiritual and Christian people.

As for the unction by a pope or a bishop, tonsure, ordination, consecration, and clothes differing from those of laymen—all this may make a hypocrite or an anointed puppet, but never a Christian or a spiritual man. Thus we are all consecrated as priests by baptism, as St Peter says: 'Ye are a royal priesthood, a holy nation' (1 Pet. ii. 9); and in the Book of Revelation: 'and hast made us unto God (by Thy blood) kings and priests' (Rev. v. 10). For, if we had not a higher consecration in us than pope or bishop can give, no priest could ever be made by the consecration of pope or bishop, nor could he say the mass or preach or absolve. Therefore the bishop's consecration is just as if in the name of the whole congregation he took one person out of the community, each member of which has equal power, and commanded him to exercise this power for the rest; just as if ten brothers, co-heirs as king's sons, were to choose one from among them to rule over their inheritance, they would all of them still remain kings and have equal power, although one is appointed to govern.

And to put the matter more plainly, if a little company of pious Christian laymen were taken prisoners and carried away to a desert, and had not among them a priest consecrated by a bishop, and were there to agree to elect one of them ... and were to order him to baptize, to celebrate the mass, to absolve and to preach, this man would as truly be a priest, as if all the bishops and all the popes had consecrated him. That is why, in cases of necessity, every man can baptize and absolve, which would not be possible if we were not all priests. This great grace and virtue of baptism and of the Christian estate they have annulled and made us forget by their ecclesiastical law. ...

Since then the 'temporal power' is as much baptized as we, and has the same faith and Gospel, we must allow it to be priest and bishop, and account its office an office that is proper and useful to the Christian community. For whatever has undergone baptism may boast that it has been consecrated priest, bishop, and pope, although it does not beseem every one to exercise these offices. For, since we are all priests alike, no man may put himself forward, or take upon himself without our consent and election, to do that which we have all alike power to do. For if a thing is common to all, no man may take it to himself without the wish and command of the community. And if it should happen that a man were appointed to one of these offices and deposed for abuses, he would be just what he was before. Therefore a priest should be nothing in Christendom but a functionary; as long as he holds his office, he has precedence; if he is deprived of it, he is a peasant or a citizen like the rest. Therefore a priest is verily no longer a priest after deposition. But now they have invented *characteres indelibiles*, and pretend that a priest after deprivation still differs from a mere layman. They even imagine that a priest can never be anything but a priest—that is, that he can never become a layman. All this is nothing but mere talk and a figment of human invention.

It follows, then, that between laymen and priests, princes and bishops, or, as they call it, between 'spiritual' and 'temporal' persons, the only real difference is one of office and function, and not of estate. ...

But what kind of Christian doctrine is this, that the 'temporal power' is not above the 'spiritual,' and therefore cannot punish it! As if the hand should not help the eye, however much the eye be suffering. ... Nay, the nobler the member the more bound the others are to help it. ...

Therefore I say, Forasmuch as the temporal power has been ordained by God for the punishment of the bad and the protection of the good, we must let it do its duty throughout the whole Christian body, without respect of persons, whether it strike popes, bishops, priests, monks, nuns, or whoever it may be. ...

Whatever the ecclesiastical law has said in opposition to this is merely the invention of Romanist arrogance. ...

Now, I imagine the first paper wall is overthrown, inasmuch as the 'temporal' power has become a member of the Christian body; although its work relates to the body, yet does it belong to the 'spiritual estate.' ...

It must indeed have been the archfiend himself who said, as we read in the canon law, 'Were the pope so perniciously wicked as to be dragging hosts of souls to the devil, yet he could not be deposed.'[1] This is the accursed, devilish foundation on which they build at Rome, and think

---

[1] If the pope be found to neglect his own salvation and that of his brethren ... and if, as hell's chief slave, he should drag with him innumerable multitudes to suffer manifold and everlasting torment; still no man may presume to reprove him, for he is appointed judge over all and is judged by none—unless perchance he is found to err from the way of faith' (Gratian, *Decretum*, I. xl. 6; *Si papa*, quoted by Robinson). This passage was ascribed to S. Boniface.

the whole world may go to the devil rather than that they should be opposed in their knavery. If a man were to escape punishment simply because he was above his fellows, then no Christian might punish another, since Christ has commanded that each of us esteem himself the lowest and humblest of all (Matt. xviii. 4; Luke ix. 48).

The second wall is even more tottering and weak: namely their claim to be considered masters of the Scriptures. ... If the article of our faith is right, 'I believe in the holy Christian Church,' the Pope cannot alone be right; else we must say, 'I believe in the Pope of Rome,' and reduce the Christian Church to one man, which is a devilish and damnable heresy. Besides that, we are all priests, as I have said, and have all one faith, one Gospel, one Sacrament; how then should we not have the power of discerning and judging what is right or wrong in matters of faith? ...

The third wall falls of itself, as soon as the first two have fallen; for if the Pope acts contrary to the Scriptures, we are bound to stand by the Scriptures to punish and to constrain him, according to Christ's commandment ... 'tell it unto the Church' (Matt. xviii. 15–17). ... If then I am to accuse him before the Church, I must collect the Church together. ... Therefore when need requires, and the Pope is a cause of offence to Christendom, in these cases whoever can best do so, as a faithful member of the whole body, must do what he can to procure a true free council. This no one can do so well as the temporal authorities, especially since they are fellow-Christians, fellow-priests. ...

[Luther proceeds to treat of matters to be discussed at the Council.]

What is the use in Christendom of those who are called 'cardinals'? I will tell you. In Italy and Germany there are many rich convents, endowments, holdings, and benefices; and as the best way of getting these into the hands of Rome they created cardinals, and gave to them the bishoprics, convents, and prelacies, and thus destroyed the service of God. That is why Italy is almost a desert now: the convents are destroyed, the sees consumed, the revenues of the prelacies and of all the churches drawn to Rome; towns are decayed, and the country and the people ruined because there is no more any worship of God or preaching. Why? Because the cardinals must have all the wealth. The Turk himself could not have so desolated Italy and so overthrown the worship of God.

Now that Italy is sucked dry, they come to Germany. They begin in a quiet way, but we shall soon see Germany brought into the same state as Italy. We have a few cardinals already. What the Romanists really mean to do, the 'drunken' Germans are not to see until they have lost everything. ...

Now this devilish state of things is not only open robbery and deceit and the prevailing of the gates of hell, but it is destroying the very life and soul of Christianity; therefore we are bound to use all our diligence to ward off this misery and destruction. If we want to fight Turks, let us begin here—we cannot find worse ones. If we rightly hang thieves and behead robbers, why do we leave the greed of Rome unpunished? For Rome is the greatest thief and robber that has ever appeared on earth, or ever will; and all in the holy names of Church and St Peter. ...

[Luther proceeds to outline '57 Articles for the Reformation of Christendom,' including restrictions on the sending of contributions to Rome, reduction of the number of monks and mendicants, and the reformation of schools and universities.]

... Poor Germans that we are—we have been deceived! We were born to be masters, and we have been compelled to bow the head beneath the yoke of our tyrants, and to become slaves. Name, title, outward signs of royalty, we possess all these; force, power, right, liberty, all these have gone over to the popes, who have robbed us of them. They get the kernel, we get the husk. ... It is time the glorious Teutonic people should cease to be the puppet of the Roman pontiff. Because the pope crowns the emperor, it does not follow that the pope is superior to the emperor. Samuel, who crowned Saul and David, was not above these kings, nor Nathan above Solomon, whom he consecrated. ... Let the emperor then be a veritable emperor, and no longer allow himself to be stripped of his sword or of his sceptre! ...

2. The Babylonish Captivity of the Church   *Op. Lat.* v. 16. Extracts in Kidd, 36

[Luther followed his political effort with a doctrinal attack, addressed in Latin to theologians. It was an attack on the whole medieval sacramental system. Henry VIII earned the title *Defensor Fidei* for his answer to this treatise.]

... In the first place I must deny the existence of seven sacraments, and must for the time being assert three only, baptism, penance, and the bread; and that these have been led into pitiable bondage for us by the Roman Curia, and the Church despoiled of all her liberty. ...

[Concerning the Lord's Supper] ... The first captivity of this sacrament is in respect of its substance or integrity, which the Roman tyranny has taken from us. Not that they sin against Christ who avail themselves of the one species ... but because they sin who by this ruling forbid the giving of both species to those who wish to avail themselves of both. ...

The second captivity of the same sacrament is less harsh as regards conscience; but to handle it, to say nothing of condemning it, is the most perilous of undertakings! ... The lord Cardinal of Cambrai [Pierre d'Ailly] once gave me food for reflexion, at a time when I was drinking in scholastic theology, by that passage in the 4th book of his 'Propositions,' where he argues most acutely that it would be much more plausible and would entail fewer redundant miracles it if were asserted that not only the accidents but also the reality of bread and wine remained in the sacrament of the altar—had not the church determined otherwise! Afterwards, when I realized what that church was which so determined, namely the Thomist, i.e. the Aristotelian, Church, I grew more bold. I had been hesitating between the devil and the deep sea, but now at last I brought my conscience to rest in my former opinion; which was, that the bread and wine are really bread and wine and the true flesh and blood of Christ is in them in the same fashion and the same degree as they hold them to be beneath their accidents. I took this step because I saw that the Thomist opinions, whether they be approved by pope or by council, remain opinions and do not become articles of faith, even if an angel from heaven should decide otherwise. For that which is asserted without the authority of Scripture or of proven revelation may be held as an opinion, but there is no obligation to believe it. ... Transubstantiation ... must be considered as an invention of human reason, since it is based neither on Scripture nor sound reasoning. ...

Why could not Christ confine his body within the substance of bread, just as in the accidents? Fire and iron are two substances; yet they are so mingled in red-hot iron [*ferro ignito*] that any part is at once iron and fire. What prevents the glorious body of Christ from being in every part of the substance of bread? ...

The third captivity of this sacrament is that most sacrilegious abuse by which it has come about that at this day there is nothing in the church more generally received or more widely held than that the mass is a good work and a sacrifice. This abuse has brought an endless flood of other abuses, until faith in the sacrament has been utterly extinguished and a divine sacrament has been turned into an article of trade, the subject of bargaining and business deals. Hence arise fellowships, fraternities, intercessions, merits, anniversaries, memorials; and such like pieces of business are bought and sold, and contracts and bargains are made about them. The entire maintenance of priests and monks depends on such things. ...

Another scandal must be removed ... namely the general belief that the mass is a sacrifice which is offered to God. This opinion seems to be in harmony with the words of the Canon; 'These gifts, these offerings, these holy sacrifices'; and later, 'This oblation.' And then there is the unambiguous prayer that 'this sacrifice may be accepted just as the sacrifice of Abel, etc.' Hence Christ is called the victim of the altar. And besides these the sayings of the Holy Fathers are adduced, and many precedents and the universal and uninterrupted observance of this way of speaking.

Because they take their stand so obstinately on these grounds we must with equal steadfastness set against them the words of Christ. ... For in them there is no mention of a 'work' [*opus*] or a 'sacrifice.' ... The offering of a sacrifice is incompatible with the distribution of a testament or the reception of a promise [and, according to L., the mass is a promise or a testament, in the words of Christ]; the former we receive, the latter we give. The same thing cannot be at once received and offered, nor be given and accepted by the same person at the same time. ...

[Concerning the Sacrament of Baptism]. ... When Satan found himself unable to destroy the virtue of baptism in infants he still had power to destroy it in adults; so that there is now scarcely anyone who recalls that he is baptized—to say nothing of glorying in his baptism— since so many other ways have been devised for securing remission of sins and entrance into the kingdom of Heaven. The occasion for such opinions was given by that dangerous remark of S. Jerome (whether the mistake lay in its utterance or in its interpretation), in which he calls repentance the 'second plank after shipwreck,' as if baptism were not repentance. For hence those who have fallen into sin despair of their first plank, or ship, as if it were lost, and begin to rely on the second alone, that is on repentance. Hence have arisen those endless burdens of vows, professions, works, satisfactions, pilgrimages, indulgences, sects, and from them those oceans of books, questions, opinions, human traditions, which the whole world cannot now contain; so that the Church of God is now under a tyranny incomparably worse than that of any synagogue or any nation whatsoever. ...

First the divine promise must be noted: 'He who believes and is baptized shall be saved.' ...

[Concerning the Sacrament of Penance] ... The first and fundamental evil of this sacrament is that they have wholly abolished the sacrament itself, leaving no trace of it. For, like the other, it consists in two things: on God's side a word of promise, on ours, faith. They have overthrown both of these. The word of promise [Matt. xvi. 19, xviii. 18; John xxi.] ... they have made use of to support their tyranny. ... They do not speak of the saving faith of the people, but babble solely of the unlimited power of the pontiff, although Christ always acts through faith, not through power. ...

Not content with this, our Babylon has so done away with faith that she has the impudence to deny that faith is necessary in that sacrament, nay with the blasphemy of Anti-christ she lays it down that it is heresy to assert the necessity of faith. ...

... Private confession, which alone is practised, though it cannot be proved from Scripture, is wholly commendable, useful and indeed necessary. I would not have it cease, but rather I rejoice that it exists in the Church of Christ, for it is the one and only remedy for troubled consciences. ... The one thing that I abhor is the employment of confession to further the despotism and the exactions of the pontiffs. ...

f. The Diet of Worms, 1521

Luther's Final Answer, 18 April   *Op. Lat.* vi. 8. Kidd, 42

[Leo's excommunication of Luther, in the Bull *Exsurge Domine*, was published in Saxony in the autumn of 1520. But the Elector refused to carry it out. Luther finally repudiated the Pope and burned the Bull publicly. In January 1521 the Pope issued another and stronger Bull, and called upon the Emperor to put it into effect. Charles V wished to secure himself against Francis I by using the threat of Luther to bring the Pope to heel, and at the same time to assert his independence of the Pope, and to grant Luther a show of justice sufficient to satisfy the anti-papal sentiment in Germany. A diet was summoned, the papal case was stated, and Luther was given his chance to recant. After this final answer of Luther, Charles announced his intention of suppressing heresy and secured his alliance with Leo. The Edict of Worms put Luther under the Imperial ban, and forbade the printing of his works or the proclamation or defence of his opinions.]

... [Eck, Official of the Archbishop of Trier, asked Luther.] Do you wish to defend the books which are recognized as your work? Or to retract anything contained in them? ...

... [Luther replied.] Most Serene Lord Emperor, Most illustrious Princes, Most Gracious Lords ... I beseech you to grant a gracious hearing to my plea, which, I trust, will be a plea of justice and truth; and if through my inexperience I neglect to give to any their proper titles or in any way offend against the etiquette of the court in my manners or behaviour, be kind enough to forgive me, I beg, since I am a man who has spent his life not in courts but in the cells of a monastery; a man who can say of himself only this, that to this day I have thought and written in simplicity of heart, solely with a view to the glory of God and the pure instruction of Christ's faithful people. ...

... Your Imperial Majesty and Your Lordships: I ask you to observe that my books are not all of the same kind.

There are some in which I have dealt with piety in faith and morals with such simplicity and so agreeably with the Gospels that my adversaries themselves are compelled to admit them useful, harmless, and clearly worth reading by a Christian. Even the Bull, harsh and cruel though it is, makes some of my books harmless, although it condemns them also, by a judgement downright monstrous. If I should begin to recant here, what, I beseech you, should I be doing but condemning, alone among mortals, that truth which is admitted by friends and foes alike, in an unaided struggle against universal consent?

The second kind consists in those writings levelled against the papacy and the doctrine of the papists, as against those who by their wicked doctrines and precedents have laid waste Christendom by doing harm to the souls and the bodies of men. No one can either deny or conceal this, for universal experience and world-wide grievances are witnesses to the fact that through the Pope's laws and through man-made teachings the consciences of the faithful have been most pitifully ensnared, troubled, and racked in torment, and also that their goods and possessions have been devoured (especially amongst this famous German nation) by unbelievable tyranny, and are to this day being devoured without end in shameful fashion); and that though they themselves by their own laws take care to provide that the Pope's laws and doctrines which are contrary to the Gospel or the teachings of the Fathers are to be considered as erroneous and reprobate. If then I recant these, the only effect will be to add strength to such tyranny, to open not the windows but the main doors to such blasphemy, which will thereupon stalk farther and more widely than it has hitherto dared. ...

The third kind consists of those books which I have written against private individuals, so-called; against those, that is, who have exerted themselves in defence of the Roman tyranny and to the overthrow of that piety which I have taught. I confess that I have been more harsh against them than befits my religious vows and my profession. For I do not make myself out to be any kind of saint, nor am I now contending about my conduct but about Christian doctrine. But it is not in my power to recant them, because that recantation would give that tyranny and blasphemy an occasion to lord it over those whom I defend and to rage against God's people more violently than ever.

However, since I am a man and not God, I cannot provide my writings with any other defence than that which my Lord Jesus Christ provided for his teaching. When he had been interrogated concerning his teaching before Annas and had received a buffet from a servant, he said: 'If I have spoken evil, bear witness of the evil.' If the Lord himself, who knew that he could not err, did not refuse to listen to witness against his teaching, even from a worthless slave, how much more ought I, scum that I am, capable of naught but error, to seek and to wait for any who may wish to bear witness against my teaching.

And so, through the mercy of God, I ask Your Imperial Majesty, and Your Illustrious Lordships, or anyone of any degree, to bear witness, to overthrow my errors, to defeat them by the writings of the Prophets or by the Gospels; for I shall be most ready, if I be better instructed, to recant any error, and I shall be the first in casting my writings into the fire. ...

Thereupon the Orator of the Empire, in a tone of upbraiding, said that his answer was not to the point, and that there should be no calling into question of matters on which condemnations and decisions had before been passed by Councils. He was being asked for a plain reply, without subtlety or sophistry, to this question: Was he prepared to recant, or no?

Luther then replied: Your Imperial Majesty and Your Lordships demand a simple answer. Here it is, plain and unvarnished. Unless I am convicted of error by the testimony of Scriptures or (since I put no trust in the unsupported authority of Pope or of councils, since it is plain that they have often erred and often contradicted themselves) by manifest reasoning I stand convicted by the Scriptures to which I have appealed, and my conscience is taken captive by God's word, I cannot and will not recant anything, for to act against our conscience is neither safe for us, nor open to us.

On this I take my stand. I can do no other. God help me. Amen.[1] ...

g. The Short Catechism, 1529   Wace and Buchheim *Primary Works*

[This superseded the Greater Catechism of 1528 and became the standard book of instruction for Southern Germany.]

PREFACE

Martin Luther to all faithful, pious pastors, and preachers: Grace, mercy, and peace, in Jesus Christ our Lord.

In setting forth this Catechism or Christian doctrine in such a simple, concise, and easy form, I have been compelled and driven by the wretched and lamentable state of affairs which I discovered lately when I acted as inspector. Merciful God, what misery I have seen, the common people knowing nothing at all of Christian doctrine, especially in the villages! and unfortunately many pastors are wellnigh unskilled and incapable of teaching; and though all are called Christians and partake

---

[1] The last words are given in German: Hie stehe ich. Ich kan nicht anders. Gott helff mir. Amen.

of the Holy Sacrament, they know neither the Lord's Prayer, nor the Creed, nor the Ten Commandments, but live like the poor cattle and senseless swine, though, now that the Gospel is come, they have learnt well enough how they may abuse their liberty.

O ye bishops, how will ye ever answer for it to Christ that ye have so shamefully neglected the people, and have not attended for an instant to your office? May all evil be averted from you! Ye forbid the taking of the Sacrament in one kind, and insist on your human laws, but never inquire whether they know the Lord's Prayer, the Belief, the Ten Commandments, or any of the words of God. Oh, woe upon you for evermore!

Therefore I pray you for God's sake, my good masters and brethren who are pastors or preachers, to attend to your office with all your heart, to take pity on your people, who are commended to your charge, and to help us to introduce the Catechism among the people, especially among the young; and let those who cannot do better take these tables and forms, and instruct the people in them word for word; in this wise:

First, the preacher must above all things beware of and avoid the use of various and different texts and forms of the Commandments, Lord's Prayer, Belief, Sacrament, &c.; he must take one form and keep to it, and constantly teach the same, year after year. For the young and simple folk must be taught one definite text and version, else they will easily become confused, if to-day we teach thus and next year thus, as though we wanted to improve it, and so all our labour and toil is lost.

This was clearly seen by the worthy fathers, who used the Lord's Prayer, the Belief, the Ten Commandments, all in one form. Therefore we must always teach the young and simple folk in such a manner that we do not alter one syllable, or preach to-morrow differently from today.

Therefore choose whatever form thou wilt, and ever keep to it. But if though preachest to scholars or wise men, thou mayest show thy skill, and vary these articles, and twist them as subtly as thou canst. But with the young keep always to one form, and teach them first of all these articles, namely, the Ten Commandments, the Belief, the Lord's Prayer, &c., according to the text, word for word, so that they may repeat them and learn them by heart.

But as for those who will not learn, let them be told that they deny Christ and are no Christians, and let them not be admitted to the Sacrament, be sponsors to any child, or enjoy any of the liberty of Christians, but be handed over simply to the Pope and his officers, yea, to the devil himself. Besides this, let their parents or masters refuse them food and drink, and tell them that the prince will have such rude people driven from the land.

For though we cannot and may not force any to believe, yet we must train and urge the multitude so that they may know what is right and wrong among those with whom they have their dwelling, food, and life. For whoever would dwell in a town must know and keep the law of which he would enjoy the privileges, whether he believe it, or be a rogue and good-for-nothing in his heart.

Secondly, when they know the text well, teach them next to understand it, so that they know what it means, and take once more the method of these tables, this or some other short method, whichever thou wilt, and keep to it, and do not alter one syllable, just as we said of the text, and take time and leisure over it. For it is not necessary to expound all at once, but one thing after the other. When they understand the First Commandment well, then take the Second, and so on, else they will be overwhelmed and retain none.

Thirdly, now when thou hast taught them this short Catechism, then take the larger Catechism, and give them a deeper and fuller explanation. Explain every commandment, petition, and article, with its various works and uses, its dangers and abuses, as thou wilt find them in abundance in the many little books written about them. And especially dwell on that commandment that is most neglected among thy people. For example, the Seventh[1] Commandment, about stealing, must be vehemently urged among artisans, tradesmen, and also among peasants and servants, for among such people there is all manner of unfaithfulness and thieving. Again, the Fourth Commandment must be specially urged upon children and the common people, that they may be quiet, faithful, obedient, peaceful; and thou must always adduce many examples from the Bible of how God punished or blessed such people.

Especially urge authorities and parents that they govern well and send the children to school, and admonish them how it is their duty to do this, and what an accursed sin they commit if they neglect it. For thereby they overthrow and desolate both God's kingdom and the world's, as the worst enemies both of God and man. Lay also great stress on the horrible injury they do, if they do not help to train children for pastors, preachers, clerks, &c., and that God will punish them terribly. For it is very necessary to preach on this subject. Parents and magistrates now sin in this matter more than we can say. The devil has also most evil designs therein.

---

[1] i.e. the Eighth, as we number them; and so the Fourth, presently mentioned, is our Fifth.

Finally, because the tyranny of the Pope is past, they will no longer come to the Sacrament, and despise it. Accordingly it is necessary to urge them, but with this caution: we must not force any one to belief or to the Sacrament, nor make any law prescribing time or place; but we ought to preach so that they come without our laws and, as it were, force us, their pastors, to give them the Sacrament. This we may do by saying to them, 'Whoever does not seek or desire the Sacrament, or demand it, at least once or four times a year, it is to be feared that he despises the Sacrament and is no Christian, just as he is no Christian who does not believe in or listen to the gospel; for Christ did not say, "Omit or despise this," but "*This do as oft as ye drink it*," etc.' He will surely have it done, and on no account neglected or despised. '*This do*,' He says.

But if there be any one who does not greatly prize the Sacrament, that is a sign that he has no sin, no flesh, no devil, no world, no death, no danger, no hell; that is, he believes in none, though he is head over ears therein and is doubly the devil's. On the other hand, he needs no mercy, life, paradise, kingdom of heaven, Christ, God, or anything that is good. For if he believed that he had so much evil and needed so much good, he would not neglect the Sacrament, in which so much help is given against evil, and so much good is bestowed. We should not then need to drive him to the Sacrament by any law, but he would come running and hurrying thither of his own accord, constrain himself, and urge you, that you should give him the Sacrament.

So thou must not establish any law herein like the Pope. Only dwell on the good and harm, necessity and blessing, the danger and salvation, in the Sacrament, and then they will come of their own accord, without your constraining them. But if they do not come, let them go their ways, and tell them they are the devil's, since they neither regard nor feel their own great need and God's gracious help. But if thou do not dwell on this, or if thou make a law and poison of it, then it is thy fault that they despise the Sacrament. How can they be otherwise than indifferent if thou sleep or keep silence? Therefore see to it, pastor and preacher! Our office has now become a different thing from what it was under the Pope: it has now become a real and saving office. Therefore it is more troublesome and full of labour, and is more encompassed by danger and temptation, and, moreover, brings little reward and thanks in this world. But Christ Himself will be our reward if we work faithfully. And so may the Father of all mercy help us, to whom be praise and thanks everlasting, through Christ our Lord. Amen.

[1. THE TEN COMMANDMENTS]

2. THE CREED

How the master of the house is to explain it as simply as possible to his household.

The First Article: of the Creation

I believe in God the Father Almighty, Maker of heaven and earth.

What does that mean?

Answer. I believe that God has created me and all other creatures, and has given me, and preserves for me, body and soul, eyes, ears, and all my limbs, my reason and all my senses; and that daily He bestows on me clothes and shoes, meat and drink, house and home, wife and child, fields and cattle, and all my goods, and supplies in abundance all needs and necessities of my body and life, and protects me from all perils, and guards and defends me from all evil. And this He does out of pure fatherly and Divine goodness and mercy, without any merit or worthiness in me; for all which I am bound to thank Him and praise Him, and, moreover, to serve and obey Him. This is a faithful saying.

The Second Article: of the Redemption

And in Jesus Christ, His only Son, our Lord, who was conceived by the Holy Ghost, born of the Virgin Mary; suffered under Pontius Pilate; was crucified, dead, and buried, He descended into hell; the third day He rose again from the dead; He ascended into heaven, and sitteth at the right hand of the Father Almighty; from thence He shall come to judge the quick and the dead.

What does that mean?

Answer. I believe that Jesus Christ, very God, born of the Father in eternity, and also very man, born of the Virgin Mary, is my Lord, who has redeemed me, a lost and damned man, and has won and delivered me from all sins, from death, and from the power of the devil, not with gold and silver, but with his His holy and precious blood and with His innocent passion and death, so that I might be His own, and might live under Him in His kingdom, and serve him in everlasting righteousness, innocence, and blessing, just as He rose from the dead, and lives and reigns in all eternity. This is a faithful saying.

The Third Article: of the Sanctification

I believe in the Holy Ghost, a holy Christian Church, the communion of saints, the forgiveness of sins, the resurrection of the body, and the life everlasting. Amen.

What does that mean?

Answer. I believe that I cannot of my own understanding and strength believe in or come to Jesus Christ my Lord, but that the Holy Ghost has called me by the Gospel, and illuminated me with His gifts, and sanctified and preserved me in the true faith, just as He calls, gathers together, illuminates, sanctifies, and preserves in Jesus Christ all Christendom throughout the earth in the one true faith; in which Christendom He daily bestows abundantly on me and all believers forgiveness of sins; and on the last day He will awaken me and all the dead, and will give to me and all that believe in Christ eternal life. This is a faithful saying.

[3. THE LORD'S PRAYER]

[4. THE SACRAMENT OF HOLY BAPTISM]

5. HOW THE SIMPLE FOLKS SHOULD BE TAUGHT TO CONFESS

Confession consists of two parts: first, to confess our sins, and secondly, to receive the absolution or forgiveness bestowed by the confessor, as from God Himself, and not to doubt thereof, but firmly to believe that our sins are thereby forgiven in the sight of God in heaven.

What sins should we confess?

To God we are to confess all sins, even those that we do not recognize, as we do in the Lord's Prayer; but to the confessor we are only to confess such sins as we know and feel guilty of in our hearts.

Which are they?

Examine thyself according to the Ten Commandments, whether thou art father, mother, son, daughter, master, mistress, manservant or maidservant, and see if thou hast been disobedient, unfaithful, and idle, whether thou hast done any one an injury by word or deed, whether thou hast been dishonest, negligent, slothful, or has otherwise caused harm.

I pray thee, friend, tell me a short form of confession.

Answer. Say thus to thy confessor: Worthy reverend master, I pray you hear my confession, and declare absolution to me for God's sake.

Say thus: I, a poor sinner, confess myself guilty of all sins before God; in particular I confess to you that I am a manservant or a maidservant, etc., but, alas! I serve my master unfaithfully, for at such and such a time I have not done what they bade me, but angered them and moved them to swear; I have neglected my work and caused damage; I have been forward in word and deed; I have been angry with my fellows, sullen to my wife, and I have sworn at her. All this I repent of, and I pray for mercy, and will seek to amend.

A master or mistress must say as follows:—

Especially I acknowledge to you that I have not faithfully trained my children and servants and my wife to the glory of God; I have sworn, and given a bad example with unchaste words and deeds; I have done injury to my neighbour, spoken ill of him, sold too dear, given short measure and false weight—and whatever else he may have done contrary to the commandments of God and his state in life.

But if any shall find that he is not burdened with similar or greater sins, he shall not be anxious or seek or invent further sins, and thus turn confession into a torture, but he must recount the one or two sins that he may remember. Thus: I confess especially that once I swore, also that I used unseemly words, neglected this or that duty. Let this suffice.

But if thou know of none (though this is wellnigh impossible), then mention none in particular, but receive forgiveness upon the general confession which thou makest to the confessor before God.

Thereupon the confessor shall say,—

God be merciful to thee, and strengthen thy faith. Amen.

Further:—

Dost thou believe that my forgiveness is God's forgiveness?

Answer. Yea, reverend sir.

Then let him say,—

As thou believest, so be it unto thee. And, by command of our Lord Jesus Christ, I forgive thee thy sins, in the name of the Father, the Son, and the Holy Ghost. Amen. Go in peace.

But if any are sorely afflicted in their conscience, or sorely grieved and tempted, the confessor will know how to comfort them with various words of Scripture, and how to lead them to faith. This is merely to serve as a general mode of confession for the simple folk.

6. THE SACRAMENT OF THE ALTAR

How the master of the house should explain it simply to his household.

What is the Sacrament of the Altar?

Answer. It is the very Body and Blood of our Lord Jesus Christ, under the Bread and Wine, for us Christians to eat and to drink, under the institution of Christ Himself.

Where is this written?

Answer. Thus say the holy Evangelists Matthew, Mark, Luke, and St Paul:—

The Lord Jesus, in the same night in which he was betrayed, took bread, and when He had given thanks, He brake it, and gave it to His disciples, and said, Take; eat. This is My body, which is given for you; this do in remembrance of Me.

After the same manner also He took the cup when He had supped, and gave it to them, saying, Take this and drink ye all of it. This cup is the new testament in My blood, which is shed for you for the forgiveness of sins; this do ye, as oft as ye drink it, in remembrance of Me.

What avails it to eat and drink thus?

Answer. This is shown by the words, '*Given for you and shed for you for the remission of sins.*' That is to say, that in the Sacrament forgiveness of sins, life, and salvation are bestowed on us by these words. For where forgiveness of sins is, there is also life and salvation.

How can bodily eating and drinking accomplish these great things?

Answer. Eating and drinking do not indeed accomplish this, but the words which stand there, '*Given for you and shed for you for the remission of sins.*' These words, together with the bodily eating and drinking, are the most important part of this Sacrament, and whoever believes these words, he has what they say, and as they speak, namely, remission of sins.

Who, then, are they who receive this Sacrament worthily?

Answer. Fasting and bodily preparation are in truth a good external discipline, but he is truly worthy and prepared who believes the words, '*Given for you and shed for the remission of sins.*' But he who does not believe them is unworthy and not prepared. For the words, '*for you,*' demand truly believing hearts.

APPENDIX I

How the master of the house should teach his household to commend themselves to God both night and morning.

The Morning Blessing

In the morning, when thou risest from thy bed, sign thyself with the Holy Cross, and say,—

In the name of the Father, the Son, and the Holy Ghost. Amen.

Then, kneeling or standing, repeat the Creed and the Lord's Prayer. If thou wilt, thou mayest also say this short prayer:—

I thank Thee, my heavenly Father, through Jesus Christ, Thy dear Son, that Thou hast preserved me through this night from all harm and danger, and I beseech Thee Thou wouldest protect me this day from sin and all evil, that all my deeds and my life may be pleasing in Thy sight. For I commend myself, my body and soul, and all, into Thy hands. Let Thy holy angel be with me, that the evil one may have no power over me. Amen.

And then go joyfully to thy work, and sing, if thou wilt, a hymn, the Ten Commandments, or whatever else thy devotion suggests.

The Evening Blessing

At night, when thou goest to bed, sign thyself with the Holy Cross, and say,—

In the name of the Father, the Son, and the Holy Ghost. Amen.

Then, kneeling or standing, repeat the Creed and the Lord's Prayer. If thou wilt, thou mayest add this short prayer:—

I thank Thee, my heavenly Father, through Jesus Christ, Thy dear Son, that Thou hast graciously protected me through this day; and I beseech Thee Thou wouldest forgive me all my sins wherever I have done wrong, and mercifully guard me this night. For I commend myself, my body and soul, and all, into Thy hands. Let Thy holy angel be with me, that the evil one may have no power over me. Amen.

And then to sleep quickly and cheerfully.

How the master of the house should teach his household to say the Benedicite and the Gratias.

The children and servants are to fold hands, modestly approach the table, and say,—

The eyes of all wait upon Thee, and Thou givest them their meat in due season. Thou openest Thine hand, and satisfiest the desire of every living thing.

Note.—Satisfaction signifies that all creatures get so much to eat that they are cheerful and happy over it, for care and greed prevent such satisfaction.

Then the Lord's Prayer and the following prayer:—

Lord God, our heavenly Father, bless us and these Thy gifts, which we accept from Thy merciful goodness, through Jesus Christ our Lord. Amen.

The Gratias

After the meal they shall do likewise, and speak modestly with folded hands.

Give thanks unto the Lord, for He is gracious, and His mercy endureth for ever. He giveth fodder unto the cattle, and feedeth the young ravens that call upon Him. He hath no pleasure in the strength of an horse, neither delighteth He in any man's legs. But the Lord's delight is in them that fear Him and put their trust in His mercy.

Then the Lord's Prayer and the following prayer:—

We thank Thee, Lord God our Father, through Jesus Christ our Lord, for all Thy mercies, who livest and reignest for ever and ever. Amen.

To All

Thou shalt love they neighbour as thyself; in this saying all command-ments are comprehended (Rom. xiii). I exhort therefore that first of all supplications, prayers, intercessions, and giving of thanks be made for all men (i Tim. ii).

> Let each one learn his lesson well;
> Then in the house content will dwell.

> 𝕰in ieder lern fein 𝕾ection
> 𝕲u wird es wohl im haufe ftohn.

> Cuique sit imprimis magnae sua lectio curae
> Ut domus officiis stet decorata suis.

> Πᾶς ἰδίην ἀνάγνωσιν ἑῆς πραπίδεσιν
> ἀθρήσας οἶκον ἔχει πυκινῶν εὐπορέοντα καλῶν.

h. The Confession of Augsburg, *1530* *Corpus Reformatorum*, xxvi. 263 ff.
Kidd, 116

[The first of Lutheran symbolical statements arise as the result of the Colloquy at Marburg, an abortive attempt by Philip of Hesse to reconcile the positions of Luther and Zwingli. Luther drew up fifteen articles as a basis of reunion, and on the failure of the conference these were revised as the Articles of Schwabach and became the basis of Lutheran doctrine. In 1530 they were expanded into the Confession of Augsburg, written by Melanchthon as a statement of the Lutheran case at the Diet summoned by Charles V. The Confession is a lengthy document and it is only possible to include here a few of its statements on points which were the principal matters of controversy at the time.]

II. *Of Original Sin*

They teach that after the fall of Adam all men, born according to nature, are born with sin, that is, without the fear of God, without confidence towards God and with concupiscence, and that this original disease or flaw is truly a sin, bringing condemnation and also eternal death to those who are not reborn through baptism and the Holy Spirit.

They condemn Pelagians and others who say that the original flaw is not a sin and who argue that man can be justified in God's sight by his own strength of reason, so as to lessen the glory of the merit and the benefits of Christ.

IV. *Of Justification*

They teach that men cannot be justified in the sight of God by their own strength, merits or works, but that they are justified freely on account of Christ through faith, when they believe that they are received into grace and that their sins are remitted on account of Christ who made satisfaction for sins on our behalf by his death. God imputes this faith for righteousness in his own sight (Romans iii and iv).

VII. *Of the Church*

They teach that the one Holy Church will remain for ever. Now this Church is the congregation of the saints, in which the Gospel is rightly taught and the sacraments rightly administered.

And for that true unity of the Church it is enough to have unity of belief concerning the teaching of the Gospel and the administration of the sacraments. It is not necessary that there should everywhere be the same traditions of men, or the same rites and ceremonies devised by men. ...

X. *Of the Lord's Supper*

They teach that the body and blood of Christ are truly present and are distributed to those who partake in the Lord's Supper; and they reject those that teach otherwise.

XI. *Of Confession*

They teach that private absolution is to be retained in the churches although it is not necessary to enumerate all sins in confession, because it is impossible, as the psalmist says 'Who understands his offences?'

XIV. *Of Orders*

They teach that no one ought to teach publicly in churches or to administer the sacraments, unless duly called.

XV. *Of the Rites of the Church*

They teach that those rites are to be preserved which can be preserved without sin and which are of service for tranquility and good order in the Church, as fixed holy days, feast-days and such like.

But men are warned not to burden their consciences in such matters, as if such observance were necessary to salvation.

They are also warned that traditions devised by man to propitiate God and to acquire grace and make satisfaction for sins are opposed to the Gospel and the teaching of faith. Wherefore vows and traditions concerning foods and days, etc., devised for the production and grace and satisfaction for sins, are useless and contrary to the Gospel.

XVIII. *Of Free Choice*

They teach that human will has some liberty in the accomplishment of civil righteousness and in the choice of things which are subject to reason. But without the Holy Spirit it has no power of accomplishing the righteousness of God, or spiritual righteousness 'because animal man does not perceive the things which belong to the spirit of God': but these came into being in our hearts when the Holy Spirit is conceived through the Word. ...

They condemn Pelagians and others who teach that we can love God above all things by the strength of our nature alone, without the Holy Spirit; and that we can perform the commands of God in respect of the *substance* of the actions. For although nature may in some way be able to accomplish the external works (for it can restrain the hands from thefts or from murder), nevertheless it cannot gain the interior motions—fear of God, confidence towards God, chastity, patience, etc.

XIX. *Of the Cause of Sin*

They teach that although God is the creator and preserver of nature, yet the cause of sin is the will of evil persons, namely of the devil and impious men, which, without God's help, turns itself away from God. ...

XX. *Of Faith and Good Works*

Our people are falsely accused of forbidding good works. For their writings on the Ten Commandments and other matters of similar import bear witness that they give useful teaching concerning all kinds of life and the various duties—what kinds of life and what works in each creation are pleasing to God. The popular preachers [*concionatores*] in former times taught too little on these subjects; for they only stressed certain childish and unnecessary works—fixed holidays and fasts, fraternities, pilgrimages, worship of saints, rosaries, monasticism and such-like.

A. Of Faith

... Our works cannot reconcile us to God or merit remission of sins and grace and justification. This we obtain only by faith, when we believe that we are received into grace on account of Christ. ...

... Men are warned that the word *faith* does not signify merely the knowledge of an event (the devils and impious men have that), but it signifies a faith which believes not in an event merely, but also in the effect of an event, namely this article, the remission of sins, i.e. that we have, through Christ, grace, righteousness, and remission of sins. ...

B. Of Good Works

Moreover our people teach that it is necessary to do good works, not in order to trust to merit grace thereby, but because of the will of God. ... Because the Holy Spirit is received through faith, and hearts are renewed and put on new affections so that they can accomplish good works. For Ambrose says: 'Faith is the mother of good will and righteous action.' ...

Hence it is readily seen that this doctrine is not to be accused of preventing good works, but much rather to be praised because it shows how we can do good works. ...

II. CALVINISM

Christianae Religionis Institutio   *Calvini Op.* ii. 31–2 (edition of 1559)
Extracts in Kidd, 273

[The first edition of the *Institutio* was published in 1536, when Calvin was twenty-six. It was several times revised, but there was no development in Calvin's thought after the first edition. Calvin's genius was for organization rather than theological speculation.]

Book II. chap. i. ... Therefore original sin is seen to be an hereditary depravity and corruption of our nature, diffused into all parts of the soul ... wherefore those who have defined original sin as the lack of the original righteousness with which we should have been endowed, no doubt include, by implication, the whole fact of the matter, but they have not fully expressed the positive energy of this sin. For our nature is not merely bereft of good, but is so productive of every kind of evil that it cannot be inactive. Those who have called it concupiscence have used a word by no means wide of the mark, if it were added (and this is what many do not concede) that whatever is in man, from intellect to will, from the soul to the flesh, is all defiled and crammed with concupiscence; or, to sum it up briefly, that the whole man is in himself nothing but concupiscence. ...

Chap. iv. ... The old writers often shrink from the straightforward acknowledgement of the truth in this matter, from motives of piety. They are afraid of opening to the blasphemers a window for their slanders concerning the works of God. While I salute their restraint, I consider that there is very little danger of this if we simply hold to the teaching of Scripture. Even Augustine is not always emancipated from that superstitious fear; as when he says [Of Predestination and Grace, §§4, 5] that 'hardening' and 'blinding' refer not to the operation of God, but to his foreknowledge. But there are so many sayings of Scripture which will not admit of such fine distinctions; for they clearly indicate that God's intervention consists in something more than his foreknow-ledge. ... In the same way their suggestions as to God's 'permission' are too weak to stand. It is very often said that God blinded and hardened the reprobate, that he turned, inclined, or drove on their hearts. ... And no explanation of such statements is given by taking refuge in 'foreknow-ledge' or 'permission.' We therefore reply that this [process of hardening or blinding] comes about in two ways. When his light is removed, nothing remains but darkness and blindness; when his Spirit is taken away, our hearts harden into stone; when his guidance ceases, we are turned from the straight path. And so he is rightly said to blind, to harden, to turn, those from whom he takes away the ability to see, to obey, to keep on the straight path. But the second way is much nearer the proper meaning of the words; that to carry out his judgements he directs their councils and excites their wills, in the direction which he has decided upon, through the agency of Satan, the minister of his wrath. ...

Book III. chap. xxi. No one who wishes to be thought religious dares outright to deny predestination, by which God chooses some for the hope of life, and condemns others to eternal death. But men entangle it with captious quibbles; and especially those who make foreknowledge the ground of it. We indeed attribute to God both predestination and foreknowledge; but we call it absurd to subordinate one to the other.

When we attribute foreknowledge to God we mean that all things have ever been, and eternally remain, before his eyes; so that to his knowledge nothing is future or past, but all things are present; and present not in the sense that they are reproduced in imagination (as we are aware of past events which are retained in our memory), but present in the sense that he really sees and observes them placed, as it were, before his eyes. And this foreknowledge extends over the whole universe and over every creature. By predestination we mean the eternal decree of God, by which he has decided in his own mind what he wishes to happen in the case of each individual. For all men are not created on an equal footing, but for some eternal life is pre-ordained, for others eternal damnation. ...

Book IV. chap xiv. *Concerning Sacraments.* ... It is convenient first of all to notice what a Sacrament is. Now the following seems to me to be a simple and proper definition of a Sacrament. An external symbol by which the Lord attests in our consciences his promises of goodwill towards us to sustain the inferiority of our faith, and we on our part testify to our piety towards him as well in his presence and before the angels as in the sight of men. Another way of putting it, more condensed but equally sound, would be: A testimony of God's grace to us confirmed by an external sign, with our answering witness of piety towards him. ...

Chap. xvii. *Concerning the Sacred Supper of Christ.* ... That sacred communication of his own flesh and blood by which Christ pours his life into us, just as if he were to penetrate into the marrow of our bones, he witnesses and attests in the Supper. And that he does not by putting before us a vain or empty sign, but offering there the efficacy of his Spirit, by which he fulfils his promise. And in truth he offers and displays the thing there signified to all who share that spiritual feast; though only by the faithful is it perceived and its fruits enjoyed. ... If it is true that the visible sign is offered to us to attest the granting of the invisible reality, then, on receiving the symbol of the body, we may be confident that the body itself is no less given to us. ...

III. THE PEACE OF AUGSBURG, 1555
Translation, Kidd, 148

[In 1547 Charles V had passed through the Diet the *Interim of Augsburg* intended as a compromise pending a General Council. It conceded the cup to the laity and marriage to clergy, but the doctrine contained in its articles was purely Roman. Paul III agreed to it on his death-bed, and Charles sought to enforce it on the cities. But Maria of Saxony allied with Henry II of France, and in 1555 Charles was compelled to agree to a settlement—a diffuse document of which the following are the most important provisions.]

In order to bring peace into the holy empire of the Germanic Nation, between the Roman Imperial Majesty and the Electors, Princes, and Estates: let neither his Imperial Majesty nor the Electors, Princes, etc., do any violence or harm to any estate of the Empire on account of the Augsburg Confession, but let them enjoy their religious belief, liturgy and ceremonies as well as their estates and other rights and privileges in peace; and complete religious peace shall be obtained only by Christian means of amity, or under threat of the punishment of the imperial ban.

Likewise the Estates espousing the Augsburg Confession shall let all the Estates and Princes who cling to the old religion live in absolute peace and in the enjoyment of all their estates, rights and privileges.

However all such as do not belong to the two above-mentioned religions shall not be included in the present peace but be totally excluded from it.

... Where an archbishop, bishop, or prelate or any other priest of our old religion shall abandon the same, his archbishopric, bishopric, prelacy, and other benefices, together with all their income and revenues which he has so far possessed, shall be abandoned by him without any further objection or delay. The chapters and such as are entitled to it by common law or the custom of the place shall elect a person espousing the old religion, who may enter on the possession and enjoyment of all the rights and incomes of the place without any further hindrance and without prejudging any ultimate amicable settlement of religion. ...

In case our subjects, whether belonging to the old religion or to the Augsburg Confession, should intend leaving their homes, with their wives and children, in order to settle in another place, they shall neither be hindered in the sale of their estates after due payment of the local taxes nor injured in their honour. ...

IV. THE EDICT OF NANTES, 1598
Dumont, *Corps universel diplomatique*, v. 544 ff.

[This Edict was really a treaty between Henry IV and the Huguenots, who were granted religious liberty on condition of renouncing all foreign alliances. The concessions were withdrawn, by Louis XIV, when the king was strong enough to subdue rebellion by force.]

III. We ordain that the Catholic, Apostolic and Roman faith be restored and re-established in all those districts and places of this our Realm. ... in which its exercise has been interrupted, there to be freely and peaceably exercised. ...

VI. And to leave no occasion for trouble or difference among our subjects: We permit those of the so-called Reformed Religion to live and abide in all the towns and districts of this our Realm ... free from inquisition, molestation or compulsion to do anything in the way of Religion, against their conscience ... provided that they observe the provisions of this Edict. ...

IX. We also permit those of the aforesaid Religion to practise it in all the towns and districts of our dominion, in which it had been established and publicly observed by them on several distinct occasions during the year 1596 and the year 1597 up to the end of August, all decrees and judgements to the contrary notwithstanding.

XIII. We most expressly forbid to those of this religion the practice thereof, in respect of ministry, organization, discipline or the public instruction of children, or in any respect, in our realm and dominion, save in the places permitted and granted by this edict.

XIV. The practice of this religion is forbidden in our court and suite, in our domains beyond the mountains, in our city of Paris, or within five leagues thereof.

XVIII. We forbid all our subjects, of whatever rank or condition, to take children of this religion, by force or persuasion, to be baptized or confirmed in the Catholic Apostolic and Roman Church; the same being forbidden to those of the so-called Reformed Religion, under penalty of exceptionally severe punishment.

XXI. Books concerning this religion are not to be printed and exposed for sale save in towns and districts where the public practice of the said religion is allowed.

XXII. No distinction is to be made with regard to this religion, in the reception of pupils for education in universities, colleges and schools, nor in the reception of the sick and needy into hospitals, almshouses or public charities.

XXVII. Members of this religion are capable of holding any office or position in this Realm....

V. THE PEACE OF WESTPHALIA, 1648

Analysis from Reddaway, *Select Documents, 1492–1715*, 131–2
Text in Dumont, *Corps universel diplomatique*, vi. 469 ff.

[The Thirty Years War ended with a peace which recognized the independence of the German States, the Swiss cantons, and the United Netherlands, and gave to Protestants the right of worship and of admission to offices. It marks the end of medieval Europe. Innocent X, in his Bull, *Zelo domus Dei*, denounced its religious provisions as 'null and void, invalid, iniquitous, unjust, condemned, rejected, absurd, without force or effect.']

V. Religious Grievances.

1. Confirmation of the Convention of Passau and the Peace of Augsburg.

15. The Ecclesiastical Reservation. Catholics or Lutherans holding an ecclesiastical dignity to vacate it and its income if they change their religion.

21. The investiture of Protestant Prelates to take place when they have taken the due oaths.

34. Toleration given to those who, in 1624, had not the right to exercise their religion, being subjects of a lord of the other faith.

35. Subjects whose religion differs from that of their prince are to have equal rights with his other subjects.

36. Those emigrating for religious reasons retain the administration of their property.

43. The religious position in provinces where the lordship is contested.

50. Disputes about the religious peace of Augsburg and the peace of Westphalia to be carried before the Diet. All doctrines contrary to these treaties are forbidden.

VI. The independence of the Swiss is acknowledged.

VII. 1. The Reformed [Calvinists] are to have equal rights in religion and other matters with the other states and subjects.

2. ... but, besides the religions named [Catholic, Lutheran, Calvinist] above, no other shall be accepted or tolerated in the Holy Roman Empire.

SECTION IX

The Reformation in England

I. THE REFORMATION UNDER HENRY VIII

a. The Submission of the Clergy, 1532   *S.P.* Henry VIII. v. no. 1023, i
[a slightly different form in 1023, ii]

[In 1531 Henry imposed a fine on the Convocations for having committed a breach of the Praemunire Statute in accepting the legatine authority of Wolsey. At the same the two Houses had to recognize the King as Supreme Head of the Church in England (see below, pp. 242–3). In the next year, from which the English Reformation is usually dated, the following submission was made by Convocation, which was later embodied in the legislation of 1534, and, with that legislation, repealed by Mary and revived by Elizabeth.]

We your most humble subjects, daily orators and bedesmen of your clergy of England, having our special trust and confidence in your most excellent wisdom, your princely goodness and fervent zeal to the promotion of God's honour and Christian religion, and also in your learning, far exceeding, in our judgement, the learning of all others kings and princes that we have read of, and doubting nothing but that the same shall still continue and daily increase in your majesty—

First, do offer and promise, *in verbo sacerdotii*, here unto your highness, submitting ourselves most humbly to the same, that we will never from henceforth enact, put in use, promulge, or execute, any new canons or constitutions provincial, or any other new ordinance, provincial or synodal, in our Convocation or synod in time coming, which Convocation is, always has been, and must be, assembled only by your highness' commandment of writ, unless your highness by your royal assent shall license us to assemble our Convocation, and to make, promulge, and execute such constitutions and ordinances as shall be made in the same; and thereto give your royal assent and authority.

Secondly, that whereas divers of the constitutions, ordinances, and canons, provincial or synodal, which have been heretofore enacted, be thought to be not only much prejudicial to your royal prerogative, but also overmuch onerous to your highness' subjects, your clergy aforesaid is contented, if it may stand so with your highness' pleasure, that it be committed to the examination and judgement of your grace, and of thirty-two persons, whereof sixteen to be of the upper and nether house of the temporalty, and other sixteen of the clergy, all to be chosen and appointed by your most noble grace. So that, finally, whichsoever of the said constitutions, ordinances, or canons, provincial or synodal, shall be thought and determined by your grace and by the most part of the said thirty-two persons not to stand with God's laws and the laws of your realm, the same to be abrogated and repealed by your grace and the clergy; and such of them as shall seem to your grace, and by the most part of the said thirty-two persons, to stand with God's laws and the laws of your realm, to stand in full strength and power, your grace's most royal assent and authority once impetrate and fully given to the same.

b. The Legal Principle—The Restraint of Appeals, 1533   24 Henry VIII, cap. 12: *Statutes of Realm*, iii. 427. [G. and H. li]

[By the Act of Praemunire (above, p. 181) appeals to Rome were forbidden save with the king's consent. They were now unconditionally forbidden. This Act was repeated in 1534, repealed under Mary, and revived under Elizabeth.]

Whereas by divers sundry old authentic histories and chronicles, it is manifestly declared and expressed, that this realm of England is an empire, and so hath been accepted in the world, governed by one supreme head and king, having the dignity and royal estate of the imperial crown of the same, unto whom a body politic, compact of all sorts and degrees of people divided in terms and by names of spiritualty and temporalty, be bounden and ought to bear, next to God, a natural and humble obedience: he being also institute and furnished, by the goodness and sufferance of Almighty God, with plenary, whole, and entire power, pre-eminence, authority, prerogative and jurisdiction, to render and yield justice, and final determination to all manner of folk, residents, or subjects within this his realm, in all causes, matters, debates, and contentions, happening to occur, insurge, or begin within the limits thereof, without restraint, or provocation[1] to any foreign princes or potentates of the world; the body spiritual whereof having power when any cause of the law divine happened to come in question or of spiritual learning it was declared, interpreted, and showed by that part of the said body politic, called the spiritualty, now being usually called the English Church, which always hath been reputed, and also found of that sort, that both for knowledge, integrity, and sufficiency of number, it hath been always thought, and is also at this hour, sufficient and meet of itself, without the intermeddling of any exterior person or persons, to declare and determine all such doubts, and to administer all such offices and

---

[1] i.e. appeal.

duties, as to their rooms spiritual doth appertain; for the due administration whereof, and to keep them from corruption and sinister affection, the king's most noble progenitors, and the antecessors of the nobles of this realm, having sufficiently endowed the said Church, both with honour and possessions; and the laws temporal, for trial of property of lands and goods, and for the conservation of the people of this realm in unity and peace, without ravin or spoil, was and yet is administered, adjudged, and executed by sundry judges and ministers of the other part of the said body politic, called the temporalty; and both their authorities and jurisdictions do conjoin together in the due administration of justice, the one to help the other.

And whereas the king, his most noble progenitors, and the Nobility and Commons of this said realm, at divers and sundry Parliaments, as well in the time of King Edward I, Edward III, Richard II, Henry IV, and other noble kings of this realm, made sundry ordinances, laws, statutes, and provisions for the entire and sure conservation of the prerogatives, liberties, and pre-eminences of the said imperial crown of this realm, and of the jurisdiction spiritual and temporal of the same, to keep it from the annoyance as well of the see of Rome, as from the authority of other foreign potentates, attempting the diminution or violation thereof, as often, and from time to time, as any such annoyance or attempt might be known or espied.

And notwithstanding the said good statutes and ordinances ... divers and sundry inconveniences and dangers, not provided for plainly by the said former acts, statutes, and ordinances, have arisen and sprung by reason of appeals sued out of this realm to the see of Rome, in causes testamentary, causes of matrimony and divorces, right of tithes, oblations and obventions, not only to the great inquietation, vexation, trouble, cost and charges of the king's highness, and many of his subjects and residents in this his realm, but also to the great delay and let to the true and speedy determination of the said causes; for so much as the parties appealing to the said Court of Rome most commonly do the same for the delay of justice.

And forasmuch as the great distance of way is so far out of this realm, so that the necessary proofs, nor the true knowledge of the cause, can neither there be so well known, nor the witnesses there so well examined, as within this realm, so that the parties grieved by means of the said appeals be most times without remedy:

In consideration whereof the king's highness, his nobles and Commons, considering the great enormities, dangers, long delays and hurts, that as well to his highness, as to his said nobles, Commons, and residents of this his realm, in the said causes testamentary, etc. … do daily ensue, does therefore by his royal assent, and by the assent of the lords spiritual and temporal, and the Commons, in this present Parliament assembled, and by authority of the same, enact, establish, and ordain, that all causes testamentary, etc. (the knowledge whereof by the goodness of princes of this realm, and by the laws and customs of the same, appertaineth to the spiritual jurisdiction of this realm) already commenced, moved, depending, being, happening, or hereafter coming in contention, debate, or question within this realm, or within any the king's dominions, or marches of the same, or else-where, whether they concern the king our sovereign lord, his heirs and successors, or any other subjects or residents within the same, of what degree soever they be, shall be from henceforth heard, examined, discussed, clearly, finally, and definitively adjudged and determined within the king's jurisdiction and authority, and not elsewhere, in such courts spiritual and temporal of the same, as the natures, conditions, and qualities of the causes and matters aforesaid in contention, or hereafter happening in contention, shall require, without having any respect to any custom, use, or sufferance, in hindrance, let, or prejudice of the same, or to any other thing used or suffered to the contrary thereof by any other manner of person or persons in any manner of wise; any foreign inhibitions, appeals, sentences, summons, citations, suspensions, interdictions, excommunications, restraints, judgements, or any other process or impediments, of what natures, names, qualities, or conditions soever they be, from the see of Rome, or any other foreign courts or potentates of the world, or from and out of this realm, or any other the king's dominions, or marches of the same, to the see of Rome, or to any other foreign courts or potentates, to the let or impediment thereof in any wise notwithstanding.

And that it shall be lawful to the king our sovereign lord, and to his heirs and successors, and to all other subjects or residents within this realm, or within any the king's dominions, or marches of the same— notwithstanding that hereafter it should happen any excommengement, excommunications, interdictions, citations, or any other censures, or foreign process out of any outward parts, to be fulminate, provulged, declared, or put in execution within this said realm, or in any other place or places, for any of the causes before rehearsed, in prejudice, derogation, or contempt of this said Act, and the very true meaning and execution thereof—may and shall nevertheless as well pursue, execute, have, and enjoy the effects, profits, benefits, and commodities of all such processes, sentences, judgements, and determinations done, or hereafter to be done, in any of the said courts spiritual or temporal, as the cases shall require, within the limits, power, and authority of this the king's said realm, and dominions and marches of the same, and those only, and none other to take place, and to be firmly observed and obeyed within the same.

As also, that all the spiritual prelates, pastors, ministers, and curates within this realm, and the dominions of the same, shall and may use, minister, execute and do, or cause to be used, ministered, executed and done, all sacraments, sacramentals, divine services, and all other things within the said realm and dominions, unto all the subjects of the same, as catholic and Christian men ought to do; any former citations, processes, inhibitions, suspensions, interdictions, excommunications, or appeals, for or touching the causes aforesaid, from or to the see of Rome, or any other foreign prince or foreign courts, to the let or contrary thereof in any wise notwithstanding.

And if any of the said spiritual persons, by the occasion of the said fulminations of any of the same interdictions, censures, inhibitions, excommunications, appeals, suspensions, summons, or other foreign citations for the causes beforesaid, or for any of them, do at any time hereafter refuse to minister, or cause to be ministered, the said sacraments and sacramentals, and other divine services, in form as is aforesaid, shall for every such time or times that they or any of them do refuse so to do, or cause to be done, have one year's imprisonment, and to make fine and ransom at the king's pleasure.

And it is further enacted by the authority aforesaid, that if any person or persons inhabiting or resident within this realm, or within any of the king's said dominions, or marches of the same, or any other person or persons, of what estate, condition, or degree soever he or they be, at any time hereafter, for or in any the causes aforesaid, do attempt, move, purchase, or procure, from or to the see of Rome, or from or to any other foreign court or courts out of this realm, any manner foreign process, inhibitions, appeals, sentences, summons, citations, suspensions, interdictions, excommunications, restraints, or judgements, of what nature, kind, or quality soever they be, or execute any of the same process, or do any act or acts to the let, impediment, hindrance, or derogation of any process, sentence, judgement, or determination had, made, done, or hereafter to be had, done, or made, in any courts of this realm, or the king's said dominions, or marches of the same, for any of the causes aforesaid, contrary to the true meaning of this present Act, and the execution of the same, that then every such person or persons so doing, and their fautors, comforters, abettors, procurers, executors, and counsellors, and every of them, being convicted of the same, for every such default shall incur the same pains, penalties, and forfeitures, ordained and provided by the Statute of Provision and Praemunire, made in the sixteenth year of the reign of the right noble prince King Richard II, against such as attempt, procure, or make provision to the see of Rome, or elsewhere, for any thing or things, to the derogation, or contrary to the prerogative or jurisdiction of the crown and dignity of this realm.

And furthermore, in eschewing the said great enormities, inquietations, delays, charges, and expenses hereafter to be sustained in pursuing of such appeals, and foreign process, for and concerning the causes aforesaid, or any of them, do therefore by authority aforesaid, ordain and enact, that in such cases where heretofore any of the king's subjects or residents have used to pursue, provoke, or procure any appeal to the see of Rome, and in all other cases of appeals, in or for any of the causes aforesaid, they may and shall from henceforth take, have, and use their appeals within this realm, and not elsewhere, in manner and form as hereafter ensueth, and not otherwise; that is to say, first from the archdeacon, or his official, if the matter or cause be there begun, to the bishop diocesan of the said see, if in case any of the parties be grieved. And in like wise if it be commenced before the bishop diocesan, or his commissary, from the bishop diocesan, or his commissary, within fifteen days next ensuing the judgement or sentence thereof there given, to the Archbishop of the province of Canterbury, if it be within his province; and if it be within the province of York, then to the Archbishop of York; and so likewise to all other archbishops in other the king's dominions, as the case by order of justice shall require; and there to be definitively and finally ordered, decreed, and adjudged, according to justice, without any other appellation or provocation to any other person or persons, courts or courts. ...

[Appeals to be made within fifteen days. Suits before an archbishop to be determined by him, without appeal—saving the prerogative of the Archbishop of Canterbury in cases where appeal to him has been customary. Appeals in cases touching the king to be decided by the Upper House of Convocation.]

c. The Ecclesiastical Principle—The Dispensations Act, 1534 25 Henry VIII, cap. 21: *Statutes of the Realm*, iii. 464. [G. and H. liii]

Most humbly beseeching your most Royal Majesty, your obedient and faithful subjects, the Commons of this your present Parliament assembled, by your most dread commandment, that where your subjects of this your realm, and of other countries and dominions, being under your obeisance, by many years past have been, and yet be greatly decayed and impoverished, by such intolerable exactions of great sums of money as have been claimed and taken, and yet continually be claimed to be taken out of this your realm, and other your said countries and dominions, by the Bishop of Rome, called the pope, and the see of Rome, as well in pensions, censes, Peter-pence, procurations, fruits, suits for provisions, and expeditions of bulls for archbishoprics and bishoprics, and for delegacies, and rescripts in causes of contentions and appeals, jurisdictions legatine, and also for dispensations, licences, faculties, grants, relaxations, writs called *perinde valere*, rehabilitations, abolitions, and other infinite sorts of bulls, briefs, and instruments of sundry natures, names, and kinds, in great numbers heretofore practised and obtained otherwise than by the laws, laudable uses, and customs of this realm should be permitted, the specialities whereof be over long, large in number, and tedious here particularly to be inserted; wherein the Bishop of Rome aforesaid has not been only to be blamed for his usurpation in the premises, but also for his abusing and beguiling your subjects, pretending and persuading to them that he has full power to dispense with all human laws, uses, and customs of all realms, in all causes which be called spiritual, which matter has been usurped and practised by him and his predecessors by many years, in great derogation of your Imperial Crown and authority royal, contrary to right and conscience:

For where this your grace's realm recognizing no superior under God, but only your grace, has been and is free from subjection to any man's laws, but only to such as have been devised, made, and ordained within this realm, for the wealth of the same, or to such other as, by sufferance of your grace and your progenitors, the people of this your realm have taken at their free liberty, by their own consent to be used amongst them, and have bound themselves by long use and custom to the observance of the same, not as to the observance of the laws of any foreign prince, potentate, or prelate, but as to the accustomed and ancient laws of this realm, originally established as laws of the same, by the said sufferance, consents, and custom, and none otherwise:

It therefore stands with natural equity and good reason, that in all and every such laws human made within this realm, or induced into this realm by the said sufferance, consents, and custom, your Royal Majesty, and your Lords spiritual and temporal, and Commons, representing the whole state of your realm, in this your most High Court of Parliament, have full power and authority, not only to dispense, but also to authorize some elect person or persons to dispense with those, and all other human laws of this your realm, and with every one of them, as the quality of the persons and matters shall require; and also the said laws, and every of them, to abrogate, annul, amplify, or diminish, as it shall be seen unto your majesty, and the nobles and Commons of your realm present in your Parliament, meet and convenient for the wealth of your realm, as by divers good and wholesome Acts of Parliaments, made and established as well in your time, as in the time of your most noble progenitors, it may plainly and evidently appear:

And because that it is now in these days present seen, that the state, dignity, superiority, reputation, and authority of the said Imperial Crown of this realm, by the long sufferance of the said unreasonable and uncharitable usurpations and exactions practised in the times of your most noble progenitors, is much and sore decayed and diminished, and the people of this realm thereby impoverished, and so or worse be like to continue, if remedy be not therefore shortly provided:

It may therefore please your most noble majesty, for the honour of Almighty God, and for the tender love, zeal, and affection that ye bear, and always have borne to the wealth of this your realm and subjects of the same, forasmuch as your majesty is supreme head of the Church of England, as the prelates and clergy of your realm, representing the said Church, in their synods and convocations have recognized, in whom consisteth full power and authority, upon all such laws as have been made and used within this realm, to ordain and enact, by the assent of your lords spiritual and temporal, and the Commons in this your present Parliament assembled, and by authority of the same, that no person or persons of this your realm, or of any other your dominions, shall from henceforth pay any pensions, censes, portions, Peter-pence or any other impositions, to the use of the said bishop, or the see of Rome, like as heretofore they have used, by usurpation of the said Bishop of Rome and his predecessors, and sufferance of your highness, and your most noble progenitors, to do; but that all such pensions, censes, portions and Peter-pence, which the said Bishop of Rome, otherwise called the pope, has heretofore taken and perceived, or caused to be taken and perceived to his use, and his chambers which he calls apostolic, by usurpation and sufferance, as is above said, within this your realm, or any other your dominions, shall from henceforth clearly surcease, and never more be levied, taken, perceived, nor paid to any person or persons in any manner of wise; any constitution, use, prescription, or custom to the contrary thereof notwithstanding.

And be it further enacted by the authority aforesaid, that neither your highness, your heirs nor successors, kings of this realm, nor any your subjects of this realm, nor of any other your dominions, shall from henceforth sue to the said Bishop of Rome, called the pope, or to the see of Rome, or to any person or persons having or pretending any authority by the same, for licences, dispensations, compositions, faculties, grants, rescripts, delagacies, or any other instruments or writings, of what kind, name, nature, or quality soever they be of, for any cause or matter, for the which any licence, dispensation, composition, faculty, grant, rescript, delegacy, instrument, or other writing, heretofore has been used and accustomed to be had and obtained at the see of Rome, or by authority thereof, or of any prelate of this realm; nor for any manner of other licences, etc. ... that in causes of necessity may lawfully be granted without offending of the Holy Scriptures and laws of God:

But that from henceforth every such licence, etc., ... necessary for your highness, your heirs or successors, and your and their people and subjects, upon the due examinations of the causes and qualities of the persons procuring such licences, etc., ... shall be granted, had, and obtained, from time to time, within this your realm, and other your dominions, and not elsewhere, in manner and form following, and none otherwise; that is to say:

The Archbishop of Canterbury for the time being, and his successors, shall have power and authority, from time to time, by their discretions, to give, grant, and dispose, by an instrument under the seal of the said archbishop, unto your majesty, and to your heirs and successors, kings of this realm, as well all manner such licences, etc., ... for causes not being contrary or repugnant to the Holy Scriptures and laws of God, as heretofore has been used and accustomed to be had and obtained by your highness, or any your most noble progenitors, or any of your or their subjects, at the see of Rome, or any person or persons by authority of the same; and all other licences, dispensations, faculties, compositions, grants, rescripts, delegacies, instruments, and other writings, in, for, and upon all such causes and matters as shall be convenient and necessary to be had, for the honour and surety of your highness, your heirs and successors, and the wealth and profit of this your realm; so that the said archbishop, or any of his successors, in no manner wise shall grant any dispensation, licence, rescript, or any other writing afore rehearsed, for any cause or matter repugnant to the law of Almighty God.

Be it also enacted by authority aforesaid, that the said archbishop and his successors, after good and due examination, by them had, of the causes and qualities of the persons procuring for licences, dispensations, compositions, faculties, delegacies, rescripts, instruments, or other writings, shall have full power and authority by themselves, or by their sufficient and substantial commissary or deputy, by their discretions, from time to time, to grant and dispose, by an instrument under the name and seal of the said archbishop, as well as to any of your subjects, as to the subjects of your heirs and successors, all manner licences, dispensations, faculties, compositions, delegacies, rescripts, instruments, or other writings, for any such cause or matter, whereof heretofore such licences, dispensations, compositions, faculties, delegacies, rescripts, instruments, or writings, have been accustomed to be had at the see of Rome, or by authority thereof, or of any prelate of this realm. ...

And be it further enacted, that if the aforesaid Archbishop of Canterbury for the time being, or the said guardian of the spiritualities for the time being, hereafter refuse or deny to grant any licences, dispensations, faculties, instruments, or other writings, which they be authorized to do by virtue and authority of this Act, in such manner and form as is afore remembered, to any person or persons that ought, of a good, just, and reasonable cause, to have the same, by reason whereof this present Act, by their wilfulness, negligence, or default, should take no effect; then the Chancellor of England, or the lord keeper of the great seal for the time being, upon any complaint thereof made, shall direct the king's writ to the said archbishop or guardian denying or refusing to grant such licences, etc., enjoining him by the said writ, upon a certain pain therein to be limited by the discretion of the said chancellor or keeper of the great seal, that he shall in due form grant such licence, dispensation, faculty, or other writing, according to the request of the procurers of the same, or else signify unto your highness, your heirs or successors, in the Court of Chancery, at a certain day, for what occasion or cause he refused and denied to grant such licences, etc. ...

Provided always, that this Act, nor any thing or things therein contained, shall be hereafter interpreted or expounded, that your grace, your nobles and subjects, intend, by the same, to decline or vary from the congregation of Christ's Church in any things concerning the very articles of the Catholic faith of Christendom, or in any other things declared, by Holy Scripture and the word of God, necessary for your and their salvations, but only to make an ordinance by policies necessary and convenient to repress vice, and for good conservation of this realm in peace, unity, and tranquillity, from ravin and spoil, ensuing much the old ancient customs of this realm in that behalf; not minding to seek for any relief, succours, or remedies for any worldly things and human laws, in any cause of necessity, but, within this realm, at the hands of your highness, your heirs and successors, kings of this realm, which have and ought to have an imperial power and authority in the same, and not obliged, in any worldly causes, to any other superior.

Provided alway, that the said Archbishop of Canterbury, or any other person or persons, shall have no power or authority by reason of this Act, to visit or vex any monasteries, abbeys, priories, colleges, hospitals, houses, or other places religious, which be or were exempt, before the making of this Act, anything in this Act to the contrary thereof notwithstanding; but that redress, visitation, and confirmation shall be had by the king's highness, his heirs and successors, by commission under the great seal, to be directed to such persons as shall be appointed requisite for the same, in such monasteries, colleges, hospitals, priories, houses, and places religious exempt; so that no visitation nor confirmation shall from thenceforth be had nor made, in or at any such monasteries, colleges, hospitals, priories, houses, and places religious exempt, by the said Bishop of Rome, nor by any of his authority, nor by any out of the king's dominions; nor that any person, religious or other, resident in any the king's dominions shall henceforth depart out of the king's dominions to or for any visitation, congregation or assembly for religion, but that all such visitations, etc. shall be within the king's dominions. ...

d. The Supremacy Act, 1534   26 Henry VIII, cap. 1: *Statutes of the Realm*, iii. 492 [G. H. lv]

[In 1531 the Convocations recognized Henry as Supreme Head of the Church of England 'as far as the Law of Christ allows'—and they had given their assent to this by silence. The Supremacy Act dropped the saving clause. It was repealed by Mary, and confirmed, with altered wording, by Elizabeth (see below, p. 250).]

Albeit the king's majesty justly and rightfully is and ought to be the supreme head of the Church of England, and so is recognized by the clergy of this realm in their Convocations, yet nevertheless for corroboration and confirmation thereof, and for increase of virtue in Christ's religion within this realm of England, and to repress and extirp all errors, heresies, and other enormities and abuses heretofore used in the same; be it enacted by authority of this present Parliament, that the king our sovereign lord, his heirs and successors, kings of this realm, shall be taken, accepted, and reputed the only supreme head in earth of the Church of England, called *Anglicana Ecclesia*; and shall have and enjoy, annexed and united to the imperial crown of this realm, as well the title and style thereof, as all honours, dignities, pre-eminences, jurisdictions, privileges, authorities, immunities, profits and commodities to the said dignity of supreme head of the same Church belonging and appertaining; and that our said sovereign lord, his heirs and successors, kings of this realm, shall have full power and authority from time to time to visit, repress, redress, reform, order, correct, restrain, and amend all such errors, heresies, abuses, offences, contempts, and enormities, whatsoever they be, which by any manner spiritual authority or jurisdiction ought or may lawfully be reformed, repressed, ordered, redressed, corrected, restrained, or amended, most to the pleasure of Almighty God, the increase of virtue in Christ's religion, and for the conservation of the peace, unity, and tranquillity of this realm; any usage, custom, foreign law, foreign authority, prescription, or any other thing or things to the contrary hereof notwithstanding.

e. Abjuration of Papal Supremacy by the Clergy, 1534   G. and H. lviii

(1) By the Convocation of Canterbury, *Wilkins, iii. 769*

On the last day of March, in the presence of the most reverend Ralph Pexsall, the clerk of the crown in the chancery of the lord the king, in the name of the said king, presented a royal writ for summoning Convocation and proroguing it to the fourth day of November following. And afterwards was exhibited a writing by William Saye, notary public, concerning the answer of the Lower House to the question, viz. 'Whether the Roman pontiff has any greater jurisdiction bestowed on him by God in the Holy Scriptures in this realm of England, than any other foreign [*externus*] bishop?' Noes 34, doubtful 1, ayes 4.

(2) By the Convocation of York, *Wilkins, iii. 782*

By virtue of a royal writ this synod, convened on the fifteenth day of May, sent to the lord the king, by the archbishop's certificate, the sentence of their decision against the pope's supremacy: 'To the most illustrious and excellent prince and lord, the lord Henry VIII, by the grace of God king of England and France, defender of the faith, and lord of Ireland, Edward, by Divine permission archbishop of York, primate of England, and metropolitan, greeting. We make known and declare to your royal highness, by the tenor of the presents, that when according to the mandate of your royal majesty, the following conclusion was proposed in the presence of the prelates and clergy of the province of York, gathered together in the sacred synod of the province or Convocation of the prelates and clergy of the same province of York, held in the Chapter House of the metropolitan church of York, on the fifth day of May, in the present year of our Lord 1534, and continued from day to day: "That the Bishop of Rome has not, in Scripture, any greater jurisdiction in the kingdom of England than any other foreign bishop." And when further, on behalf of the presidents deputed by you in the same synod, the said prelates and clergy were asked and demanded to confirm and endorse that opinion by their consent, if they thought or judged it consonant to the truth and not repugnant to the Holy Scriptures; at length the said prelates and clergy of the province of York aforesaid, after careful discussion had in that behalf, and mature deliberation, unanimously and concordantly, with no dissentient, affirmed the conclusion above-mentioned to have been and to be true, and concordantly consented to the same. Which all and singular we notify to your highness by the tenor of the presents. In testimony of which, all and singular, we have caused our seal to be affixed to the presents. Given in our castle of Cawood, the second day of June, in the year of our Lord 1534, and the third of our consecration.'

f. **The Pope's Condemnation of Henry, 1535**   Bull of Paul III, *Eius qui immobilis*, dated 30 August 1535. *B.R.* vi. 195 ff.; Mirbt, 426 (selections)

[The Bull was not published in 1535, and it is doubtful if it ever achieved promulgation, for the Pope had difficulty in finding any prince prepared to carry it into effect.]

... § 7. But if King Henry and the others warned above shall not, within the aforesaid limits appointed for each of them, have appeared and if they have borne (which God forbid) with a hardened spirit the aforesaid sentence of excommunication for three days after the passing of the said limits, we lay upon them successively weightier censures. [We proclaim] that King Henry has incurred the penalty of deprivation of his kingdom and that they have been sundered for ever from all faithful Christians and their goods. And if meanwhile he depart from this life we decree and declare, with the authority and fullness of power aforesaid, that he ought to be deprived of Church burial and we smite them with the sword of anathema, malediction and eternal damnation. ...

§ 9. And let the sons of King Henry, his accomplices, abettors, etc. be partakers of the punishment, as in this case is equitable. We decree and declare that all the sons of King Henry, by the said Anne, and the sons of all the others aforementioned, born or to be born, and the rest of their descendants to that degree to which the penalties of wrath extend in cases of this kind (with no exception, and no consideration being taken of minority or sex or ignorance or any other excuse whatsoever), are deprived of all dignities and honours whatsoever in which they have been set, in which they rejoice, which they employ or have in possession or by which they are hedged about, together with the privileges, concessions, graces, indulgences, immunities, remissions, liberties and favours, also their domains, realms, castles, lands, estates, towns and all other possessions, moveable and immoveable, rights and activities in any way to them pertaining ... and we likewise decree and declare them incapable of holding these and such like in the future.

§ 10. ... And all the subjects of the same King Henry we do absolve and utterly release from their oath of fidelity, from their allegiance and from all kind of subjection to the King and the other persons aforementioned. Commanding them nevertheless, on pain of excommunication, that they utterly and entirely withdraw themselves from obedience to the said King Henry, his officials, judges and magistrates, and do not regard them as superiors nor obey their commands.

§ 11. And that the rest, terrified by their example, may learn to abstain from such excesses, we will and decree ... that King Henry, his accomplices, etc. ... together with the aforesaid descendants, be thereafter void of civil rights [*infames*] and be not admitted to testimony, be unable to leave or make wills, codicils or other dispositions, even among the living; and shall be incapable of succeeding to anything by will or from intestacy, and also incapable as regards jurisdiction, or the power of judging, the office of notary and all legal acts whatsoever (so that their processes or instruments and other acts whatsoever shall have no strength or validity); and none shall be held bound of right to make answer to the said Henry and the said other persons, in the matter of any debt or any matter, whether civil or criminal.

g. The Royal Injunctions (1) 1536. Cranmer's *Register*, fo. 97*b*. [G. and H. lxii]

[In 1536 the Ten Articles were drawn up by the King and approved by Convocation. In the same year Henry fulfilled his functions as 'supreme head' in the publication by Cromwell, as Vicar-General, of injunctions which had never been submitted to Convocation, as had been all his previous ecclesiastical measures.]

In the name of God, Amen. In the year of our Lord God 1536, and of the most noble reign of our sovereign lord Henry VIII, king of England and of France, the twenty-eighth year, and the —— day of ——, I, Thomas Cromwell, knight, Lord Cromwell, keeper of the privy seal of our said sovereign lord the king, and vicegerent unto the same, for and concerning all his jurisdiction ecclesiastical within this realm, visiting by the king's highness's supreme authority ecclesiastical the people and clergy of this deanery of —— by my trusty commissary —— lawfully deputed and constituted for this part, have to the glory of Almighty God, to the king's highness's honour, the public weal of this his realm, and increase of virtue in the same, appointed and assigned these injunctions ensuing, to be kept and observed of the dean, parsons, vicars, curates, and stipendiaries resident or having cure of souls, or any other spiritual administration within this deanery, under the pains hereafter limited and appointed.

The first is, that the dean, parsons, vicars, and others having cure of souls anywhere within this deanery, shall faithfully keep and observe, and as far as in them may lie, shall cause to be observed and kept of other, all and singular laws and statutes of this realm made for the abolishing and extirpation of the Bishop of Rome's pretensed and usurped power and jurisdiction within this realm, and for the establishment and confirmation of the king's authority and jurisdiction within the same, as of the supreme head of the Church of England, and shall to the uttermost of their wit, knowledge, and learning, purely, sincerely, and without any colour or dissimulation declare, manifest, and open for the space of one quarter of a year now next ensuing, once every Sunday, and after that at the leastwise twice every quarter, in their sermons and other collations, that the Bishop of Rome's usurped power and jurisdiction, having no establishment nor ground by the law of God, was of most just causes taken away and abolished; and therefore they owe unto him no manner of obedience or subjection, and that the king's power is within his dominion the highest power and potentate under God, to whom all men within the same dominion by God's commandment owe most loyalty and obedience, afore and above all other powers and potentates in earth.

Item, whereas certain Articles were lately devised and put forth by the king's highness's authority, and condescended upon by the prelates and clergy of this his realm, in Convocation, whereof part are necessary to be holden and believed for our salvation, and the other part do concern and touch certain laudable ceremonies, rites, and usages of the Church meet and convenient to be kept and used for a decent and a politic order in the same; the said dean, parsons, vicars, and other curates shall so open and declare in their said sermons and other collations the said Articles unto them that be under their cure, that they may plainly know and discern which of them be necessary to be believed and observed for their salvation; ...

Besides this, to the intent that all superstition and hypocrisy, crept into divers men's hearts, may vanish away, they shall not set forth or extol any images, relics, or miracles for any superstition or lucre, nor allure the people by any enticements to the pilgrimage of any saint, otherwise than is permitted in the Articles lately put forth by the authority of the king's majesty and condescended upon by the prelates and clergy of this his realm in Convocation, as though it were proper or peculiar to that saint to give commodity or that, seeing all goodness, health, and grace ought to be both asked and looked for only of God, as of the very Author of the same, and of none other, for without Him that cannot be given; but they shall exhort as well their parishioners as other pilgrims, that they do rather apply themselves to the keeping of God's commandments and fulfilling of His works of charity, persuading them that they shall please God more by the true exercising of their bodily labour, travail, or occupation, and providing for their families, than if they went about to the said pilgrimages; and that it shall profit more their soul's health, if they do bestow that on the poor and needy, which they would have bestowed upon the said images or relics. ...

(2) 1538. Ibid. *fo. 215*b. *[G. H. lxiii]*

[Drawn up by Cromwell, submitted to Cranmer, and sent by him to the archdeacons.]

Item, that you shall provide on this side the feast of Easter next coming, one book of the whole Bible of the largest volume,[1] in English, and the same set up in some convenient place within the said church that you have cure of, whereas your parishioners may most commodiously resort to the same, and read it; the charges of which book shall be rateably borne between you, the parson, and the parishioners aforesaid, that is to say, the one half by you, and the other half by them.

Item, that you shall discourage no man privily or apertly from the reading or hearing of the said Bible, but shall expressly provoke, stir, and exhort every person to read the same, as that which is the very lively word of God, that every Christian man is bound to embrace, believe, and follow, if he look to be saved; admonishing them nevertheless, to avoid all contention and altercation therein, and to use an honest sobriety in the inquisition of the true sense of the same, and refer the explication of obscure places to men of higher judgement in Scripture.

Item, that you shall every Sunday and holy day through the year openly and plainly recite to your parishioners twice or thrice together, or oftener, if need require, one particle or sentence of the 'Pater noster' or Creed, in English, to the intent they may learn the same by heart, and so from day to day to give them one like lesson or sentence of the same till they have learned the whole 'Pater noster' and Creed, in English, by rote; and as they be taught every sentence of the same by rote, you shall

---

[1] i.e. Cranmer's revision of Matthew's transaltion (based on Tyndale) of 1537; the source of the version of the psalms in the BCP.

expound and declare the understanding of the same unto them, exhorting all parents and householders to teach their children and servants the same, as they are bound in conscience to do, and that done, you shall declare unto them the Ten Commandments, one by one, every Sunday and holy day, till they be likewise perfect in the same.

Item, that you shall in confessions every Lent examine every person that comes to confession to you, whether they can recite the Articles of our faith and the 'Pater noster,' in English, and hear them say the same; particularly wherein if they be not perfect, you shall declare to the same; particularly wherein if they be not perfect, you shall declare to the same that every Christian person ought to know the same before they should receive the blessed Sacrament of the altar, and monish them to learn the same more perfectly by the next year following, or else like as they ought not to presume to come to God's board without perfect knowledge of the same; and if they do, it is to the great peril of their souls: so you shall declare unto them, that you look for other injunctions from the king's highness by that time, to stay and repel all such from God's board, as shall be found ignorant in the premises; whereof you do thus admonish them, to the intent they should both eschew the peril of their souls, and also the worldly rebuke that they might incur hereafter by the same.

Item, that you shall make, or cause to be made in the said church, and every other cure you have, one sermon every quarter of the year at the least, wherein you shall purely and sincerely declare the very gospel of Christ, and in the same exhort your hearers to the works of charity, mercy, and faith, specially prescribed and commanded in Scripture, and not to repose their trust of affiance in any other works devised by men's phantasies beside Scripture; as in wandering to pilgrimages, offering of money, candles, or tapers to images or relics, or kissing or licking the same, saying over a number of beads, not understood or minded on, or in such-like superstition, for the doing whereof you not only have no promise of reward in Scripture, but contrariwise, great threats and maledictions of God, as things tending to idolatry and superstition, which of all other offences God Almighty does most detest and abhor, for that the same diminishes most His honour and glory.

Item, that such feigned images as you know in any of your cures to be so abused with pilgrimages or offerings of anything made thereunto, you shall for avoiding that most detestable offence of idolatry forthwith take down and delay, and shall suffer from henceforth no candles, tapers, or images of wax to be set afore any image or picture, but only the light that commonly goeth across the church by the rood loft, the light before the

Sacrament of the altar, and the light about the sepulchre, which for the adorning of the church and divine service you shall suffer to remain; still admonishing your parishioners that images serve for none other purpose but as to be books of unlearned men that cannot know letters, whereby they might be otherwise admonished of the lives and conversation of them that the said images do represent; which images, if they abuse for any other intent than for such remembrances, they commit idolatry in the same to the great danger of their souls: and therefore the king's highness, graciously tendering the weal of his subjects' souls, has in part already, and more will hereafter travail for the abolishing of such images, as might be occasion of so great an offence to God, and so great a danger to the souls of his loving subjects.

h. The Six Articles, 1539   From the Six Articles Act, 31 Henry VIII, cap. 14: *Statutes of the Realm*, iii. 739. [G. and H. lxv]

[These Articles, 'the bloody whip with six strings,' were passed through Parliament in the presence and through the authority of the King. Cranmer opposed them, but he submitted and put away his wife. The attitude of the King, shown in these and in the Ten Articles, made any further advance in doctrinal reform impossible during his reign.]

First, that in the most blessed Sacrament of the altar, by the strength and efficacy of Christ's mighty word (it being spoken by the priest), is present really, under the form of bread and wine, the natural body and blood of our Saviour Jesus Christ, conceived of the Virgin Mary; and that after the consecration there remaineth no substance of bread or wine, nor any other substance, but the substance of Christ, God and man.

Secondly, that communion in both kinds is not necessary *ad salutem*, by the law of God, to all persons; and that it is to be believed, and not doubted of, but that in the flesh, under the form of bread, is the very blood; and with the blood, under the form of wine, is the very flesh; as well apart, as though they were both together.

Thirdly, that priests after the order of priesthood received, as afore, may not marry, by the law of God.

Fourthly, that vows of chastity or widowhood, by man or woman made to God advisedly, ought to be observed by the law of God; and that it exempts them from other liberties of Christian people, which without that they might enjoy.

Fifthly, that it is meet and necessary that private masses be continued and admitted in this the king's English church and congregation, as whereby good Christian people, ordering themselves accordingly, do receive both godly and goodly consolations and benefits; and it is agreeable also to God's law.

Sixthly, that auricular confession is expedient and necessary to be retained and continued, used and frequented in the Church of God.

II. THE ELIZABETHAN SETTLEMENT

a. **The Supremacy Act, 1559**   1 Elizabeth, cap. 1: *Statutes of the Realm*, iv, pt. i. 350. [G. and H. lxxix]

[This Act repealed the Heresy Act of Philip and Mary and their Repealing Act, revived ten Acts of Henry VIII, including those on Annates and Appeals, and renewed the Supremacy Act, but with the change of title from Supreme *Head* to Supreme *Governor*, with the implication rather of administrative than of legislative power.]

And to the intent that all usurped and foreign power and authority, spiritual and temporal, may for ever be clearly extinguished, and never to be used or obeyed within this realm, or any other your majesty's dominions or countries, may it please your highness that it may be further enacted by the authority aforesaid, that no foreign prince, person, prelate, state, or potentate, spiritual or temporal, shall at any time after the last day of this session of Parliamant, use, enjoy, or exercise any manner of power, jurisdiction, superiority, authority, pre-eminence or privilege, spiritual or ecclesiastical, within this realm, or within any other your majesty's dominions or countries that now be, or hereafter shall be, but from thenceforth the same shall be clearly abolished out of this realm, and all other your highness's dominions for ever; any statute, ordinance, custom, constitutions, or any other matter or cause whatsoever to the contrary in any wise notwithstanding.

And for the better observation and maintenance of this Act, may it please your highness that it may be further enacted by the authority aforesaid, that all and every archbishop, bishop, and all and every other ecclesiastical person, and other ecclesiastical officer and minister, of what estate, dignity, pre-eminence, or degree soever he or they be or shall be, and all and every temporal judge, justice, mayor, and other lay or temporal officer and minister, and every other person having your highness's fee or wages, within this realm or any your highness's dominions, shall make, take, and receive a corporal oath upon the evangelist, before such person or persons as shall please your highness, your heirs or successors, under the great seal of England to assign and name, to accept and to take the same according to the tenor and effect hereafter following, that is to say:

'I, *A. B.*, do utterly testify and declare in my conscience, that the queen's highness is the only supreme governor of this realm, and of all other her highness's dominions and countries, as well in all spiritual or ecclesiastical things or causes, as temporal, and that no foreign prince, person, prelate, state or potentate, has, or ought to have, any jurisdiction, power, superiority, pre-eminence, or authority ecclesiastical or spiritual, within this realm; and therefore I do utterly renounce and forsake all foreign jurisdictions, powers, superiorities, and authorities, and do promise that from henceforth I shall bear faith and true allegiance to the queen's highness, her heirs and lawful successors, and to my power shall assist and defend all jurisdictions, pre-eminences, privileges, and authorities granted or belonging to the queen's highness, her heirs and successors, or united and annexed to the imperial crown of this realm. So help me God, and by the contents of this book.'

b. Elizabeth's Act of Uniformity, 1559   1 Elizabeth, cap. 2: *Statues of the Realm*, iv, pt. i. 355. [G and H. lxxx]

[This was passed immediately after the Supremacy Act, to accompany the publication of the Prayer Book, which was the 1552 book with certain objectionable features removed. This Act was passed by Parliament without consulting Convocation: and all the spiritual peers in the Lords voted against it.]

Where at the death of our late sovereign lord King Edward VI there remained one uniform order of common service and prayer, and of the administration of sacraments, rites, and ceremonies in the Church of England, which was set forth in one book, intituled: The Book of Common Prayer, and Administration of Sacraments, and other rites and ceremonies in the Church of England; authorized by Act of Parliament holden in the fifth and sixth years of our said late sovereign lord King Edward VI, intituled: An Act for the uniformity of common prayer and administration of the sacraments; the which was repealed and taken away by Act of Parliament in the first year of the reign of our late sovereign lady Queen Mary, to the great decay of the due honour of God, and discomfort to the professors of the truth of Christ's religion:

Be it therefore enacted by the authority of this present Parliament, that the said statute of repeal, and everything therein contained, only concerning the said book, and the service, administration of sacraments, rites, and ceremonies contained or appointed in or by the said book, shall be void and of none effect, from and after the feast of the Nativity of St John Baptist next coming; and that the said book, with the order of service, and of the administration of sacraments, rites, and ceremonies, with the alterations and additions therein added and appointed by this statute, shall stand and be, from and after the said feast of the Nativity of St John Baptist, in full force and effect, according to the tenor and effect of this statute; anything in the aforesaid statute of repeal to the contrary notwithstanding.

And further be it enacted by the queen's highness, with the assent of the Lords and Commons in this present Parliament assembled, and by authority of the same, that all and singular ministers in any cathedral or Parish church, or other place within this realm of England, Wales, and the marches of the same, or other the queen's dominions, shall from and after the feast of the Nativity of St John Baptist next coming be bounden to say and use the Matins, Evensong, celebration of the Lord's Supper and administration of each of the sacraments, and all their common and open prayer, in such order and form as is mentioned in the said book, so authorized by Parliament in the said fifth and sixth years of the reign of King Edward VI, with one alteration or addition of certain lessons to be used on every Sunday in the year,[1] and the form of the Litany altered and corrected,[2] and two sentences only added in the delivery of the sacrament to the communicants,[3] and none other or otherwise.

And that if any manner of parson, vicar, or other whatsover minister, that ought or should sing or say common prayer mentioned in the said book, or minister the sacraments, from and after the feast of the Nativity of St John Baptist next coming, refuse to use the said common prayers, or to minister the sacraments in such cathedral or parish church, or other places as he should use to minister the same, in such order and form as they be mentioned and set forth in the said book, or shall, wilfully or obstinately standing in the same, use any other rite, ceremony, order, form, or manner of celebrating of the Lord's Supper, openly or privily, or Matins, Evensong, administration of the sacraments, or other open prayers, than is mentioned and set forth in the said book (open prayer in and throughout this Act, is meant that prayer which is for other to

---

[1] Proper Lessons for Sundays were given in 1st PB of Edw. VI (1549), but omitted in the 1552 Book.

[2] The more important changes were: the omission of the deprecation, 'From the tyranny of the bishop of Rome and all his detestable enormities,' which appeared in 1549 and 1552, and the inclusion of the *Prayer of the Queen's Majesty*, and the *Prayer for the Clergy and People*, which have been, since 1662, included in Morning and Evening Prayer.

[3] In the 1549 Book the words of administration were, 'The body (blood) of our Lord Jesus Christ which was given (shed) for thee, preserve thy body and soul unto everlasting life.' In 1552 there was substituted, 'Take and eat this (Drink this) in remembrance that Christ died (Christ's blood was shed) for thee, and feed on him in thy heart by faith with thanksgiving (and be thankful).' The two forms were combined in 1559 and retained thus in 1662.

come unto, or hear, either in common churches or private chapels or oratories, commonly called the service of the Church), or shall preach, declare, or speak anything in the derogation or depraving of the said book, or anything therein contained, or of any part thereof, and shall be thereof lawfully convicted, according to the laws of this realm, by verdict of twelve men, or by his own confession, or by the notorious evidence of the fact, shall lose and forfeit to the queen's highness, her heirs and successors, for his first offence, the profit of all his spiritual benefices or promotions coming or arising in the one whole year next after his conviction; and also that the person so convicted shall for the same offence suffer imprisonment by the space of six months, without bail or mainprize.

And if any such person once convicted of any offence concerning the premises, shall after his first conviction eftsoons offend, and be thereof, in form aforesaid, lawfully convicted, that then the same person shall for his second offence suffer imprisonment by the space of one whole year, and also shall therefor be deprived, *ipso facto*, of all his spiritual promotions; and that it shall be lawful to all patrons or donors of all and singular the same spiritual promotions, or of any of them, to present or collate to the same, as though the person and persons so offending were dead.

And that if any such person or persons, after he shall be twice convicted in form aforesaid, shall offend against any of the premises the third time, and shall be thereof, in form aforesaid, lawfully convicted, that then the person so offending and convicted the third time, shall be deprived, *ipso facto*, of all his spiritual promotions, and also shall suffer imprisonment during his life.

And if the person that shall offend, and be convicted in form aforesaid, concerning any of the premises, shall not be beneficed, nor have any spiritual promotion, that then the same person so offending and convicted shall for the first offence suffer imprisonment during one whole year next after his said conviction, without bail or mainprize. And if any such person, not having any spiritual promotion, after his first conviction shall eftsoons offend in anything concerning the premises, and shall be, in form aforesaid, thereof lawfully convicted, that then the same person shall for his second offence suffer imprisonment during his life.

And it is ordained and enacted by the authority aforesaid, that if any person or persons whatsoever, after the said feast of the Nativity of St John Baptist next coming, shall in any interludes, plays, songs, rhymes, or by other open words, declare or speak anything in the derogation, depraving, or despising of the same book, or of anything therein contained, or any part thereof, or shall, by open fact, deed, or by open threatenings, compel or cause, or otherwise procure or maintain, any parson, vicar, or other minister in any cathedral or parish church, or in chapel, or in any other place, to sing or say any common or open prayer, or to minister any sacrament otherwise, or in any other manner and form, than is mentioned in the said book; or that by any of the said means shall unlawfully interrupt or let any parson, vicar, or other minister in any cathedral or parish church, chapel, or any other place, to sing or say common and open prayer, or to minister the sacraments or any of them, in such manner and form as is mentioned in the said book; that then every such person, being thereof lawfully convicted in form abovesaid, shall forfeit to the queen our sovereign lady, her heirs and successors, for the first offence a hundred marks.

And if any person or persons, being once convicted of any such offence, eftsoons offend against any of the last recited offences, and shall, in form aforesaid, be thereof lawfully convicted, that then the same person so offending and convicted shall, for the second offence, forfeit to the queen our sovereign lady, her heirs and successors, four hundred marks.

And if any person, after he, in form aforesaid, shall have been twice convicted of any offence concerning any of the last recited offences, shall offend the third time, and be thereof, in form abovesaid, lawfully convicted, that then every person so offending and convicted shall for his third offence forfeit to our sovereign lady the queen all his goods and chattels, and shall suffer imprisonment during his life.

And if any person or persons, that for his offence concerning the premises shall be convicted, in form aforesaid, do not pay the sum to be paid by virtue of his conviction, in such manner and form as the same ought to be paid, within six weeks next after his conviction; that then every person so convicted, and so not paying the same, shall for the same first offence, instead of the said sum, suffer imprisonment by the space of six months, without bail or mainprize. And if any person or persons, that for his second offence concerning the premises shall be convicted in form aforesaid, do not pay the said sum to be paid by virtue of his conviction and this statute, in such manner and form as the same ought to be paid, within six weeks next after his said second conviction; that then every person so convicted, and not so paying the same, shall, for the same second offence, in the stead of the said sum, suffer imprisonment during twelve months, without bail or main-prize.

And that from and after the said feast of the Nativity of St John Baptist next coming, all and every person and persons inhabiting within this realm, or any other the queen's majesty's dominions, shall diligently and faithfully, having no lawful or reasonable excuse to be absent, endeavour themselves to resort to their parish church or chapel accustomed, or upon reasonable let thereof, to some usual place where common prayer and such service of God shall be used in such time of let, upon every Sunday and other days ordained and used to be kept as holy days, and then and there to abide orderly and soberly during the time of the common prayer, preachings, or other service of God there to be used and ministered; upon pain of punishment by the censures of the Church, and also upon pain that every person so offending shall forfeit for every such offence twelve pence, to be levied by the churchwardens of the parish where such offence shall be done, to the use of the poor of the same parish, of the goods, lands, and tenements of such offender, by way of distress.

And for due execution hereof, the queen's most excellent majesty, the Lords temporal (*sic*), and all the Commons, in this present Parliament assembled, do in God's name earnestly require and charge all the arch-bishops, bishops, and other ordinaries, that they shall endeavour them-selves to the uttermost of their knowledges, that the due and true execution hereof may be had throughout their dioceses and charges, as they will answer before God, for such evils and plagues wherewith Almighty God may justly punish His people for neglecting this good and wholesome law. ...

c. **Parker's 'Advertisements', 1566** G. and H. lxxxi

[The *Advertisements* were an attempt to enforce a minimum observance upon all, with reference to the 'Vestiarian Controversy,' between the Puritans, who sought to do away with all ecclesiastical vestments as with all other outward symbols, and those who sought to maintain at least enough of the ancient usages to point to the continuity of the Church of England with the past. The *Advertisements* appear to have been issued on Parker's own authority as Archbishop.]

Articles for Doctrine and Preaching

First, that all they, which shall be admitted to preach, shall be diligently examined for their conformity in unity of doctrine, established by public authority; and admonished to use sobriety and discretion in teaching the people, namely, in matters of controversy; and to consider the gravity of their office, and to foresee with diligence the matters which they will speak, to utter them to the edification of the audience.

Item, that they set out in their preaching the reverent estimation of the holy sacraments of Baptism and the Lord's Supper, exciting the people to the often and devout receiving of the Holy Communion of the Body and Blood of Christ, in such form as is already prescribed in the Book of Common Prayer, and as it is further declared in a Homily concerning the virtue and efficacy of the said sacraments. ...

Articles for Administration of Prayer and Sacraments

First, that the common prayer be said or sung decently and distinctly, in such place as the ordinary shall think meet for the largeness and straitness of the church and choir, so that the people may be most edified.

Item, that no parson or curate, not admitted by the bishop of the diocese to preach, do expound in his own cure, or elsewhere, any Scripture or matter of doctrine, or by the way of exhortation, but only study to read gravely and aptly, without any glossing of the same, or any additions, the Homilies already set out, or other such necessary doctrine as is or shall be prescribed for the quiet instruction and edification of the people. ...

Item, in the ministration of the Holy Communion in cathedral and collegiate churches, the principal minister shall use a cope with gospeller and epistoler agreeably; and at all other prayers to be said at the Communion Table, to use no copes but surplices.

Item, that the dean and prebendaries wear a surplice with a silk hood in the choir; and when they preach in the cathedral or collegiate church, to wear their hood.

Item, that every minister saying any public prayers, or ministering the sacraments or other rites of the Church, shall wear a comely surplice with sleeves, to be provided at the charges of the parish; and that the parish provide a decent table standing on a frame for the Communion Table.

Item, that they shall decently cover with carpet, silk, or other decent covering, and with a fair linen cloth (at the time of the ministration) the Communion Table, and to set the Ten Commandments upon the east wall over the said table.

Item, that all communicants do receive kneeling, and as is appointed by the laws of the realm and the queen's majesty's Injunctions. ...

d. The Papal Bull against Elizabeth, 1570 Bull of Pius V, *Regnans in excelsis: B.R.* vii. 810ff. Extracts in Mirbt, 491

[The Pope called upon France and Spain to carry out this Bull. 'From that moment until the defeat of the Spanish Armada in 1588 there was war, more or less overt, between England and the counter-reformation. On the one side was the unconquerable patriotism of Englishmen, on the other the combined forces of political ambition and religious enthusiasm' (H. O. Wakeman, *History of the Church of England*, 335).]

He that reigns in the highest, to whom has been given all power in heaven and earth, entrusted the government of the one Holy Catholic and Apostolic Church (outside which there is no salvation) to one man alone on the earth, namely to Peter, the chief of the Apostles, and to Peter's successor, the Roman pontiff, in fullness of power [*potestatis plenitudo*]. This one man he set up as chief over all nations and all kingdoms, to pluck up, destroy, scatter, dispose, plant and build. ...

§ 3. ... Resting then upon the authority of him who has willed to place us (albeit unequal to such a burden) in this supreme throne of justice, we declare the aforesaid Elizabeth a heretic and an abettor of heretics, and those that cleave to her in the aforesaid matters to have incurred the sentence of anathema, and to be cut off from the unity of Christ's body.

§ 4. Moreover we declare her to be deprived of her pretended right to the aforesaid realm, and from all dominion, dignity and privilege whatsoever.

§ 5. And the nobles, subjects and peoples of the said realm, and all others who have taken an oath of any kind to her we declare to be absolved for ever from such oath and from all dues of dominion, fidelity and obedience, as by the authority of these presents we do so absolve them; and we deprive the said Elizabeth of her pretended right to the realm and all other things aforesaid: and we enjoin and forbid all and several the nobles, etc. ... that they presume not to obey her and her admonitions, commands, and laws. All who disobey our command we involve in the same sentence of anathema.

e. Act against Jesuits and Seminarists, 1585   27 Elizabeth, cap. 2: *Statutes of the Realm*, iv, pt. i. 706. [G. and H. lxxxv]

[The Bull *Regnans in excelsis* (above) had made all Romanists potential traitors. In 1568 the seminary at Douai was founded to train missionaries for England, and in 1580 the Jesuits Campion and Parsons landed.]

Whereas divers persons called or professed Jesuits, seminary priests, and other priests, which have been, and from time to time are, made in the parts beyond the seas, by or according to the order and rites of the Romish Church, have of late years come and been sent, and daily do come and are sent, into this realm of England and other the queen's majesty's dominions, of purpose (as has appeared, as well by sundry of their own examinations and confessions, as by divers other manifest means and proofs) not only to withdraw her highness's subjects from their due obedience to her majesty, but also to stir up and move sedition, rebellion, and open hostility within the same her highness's realms and dominions, to the great endangering of the safety of her most royal person, and to the utter ruin, desolation, and overthrow of the whole realm, if the same be not the sooner by some good means foreseen and prevented:

For reformation whereof be it ordained, established, and enacted by the queen's most excellent majesty, and the Lords spiritual and temporal, and the Commons, in this present Parliament assembled, and by the authority of the same Parliament, that all and every Jesuits, seminary priests, and other priests whatsoever made or ordained out of the realm of England or other her highness's dominions, or within any of her majesty's realms or dominions, by any authority, power, or jurisdiction derived, challenged, or pretended from the see of Rome, since the feast of the Nativity of St John Baptist in the first year of her highness's reign, shall within forty days next after the end of this present session of Parliament depart out of this realm of England, and out of all other her highness's realms and dominions, if the wind, weather, and passage shall serve for the same, or else so soon after the end of the said forty days as the wind, weather, and passage shall so serve. ...

Provided also, that this Act, or anything therein contained, shall not in anywise extend to any such Jesuit, seminary priest, or other such priest, deacon, or religious or ecclesiastical person as is before mentioned, as shall at any time within the said forty days, or within three days after that he shall hereafter come into this realm, or any other her highness's dominions, submit himself to some archbishop or bishop of this realm, or to some justice of peace within the country where he shall arrive or land, and do thereupon truly and sincerely, before the same archbishop, bishop, or such justice of peace, take the said oath set forth in *anno primo*, and by writing under his hand confess and acknowledge, and from thenceforth continue, his due obedience unto her highness's laws, statutes, and ordinances. ...

f. **Act against Puritans, 1593**   35 Elizabeth, cap i: *Statutes of the Realm*, iv, pt. ii. 841. [G. and H. lxxxvi]

For the preventing and avoiding of such great inconveniences and perils as might happen and grow by the wicked and dangerous practices of seditious sectaries and disloyal persons; be it enacted by the Queen's most excellent majesty, and by the Lords spiritual and temporal, and the Commons, in this present Parliament assembled, and by the authority of the same, that if any person or persons above the age of sixteen years, which shall obstinately refuse to repair to some church, chapel, or usual place of common prayer, to hear divine service established by her majesty's laws and statutes in that behalf made, and shall forbear to do the same by the space of a month next after, without lawful cause, shall at any time after forty days next after the end of this session of Parliament, by printing, writing, or express words or speeches, advisedly and purposely practise or go about to move or persuade any of her majesty's subjects, or any other within her highness's realms or dominions, to deny, withstand, and impugn her majesty's power and authority in causes ecclesiastical, united, and annexed to the imperial crown of this realm; or to that end or purpose shall advisedly and maliciously move or persuade any other person whatsoever to forbear or abstain from coming to church to hear divine service, or to receive the communion according to her majesty's laws and statutes aforesaid, or to come to or be present at any unlawful assemblies, conventicles, or meetings, under colour or pretence of any exercise of religion, contrary to her majesty's said laws and statutes; or if any person or persons which shall obstinately refuse to repair to some church, chapel, or usual place of common prayer, and shall forbear by the space of a month to hear divine service, as is aforesaid, shall after the said forty days, either of him or themselves, or by the motion, persuasion, enticement, or allurement of any other, willingly join, or be present at, any such assemblies, conventicles, or meetings, under colour or pretence of any such exercise of religion, contrary to the laws and statutes of this realm, as is aforesaid, that then every such person so offending as aforesaid, and being thereof lawfully convicted, shall be committed to prison, there to remain without bail or mainprize, until they shall conform and yield themselves to come to some church, chapel, or usual place of common prayer, and hear divine service, according to her majesty's laws and statutes aforesaid, and to make such open submission and declaration of their said conformity, as hereafter in this Act is declared and appointed.

g. Act against Recusants, 1593   35 Elizabeth, cap. 2: *Statutes of the Realm*, iv, pt. ii. 843 [G. and H. lxxxvii]

[The culmination of the Elizabethan anti-Roman legislation.]

For the better discovering and avoiding of all such traitorous and most dangerous conspiracies and attempts as are daily devised and practised against our most gracious sovereign lady the queen's majesty and the happy estate of this commonweal, by sundry wicked and seditious persons, who, terming themselves Catholics, and being indeed spies and intelligencers, not only for her majesty's foreign enemies, but also for rebellious and traitorous subjects born within her highness's realms and dominions, and hiding their most detestable and devilish purposes under a false pretext of religion and conscience, do secretly wander and shift from place to place within this realm, to corrupt and seduce her majesty's subjects, and to stir them to sedition and rebellion:

Be it ordained and enacted by our sovereign lady the queen's majesty, and the Lords spiritual and temporal, and the Commons, in this present Parliament assembled, and by the authority of the same, that every person above the age of sixteen years, born within any of the queen's majesty's realms and dominions, or made denizen, being a popish recusant, and before the end of this session of Parliament, convicted for not repairing to some church, chapel, or usual place of common prayer, to hear divine service there, for forbearing the same, contrary to the tenor of the laws and statutes heretofore made and provided in that behalf, and having any certain place of dwelling and abode within this realm, shall within forty days next after the end of this session of Parliament (if they be within this realm, and not restrained or stayed either by imprisonment, or by her majesty's commandment, or by order and direction of some six or more of the privy council, or by such sickness or infirmity of body, as they shall not be able to travel without imminent danger of life, and in such cases of absence out of the realm, restraint, or stay, then within twenty days next after they shall return into the realm, and be enlarged of such imprisonment or restraint, and shall be able to travel) repair to their place of dwelling where they usually heretofore made their common abode, and shall not, any time after, pass or remove above five miles from thence. ...

And furthermore be it enacted by the authority of this present Parliament, that if any person, or persons, that shall at any time hereafter offend against this Act, shall before he or they shall be thereof convicted come to some parish church on some Sunday or other festival day, and then and there hear divine service, and at service-time, before the sermon, or reading of the gospel, make public and open submission and declaration of his and their conformity to her majesty's laws and statutes, as hereafter in this Act is declared and appointed; that then the same offender shall thereupon be clearly discharged of and from all and every pains and forfeitures inflicted or imposed by this Act for any of the said offences in this Act contained: the same submission to be made as hereafter follows, that is to say:

'I, *A. B.*, do humbly confess and acknowledge, that I have grievously offended God in contemning her majesty's godly and lawful government and authority, by absenting myself from church, and from hearing divine service, contrary to the godly laws and statutes of this realm: and I am heartily sorry for the same, and do acknowledge and testify in my conscience, that the bishop or see of Rome has not, nor ought to have, any power or authority over her majesty, or within any her majesty's realms or dominions: and I do promise and protest, without any dissimulation, or any colour or means of any dispensation, that from henceforth I will from time to time obey and perform her majesty's laws and statutes, in repairing to the church, and hearing divine service, and do my uttermost endeavour to maintain and defend the same.'

And that every minister or curate of every parish, where such submission and declaration of conformity shall hereafter be so made by any such offender as aforesaid, shall presently enter the same into a book to be kept in every parish for that purpose, and within ten days then next following shall certify the same in writing to the bishop of the same diocese. ...

SECTION X

The Roman Catholic Church from the Counter-Reformation to the Second Vatican Council

I. THE JESUITS

[The Society of Jesus, founded by Ignatius Loyola (1491–1556), was skilfully organized into a great force for the conservation and propagation of the Roman Catholic Church. The Society started with six friends, in 1534, but it was not until 1540 that Pope Paul III could be induced to give his approval. The following extracts are given to show the spirit of obedience which served to make the Society such a mighty influence of propaganda.]

a. Rules for Thinking with the Church Ignatius Loyola, *Spiritual Exercises*, part ii

1. Always to be ready to obey with mind and heart, setting aside all judgement of one's own, the true spouse of Jesus Christ, our holy mother, our infallible and orthodox mistress, the Catholic Church, whose authority is exercised over us by the hierarchy.

2. To commend the confession of sins to a priest as it is practised in the Church; the reception of the Holy Eucharist once a year, or better still every week, or at least every month, with the necessary preparation.

3. To commend to the faithful frequent and devout assistance at the holy sacrifice of the Mass, the ecclesiastical hymns, the divine office, and in general the prayers and devotions practised at stated times, whether in public in the churches or in private.

4. To have a great esteem for the religious orders, and to give the preference to celibacy or virginity over the married state.

5. To approve of the religious vows of chastity, poverty, perpetual obedience, as well as to the other works of perfection and supererogation. Let us remark in passing, that we must never engage by vow to take a state (such e.g. as marriage) that would be an impediment to one more perfect. ...

6. To praise relics, the veneration and invocation of Saints: also the stations, and pious pilgrimages, indulgences, jubilees, the custom of lighting candles in the churches, and other such aids to piety and devotion.

7. To praise the use of abstinence and fasts as those of Lent, of Ember Days, of Vigils, of Friday, of Saturday, and of others undertaken out of pure devotion: also voluntary mortifications, which we call penances, not merely interior, but exterior also.

8. To commend moreover the construction of churches, and ornaments; also images, to be venerated with the fullest right, for the sake of what they represent.

9. To uphold especially all the precepts of the Church, and not censure them in any manner; but, on the contrary, to defend them promptly, with reasons drawn from all sources, against those who criticize them.

10. To be eager to commend the decrees, mandates, traditions, rites and customs of the Fathers in the Faith or our superiors. As to their conduct; although there may not always be the uprightness of conduct that there ought to be, yet to attack or revile them in private or in public tends to scandal and disorder. Such attacks set the people against their princes and pastors; we must avoid such reproaches and never attack superiors before inferiors. The best course is to make private approach to those who have power to remedy the evil.

11. To value most highly the sacred teaching, both the Positive[1] and the Scholastic, as they are commonly called. ...

---

[1] i.e. dogmatic, defined in formularies and decrees, as opposed to the philosophical speculations of scholasticism.

12. It is a thing to be blamed and avoided to compare men who are still living on the earth (however worthy of praise) with the Saints and Blessed, saying: This man is more learned than St Augustine, etc. ...

13. That we may be altogether of the same mind and in conformity with the Church herself, if she shall have defined anything to be black which to our eyes appears to be white, we ought in like manner to pronounce it to be black. For we must undoubtingly believe, that the Spirit of our Lord Jesus Christ, and the Spirit of the Orthodox Church His Spouse, by which Spirit we are governed and directed to Salvation, is the same; ...

14. It must also be borne in mind, that although it be most true, that no one is saved but he that is predestinated, yet we must speak with circumspection concerning this matter, lest perchance, stressing too much the grace or predestination of God, we should seem to wish to shut out the force of free will and the merits of good works; or on the other hand, attributing to these latter more than belongs to them, we derogate meanwhile from the power of grace.

15. For the like reason we should not speak on the subject of predestination frequently; if by chance we do so speak, we ought so to temper what we say as to give the people who hear no occasion of erring and saying, 'If my salvation or damnation is already decreed, my good or evil actions are predetermined'; whence many are wont to neglect good works, and the means of salvation.

16. It also happens not unfrequently, that from immoderate preaching and praise of faith, without distinction or explanation added, the people seize a pretext for being lazy with regard to any good works, which precede faith, or follow it when it has been formed by the bond of charity.

17. Nor any more must we push to such a point the preaching and inculcating of the grace of God, as that there may creep thence into the minds of the hearers the deadly error of denying our faculty of free will. We must speak of it as the glory of God requires ... that we may not raise doubts as to liberty and the efficacy of good works.

18. Although it is very praiseworthy and useful to serve God through the motive of pure charity, yet we must also recommend the fear of God; and not only filial fear, but servile fear, which is very useful and often even necessary to raise man from sin. ... Once risen from the state, and free from the affection of mortal sin, we may then speak of that filial fear which is truly worthy of God, and which gives and preserves the union of pure love.

b. Obedience of the Jesuits   *Const.* vi. 1 [Institutum I, 407 f.]: Mirbt, 431

Let us with the utmost pains strain every nerve of our strength to exhibit this virtue of obedience, firstly to the Highest Pontiff, then to the Superiors of the Society; so that in all things, to which obedience can be extended with charity, we may be most ready to obey his voice, just as if it issued from Christ our Lord ... , leaving any work, even a letter, that we have begun and have not yet finished; by directing to this goal all our strength and intention in the Lord, that holy obedience may be made perfect in us in every respect, in performance, in will, in intellect; by submitting to whatever may be enjoined on us with great readiness, with spiritual joy and perseverance; by persuading ourselves that all things [commanded] are just; by rejecting with a kind of blind obedience all opposing opinion or judgement of our own; and that in all things which are ordained by the Superior where it cannot be clearly held [*definiri*] that any kind of sin intervenes. And let each one persuade himself that they that live under obedience ought to allow themselves to be borne and ruled by divine providence working through their Superiors exactly as if they were a corpse which suffers itself to be borne and handled in any way whatsoever; or just as an old man's stick which serves him who holds it in his hand wherever and for whatever purpose he wish to use it. ...

II. THE COUNCIL OF TRENT, 1545–63

[The Popes were for long unwilling to agree to a Council, but the Empire threatened a Council on German soil, and the Pope agreed. Trent was fixed on as an Imperial city. The Council had three distinct periods, 1545–50, 1550–52 (during which Protestant deputations from Germany were admitted), and after Charles's abdication and the Peace of Augsburg, 1562–64.]

a. On Scripture and Tradition

Session IV, 8 April 1546   *Concilium Tridentinum, Diariorum, etc. Nova Collectio* (Freiburg, 1901–), v. 91. Denzinger, 783

The Holy, Oecumenical and General Synod of Trent ... having this aim always before its eyes, that errors may be removed and the purity of the Gospel be preserved in the Church, which was before promised through the prophets in the Holy Scriptures and which our Lord Jesus Christ the Son of God first published by his own mouth and then commanded to be preached through his Apostles to every creature as a source of all saving truth and of discipline of conduct; and perceiving that this truth and this discipline are contained in written books and in unwritten traditions, which were received by the Apostles from the lips of Christ himself, or, by the same Apostles, at the dictation of the Holy Spirit, and were handed on and have come down to us; following the example of the orthodox Fathers, this Synod receives and venerates, with equal pious affection and reverence, all the books both of the New and the Old Testaments, since one God is the author of both, together with the said Traditions, as well those pertaining to faith as those pertaining to morals, as having been given either from the lips of Christ or by the dictation of the Holy Spirit and preserved by unbroken succession in the Catholic Church. ...

b. On Original Sin

Session V, 17 June 1546 *C. Tr.* v. 238 ff. Denzinger, 788 ff.

1. If any one does not confess that the first man Adam, when he had transgressed the command of God in Paradise, straightway lost that holiness and righteousness in which he had been established, and through the offence of this disobedience incurred the wrath and indignation of God, and therefore incurred death, which God had before threatened to him, and with death, captivity under the power of him who thereafter had the power of death, namely the devil, and that the whole of Adam, through the offence of that disobedience, was changed for the worse in respect of body and soul: let him be anathema.

2. If any one asserts that the disobedience of Adam injured only himself and not his offspring ... or that ... only death and the pains of the body were transferred to the whole human race, and not the sin also, which is the death of the soul: let him be anathema [Rom. v. 12].

3. If any one asserts that the sin of Adam—which in origin is one and which has been transmitted to all mankind by propagation, not through imitation, and is in every man and belongs to him—can be removed either by man's natural powers or by any other remedy than the merit of the one mediator our Lord Jesus Christ ...

4. If any one denies that infants who have just issued from their mother's womb are to be baptized, even if born of baptized parents, or says that they are indeed baptized for the remission of sins but that they are not infected with any original sin from Adam such as would need expiation by the laver of regeneration for the attainment of eternal life; whence it follows that in regard to them the formula of baptism for remission of sins is to be understood not in its true but in a false sense ...

c. On Justification

Session VI, January 1547   *C. Tr.* v. 797 ff. Denzinger, 811 ff.

Canons on Justification

[The following propositions, among others, were anathematized.]

1. That man can be justified before God by his own works, which are done either in the strength of human nature or through the teaching of the law, apart from the divine grace through Jesus Christ.

2. That this grace is given through Jesus Christ solely to the end that a man may be able more easily to live justly and to earn eternal life, as if he could, though with great difficulty, do both these through his free will, without grace.

3. That without the prevenient inspiration of the Holy Spirit and his aid a man can believe, hope and love, or can repent, as he should, so that on him the grace of justification may be conferred.

4. That the free will of man, moved and aroused by God, does not co-operate at all by responding to the awakening call of God, so as to dispose and prepare itself for the acquisition of the grace of justification, nor can it refuse that grace, if it so will, but it does nothing at all, like some inanimate thing, and is completely passive.

5. That man's free will has been wholly lost and destroyed after Adam's sin.

6. That it is not in the power of man to make his ways evil, but that evil works as well as good are wrought by God, not just by way of permission but even by his own personal activity; so that the betrayal of Judas is no less his work than the calling of Paul.

7. That all works before justification, for whatever reason they were done, are in truth sins and deserve the hatred of God, or that the more strongly a man strives to dispose himself to receive Grace, the more grievously he sins.

9. That the impious is justified by faith alone—if this means that nothing else is required by way of co-operation in the acquisition of the grace of justification, and that it is in no way necessary for a man to be prepared and disposed by the motion of his own will.

15. That a man reborn and justified is bound by faith to believe that he is assuredly in the number of the predestinate.

23. That a man once justified can no more sin, nor can he lose the grace, and so he that falls into sin was never truly justified; or that it is possible altogether to avoid all sins, even venial sins. ...

24. That justification once received is not preserved and even increased in the sight of God through good works; but that these same works are only fruits and signs of justification, not causes of its increase.

d. On the Eucharist

Session XIII, October 1551   *C. Tr.* v. 996. Denzinger, 874 ff.

Chapter 4. *On Transubstantiation*

Since Christ our Redeemer said that that which he offered under the appearance of bread was truly his body, it has therefore always been held in the Church of God, and this holy Synod now declares anew, that through consecration of the bread and wine there comes about a conversion of the whole substance of the bread into the substance of the body of Christ our Lord, and of the whole substance of the wine into the substance of his blood. And this conversion is by the Holy Catholic Church conveniently and properly called transubstantiation.

Chapter 5. *On the worship and veneration of the Holy Eucharist*

And so no place is left for doubting that all Christ's faithful should in their veneration display towards this most Holy Sacrament the full worship of adoration [*latriae cultum*] which is due to the true God, in accordance with the custom always received in the Catholic Church. For it is not the less to be adored because it was instituted by Christ the Lord that it might be taken and eaten.

Canons on the Holy Eucharist

Mansi, xxxiii. 84 C f. Denzinger, 883 ff.

3. On the Eucharist. If any one denies that in the venerable sacrament of the Eucharist the whole Christ is contained under each species and in each separate part of each species: let them be anathema.

9. If any one denies that each and all of Christ's faithful, of either sex, having come to years of discretion, is bound to communicate at least once a year in Eastertide, in accordance with the precept of Holy Mother Church: let him be anathema.

e. On Penance

Session XIV, November 1551　　Mansi, xxxiii. 99 C. ff. Denzinger, 911 ff.

Canons on the Sacrament of Penance

[The following propositions, among others, are anathematized.]

1. That penance is not truly and properly a sacrament in the Catholic Church, instituted for the faithful by Christ our Lord, for their reconciliation to God whenever they fall into sin after baptism.

2. That baptism itself is the sacrament of penance (as if there were not two distinct sacraments) and that therefore it is not right to call penance the 'second plank after shipwreck.'[1]

3. That the words of our Lord and Saviour, 'Whosesoever sins', etc. [John xx. 22], are not to be understood of the power of remitting or retaining sins in the sacrament of penance, as the Catholic Church has always, from the first, understood them: but ... that they refer to the authority to preach the Gospel.

4. That for entire and perfect remission of sins three acts are not required in a penitent, to be as it were the matter of the sacrament, namely contrition, confession and satisfaction.

6. That sacramental confession was neither instituted by divine authority, nor is it necessary to salvation by divine authority; or that the method of private confession to a priest alone, a method always observed from the first down to this day by the Catholic Church, is alien from the institution and command of Christ, and is a human invention.

f. On the Most Holy Sacrifice of the Mass

Session XXII, September 1562　　*C. Tr.* viii. 699 f. Denzinger, 938 ff.

Chapter 2. And since in this divine Sacrifice which is performed in the Mass, that same Christ is contained in a bloodless sacrifice who on the altar of the cross once offered himself with the shedding of his blood: the holy Synod teaches that this sacrifice is truly propitiatory, and through it it comes about that if with true hearts and right faith, with fear and reverence, with contrition and penitence, we approach God we 'attain mercy and find grace and help in time of need' [Hebrews iv. 16]. For God, propitiated by the oblation of this sacrifice, granting us grace and the gift of penitence, remits our faults and even our enormous sins. For there is one and the same victim, now offering through the ministry of the priesthood, who then offered himself on the cross; the only difference is

---

[1] As Luther maintained, see p. 211 above.

in the method of the offering. The fruits of this (the bloody) oblation are perceived most fully through this bloodless oblation; so far is it from taking any honour from the former. Wherefore it is rightly offered, in accordance with the tradition of the Apostles, not only for the sins, penances, satisfactions and other necessities of the faithful living, but also for the dead in Christ, whose purification is not yet accomplished.

g. On Purgatory and Invocation of Saints

Session XXV, December 1563   *C. Tr.* ix. 1077 f. Denzinger, 983 f.

Since the Catholic Church, taught by the Holy Spirit from the Sacred writings and the ancient traditions of the Fathers, has taught, in holy Councils and lately in this oecumenical Synod, that there is a purgatory and that souls there detained are helped by the intercessions of the faithful, but most of all by the acceptable sacrifice of the altar, this sacred Synod instructs bishops to take earnest care that the sound doctrine concerning purgatory handed down by the holy Fathers and sacred Councils be by Christ's faithful believed, held, taught and everywhere preached. But among the unlettered folk let the more difficult and subtler questions, which do not tend to edification [1 Tim. i. 4] and from which no increase of piety is wont to arise, be excluded from public preaching. And let them not permit any public handling of matters uncertain or those which labour under an appearance of falsehood. And let them prohibit, as scandals and sources of offence to the faithful, things which pander to curiosity and superstition or which savour of base lucre.

The holy Synod enjoins on all bishops and others on whom is laid the duty and charge of teaching, that they diligently instruct the faithful, in accordance with the use of the Catholic and Apostolic Church (received from the earliest age of the Christian religion), the consensus of the holy Fathers and the decrees of the Sacred Councils, firstly concerning the intercession of saints, the invocation of saints, the honour due to relics, and the lawful use of images; teaching them that the Saints who reign with Christ offer their prayers to God on behalf of men, that it is good and useful to invoke them in supplication and to have recourse to their prayers, their help and their succour for the obtaining of benefits from God through his son, Jesus Christ our Lord, who is our only Saviour and Redeemer. ...

h. On Indulgences

Session XXV   *C.Tr.* ix. 1105. Denzinger, 989

Since the power of conferring indulgences has been granted to the Church by Christ, and since the Church has made use of this divinely given power even from the earliest times, the holy Synod teaches and enjoins that the use of indulgences, which is greatly salutary for Christian people and has been approved by the authority of sacred Councils, is to be retained in the Church. ...

III.   THE TRIDENTINE PROFESSION OF FAITH, 1564
From the Bull of Pius IV, *Injunctum nobis*, November 1564:
Mansi, xxxiii. 220 B ff. Denzinger, 994 ff.

[Issued to be recited publicly by all bishops and beneficed clergy. It was the symbol imposed on all converts to Roman Catholicism.]

I, N, with steadfast faith believe and profess each and all the things contained in the Symbol of faith which the holy Roman Church uses, namely 'I believe in One God, etc. [The Nicene Creed].'

I most firmly acknowledge and embrace the Apostolic and ecclesiastical traditions and other observances and constitutions of the same Church. I acknowledge the sacred Scripture according to that sense which Holy Mother Church has held and holds, to whom it belongs to decide upon the true sense and interpretation of the holy Scriptures, nor will I ever receive and interpret the Scripture except according to the unanimous consent of the Fathers.

I profess also that there are seven sacraments. ... I embrace and receive each and all of the definitions and declarations of the sacred Council of Trent on Original Sin and Justification.

I profess likewise that true God is offered in the Mass, a proper and propitiatory sacrifice for the living and the dead, and that in the most Holy Eucharist there are truly, really and substantially the body and blood, together with the soul and divinity of Our Lord Jesus Christ, and that a conversion is made of the whole substance of bread into his body and of the whole substance of wine into his blood, which conversion the Catholic Church calls transubstantiation. I also confess that the whole and entire Christ and the true sacrament is taken under the one species alone.

I hold unswervingly that there is a purgatory and that the souls there detained are helped by the intercessions of the faithful; likewise also that the Saints who reign with Christ are to be venerated and invoked; that they offer prayers to God for us and that their relics are to be venerated. I firmly assert that the images of Christ and of the ever-Virgin Mother of God, as also those of other Saints, are to be kept and retained, and that due honour and veneration is to be accorded them; and I affirm that the power of indulgences has been left by Christ in the Church, and that their use is very salutary for Christian people.

I recognize the Holy Catholic and Apostolic Roman Church as the mother and mistress of all churches; and I vow and swear true obedience to the Roman Pontiff, the successor of blessed Peter, the chief of the Apostles and the representative [*vicarius*] of Jesus Christ.

I accept and profess, without doubting, the traditions, definitions and declarations of the sacred Canons and Oecumenical Councils and especially those of the holy Council of Trent;[1] and at the same time I condemn, reject and anathematize all things contrary thereto, and all heresies condemned, rejected and anathematized by the Church. This true Catholic Faith (without which no one can be in a state of salvation), which at this time I of my own will profess and truly hold, I, *N*, vow and swear, God helping me, most constantly to keep and confess entire and undefiled to my life's last breath, and that I will endeavour, as far as in me shall lie, that it be held, taught and preached by my subordinates or by those who shall be placed under my care: so help me God and these Holy Gospels of God.

IV. ARMINIANISM

The Five Articles of the Remonstrants   Schaff, *Creeds of Christendom*, III

[Jacobus Arminius, Professor of Divinity in the University of Leyden, 1603, charged the Calvinist theory of predestination (incorporated in the *Confessio Belgica*) with making God the author of sin. His developed views on this point were very similar to those of the Council of Trent. Though he did not deny election he based it not on a divine arbitrary decree, but upon God's foreknowledge of man's merit. In 1618 these views, expressed in the Five Articles, were condemned by a synod at Dort, and the Remonstrants were compelled to leave the national Reformed Church.]

I. That God, by an eternal and unchangeable purpose in Jesus Christ his Son, before the foundations of the world were laid, determined to save, out of the human race which had fallen into sin, in Christ, for Christ's sake and through Christ, those who through the grace of the Holy Spirit shall believe on the same his Son and shall through the same grace persevere in this same faith and obedience of faith even to the end; and on the other hand to leave under sin and wrath the contumacious and unbelieving and to condemn them as aliens from Christ, according to the word of the Gospel in John iii. 36, and other passages of Scripture.

---

[1] By a decree of 1877 there is here added 'and of the oecumenical Vatican Council [i.e. of 1870], especially the definitions concerning the Primacy of the Roman Pontiff and his infallible authority [*magisterio*].'

II. That, accordingly, Jesus Christ, the Saviour of the world, died for all men and for every man, so that he has obtained for all, by his death on the cross, reconciliation and remission of sins; yet so that no one is partaker of this remission except the believers [John iii. 16; 1 John ii. 2].

III. That man has not saving grace of himself, nor of the working of his own free-will, inasmuch as in his state of apostasy and sin he can for himself and by himself think nothing that is good—nothing, that is, truly good, such as saving faith is, above all else. But that it is necessary that by God, in Christ and through his Holy Spirit he be born again and renewed in understanding, affections and will and in all his faculties, that he may be able to understand, think, will and perform what is truly good, according to the Word of God [John xv. 5].

IV. That this grace of God is the beginning, the progress and the end of all good; so that even the regenerate man can neither think, will nor effect any good, nor withstand any temptation to evil, without grace precedent (or prevenient), awakening, following and cooperating. So that all good deeds and all movements towards good that can be conceived in thought must be ascribed to the grace of God in Christ.

But with respect to the mode of operation, grace is not irresistible; for it is written of many that they resisted the Holy Spirit [Acts vii and elsewhere *passim*].

V. That those who are grafted into Christ by a true faith, and have thereby been made partakers of his life-giving Spirit, are abundantly endowed with power to strive against Satan, sin, the world and their own flesh, and to win the victory; always, be it understood, with the help of the grace of the Holy Spirit, with Jesus Christ assisting them in all temptations, through his Spirit; stretching out his hand to them and (provided only that they are themselves prepared for the fight, that they entreat his aid and do not fail to help themselves) propping and upholding them so that by no guile or violence of Satan can they be led astray or plucked from Christ's hands [John x. 28]. But for the question whether they are not able through sloth or negligence to forsake the beginning of their life in Christ, to embrace again this present world, to depart from the holy doctrine once delivered to them, to lose their good conscience and to neglect grace—this must be the subject of more exact inquiry in the Holy Scriptures, before we can teach it with full confidence of our mind.

These Articles thus set out and delivered the Remonstrants deem agreeable to the word of God, suitable for edification and, on this subject, sufficient for salvation. So that it is not needful, and tends not to edification, to rise higher or to descend lower.

V. JANSENISM. THE 'FIVE PROPOSITIONS', 1653
Innocent X, *Cum occasione*, 1653: *B.R.* XV. 720 f.

[[1]Jansen, Bishop of Ypres, died in 1638. He had been a great admirer of Augustine and had written a book, *Augustinus*, which was published in 1640 and was studied at Port Royal by Arnauld (brother of Mère Angelique, the superior of the convent), Le Maistre, and Pascal. When they had aroused the enmity of the Jesuits by their education experiments their rivals extracted five propositions from the writings of Arnauld and secured their condemnation by Innocent X. Arnauld gave way, and the Jesuits thereupon declared that the propositions were taken from Jansen. This was to accuse Arnauld of Calvinism, and the Port Royalists refused to admit the allegation. But Pascal and his fellow-students were turned out of their house near the convent and the nuns were dispersed. In 1668 the quarrel was patched up, but in 1713 the Jesuits secured the condemnation of the works of Père Quesnel, the director of Port Royal, and the convent was finally dissolved. An important result of the quarrel was the arousing of Pascal to attack the Jesuits in the *Provincial Letters*.]

1. Some commandments of God to men wishing and striving to be righteous are impossible with regard to the present strength that they possess; and they lack the grace by which they may become possible.

2. Interior grace is never resisted in the state of fallen nature.

3. For merit or demerit in the state of fallen nature freedom from necessity is not required in man but freedom from compulsion.

4. Semipelagians admit the necessity of prevenient interior grace for single acts, even for the beginning of faith; and they are heretics in this, that they wish grace to be of such a kind as human will can resist or obey.

5. It is Semipelagian to say that Christ died and shed his blood for all men.

VI. THE GALLICAN DECLARATION, 1682
Reddaway, *Select Documents*, 155. Mirbt, 535

[Louis XIV came into collision with Innocent XI over his habit of drawing the revenues of vacant bishoprics and his claim to the right of nomination to the sees. The Pope refused to admit the claim and declared invalid the acts of bishops so appointed. In a General Assembly of 1681 the clergy supported the king and in the next year the Gallican declaration was drawn up by Bossuet. It was condemned by Alexander VIII in 1690 and retracted by Louis in 1693. In 1786, Ricci, Bishop of Pistoia, persuaded a synod there to accept the Articles—but he was driven to resign on the charge of Jansenism.]

---

[1] Abridged from Wand, *Hist. of the Modern Church*, 114 ff.

Many people are striving to overthrow the decrees of the Gallican Church ... and to destroy the foundations of its liberties, which are based on the sacred canons and on the tradition of the Fathers; others, under the pretext of defending them, have the audacity to attack the supremacy of St Peter and his successors, the Popes of Rome. ... The heretics, for their part, are doing their utmost to make this power, which keeps the peace of the Church, intolerable to kings and peoples. ...

Wishing to remedy this state of affairs ...

Article I. ... We declare that Kings and Sovereigns are not, by God's command, subject to any ecclesiastical power in temporal matters; that they cannot be deposed, directly or indirectly, by the authority of the heads of the Church; that their subjects cannot be dispensed from obedience, nor absolved from the oath of allegiance. ...

Article II. [The plenitude of power in spiritual matters possessed by St Peter and his successors, none the less remains, as laid down by the decrees of the Council of Constance.]

Article III. Thus the use of the apostolic power must be regulated, by following the canons made by the Holy Spirit and sanctified by universal reverence. The rules, customs and constitutions, accepted in the realm and Church of France must have their strength and virtue ... since the greatness of the Holy See requires that the laws and customs established with its consent and that of the Churches remain invariable.

Article IV. Although the Pope has the chief voice in questions of faith, and his decrees apply to all churches and to each particular church, yet his decision is not unalterable unless the consent of the Church is given.

Article V. [These maxims sent to all the French bishops and churches that they may be unanimous.]

VII. THE DOCTRINE OF THE IMMACULATE CONCEPTION, 1854
From the Bull *Ineffabilis Deus* of Pius IX. *Acta et Decreta,*
Collectio Lacensis, vi. 842 f. Extract in Denzinger, 1641

[The question whether the Virgin was conceived without taint of original sin had been debated for centuries. Anselm held that the Virgin was conceived and born in sin (*Cur deus homo,* ii. 16); Bernard that she was conceived in sin but sanctified before birth (*Ep.* clxxiv. 58); the Dominicans followed Aquinas (*S.T.* III. xxvii. 1, 2) in agreeing with Bernard; Duns Scotus (*Sent.* III. iii. 1) and the Franciscans argued for the sinless conception. In 1483 Pope Sixtus IV in the bull *Grave nimis* censured both those who attacked the preacher of the Immaculate Conception and those who accused such attackers of heresy 'since the matter has not yet been decided by the Roman Church and the Apostolic See' (Mirbt, 407; Denzinger, 735). The promulgation of the dogma was one of the fruits of that Ultramontanism, encouraged by the restored Jesuits, which in the pontificate of Pius XI produced also the Syllabus of Errors and the Decree of Infallibility.]

... To the honour of the Holy and Undivided Trinity, to the glory and adornment of the Virgin Mother of God, to the exaltation of the Catholic Faith and the increase of the Christian religion, we, with the authority of our Lord Jesus Christ, the blessed Apostles Peter and Paul, and with our own, do declare, pronounce and define that the doctrine which holds that the Virgin Mary was, in the first instant of her conception, preserved untouched by any taint of original guilt, by a singular grace and privilege of Almighty God, in consideration of the merits of Christ Jesus the Saviour of mankind—that this doctrine was revealed by God and therefore is to be firmly and steadfastly believed by all the faithful. Wherefore if any shall presume (which God forbid) to think in their hearts anything contrary to this definition of ours, let them realize and know well that they are condemned by their own judgement, have suffered shipwreck concerning the faith and have revolted from the unity of the Church, and that besides this they do by this subject themselves to the lawful penalties if they shall dare to signify, by word or writing or any other external means, what they think in their hearts.

VIII. THE SYLLABUS OF ERRORS, 1864
Acta Sanctae Sedis, 3 (1867), 168 ff. Denzinger, 1701 ff.

§ 1. Pantheism, Naturalism, and Absolute Rationalism

'That there exists no Divine Power, Supreme Being, Wisdom and Providence, distinct from the Universe. ... That the prophecies and miracles narrated in Holy Scripture are the fictions of poets. ... '

§ 2. Moderate Rationalism

' ... That the Church ought to tolerate the errors of philosophy; leaving to philosophy the care of their correction. That the decrees of the Apostolic See and of the Roman Congregations fetter the free progress of science. That the method and principles, by which the old scholastic Doctors cultivated Theology, are no longer suitable to the demands of the age. ... '

§ 3. Indifferentism and Toleration

'That every man is free to embrace and profess the religion he shall believe true, guided by the light of reason. ... That the eternal salvation may (at least) be hoped for, of all those who are not at all in the true Church of Christ. That Protestantism is nothing more than another form of the same true Christian religion; in which it is possible to please God equally as in the Catholic Church.'

§ 4. Socialism, Biblical Societies, Clerico-Liberal Societies, etc.

Pests of this description are frequently rebuked in the severest terms, in the Encycl. *Qui pluribus*, etc.

§ 5. Errors concerning the Church and her Rights

'That the Roman Pontiffs and Oecumenical Councils have exceeded the limits of their power, have usurped the rights of princes, and have even committed errors in defining matters of faith and morals. That the Church has not the power of availing herself of force, or of any direct or indirect temporal power. ... That ecclesiastical jurisdiction for the temporal causes—whether civil or criminal—of the clergy, ought by all means to be abolished. ... That National Churches can be established, after being withdrawn and separated from the authority of the holy Pontiff. That many Pontiffs have, by their arbitrary conduct, contributed to the division of the Church into Eastern and Western.'

§ 6. Errors about Civil Society, etc.

' ... That the civil government—even when exercised by an infidel sovereign—possesses an indirect and negative power over religious affairs; and possesses, not only the right called that of *exequatur*, but also that of the (so-called) *appellatio ab abusu*. ... That the best theory of civil society requires that popular schools, open to the children of all classes, should be freed from all ecclesiastical authority. ... That the Church ought to be separated from the State, and the State from the Church.'

§ 7. Errors concerning Natural and Christian Ethics

' ... That knowledge of philosophical matters, and of morals, and civil laws, may be and should be independent of Divine and ecclesiastical authority. ... That is allowable to refuse obedience to legitimate princes; nay more, to rise in insurrection against them. ... '

§ 9. Errors regarding the Civil Power of the Sovereign Pontiff

' ... That the abrogation of the temporal power of which the Apostolic See is possessed, would be the greatest contribution to the liberty and prosperity of the Church. ... '

§ 10. Errors relating to Modern Liberalism

'That in the present day, it is no longer necessary that the Catholic religion be held as the only religion of the State, to the exclusion of all other modes of worship: whence it has been wisely provided by the law, in some countries nominally Catholic, that persons coming to reside therein shall enjoy the free exercise of their own worship. ... That the Roman Pontiff can, and ought to, reconcile himself to, and agree with, progress, liberalism, and modern civilization.'

IX. THE DOCTRINE OF PAPAL INFALLIBILITY, 1870
Vatican Council, Session IV, cap. 4. *Collectio Lacensis*, viii. 482 f.
Denzinger, 1832 ff.

[The decree aroused much opposition in the Church, notably that of Döllinger of Munich, who refused to submit and was excommunicated. Some of the opponents united to found the 'Old Catholic Church'.]

... We [i.e. Pope Pius IX], adhering faithfully to the tradition received from the beginning of the Christian faith—with a view to the glory of our Divine Saviour, the exaltation of the Catholic religion, and the safety of Christian peoples (the sacred Council approving), teach and define as a dogma divinely revealed: That the Roman Pontiff, when he speaks *ex cathedra* (that is, when—fulfilling the office of Pastor and Teacher of all Christians—on his supreme Apostolical authority, he defines a doctrine concerning faith or morals to be held by the Universal Church), through the divine assistance promised him in blessed Peter, is endowed with that infallibility, with which the Divine Redeemer has willed that His Church—in defining doctrine concerning faith or morals—should be equipped: And therefore, that such definitions of the Roman Pontiff of themselves—and not by virtue of the consent of the Church—are irreformable. If any one shall presume (which God forbid!) to contradict this our definition; let him be anathema.

X. POPE LEO XIII ON ANGLICAN ORDERS
From the Epistle *Apostolicae curae*, 13 September 1896. *Acta Sanctae Sedis* (96/97), 198 ff. Extract in Denzinger, 1963 ff.

[In 1894, largely through the efforts of Lord Halifax, Leo XIII appointed a commission to inquire into Anglican Orders. Some members of the commission were convinced of their validity, but a further commission of Cardinals laid down the view which the Pope published in his letter. The archbishops of the Church of England responded to *Apostolicae curae* in their own *Responsio* of February 1897.]

... In the rite of the accomplishment and administration of any sacrament we rightly distinguish between the ceremonial part and essential part, which are usually called the matter and the form. And all are aware that the sacraments of the new law, being sensible signs and signs efficacious of invisible grace, ought both to signify the grace which they effect and to effect the grace they signify. ... Now the words which up to the last generation were universally held by Anglicans to be the proper form of ordination to the priesthood. viz. *Receive the Holy Ghost*, are surely far from the precise signification of the order of the priesthood, or its grace and power, which is especially the power of consecrating and offering the true body and blood of the Lord in that sacrifice which is no mere commemoration of the sacrifice accomplished on the cross. This form was indeed afterwards augmented by the words *for the Office and work of a priest*, but this rather proves that Anglicans saw that the first form was defective and inadequate. And the addition, even if it were able to give the necessary significance to the form, was brought in too late, for a century had elapsed after the acceptance of the Edwardian Ordinal: the hierarchy had died out and there remained no power to ordain.

Similarly in the case of episcopal consecration. For to the formula *Receive the Holy Ghost* the words *for the office and work of a bishop* were not only added too late but, as we shall soon remark, a different interpretation is to be placed on them than [is understood] in the catholic rite. ... So it came about that, since the sacrament of ordination and the true Christian priesthood has been utterly cast out of the Anglican rite, and thus in the consecration of bishops of the said rite no priesthood is conferred, so no episcopacy can be truly or rightly conferred. ...

With this deep-seated defect of form is joined a defect of intention, which is equally necessary for the performance of a sacrament.[1] ... And so ... we pronounce and declare that ordinations performed according to the Anglican rite are utterly invalid and altogether void.

---

[1] *Intention*, according to Aquinas (*S.T.* III. lxiv. 8, 10), means that the action of the minister in a sacrament should be directed to the effecting of the sacrament; this requirement is fulfilled if he utters the words which express the Church's intention, unless he is openly aiming at mockery. According to the Council of Trent (Session VII, Canon II) the minimum requirement is that the minister shall 'intend to do what the Church does'. The extension of the doctrine implied in *Apostolicae curae*, which would make 'right intention' include a true belief about the sacrament, savours of Donatist theory, and finds no support in Roman theology before the nineteenth century.

XI. THE ROMAN CATHOLIC CHURCH
AND SOCIAL PROBLEMS

[Under Pius IX the Roman Catholic Church seemed to many to have set its face against the modern world. Leo XIII showed a desire to come to terms with the contemporary situation, and his encyclical *De Condicione Opificum* ('Rerum Novarum') displayed the Church's concern for social justice. Though attacked from the Right as subversive, from the Left as timid, this encyclical has had great influence; and its teaching has been underlined and developed by Pius XI in *Quadragesimo Anno*, on the fortieth anniversary of its publication, and thirty years later in *Mater et Magistra*, by John XXIII.]

a. From the encyclical *Rerum Novarum* of Leo XIII, 15 May 1891

Acta Santae Sedis 23 (90/91) and 99 f., *Acta Leonis XIII*, 100 f. Extracts in Denzinger 1938 f.

Property

The possession of private property is a right given to man by nature. ... There is no reason why the directing power of the state should be brought in; for man is prior to the state, and therefore he must have had by nature the right to preserve his life and person before any community was organized. ... The necessary materials for the preservation of life are lavishly supplied by the earth; but the earth could not supply them by itself without man's cultivation, and since man applies the activity of his mind and the strength of his body in the production of the good things of nature, it follows that he claims for himself the portion of physical nature which he has himself tended, which he has in a sense stamped with his own personal impress. And so it should be altogether right for that portion to be possessed by him as his personal property; nor should anyone be allowed to violate that right in any way. ... The force of these arguments is so obvious that it seems strange that they are opposed by some people who seek to re-establish worn-out doctrines; who allow individuals the use of the soil and the different products of lands, but say that it is not right that a man should possess, as an owner, the land on which he has built, or the estate which he has cultivated. ...

Wages

Man's labour has two inherent natural characteristics; it is *personal*, since the active force is attached to a person, and is completely the personal possession of the man by whom it is exercised, and is by nature designed for his advantage: and secondly, it is *necessary*, for this reason, that man requires the fruit of his labour for the preservation of his life, and the duty of self-preservation is grounded in the natural order. It follows that if we consider merely the *personal* aspect there is no doubt that it is open to the worker to reduce the agreed wage to narrow dimensions. He gives his services of his free will, and he can, of free will, content himself with a slender reward, or even with none at all. But a very different conclusion is reached when we combine the *necessary* with the *personal* element, and indeed they are only separable in thought, not in reality. To remain alive is a duty incumbent on all alike, in fact, and to fail in this duty is a crime. Hence arises of necessity the right of acquiring the materials for the support of life; and it is only by the wage earned with their labour that the lower orders are supplied with these means. Therefore the worker and the employer should freely come to agreement, especially in regard to the level of wages. ... But there is an underlying condition which arises from natural laws, namely that the wage should be sufficient to support the worker, provided he is thrifty and well behaved. If the worker is compelled to accept harsher terms, or is induced to do so by fear of worse hardships, and these have to be accepted because they are imposed by a master or employer, this is submission to force and therefore repugnant to justice. ... If the worker receives sufficient payment to maintain himself, his wife, and his children, in comfort, he will be ready to practise thrift, if he is sensible, and will follow the prompting of nature by reducing his expenditure to ensure some surplus by means of which he may attain a modest property. ... The right of private property ought to be inviolate. ... For the attainment of these advantages it is an essential condition that private property should not be exhausted by inordinate taxation. The right of personal possessions is not based on human law; it is given by nature. Therefore public authority cannot abolish it; it can only control its use and adjust it to the common good.

Trade Unions

That men should commonly unite in associations of this kind [trade unions and the like], whether made up wholly of workers or of both classes together, is to be welcomed. ... Natural law grants man the right to join particular associations, and the state is appointed to support natural law, not to destroy it. ... and the state arises from the same principle which produces particular societies, the fact that men are by nature gregarious. But circumstances sometimes arise when it is right for the laws to check associations of this kind; this happens if ever these associations deliberately adopt aims which are in open conflict with honesty, with justice, and with the well-being of the community.

b. From *Quadragesimo Anno,* the encyclical of Pius XI, 15 May 1931

Acta Apostolicae Sedis, 23 (1931) 118 ff. Extracts from Denzinger, 2253 ff.

Ownership and Right of Property

It must be taken as an established fact that neither Leo nor those theologians who were taught under the guidance and the leadership of the Church have ever denied or questioned the two-fold character of ownership, personal and social. ... They have always united in affirming that the right of private ownership has been granted to men by nature or by the Creator himself in order that each man may be able to make provision for himself and his family, and at the same time that with the aid of this institution the goods which the Creator intended for the whole human family should in fact serve this purpose. These ends cannot be attained unless a fixed and defined order is observed. ...

The Obligations of Ownership. ... We must take as a fundamental premise the ruling of Leo XIII, that the right of property is to be distinguished from its use. For what is called 'commutative justice' demands that the distribution of possessions should be preserved without violation, and forbids a man to invade another's right by exceeding the limits of his own rights of ownership: But the question of the right use of property does not belong to this kind of justice. This falls under other virtues and there exists no right of demanding their exercise by process of law. Therefore there is no justification for the assertion made by some, that ownership and its right use are contained within the same limits: it is much further from the truth to assert that the right of property is destroyed or lost by its abuse or non-use.

The Power of the State. From the double character of ownership—personal and social—it follows that in this matter men must take account not only of their own advantage but also of the common good. To define these duties in detail, when necessity demands, and natural law itself does not give guidance, belongs to those in authority in the State. Therefore public authority can decide more accurately what is permissible and what is forbidden to owners of property in the use of their possessions, in the consideration of the governing demands of the common good—always in the light of the teaching of natural and divine law. Indeed Leo XIII wisely taught that 'the control of private possessions has been entrusted by God to the skill of men and the laws of nations'. ... However, it is clear that the state is not permitted to exercise its prerogative in an arbitrary manner. For the natural right of private property and of hereditary transmission must be kept intact and inviolate as a right which the state cannot take away 'because man is prior to the state' and 'the family is prior to the civil community in thought and in fact'. Hence that wisest of pontiffs laid it down that it was utterly wrong for the state to exhaust private incomes by inordinate taxation. 'The right of private property is given by nature, not by human law. Public authority has therefore merely the power of controlling its use and of adjusting it with the common good, it has no right to abolish it.' ...

Capital and Labour

[Capital and labour need each other] ... Wealth which is continually increased by economic-social gains should be assigned to individuals and classes in such a way as to secure ... the common good of the whole community. By this law of social justice it is forbidden that one class should exclude the other from sharing the profits. This law is violated when the rich ... consider the just state of affairs to be that by which they receive all the profit and the workers receive none, and equally when the working class ... claims that all things are the result of its manual labour, and therefore attacks and strives to abolish all ownership and all returns and profits which are not acquired by labour. ...

The Just Wage

The Personal and Social Character of Labour. ... Unless the social and juridical order safeguards the exercise of labour ... unless intelligence, money and labour are allied and united, the activity of man is unable to produce its proper results. If the social and personal nature of labour be disregarded it cannot be justly valued nor equitably recompensed.

Three Principles

(*a*) The worker should receive a wage adequate for the support of himself and his family. ... It is the worst of abuses ... that mothers should be compelled, because of the inadequacy of the father's wage, to earn money outside the home, to the neglect of their particular duties and responsibilities, especially the care of their children. ...

(*b*) In deciding the level of wages the condition of the productive organization must be taken into account. It is unjust to demand excessive payment which the business cannot stand without disaster to itself and subsequent ruin to its workers. But technical and economic inefficiency ... is not to be considered an excuse for reducing wages. ...

(*c*) The level of wages must be adjusted to the public economic good. ... Wages should be so regulated, as far as possible by consent, that as many as possible may be able to hire their labour and receive suitable reward for their livelihood. ...

The Right Order of Society

The State's Responsibility. ... Public authority should delegate to subordinate bodies the task of dealing with problems of minor importance so that it may carry out ... the duties peculiarly incumbent upon it ... [of promoting the common good, regulating the 'hierarchical order' of these free associations of bodies autonomous in their economic and professional spheres, and encouraging a 'harmony of orders' in place of a 'rivalry of classes'.]

The Governing Economic Principle. ... The unity of human society cannot be based on the opposition of 'classes'; the establishment of a right economic order cannot be left to a free trial of strength ... economic power must be controlled by social justice and social charity. ...

[Changes since *Rerum Novarum.*] ... There has been not merely an accumulation of wealth but a huge concentration of power and of economic dictatorship in the hands of a few who are for the most part not the owners but merely the trustees and administrators of invested property, handling such funds at their arbitrary pleasure. ... This irresponsible power is the natural fruit of unlimited free competition, which leaves surviving only the most powerful, which often means the most violent and unscrupulous fighters. ...

Socialism and Communism

[Since *Rerum Novarum* socialism has divided into two parties.]

(a) *Communism.* ... Communism teaches the fiercest warfare between classes and aims at the total abolition of private ownership ... it shrinks from nothing in the pursuit of its aims ... and when it seizes power it displays incredible cruelty and inhumanity ... its open enmity to Holy Church and to God himself is, alas, all too clearly proved by its actions. ...

(b) *Socialism.* The other party, which keeps the name 'Socialism' is milder. It professes to abjure violence, and if it does not do away with class warfare and the abolition of private property, it does in some degree soften and ameliorate those conceptions. ... One might say that socialism in some way approaches the truths which Christian tradition has always held. ... But whether considered as a doctrine, or as a historical fact, or an as activity, socialism, while it remains truly socialism, cannot be harmonized with the dogmas of the Catholic Church, even after the concessions made to truth and justice. ... The picture it draws of society is utterly remote from Christian truth. For the Christian teaching is that man, endowed with a social nature, is placed on this earth to live his life in society and under the authority ordained by God (cf. Rom. xiii. 1), and to cultivate and develop all his powers to the full for the praise and glory of his Creator, and by the faithful fulfilment of his duty in his craft or other vocation to attain both temporal and eternal happiness. While socialism neither knows nor cares anything at all about this sublime end of man and of society, and considers that human fellowship is instituted solely for convenience. ... 'Religious socialism,' 'Christian socialism' are contradictions; no-one can be at once a true Catholic and a socialist, in the proper meaning of the term. ...

c. From *Mater et Magistra,* encyclical of John XXIII, 15 May 1961
  Acta Apostolicae Sedis 53 (1961) 401 ff.

[The letter surveys the social teaching of *Rerum Novarum* and *Quadragesimo Anno* and explains and develops it in view of the great changes, scientific, technological, social and political, of the last thirty years. Under the heading of renunciation, it takes up the suggestions of Pius XII on co-partnerships.]

In many economies today, organizations of moderate and large size often effect swift and extensive increases in productive capacity by methods of financing themselves. We hold that in such cases the workers should acquire shares in the firms which employ them, especially when they earn only the minimum salary. ... The workers should be able to share in the ownership of the business. ... [Noting the increasing danger of the loss of the sense of responsibility in those engaged in the large impersonal enterprises, the encyclical develops the directive of *Quadragesimo Anno*; 'businesses of small or moderate size ... should be helped and encouraged by means of cooperative enterprises: in the larger firms it should be made possible to modify the contract of work into something like a contract of partnership'.] The workers should have a voice and a share in the running and development of their business. ... Unity of direction must be procured, and the authority essential for efficiency ... but the workers must not be reduced to mere 'hands' without a voice, and without the opportunity of applying their experience; they must not be kept entirely passive in respect of the decisions which guide their employment. ...

There has been a wide development in recent times of associations of workers, and a general recognition of them in the legal codes of various countries, and also on the international level, for the specific purpose of cooperation, particularly in the form of collective bargaining. But ... workers should exert effective influence beyond the boundaries of their particular businesses, and at all levels, for the particular businesses, however extensive and efficient, belong to the social-economic complex of their political communities and are controlled by it. Thus the greatest importance rests, not in the decisions within the individual businesses, but in those made by public authorities, or by agencies acting on a world-wide, regional, or national scale. ... We are glad to express whole-hearted approval of the work of the International Labour Organization which for decades has been making an effective and valuable contribution to the establishment in the world of an economic and social order characterized by justice and humanity, where the legitimate claims of the workers find expression.

XII. THE DOCTRINE OF THE ASSUMPTION OF THE BLESSED VIRGIN MARY, 1950

From the Apostolic Constitution *Munificentissimus Deus*, 1 November 1950. *Acta Apostolicae Sedis*, 42 (1950) 767 ff. Extract in Denzinger, 3031 ff.

[The assertion that the Blessed Virgin Mary had been taken up to glory in soul and body is first found in New Testament apocrypha of the fourth century. From the sixth century it gained support in both East and West, and by the end of the eighth century it was generally held, and the feast of the Assumption (or in the East the *Koimesis*, 'falling asleep') observed on 15 August. The medieval school-men provided theological defence for the popular devotion, but it lacked official definition as a dogma, and in the eighteenth century Benedict XIV classed it among probable opinions. At the Vatican Council of 1870 there was pressure for dogmatic declaration, which continued until Pius XII defined the doctrine as *de fide* and provided a new mass for the feast.]

... Holy Scripture sets as it were before our eyes the bounteous Mother of God as most closely united with her Divine Son, and always sharing His lot. Therefore it seems scarcely possible to suppose that she who conceived and bore Christ, who nursed Him with her own milk, who held Him in her arms and clasped Him to her breast, was after this life on earth separated from Him in body, even though not in soul. Since our Redeemer is the Son of Mary, he could not fail, being the most perfect observer of the divine law, to honour, besides His Eternal Father, His most beloved Mother. In fact, since He was able to do her so great an honour as to keep her safe from the corruption of the tomb, we must believe that He actually did so. ...

Therefore the majestic Mother of God, from all eternity united in a mysterious way with Jesus Christ by 'one and the same decree'[1] of predestination, immaculate in her conception, in her divine motherhood a most unspotted virgin, the noble ally of the Divine Redeemer who bore

---

[1] A quotation from the bull *Ineffabilis Deus*, defining the Immaculate Conception (see above p. 274).

off the triumph over sin and its supporters, finally achieved, as the supreme crown of her privileges, that she should be preserved immune from the corruption of the tomb, and, like her Son before her, having conquered death, should be carried up, in body and soul, to the celestial glory of Heaven, to reign there as Queen at the right hand of her Son, the immortal King of the ages. ...

Therefore we ... declare and define, as a dogma revealed by God, that the Immaculate Mother of God, ever-Virgin Mary, on the completion of the course of her earthly life, has been taken up, in body and soul, to the glory of heaven.

SECTION XI

The British Churches in the Seventeenth Century

I. ANGLICANISM OF THE SEVENTEENTH CENTURY

[In the period between 1594, the date of the publication of the first four books of Hooker's *Ecclesiastical Polity*, and the accession of William and Mary, with the consequent schism of the Non-Jurors, there flourished a number of divines whose writings are among the chief glories of the Church of England. It was then that there came into being what is termed Anglicanism, a belief in and a love for the Church of England based on more than mere repudiation of Rome and Dissent, a conviction of her position as a member of the Catholic Church, of her continuity with the past and of her responsibility to the present and the future of Christendom. These few extracts are designed to show some of the characteristic ideas of Anglicanism. But it must not be supposed that the term denotes one fixed and accepted body of beliefs—apart from the acceptance of the Church's doctrine contained in the English formularies; Anglicanism is more a loyalty than a docrinal position.

These extracts are all to be found in More and Cross, *Anglicanism*.]

a. The Church of England

Jeremy Taylor (1613–67): Bishop of Down and Connor, 1661–7   From *A Letter to a Gentleman Seduced to the Church of Rome*. *Works* (Heber's edition), xi. 185

What can be supposed wanting [in the Church of England] in order to salvation? We have the Word of God, the Faith of the Apostles, the Creeds of the Primitive Church, the Articles of the four first General Councils, a holy liturgy, excellent prayers, perfect Sacraments, faith and repentance, the Ten Commandments, and the sermons of Christ, and all the precepts and counsels of the Gospel. We teach the necessity of good works, and require and strictly exact the severity of a holy life. We live in obedience to God, and are ready to die for Him, and do so when He requires us so to do. We speak honourably of His most Holy Name. We worship Him at the mention of His Name. We confess His attributes. We love His servants. We pray for all men. We love all Christians, even our most erring brethren. We confess our sins to God and to our brethren whom we have offended, and to God's ministers in cases of scandal or of a troubled conscience. We communicate often. We are enjoined to receive the Holy Sacrament thrice every year at least. Our priests absolve the penitent. Our Bishops ordain priests, and confirm baptized persons, and bless their people and intercede for them. And what could here be wanting to salvation?

b. The Catholic Church

1. *William Sherlock, 1641–1707: Dean of St Paul's, 1691* From *A Vindication of the Doctrine of the Trinity* (1690), 35 f.

The Catholic Faith, I grant, is so called with relation to the Catholic Church, whose Faith it is, and the Catholic Church is the Universal Church, or all the true churches in the world, which are all but one whole Church, united in Christ their Head. The profession of the true Faith and Worship of Christ makes a true Church, and all true churches are the One Catholic Church, whether they be spread over all the world, or shut up in any one corner of it, as at the first preaching of the Gospel the Catholic Church was nowhere but in Judaea. Now as no Church is the Catholic Church of Christ, how far soever it has spread itself over the world, unless it profess the true Faith of Christ, no more is any Faith the Catholic Faith, how universally soever it be professed, unless it be the true Faith of Christ. Nor does the true Christian Faith cease to be Catholic, how few soever there be who sincerely profess it. It is downright Popery to judge of the Catholic Church by its multitudes or large extent, or to judge of the Catholic Faith by the vast numbers of its professors. Were there but one true Church in the world, that were the Catholic Church, because it would be the whole Church of Christ on earth, and were the true Christian Faith professed but in one such Church it would be the Catholic Faith still, for it is the Faith of the whole true Church of Christ, the sincere belief and profession of which makes a Catholic Church.

2. *Richard Hooker, 1554–1600: Master of the Temple, 1585*   From *The Laws of Ecclesiastical Polity*, Book III, i, § 14. *Works*, ed. J. Keble, i. 351

By the Church ... we understand no other than only the visible Church. For preservation of Christianity there is not any thing more needful, than that such as are of the visible Church have mutual fellowship and society one with another. In which consideration, as the main body of the sea being one, yet within divers precincts hath divers names, so the Catholic Church is in like sort divided into a number of distinct Societies, every of which is termed a Church within itself. In this sense the Church is always a visible society of men; not an assembly, but a Society. For although the name of the Church be given unto Christian assemblies, although any multitude of Christian men congregated may be termed by the name of a Church, yet assemblies properly are rather things that belong to a Church. Men are assembled for performance of public actions; which actions being ended, the assembly dissolveth itself and is no longer in being, whereas the Church which was assembled doth no less continue afterwards than before.

3. *Richard Field, 1561–1616*   From *Of the Church*, Book II, ii: ed. E.H.S., Cambridge, 1847, i. 65

This entire profession of the truth revealed in Christ, though it distinguish right believers from heretics, yet it is not proper to the happy number and blessed company of Catholic Christians, because schismatics may and sometimes do hold an entire profession of the truth of God revealed in Christ. It remaineth, therefore, that we seek out those things that are so peculiarly found in the companies of right believing and Catholic Christians, that they may serve as notes of difference to distinguish them from all, both Pagans, Jews, heretics and schismatics. These are of two sorts; for either they are such as only at some times and not perpetually, or such as do perpetually and ever, sever the true Church from all conventicles of erring and seduced miscreants. Of the former sort was multitude, largeness of extent, and the name of 'Catholic,' esteemed a Note of the Church in the time of the Fathers. The Notes of the latter sort, that are inseparable, perpetual, and absolutely proper and peculiar, which perpetually distinguish the true Catholic Church from all other societies of men and professions of religions in the world, are three: First, the entire profession of those supernatural verities, which God hath revealed in Christ His Son; Secondly, the use of such holy ceremonies and Sacraments as He hath instituted and appointed to serve as provocations to godliness, preservations from sin, memorials of the benefits of Christ, warrants for the greater security of our belief, and marks of distinction to separate His Own from strangers; Thirdly, an union or connexion of men in this profession and use of these Sacraments under lawful pastors and guides, appointed, authorized, and sanctified, to direct and lead them in the happy ways of eternal salvation. That these are Notes of the Church it will easily appear by consideration of all those conditions that are required in the nature of Notes. They are inseparable, they are proper, and they are essential, and such things as give being to the Church, and therefore are in nature more clear and evident, and such as that from them the perfect knowledge of the Church may and must be derived.

c. **Roman Catholicism**

John Cosin, 1594–1672: Bishop of Durham, 1660   From 'A Letter to the Countess of Peterborough': *Works*, ed. L.A.C.T., iv. 332–6

The Differences, in the Chief Points of Religion, between the Roman Catholics and us of the Church of England; together with the Agreements, which we for our parts profess, and are ready to embrace, if they for theirs were as ready to accord with us in the same.

The Differences

We that profess the Catholic Faith and Religion in the Church of England do not agree with the Roman Catholics in any thing whereunto they now endeavour to convert us. But we totally differ from them (as they do from the ancient Catholic Church) in these points:

1. That the Church of Rome is the Mother and Mistress of all other Churches in the world.

2. That the Pope of Rome is the vicar-general of Christ, or that he hath an universal jurisdiction over all Christians that shall be saved.

3. That either the Synod of Trent was a General Council or that all the canons thereof are to be received as matters of Catholic Faith under pain of damnation.

4. That Christ hath instituted seven true and proper Sacraments in the New Testament, neither more nor less, all conferring grace and all necessary to salvation.

5. That the priests offer up our Saviour in the Mass, as a real, proper, and propitiatory sacrifice for the quick and the dead, and that whosoever believes it not is eternally damned.

6. That, in the Sacrament of the Eucharist, the whole substance of bread is converted into the substance of Christ's Body, and the whole

substance of wine into His Blood, so truly and properly, as that after Consecration there is neither any bread nor wine remaining there; which they call Transubstantiation, and impose upon all persons under pain of damnation to be believed.

7. That the communion under one kind is sufficient and lawful (notwithstanding the institution of Christ under both), and that whosoever believes or holds otherwise is damned.

8. That there is a purgatory after this life, wherein the souls of the dead are punished, and from whence they are fetched out by the prayers of offerings of the living; and that there is no salvation possibly to be had by any that will not believe as much.

9. That all the old saints departed, and all those dead men and women whom the Pope hath of late canonized for saints or shall hereafter do so, whosoever they be, are and ought to be invocated by the religious prayers and devotions of all persons; and that they who do not believe this as an article of their Catholic Faith cannot be saved.

10. That the relics of all these true or reputed saints ought to be religiously worshipped; and that whosoever holdeth the contrary is damned.

11. That the images of Christ and the Blessed Virgin and of the other saints ought not only to be had and retained, but likewise to be honoured and worshipped, according to the use and practices of the Roman Church; and that this is to be believed as of necessity to salvation.

12. That the power and use of indulgences, as they are now practised in the Church of Rome, both for the living and the dead, is to be received and held of all, under pain of eternal perdition.

13. That all the ceremonies used by the Roman Church in the administration of the Sacraments (such as are spittle and salt at Baptism, the five crosses upon the Altar and Sacrament of the Eucharist, the holding of that Sacrament over the Priest's head to be adored, the exposing of it in their churches to be worshipped by the people, the circumgestation and carrying of it abroad in procession upon their Corpus Christi Day, and to their sick for the same, the oil and chrism in Confirmation, the anointing of the ears, the eyes, and noses, the hands, the reins, of those that are ready to die, the giving of an empty chalice and paten to them that are to be ordained Priests, and many others of this nature now in use with them) are of necessity to salvation to be approved and admitted by all other Churches.

14. That all the ecclesiastical observations and constitutions of the same Church (such as are their laws of forbidding all Priests to marry, the appointing several orders of monks, friars, and nuns, in the Church,

the service of God in an unknown tongue, the saying of a number of Ave-Marias by tale upon their chaplets, the sprinkling of themselves and the dead bodies with holy water as operative and effectual to the remission of venial sins, the distinctions of meats to be held for true fasting, the religious consecration and incensing of images, the baptizing of bells, the dedicating of divers holidays for the Immaculate Conception and the Bodily Assumption of the blessed Virgin, and for Corpus Christi or Transubstantiation of the Sacrament, the making of the Apocryphal books to be as Canonical as any of the rest of the holy and undoubted Scriptures, the keeping of those Scriptures from the free use and reading of the people, the approving of their own Latin translation only, and divers other matters of the like nature) are to be approved, held, and believed, as needful to salvation; and that whoever approves them not is out of the Catholic Church, and must be damned.

All which, in their several respects, we hold, some to be pernicious, some unnecessary, many false, and many fond, and none of them to be imposed upon any Church, or any Christian, as the Roman Catholics do upon all Christians and all Churches whatsoever, for matters needful to be approved for eternal salvation.

Our Agreements

If the Roman Catholics would make the essence of their Church (as we do ours) to consist in these following points, we are at accord with them in the reception and believing of:

1. All the two and twenty canonical books of the Old Testament, and the twenty-seven of the New, as the only foundation and perfect rule of our faith.

2. All the apostolical and ancient Creeds, especially those which are commonly called the Apostles' Creed, the Nicene Creed, and the Creed of St. Athanasius; all which are clearly deduced out of the Scriptures.

3. All the decrees of faith and doctrine set forth, as well in the first four General Councils, as in all other Councils, which those first four approved and confirmed, and in the fifth and sixth General Councils besides (than which we find no more to be General), and in all the following Councils that be thereunto agreeable, and in all the anathemas and condemnations given out by those Councils against heretics, for the defence of the Catholic Faith.

4. The unanimous and general consent of the ancient Catholic Fathers and the universal Church of Christ in the interpretation of the Holy Scriptures, and the collection of all necessary matters of Faith from them during the first six hundred years, and downwards to our own days.

5. In acknowledgement of the Bishop of Rome, if he would rule and be ruled by the ancient canons of the Church, to be the Patriarch of the West, by right of ecclesiastical and imperial constitution, in such places where the kings and governors of those places had received him, and found it behooveful for them to make use of his jurisdiction, without any necessary dependence upon him by divine right.

6. In the reception and use of the two blessed Sacraments of our Saviour; in the Confirmation of those persons that are to be strengthened in their Christian Faith, by prayer and imposition of hands, according to the examples of the holy Apostles and ancient Bishops of the Catholic Church; in the public and solemn benediction of persons that are to be joined together in Holy Matrimony; in public or private absolution of penitent sinners; in the consecrating of Bishops, and the ordaining of Priests and Deacons, for the service of God in His Church by a lawful succession; and in visiting the sick, by praying for them, and administering the Blessed Sacrament to them, together with a final absolution of them from their repented sins.

7. In commemorating at the Eucharist the Sacrifice of Christ's Body and Blood once truly offered for us.

8. In acknowledging His sacramental, spiritual, true, and real Presence there to the souls of all them that come faithfully and devoutly to receive Him according to His own institution in that Holy Sacrament.

9. In giving thanks to God for them that are departed out of this life in the true Faith of Christ's Catholic Church; and in praying to God, that they may have a joyful resurrection and a perfect consummation of bliss, both in their bodies and souls, in His eternal kingdom of glory.

10. In the historical and moderate use of painted and true stories, either for memory or ornament, where there is no danger to have them abused or worshipped with religious honour.

11. In the use of indulgences, or abating the rigour of the canons imposed upon offenders, according to their repentance, and their want of ability to undergo them.

12. In the administration of the two Sacraments, and other rites of the Church, with ceremonies of decency and order, according to the precept of the Apostle, and the free practice of the ancient Christians.

13. In observing such Holy days and times of fasting as were in use in the first ages of the Church, or afterwards received upon just grounds, by public or lawful authority.

14. Finally, in the reception of all ecclesiastical constitution and canons made for the ordering of our Church; or others which are not repugnant either to the Word of God, or the power of kings, or the laws established by right authority in any nation.

d. Justification

William Beveridge (1637–1708): Bishop of S. Asaph, 1704   From *Ecclesia Anglicana Ecclesia Catholica*. On Article XVII, 'Of Predestination and Election.' *Works*, ed. L.A.C.T., vii. 343 f.

Though in the other [i.e. of the Thirty-Nine] Articles we may make use of reason as well as Scripture and Fathers, yet in this [XVIIth] we must make use of Scripture and Fathers only, and not of reason. For as the ordinary priests were not to enter into the Holy of Holies, so neither is carnal reason to venture upon this mystery of mysteries. For it concerns God's Predestination, which must needs be infinitely above man's apprehension. So that a cockle-fish may as soon crowd the ocean into its narrow shell, as vain man ever comprehend the decrees of God. And hence it is that both in public and private I have still endeavoured to shun discourses of this nature; and now that I am unavoidably fallen upon it, I shall speak as little as possibly I can unto it, especially considering how many other truths are still behind to be insisted upon. And in that little that I shall speak, I shall labour to make use of a few of my own words as by any means I can, speaking nothing concerning this great mystery but what Scripture and Fathers have expressly delivered unto me.

e. The Eucharist

I. *Lancelot Andrewes, 1555–1626: Bishop of Winchester, 1619*   From Responsio ad Apologiam Bellarmini. *Translated Stone,* History of the Doctrine of the Holy Eucharist, ii. 264–6

Christ said. 'This is My Body.' He did not say, 'This is My Body in this way.' We are in agreement with you as to the end; the whole controversy is as to the method. As to the 'This is,' we hold with firm faith that it is. As to the 'This is in this way' (namely, by the Transubstantiation of the bread into the Body), as to the method whereby it happens that it is, by means of In or With or Under or By transition, there is no word expressed. And because there is no word, we rightly make it not of faith; we place it perhaps among the theories of the school, but not among the articles of the faith. ... We believe no less than you that the presence is real. Concerning the method of the presence, we define nothing rashly, and, I add, we do not anxiously inquire, any more than how the Blood of Christ washes us in our Baptism, any more than how the Human and Divine Natures are united in one Person in the Incarnation of Christ. ...

It is perfectly clear that Transubstantiation, which has lately been born in the last four hundred years, never existed in the first four hundred. ... In opposition to the Jesuit, our men deny that the Fathers had anything to do with the fact of Transubstantiation, any more than with the name. He regards the fact of Transubstantiation as a change in substance (*substantialis transmutatio*). And he calls certain witnesses to prove this. And yet on this point, whether there is there a conversion in substance, not long before the Lateran Council the Master of the Sentences[1] himself says 'I am not able to define.' But all his witnesses speak of some kind of change (*promutatione, immutatione, transmutatione*). But there is no mention there of a change in substance, or of the substance. But neither do we deny in this matter the preposition *trans*; and we allow that the elements are changed (*transmutari*). But a change in substance we look for, and we find it nowhere. ...

At the coming of the almighty power of the Word, the nature is changed so that what before was the mere element now becomes a Divine Sacrament, the substance nevertheless remaining what it was before. ... There is that kind of union between the visible Sacrament and the invisible reality (*rem*) of the Sacrament which there is between the manhood and the Godhead of Christ, where unless you want to smack of Eutyches,[2] the Manhood is not transubstantiated into the Godhead. ...

About the adoration of the Sacrament he stumbles badly at the very threshold. He says 'of the Sacrament, that is, of Christ the Lord present by a wonderful but real way in the Sacrament.' Away with this. Who will allow him this? 'Of the Sacrament, that is, of Christ in the Sacrament.' Surely, Christ Himself, the reality (*res*) of the Sacrament, in and with the Sacrament, outside and without the Sacrament, wherever He is, is to be adored. Now the King [i.e. James I] laid down that Christ is really present in the Eucharist, and is really to be adored, that is, the reality (*rem*) of the Sacrament; but not the Sacrament, that is, the 'earthly part,' as Irenaeus[3] says, the 'visible,' as Augustine says. We also, like Ambrose, 'adore the flesh of Christ in the mysteries,'[4] and yet not it but Him Who is worshipped on the altar. For the Cardinal puts his question badly, 'What is there worshipped?' since he ought to ask, 'Who?', as Nazianzen[5] says, 'Him,' not 'it.' And, like Augustine, we 'do not eat the flesh without first adoring.'[6] And yet we none of us adore the Sacrament. ...

Our men believe that the Eucharist was instituted by the Lord for a memorial of Himself, even of His Sacrifice, and, if it be lawful so to speak, to be a commemorative sacrifice, not only to be a Sacrament and for spiritual nourishment. Though they allow this, yet they deny that either

---

[1] Peter Lombard, Bishop of Paris, mid-12th cent., *Libri Sententiarum*, IV. xi (see p. 156).
[2] See pp. 51 ff.   [3] See p. 79.   [4] *De Spirit. Sanct.*, iii. 79.
[5] Gregory of Nazianzus, *Orat.* viii. 18.   [6] Enarr. in Ps. xcviii. 9.

of these uses (thus instituted by the Lord together) can be divided from the other by man, either because of the negligence of the people or because of the avarice of the priests. The Sacrifice which is there is Eucharistic, of which Sacrifice the law is that he who offers it is to partake of it, and that he partake by receiving and eating, as the Saviour ordered. For to 'partake by sharing in the prayer,' that indeed is a fresh and novel way of partaking, much more even than the private Mass itself. ... Do you take away from the Mass your Transubstantiation; and there will not long be any strife with us about the Sacrifice. Willingly we allow that a memory of the Sacrifice is made there. That your Christ made of bread is sacrificed there we will never allow.

2. *Jeremy Taylor,* The Great Exemplar, III. XV. *Works* (Heber), iii. 296 ff.

As it is a Commemoration and Representation of Christ's death, so it is a Commemorative Sacrifice. As we receive the symbols and the mystery, so it is a Sacrament. In both capacities, the benefit is next to infinite. First, for whatsoever Christ did at the Institution, the same He commanded the Church to do in remembrance and repeated rites; and Himself also does the same thing in Heaven for us, making perpetual intercession for His Church, the Body of His redeemed ones, by representing to His Father His Death and Sacrifice. There He sits, a High Priest continually, and offers still the same one perfect Sacrifice; that is, still represents it as having been once finished and consummate, in order to perpetual and never failing events. And this also His ministers do on earth. They offer up the same Sacrifice to God, the Sacrifice of the Cross by prayers, and a commemorating rite and representment, according to His holy Institution. ... Our very holding up the Son of God and representing Him to his Father is the doing an act of mediation and advantage to ourselves in the virtue and efficacy of the Mediator. As Christ is a Priest in Heaven for ever and yet does not sacrifice Himself afresh, nor yet without a Sacrifice could He be a Priest, but by a daily ministration and intercession represents His Sacrifice to God and offers Himself as sacrificed, so He does upon earth by the ministry of His servants. He is offered to God; that is, He is by prayers and the Sacrament represented or offered up to God as sacrificed, which in effect is a celebration of His Death, and the applying it to the present and future necessities of the Church as we are capable by a ministry like to His in Heaven. It follows, then, that the celebration of this Sacrifice be in its proportion an instrument of applying the proper Sacrifice to all the purposes which it first designed. It is ministerially and by application an instrument propitiatory; it is eucharistical; it is an homage and an act of adoration; and it is impetratory and obtains for us and for the whole church all the benefits of the Sacrifice, which is now celebrated and applied. That is, as this rite is the remembrance and ministerial celebration of Christ's Sacrifice, so it is destined to do honour to God, to express the homage and duty of His servants, to acknowledge His supreme dominion, to give Him thanks and worship, to beg pardon, blessings, and supply of all our needs. And its profit is enlarged not only to the persons celebrating, but to all to whom they design it, according to the nature of sacrifices and prayers and all such solemn actions of religion.

f. Confession

John Cosin [?]. From the Notes appended to Nicholls' *Commentary on the Book of Common Prayer.*   Cosin's *Works*, ed. L.A.C.T., v. 163 f. [Authorship uncertain.]

The Church of England, howsoever it holdeth not Confession and Absolution Sacramental that is made unto and received from a Priest to be so absolutely necessary, as without it there can be no remission of sins, yet by this place[1] it is manifest what she teacheth concerning the virtue and force of this sacred action. The Confession is commanded to be special. The Absolution is the same that the ancient Church and the present Church of Rome useth. What would they more? Maldonate, their greatest divine that I meet with, *De Paenit*, p. 19, saith thus *Ego autem sic respondendum puto, non esse necesse, ut semper peccata remittantur per sacramentum paenitentiae, sed ut ipsum sacramentum natura sua possit peccata remittere, si inveniat peccata, et non inveniat contrarium impedimentum.*[2] And so much we acknowledge. Our 'if he feel his conscience troubled' is no more than his *si inveniat peccata*; for if he be not troubled with sin, what needs either Confession or Absolution? Venial sins that separate not from the grace of God need not so much to trouble a man's conscience; if he hath committed any mortal sin, then we require Confession of it to a Priest, who may give him, upon his true contrition and repentance, the benefit of Absolution, which takes effect according to his disposition that is absolved. And therefore the Church of Rome adds to the Form of Absolution, *Quantum in me est, et de jure possum, ego te*

---

[1] i.e. in the Office for the Visitation of the Sick.

[2] 'I think the reply should be: It is not necessary that sins should always be remitted through the sacrament of penance, but that the sacrament should of its own nature have power to remit sins if it meet with sin, and meet not with a contrary impediment.'

absolvo;[1] not absolutely, lest the doctrine should get head, that some of their ignorant people believe, that be the party confessed never so void of contrition the very act of Absolution forgives him his sins. The truth is, that in the Priest's Absolution there is the true power and virtue of forgiveness, which will most certainly take effect, *Nisi ponitur obex,*[2] as in Baptism.

g. Prayer for the Dead

Herbert Thorndike, 1598–1672 From *Just Weights and Measures; That is, The Present State of Religion Weighed in the Balance, and Measured by the Standard of the Sanctuary,* xvi. §§ 1–3.   Works, ed. L.A.C.T., v. 186 f.

The practice of the Church in interceding for them [i.e. for the Departed] at the Celebration of the Eucharist is so general and so ancient, that it cannot be thought to have come in upon imposture, but that the same aspersion will seem to take hold of the common Christianity.

But to what effect this intercession was made, that is, indeed, the due point of difference. For they, who think that the ancient Church prayed, and do themselves pray, for the removing of them from a place of purgatory-pains into perfect happiness by the clear sight of God, offend against the ancient Church, as well as against the Scripture, both ways. For Justin Martyr makes it a part of the Gnostics' heresy, that the soul without the body is in perfect happiness. They indeed held it, because they denied the resurrection. But the Church therefore, believing the resurrection, believes no perfect happiness of the soul before it. And the great consent of the ancient Church in this point is acknowledged by divers learned writers in the Church of Rome. Neither is the consent of it less evident in this, that there is no translating of souls into a new estate before the great trial of the general judgement.

In the meantime, then, what hinders them to receive comfort and refreshment, rest and peace and light (by the visitation of God, by the consolation of His Spirit, by His good Angels), to sustain them in the expectation of their trial, and the anxieties they are to pass through during the time of it? And though there be hope for those that are most solicitous to live and die good Christians, that they are in no such suspense, but within the bounds of the Heavenly Jerusalem, yet because their condition is uncertain and where there is hope of the better there is fear of the worse, therefore the Church hath always assisted them with

---

[1] 'As far as in me lies, and to the extent of my lawful power, I absolve thee.'
[2] 'Unless an obstacle is put in the way.'

the prayers of the living, both for their speedy trial (which all blessed souls desire), and for their easy absolution and discharge with glory before God, together with the accomplishment of their happiness in the receiving of their bodies.

II. JAMES I AND THE PURITANS

a. The Millenary Petition, 1603   Fuller, *Church History*, 1655, bk. x. 21

[This petition—which was given its name because of the doubtless exaggerated claim that it represented 1000 clergy—was presented to James on his way to London after his accession. James promised a conference, which was held at Hampton Court the following year. The Puritans then increased their demands, but few concessions were made to them. The Prayer Book was issued with a few explanations for the benefit of the Puritans, and conformity was enjoined.]

Most gracious and dread sovereign,—Seeing it has pleased the Divine majesty, to the great comfort of all good Christians, to advance your highness, according to your just title, to the peaceable government of this Church and Commonwealth of England, we, the ministers of the gospel in this land, neither as factious men affecting a popular parity in the Church, nor as schismatics aiming at the dissolution of the State ecclesiastical, but as the faithful servants of Christ and loyal subjects to your majesty, desiring and longing for the redress of divers abuses of the Church, could do no less in our obedience to God, service to your majesty, love to His Church, than acquaint your princely majesty with our particular griefs; for as your princely pen writeth, 'the king, as a good physician, must first know what peccant humours his patient naturally is most subject unto, before he can begin his cure'; and although divesrs of us that sue for reformation have formerly, in respect of the times, subscribed to the book—some upon protestation, some upon exposition given them, some with condition rather than the Church should have been deprived of their labour and ministry—yet now we, to the number of more than a thousand of your majesty's subjects and ministers, all groaning as under a common burden of human rites and ceremonies, do with one joint consent humble ourselves at your majesty's feet, to be eased and relieved in this behalf. Our humble suit, then, unto your majesty is that these offences following, some may be removed, some amended, some qualified:

(1) In the Church service: that the cross in baptism, interrogatories ministered to infants, confirmation, as superfluous, may be taken away; baptism not to be ministered by women, and so explained; the cap and surplice not urged; that examination may go before the communion;

that it be ministered with a sermon; that divers terms of priests, and absolution, and some other used, with the ring in marriage, and other such like in the book, may be corrected; the longsomeness of service abridged, Church songs and music moderated to better edification; that the Lord's Day be not profaned; the rest upon holy days not so strictly urged; that there may be a uniformity of doctrine prescribed; no popish opinion to be any more taught or defended; no ministers charged to teach their people to bow at the name of Jesus; that the canonical Scriptures only be read in the Church.

(2) Concerning Church ministers: that none hereafter be admitted into the ministry but able and sufficient men, and those to preach diligently and especially upon the Lord's day; that such as be already entered and cannot preach, may either be removed, and some charitable course taken with them for their relief, or else be forced, according to the value of their livings, to maintain preachers; that non-residency be not permitted; that King Edward's statute for the lawfulness of ministers' marriages be revived; that ministers be not urged to subscribe, but according to the law, to the Articles of Religion, and the king's supremacy only.

(3) For Church livings and maintenance: that bishops leave their commendams, some holding parsonages, some prebends, some vicarages, with their bishoprics; that double-beneficed men be not suffered to hold some two, some three benefices with cure, and some two, three, or four dignities besides; that impropriations annexed to bishoprics and colleges be demised only to the preachers incumbents, for the old rent; that the impropriations of laymen's fees be charged, with a sixth or seventh part of their worth, to the maintenance of the preaching minister.

(4) For Church discipline: that the discipline and excommunication may be administered according to Christ's own institution, or, at the least, that enormities may be redressed, as namely, that excommunication come not forth under the name of lay persons, chancellors, officials, etc.; that men be not excommunicated for trifles and twelve-penny matters; that none be excommunicated without consent of his pastor; that the officers be not suffered to extort unreasonable fees; that none having jurisdiction or registers' places, put out the same to farm; that divers popish canons (as for restraint of marriage at certain times) be reversed, that the longsomeness of suits in ecclesiastical courts (which hang sometimes two, three, four, five, six, or seven years) may be restrained; that the oath *Ex Officio*, whereby men are forced to accuse themselves, be more sparingly used; that licences for marriages without banns asked, be more cautiously granted:

These, with such other abuses yet remaining and practised in the Church of England, we are able to show not to be agreeable to the Scriptures, if it shall please your highness further to hear us, or more at large by writing to be informed, or by conference among the learned to be resolved; and yet we doubt not but that, without any further process, your majesty (of whose Christian judgement we have received so good a taste already) is able of yourself to judge of the equity of this cause. God, we trust, has appointed your highness our physician to heal these diseases; and we say with Mordecai to Esther, 'Who knoweth whether you are come to the kingdom for such a time?' Thus your majesty shall do that which we are persuaded shall be acceptable to God, honourable to your majesty in all succeeding ages, profitable to His Church, which shall be thereby increased, comfortable to your ministers, which shall be no more suspended, silenced, disgraced, imprisoned for men's traditions, and prejudicial to none but to those that seek their own quiet, credit and profit in the world.

Thus, with all dutiful submission, referring ourselves to your majesty's pleasure for your gracious answer, as God shall direct you, we most humbly recommend your highness to the Divine majesty, whom we beseech, for Christ His sake, to dispose your royal heart to do herein what shall be to His glory, the good of His Church, and your endless comfort.

Your majesty's most humble subjects, the ministers of the Gospel that desire not a disorderly innovation, but a due and godly reformation.

b. *The Book of Sports,* 1618   G. and H. xciii

[Then, as now, the Puritan party mistakenly supposed that Sunday was to be identified with the Jewish Sabbath. Their views had aroused great opposition, and James, who seems to have liked the sound of his own words, ordered the *Book of Sports* to be read from the pulpit. But so many of the clergy refused that he was forced to withdraw his order. The manifesto was reissued by Charles I in 1633.]

Whereas upon our return the last year out of Scotland, we did publish our pleasure touching the recreations of our people in those parts under our hand; for some causes us thereunto moving, we have thought good to command these our directions then given in Lancashire, with a few words thereunto added, and most applicable to these parts of our realms, to be published to all our subjects.

Whereas we did justly in our progress through Lancashire rebuke some Puritans and precise people, and took order that the like unlawful carriage should not be used by any of them hereafter, in the prohibiting and unlawful punishing of our good people for using their lawful recreations and honest exercises upon Sundays, and other holy days, after the afternoon sermon or service, we now find that two sorts of people wherewith that country is much infected, we mean Papists and Puritans, have maliciously traduced and calumniated those our just and honourable proceedings: and therefore lest our reputation might upon the one side (though innocently) have some aspersion laid upon it, and that upon the other part our good people in that country be misled by the mistaking and misinterpretation of our meaning, we have therefore thought good hereby to clear and make our pleasure to be manifested to all our good people in those parts.

It is true that at our first entry to this crown and kingdom we were informed, and that too truly, that our county of Lancashire abounded more in popish recusants than any county of England, and thus hath still continued since, to our great regret, with little amendment, save that, now of late, in our last riding through our said country, we find both by the report of the judges, and of the bishop of that diocese, that there is some amendment now daily beginning, which is no small contentment to us.

The report of this growing amendment amongst them made us the more sorry, when with our own ears we heard the general complaint of our people, that they were barred from all lawful recreation and exercise upon the Sunday's afternoon, after the ending of all divine service, which cannot but produce two evils: the one the hindering of the conversion of many, whom their priests will take occasion hereby to vex, persuading them that no honest mirth or recreation is lawful or tolerable in our religion, which cannot but breed a great discontentment in our people's hearts, especially of such as are peradventure upon the point of turning: the other inconvenience is, that this prohibition barreth the common and meaner sort of people from using such exercises as may make their bodies more able for war, when we or our successors shall have occasion to use them; and in place thereof sets up filthy tipplings and drunkenness, and breeds a number of idle and discontented speeches in their alehouses. For when shall the common people have leave to exercise, if not upon the Sundays and holy days, seeing they must apply their labour and win their living in all working-days?

Our express pleasure therefore is, that the laws of our kingdom and canons of our Church be as well observed in that county, as in all other places of this our kingdom: and on the other part, that no lawful recreation shall be barred to our good people, which shall not tend to the breach of our aforesaid laws and canons of our Church: which to express more particularly, our pleasure is, that the bishop, and all other inferior churchmen and churchwardens, shall for their parts be careful and diligent, both to instruct the ignorant, and convince and reform them that are misled in religion, presenting them that will not conform themselves, but obstinately stand out, to our judges and justices: whom we likewise command to put the law in due execution against them.

Our pleasure likewise is, that the bishop of that diocese take the like strait order with all the Puritans and Precisians within the same, either constraining them to conform themselves or to leave the county, according to the laws of our kingdom and canons of our Church, and so to strike equally on both hands against the contemners of our authority and adversaries of our Church: and as for our good people's lawful recreation, our pleasure likewise is, that after the end of divine service our good people be not disturbed, letted or discouraged from any lawful recreation, such as dancing, either men or women; archery for men, leaping, vaulting, or any other such harmless recreation, nor from having of May-games, Whitsun-ales, and Morris-dances; and the setting up of May-poles and other sports therewith used: so as the same be had in due and convenient time, without impediment or neglect of divine service; and that women shall have leave to carry rushes to the church for the decorating of it, according to their old custom; but withal we do here account still as prohibited all unlawful games to be used upon Sundays only, as bear and bull-baitings, interludes, and at all times in the meaner sort of people by law prohibited, bowling.

And likewise we bar from this benefit and liberty all such known as recusants, either men or women, as will abstain from coming to church or divine service, being therefore unworthy of any lawful recreation after the said service, that will not first come to the church and serve God: prohibiting in like sort the said recreations to any that, though [they] conform in religion, are not present in the church at the service of God, before their going to the said recreations. Our pleasure likewise is, that they to whom it belongeth in office, shall present and sharply punish all such, as in abuse of this our liberty, will use these exercises before the ends of all divine services for that day: and we likewise straitly command that every person shall resort to this own parish church to hear divine service, and each parish by itself to use the said recreation after divine service: prohibiting likewise any offensive weapons to be carried or used in the said times of recreation: and our pleasure is, that this our declaration shall be published by order from the bishop of the diocese, through all the parish churches, and that both our judges of our circuit, and our justices of our peace be informed thereof. ...

III. THE SOLEMN LEAGUE AND COVENANT, 1643
Rushworth, *Hist Coll.* v. 478

[This was based on the National Covenant signed by the Scots in 1639, after the attempt, in 1637, to force the English Prayer Book upon Scotland. In 1644, in return for military help from Scotland, it was imposed on all Englishmen over 18 years of age.]

A solemn league and covenant for reformation and defence of religion, the honour and happiness of the king, and the peace and safety of the three kingdoms of England, Scotland, and Ireland.

We noblemen, barons, knights, gentlemen, citizens, burgesses, ministers of the gospel, and commons of all sorts in the kingdoms of England, Scotland, and Ireland, by the providence of God living under one king, and being of one reformed religion; having before our eyes and glory of God, and the advancement of the kingdom of our Lord and Saviour Jesus Christ, the honour and happiness of the king's majesty and his posterity, and the true public liberty, safety, and peace of the kingdoms, wherein every one's private condition is included; and calling to mind the treacherous and bloody plots, conspiracies, attempts, and practices of the enemies of God against the true religion and professors thereof in all places, especially in these three kingdoms, even since the reformation of religion, and how much their rage, power, and presumption are of late, and at this time, increased and exercised, whereof the deplorable estate of the Church and kingdom of Ireland, the distressed estate of the Church and kingdom of England, and the dangerous estate of the Church and kingdom of Scotland, are present and public testimonies: we have (now at last), after other means of supplication, remonstrance, protestations, and sufferings, for the preservation of ourselves and our religion from utter ruin and destruction, according to the commendable practice of these kingdoms in former times, and the example of God's people in other nations, after mature deliberation, resolved and determined to enter into a mutual and solemn league and covenant, wherein we all subscribe, and each one of us for himself, with our hands lifted up to the most high God, do swear:

1

That we shall sincerely, really and constantly, through the grace of God, endeavour in our several places and callings, the preservations of the reformed religion in the Church of Scotland, in doctrine, worship, discipline, and government, against our common enemies; the reformation of religion in the kingdoms of England and Ireland, in doctrine, worship, discipline, and government, according to the word of God and the example of the best reformed Churches; and we shall endeavour to bring the Churches of God in the three kingdoms to the nearest conjunction and uniformity in religion, confession of faith, form of Church government, directory for worship and catechizing, that we, and our posterity after us, may, as brethren, live in faith and love, and the Lord may delight to dwell in the midst of us.

2

That we shall in like manner, without respect of persons, endeavour the extirpation of popery, prelacy (that is, Church government by archbishops, bishops, their chancellors and commissaries, deans, deans and chapters, archdeacons, and all other ecclesiastical officers depending on that hierarchy), superstition, heresy, schism, profaneness, and whatsoever shall be found to be contrary to sound doctrine and the power of godliness, lest we partake in other men's sins, and thereby be in danger to receive of their plagues; and that the Lord may be one, and His name one in the three kingdoms.

3

We shall, with the same sincerity, reality and constancy, in our several vocations, endeavour with our estates and lives mutually to preserve the rights and privileges of the Parliaments and the liberties of the kingdoms, and to preserve and defend the king's majesty's person and authority, in the preservation and defence of the true religion and liberties of the kingdoms, that the world may bear witness with our consciences of our loyalty, and that we have no thoughts or intentions to diminish his majesty's just power and greatness.

4

We shall also with all faithfulness endeavour the discovery of all such as have been or shall be incendiaries, malignants, or evil instruments, by hindering the reformation of religion, dividing the king from his people, or one of the kingdoms from another, or making any faction or parties amongst the people, contrary to the league and covenant, that they may be brought to public trial and receive condign punishment, as the degree of their offences shall require or deserve, or the supreme judicatories of both kingdoms respectively, or others having power from them for that effect, shall judge convenient.

5

And whereas the happiness of a blessed peace between these kingdoms, denied in former times to our progenitors, is by the good providence of God granted to us, and hath been lately concluded and settled by both Parliaments: we shall each one of us, according to our places and interest, endeavour that they may remain conjoined in a firm peace and union to all posterity, and that justice may be done upon the wilful opposers thereof, in a manner expressed in the precedent articles.

6

We shall also, according to our places and callings, in the common cause of religion, liberty and peace of the kingdom, assist and defend all those that enter into this league and covenant, in the maintaining and pursuing thereof; and shall not suffer ourselves, directly or indirectly, by whatsoever combination, persuasion, or terror, to be divided and withdrawn from this blessed union and conjunction, whether to make defection to the contrary part, or give ourselves to a detestable indifference or neutrality in this cause, which so much concerneth the glory of God, the good of the kingdoms and honour of the king; but shall all the days of our lives zealously and constantly continue therein, against all opposition, and promote the same according to our power, against all lets and impediments whatsoever; and what we are not able ourselves to suppress or overcome we shall reveal and make known, that it may be timely prevented or removed: all which we shall do as in the sight of God.

And because these kingdoms are guilty of many sins and provocations against God and His Son Jesus Christ, as is too manifest by our present distresses and dangers, the fruits thereof: we profess and declare, before God and the world, our unfeigned desire to be humbled for our sins, and for the sins of these kingdoms; especially that we have not as we ought valued the inestimable benefit of the gospel; that we have not laboured for the purity and power thereof; and that we have not endeavoured to receive Christ in our hearts, not to walk worthy of Him in our lives, which are the causes of other sins and transgressions so much abounding amongst us, and our true and unfeigned purpose, desire, and endeavour, for ourselves and all others under power and charge, both in public and in private, in all our duties we owe to God and man, to amend our lives, and each one to go before another in the example of a real reformation, that the Lord may turn away His wrath and heavy indignation, and establish these Churches and kingdoms in truth and peace. And this covenant we make in the presence of Almighty God, the Searcher of all hearts, with a true intention to perform the same, as we shall answer at that great day when the secrets of all hearts shall be disclosed; most humbly beseeching the Lord to strengthen us by His Holy Spirit for this end, and to bless our desires and proceedings with such success as may be a deliverance and safety to His people, and encouragement to the Christian Churches groaning under or in danger of the yoke of antichristian tyranny, to join in the same or like association and covenant, to the glory of God, the enlargement of the kingdom of Jesus Christ, and the peace and tranquillity of Christian kingdoms and commonwealths.

IV. PRESBYTERIANISM

The Westminster Confession of Faith, 1643   Schaff, *Creeds of Christendom*, III, etc.

[The Westminster Confession was drawn up in 1643 by the Assembly of Divines to which was entrusted the task of organizing the new Establishment. In 1689, when Episcopacy was abolished in the Church of Scotland, it became the official formulary of that Church, to which, until 1910, all ministers had to subscribe. Subscription is now made to the 'fundamental doctrines' of the Confession as a 'subordinate standard' of the faith. (See pp. 403–5.) It holds an historic place in English-speaking Presbyterianism.]

I. Of the Holy Scripture

... The authority of the Holy Scripture ... dependeth not on the testimony of any man or Church; but wholly upon God (who is truth itself) the author thereof. ... Our full persuasion and assurance of the infallible truth and divine authority thereof is from the inward work of the Holy Spirit, bearing witness, by and with the Word, in our hearts. ... Nothing is at any time to be added—whether by new revelations of the Spirit or traditions of men. ... The Church is finally to appeal to them. ... The infallible rule of interpretation of Scripture is the Scripture itself. ...

II. *Of God and of the Holy Trinity*

III. *Of God's Eternal Decree*

God from all eternity did, by the most wise and holy counsel of His own will, freely and unchangeably ordain whatsoever comes to pass. Yet so as thereby neither is God the author of sin or is violence offered to the will of the creatures. ... By the decree of God, for the manifestation of His glory, some men and angels are predestinated unto everlasting life, and others foreordained to everlasting death. ... Neither are any redeemed by Christ ... but the elect only. The rest of mankind God was pleased ... to pass by, and to ordain them to dishonour and wrath. ...

IV. *Of Creation*

V. *Of Providence*

VI. *Of the Fall of Man, etc.*

Our first parents ... so became dead in sin and wholly defiled in all the faculties and parts of soul and body. They being the root of all mankind, the guilt of this sin was imputed, and the same death in sin and corrupted nature conveyed, to all their posterity ... whereby we are utterly indisposed, disabled, and made opposite to all good, and wholly inclined to all evil. ...

VII. *Of God's Covenant with Man*

VIII. *Of Christ the Mediator*

IX. *Of Free-Will*

... Man, by his fall into a state of sin, hath wholly lost all ability of will to any spiritual good. ... When God converts a sinner and translates him into the state of grace, He freeth him from his natural bondage under sin; and by His grace alone enables him freely to will and to do that which is spiritually good. ...

X. *Of Effectual Calling*

All those whom God hath predestinated unto life—and those only—He is pleased, in His appointed and accepted time, effectually to call by His Word and Spirit ... not from anything foreseen in man, who is altogether passive therein. ... Elect infants, dying in infancy, are regenerated and saved by Christ through the Spirit, who worketh when, where, and how He pleaseth. ...

XI. *Of Justification*

Those whom God effectually calleth, He also freely justifieth ... by imputing the obedience and satisfaction of Christ unto them. ... They are not justified, until the Holy Spirit doth in due time actually apply Christ until them. ... Although they can never fall from the state of justification, yet they may by their sins fall under God's fatherly displeasure. ...

XII. *Of Adoption*

XIII. *Of Sanctification*

XIV. *Of Saving Faith*

XV. *Of Repentance unto Life*

XVI. *Of Good Works*

Good works are only such as God hath commanded in His holy Word—and not such as, without the warrant thereof, are devised by men out of blind zeal or upon any pretence of good intention. ... Works done by unregenerate men—although, for the matter of them, they may be things which God commands ... are sinful and cannot please God. ... And yet their neglect of them is more sinful and displeasing unto God.

XVII. *Of the Perseverance of the Saints*

They whom God hath accepted ... can neither totally nor finally fall away from the state of grace; but shall certainly persevere therein to the end and be eternally saved. ...

XVIII. *Of Assurance of Grace and Salvation*

... This certainly is not a bare conjecture and probable persuasion grounded upon fallible hope, but an infallible assurance of faith—founded upon the divine truth of the promises of salvation, the inward evidence of those graces unto which the promises are made, the testimony of the spirit of adoption witnessing with our spirits. ...

XIX. *Of the Law of God*

XX. *Of Christian Liberty, and Liberty of Conscience*

... God alone is Lord of the conscience; and hath left it free from the doctrines and commandments of men, which are in anything contrary to His Word—or beside it, if matters of faith or worship. So that to believe such doctrines or to obey such commands out of conscience, is to betray true liberty of conscience. ... For their publishing to such opinions or maintaining of such practices as ... are destructive to the external peace and order which Christ hath established in the Church, they may lawfully be called to account, and proceeded against by the censures of the Church and by the power of their civil magistrate.

XXI. *Of Religious Worship, and the Sabbath Day*

XXII. *Of Lawful Oaths and Vows*

XXIII. *Of the Civil Magistrate*

... It is his duty to take order that unity and peace be preserved in the Church, that the truth of God be kept pure and entire, that all blasphemies and heresies be suppressed, all corruptions and abuses in worship and discipline prevented and reformed, and all ordinances of God duly settled, administered and observed. For the better effecting whereof, he hath power to call synods, to be present at them, and to provide that whatsoever is transacted within be according to the mind of God. ...

XXIV. *Of Marriage and Divorce*

XXV. *Of the Church*

The Catholic or universal Church, which is invisible, consists of the whole number of the elect. ... The visible Church, which is also Catholic or universal under the Gospel, consists of all those throughout the world that profess the true religion, together with their children. ... This Catholic Church hath been sometimes more, sometimes less, visible; and particular Churches—which are members thereof—are more or less pure. ... There is no other head of the Church but the Lord Jesus Christ. Nor can the Pope of Rome in any sense be head thereof; but is that Antichrist, that man of sin, and son of perdition that exalteth himself in the Church against Christ and all that is called God.

XXVI. *Of the Communion of Saints*

XXVII. *Of the Sacraments*

XXVIII. *Of Baptism*

... Not only those that do actually profess faith and obedience unto Christ, but also the infants of one or both believing parents, are to be baptized. ... Grace and salvation are not so inseparably annexed to it, as that ... all that are baptized are undoubtedly regenerated. ...

XXIX. *Of the Lord's Supper*

... In this Sacrament Christ is not offered up to his Father, nor any real sacrifice made at all. ... Worthy receivers, outwardly partaking of the visible elements ... do then inwardly by faith, really and indeed, yet not carnally and corporally, but spiritually, receive and feed upon Christ crucified.

XXX. *Of Church Censures*

XXXI. *Of Synods and Councils*

XXXII. *Of the State of Men after Death*

XXXIII. *Of the Last Judgement*

V. BAPTIST CONFESSIONS OF FAITH

a. The First Confession, 1646   Schaff, *Creeds of Christendom*, III

[This confession was drawn up by seven congregations in London in 1646. It contains fifty-two articles.]

... (III) ... God hath, before the foundation of the world, foreordained some men to eternal life through Jesus Christ, to the praise and glory of

His grace: leaving the rest in their sin, to their just condemnation, to the praise of His justice. ... (VIII) The rule of this knowledge, faith, and obedience, concerning the worship of God,—in which is contained the whole duty of man,—is (not men's laws, or unwritten traditions, but) only the Word of God contained in the Scriptures; ... which are the only rule of holiness and obedience for all saints, at all times, in all places to be observed. ... (XXI) Jesus Christ by His death did purchase salvation for the elect that God gave unto Him; these only have interest in Him and fellowship with Him. ... The free gift of eternal life is given to them, and none else. ... (XXIII) All those that have this precious faith wrought in them by the Spirit, can never finally nor totally fall away. ... (XXXIII) The Church is a company of visible saints, called and separated from the world by the Word and Spirit of God, to the visible profession of the faith of the Gospel; being baptized into that faith. ... (XXXV) And all His servants ... are to lead their lives in this walled sheepfold and watered garden, ... to supply each other's wants, inward and outward. ... (XXXVI) Being thus joined, every Church hath power given them from Christ, for their well-being to choose among themselves meet persons for elders and deacons ... and none have power to impose on them either these or any other. ... (XXXIX) Baptism is an ordinance of the New Testament, given by Christ, to be dispensed upon persons *professing faith*, or that are made disciples; who, upon profession of faith, ought to be baptized and after to partake of the Lord's Supper. ... (XL) The way and manner of dispensing this ordinance, is *dipping or plunging the body under water*. It, being a sign, must answer the things signified; which is, that interest the saints have in the death, burial, and resurrection of Christ, and that as certainly as the body is buried under water, and risen again, so certainly shall the bodies of the saints be raised by the power of Christ, in the day of the resurrection, to reign with Christ. (XLVIII) ... We acknowledge with thankfulness, that God hath made this present king and parliament honourable in throwing down the prelatical hierarchy ... and concerning the worship of God, there is but one lawgiver ... Jesus Christ; who hath given laws and rules sufficient, in His Word, for His worship; and to make any more, were to charge Christ with want of wisdom or faithfulness, or both. ... It is the magistrates' duty to tender the liberty of men's consciences ... without which all other liberties will not be worth the naming. ... Neither can we forbear the doing of that, which our understandings and consciences bind us to do. And if the magistrates should require us to do otherwise, we are to yield our persons in a passive way to their power ... (The conclusion). Thus we desire to give unto Christ that which is His. ... Also we confess, that we know but in part, and that we are ignorant of many things which we desire and seek to know. And if any shall do us that friendly part, to shew us from the Word of God that we see not, we shall have cause to be thankful to God and to them. But if any man shall impose on us anything that we see not to be commanded by our Lord Jesus Christ, we should rather ... die a thousand deaths, than to do anything ... against the light of our own consciences.

b. The Second Confession, 1677 *Ibid.*

[This is modelled on the Westminster Confession. It was published, in thirty-two chapters, in 1677, and republished in 1689 with the recommendation of more than one hundred congregations.]

I. The Holy Scripture is the only sufficient, certain, and infallible rule of all saving knowledge, faith, and obedience. ... Nothing is at any time to be added, whether by new revelation of the Spirit or traditions of men. Nevertheless, we acknowledge that ... there are some circumstances concerning the worship of God and government of the Church, common to human actions and societies, which are to be ordered by the light of nature and Christian prudence, according to the general rules of the Word, which are always to be observed. ... The infallible rule of interpretation of Scripture is the Scripture itself. ...

III. [On Predestination, repeating Article III of the First Confession.]

X. ... Infants dying in infancy are regenerated and saved by Christ, through the Spirit; who worketh when, where and how He pleaseth; so also are all elect persons, who are incapable of being outwardly called by the ministry of the Word. Others, not elected, though they may be called by the ministry of the Word ... neither will nor can truly come to Christ, and therefore cannot be saved. ...

XIX. The grace of faith, whereby the elect are enabled to believe ... is ordinarily wrought by the ministry of the Word; by which also, and by the administration of Baptism and the Lord's Supper, prayer, and other means appointed of God, it is increased and strengthened. ...

XXVI. The Catholic or universal Church, which (with respect to the internal work of the spirit and truth of grace) may be called invisible, consists of the whole number of the elect. ... The officers appointed by Christ to be chosen and set apart by the Church ... are bishops or elders and deacons. ...

XXIX. [On Baptism, repeating XXIX of the First Confession.]

VI. SELECTIONS FROM THE AGREEMENT
OF THE PEOPLE, 1649

Gardiner, *Constitutional Documents*, 270 [G. and H. cviii]

[By the acceptance of the Solemn League and Covenant episcopacy was abolished. In 1645 the 'Directory' displaced the Prayer Book, and in the next year a
presbyterian system was imposed on an unwilling country. Thereafter, until the
Protectorate, the inquisitorial Calvinism of Parliament succeeded only in producing a general anarchy in the Church. In 1649, at the close of the Civil War,
there was put forward this proposal for liberty—for all but papists and prelatists.
But it was not implemented until Cromwell was given supreme power.]

*An agreement of the people of England, and the places therewith incorporated,
for a secure and present peace, upon grounds of common right, freedom and
safety.*

9. *Concerning religion, we agree as followeth:*

(1) It is intended that the Christian religion be held forth and recommended as the public profession in this nation, which we desire may, by
the grace of God, be reformed to the greatest purity in doctrine, worship,
and discipline, according to the word of God; the instructing the people
thereunto in a public way, so it be not compulsive; as also the maintaining of able teachers for that end, and for the confutation or discovering of
heresy, error, and whatsoever is contrary to sound doctrine, is allowed to
be provided for by our representatives; the maintenance of which teachers may be out of a public treasury, and we desire, not by tithes:
provided that popery or prelacy be not held forth as the public way or
profession in this nation. (2) That, to the public profession so held forth,
none be compelled by penalties or otherwise; but only may be endeavoured to be won by sound doctrine, and by the example of good
conversation. (3) That such as profess faith in God by Jesus Christ,
however differing in judgement from the doctrine, worship, or discipline
publicly held forth as aforesaid, shall not be restrained from, but shall be
protected in, the profession of their faith and exercise of religion, according to their consciences, in any place except such as shall be set apart for
the public worship; where we provide not for them, unless they have
leave, so as they abuse not this liberty to the civil injury of others, or to
actual disturbance of the public peace on their parts. Nevertheless it is
not intended to be hereby provided that this liberty shall necessarily
extend to popery or prelacy. (4) That all laws, ordinances, statutes, and
clauses in any law, statute, or ordinance to the contrary of the liberty
herein provided for, in the two particulars next preceding concerning
religion, be, and are hereby, repealed and made void.

VII. SELECTIONS FROM THE INSTRUMENT
OF GOVERNMENT, 1653

Gardiner, *Constitutional Documents*, 314. [Selections from G. and H. cx]

[In December 1653 Cromwell was appointed Lord Protector and his power and duties defined in the Instrument of Government. The following clauses relate to religion.]

35. That the Christian religion, as contained in the scriptures, be held forth and recommended as the public profession of these nations; and that, as soon as may be, a provision, less subject to scruple and contention, and more certain than the present, be made for the encouragement and maintenance of able and painful teachers, for the instructing the people, and for the discovery and confutation of error, heresy, and whatever is contrary to sound doctrine; and until such provision be made, the present maintenance shall not be taken away or impeached.

36. That to the public profession held forth none shall be compelled by penalties or otherwise; but that endeavours be used to win them by sound doctrine and the example of a good conversation.

37. That such as profess faith in God by Jesus Christ (though differing in judgement from the doctrine, worship, or discipline publicly held forth) shall not be restrained from, but shall be protected in, the profession of the faith and exercise of their religion, so as they abuse not this liberty to the civil injury of others and to the actual disturbance of the public peace on their parts: provided this liberty be not extended to popery or prelacy, nor to such as, under the profession of Christ, hold forth and practise licentiousness.

38. That all laws, statutes, and ordinances, and clauses in any law, statute, or ordinance to the contrary of the aforesaid liberty, shall be esteemed as null and void.

39. That the Acts and ordinances of Parliament made for the sale or other disposition of the lands, rents, and hereditaments of the late king, queen, and prince, of archbishops and bishops, etc., deans and chapters, shall remain good and firm. ...

VIII. 'THE HUMBLE PETITION AND ADVICE', 1657
Scobell, *Acts and Ordinances of Parliament*, ii. 878.
[Selections in G. and H. cxiii]

[This petition, on passing into law, superseded the Instrument of Government. The Protectorate became practically a monarchy, and Independency the established religion. Church festivals were abolished, dancing was forbidden, churches were despoiled and desecrated.]

To his highness the lord protector of the commonwealth of England, Scotland, and Ireland, and the dominion thereto belonging, the humble petition and advice of the knights, citizens, and burgesses now assembled in the Parliament of this commonwealth: ...

10. And whereas your highness out of your zeal to the glory of God and the propagation of the gospel of the Lord Jesus Christ, has been pleased to encourage a godly ministry in these nations, we earnestly desire that such as do openly revile them or their assemblies, or disturb them in the worship or service of God to the dishonour of God, scandal of good men, or breach of the peace, may be punished according to law; and where the laws are defective that your highness will give consent to such laws as shall be made in that behalf.

11. That the true Protestant Christian religion, as it is contained in the Holy Scriptures of the Old and New Testament, and no other, be held forth and asserted for the public profession of these nations; and that a confession of faith, to be agreed by your highness and the Parliament, according to the rule and warrant of the Scriptures, be asserted, held forth, and recommended to the people of these nations, that none may be suffered or permitted, by opprobrious words or writing, maliciously or contemptuously to revile or reproach the confession of faith to be agreed upon as aforesaid; and such who profess faith in God the Father, and in Jesus Christ His eternal Son, the true God, and in the Holy Spirit, God coequal with the Father and the Son, one God blessed for ever, and do acknowledge the Holy Scriptures of the Old and New Testament to be the revealed Will and Word of God, and shall in other things differ in doctrine, worship, or discipline from the public profession held forth, endeavours shall be used to convince them by sound doctrine and the example of a good conversation; but that they may not be compelled thereto by penalties, nor restrained from their profession, but protected from all injury and molestation in the profession of the faith and exercise of their religion, whilst they abuse not this liberty to the civil injury of others, or the disturbance of the public peace; so that this liberty be not extended to popery or prelacy, or to the countenancing such who publish horrible blasphemies or practise or hold forth licentiousness or profaneness under the profession of Christ; and that those ministers or pubic preachers who shall agree with the public profession aforesaid in matters of faith, although in their judgement and practice they differ in matters of worship and discipline, shall not only have protection in the way of their churches and worship respectively, but be esteemed fit and capable, notwithstanding such difference (being otherwise duly qualified and duly approved), of any trust, promotion, or employment whatsoever in these

nations, that any ministers who agree in doctrine, worship, and discipline with the public profession aforesaid are capable of; and all others who agree with the public profession in matters of faith, although they differ in matters of worship and discipline as aforesaid, shall not only have protection as aforesaid, but be esteemed fit and capable, notwithstanding such difference (being otherwise duly qualified), of any civil trust, employment, or promotion in these nations: but for such persons who agree not in matters of faith with the public profession aforesaid, they shall not be capable of receiving the public maintenance appointed for the ministry.

Provided that this clause shall not be construed to extend to enable such minister or public preachers or pastors of congregations; but that they be disenabled, and they are hereby disenabled, to hold any civil employment which those in orders were or are disenabled to hold, by an Act, entitled: 'An Act for disenabling all Persons in Holy Orders to exercise any temporal jurisdiction or authority.' And that your highness will give your consent that all laws, statutes, ordinances, and clauses in any law, statute, and ordinance, so far as they are contrary to the aforesaid liberty, be repealed.

IX. THE INDEPENDENTS (CONGREGATIONALISM)

The Savoy Declaration of Faith and Order, 1658

[A few Independent divines were included in the Westminster Assembly, where they became known as the 'Dissenting Brethren' in a body mainly Presbyterian. But when the Assembly came to an end, as also did the king, and the army took control, the Scots, and with them the Presbyterians, were defeated. An Independent became Protector, and the Independents became the dominant party in the state. A conference of ministers was held at the Savoy Palace to define the Independent position: the Westminster Confession of Faith was adopted, with its Calvinism somewhat mitigated by omissions and alterations, and to it was added a preface of some prolixity, and thirty chapters on Order, which state the principles of Congregationalism.]

The Preface

... *Confessions* when *made by a company* of professors of Christianity jointly meeting to that end, the most genuine and natural use of such *Confessions* is, That under the same form of words, they express the substance of the same *common salvation,* or *unity of their faith*: whereby *speaking the same things, they shew themselves perfectly joyned in the same minde, and in the same judgement.*

And accordingly such a transaction is to be looked upon but as a meet or fit *medium* or *means* whereby to express that their *common faith and salvation*, and no way to be made use of as an *imposition* upon any: Whatever is of force or constraint in matters or this nature causeth them to degenerate from the *name* and *nature* of *Confessions*, and turns them from being *Confessions of Faith.* into *exactions* and *impositions of Faith.* ...

We have all along this season held forth (though quarreled with for it by our brethren) this great principle of these times, That amongst all Christian States and Churches, there ought to be vouchsafed a forebearance and mutual indulgence unto Saints of all persuasions, that keep unto, and hold fast the necessary foundation of faith and holiness, in all matters extrafundamental, whether of Faith or Order. ...

Of the INSTITUTION of CHURCHES and the ORDER Appointed in them by JESUS CHRIST

II. II. ... The Lord Jesus calleth out of the World unto Communion with himself, those that are given unto him by his Father. ...

III. Those thus called ... he commandeth to walk together in particular Societies or Churches, for their mutual edification. ...

IV. To each of these churches thus gathered, according to his minde declared in his Word, he hath given all that Power and Authority, which is any way needful for their carrying on that Order in Worship and Discipline, which he hath instituted for them to observe with Commands and Rules, for the due and right exerting and executing of that Power.

V. These particular Churches thus appointed by the Authority of Christ, and intrusted with power from him for the ends before expressed, are each of them as unto these ends, the seat of that Power which he is pleased to communicate to his Saints or Subjects in this world, so that as such they receive it immediately from himself.

VI. Besides these particular Churches, there is not instituted by Christ any Church more extensive or Catholique intrusted with power for the administration of his Ordinances, or the execution of any authority in his name.

VII. A particular Church gathered and completed according to the minde of Christ, consists of Officers and Members: The Lord Christ having given to his called ones (united according to his appointment in Church-order) Liberty and power to choose Persons fitted by the holy Ghost for that purpose, to be over them, and to minister to them in the Lord.

IX. The Officers appointed by Christ to be chosen and set apart by the Church so called, and gathered for the peculiar administration of the

Ordinances, and execution of Power or Duty which he intrusts them with, or calls them to, to be continued to the end of the World, are Pastors, Teachers, Elders, and Deacons.

XI. The way appointed by Christ for the calling of any person, fitted and gifted by the Holy Ghost, unto the Office of Pastor, Teacher or Elder in a Church, is, that he be chosen thereunto by the suffrage of the Church itself, and solemnly set apart by Fasting and Prayer, with the Imposition of Hands of the Eldership of that Church, if there be any before constituted therein: And of a Deacon, that he be chosen by the like suffrage, and set apart by Prayer, and the like Imposition of Hands.

XII. The Essence of this Call ... consists in the Election of the Church, together with the acceptance of it, and separation by *Fasting* and *Prayer*. And those who are so chosen, though not set apart by Imposition of Hands, are rightly constituted Ministers of Jesus Christ. ...

XXVI. In cases of Difficulties or Differences, either in point of Doctrine or Administrations ... it is according to the minde of Christ that many Churches holding communion together, do by their messengers meet in a Synod or Councel, to consider and give their advice ... Howbeit these Synods ... are not intrusted with any Church-Power, or with any jurisdiction over the Churches themselves. ...

XXVII. Besides these occasional Synods or Councels, there are not instituted by Christ any stated Synods in a fixed Combination of Churches, or their Officers in lesser or greater Assemblies. ...

XXX. Churches gathered and walking according to the minde of Christ, judging other Churches (though less pure) to be true Churches, may receive into occasional communion with them, such Members of those Churches as are credibly testified to be godly, and to live without offence.

X. THE CLARENDON CODE

[Three Acts aimed at the abolition of Nonconformity, issued under Lord Chancellor Clarendon.]

a. The Corporation Act, 1661   13 Charles II, stat. 2, cap. I: *Statutes of the Realm*, v. 321. [G. and H. cxvi]

... Be it enacted by the authority aforesaid, that all persons who upon the four-and-twentieth day of December, 1661, shall be mayors, alderman, recorders, bailiffs, town-clerks, common council-men, and other persons then bearing any office or offices of magistracy, or places, or trusts, or other employment relating to or concerning the government of the said respective cities, corporations and boroughs, and Cinque ports and their members, and other port-towns, shall at any time before the five-and-twentieth day of March, 1663, when they shall be thereunto required by the said respective commissioners or any three or more of them, take the oaths of allegiance and supremacy, and this oath following:

'I, A. B., do declare and believe that it is not lawful, upon any pretence whatsoever, to take arms against the king; and that I do abhor that traitorous position of taking arms by his authority against his person, or against those that are commissioned by him: so help me God.'

And also at the same time shall publicly subscribe, before the said commissioners or any three of them, this following declaration:

'I, A. B., do declare that I hold that there lies no obligation upon me or any other person, from the oath commonly called the Solemn League and Covenant; and that the same was in itself an unlawful oath, and imposed upon the subjects of this realm against the known laws and liberties of the kingdom.'

And that all such of the said mayors and other the persons aforesaid, by whom the said oaths are to be taken, and declaration subscribed as aforesaid, who shall refuse to take and subscribe the same within the time and in manner aforesaid, shall, from and immediately after such refusal, be by authority of this Act (*ipso facto*) removed and displaced of and from the said offices and places respectively; ...

Provided also, and be it enacted by the authority aforesaid, that from and after the expiration of the said commissions, no person or persons shall for ever hereafter be placed, elected, or chosen, in or to any the offices or places aforesaid, that shall not have, within one year next before such election or choice, taken the Sacrament of the Lord's Supper, according to the rites of the Church of England; and that every such person and persons so placed, elected, or chosen, shall likewise take the aforesaid three oaths, and subscribe the said declaration, at the same time when the oath for the due execution of the said places and offices respectively shall be administered; and in default hereof, every such placing, election, and choice is hereby enacted and declared to be void. ...

b. The Conventicle Act, 1664–70   22 Charles II, cap. I: *Statutes of the Realm*, v. 648. [G. and H. cxix]

[The modified form of 1670.]

For providing further and more speedy remedies against the growing and dangerous practices of seditious sectaries and other disloyal persons, who, under pretence of tender consciences, have or may at their meetings contrive insurrections (as late experience has shown), be it enacted by the king's most excellent majesty, by and with advice and consent of the Lords spiritual and temporal, and Commons, in this present Parliament assembled, and by authority of the same, that if any person of the age of sixteen years or upwards, being a subject of this realm, at any time after the tenth day of May next shall be present at any assembly, conventicle, or meeting, under colour or pretence of any exercise of religion, in other manner than according to the liturgy and practice of the Church of England, in any place within the kingdom of England, dominion of Wales, or town of Berwick-upon-Tweed, at which conventicle, meeting, or assembly there shall be five persons or more assembled together, over and besides those of the same household, if it be in a house where there is a family inhabiting, or if it be in a house, field, or place where there is no family inhabiting, then where any five persons or more are so assembled as aforesaid, it shall and may be lawful to and for any or more justices of the peace of the country, limit, division, corporation, or liberty wherein the offence aforesaid shall be committed, or for the chief magistrate of the place where such offence aforesaid shall be committed, and he and they are hereby required and enjoined, upon proof to him or them respectively made of such offence, either by confession of the party or oath of two witnesses (which oath the said justice and justices of the peace, and chief magistrate respectively, are hereby empowered and required to administer), or by notorious evidence and circumstances of the fact, to make a record of every offence under his or their hands and seals respectively; …

[Penalties to be 5s. for first offence; for subsequent offences 10s.]

And be it further enacted by the authority aforesaid, that the justice, justices of the peace, and chief magistrate respectively, or the respective constables, headboroughs, and tithingmen, by warrant from the said justice, justices, or chief magistrate respectively, shall and may, with what aid, force, and assistance they shall think fit, for the better execution of this Act, after refusal or denial to enter, break open and enter into any house or other place where they shall be informed any such conventicle as aforesaid is or shall be held, as well within liberties as without, and take into their custody the persons there unlawfully assembled, to the intent they may be proceeded against according to this Act; and that the lieutenants or deputy-lieutenants, or any commissionated officer of the militia, or other of his majesty's forces, with such troops or companies of horse and foot, and also the sheriffs, and other magistrates and minister of justice, or any of them, jointly or severally, within any the counties or places within this kingdom of England, dominion of Wales, or town of Berwick-upon-Tweed, with such other assistance as they shall think meet, or can get in readiness with the soonest, on certificate made to them respectively under the hand and seal of any one justice of the peace or chief magistrate, or of his particular information or knowledge of such unlawful meeting or conventicle held or to be held in their respective countries or places, and that he, with such assistance as he can get together, is not able to suppress and dissolve the same, shall and may, and are hereby required and enjoined to repair unto the place where they are so held or to be held, and, by the best means they can, to dissolve, dissipate, or prevent all such unlawful meetings, and take into their custody such and so many of the said persons so unlawfully assembled as they shall think fit, to the intent they may be proceeded against according to this Act.

c. The Five-Mile Act, 1665   17 Charles II, cap. 2. [G. and H. cxviii]

Whereas divers parsons, vicars, curates, lecturers, and other persons in Holy Orders, have not declared their unfeigned assent and consent to the use of all things contained and prescribed in the Book of Common Prayer and Administration of the Sacraments, and other Rites and Ceremonies of the Church, according to the Use of the Church of England, or have not subscribed the declaration or acknowledgement contained in a certain Act of Parliament made in the fourteenth year of his majesty's reign, and entitled 'An Act for the uniformity of public prayers and administration of Sacraments and other rites and ceremonies, and for the establishing the form of making, ordaining, and consecrating of bishops, priests, and deacons in the Church of England,' according to the said Act or any other subsequent Act; and whereas they or some of them, and divers other person and persons not ordained according to the form of the Church of England, and as have since the Act of Oblivion taken upon them to preach in unlawful assemblies, conventicles, or meetings, under colour or pretence of exercise of religion, contrary to the laws and statutes of this kingdom, have settled themselves in divers corporations in England, sometimes three or more of them in a place, thereby taking an opportunity to distil the poisonous principles of schism and rebellion into the hearts of his majesty's subjects, to the great danger of the Church and kingdom:

Be it therefore enacted by the king's most excellent majesty, by and with the advice and consent of the Lords spiritual and temporal, and the Commons, in this present Parliament assembled, and by the authority of the same, that the said parsons, vicars, curates, lecturers, and other persons in Holy Orders, or pretended Holy Orders, or pretending to Holy Orders, and all stipendaries and other persons who have been possessed of any ecclesiastical or spiritual promotion, and every of them, who have not declared their unfeigned assent and consent as aforesaid, and subscribed the declaration aforesaid, and shall not take and subscribe the oath following:

'I, *A. B.*, do swear that it is not lawful upon any pretence whatsoever to take arms against the king; and that I do abhor that traitorous position of taking arms by his authority against his person, or against those that are commissionated by him in pursuance of such commissions; and that I will not at any time endeavour any alteration of government, either in Church or State.'

And all such person and persons as shall take upon them to preach in any unlawful assembly, conventicle, or meeting, under colour or pretence of any exercise of religion, contrary to the laws and statutes of this kingdom, shall not at any time, from and after the four-and-twentieth day of March which shall be in this present year of our Lord God, 1665, unless only in passing upon the road, come or be within five miles of any city or town corporate, or borough that sends burgesses to the Parliament, within his majesty's kingdom of England, principality of Wales, or of the town of Berwick-upon-Tweed, or within five miles of any parish, town, or place wherein he or they have since the Act of Oblivion been parson, vicar, curate, stipendiary, or lecturer, or taken upon them to preach in any unlawful assembly, conventicle, or meeting, under colour or pretence of any exercise of religion, contrary to the laws and statutes of this kingdom, before he or they have taken and subscribed the oath aforesaid, before the justices of peace at their quarter sessions to be holden for the county, riding, or division next unto the said corporation, city or borough, parish, place or town, in open court (which said oath the said justices are hereby empowered there to administer); upon forfeiture of (*sic*) every such offence the sum of forty pounds of lawful English money, the one third part thereof to his majesty and his successors, the other third part to the use of the poor of the parish where the offence shall be committed, and the other third part thereof to such person or persons as shall or will sue for the same by action of debt, plaint, bill, or information, in any court of record at Westminster, or before any justices of assize, *oyer* and *terminer*, or gaol delivery, or before any justices of the counties palatine of Chester, Lancaster, or Durham, or the justices of the great sessions in Wales, or before any justices of peace in their quarter sessions, wherein no essoin, protection, or wager of law shall be allowed. ...

XI.   THE TEST ACT, 1673
25 Charles II, cap. 2. [G.H. cxx]

For preventing dangers which may happen from popish recusants, and quieting the minds of his majesty's good subjects, be it enacted by the king's most excellent majesty, by and with the advice and consent of the Lords spiritual and temporal, and the Commons, in this present Parliament assembled, and by authority of the same, that all and every person or persons, as well peers as commoners, that shall bear any office or offices, civil or military, or shall receive any pay, salary, fee, or wages by reason of any patent or grant from his majesty, or shall have command or place of trust from or under his majesty, or from any of his majesty's predecessors, or by his or their authority, or by authority derived from him or them, within the realm of England, dominion of Wales, or town of Berwick-upon-Tweed, or in his majesty's navy, or in the several islands of Jersey and Guernsey, or shall be of the household or in the service of employment of his majesty, or of his royal highness the Duke of York, who shall inhabit, reside, or be within the city of London or Westminster, or within thirty miles distant from the same, on the first day of Easter term, that shall be in the year of our Lord 1673, or at any time during the said term, all and every the said person and persons shall personally appear before the end of the said term, or of Trinity term next following, in his majesty's High Court of Chancery, or in his majesty's Court of King's Bench, and there in public and open court, between the hours of nine of the clock and twelve in the forenoon, take the several oaths of supremacy and allegiance—which oath of allegiance is contained in a statute made in the third year of King James—by law established; and during the time of the taking thereof by the said person and persons, all pleas and proceedings in the said respective courts shall cease: and that all and every of the said respective persons and officers, not having taken the said oaths in the said respective courts aforesaid, shall on or before the first day of August, 1673, at the quarter sessions for that county or place where he or they shall be, inhabit, or reside on the twentieth day of May, take the said oaths in open court between the said hours of nine and twelve of the clock in the forenoon; and the said respective officers aforesaid shall also receive the sacrament of the Lord's Supper, according to the usage of the Church of England, at or before the first day of August in the year of our Lord 1673, in some parish church, upon some Lord's day, commonly called Sunday, immediately after divine service and sermon.

And be it further enacted by the authority aforesaid, that at the same time when the persons concerned in this Act shall take the aforesaid oaths of supremacy and allegiance, they shall likewise make and subscribe this declaration following, under the same penalties and forfeitures as by this Act is appointed:

'I, *A. B.*, do declare that I do believe that there is not any transubstantiation in the Sacrament of the Lord's Supper, or in the elements of bread and wine, at or after the consecration thereof by any person whatsoever.'

Of which subscription there shall be the like register kept, as of the taking the oaths aforesaid.

XII. THE QUAKERS

The Chief Principles of the Christian religion, as professed by the people Called the Quakers

[These fifteen propositions were drawn up in 1678 by Robert Barclay, an educated disciple of George Fox. They form the headings of the fifteen chapters of his *Apology for the Quakers*.]

I. *Concerning the True Foundations of Knowledge*

Seeing the height of all happiness is placed in the true knowledge of God ... the right understanding of this foundation and ground of knowledge is that which is most necessary to be known and believed in the first place.

II. *Concerning Immediate Revelation*

Seeing no man knoweth the Father but the Son, and he to whom the Son revealeth Him; and seeing the revelation of the Son is in and by the Spirit; therefore the testimony of the Spirit is that alone by which the true knowledge of God hath been, is and can be only revealed; ... by the revelation of the same Spirit He hath manifested Himself all along unto the sons of men, both patriarchs, prophets, and apostles; which revelations of God by the Spirit, whether by outward voices and appearances, dreams, or inward objective manifestations in the heart, were of old the formal object of their faith, and remain yet so to be; since the object of the saints' faith is the same in all ages, though set forth under divers administrations. Moreover, these divine inward revelations, which we make absolutely necessary for the building up of true faith, neither do nor can contradict the outward testimony of the Scriptures, or right and sound reason. Yet from hence it will not follow that these divine revelations are to be subjected to the examination either of the outward testimony of the Scriptures, or of the natural reason of man, as to a more noble or certain rule and touchstone; for this divine revelation, and inward illumination, is that which is evident and clear of itself, forcing, by its own evidence and clearness, the well-disposed understanding to assent, irresistibly moving the same thereunto. ...

III. *Concerning the Scriptures*

From these revelations of the Spirit of God to the saints have proceeded the Scriptures of truth, ... nevertheless, because they are only a declaration of the fountain, and not the fountain itself, therefore they are not to be esteemed the principal ground of all truth and knowledge, nor yet the adequate primary rule of faith and manners. Nevertheless, as that which giveth a true and faithful testimony of the first foundation, they are and may be esteemed a secondary rule, subordinate to the Spirit from which they have all their excellency and certainty. ...

IV. *Concerning the Condition of Man in the Fall*

All Adam's posterity (or mankind) both Jews and Gentiles, as to the first Adam or earthly man, is fallen, degenerated, and dead, deprived of the sensation or feeling of this inward testimony or seed of God; and is subject unto the power, nature, and seed of the serpent. ... Hence are rejected the Socinian and Pelagian errors, in exalting a natural light; as also those of the Papists, and most Protestants, who affirm that man, without the true grace of God, may be a true minister of the Gospel. Nevertheless, this seed is not imputed to infants, until by transgression they actually join themselves therewith: for 'they are by nature the children of wrath, who walk according to the power of the prince of the air.' ...

V. and VI. *Concerning the Universal Redemption by Christ, and also the Saving and Spiritual Light wherewith every man is enlightened.*

God out of His infinite love, who delighteth not in the death of a sinner, but that all should live and be saved, hath so loved the world, that He hath given His only Son a light, that whosoever believeth in Him should be saved; who enlighteneth every man that cometh into the world. ...

... Therefore Christ hath tasted death for every man; not only for some kinds of men, as some vainly talk, but for every one, of all kinds; the benefit of whose offering is not only extended to such who have the distinct outward knowledge of His death and sufferings, as the same is declared in the Scriptures, but even unto those who are necessarily excluded from the benefits of this knowledge by some inevitable accident; which knowledge we willingly confess to be very profitable and comfortable, but not absolutely needful unto such from whom God himself hath withheld it.

VII. *Concerning Justification*

As many as resist not this light, but receive the same, in them is produced a holy, pure and spiritual birth; bringing forth holiness, righteousness, purity, and all those other blessed fruits which are acceptable to God. By which holy birth (to wit, Jesus Christ formed within us, and working his works in us) as we are sanctified, so are we justified in the sight of God. ...

VIII. *Concerning Perfection*

In whom this holy and pure birth is fully brought forth, the body of death and sin comes to be crucified and removed, and their hearts united and subjected to the truth, so as not to obey any suggestion or temptation of the evil one, but to be free from actually sinning and transgressing of the law of God, and in that respect perfect. Yet does this perfection still admit of a growth; and there remaineth a possibility of sinning. ...

IX. *Concerning Perseverance and the Possibility of Falling from Grace*

X. *Concerning the Ministry*

As by this gift, or light of God, all true knowledge in things spiritual is received and revealed ... by the leading, moving and drawing hereof ought every Evangelist and Christian pastor to be led and ordered in his labour and work of the Gospel, both as to the place where, as to the persons to whom, and as to the times when, he is to minister. Moreover, those who have this authority may and ought to preach the Gospel, though without human commission or literature, as, on the other hand, those who want the authority of this divine gift, however learned or authorized by the commissions of men and churches, are to be esteemed but as deceivers, and not true ministers of the Gospel. Also, those who have received this holy and unspotted gift, as they have freely received, so are they freely to give, without hire or bargaining, far less to use it as a trade to get money by it.

XI. *Concerning Worship*

All true and acceptable worship to God is offered in the inward and immediate moving and drawing of His own Spirit, which is neither limited to places, times, or persons: for though we be to worship Him always, in that we are to fear before Him; yet as to the outward significa- tion thereof in prayers, praises and preaching, we ought not to do it where and when we will, but where and when we are moved thereunto by the secret inspiration of His Spirit in our hearts; ... All other worship then, both praises, prayers and preachings, which man sets about in his own will, and at his own appointment, which he can both begin and end at his pleasure, do or leave undone as himself sees meet; whether they be a prescribed form, as a liturgy, or prayers conceived extemporarily, by the natural strength and faculty of the mind; they are all but super- stitions, will-worship, and abominable idolatry, in the sight of God; which are to be denied, rejected, and separated from in this day of His spiritual arising.

XII. *Concerning Baptism*

As there is one Lord and one faith, so there is one baptism; which is not the putting away the filth of the flesh, but the answer of a good con- science before God, by the resurrection of Jesus Christ. And this baptism is a pure and spiritual thing, to wit, the baptism of the Spirit and fire, by which we are buried with Him, that being washed and purged from our sins, we may walk in newness of life; of which the baptism of John was a figure which was commanded for a time, and not to continue for ever. As to the baptism of infants, it is a mere human tradition, for which neither precept nor practice is to be found in all the Scripture.

XIII. *Concerning the Communion, or Participation of the Body and Blood of Christ*

The Communion of the Body and Blood of Christ is inward and spiri- tual, which is the participation of His flesh and blood, by which the inward man is daily nourished in the hearts of those in whom Christ dwells; of which things the breaking of bread by Christ with His disciples was a figure, which they even used in the Church for a time, who had received the substance, for the cause of the weak; even as abstaining from things strangled, and from blood, the washing one another's feet and the anointing of the sick with oil; all of which are commanded with no less authority and solemnity than the former; yet seeing they are but the shadows of better things, they cease in such as have obtained the substance.

XIV. *Concerning the Power of the Civil Magistrate in Matters purely Religious and pertaining to the Conscience*

Since God hath assumed to himself the power and dominion of the conscience, who alone can rightly instruct and govern it, therefore it is not lawful for any whatsoever, by virtue of any authority or principality they bear in the government of this world, to force the consciences of others; ... provided always, that in man, under the pretence of conscience, prejudice his neighbour in his life or estate; or do anything destructive to, or inconsistent with, human society; in which case the law is for the transgressor, and justice to be administered upon all, without respect of persons.

XV. *Concerning Salutations and Recreations, etc.*

Seeing the chief end of all religion is to redeem man from the spirit and vain conversation of this world, and to lead into inward communion with God, before whom if we fear always, we are accounted happy, therefore all the vain customs and habits hereof, both in word and deed, are to be rejected and forsaken; such as the taking off the hat to a man, the bowing and cringings of the body, and such other salutations of that kind, with all the foolish and superstitious formalities attending them. ...

XIII. THE DECLARATION OF INDULGENCE, 1688

Patent Roll, 3 James II, 3, 18

[This declaration, giving rights of public worship to Nonconformists, both Protestant and Roman, was ordered to be read in all churches. Seven bishops drew up a petition against such an unconstitutional command. They were put on trial on a charge of seditious libel, but acquitted, and James, warned of the intended invasion of William of Orange, fled the country.]

It having pleased Almighty God not only to bring us to the imperial crown of these kingdoms through the greatest difficulties, but to preserve us by a more than ordinary providence upon the throne of our royal ancestors, there is nothing now that we so earnestly desire as to establish our government on such a foundation as may make our subjects happy, and unite them to us by inclination as well as duty. Which we think can be done by no means so effectually as by granting to them the free exercise of their religion for the time to come, and add that to the perfect enjoyment of their property, which has never been in any case invaded by us since our coming to the crown. Which being the two things men value most, shall ever be preserved in these kingdoms, during our reign over them, as the truest methods of their peace and our glory. We cannot but heartily wish, as it will easily be believed, that all the people of our dominions were members of the Catholic Church; yet we humbly thank Almighty God, it is and has of long time been our constant sense and opinion (which upon divers occasions we have declared) that conscience ought not to be constrained nor people forced in matters of mere religion: it has ever been directly contrary to our inclination, as we think it is to the interest of government, which it destroys by spoiling trade, depopulating countries, and discouraging strangers, and finally, that it never obtained the end for which it was employed. And in this we are the more confirmed by the reflections we have made upon the conduct of the four last reigns. For after all the frequent and pressing endeavours that were used in each of them to reduce this kingdom to an exact conformity in religion, it is visible the success has not answered the design, and that the difficulty is invincible.

We therefore, out of our princely care and affection unto all our loving subjects, that they may live at ease and quiet, and for the increase of trade and encouragement of strangers, have thought fit by virtue of our royal prerogative to issue forth this our declaration of indulgence, making no doubt of the concurrence of our two Houses of Parliament when we shall think it convenient for them to meet.

In the first place, we do declare that we will protect and maintain our archbishops, bishops, and clergy, and all other our subjects of the Church of England in the free exercise of their religion as by law established, and in the quiet and full enjoyment of all their possessions, without any molestation or disturbance whatsoever.

We do likewise declare, that it is our royal will and pleasure that from henceforth the execution of all and all manner of penal laws in matters ecclesiastical, for not coming to church, or not receiving the Sacrament, or for any other nonconformity to the religion established, or for or by reason of the exercise of religion in any manner whatsoever, be immediately suspended; and the further execution of the said penal laws and every of them is hereby suspended.

And to the end that by the liberty hereby granted the peace and security of our government in the practice thereof may not be endangered, we have thought fit, and do hereby straitly charge and command all our loving subjects, that—as we do freely give them leave to meet and serve God after their own way and manner, be it in private houses or places purposely hired or built for that use, so that they take especial care that nothing be preached or taught amongst them, which may any way tend to alienate the hearts of our people from us or our government, and that their meetings and assemblies be peaceably, openly, and publicly held, and all persons freely admitted to them, and that they do signify and make known to some one or more of the next justices of the peace what place or places they set apart for those uses, and that all our subjects may enjoy such their religious assemblies with greater assurance and protection—we have thought it requisite, and do hereby command, that no disturbance of any kind be made or given unto them, under pain of our displeasure, and to be further proceeded against with the utmost severity.

And forasmuch as we are desirous to have the benefit of the service of all our loving subjects, which by the law of nature is inseparably annexed to and inherent in our royal person, and that none of our subjects may for the future be under any discouragement or disability (who are otherwise well inclined and fit to serve us) by reason of some oaths or tests that have been usually administered on such occasions, we do hereby further declare, that it is our royal will and pleasure that the oaths commonly called 'The oaths of supremacy and allegiance,' and also the several tests and declarations mentioned in the Acts of Parliament made in the five-and-twentieth and thirtieth years of the reign of our late royal brother, King Charles II, shall not at any time hereafter be required to be taken, declared, or subscribed by any person or persons whatsoever, who is or shall be employed in any office or place of trust, either civil or military, under us or in our government. And we do further declare it to be our pleasure and intention from time to time hereafter, to grant our royal dispensations under our great seal to all our loving subjects so to be employed, who shall not take the said oaths, or subscribe or declare the said tests or declarations in the above-mentioned Acts and every of them.

And to the end that all our loving subjects may receive and enjoy the full benefit and advantage of our gracious indulgence, hereby intended, and may be acquitted and discharged from all pains, penalties, forfeitures, and disabilities by them or any of them incurred or forfeited, or which they shall or may at any time hereafter be liable to, for or by reason of their nonconformity, or the exercise of their religion, and from all suits, troubles, or disturbances for the same; we do hereby give our free and ample pardon unto all nonconformists, recusants, and other our loving subjects, for all crimes and things by them committed or done contrary to the penal laws, formerly made relating to religion, and the profession or exercise thereof; hereby declaring that this our royal pardon and indemnity shall be as good and effectual to all intents and purposes, as if every individual person had been therein particularly named, or had particular pardons under our great seal, which we do likewise declare shall from time to time be granted unto any person or persons desiring the same: willing and requiring our judges, justices, and other officers to take notice of and obey our royal will and pleasure hereinbefore declared.

And although the freedom and assurance we have hereby given in relation to religion and property might be sufficient to remove from the minds of our loving subjects all fears and jealousies in relation to either, yet we have thought fit further to declare that we will maintain them in all their properties and possessions, as well of church and abbey lands, as in any other their lands and properties whatsoever. Given at our court at Whitehall the fourth day of April 1687, in the third year of our reign.

SECTION XII

The British Churches in the Eighteenth and Nineteenth Centuries

I. THE DEISTIC CONTROVERSY OF THE EIGHTEENTH CENTURY

[These extracts are typical of the kind of argument used by the eighteenth-century rationalists.[1] They are taken from Creed and Boys Smith, *Religious Thought in the Eighteenth Century*, 1934.]

(1) From *Christianity as Old as the Creation, or the Gospel a Republication of the Religion of Nature* (1730), by Matthew Tindal (1637–1753), Fellow of All Souls College, Oxford.

c. 12. Revelation a Republication of the Religion of Nature

... If nothing but Reasoning can improve Reason, and no Book can improve my Reason in any Point, but as it gives me convincing Proofs of its Reasonableness; a Revelation, that will not suffer us to judge of its Dictates by our Reason, is so far from improving Reason, that it forbids the Use of it; and reasoning Faculties, unexercis'd, will have as little Force, as unexercis'd Limbs; he that is always carry'd, will at length be

---

[1] Deism, in contrast with Theism, would confine God's activity to the primal act of creation, and exclude the supernatural as contrary to reason.

unable to go: And if the *Holy Ghost*, as Bishop Taylor says, *works by heightening, and improving our natural Faculties*; it can only be by using such Means as will improve them, in proposing Reasons and Arguments to convince our Understanding; which can only be improv'd, by studying the Nature and Reason of Things: *I apply'd my Heart* (says the wisest of Men) *to know, and to search, and to seek out Wisdom, and the Reason of Things* (Eccles. vii. 25).

So that the Holy Ghost can't deal with Men as rational Creatures, but by proposing Arguments to convince their Understandings, and influence their Wills, in the same manner as if propos'd by other Agents; for to go beyond this, would be making Impressions on men, as a Seal does on Wax; to the Confounding of their Reasons, and their Liberty in choosing; and the Man would then be merely passive, and the Action would be the Action of another Being acting upon him; for which he could be in no way accountable; but if the Holy Ghost does not act thus, and Revelation itself be not arbitrary; must it not be founded on the Reason of Things? And consequently, be a Republication, or Restoration of the Religion of Nature?

(2) From *Christianity not Mysterious* (1696), by John Toland (1670–1722)

The Doctrines of the Gospel not Contrary to Reason

After having said so much of *Reason*, I need not operosely shew what it is to be contrary to it; for I take it to be very intelligible from the precedent Section, that *what is evidently repugnant to clear and distinct Ideas, or to our common Notions, is contrary to Reason*: I go on therefore to prove, that *the Doctrines of the Gospel*, if it be the Word of God, *cannot be so*. But if it be objected, that very few maintain they are: I reply, that no *Christian* I know of now (for we shall not disturb the Ashes of the Dead) expressly says *Reason* and the *Gospel* are contrary to one another. But, which returns to the same, very many affirm, that though the Doctrines of the latter cannot in themselves be contradictory to the Principles of the former, as proceeding both from God; yet, that according to our Conceptions of them, *they may see directly to clash*: And that though we cannot reconcile them by reason of our corrupt and limited Understandings; yet from the Authority of *Divine Revelation*, we are bound to believe and acquiesce in them; or, as the *Fathers* taught 'em to speak, to *adore what we cannot comprehend*.

This famous and admirable Doctrine is the undoubted Source of all the *Absurdities* that ever were seriously vented among *Christians*. Without the Pretence of it, we should never hear of the *Transubstantiation*, and other ridiculous Fables of the Church of *Rome*; nor of any of the *Eastern Ordures*, almost all receiv'd into this *Western Sink*: Nor should we be ever banter'd with the *Lutheran Impanation*, or the *Ubiquity* it has produc'd as one Monster ordinarily begets another. And tho the *Socinians* disown this Practice, I am mistaken if either they or the *Arians* can make their Notions of a *dignifi'd and Creature-God capable of Divine Worship*, appear more reasonable than the Extravagancies of other Sects touching the Article of the *Trinity*. ...

Faith and Knowledge

But 'tis affirmed, that God *has a Right to require the Assent of his Creatures to what they cannot comprehend*; and, questionless, he may command whatever is just and reasonable, for to act Tyrannically do's only become the *Devil*. But I demand what end should God require us to believe what we cannot understand? To exercise, some say, our Diligence. But this at first sight looks ridiculous, as if the plain Duties of the *Gospel* and our necessary Occupations were not sufficient to employ all our time. But how exercise our Diligence? Is it possible for us to understand those *Mysteries* at last, or not? If it be, then all I contend for is gain'd; for I never pretended that the *Gospel* could be understood without due Pains and Application, no more than any other Book. But if it be impossible after all to understand them, this is such a piece of Folly and Impertinence as no sober Man would be guilty of, to puzzle Peoples Heads with what they could never conceive, to exhort to and command the Study of them; and all this to keep 'em from Idleness, when they can scarce find leisure enough for what is on all hands granted to be intelligible.

Other say that God has enjoin'd the Belief of *Mysteries* to make us more humble. But how? By letting us see the small extent of our knowledg. But this extraordinary Method is quite needless, for Experience acquaints us with that every day. ...

From all these Observations, and what went before, it evidently follows that *Faith* is so far from being an implicate Assent to any thing above Reason, that this Notice directly contradicts the Ends of Religion, the Nature of Man, and the Goodness and Wisdom of God. But at this rate, some will be apt to say, *Faith* is no longer *Faith* but *Knowledg*. I answer, that if *Knowledg* be taken for a present and immediate view of things, I have no where affirm'd any thing like it, but the contrary in many Places. But if by *Knowledg* be ment understanding what is believ'd, then I stand by it that *Faith* is *Knowledg*: I have all along maintain'd it, and the very Words are promiscuously us'd for one another in the

Gospel. We know, i.e. we believe, *that this is indeed the Christ, the Saviour of the World*, Joh. 4. 42. *I know and am persuaded by the Lord Jesus that there is nothing unclean of itself*, Rom. 14. 14. *You know that your Labour is not in vain in the Lord*, 1 Cor. 15. 58.

Others will say that his Notion of *Faith* makes *Revelation* useless. But, pray, how so? for the Question is not, whether we could discover all the Objects of our *Faith* by Ratiocination: I have prov'd on the contrary, that no Matter of Fact can be known without *Revelation*. But I assert, that what is once reveal'd we must as well understand as any other Matter in the World, *Revelation* being only of use to enform us, while the Evidence of its Subject perswades us. Then, reply they, *Reason* is of more Dignity than *Revelation*. I answer, Just as much as a *Greek Grammar* is superior to the *New Testament*; for we make use of *Grammar* to understand the *Language*, and of *Reason* to comprehend the Sense of that Book. But, in a word, I see no need of Comparisons in this Case, for Reason is not less from God than *Revelation*; 'tis the Candle,[1] the Guide, the Judg he has lodg'd within every Man that cometh into this World. ...

How Mysteries were Brought into Christianity

The End of the LAW being Righteousness, Rom. 10. 4, *JESUS CHRIST came not to destroy, but to fulfil it*, Mat. 5. 17: for he fully and clearly preach'd the purest Morals, he taught that reasonable Worship, and those just Conceptions of Heaven and Heavenly Things, which were more obscurely signifi'd or design'd by the Legal Observations. So having stripp'd the Truth of all those external Types and Ceremonies which made it difficult before, he rendred it easy and obvious to the meanest Capacities.

His Disciples and Followers kept to this Simplicity for some considerable time, tho very early divers Abuses began to get footing amongst them. The converted *Jews*, who continu'd mighty fond of their *Levitical* Rites and Feasts, would willingly retain them and be Christians too. Thus what at the Beginning was but only tolerated in weaker Brethren, became afterwards a part of Christianity itself, under the Pretence of *Apostolick* Prescription or Tradition.

But this was nothing compar'd to the Injury done to Religion by the *Gentiles*; who, as they were proselyted in greater number than the *Jews*, so the Abuses they introduc'd were of more dangerous and universal Influence. They were not a little scandaliz'd at the plain Dress of the

---

[1] 'The spirit of man is the candle of the Lord,' Prov. 20: 27.

Gospel, with the wonderful Facility of the Doctrines it contain'd, having been accustom'd all their lives to the pompous Worship and secret *Mysteries* of Deities without Number. The *Christians* on the other hand were careful to remove all Obstacles lying in the way of the *Gentiles*. They thought the most effectual way of gaining them over to their side was by compounding the Matter, which led them to unwarrantable Compliances, till at length they likewise set up for *Mysteries*. Yet not having the least Precedent for any Ceremonies from the *Gospel*, excepting *Baptism* and the *Supper*, they strangely disguiz'd and transform'd these by adding to them the Pagan Mystick Rites. They administered them with the strictest Secrecy; and, to be inferiour to their Adversaries in no Circumstance, they permitted none to assist at them, but such as were antecedently prepar'd or *initiated*. And to inspire their *Catechumens* with most ardent Desires of Participation, they gave out that what was so industriously hid were *tremendous and unutterable Mysteries*.

Thus lest *Simplicity*, the noblest *Ornament* of the Truth, should expose it to the Contempt of Unbelievers, *Christianity* was put upon an equal Level with the *Mysteries of Ceres*, or the *Orgies of Bacchus*. Foolish and mistaken Care! as if the most impious Superstitions could be sanctifi'd by the Name of Christ. But such is always the Fruit of prudential and condescending Terms of Conversion in Religion, whereby the Number and not the Sincerity of Professors in mainly intended.

[Though Deism may be regarded as a typical fruit of the eighteenth century, and though Latitudinarian churchmanship was fashionable and profitable, the Anglican tradition was carried on by the non-jurors and by such men as Sherlock[1] and Waterland. And Deism had beneficial reactions; for Toland's work prompted Butler to the writing of his *Analogy*, while William Law responded to Tindal with the *Case of Reason*, and to the deadness of the Latitudinarian church with his works of piety, which became the devotional handbooks of the Evangelical, as later of the Catholic, Revival.]

II.   THE ORGANIZATION OF THE METHODISTS

a. The Deed of Declaration, 1784

[Drawn up by Wesley and entered in His Majesty's High Court of Chancery. There is obviously here no intention of making Methodism anything more than a movement for spiritual revival *in* the Church of England.]

---

[1] Thomas, son of William Sherlock (p. 287), 1678–1761.

To all to whom these presents shall come, John Wesley—late of Lincoln College, Oxford, but now of the City Road, London, Clerk—sendeth greeting. Whereas divers buildings, commonly called chapels, with a messuage and dwelling-house, or other appurtenances, to each of the same belonging, situate in various parts of Great Britain, have been given and conveyed from time to time ... upon trust, that the trustees ... should permit and suffer such persons ... as should be appointed at the yearly Conference of the people called Methodists ..., and no others, to have and enjoy the said premises for the purposes aforesaid: ... Now, therefore, the said John Wesley doth hereby declare that the Conference ... hath always heretofore consisted of the preachers and expounders of God's Holy Word ... whom he hath thought expedient, year after year, to summon to meet him, to advise with them for the promotion of the Gospel of Christ, ... and for the expulsion of unworthy and admission of new persons under his care, and into his connexion, to be preachers and expounders as aforesaid. ... And these presents further witness, that the several persons hereinafter named [one hundred in number], ... now are the members of the said Conference ... subject to the regulations hereinafter prescribed: that is to say, ... No act of the Conference shall be had, taken, or be the act of the Conference, ... until all the vacancies occasioned by death, or absence, shall be filled up by the election of new members [by co-optation], *so as to make up the number of one hundred*: and during the assembly of the Conference, there shall always be forty members present at the doing of any act. ... The duration of the yearly assembly of the Conference shall not be less than five days, nor more than three weeks. ... The Conference shall and may expel and put out from being a member thereof, or from being in connexion therewith, or from being upon trial, any person ..., from any cause which to the Conference may seem fit and necessary. ... The Conference shall not appoint any person, *for more than three years successively*, to the use and enjoyment of any chapels and premises, ... except ordained ministers of the Church of England. ... Whenever the said Conference shall be reduced under the number of forty members, and continue so reduced for three yearly assemblies thereof successively—or whenever the members thereof shall decline or neglect to meet together annually for the purposes aforesaid during the space of three years—then the Conference of the people called Methodists shall be extinguished, ... and the said chapels, etc., shall vest in the trustees for the time being ..., upon trust that they shall appoint such persons to preach therein ... as to them shall seem proper. ...

b. The Plan of Pacification, 1795

[Wesley died in 1791, and four years after his death his followers—setting aside Wesley's words 'I live and die a member of the Church of England; and none who regard my judgement will ever separate from it' (*Arminian Magazine*, April 1790)—formed themselves into a dissenting body.]

The sacrament of the Lord's Supper shall not be administered in any chapel, except a majority of the trustees of that chapel ..., and of the stewards and leaders belonging to that chapel (as the best qualified to give the sense of the people), allow of it. Nevertheless, in all cases, the consent of the Conference shall be first obtained. ... Provided that, *in all chapels where the Lord's Supper has been already peaceably administered, the administration of it shall continue in future.* ... We agree that the Lord's Supper be administered among us, on Sunday evenings only; except where the majority of the stewards and leaders desire it in Church hours. ... Nevertheless, it shall never be administered on those Sundays on which it is administered in the parish Church. The Lord's Supper shall always be administered in England, *according to the form of the Established Church*: but the person who administers shall have liberty to give out hymns, to use exhortation, and extemporary prayer. Wherever Divine Service is performed in England on the Lord's day, in Church hours, the officiating preacher shall read either the service of the Church, our venerable father's abridgement, or at least the lessons appointed by the calendar. But we recommend either the full service or the abridgement. The appointment of the preachers shall remain solely with the Conference. ... The hundred preachers mentioned in the enrolled deed, and their successors, are the only legal persons who constitute the Conference. And we think the junior brethren have no reason to object to this proposition, as they are regularly elected according to seniority.

c. The Model Trust Deed, 1832

[Giving a model contract for the purchase of land for a chapel. The important point is that it establishes Wesley's Sermons and Notes on the New Testament as the standard of Wesleyan Orthodoxy.]

... upon trust, to permit the said chapel and premises to be used as a place of worship for the people called Methodists ... and to allow such persons only to preach and expound therein, as should be duly appointed by Conference, or by the superintendent preacher for the time being ... [who shall] have the direction and control of the said worship. ... Provided always, that no person shall be permitted to preach or expound in the said chapel or premises, who shall teach any doctrine contrary to what is contained in certain *Notes to the New Testament* by the late John Wesley, and the *first four volumes of Sermons* reputed to be written by him. ...

III. JOHN KEBLE'S ASSIZE SERMON, 1833

['The following Sunday, July 14th, Mr Keble preached the Assize Sermon in the University Pulpit. ... I have ever considered, and kept the day, as the start of the religious movement of 1833.'—Newman, *Apologia pro Vita Sua*, end of chapter I.]

'National Apostasy', no. 6 of *Sermons Academical and Occasional* (2nd edn.), Oxford, 1848. Preached at S. Mary's, Oxford, before his Majesty's Judges of Assize, 14 July 1833.

[From the Advertisement to the First Edition:

'Since the following pages were prepared for the press, the calamity in anticipation of which they were written, has actually overtaken this portion of the Church of God. The Legislature of England and Ireland (*the members of which are not even bound to profess belief in the Atonement*), this body has virtually usurped the commission of those whom our Saviour entrusted with *at least one voice* in making ecclesiastical laws, on matters wholly or partly spiritual.[1] The same legislature has also ratified, to its full extent, this principle,—that the Apostolical Church in this realm is henceforth only to stand, in the eye of the State, as *one sect among many*, depending, for any preeminence she may still appear to retain, merely upon the accident of her having a strong party in the country.

'It is a moment, surely, full of deep solicitude to all those members of the Church who still believe in her authority divine, and the oaths and obligations, by which they are bound to her, undissolved and indissoluble by calculations of human expediency. Their anxiety turns not as much on the consequences, to the State, of what has been done (*they* are but too evident) as on the line of conduct which they are bound themselves to pursue. How may they continue their communion with the Church established, (hitherto the pride and comfort of their lives) without any taint of those Erastian principles on which she is now assumed to be governed? What answer can we make henceforth to the partisans of the bishop of Rome, when they taunt us with being a mere Parliament Church? And how, consistently with our present relations to the State, can even the doctrinal purity and integrity of the MOST SACRED ORDER be preserved? ... July 22, 1833.']

1 Samuel xii. 23. 'As for me, God forbid that I should sin against the Lord in ceasing to pray for you.'

... What are the symptoms by which we may judge most fairly, whether or no a nation, as such, is becoming alienated from God and Christ?

---

[1] In the suppression of certain Irish sees, contrary to the suffrages of the bishops of England and Ireland.

And what are the particular duties of sincere Christians, whose lot is cast, by divine Providence, in such a time of calamity?

The conduct of the Jews, in asking for a king, may furnish an example of the first point: the behaviour of Samuel, then and afterwards, supplies as perfect a pattern of the second as can be expected from human nature.

I. The case is at least possible, of a nation, having for centuries acknowledged, as an essential part of its theory of government, that, as a Christian nation, she is also part of Christ's Church, and bound, in all her legislation and policy, by the fundamental rules of that Church—the case is, I say, conceivable, of a government and people, so constituted, throwing off the restraint which in many respects such a principle would impose on them, nay, disowning the principle itself; and that, on the plea that other states, as flourishing or more so in regard of wealth and dominion, do well enough without it. Is not this desiring, like the Jews, to have an earthly king over them, when the Lord their God is their King? ...

To such a change, whenever it takes place, the immediate impulse will probably be given by some pretence of danger from without ... but in reality the movement will always be traceable to the same decay and want of faith, the same deficiency in Christian resignation and thankfulness, which leads so many, as individuals, to disdain and forfeit the blessings of the Gospel. ...

One of the most alarming [omens of an Apostate mind in a nation] is the growing indifference, in which men indulge themselves, to other men's religious sentiments. Under the guise of charity and toleration we are come almost to this pass; that no difference, in matters of faith, is to disqualify for our approbation and confidence, whether in public or domestic life. Can we conceal it from ourselves, that every year the practice is becoming more and more common, of trusting men unreservedly in the most delicate and important matters, without one serious inquiry, whether they do not hold principles which make it impossible for them to be loyal to their Creator, Redeemer and Sanctifier? Are not offices conferred, partnerships formed, intimacies entered upon—nay, (what is almost too painful to think of) do not parents commit their children to be educated, do they not encourage them to intermarry, in houses on which Apostolical Authority would rather teach them to set a mark, as unfit to be entered by a faithful servant of Christ?

I do not now speak of public measures only or chiefly; many things of that kind may be thought, whether wisely or no, to become from time to time necessary, which are in reality as little desired by those who lend them a seeming concurrence, as they are, in themselves, undesirable. But I speak of the spirit which leads men to exult in every step of that kind, to congratulate one another on the supposed decay of what they call an exclusive system.

Very different are the feelings with which it seems natural for a true Christian to regard such a state of things, from those which would arise in his mind on witnessing the mere triumph of any given set of adverse opinions, exaggerated or even heretical as he might deem them. He might feel as melancholy,—he could hardly feel so indignant.

But this is not a becoming place, nor are these safe topics, for the indulgence of mere feeling. The point really to be considered is, whether, according to the coolest estimate, the fashionable liberality of this generation be not ascribable, in a great measure, to the same temper which led the Jews voluntarily to set about degrading themselves to a level with the idolatrous Gentiles? And if it be true anywhere that such enactments are forced on the legislature by public opinion, is APOSTASY too hard a word to describe the temper of the nation? ...

... They [*sc.* professing Christians who disregard Christian principles in their public conduct] will have more reason to suspect themselves [of disregarding God] in proportion, as they see and feel more of that impatience under pastoral authority which our Saviour himself has taught us to consider as a never-failing symptom of an un-Christian temper. 'He that despiseth you, despiseth me' [Luke x. 16]. These words of divine truth put beyond all sophistical exception what common sense would lead us to infer, and what daily experience teaches;—that disrespect to the Successors of the Apostles, as such, is an unquestionable symptom of enmity to Him who gave them their commission at first and has pledged himself to be with them for ever. Suppose such disrespect general and national, suppose it also avowedly grounded not on any fancied tenet of religion, but on mere human reasons of popularity and expediency; either there is no meaning at all in these emphatic declarations of our Lord, or that nation, how highly soever she may think of her own religion and morality, stands convicted in his sight of direct disavowal of his Sovereignty. ...

II. [The duties of the Church are intercession and remonstrance, as indicated in the text.]

IV. TRACT XC

[This was the last of the Tracts for the Times. The general public, whose suspicions of the good faith of the Tractarians had been aroused by Isaac Williams' tract 'On Reserve in Communicating Religious Knowledge,' were really alarmed by the 'Jesuitry' of the suggested interpretations of the Articles. The heads of houses at Oxford made a protest; questions were asked in Parliament; the Bishop of Oxford intervened, and Newman brought the tracts to an end. In 1843 he resigned his living and in 1845 he was received into the Roman Catholic Church.]

Remarks on Certain Passages in the Thirty-Nine Articles, London, 1841

Introduction

It is often urged, and sometimes felt and granted, that there are in the Articles propositions or terms inconsistent with the Catholic faith. ... The following tract is drawn up with the view of showing how groundless the objection is. ... That there are real difficulties to a Catholic Christian in the Ecclesiastical position of our Church at this day, no one can deny; but the statements of the Articles are not in this number: and it may be right at the present moment to insist upon this. If in any question it is supposed that persons who profess to be disciples of the early Church will silently concur with those of very opposite sentiments in furthering a relaxation of subscriptions which, it is imagined, are galling to both parties, though for different reasons, and that they will do this against the wish of the great body of the Church, the writer of the following pages would raise one voice, at least, in protest against any such anticipation. ...

... Our present scope is merely to show that while our Prayer Book is acknowledged on all hands to be of Catholic origin, our Articles also, the offspring of an un-Catholic age, are, through God's good providence, to say the least, not un-Catholic, and may be subscribed by those who aim at being Catholic in heart and doctrine.

[Articles discussed: 6 and 20, 11, 12 and 13, 19, 21, 22, 25, 28, 31, 32, 35, 37.]

§ 1. Holy Scripture and the Authority of the Church

Articles vi and xx

... Not a word is said ... in favour of Scripture having no rule or method to fix interpretation by, or, as is commonly expressed, being *the sole rule of faith*.

[There follow quotations from Anglican divines, to show that they held the decisions of the first four General Councils, together with the tradition of the Church, to form, with Scripture, the Rule of Faith.]

.   .   .   .

§ 6. Purgatory, Pardons, Images, Relics, Invocation

Article xxii

Now the first remark that occurs on perusing this Article is, that the doctrine objected to is 'the *Romish* doctrine.' For instance, none would suppose that the Calvinistic doctrine concerning purgatory, pardons and image worship is spoken against. Not every doctrine on these matters is 'a fond thing,' but the *Romish* doctrine. Accordingly the *Primitive* doctrine is not condemned in it, unless, indeed, the Primitive doctrine be the Romish, which must not be supposed. Now there *was* a Primitive doctrine on all these points—how far Catholic or universal, is another question—but still so widely received and so respectably supported that it may well be entertained as a matter of opinion by a theologian now: this then, whatever be its merits, is not condemned by this Article.

This is clear without proof on the face of the matter, at least as regards pardons. Of course, the Article never meant to make light of *every* doctrine about pardons, but a certain doctrine, the *Romish* doctrine [as indeed the plural form itself shows].[1]

... And further, by 'the Romish doctrine' is not meant the Tridentine [statement], because this Article was drawn up before the decree of the Council of Trent. What is opposed is the *received doctrine* of the day, and unhappily of this day too, or the doctrine of the *Roman schools*. ...

If then the doctrine condemned in this Article be not the primitive doctrine, nor the Catholic doctrine, nor the Tridentine [statement] but the Romish, *doctrina Romanensium*, let us next consider *what* in matter of fact it is. And—

I. As to the doctrine of the Romanists concerning Purgatory.

Now here there was a primitive doctrine ... that the conflagration of the world, or the flames that attend the Judge, will be an ordeal through which all men will pass; that great saints, such as S. Mary, will pass it unharmed; that others will suffer loss; but none will fail under it who are built on the right foundation. Here is one [purgatorian doctrine] not 'Romish'.

---

[1] Passages in square brackets—apart from notes in small type—are not contained in the first edition.

Another ... is that said to be maintained by the Greeks at Florence, that the cleansing, though a punishment, was but a *poena damni*, not a *poena sensûs*; not a positive sensible infliction, much less the torment of fire, but the absence of God's presence. And another purgatory is that in which the cleansing is but a progressive sanctification, and has no pain at all.

None of these doctrines does the Article condemn; any of them may be held by the Anglo-Catholic as a matter of private belief: not that they are here advocated, one or other, but they are adduced as an *illustration* of what the Article does *not* mean, and to vindicate our Christian liberty in a matter where the Church has not confined it. ...

[Pardons, etc., are then dealt with on similar lines.]

§ 8. Transubstantiation

Article xxviii

... We see then[1] that by transubstantiation our article does not confine itself to any abstract theory, nor aim at any definition of the word substance, nor, in rejecting it, rejects a word, nor in denying a *mutatio panis et vini* is denying *every kind* of change, but opposes itself to a certain plain and unambiguous statement, not of this or that council, but one generally received or taught both in the schools and in the multitude, that the material elements are changed into an earthly, fleshly, and organized body, extended in size, distinct in its parts, which is there where the outward appearances of bread and wine are, and only does not meet the senses, nor even that always.

§ 9. Masses

Article xxi

Nothing can show more clearly than this passage that the Articles are not written against the creed of the Roman Church, but against actual existing errors in it, whether taken into its system or not. Here the sacrifice of the *Mass* is not spoken of ... but the sacrifice of *Masses*. ... On the whole then, it is conceived that the Article before us neither speaks against the Mass in itself nor against its being [an offering though commemorative][2] for the quick and dead for the remission of sins; [(especially since the decree of Trent says that 'the fruits of the Bloody

---

[1] From quotations from Anglican divines giving examples of grossly corporal doctrines of Roman Catholics.

[2] 'An offering for the quick, etc.' 1st edn.

Oblation are through this most abundantly obtained: so far is the latter from detracting in any way from the former';)] but against its being viewed, on the one hand, as independent of or distinct from the Sacrifice on the cross, which is blasphemy, and, on the other, its being directed to the emoluments of those to whom it pertains to celebrate it, which is imposture in addition.

. . . .

Conclusion

It may be objected that the tenor of the above explanation is anti-Protestant, whereas it is notorious that the Articles were drawn up by Protestants and intended for the establishment of Protestantism; accordingly that it is an evasion of their meaning to give them any other than a Protestant drift, possible as it may be to do so grammatically, or in each separate part.

But the answer is simple:

1. In the first place it is a *duty* which we owe both to the Catholic Church and to our own, to take our reformed confessions in the most Catholic sense they will admit; we have no duties towards their framers. ...

2. In giving the Articles a Catholic interpretation, we bring them into harmony with the Book of Common Prayer, an object of the most serious moment in those who have given their assent to both formularies.

3. Whatever be the authority of the [Declaration] prefixed to the Article, so far as it has any weight at all, it sanctions the mode of interpreting them above given. For its injoining the 'literal and grammatical sense,' relieves us from the necessity of making the known opinions of their framers a comment upon their text; and its forbidding any person to 'affix any *new* sense to any Article,' was promulgated at a time when the leading men of our Church were especially noted for those Catholic views which have been here advocated.

. . . .

5. Further: the Articles are evidently framed on the principle of leaving open large questions on which the controversy hinges. They state broad extreme truths, and are silent upon their adjustment.

. . . .

7. Lastly, their framers constructed them in such a way as best to comprehend those who did not go so far in Protestantism as themselves. Anglo-Catholics then are but the successors and representatives of those moderate reformers; and their case has been directly anticipated in the

wording of the Articles. It follows that they are not perverting, they are using them, for an express purpose for which among others their authors framed them. ...

... The Protestant Confession was drawn up with the purpose of including Catholics, and Catholics now will not be excluded. What was an economy in the reformers, is a protection to us. What would have been a perplexity to us then, is a perplexity to Protestants now. We could not then have found fault with their words: they cannot now repudiate our meaning.

[J.H.N.]

Oxford, Feast of Conversion of S. Paul, 1841
  (2nd edition)

SECTION XIII

The Roman Catholic Church at the Second Vatican Council

I. CONSTITUTION ON THE SACRED LITURGY

Sacrosanctum Concilium, 4 December 1963, paras. 47–56

Flannery, *Vatican II: Constitutions*, 134–7

[The Second Vatican Council was called by Pope John XXIII—although Paul VI was pope by the time the documents quoted here were published—and met from 1962 to 1965 with observers from other denominations. It 'opened the windows of the Vatican and let in some air', in words attributed to Pope John, and represented *aggiornamento*, a 'bringing up to date' of the Roman Catholic Church. The Constitution on the Liturgy paved the way for the celebration of the Mass in the vernacular rather than Latin (although Latin remained the universal liturgical and doctrinal language of Roman Catholicism). The new emphasis—inspired by the 'liturgical movement' of the twentieth century which attempted to rediscover the worship of the early Church—was on communal celebration of the liturgy rather than clerical exclusivism; hence the priest was to face the congregation, and the altar rails were to be removed. The reading of scripture and the homily were to be given a more prominent role in the Mass. All of these changes came in gradually but surely over the following decade. This excerpt from chapter 2 summarizes the main points of revision in the Mass.]

47. At the last supper, on the night he was betrayed, our Savior instituted the eucharistic sacrifice of his body and blood. This he did in order to perpetuate the sacrifice of the cross throughout the ages until he should

come again, and so to entrust to his beloved spouse, the church, a memorial of his death and resurrection: a sacrament of love, a sign of unity, a bond of charity, 'a paschal banquet in which Christ is received, the mind is filled with grace, and a pledge of future glory is given to us.'

48. The church, therefore, spares no effort in trying to ensure that, when present at this mystery of faith, Christian believers should not be there as strangers or silent spectators. On the contrary, having a good grasp of it through the rites and prayers, they should take part in the sacred action, actively, fully aware, and devoutly. ...

50. The rite of the Mass is to be revised in such a way that the intrinsic nature and purpose of its several parts, as well as the connection between them, may be more clearly shown, and that devout and active participation by the faithful may be more easily achieved. ...

51. The treasures of the Bible are to be opened up more lavishly so that a richer fare may be provided for the faithful at the table of God's word. ...

52. By means of the homily, the mysteries of the faith and the guiding principles of the christian life are expounded from the sacred text during the course of the liturgical year. The homily is strongly recommended since it forms part of the liturgy itself. ...

53. The 'common prayer' or 'prayer of the faithful' is to be restored after the gospel and homily, especially on Sundays and holydays of obligation. ...

54. A suitable place may be allotted to the vernacular in Masses which are celebrated with the people, especially in the readings and 'the common prayer'. ...

55. The more perfect form of participation in the Mass whereby the faithful, after the priest's communion, receive the Lord's Body from the same sacrifice, is warmly recommended.

The dogmatic principles about communion of the faithful which were laid down by the Council of Trent are confirmed, yet communion under both kinds may be granted when the bishops think fit, not only to clerics and religious but also to the laity. ...

56. The two parts which in a sense go to make up the Mass, viz. the liturgy of the word and the eucharistic liturgy, are so closely connected with each other that they form but one single act of worship. Accordingly this sacred synod strongly urges pastors of souls that, when instructing the faithful, they take care to teach them to take their part in the entire Mass, especially on Sundays and holydays of obligation. ...

II. DOGMATIC CONSTITUTION ON THE CHURCH

Lumen Gentium, 21 November 1964, paras. 9–10, 22, 60, 62

Flannery, *Vatican II: Constitutions,* 12–15, 29–31, 85–6

[These excerpts from *Lumen Gentium* illustrate the following important em-
phases in the document: (*a*) in chapter 2, there is the description of the whole
'People of God', that is, clergy and laity together as one community in the divine
covenant; (*b*) in chapter 3, while the papacy retains its authority, equally important is 'collegiality', the communion of all the bishops as leaders; (*c*) chapter
8 includes Mary in the doctrine of the Church countering a very high mariology
that could cause difficulties for ecumenism.

The setting of mariology within the Constitution on the Church, rather than
giving it a more traditional separate section, was the result of the closest vote of the
Council. The mariology of the Roman Catholic Church was further developed in
Marialis Cultus (1974), in which Paul VI tried to accommodate the view of the
'modern woman'—understanding Mary as a woman of initiative, strength, and
prophetic vision, not rejecting the married state, and 'the perfect model of the
disciple of the Lord'—and later in John Paul II's *Redemptoris Mater* (1987). Yet
feminist and liberation theology continued to demand a Mary of the common
people more in line with a liberating view of womanhood and sexuality—see, for
example, Balasuriya in Section XIV, v. d below.]

a. The 'People of God'

9. At all times and in every nation, anyone who fears God and does what
is right has been acceptable to him (see Acts 10: 35). He has, however,
willed to make women and men holy and to save them, not as individuals
without any bond between them, but rather to make them into a people
who might acknowledge him and serve him in holiness. ... Christ
instituted this new covenant, the new covenant in his blood (see 1 Cor
11: 25); he called a people together made up of Jews and Gentiles which
would be one, not according to the flesh, but in the Spirit, and it would be
a new People of God. ...

10. Christ the Lord, high priest taken from the midst of humanity
(see Heb. 5: 1–5), made the new people 'a kingdom of priests to his God
and father' (Apoc. 1: 6; see 5: 9–10). The baptized, by regeneration and
the anointing of the holy Spirit, are consecrated as a spiritual house and a
holy priesthood, that through all their christian activities they may offer
spiritual sacrifices and proclaim the marvels of him who has called them
out of darkness into his wonderful light (see 1 Pet. 2: 4–10). ...

Though they differ essentially and not only in degree, the common
priesthood of the faithful and the ministerial of hierarchical priesthood

are none the less interrelated; each in its own way shares in the one priesthood of Christ. The ministerial priest, by the sacred power that he has, forms and governs the priestly people; in the person of Christ he brings about the Eucharistic sacrifice and offers it to God in the name of all the people. The faithful indeed, by virtue of their royal priesthood, participate in the offering of the Eucharist. They exercise that priesthood, too, by the reception of the sacraments, by prayer and thanksgiving, by the witness of a holy life, self-denial and active charity. ...

b. Collegiality

22. Just as, in accordance with the Lord's decree, St Peter and the other apostles constitute one apostolic college, so in like fashion the Roman Pontiff, Peter's successor, and the bishops, the successors of the apostles, are joined together. Indeed, the collegiate character and structure of the episcopal order is clearly shown by the very ancient discipline whereby the bishops installed throughout the whole world lived in communion with one another and with the Roman Pontiff in a bond of unity, charity and peace; it is also shown in the holding of councils in order to reach agreement on questions of major importance, a balanced decision being made possible thanks to the number of those giving counsel. It is made abundantly clear by the ecumenical councils which have been held over the centuries. ...

The college or body of bishops has no authority, however, other than the authority which it is acknowledged to have in union with the Roman Pontiff, Peter's successor, as its head, his primatial authority over everyone, pastors of faithful, remaining intact. For the Roman Pontiff, by reason of his office as Vicar of Christ and as pastor of the entire church, has full, supreme and universal power over the whole church, a power which he can always exercise freely. ...

c. The Role of Mary

60. In the words of the apostle there is but one mediator..(1 Tim. 2: 5–6). But Mary's function as mother of humankind in no way obscures or diminishes this unique mediation of Christ, but rather shows its power. All the Blessed Virgin's salutary influence on men and women originates not in any inner necessity but in the disposition of God. It flows forth from the superabundance of the merits of Christ, rests on his mediation, depends entirely on it and draws all its power from it. It does not hinder

in any way the immediate union of the faithful with Christ but on the contrary fosters it. ...

62. Therefore the Blessed Virgin is invoked in the Church under the titles of advocate, helper, benefactress, and mediatrix. This, however, is so understood in such a way that it neither takes away anything from nor adds anything to, the dignity and efficacy of Christ the one mediator. ...

III. DECREE ON THE CATHOLIC EASTERN CHURCHES

Orientalium Ecclesiarum, 21 November 1965, paras. 5–6

Flannery, *Vatican II: Constitutions*, 527

[Vatican II encouraged a move from the highly centralized Church which developed between Trent and the nineteenth century to one in which local customs and liturgical styles were valued. The process by which this occurs is known as 'inculturation'. In this spirit, the Council was concerned to clarify the situation regarding the churches in Eastern Europe, the Middle East, and Asia who did not use the Latin form of the liturgy, and sometimes followed the eastern patriarchal form of church government, but who nevertheless remained in communion with Rome. Their spiritual heritage was to be preserved, not suppressed by the centre. The document also opened the way for a reunion with the Eastern Orthodox which would not violate the separate traditions of the latter. However, the relations between Rome and Orthodoxy remained strained in the post-conciliar period because of the Eastern Catholic tendency to proselytize the Orthodox: see Section XVI, vii. b below.]

5. History, tradition and very many ecclesiastical institutions give clear evidence of the great debt owed to the eastern churches by the church universal. Therefore this holy council not merely praises and appreciates as is due this ecclesiastical and spiritual heritage, but also insists on viewing it as the heritage of the whole church of Christ. For that reason this council solemnly declares that the churches of the east like those of the west have the right and duty to govern themselves according to their own special disciplines. For these are guaranteed by ancient tradition, and seem to be better suited to the customs of their faithful and better fitted for bringing about the good of their souls.

6. All members of the eastern churches should be firmly convinced that they can and ought always preserve their own legitimate liturgical rites and ways of life, and that changes are to be introduced only to forward their own organic development. ...

IV. DECREE ON ECUMENISM

Unitatis Redintegratio, 21 November 1964, para. 3

Flannery, *Vatican II: Constitutions*, 502–3

[Just as the Council drew on the 'liturgical movement' of the twentieth century to revise its liturgy—see Section XIII, i above—it also accepted the broad principles of the 'ecumenical movement'. The excerpt below shows how the Council envisioned a Church wider than Roman Catholicism; the old principle *extra ecclesiam non salus est* ('there is no salvation outside the (Catholic) Church') had been superseded by the more inclusive theology of, for example, Karl Rahner. The Council also accepted that the Roman Catholic Church bore some of the responsibility for the divisions of the past. Nevertheless—see the last paragraph—the Roman Catholic Church in communion with the Pope was still to be normative.]

. ... 3. In this one and only Church of God from its very beginnings there arose certain rifts, which the Apostle strongly censures as damnable. But in subsequent centuries much more serious dissensions appeared and large communities became separated from full communion with the Catholic Church—for which, often enough, people on both sides were to blame. However, one cannot charge with the sin of the separation those who at present are born into these communities and in them are brought up in the faith of Christ, and the Catholic Church accepts them with respect and affection as brothers and sisters. For those who believe in Christ and have been properly baptized are put in some, though imperfect, communion with the Catholic Church. ...

Moreover, some, even very many, of the most significant elements and endowments which together go to build up and give life to the church itself, can exist outside the visible boundaries of the Catholic Church: the written Word of God; the life of grace; faith, hope and charity, with the other interior gifts of the Holy Spirit, as well as visible elements. All of these, which come from Christ and lead back to Christ, belong by right to the one Church of Christ.

Our separated brothers and sisters also carry out many liturgical actions of the christian religion. In ways that vary according to the condition of each church or community, these liturgical actions most certainly can truly engender a life of grace, and, one must say, are capable of giving access to that communion in which is salvation. ...

Nevertheless .. it is through Christ's Catholic Church alone, which is the universal help towards salvation, that the fullness of the means of salvation can be obtained. ...

V. DECLARATION ON THE RELATION OF THE CHURCH
TO NON-CHRISTIAN RELIGIONS

Nostra Aetate, **28 October 1965, para. 4** Flannery, *Vatican II: Constitutions*, 572–3

[The Council promoted dialogue with other faiths as well as with other Christian denominations. Looking towards Eastern faiths, it stated that 'the Catholic Church rejects nothing of what is true and holy in these religions' (para. 2, pp. 570–1). While holding to the belief that Christ is the way, truth, and life (John 14: 6), the Declaration speaks in warm terms about other faiths. Muslims stand in the tradition of Abraham, and venerate Jesus and Mary. However, the longest section, part of which is reproduced here, is reserved for the Jews. Like other Christian churches, Roman Catholicism had to come to terms with its own responsibility for the *Shoah* or Holocaust and reconsider its relationship to the history and tradition of the Jewish people. See other aspects of Christian–Jewish post-war relations in Section XV below.]

.... . 4. Sounding the depths of the mystery which is the church, this sacred council remembers the spiritual ties which link the people of the new covenant to the stock of Abraham. ... the church cannot forget that it received the revelation of the Old Testament by way of that people with whom God in his inexpressible mercy established the ancient covenant. ...

Since Christians and Jews have such a common spiritual heritage, this sacred council wishes to encourage and further mutual understanding and appreciation. This can be achieved, especially, by way of biblical and theological enquiry and through friendly discussions.

Even though the Jewish authorities and those who followed their lead pressed for the death of Christ (see John 19: 6), neither all Jews indiscriminately at that time, nor Jews today, can be charged with the crimes committed during his passion. It is true that the church is the new people of God, yet the Jews should not be spoken of as rejected or accursed as if this followed from holy scripture. Consequently, all must take care, lest in catechizing or in preaching the Word of God, they teach anything which is not in accord with the truth of the Gospel message or the spirit of Christ.

Indeed, the Church reproves every form of persecution against whomsoever it may be directed. Remembering, then, its common heritage with the Jews and moved not by any political consideration, but solely by the religious motivation of christian charity, it deplores all hatreds, persecutions, displays of antisemitism levelled at any time or from any source against the Jews. ...

VI. DECLARATION ON RELIGIOUS LIBERTY

Dignitatis Humanae, 7 December 1965, para. 2

Flannery, *Vatican II: Constitutions,* 552–3

[After the republican and communist revolutions in Europe and elsewhere, Roman Catholicism had good reason to promote religious liberty. Its people, like those of other denominations, had suffered persecution in several countries. The Council, in this and other instances, turned its back on the hard line of the *Syllabus of Errors* (1864, Section X, VIII above), which had rejected religious toleration.]

2. The Vatican council declares that the human person has a right to religious freedom. Freedom of this kind means that everyone should be immune from coercion by individuals, social groups and every human power so that, within due limits, no men or women are forced to act against their convictions nor are any persons to be restrained from acting in accordance with their convictions in religious matters in private or in public, alone or in association with others. The council further declares that the right to religious freedom is based on the very dignity of the human person as known through the revealed word of God and by reason itself. This right of the human person to religious freedom must be given such recognition in the constitutional order of society as will make it a civil right. ...

VII. PASTORAL CONSTITUTION ON THE CHURCH
IN THE MODERN WORLD

Gaudium et Spes, 7 December 1965, paras. 3, 4, 26, 29, 80

Flannery, *Vatican II: Constitutions,* 164–5, 191–2, 194, 266–7

[*Gaudium et Spes* was the most substantial and arguably the most radical document of the Council. Its teaching on human rights, dignity, and social justice stands in a modern tradition of Roman Catholic social teaching from *Rerum Novarum* (1891), *Quadgragesimo Anno* (1931), and *Mater et Magistra* (1961) (Section X, xi above) to *Populorum Progressio* (1967) (Section XIV, iv. a below) and *Sollicitudo Rei Socialis* (1987). The concern for peace has a parallel in *Pacem in Terris* (1963) (Section XIV, i. below).

The five sections here illustrate the Council's teaching on issues of justice and peace. There is (*a*) the importance of dialogue with all people of conscience in the effort to solve the world's problems; (*b*) the responsibility of reading the 'signs of the times'; (*c*) the concept of the 'common good'; (*d*) equality and the denial of discrimination; (*e*) an abhorrence of the potential of modern weapons for mass destruction. In all these things, the Church is to be a servant to the human race and to proclaim the presence and justice of God in the modern world.]

a. The Church in Dialogue and Service

3. Though proud of its discoveries and its power, humanity is often concerned about current developments in the world, about humanity's place and role in the universe, about the meaning of individual and collective endeavor, and finally about the destiny of nature and of humanity. And so the council, as witness and guide to the faith of all God's people, gathered together by Christ, can find no more eloquent expression of this people's solidarity, respect and love for the whole human family, of which it forms part, than to enter into dialogue with it about all these various problems. ... The church is not motivated by earthly ambition but is interested in one thing only—to carry on the work of Christ under the guidance of the Holy Spirit, who came into the world to bear witness to the truth, to save and not to judge, to serve and not to be served.

b. The 'Signs of the Times'

4. In every age, the church carries the responsibility of reading the signs of the times and of interpreting them in the light of the Gospel, if it is to carry out its task. In language intelligible to every generation, it should be able to answer the ever recurring questions which people ask about the meaning of this present life and of the life to come, and how one is related to the other. We must be aware of and understand the aspirations, the yearnings, and the often dramatic features of the world in which we live. ...

c. The 'Common Good'

26. Because of the increasingly close interdependence which is gradually spreading to the entire world, we are today witnessing an extension of the role of the common good, which is the sum total of social conditions which allow people, either as groups or as individuals, to reach their fulfillment more fully and easily. The resulting rights and obligations are consequently the concern of the entire human race. Every group must take into account the needs and legitimate aspirations of every other group, and even those of the human family as a whole.

At the same time, however, there is a growing awareness of the sublime dignity of human persons, who stand above all things and whose rights and duties are universal and inviolable. They ought, therefore, to have ready access to all that is necessary for living a genuinely human life: for example, food, clothing, housing, the right freely to choose their state of life and set up a family, the right to education, work, to their good name, to respect, to proper knowledge, the right to act according to the dictates of conscience and to safeguard their privacy, and rightful freedom, including freedom of religion. ...

d. Equality and Social Justice

29. All women and men are endowed with a rational soul and are created in God's image; they have the same nature and origin and, being redeemed by Christ, they enjoy the same divine calling and destiny; there is here a basic equality between all and it must be accorded ever greater recognition. Undoubtedly not all people are alike as regards physical capacity and intellectual and moral powers. But any kind of social or cultural discrimination in basic personal rights on the grounds of sex, race, color, social conditions, language or religion, must be curbed and eradicated as incompatible with God's design. It is deeply to be deplored that these basic personal rights are not yet being respected everywhere, as is the case with women who are denied the chance freely to choose a husband, or a state of life, or to have access to the same educational and cultural benefits as are available to men.

Furthermore, while there are just differences between people, their equal dignity as persons demands that we strive for fairer and more humane conditions. Excessive economic and social disparity between individuals and peoples of the one human race is a source of scandal and militates against social justice, equity, human dignity, as well as social and international peace. ...

e. Total Warfare

80. The proliferation of scientific weapons has immeasurably magnified the horror and wickedness of war. Warfare conducted with such weapons can inflict immense and indiscriminate havoc which goes far beyond the bounds of legitimate defense. Indeed if the kind of weapons now stocked in the arsenals of the great powers were to be employed to the fullest, the result would be the almost complete reciprocal slaughter of one side by the other, not to speak of the widespread devastation that would follow in the world and the deadly after-effects resulting from the use of such weapons.

All these factors force us to undertake a completely fresh appraisal of war. People of the present generation should realize that they will have to render an account of their warlike behavior; the destiny of generations to come depends largely on the decisions they make today.

With these considerations in mind the council, endorsing the condemnations of total warfare issued by recent popes, declares: Every act of war directed to the indiscriminate destruction of whole cities or vast areas with their inhabitants is a crime against God and humanity, which merits firm and unequivocal condemnation. ...

SECTION XIV

The Twentieth-Century Churches: Justice, Peace, and the Environment

I.   THE CALL FOR PEACE

a. 'Quakers against World War'   Statement issued by the Quaker London
Yearly Meeting 1915, *Quaker Faith and Practice*, para. 24.08

[The concern for peace among Christians has intensified during a twentieth century in which the world has been torn apart by warfare and destruction on a scale greater than ever before. The Quakers' 300-year-old tradition of pacifism resonated with other pacifist voices during the First World War, and Quakers—and the Quaker-inspired Peace Pledge Union—have been at the forefront of protest against warfare and nuclear weapons throughout the century.]

Meeting at a time when the nations of Europe are engaged in a war of unparalleled magnitude, we have been led to recall the basis of the peace testimony of our religious Society. It is not enough to be satisfied with a barren negative witness, a mere proclamation of non-resistance. We must search for a positive, vital, constructive message. Such a message, a message of supreme love, we find in the life and death of our Lord Jesus Christ. We find it in the doctrine of the indwelling Christ, that rediscovery of the early Friends, leading as it does to a recognition of the brotherhood of all men. Of this doctrine our testimony as to war and peace is a necessary outcome, and if we understand the doctrine aright, and follow it in its wide implications, we shall find that it calls to the peaceable spirit and the rule of love in all the broad and manifold relations of life.

Thus while love, joy, peace, gentleness and holiness are the teaching of the life and death of our Lord, it is to these that we are also impelled by the indwelling of the Divine in men. As this spirit grows within us, we shall realise increasingly what it is to live in the virtue of that life and power which takes away the occasion of all wars.

b. *Pacem in Terris,* 1963 *Pacem in Terris,* John XXIII, II April 1963, paras.
126–9, p. 121

[In the last year of his life, during the Second Vatican Council, John XXIII
followed his recent predecessors (notably Benedict XV in the First World War)
in championing the cause of peace. The 1960s saw a deepening of the arms race,
from the Cuba crisis onwards, accompanied by an increased and widespread
public fear of nuclear war. The Roman Catholic call for peace continued in the
Council's document *Gaudium et Spes,* 1965 (see Section XIII, VII above). This
extract is entitled with Pope John's famous motto *'Signs of the Times'.*]

126. Men nowadays are becoming more and more convinced that any
disputes which may arise between nations must be resolved by negotiation and agreement, and not by recourse to arms.

127. We acknowledge that this conviction owes its origin chiefly to the
terrifying destructive force of modern weapons. It arises from fear of the
ghastly and catastrophic consequences of their use. Thus, in this age
which boasts of its atomic power, it no longer makes sense to maintain
that war is a fit instrument with which to repair the violation of justice.

128. And yet, unhappily, we often find the law of fear reigning
supreme among nations and causing them to spend enormous sums
on armaments. Their object is not aggression, so they say—and there is
no reason for disbelieving them—but to deter others from aggression.

129. Nevertheless, we are hopeful that, by establishing contact with
one another and by a policy of negotiation, nations will come to a better
recognition of the natural ties that bind them together as men. We are
hopeful, too, that they will come to a fairer realization of one of the
cardinal duties deriving from our common nature: namely, that love, not
fear, must dominate the relationships between individuals and between
nations. It is principally characteristic of love that it draws men together
in all sorts of ways, sincerely united in the bonds of mind and matter; and
this is a union from which countless blessings flow.

c. The World Council of Churches and the Nuclear Arms Race
Abrecht and Koshy, *Before It's Too Late,* WCC, 1984, 32–4

[The World Council of Churches organized a public hearing on the question of
the nuclear arms race in November 1981. This included participants 'representing
a wide variety of theological, political, scientific and military backgrounds and
including popular peace and public interest movements' (p. 3), as well as observers from churches and other organizations. The following excerpt appears in
the resulting Report, and represents a call for action by churches worldwide.]

. . . . 1. We believe that the time has come when the churches must unequiv-
ocally declare that the production and deployment as well as the use of

Justice, Peace, and the Environment

nuclear weapons are a crime against humanity and that such activities must
be condemned on ethical and theological grounds. The nuclear weapons
issue is, in its import and threat to humanity, a question of Christian
discipline and faithfulness to the Gospel. We recognise that nuclear weapons
will not disappear because of such an affirmation by the churches. But it will
involve the churches and their members in a fundamental examination of
their own implicit or explicit support of policies which, implicitly or explicitly, are based on the possessions and use of these weapons. Further, the
churches must become involved in whatever ways are appropriate in active
and effective programmes for disarmament. ...

5. Increasing popular resistance to nuclear weapons in many
countries, both East and West, is creating a political climate in which
the issues of disarmament and arms control have become matters of
central concern. Some movements include wider consideration about the
relationship between disarmament and development. We support such
movements, both as expressions of effective participation by large numbers of people in matters of vital importance to them, and as opportunities for popular education about peace, justice and security. We have
received striking evidence of the effectiveness of some of these movements, particularly those in which the tradition of education extends
over many years, and we urge churches and Christian individuals, where
appropriate, to play a responsible part within them.

6. The churches have a particular responsibility to remind public
opinion of the close links between disarmament and development policies, and to associate the efforts for disarmament with the wider issues
of justice, nationally and globally.

7. We cannot here make detailed proposals for the specific actions of
the churches in particular countries. However, in light of the principles
enunciated above and in view of the suggestions received at the Hearing
we urge consideration of the following proposals:

a. encourage the spread of information to remove the myths surrounding, and to challenge the legitimacy of, nuclear weapons and the
   driving forces behind the arms race;
b. help political, military and scientific workers to understand the moral
   implications of what they are doing;
c. explore ways of co-operating with other organizations and movements in the field of peace and disarmament and co-operate with
   peoples of other faiths;
d. support the victims of weapons testing, development and production;
   this will involve acts of international solidarity, e.g. support for the

campaign of the Pacific Islands for an end to nuclear testing; work on such specific concerns could also help to strengthen political determination to achieve a Comprehensive Test Ban Treaty.

II. RESISTANCE IN NAZI GERMANY

a. Barth's Prophetic Theology Karl Barth, *The Epistle to the Romans*, 6th edn., 1928 (1968, 28, 113)

[The courageous resistance of a minority of Christians in Germany to the Nazi state inspired many afterwards to take up the struggle for justice. The Swiss Reformed churchman Karl Barth was one of the architects of the Barmen declaration (b, below) and one of the outstanding theologians of the century. His theology, first made famous in his commentary on Romans, was rooted in a sense of despair over the First World War; it represented a rejection of any identification of the gospel with European culture, even in its greatest moral achievements. God is 'wholly Other' over against human culture and religion. Thus, later, Barth was theologically well equipped to stand against the Nazi attempt to dominate German Christianity.]

[On Romans 1: 1–2]. ... Paul is authorized to deliver—**the Gospel of God**. He is commissioned to hand over to men something quite new and unprecedented, joyful and good—the truth of God. Yes, precisely—of God! The Gospel is not a religious message to inform mankind of their divinity or to tell them how they may become divine. The Gospel proclaims a God utterly distant from men. ...

[On Romans 3: 29, 30]. ... It then becomes clear that God is the God of all men, the God of the Gentiles and of the Jews; He is not an element in spiritual experience or in the course of history; He is, rather, the ground of all elements, by whom they are measured and in whom they are contained. He differs absolutely from all our light and properties and abilities. This being so, the *everlasting power and divinity* (1: 20) of God shines forth ever more clearly. When therefore we use the word 'God', we do not say something but everything, not the last truth but one, but the last truth of all. It is the word of judgement, of challenge, of hope; it is directed, to all, and is significant— of supreme significance—for all. ...

b. The Barmen Declaration, 1934 The Barmen Declaration ('*A Theological Declaration to the Present State of the German Evangelical Church*', 1934), E. H. Robertson, Christians against Hitler, 48–52

[Barth and the other writers of the 'Barmen Declaration' rejected the Nazi claim on the life and theology of the German churches made by means of the 'German Christians'. The persecution of Jews who had converted to become Christian pastors was the first indication of the danger. For the Christian resistance, this widened out to become a general rejection of antisemitism. The Barmen

Declaration gave rise to the 'Confessing Church', in which the Christian resistance, most famously Dietrich Bonhoeffer, stood together until the end of the war and the collapse of Nazism in 1945.]

... . We, assembled representatives of Lutheran, Reformed and United churches, independent synods, *Kirchentage* and local church groups, hereby declare that we stand together on the foundation of the German Evangelical Church as a federal union of German confessional churches. We are held together by confession of the one Lord of the one, holy, universal and apostolic church.

We declare, before the public view of all the Evangelical Churches of Germany, that the unity of this confession and thereby also the unity of the German Evangelical Church is severally threatened. In this year of the existence of the German Evangelical Church it is endangered by the more and more clearly evident style of teaching and action of the ruling ecclesiastical party of the German Christians and the church government which they run. ...

Jesus Christ, as he is testified to us in Holy Scripture, is the one Word of God, which we are to hear, which we are to trust and obey and in life and in death.

We repudiate the false teaching that the Church can and must recognize yet other happenings and powers, personalities and truths as divine revelation alongside this one Word of God, as a source of her preaching. ...

We repudiate the false teaching that there are areas of our life in which we belong not to Jesus Christ but another lord, areas in which we do not need justification and sanctification through him. ...

We repudiate the false teaching that the Church can turn over the form of her message and ordinances at will or according to some dominant ideological and political convictions. ...

The various offices in the Church establish no rule of one over the other but the exercise of the service entrusted and commanded to the whole congregation.

We repudiate the false teaching that the Church can and may, apart from this ministry, set up or accept special leaders (*Führer*) equipped with powers to rule. ...

We repudiate the false teaching that the State can and should expand beyond its special responsibility to become the single and total order of human life, and also thereby fulfil the commission of the Church.

We repudiate the false teaching that the Church can and should expand beyond its special responsibility to take on the characteristics, functions and dignities of the State, and thereby become itself an organ of the State. ...

We repudiate the false teaching that the Church, in human self-esteem, can put the word and work of the Lord in the service of some wishes, purposes and plans or other, chosen according to desire. ...

c. **Dietrich Bonhoeffer in Tegel Prison, 1944** Letter from Tegel, 21 July 1944 *Letters and Papers from Prison*, 1971, 369–70

[Bonhoeffer's part in the resistance came to a head in 1943, when he was arrested. He was able to send letters from prison, most notably to his friend Eberhard Bethge. The failure of the plot to assassinate Hitler on 20 July 1944 sealed Bonhoeffer's fate, and he was executed just before the end of the war, on 9 April 1945. However, in his letters he had sketched a radical and creative theology born in the desperation of imprisonment, a theology drawing upon and developing Karl Barth's concept of 'religionless Christianity'. This was to inspire later theologians who saw the gospel as a truth to be acted out in the struggle for justice in the secular world, not kept apart as a religious artefact.]

.... . During the last year or so I've come to know and understand more and more the profound this-worldliness of Christianity. The Christian is not a *homo religiosus*, but simply a man, as Jesus was a man—in contrast, shall we say, to John the Baptist. I don't mean the shallow and banal this-worldliness of the enlightened, the busy, the comfortable, or the lascivious, but the profound this-worldliness, characterized by discipline and the constant knowledge of death and resurrection. I believe Luther lived a this-worldy life in this sense. ...

I discovered later, and I'm still discovering right up to this moment, that is it only by living completely in this world that one learns to have faith. One must completely abandon any attempt to make something of oneself, whether it be a saint, or a converted sinner, or a churchman (a so-called priestly type!), a righteous man or an unrighteous one, a sick man or a healthy one. By this worldliness I mean living unreservedly in life's duties, problems, successes and failures, experiences and helplessness. In doing so we throw ourselves completely into the arms of God, taking seriously, not our own sufferings, but those of God in the world—watching with Christ in Gethsemane. That, I think, is faith; that is *metanoia*; and that is how one becomes a man and a Christian (cf. Jer. 45!). How can success make us arrogant or failure lead us astray, when we share in God's sufferings through a life of this kind?

I think you see what I mean, even though I put it so briefly. I'm glad to have been able to learn this, and I know I've been able to do so only along the road that I've travelled. So I'm grateful for the past and the present, and content with them. ...

May God in his mercy lead us through these times; but above all, may he lead us to himself. ...

III. BLACK THEOLOGY IN THE 1960S

a. Luther King's Civil Rights Movement Martin Luther King, *Letter from Birmingham Jail*, 16 April 1963, *Why We Can't Wait*, 76–8

[The black civil rights movement of the 1960s in the USA raised profound and radical theological questions regarding the presence of Christ and the true nature of the Church, themes taken up just a little later in Latin America—see IV and V below. The black pastor Martin Luther King was the leader of the movement until his assassination in 1968. In this letter from prison he answers critical churchmen who object to his strong, but nonviolent, opposition to the racial injustice endemic in the USA. Here he articulates a perennial theme in Christian social campaigning: that its detractors are more concerned about the threat to the status quo than about the conditions which give rise to protest.]

MY DEAR FELLOW CLERGYMEN:

While confined here in the Birmingham city jail, I came across your recent statement calling my present activities 'unwise and untimely'. ... You deplore the demonstrations taking place in Birmingham. But your statement, I am sorry to say, fails to express a similar concern for the conditions that brought about the demonstrations. I am sure that none of you would want to rest content with the superficial kind of social analysis that deals merely with effects and does not grapple with underlying causes. It is unfortunate that demonstrations are taking place in Birmingham, but it is even more unfortunate that the city's white power structure left the Negro community with no alternative.

In any nonviolent campaign there are four basic steps: collection of the facts to determine whether injustices exist; negotiation; self-purification; and direct action. We have gone through all these steps in Birmingham. There can be no gainsaying the fact that racial injustice engulfs this community.

Birmingham is probably the most thoroughly segregated city in the United States. Its ugly record of brutality is widely known. Negroes have experienced grossly unjust treatment in the courts. There have been more unsolved bombings in Negro homes and churches in Birmingham than in any other city in the nation. These are the hard, brutal facts of the case. On the basis of these conditions, Negro leaders sought to negotiate with the city fathers. But the latter consistently refused to engage in good-faith negotiation.

Then, last September, came the opportunity to talk with leaders of Birmingham's economic community. In the course of the negotiations, certain promises were made by the merchants—for example, to remove the stores' humiliating racial signs. On the basis of these promises, the Reverend Fred Shuttlesworth and the leaders of the Alabama Christian Movement for Human Rights agreed to a moratorium on all demonstrations. As the weeks and months went by, we realized that we were the victims of a broken promise. A few signs, briefly removed, returned; the others remained.

As in so many past experiences, our hopes had been blasted, and the shadow of deep disappointment settled upon us. We had no alternative except to prepare for direct action, whereby we would present our very bodies as a means of laying our case before the conscience of the local and the national community. ...

b. **Black Church Leaders**   National Committee of Negro Churchmen on 'Black Power', 1966, Cone and Wilmore, *Black Theology: A Documentary History 1966–1979*, 201

[The refusal of many white-dominated civil authorities to respond to the non-violent campaign of Martin Luther King led to a more aggressive movement, that of 'Black Power', led by such figures as 'Malcolm X'. The black church leaders quoted below address American politicians in this excerpt. They do not want to condone violence, but they echo Martin Luther King in turning the attention back from riots and unrest to the conditions which aggravated them.]

It is of critical importance that the leaders of this nation listen also to a voice which says that the principle source of the threat to our nation comes neither from the riots erupting in our big cities, nor from the disagreements among the leaders of the civil rights movement, nor even from mere raising of the cry for 'black power'. These events, we believe, are but the expression of the judgement of God upon our nation for its failure to use its abundant resources to serve the real well-being of people, at home and abroad.

We give our full support to all civil rights leaders as they seek for basically American goals, for we are not convinced that their mutual reinforcement of one another in the past is bound to end in the future. We would hope that the public power of our nation will be used to strengthen the civil rights movement and not to manipulate or further fracture it.

We deplore the overt violence of riots, but we believe it is more important to focus on the real sources of the eruptions. These sources may be abetted inside the ghetto, but their basic causes lie in the silent and covert violence which white middle-class America inflicts upon the victims of the inner city. The hidden, smooth and often smiling decisions of American leaders which tie a white noose of suburbia around their necks, and which pin the backs of the masses of Negroes against the steaming ghetto walls—without jobs in a booming economy; with dilapidated and segregated educational systems in the full view of unenforced laws against it; in short: the failure of American leaders to use American power to create equal opportunity *in life* as well as *in law*— this is the real problem and not the anguished cry for 'black power'. ...

When American leaders decide to serve the real welfare of people instead of war and destruction; when American leaders are forced by the American people to quit misusing and abusing American power; then will the cry for 'black power' become inaudible, for the framework in which all power in America operates would include the power and experience of black men as well as those of white men. In that way, the fear of the power of each group would be removed. America is our beloved homeland. But, America is not God. Only God can do everything. America and the other nations of the world must decide which among a number of alternatives they will choose.

c. **Cone and Black Theology** James H. Cone, *Black Theology and Black Power*, 1969 (1997 edn., 62–3, 67, 69)

[James Cone is the most prominent of the black theologians who followed Martin Luther King. His work drew upon the spirit of the black power movement, and it is he who asks the question: who and where is Christ and his church in modern America? Thus he is the first black liberation theologian. In this excerpt he speaks of Christ as black, an important motif in the modern struggle whereby non-white Christians redefine their faith by removing the religious images of white domination. Cone's work should be seen in part as a response to the promulgation of a normative white, blue-eyed Jesus, far removed from the reality of the Incarnation.]

.... . The meaning of Black Power and its relationship to Christianity has been the focal point of our discussion thus far. It has been argued that Black Power is the spirit of Christ himself in the black-white dialogue which makes possible the emancipation of blacks from self-hatred and frees whites from their racism. Through Black Power, blacks are becoming men of worth, and whites are forced to confront them as human beings.

There is no other spirit in American life so challenging as the spirit of Black Power. We can see it affecting every major aspect of American life—economic, political, and social. In major white and black universities its spirit is manifested in the demand for more emphasis on 'black studies'. Black students have literally taken over some administration buildings in an effort to make white authorities recognize the importance of their demands. In politics, Stokely Carmichael and Charles Hamilton have given the political implications of Black Power. For them Black Power in politics means blacks controlling their political destiny by voting for black people and perhaps eventually forming a coalition with poor whites against middle-class whites. For some others it means a black nationalism. Economically it may mean boycotting, or building stores for black people. Religiously or philosophically it means an inner sense of freedom from the structures of white society which builds its economy on the labor of poor blacks and whites. It means that the slave now knows that he is a man, and thus resolves to make the enslaver recognize him. I contend that such a spirit is not merely compatible with Christianity; in America in the latter twentieth century it is Christianity ... The Church not only preaches the Word of liberation, it joins Christ in his work of liberation ...

To suggest that Christ has taken on a black skin is not theological emotionalism. If the Church is a continuation of the Incarnation, and if the Church and Christ are where the oppressed are, then Christ and his Church must totally identify with the oppressed to the extent that they too suffer for the same reasons persons are enslaved. In America, blacks are oppressed because of their blackness. It would seem, then, that emancipation could only be realized by Christ and his Church becoming black. Thinking of Christ as nonblack in the twentieth century is as theologically impossible as thinking of him as non-Jewish in the first century. God's Word in Christ not only fulfills his purposes for man through his elected people, but also inaugurates a new age in which all oppressed people become his people. In America, that people is a black people. In order to remain faithful to his Word in Christ, his present manifestation must be the very essence of blackness.

IV. THE ORIGINS OF LIBERATION THEOLOGY

a. *Populorum Progressio*, 1967 *Populorum Progressio*, Paul VI, 26 March 1967, paras. 48, 56–8, pp. 25, 28–9

[*Populorum Progressio* stands in a modern tradition of Roman Catholic social teaching—see above, Section X, XI. This encyclical and the Vatican II document *Gaudium et Spes* (Section XIII, VII) were published in the 1960s, a time of increased awareness and sensitivity to social problems and injustices, with the attendant movements for reform. Hence liberation theology, which initially regarded itself as part of the mainstream thinking of the Roman Catholic Church, was greatly inspired and encouraged by these two documents, and they are often quoted in its early works, such as *A Theology of Liberation* by Gutiérrez (c, below).

Indeed, *Populorum Progressio* is bold and radical in its condemnation of the effect that the economic grip of the more powerful nations has on the global poor. In these excerpts the charity and generosity expected of individuals is projected onto the international sphere. 'Solidarity', an important concept later in the 1980s Polish struggle against communism, is a keyword. The Pope also points to the inequity of the so-called free market, thus reinforcing the Vatican's role as critic of liberal capitalism as well as communism (although Vatican policy has consistently preferred the former to the latter).]

48. The same duty of solidarity that rests on individuals exists also for nations: 'It is the very serious duty of the developed nations to help the under-developed'. It is necessary to put this teaching of the Council into effect. Although it is normal that a nation should be the first to benefit from the gifts that Providence has bestowed on it as the fruit of the labour of its people, still no country can claim on that account to keep its wealth for itself alone. Every nation must produce more and better quality goods to give to all its inhabitants a truly human standard of living, and also to contribute to the common development of the human race. Given the increasing needs of the under-developed countries, it should be considered quite normal for an advanced country to devote a part of its production to meet their needs, and to train teachers, engineers, technicians and scholars prepared to put their knowledge and their skill at the disposal of less fortunate peoples. ...

56. The efforts which are being made to assist developing nations on a financial and technical basis, though considerable, would be illusory if their benefits were to be partially nullified as a consequence of the trade relations existing between rich and poor countries. The confidence of these latter would be severely shaken if they had the impression that what was being given them with one hand was being taken away with the other.

57. Of course, highly industrialized nations export for the most part manufactured goods, while countries with less developed economies have only food, fibres and other raw materials to sell. As a result of technical progress the value of manufactured goods is rapidly increasing and they can always find an adequate market. On the other hand, raw materials produced by under-developed countries are subject to wide and sudden fluctuations in price, a state of affairs far removed from the progressively increasing value of industrial products. As a result, nations whose industrialization is limited are faced with serious difficulties when they have to rely on their exports to balance their economy and to carry out their plans for development. The poor nations remain ever poorer while the rich ones become still richer.

58. In other words, the rule of free trade, taken by itself, is no longer able to govern international relations. Its advantages are certainly evident when the parties involved are not affected by any excessive inequalities of economic power: it is an incentive to progress and a reward for effort. That is why industrially developed countries see in it a law of justice. But the situation is no longer the same when economic conditions differ too widely from country to country; prices which are 'freely' set in the market can produce unfair results. One must recognize that it is the fundamental principal of 'liberalism', as the rule for commercial exchange, which is questioned here.

b. The Medellin Conference, 1968   Second General Conference of Latin American Bishops at Medellin, Colombia, 26 August–6 September 1968, A. T. Hennelly, *Liberation Theology: A Documentary History*, 91, 107–8

[Liberation theology was encouraged by episcopal conferences in Latin America itself. The 1968 Medellin conference drew upon *Gaudium et Spes* in looking for the 'signs of the times', that is, seeking how to live out the gospel in modern Latin America and its social and political troubles. The Church as envisaged at Medellin was a radical church, a critic of government. The Conference affirmed the 'preferential option for the poor', a key theme in liberation theology. These extracts are taken from the 'Message to the Peoples of Latin America' and the 'Document on Peace.']

. . . . As Christians we believe that this historical stage of Latin America is intimately linked to the history of salvation.

As pastors, with a common responsibility, we wish to unite ourselves with the life of all of our peoples in the painful search for adequate solutions to their multiple problems. Our mission is to contribute to the integral advancement of humankind and of human communities of the continent.

We believe that we are in a new historical era. This era requires clarity in order to see, lucidity in order to diagnose, and solidarity in order to act. In the light of the faith that we profess as believers, we have undertaken to discover a plan of God in the 'signs of the times'. We interpret the aspirations and clamors of Latin America as signs that reveal the direction of the divine plan operating in the redeeming love of Christ, which bases these aspirations on an awareness of fraternal solidarity.

Faithful to this divine plan, and in order to respond to the hopes placed in the church, we wish to offer that which we hold as most appropriate: a global vision of humanity, and the integral vision of Latin Americans in development. . . .

We refer here particularly to the implications for our countries of dependence on a center of economic power, around which they gravitate. For this reason, our nations frequently do not own their goods, or have a say in economic decisions affecting them. ...

a. **Growing distortion of international commerce.** Because of the relative depreciation of the terms of exchange, the value of raw materials is increasingly less in relation to the cost of manufactured products.

b. **Rapid flight of economic and human capital.** The search for security and individual gain leads many members of the more comfortable sectors of our countries to invest their money in foreign countries.

c. **Tax evasion and loss of gains and dividends.** Some foreign companies working in our country (also some national firms) often evade the established tax system by subterfuge.

d. **Progressive debt.** It is not surprising to find that in the system of international credits, the true needs and capabilities of our countries are not taken into account. We thus run the risk of encumbering ourselves with debts whose payment absorbs the greater part of our profits.

e. **International monopolies and international imperialism of money.** We wish to emphasize that the principal guilt for economic dependence of our countries rests with powers, inspired by uncontrolled desire for gain, which leads to economic dictatorship and the 'international imperialism of money' condemned by Pope Pius XI in *Quadragesimo Anno* and by Pope Paul VI in *Populorum Progressio*. ...

c. Gutiérrez, the Pioneer of Liberation Theology   Gustavo Gutiérrez, *A Theology of Liberation: History, Politics and Salvation*, 1971 (1988, 9–10, 54, 63)

[The work of the Peruvian priest Gutiérrez is as seminal in Latin American liberation theology as Cone's is in black theology. He argues that theology must be critical, and this means critical of Church as well as State. This, in addition to the use of Marxist concepts, laid the ground for the later dispute between liberation theologians and the Roman Catholic hierarchy. Liberation theology was the rallying cry of a grass-roots church willing to live out its faith in social—occasionally violent—revolution in the search for justice. Salvation, in this view, cannot be confined to an other-worldly paradise, but should involve the whole human being, including the social and political dimension. Thus salvation is realized in history in the liberation of the poor.]

.... . Theology must be critical reflection on humankind, on basic human principles. Only with this approach will theology be a serious discourse, aware of itself, in full possession of its conceptual elements. But we are not referring exclusively to this epistemological aspect when we talk about theology as critical reflection. We also refer to a clear and critical attitude regarding economic and socio-cultural issues in the life and reflection of the Christian community. To disregard these is to deceive both oneself and others. But above all, we intend this term to express the theory of a definite practice. Theological reflection would then necessarily be a criticism of society and the Church insofar as they are called and addressed by the Word of God; it would be a critical theory, worked out in the light of the Word accepted in faith and inspired by a practical purpose—and therefore indissolubly linked to historical praxis.

By preaching the Gospel message, by its sacraments, and by the charity of its members, the Church proclaims and shelters the gift of the Kingdom of God in the heart of human history. The Christian community professes a 'faith which works through charity'. It is—at least ought to be—real charity, action, and commitment to the service of others. Theology is reflection, a critical attitude. Theology *follows*; it is the second step. What Hegel used to say about philosophy can likewise be applied to theology: it rises only at sundown. The pastoral activity of the Church does not flow as a conclusion from theological premises. Theology does not produce pastoral activity; rather it reflects upon it. Theology must be able to find in pastoral activity the presence of the Spirit inspiring the action of the Christian community. A privileged *locus theologicus* for understanding the faith will be the life, preaching, and historical commitment of the Church.

To reflect upon the presence and action of the Christian in the world means, moreover, to go beyond the visible boundaries of the Church. This is of prime importance. It implies openness to the world, gathering the questions it poses, being attentive to its historical transformations. ...

Understood in this way, theology has a necessary and permanent role in liberation from every from of religious alienation—which is often fostered by the ecclesiastical institution itself when it impedes an authentic approach to the Word of the Lord. ...

... . Finally, theology thus understood, that is to say as linked to praxis, fulfills a prophetic function insofar as it interprets historical events with the intention of revealing and proclaiming their profound meaning. ...

To characterize Latin America as a dominated and oppressed continent naturally leads one to speak of liberation and above all to participate in the process. Indeed, *liberation* is a term which expresses a new posture of Latin Americans.

The failure of reformist efforts has strengthened this attitude. Among more alert groups today, what we have called a new awareness of Latin American reality is making headway. They believe that there can be authentic development for Latin America only if there is liberation from the domination exercised by the great capitalist countries, and especially by the most powerful, the United States of America. This liberation also implies a confrontation with these groups' natural allies, their compatriots who control the national power structure. It is becoming more evident that the Latin American peoples will not emerge from their present status except by means of a profound transformation, *a social revolution*, which will radically and qualitatively change the conditions in which they now live. The oppressed sectors within each country are becoming aware—slowly, it is true—of their class interests and of the painful road which must be followed to accomplish the breakup of the status quo. Even more slowly they are becoming aware of all that the building of a new society implies. ...

d. **The Puebla Conference, 1979**   Third General Conference of Latin American Bishops at Puebla, Mexico, 27 January–13 February 1979, A. T. Hennelly, *Liberation Theology: A Documentary History*, 234–5

[Puebla confirmed the Medellin emphasis on the 'preference for the poor' and the concerns about injustice in Latin America, but it also sounded a note of caution about the more radical elements in liberation theology, which had attracted the attention of the Vatican. Thus while the Puebla document is often spoken of in the same breath as that of Medellin, both representing the Latin American rediscovery of the radical call of the gospel, it also articulates the division between the grass-roots movement and the hierarchy, and anticipates the more public disputes of the 1980s (see v below).]

... . At the Medellin Conference we saw the elucidation of a dynamic process of integral liberation. Its positive echoes were taken up by *Evangelii Nuntiandi* and by John Paul II in his message to this conference. This proclamation imposes an urgent task on the church, and it belongs to the very core of an evangelization that seeks the authentic realization of the human being. But there are different conceptions and applications of liberation. Though they share common traits, they contain points of view that can hardly be brought together satisfactorily. The best thing to do, therefore, is to offer criteria that derive from the magisterium and that provide us with the necessary discernment regarding the original conception of Christian liberation.

There are two complementary and inseparable elements. The first is liberation from all forms of bondage, from personal and social sin, and from everything that tears apart the human individual and society; all this finds its source to be in egotism, in the mystery of iniquity. The second element is liberation for progressive growth in being through communion with God and other human beings; this reaches its culmination in the perfect communion of heaven, where God is all in all and weeping forever ceases. This liberation is gradually being realized in history, in our personal history and that of our peoples. It takes in all the different dimensions of life: the social, the political, the economic, the cultural, and all their interrelationships. Through all these dimensions must flow the transforming treasure of the gospel. ...

The sort of liberation we are talking about knows how to use evangelical means, which have their own distinctive efficacy. It does not resort to violence of any sort, to the dialectics of class struggle. Instead it relies on the vigorous energy and activity of Christians, who are moved by the Spirit to respond to the cries of countless millions of their brothers and sisters. ...

V. LIBERATION THEOLOGY AND THE VATICAN

a. The Silencing of Boff   Leonardo Boff, *Church: Charism and Power: Liberation Theology and the Institutional Church*, 1981 (1985, 62–3)

[The title of the Brazilian Franciscan Boff's book suggests criticism of the hierarchy of the Roman Catholic Church, and indeed he, like Jon Sobrino in *The True Church and the Poor*, locates the church that is true to the gospel among the poor and those marginalized by both Church and State. This excerpt shows why he attracted the displeasure of the Vatican, who censured his work and ordered his silence after an investigation. Entitled 'Ecclesiogenesis: The New Church Born of the Old', the section quoted distinguishes the old Church of the centre and the new Church of the periphery. Boff later left the Franciscan order.]

Meditating on the Gospels and with a theological reading of the signs of the times, a significant portion of the Church as institution has understood the current challenges for Christian faith and responsibly tries to respond to them. We are seeing the rising of a new Church, born in the heart of the Old Church, in the form of *comunidades de base*, communities on the peripheries of our cities, a Church of the poor, comprised of poor people, in the form of bishops, priests, and religious entering into the life of the marginalized, centers of evangelization headed by lay people, and so on. It is a Church that has definitively renounced the centralization of power; unity resides in the idea of Church as People of God, a pilgrim Church, open to the historical march of peoples, a Church that shares in all the risks and enjoys the small victories with a very deep sense of following Jesus Christ, identified with the poor, the rejected, and the disinherited of the earth. This Church is being built day by day, open to new ministries answering the needs of the community and responding to all human life and not just culture, a Church involved in the working world and living out the meaning and joy of the resurrection in the heart of the secular world. ...

This new Church, as in all renewal movements, first appears on the periphery. Given the power structure at the center, the periphery is the only place where true creativity and freedom is possible. Faith is born and made present through personal witness; it is not being watched over by the institution. Thus, there is the opportunity for a pure and evangelical authenticity not found within the institution with its bureaucratic preoccupations and its time and energy spent to justify, defend, preserve, and expand its structures.

It is to be expected that the old Church will distrust the new Church on the periphery with its gospel freedoms. It will call it a parallel Church, with its own magisterium, disobedient and disloyal to the center!. ...

The future of the institutional Church lies in this small seed that is the new Church growing in the fields of the poor and the powerless. ...

b. The First Vatican Instruction, 1984   *Instruction on Certain Aspects of the 'Theology of Liberation'*, Sacred Congregation for the Doctrine of the Faith, 6 August 1984, A. T. Hennelly, *Liberation Theology: A Documentary History*, 394

[The SCDF, led by its prefect, Cardinal Josef Ratzinger, responded to several years of dispute and hierarchical concern over liberation theology by issuing this first of two instructions on the topic. These documents (an excerpt from the second is given in c. below) attempted to identify what is acceptable and what is incorrect, from an hierarchical point of view, in the new theological current, which had now extended beyond Latin America to many locations and Christians, Catholic and non-Catholic.]

... . The Sacred Congregation for the Doctrine of the Faith does not intend to deal here with the vast theme of Christian freedom and liberation in it own right. This it intends to do in a subsequent document which will detail in a positive fashion the great richness of this theme for the doctrine and the life of the church.

The present instruction has much more limited and precise purpose: to draw the attention of pastors, theologians, and all the faithful to the deviations and risks of deviation, damaging to the faith and to Christian living, that are brought about by certain forms of liberation theology which use, in an insufficiently critical manner, concepts borrowed from various currents of Marxist thought.

This warning should in no way be interpreted as a disavowal of all those who want to respond generously and with an authentic evangelical spirit to the 'preferential option for the poor'. It should not at all serve as an excuse for those who maintain an attitude of neutrality and indifference in the face of the tragic and pressing problems of human misery and injustice. It is, on the contrary, dictated by the certitude that the serious ideological deviations which it points out tend inevitably to betray the cause of the poor. More than ever, it is important that numerous Christians, whose faith is clear and who are committed to live the Christian life in its fullness, become involved in the struggle for justice, freedom, and human dignity because of their love for their disinherited, oppressed, and persecuted brothers and sisters. More than ever, the church intends to condemn abuses, injustices, and attacks against freedom, wherever they occur and whoever commits them. It intends to struggle, by its own means, for the defence and advancement of the rights of humankind, especially of the poor.

c. **The Second Vatican Instruction, 1986** *Instruction on Christian Freedom and Liberation*, Sacred Congregation for the Doctrine of the Faith, 22 March 1986, A. T. Hennelly, *Liberation Theology: A Documentary History*, paras. 67–9, pp. 482–3

[This excerpt includes a mention of the 'base communities', grass-roots groups of radical Christians who created the paradigmatic context for liberation theology.]

67. But Jesus not only brought the grace and peace of God; he also healed innumerable sick persons; he had compassion on the crowd who had nothing to eat and he fed them; with the disciples who followed him he practiced almsgiving. Therefore the Beatitude of poverty, which he proclaimed, can never signify that Christians are permitted to ignore the poor, who lack what is necessary for human life in this world. This poverty is the result and consequence of sin and natural frailty, and it is an evil from which human beings must be freed as completely as possible.

68. ... The special option for the poor, far from being a sign of particularism or sectarianism, manifests the universality of the church's being and mission. This option excludes no one.

This is the reason why the church cannot express this option by means of reductive sociological and ideological categories which would make this preference a partisan choice and a source of conflict.

69. The new basic communities or other groups of Christians which have arisen to be witnesses to this evangelical love are a source of great

hope for the church. If they really live in unity with the local church and the universal church, they will be a real expression of communion and a means for constructing a still deeper communion. Their fidelity to their mission will depend on how careful they are to educate their members in the fullness of the Christian faith through listening to the word of God, fidelity to the teaching of the magisterium, to the hierarchical order of the church and to the sacramental life. If this condition is fulfilled, their experience, rooted in a commitment to the complete human liberation, becomes a treasure for the whole church. ...

d. The Excommunication of Balasuriya   Tissa Balasuriya, *Mary and Human Liberation*, 1990 (1997 edn., 142–3, 161–2)

[The liberation theology dispute had spread to Asian Catholicism from its Latin American origins. In Sri Lanka the struggle for social justice involves dialogue with Buddhism and Hinduism and the taking seriously of Asian concepts of salvation. In this book the social activist and Oblate of Mary Immaculate Balasuriya takes to task the conservative marian cult, influential in Sri Lanka: the traditional view of Mary, in his view, is divorced from human suffering by the image of the Virgin free of original sin and the impurity of sexuality. Hence Balasuriya's Mary, like many other contemporary approaches (see the comments on Section XIII, II) is a woman of the people; this perspective leads Balasuriya to question the traditional teaching on original sin and salvation. This was not new—Matthew Fox had already been censured for questioning the doctrine of original sin (see VIII. a. below). After disapproval by the Sri Lankan hierarchy, the Vatican took up the demand for Balasuriya to retract his work, and his request for a public debate was met instead by excommunication in January 1997. However, the resulting global outcry helped persuade the Vatican to lift the excommunication one year later.]

.... . This doctrine of original sin as developed in Christian theology also taught that humanity was in such a state of sinfulness that only Jesus Christ and his merits could achieve salvation. For many centuries this meant that everyone was called upon to acknowledge Jesus Christ as saviour, and to belong to the Catholic Church. Even today, it is generally understood to imply that salvation is, by some means or other, through Jesus Christ. ...

This claim of the Church to be the vehicle of eternal salvation has a twofold impact which I would question. First, it claims for a religious institution the power to mediate salvation beyond this life. ...

This traditional explanation of the doctrine of original sin seems also to reduce the chances of eternal salvation for people of no religion, since human conscience as a guide determining human actions, morality and spirituality was regarded as a less reliable path to salvation. ...

A second aspect of discrimination embodied in this doctrine concerns people of faiths other than Christianity. Though the Churches now affirm the possibility of salvation through other religions, the weight of the Christian tradition has been to explain original sin in such a way that the remedy for it was said to be exclusively in and through the Church, thanks to the merits of Christ.

This understanding of original sin is linked to a concept of God that is not acceptable to the other religions. In Asia, the idea of humanity being born alienated from the creator would seem an abominable concept of the divine. To believe that whole generations of entire continents lived and died with a diminished chance of salvation is repugnant to the notion of a just and loving God.

In fact one of the causes of the excess of missionary zeal against other religions was the theological perspective of 'salvation only in the Church'. ...

Marian spirituality, associated closely with the consequences of the fall and original sin, has encouraged a certain sense of weakness, dependency and powerlessness among human beings, particularly among women. Mary is presented as the refuge, consoler, mediatrix who intercedes for us with God. While it is true that human beings are finite, fallible and mortal, it is also important that our own strengths and potentialities be recognised, encouraged and developed. As innumerable prayers and hymns indicate, these human capabilities are not so much encouraged in Marian devotions as is the attitude of dependence based on a helplessness. ...

In capitalist and colonial situations, Marian devotions can also have a domesticating influence, by inducing Christians to accept hard realities as the will of God. Throughout the centuries of European colonialism, Catholic missionaries had no concerns that propagating their cult of Mary might have a revolutionary impact on the working classes or colonized peoples. ...

VI. THE ORDINATION OF WOMEN

a. **Canterbury and Rome, 1975**   Letters of Donald Coggan, Archbishop of Canterbury to Pope Paul VI and to Cardinal Willebrands, President of the Secretariat for Promoting Christian Unity, 9 July 1975

[The contemporary debate about the ordination of women to the priesthood in the Anglican and Roman Catholic churches comes in the wake of many other denominations admitting women to full equality in ministry and leadership. The opponents to this trend argue that it is inspired by secular feminism, but, on the other hand, supporters point out that secular feminism may itself owe much to radical Christian groups such as the Quakers, who championed gender equality well before the modern period.

In Anglicanism and Roman Catholicism, however, the debate revolves around discussion about the nature of priesthood. The Anglican communion worldwide had begun to ordain women before the decisive theological break-through in England in 1975, and some national Anglican churches, for example those of the USA and New Zealand, were the first to allow women bishops; in England, the measure allowing ordination to the diaconate came in 1987, and to the priesthood, in 1992. These brief extracts from the letters of the Archbishop of Canterbury to Roman Catholic leaders document the 1975 decision.]

[*To Pope Paul VI*] After our predecessor's visit to Rome in 1966, together with him you inaugurated a 'serious dialogue' between the Roman Catholic Church and the Anglican Communion. The Agreed Statements of the consequent Anglican/Roman Catholic International Commission on the Eucharist and the Ministry are not authoritative statements of faith of either the Roman Catholic Church or the Anglican Communion; nevertheless they do bear witness to the steady growth of mutual understanding and trust developing between our two traditions.

It is with this in mind that we write to inform Your Holiness of the slow but steady growth of a consensus of opinion within the Anglican Communion that there are no fundamental objections in principle to the ordination of women to the priesthood.

At the same time we are aware that action on this matter could be an obstacle to further progress along the path of unity Christ wills for his Church. ...

[*To Cardinal Willebrands*]. ... on Thursday 3rd July, the General Synod of the Church of England investigated this question and you will no doubt be interested to learn of the outcome of the debate.

A motion, moved by the Bishop of Oxford, was passed to the effect 'That this Synod considers that there are no fundamental objections to the ordination of women to the priesthood.'

Nevertheless both a motion for immediate action to remove the legal and other barriers to the Ordination of Women and a motion on behalf of the Standing Committee of the General Synod against immediate action were lost. This reflects the significant division of opinion on the matter within the Church of England at large and in the Synod itself, a division reflected in various degrees amongst laity, clergy and bishops. ...

b. Declaration on Women Priests, 1976 *Inter Insigniores (Declaration on the question of the admission of women to the ministerial priesthood)*, Sacred Congregation for the Doctrine of the Faith, 1976, 6–7, 14

[The Roman Catholic hierarchy responded to the breakthrough in England with its own statement in 1976, which articulates the contemporary Roman Catholic hierarchical position in the face of a growing movement for women's ordination in the Roman Catholic Church. The extracts here pinpoint two major issues in the argument.]

.... Jesus Christ did not call any woman to become part of the Twelve. If he acted in this way, it was not in order to conform to the customs of his time, for his attitude towards women was quite different from that of his milieu, and he deliberately and courageously broke with it. ...

The whole sacramental economy is in fact based upon natural signs, on symbols imprinted upon the human psychology: 'Sacramental signs,' says Saint Thomas, 'represent what they signify by natural resemblance.' The same natural resemblance is required for persons as for things: when Christ's role in the Eucharist is to be expressed sacramentally, there would not be this 'natural resemblance' which must exist between Christ and his minister if the role of Christ were not taken by a man: in such a case it would be difficult to see in the minister the image of Christ. For Christ himself was and remains a man. ...

VII. FEMINIST THEOLOGY

a. Ruether on Sexism in Theology   Rosemary Radford Ruether, *Sexism and God-Talk: Towards a Feminist Theology*, 1983 (1992 edn. 18–19, 205–6)

[Feminist theology has two major roots: first, the feminist movement in its general sense and, secondly, liberation theology applied to the question of sexism. It begins with the demand for inclusive language and women's leadership in the churches, but it goes further to a new vision of what it means to be the Church. Rosemary Radford Ruether, an American Roman Catholic, here articulates some foundational themes.]

.... The critical principle of feminist theology is the promotion of the full humanity of women. Whatever denies, diminishes, or distorts the full humanity of women is, therefore, appraised as not redemptive. Theologically speaking, whatever diminishes or denies the full humanity of women must be presumed not to reflect the divine or an authentic relation to the divine, or to reflect the authentic nature of things, or to be the message or work of an authentic redeemer or a community of redemption.

This negative principle also implies the positive principle: what does promote the full humanity of women is of the Holy, it does reflect true relation to the divine, it is the true nature of things, the authentic message of redemption and the mission of redemptive community. But the meaning of this positive principle—namely, the full humanity of women—is not fully known. It has not existed in history. What we have known is the negative principle of the denigration and marginalization of women's humanity. Still, the humanity of women, although diminished, has not been destroyed. It has constantly affirmed itself, often in only limited and subversive ways, and it has been a touchstone against which we test and criticize all that diminishes us. In the process we experience our larger potential that allows us to begin to imagine a world without sexism. ...

The formation of such feminist base communities does not necessarily imply a sectarian rejection of institutional churches. People who find their primary support in such feminist communities might also participate in various structures of institutional church life. Some might be lay members or even clergy of local churches, members of religious congregations, teachers in theological schools, or denominational employees, while drawing support for a more radical vision for social action from the base community. The transformed liturgies, theological reflection, and social action developed in base groups could then be brought to bear on the institutional Church. The creation of 'liberated zones' in a least some sectors of institutional churches would be seen as one of the 'fields of mission' of the base community. The exodus out of the institutional Church into the feminist base community would be for the sake of creating a freer space from which to communicate new possibilities to the institutional Church. The relationship between the two becomes a creative dialectic rather than a schismatic impasse. Indeed, precisely as one takes seriously one's responsibility to transform the historical Church, it becomes essential to have a support community that really nurtures liberated ways of living together rather than remaining crabbed and frustrated by religious experiences of alienation and negation of this vision. ...

b. Feminism and the Bible   Letty M. Russell, 'Authority and the Challenge of Feminist Interpretation', 1985, L. M. Russell, *Feminist Interpretation of the Bible*, 143–4

[The question of the interpretation of the Bible is raised in all debates about Christian authority and radical theology. Just as the liberation theologians found inspiration in a reading based on the preference for the poor, so also feminist theologians seek a new reading which frees Christianity from patriarchy. The very act of interpretation itself has, according to Russell, to be re-envisioned.]

.... . The paradigm that no longer makes sense to feminists is that of *authority as domination*. This constellation of beliefs, values, and methods shared as a common perspective tends to predominate in church and university and in most theological research and dialogue. Consciously or unconsciously, reality is seen in the form of a hierarchy, or pyramid. Ordination and every other topic are viewed in terms of super- and subordination. Things are assigned a divine order, with God at the top, men next, and so on down to dogs, plants, and 'impersonal' nature. This paradigm reinforces ideas of authority *over* community and refuses to admit the ideas and persons that do not (wish to) fit into the established hierarchies of thought or social structures. ...

This paradigm of reality is an inadequate theological perspective because it provides a religious rationale of the domination and oppression of the weak by the oppressive political, economic, and religious power elites. ...

The emerging feminist paradigm trying to make sense of biblical and theological truth claims is that of *authority as partnership*. In this view, reality is interpreted in the form of a circle of interdependence. Order is explored through inclusion of diversity in a rainbow spectrum that does not require that persons submit to the 'top' but, rather, that they participate in the common task of creating an interdependent community of humanity and nature. Authority is exercised *in* community and tends to reinforce ideas of cooperation, with contributions from a wide diversity of persons enriching the whole. When difference is valued and respected, those who have found themselves marginal to church or society begin to discover their own worth as human beings. ...

c. **Decade of Solidarity with Women**   Mercy Oduyoye, *Who Will Roll the Stone Away?* WCC, 1990, 13–14

[All churches, to some extent, accept that the equality of women—if not in ministry in some cases—is a necessary part of social reform in the latter part of the twentieth century. The World Council of Churches launched an 'Ecumenical Decade of the Churches in Solidarity with Women' for 1988–98. Mercy Oduyoye's book accompanied the launch. The disadvantage for women is intensified in the poorer countries of the world, and female theologians from the so-called Third World have become leading exponents of the call for justice (including care of the environment, see VIII. c below). The black feminist perspective—which should be distinguished from its European counterpart—is referred to as 'womanist'. The precise identification of different liberation theologies in this way gives a voice to those often overlooked by 'mainstream' traditions of theology.]

... . We as a church must recognize that in most instances women experience the worst effects of poverty, economic injustice, racism, casteism, militarism, and suffer more than others from the denial of land and minority rights. Women are the poorest of the poor, always with limited access to food, education and paid work. Women's bodies are abused by medical technology and sold into prostitution. Women are the victims of various forms of violence. Women of the world are asking: 'Who will roll the stone away?'

We as a church are not free from idolatries and power structures that oppress people. We do not always admit that we sin by creating and justifying obstacles that destroy God's purposes for the earth. We do not empower women to challenge oppressive structures in the global community, our country and our church. We as women and men are called to repent, and together we say: 'We will roll the stone away.'

We as the church celebrate the visions and commitment of women to the struggles for justice, peace and the integrity of creation in our wounded world. Women and men created in the image of God are today all invited to take part in the human responsibility of caring for all life.

During the Ecumenical Decade of the Churches in Solidarity with Women, we as a church will rise up and identify the obstacles to women's full and active participation in church and society. We will work to remove the obstacles. We will affirm women's perspectives and contributions. We will pluck up and break down, build and plant. We will participate with God in transforming the world. We will say to each other: 'We will roll the stone away'. ...

VIII.   ECOTHEOLOGY

a. Fox and Creation Spirituality   Matthew Fox, *Original Blessing: A Primer in Creation Spirituality*, 1983, (1990 edn. 26, 305, 353)

[The concern for the environment caused by modern pollution and the nuclear threat led to a new branch of liberation theology known as 'green theology' or 'creation spirituality', which criticized the Christian tradition for its legitimation of human domination over nature. The American Dominican Matthew Fox sought to replace the anthropocentric view with a theology which asserted God's blessing of and presence in nature; Fox argued that this should be emphasized above human sinfulness. His assault on the doctrine of original sin led to the disapproval of the Roman Catholic hierarchy (see also above: Boff, v. a, and Balasuriya, v. d), and he later left his order to join the American Episcopalian Church so that he could continue his work.]

.... . In religion we have been operating under the model that humanity, and especially sinful humanity, was the center of the spiritual universe. This is not so. The universe itself, blessed and graced, is the proper starting point for spirituality. Original blessing is prior to any sin, original or less than original. ...

This entire book and its journey into creation-centered spirituality also leads to a letting go of certain forms of religion, those based on fall/ redemption theologies, structures, and spiritualities. It is about a call to transformation. Religion can and must let go of a dualistic tradition and be transformed into that tradition which is more ancient, more celebrative, more justice-oriented and more like the tradition Jesus himself lived and preached. Here truly there would happen a New Pentecost, a New Creation, a spiritual awakening that all the world's peoples and all the world's religions might share in. ...

Creation Spirituality is a bridge which carries us back to an ancient past and forward with hope for the future. It is also an umbrella under which the following persons can meet and share a common language: those dedicated to feminist wisdom, Earth and animal rights, renewed education, honoring the artists in us and around us, respect for the *anawim* among us, global justice, mystical and religious renewal. ...

b. Moltmann, Creation, and the Sabbath   Jürgen Moltmann, *God in Creation: An Ecological Doctrine of Creation*, 1985, xii–xiii, 5–6

[The movement for green theology in Europe gained a champion in the influential German Lutheran theologian Jürgen Moltmann. Moltmann's theology draws upon his memories of the suffering caused by the Nazis, and he is therefore keen to re-evaluate the debt of Christianity to its Jewish heritage. Here he utilizes the Jewish tradition of the sabbath to promote an ecological doctrine of God.]

.... . By the title 'God in Creation' I mean God the Holy Spirit. God is 'the lover of life' and his Spirit is *in* all created beings. ...

I have devoted not the least part of my attention to Christian and Jewish sources. Christianity took over the doctrine of creation from Israel's Scripture, and will therefore do well to listen attentively to what Jewish interpretations of these common traditions have to tell us. The best creation wisdom is to be found in the Jewish theology and practice of the sabbath. In abandoning the sabbath, the Gentile Christian churches have lost this means of access, and we generally overlook it altogether. ...

According to the biblical traditions, creation is aligned towards its redemption from the very beginning; for the creation of the world points forward to the sabbath, 'the feast of creation'. 'Sabbath is one-sixtieth part of the world to come.' On the sabbath the creation is completed. The sabbath is the prefiguration of the world to come. So when we present creation in the light of its future—'the glory of God', 'existence as home' and the general 'sympathy of all things'—then we are developing a *sabbath doctrine of creation.* ...

c. **Chung Hyun Kyung and Eco-Feminism** Chung Hyun Kyung, 'Ecology, Feminism and African and Asian Spirituality: Towards a Spirituality of Eco-Feminism', David G. Hallman, *Ecotheology: Voices from South and North*, WCC, 1994, 176–7

[The work of theologians such as Rosemary Radford Ruether and Mary Daly bears testimony to the strong link between feminist theology and ecology; nature and the female have been associated in the Christian tradition, and both have suffered from patriarchy. Here the well-known Korean feminist Chung Hyun Kyung contributes to a World Council of Churches volume on this debate. She articulates the yearnings of Africans and Asians for freedom from a Euro-centric theology in which nature—in the same way as the people she represents—is regarded as an object to be plundered and subdued.]

... . When God becomes a white, rich European man, white European man becomes a god for all other people and beings in the universe. Therefore, eco-feminists are looking for an alternative spirituality which is able to respond to their need for affirming the sacredness of the cosmos. Where can we find the resources for this cosmic spirituality? Many agree that institutionalized, patriarchal, otherworldly religions cannot be the main source of holistic spirituality and have turned to the spirituality of indigenous people in Asia and Africa. This spirituality gives full value to creation as a dynamic and highly integrated Web of Life. It exudes life-giving values: sacredness of the land, reverence for all creatures, judicious use and conservation of the earth's resources, compassion for the weak, oppressed and marginalized. These cosmic values, rituals and practices are often considered 'superstitious'. But they capture a cosmic interwovenness that can become a healing and transforming experience for all of us.

This cosmic interwovenness is a wholesome, harmonious and compassionate web of relationships: intrapersonal and interpersonal, communal and societal, global and planetary. These relationships are based on justice: no exploitation, manipulation or oppression, but mutuality, deep respect and delicate balance. For example, when African and Asian people approach or pass rivers, trees, mountains, or when they plant, fish or harvest they often ask permission from the spirits of the land, the mountains, the plants and trees, the rivers and streams. They do not take from nature more than they need or without asking for what they need for life. They try to return to nature in some other way what they have taken, as if to repay this debt.

Therefore, when we incorporate African or Asian indigenous spirituality to eco-feminist spirituality, we begin to perceive the meaning of nature, God and humanity in a fresh new way. First of all, nature stops being a non-feeling, dead place. It becomes a God-infused and God-breathed place. We begin to feel deep respect, even a sense of awe before the life-giving, yet fragile interwovenness of the earth. The earth becomes sacred. ...

IX. SOUTH AFRICA AND THIRD WORLD SOLIDARITY

a. 'Kairos' and Apartheid The Kairos Theologians (South Africa), *Challenge to the Church: The Kairos Document*, 1985, 4–5

[The struggle for black liberation in the USA in the 1960s was also important in South Africa under its apartheid regime. The leading church figures in the social revolution that finally resulted in Nelson Mandela's presidency were the inspirational writers and preachers Desmond Tutu and Allan Boesak. In 1985 many other South African theologians drew on the liberation theology tradition to suggest that the critical time ('kairos', from the Greek New Testament) had come for the churches to speak out prophetically against the government. They should neither support the State nor opt out of the struggle for change.]

The time has come. The moment of truth has arrived. South Africa has been plunged into a crisis that is shaking the foundations and there is every indication that the crisis has only just begun and that it will deepen and become even more threatening in the months to come. It is the KAIROS or moment of truth not only for apartheid but also for the Church. ...

What the present crisis shows up, although many of us have known it all along, is that *the Church is divided*. More and more people are now saying that there are in fact two Churches in South Africa—a White Church and a Black Church. Even within the same denomination there are in fact two Churches. In the life and death conflict between different social forces that has come to a head in South Africa today, there are Christians (or at least people who profess to be Christians) on both sides of the conflict—and some who are trying to sit on the fence!. ...

There we sit in the same Church while outside Christian policemen and soldiers are beating up and killing Christian children or torturing Christian prisoners to death while yet other Christians stand by and weakly plead for peace.

The Church is divided and its day of judgement has come.

The moment of truth has compelled us to analyse more carefully the different theologies in our Churches and to speak out more clearly and boldly about the real significance of these theologies. We have been able to isolate three theologies and we have chosen to call them 'State Theology', 'Church Theology' and 'Prophetic Theology'. In our thoroughgoing criticism of the first and second theology we do not wish to mince our words. The situation is too critical for that.

b. *The Belhar Confession* *The Belhar Confession*, Reformed Church in South Africa, September 1986, section 3, http://www.rca.org/Page.aspx?pid=304 (accessed 27 May 2011)

[The Belhar Confession was formulated in South Africa under apartheid, but it is now a standard statement of social and ecclesial commitment for the Reformed Churches. The extreme nature of the racial discrimination in South Africa before 1990, and the way in which theology was used to justify it, provoked this Christian response, but the issues of unity, reconciliation and justice are applicable to all contexts.]

We believe

- that God has entrusted the church with the message of reconciliation in and through Jesus Christ, that the church is called to be the salt of the earth and the light of the world, that the church is called blessed because it is a peacemaker, that the church is witness both by word and by deed to the new heaven and the new earth in which righteousness dwells (2 Cor. 5:17–21; Matt. 5:13–16; Matt. 5:9; 2 Peter 3:13; Rev. 21–22).
- that God's lifegiving Word and Spirit has conquered the powers of sin and death, and therefore also of irreconciliation and hatred, bitterness and enmity, that God's lifegiving Word and Spirit will enable the church to live in a new obedience which can open new possibilities of life for society and the world (Eph. 4:17–6:23; Rom. 6; Col. 1:9–14; Col. 2:13–19; Col. 3:1–4:6);
- that the credibility of this message is seriously affected and its beneficial work obstructed when it is proclaimed in a land which professes to be Christian, but in which the enforced separation of people on a racial basis promotes and perpetuates alienation, hatred and enmity;
- that any teaching which attempts to legitimate such forced separation by appeal to the gospel, and is not prepared to venture on the road of obedience and reconciliation, but rather, out of prejudice, fear, selfishness and unbelief, denies in advance the reconciling power of the gospel, must be considered ideology and false doctrine.

Therefore, we reject any doctrine

• which, in such a situation, sanctions in the name of the gospel or of the will of God the forced separation of people on the grounds of race and color and thereby in advance obstructs and weakens the ministry and experience of reconciliation in Christ.

c. **Third World Theologians in Solidarity**   *The Road to Damascus: Kairos and Conversion*, a document signed by Third World theologians in July 1989, 1, 7

[The Kairos Document inspired another declaration in 1989, but this time in a global context. From the 1970s, theologians from the poorer nations had met together in the Ecumenical Association of Third World Theologians (EATWOT). The common ground was the suffering of the people of the so-called Third World countries from a global economic and political system that continued the colonial system in another guise and severely disadvantaged them. This document reflects that joint approach. The extracts are from the Preamble and paras. 19–21.]

We, the signatories of this document, are Christians from different church traditions in seven different nations: the Philippines, South Korea, Namibia, South Africa, El Salvador, Nicaragua and Guatemala. What we have in common is not only a situation of violent political conflict, but also the phenomenon of Christians on both sides of the conflict. This is accompanied by the development of a Christian theology that sides with the poor and the oppressed and the development of a Christian theology that sides with the oppressor. This is both a scandal and a crisis that challenges the Christian people of our countries. ...

19. Colonial and imperial powers have reacted to the people's resistance by devising different counter-insurgency programmes. Faced with the emergence of Third World people as new historical subjects, they have developed what they consider a more sophisticated response. It has different names—low intensity conflict (LIC), low intensity war, total war, total strategy, total security.

20. For the imperialists, it might be low intensity conflict, but for the Third World people it is total war. LIC uses all military weapons, short of nuclear arms. It employs not just rifle infantry, but artillery, helicopter gunships, armoured vehicles like casspirs in South Africa and Namibia and armadillos in Central America; it does not hesitate to bomb suspected rebel areas. It organises paramilitary groups, death squads and vigilantes to divide and destroy unarmed communities and organisations of the people.

21. Unlike traditional regular warfare, total war places a premium on psychological and ideological war. In Namibia and South Africa, this is

called 'winning hearts and minds' or WHAM. The Santa Fe Document
calls it 'cultural war'. It tries to discredit all those who work for change
by calling them 'communists', while trying to present the government as
democratic. In highly repressive and polarised situations, it promotes
reformist alternatives, or a 'third force'. This total strategy includes the
misuse of Christianity as a religious legitimisation for the West.

X. FAITH, SOCIETY, AND THE ECONOMY

a. ***Faith in the City,*** **1985**   The Archbishops' Commission on Urban Priority
Areas, *Faith in the City: A Call for Action by Church and Nation*, 1985, 359–60

[The Church of England angered the Conservative Government with the *Faith in
the City* report in 1985. The Commission which had produced the report drew
attention to the social conditions of Britain's cities, and criticized government
policy (as well as its own pastoral provisions) in the process. Though owing more
to the Anglican social theology tradition than liberation theology, the document
appealed to those who advocated a sharper and more prophetic role for the
Church to support the victims of free market capitalism. Some representatives of
the government therefore regarded the document as inspired by left-wing politics. The excerpt below is from the Conclusion (chapter 15).
  Many new local and provincial projects and the Church Urban Fund were the
fruits of the report. However, ten years later, the review document *Staying in the
City* (1995) reflected on worsening social conditions in Britain. A report on rural
areas, *Faith in the Countryside*, was produced in 1991.]

'We have found faith in the city.' (The Commission)

15.1 Chapter after chapter of our Report tells the same story: that a
growing number of people are excluded by poverty or powerlessness
from sharing in the common life of our nation. A substantial minority—
perhaps as many as one person in every four or five across the nation,
and a much higher proportion in the UPAs—are forced to live on the
margins of poverty or below the threshold of an acceptable standard of
living.

15.2 The present acute situation of our nation's Urban Priority Areas
demands an urgent response from the Church and from government.

15.3 The Archbishops' Commission on 'Church and State' concluded
its report in 1970:

  'The Church should concern itself first, and indeed second, with
  the poor and needy, whether in spirit or in body.'

15.4 We echo these words. The Church cannot supplant the market or
the state. It can, as we recommend, mobilize its own resources in a way
that accords high priority to the poor. It must by its example and its

exertions proclaim the ethic of altruism against egotism, of community against self-seeking and of charity against greed.

15.5 But we are conscious that we have only scratched the surface of some of the major concerns to have emerged from our work. To draw out the implications of some of these, such as the Church's response to the prospect of persistent long-term unemployment, will require more time and resources than have been available to us. There must also be a major national debate on the future of our cities, in which the Church must play a full part.

15.6 Perhaps the most important wider question concerns the structure of our society. One submission to us put it bluntly: 'The exclusion of the poor is pervasive and not accidental. It is organized and imposed by powerful institutions which represent the rest of us.' The critical issue to be faced is whether there is any serious political will to set in motion a process which will enable those who are at present in poverty and powerless to rejoin the life of the nation.

15.7 Here is a challenge indeed. It will call among other things for a clear resolve on the part of Church and government to have faith in the city. ...

b. Economy and Debt *Christian Faith and the World Economy Today,* WCC, 1992, 8–9, 40–1

[The Christian critique of global capitalism grew in the 1990s with the demise of communism in Eastern Europe. With the approaching Millennium in view, there was a strong Christian call, illustrated below in the World Council of Churches study document, for the cancellation of Third World debt, which devastates poor economies because of the interest due. This is supported by interpretations of the biblical tradition, particularly the Israelite tradition of 'Jubilee', referred to by Jesus as he announces his mission in Luke 4: 18–19 (see below, Section XVIII, III).]

... . Economic themes recur throughout the Bible. The Torah, in regulating and limiting the buying and selling of goods, the cultivation of land and the raising of animals, placed all economic activity within God's covenant relationships with Israel. This includes concern for the poor (e.g. Ex. 23: 6, Deut. 15: 7–11), for the stranger (e.g. Ex. 21: 21–4), the widow and orphan (e.g. Deut: 24: 19–22), and the environment (e.g. Lev. 25: 1–8). The prescription of the Jubilee year (Lev. 25: 8–55) was intended as a regular moment of release from the economic hardships of slavery and poverty and to make a new beginning. Economic matters come to the fore again in the prophets [quotes from Amos 2: 6–7, Isaiah 5: 8, Jeremiah

22: 13]. Jesus is no less forthright: [references to Matt. 6: 24, Luke 18: 18–30, Luke 16: 19–31].

The heart and key of his teaching, as of his living and dying, was the primary focus on God, on a loving response to God's will nourished by prayer, and on an unshakeable criterion of obedience to God. Any compartmentalizing of life into what was 'religious' and what was something else was unthinkable. Because God invariably came first, everything Jesus dealt with was handled in terms of God's nature, of God's love.

As the community of faith is constantly recalled to God's love and the solidarity, justice and peace that flow from it, they will shape their prayer, thought and action by looking first to the conditions of the poor and unprotected, those who are neglected or ill-treated by the dominant powers in society. ...

Especially in 1992, we can ask ourselves to what extent five hundred years of colonization has led to a historical debt of the North to the South. Although such a debt would be difficult to calculate in monetary terms, it is clear that historical developments over the last five hundred years have greatly influenced economic relationships between South and North as they exist nowadays. Many churches in the South have over the last ten years insisted that the foreign debt of the South should be cancelled or greatly reduced. ...

Under any just accounting system, the third-world debt has already been paid given the excessive debt payments made due to high real interest rates and deteriorating terms of trade (over both of which the South has no control), and capital flight from South to North. ...

However, substantial foreign debt reductions or even sheer cancellation will not prevent the problems from recurring again if this is not accompanied by comprehensive changes in political economic systems and policies at national levels both in South and North, at the level of the world economy, and within international institutions. ...

c. Unemployment   *Unemployment and the Future of Work: An Enquiry for the Churches*, Council of Churches for Britain and Ireland, London, 1997 (from *Summary*, 20)

[One aspect of modern industrial life which causes pastoral concern is unemployment, and the resulting effect on morale and family life. These questions are challenging to Christians and are tackled here by a working party reporting to the Council of Churches for Britain and Ireland.]

The Christian *work ethic* is widely misunderstood. We do not have to work to earn the love of God or to be valued by one another. On the contrary, we should see our work as, in part, a grateful recognition of what we have been given. ...

The good life requires a balanced alternation of work and rest, typified by the Sabbath laws of the Old Testament. It seems to us absurd, and also altogether unjust, that some people should be working so long and so hard, whilst other people have no paid work to do at all. As we have said, we believe that the total amount of work done could be increased, but we are also concerned about its distribution. If some people worked shorter hours more jobs might be created for others. We recognise that the scale of this effect is highly uncertain, especially in the longer term, and we feel it is a subject which needs further investigation. The case for limiting hours of work, however, does not rest only on calculations of this sort. No-one should be required to work longer than is good for their health or well-being. ...

XI. THE FALL OF COMMUNISM IN EASTERN EUROPE

[Christian churches had struggled to survive in communist Eastern Europe: in the Soviet Union from 1917, and in its conquered territories and allied countries from 1945. The different situations of churches in the various countries of Eastern Europe are too complex to be recorded here—an excellent overview can be found in Trevor Beeson's *Discretion and Valour* or in the work of Michael Bordeaux and Keston College. The range of responses of Christians to communist governments ranged from radical resistance to relatively passive acceptance of state regulations governing religious bodies.

Roman Catholics in Poland's 'Solidarity' movement were at the forefront of the resistance of the 1980s, which culminated in the fall of communism in Eastern Europe between 1989 and 1991. In East Germany Christians were very active in the democracy movement. The churches had sufficient autonomy to provide the space necessary for meetings and networks, notably the peace movement. However, as the situation became more tense, the institutional churches, protecting their own position as peacemakers and mediators, were not always radical enough to act as the spearhead for change. Many Christian activists went their own way while protesting against the passivity of the church leaders.]

a. The Role of Pope John Paul II   Jonathan Kwitny, *Man of the Century: The Life and Times of Pope John Paul II*, 1997, 324–5

[The accession of the Archbishop of Cracow, Karol Wojtyla, to the papacy as John Paul II in October 1978, made a considerable—and very probably essential—contribution to the fall of communism in Eastern Europe. His visits to Poland in 1979 and 1983 helped, firstly, to inspire the founding of the Solidarity trade union (he used the word many times both before and after its establishment) and, secondly, to maintain its momentum. Here Jonathan Kwitny describes the visit of June 1979. However, Kwitny also observes that John Paul II struggled to find sympathy with the radical stance of Archbishop Romero who was challenging a different kind of dictatorship in El Salvador, and who was assassinated after failing to elicit Vatican support in 1980. The fact that communism was imposed in Poland but was underground in Latin America seems to have prevented John Paul II from seeing the possible parallels between these contexts, and the important role that the Church might have in fostering non-violent resistance to injustice in each area.]

The most important change John Paul brought—the empowerment of the Polish people—began even before he arrived. Parish by parish, the Church organized an army of marshals to keep order during public gatherings. Ordinary lay Catholics replaced police physically and, more important, in people's minds.

'It was the first time people could gather in such masses, for their own purposes', says Ewa Krasinska, who later became a Solidarity fighter and is now a Polish diplomat. 'One could sense in the street that people were somehow united. The police stood aside. People had a feeling they could decide things for themselves'.

This mood change was precisely what the pope had aimed for, says Bohdan Cywinski, who met privately with him on the trip. 'He knew he could cause an enormous change in the way people thought. The [immediate] political results were of secondary importance.' ...

As usual, John Paul knew how to convey his message in words the communists couldn't argue with. Arriving at the airport, he thanked Gierek politely for allowing the trip, but said, 'peace and the drawing together of peoples' depended on 'respect for the basic rights of the nation ... political self-determination for its citizens and formation of its own culture and civilization.' ...

In the photographs of John Paul's open-air Mass that afternoon in the huge Victory Square Park in central Warsaw, you can't see a blade of grass, so thick are the crowds fading into the distant trees. Estimates ranged up to one million. Directing not another word of thanks to the communists, he skewered them for an hour ...

[In these extracts taken from the memoirs of East German Protestant pastors, Rainer Eppelmann—founder of 'Democratic Awakening' and future minister for disarmament and defence—in b. remembers the beginnings of the democracy movement in the churches in the 1970s. Klaus Kaden in c. recalls the massive prayer meetings during the autumn of 1989, the momentous period of peaceful revolution.]

b. **Rainer Eppelmann**   Protestant Pastor Rainer Epplemann, in Philipsen, *We Were the People: Voices from East Germany's Revolutionary Autumn of 1989*, 63

... . I began to conduct church services that were very unusual for the time, so-called 'Blues Masses'.

Perhaps it is important to point out that the common thing to do at youth masses until then had been to find a biblical theme as a motto for the month or year. ...

The topics that came up had to do with hopelessness, feeling incarcerated, fear, fear of the police, fear of the Stasi, fear of superiors—all these were topics that we tried to pick up on, even during public events. We also tried to provide answers to the best of our knowledge. When we started all this in 1976, it was extremely exotic within the conditions of the GDR.

You see, before the time when certain people began to wear the buttons 'Swords to Ploughshares' and such, citizens of the GDR only expressed what they really thought among circles of close friends, the family, or at the neighborhood bar after they got drunk.. So we were among the first who began to express such things publicly. ...

c. **Klaus Kaden**   Protestant Pastor Klaus Kaden in Philipsen, *We Were the People: Voices from East Germany's Revolutionary Autumn of 1989*, p. 219

... . But, of course, the peace prayers continued, and every Monday more and more people showed up, until we had at least 70,000 on 9 October, despite the most severe kinds of repression and most extensive forms of intimidation exercised by the party. As you know, they had used their whole arsenal of threats prior to 9 October, telling people they would use, if necessary, guns and tanks to repress the demonstration. And still, more than 70,000 people showed up. We have to keep in mind that this was about half the population of Leipzig willing to risk their lives. ...

SECTION XV

The Twentieth-Century Churches and Inter-Faith Dialogue

I. JEWISH–CHRISTIAN RELATIONS

a. **Seelisberg, 1947** *The Ten Points of Seelisberg*, published by the International Council of Christians and Jews in 1947. Croner, *More Stepping Stones to Jewish–Christian Relations*, 32–3

[The *Shoah*, or Holocaust, gave the Christian churches much cause for the searching of conscience and regret over the antisemitism of the past. The German Christian resistance (see Section XIV, II above) had challenged antisemitism in Nazi Germany, but the churches as a whole, both within Germany and internationally, had done little to prevent the genocide. Thus after the war, Protestants, Catholics, and Jews met at Seelisberg to consider antisemitism in Germany and elsewhere, and the following document was published.

In the Roman Catholic Church, Pius XI had issued an anti-Nazi encyclical *Mit Brennender Sorge*, in 1937, because of the Nazi persecution of Catholics. Yet Pius XII's greater fear of communism led him, it has often been claimed, to remain silent about the murder of the Jewish people. Later, the Roman Catholic Church dealt with its relationship with the Jews at the Second Vatican Council (see Section XIII. v above).]

1. Remember that One God speaks to us all through the Old and the New Testaments.
2. Remember that Jesus was born of a Jewish mother of the seed of David and the people of Israel, and that His everlasting love and forgiveness embraces His own people and the whole world.
3. Remember that the first disciples, the apostles and first martyrs were Jews.
4. Remember that the fundamental commandment of Christianity, to love God and one's neighbour, proclaimed already in the Old Testament and confirmed by Jesus, is binding upon both Christians and Jews in all human relationship, without any exception.
5. Avoid distorting or misrepresenting biblical or post-biblical Judaism with the object of extolling Christianity.
6. Avoid using the word *Jews* in the exclusive sense of the enemies of Jesus, and the words *The Enemies of Jesus* to designate the whole Jewish people.

7. Avoid presenting the Passion in such a way to bring the odium of the killing of Jesus upon all Jews or upon Jews alone. It was only a section of the Jews in Jerusalem who demanded the death of Jesus, and the Christian message has always been that it was the sins of mankind which were exemplified by those Jews and the sins in which all men share that brought Christ to the Cross.

8. Avoid referring to the scriptural curses, or the cry of a raging mob: *His Blood be Upon Us and Our Children*, without remembering that this cry should not count against the infinitely more weighty words of our Lord: *Father Forgive Them, for They Know not What They Do.*

9. Avoid promoting the superstitious notion that the Jewish people are reprobate, accursed, reserved for a destiny of suffering.

10. Avoid speaking of the Jews as if the first members of the Church had not been Jews.

b. The World Council of Churches, 1948   *The First Assembly of the World Council of Churches, 1948, Brockway et al., The Theology of the Churches and the Jewish People, WCC, 1988, 5*

[The newly formed World Council of Churches also dealt with the post-war repentant mood of the Christian churches at its first assembly in Amsterdam, 1948.]

A concern for the Christian approach to the Jewish people confronts us inescapably, as we meet together to look with open and penitent eyes on man's disorder and to rediscover together God's eternal purpose for His Church. This concern is ours because it is first a concern of God made known to us in Christ. No people in His one world have suffered more bitterly from the disorder of man than the Jewish people. We cannot forget that we meet in a land from which 110,000 Jews were taken to be murdered. Nor can we forget that we meet only five years after the extermination of 6 million Jews. To the Jews our God has bound us in a special solidarity linking our destinies together in His design. We call upon all our churches to make this concern their own as we share with them the results of our too brief wrestling with it. …

c. The World Council of Churches, 1988   'Final Reflections', 1988. *Brockway et al., The Theology of the Churches and the Jewish People, WCC, 1988, 183–4*

[For the forty years after the foundation of the WCC until the publishing of this volume, the issue of Jewish–Christian relations remained an important one. In these reflections, the WCC looks back over statements made. A theological analysis continued to be necessary because of attempts by some Christians to convert Jews in the belief that the conversion of the Jewish people was an essential precursor to the second coming of the Messiah.]

The statements reproduced here, and the commentary on them, reveal that the World Council of Churches and many of its member churches have arrived at some rather certain theological positions resulting from almost forty years of dialogue and conscious interaction with the Jewish people. As such, they represent a major shift in the church's understanding of the Jewish People. Among these are that:

- the covenant of God with the Jewish people remains valid;
- antisemitism is 'sin against God and man';
- coercive proselytism directed towards Jews is incompatible with Christian faith.

Although most frequently these theological positions are treated as discrete entities, they may most profitably be understood as flowing directly from the first fundamental affirmation: the covenant of God with the Jewish people remains valid. ...

... . Christian complicity in the Shoah, confessed by a number of churches soon after the end of the war, forty years later was all but universally acknowledged by Western churches. As a consequence attention increasingly was paid to the history of Christian persecution of Jews from the beginning of the church. Although many in the churches rejected antisemitism prior to the Shoah, after it such rejection became the single most unambiguous element in ecclesiastical statements about Jews and Judaism. ...

d. **Messianic Judaism**   David H. Stern, *Messianic Jewish Manifesto*, 2nd edn., 1988 (1991, 20–1)

[Jewish belief in Jesus Christ—the original form of Christianity—survived until the fourth century of the Christian era, and then disappeared for centuries. However, the nineteenth century saw examples of Jews who were also Christians (Stern names, for example, Mendelssohn and Disraeli), and the term Messianic Judaism was coined in 1895. From the 1960s, the movement gained some strength—Stern here defines what Messianic Judaism entails, a following of Jesus (Yeshua), but also adherence to Torah.]

So, then, who is a Messianic Jew? My first choice for a definition is: A person who was born Jewish or converted to Judaism, who is a "genuine believer" in Yeshua, and who acknowledges his Jewishness ...

A broader definition would also include assimilated Jews who are not interested in, or even are opposed to, acknowledging their Jewishness ...

But perhaps "Messianic Jew" makes different demands. I personally think it is a mistake to confer the term "Messianic Jew" on just any believer in Yeshua whose parents happen to be Jewish ...

There are Gentile Christians who cite verses such as Romans 2:28–29 ... and Philippians 3:3 ... as authority for calling themselves Messianic Jews. I think this is a mistake and a misuse of Scripture. A Gentile believer in Yeshua, called a "Christian" in Acts 11:26, or perhaps a "Gentile Christian" in modern terminology to distinguish him from a "Jewish Christian" (neither term is found in Scripture), is not a Messianic Jew. He may promote Messianic Judaism. He may love Messianic Jews. He may feel an affinity toward Jewish forms of worship which honor Yeshua the Messiah. He may speak of himself metaphorically as having a Jewish heart. But he is not a Jew, Messianic or otherwise. I suggest that in order to distinguish him from Gentiles who have not come to faith in the God of Abraham, Isaac and Jacob through Yeshua the Messiah, while at the same time associating him with the Messianic Jewish movement, one might call him a Messianic Gentile.

II. MUSLIM–CHRISTIAN RELATIONS
Christian–Muslim Conversations in Cartigny, Switzerland, 1969. Brown, *Meeting in Faith*, 3–4

[The WCC also instituted a series of conversations with Muslims. The long history of antagonism between the faiths, the sensitivity of the situation in the Middle East, and the growing number of Muslims in traditionally Christian countries all made such a dialogue essential. The obvious starting point was to seek common ground, namely, belief in one God, the Abrahamic faith, and shared concern over modern social problems.]

The participants of the meeting are agreed that the dialogue between Muslims and Christians is necessary, and that it should be established at various levels. This necessity arises out of several factors, e.g.:

a. the specific historical roots which the two religions have in common;
b. the attitude of self-criticism which is inherent in each religion;
c. the increased mobility and mixing of populations which has made meetings of Christians and Muslims much more common, and has increased the responsibility of the two religions to find ways of living together in same society;
d. the special present situation, especially the common responsibility of both religions with regard to the political problems in the Near East.

The aim of the dialogue consists first in leading both religions to greater mutual respect and better understanding of each other. Their relations are made difficult by a centuries-old history characterized by many misunderstandings. Further, the dialogue must aim to raise the questions which can lead each of the religions to a deepening and a renewal of its spirituality. Finally, such dialogue can lead to accepting and fulfilling common practical responsibilities. ...

The encounter of the two religions is taking place in a world which finds itself in the midst of rapid change, in which the traditional religious conceptions are being called into question. Islam and Christianity stand before the task of formulating their belief in God in the present world, and, above all, of living it in a convincing way. The dialogue contains a special promise, if it does not confine itself to a comparison of traditional positions, but rather turns to this task. The common roots can, in discussion with the modern world, appear in a special way. This discussion includes such problems of social ethics as development, peace and education. In particular, it must concern itself with the question of knowing what serves the true liberation of man. ...

III. THE PARLIAMENT OF THE WORLD'S RELIGIONS
Declaration Toward a Global Ethic, from the Parliament of the World's Religions, 1993. Küng, Yes *to a Global Ethic*, 13–15

[This gathering of world faiths celebrated the centenary of the ground-breaking Parliament in Chicago, 1893. Representatives of world faiths had met again to pray for global peace at the instigation of John Paul II, at Assisi in 1986. The editor of the volume quoted from here is the Roman Catholic dissident Hans Küng. His well-known thesis is that, without a shared approach by the world religions, important social and ethical questions could not be tackled effectively by religion, and this would render a sense of global order and shared values impossible.]

We women and men of various religions and regions of Earth therefore address all people, religious and non-religious. We wish to express the following convictions which we hold in common.

- We *all* have a *responsibility for a better global order.*
- Our involvement for the sake of human rights, freedom, justice, peace, and the preservation of Earth is absolutely necessary.
- Our different religious and cultural traditions must not prevent our common involvement in opposing all forms of inhumanity and working for greater humaneness.
- The principles expressed in this global ethic can be affirmed by all persons with ethical convictions, whether religiously grounded or not.

As *religious and spiritual persons* we base our lives on an Ultimate Reality, and draw spiritual power and hope therefrom, in trust, in prayer or mediation, in word or silence. We have a special responsibility for the welfare of all humanity and care for the planet Earth. We do not consider ourselves better than other women and men, but we trust that the ancient wisdom of our religions can point the way for the future.

After two world wars and the end of the cold war, the collapse of fascism and nazism, the shaking to the foundations of communism and colonialism, humanity has entered a new phase of its history. Today we possess sufficient economic, cultural, and spiritual resources to introduce a better global order, but old and new *ethnic, national, social, economic, and religious tensions* threaten the peaceful building of a better world. We have experienced greater technological progress than ever before, yet we see that world-wide poverty, hunger, death of children, unemployment, misery, and the destruction of nature have not diminished but rather have increased. Many peoples are threatened with economic ruin, social disarray, political marginalization, ecological catastrophe, and moral collapse. ...

On the basis of personal experiences and the burdensome history of our planet we have learned

- that a better global order cannot be created or enforced by laws, prescriptions, and conventions alone;
- that the realisation of peace, justice, and the protection of the earth depends on the insight and readiness of men and women to act justly;
- that action in favour of rights and freedoms presumes a consciousness of responsibility and duty, and that therefore both the minds and hearts of women and men must be addressed;
- that rights without morality cannot long endure, and that there will be *no better global order without a global ethic.*

By *a global ethic* we do not mean a global ideology or a *single unified religion* beyond all existing religions, and certainly not the domination of one religion over all others. By a global ethic we mean a *fundamental consensus on binding values, irrevocable standards, and personal attitudes.* Without such a fundamental consensus on an ethic, sooner or later every community will be threatened by chaos or dictatorship, and individuals will despair.

IV. CHRISTIANITY AND THE NEW AGE MOVEMENT
Methodist Conference Report on the New Age Movement, 1994, 298–9

[Many people in the modern world do not follow a traditional 'world religion', but seek new expressions of spirituality or beliefs that claim to be reconstructions of ancient religions. This tendency has been given the general label 'New Age', describing the hopes and expectations of its followers. The New Age phenomenon has caused Christianity much concern and soul-searching, particularly with the decline of committed churchgoers. However, the 1994 British Methodist Report—from which the 'Concluding Reflections' are reproduced here—tries to find a balanced policy and to avoid the denunciation and demonization of New Agers by some Christians.]

109 (i). Any over-reaction by Christians to New Agers, their beliefs and practices, is very unhelpful and unwise. Actually, New Agers often address themes which our modern society, including Western Christianity, has until recently, largely ignored: for example, the nurturing of our planet. Moreover, many Christians have tended to shun perfectly respectable practices, such as homeopathy, because New Agers have annexed them to serve their points of view. Even more controversial practices, such as yoga, are not inherently associated with non-Christian belief systems, so the determination of some Christians to shun them can seem an over-reaction.

110 (ii). Indeed, Christians would, to some extent, share three of the four cohesive features of the New Age Movement, mentioned in Part I: the spiritual as opposed to the physical; harmony and wholeness; and hopefulness. To be sure, there are major disagreements about the form of these features and in whom (or, for many New Agers, in what) they are located. In the one major area of disagreement, the New Age insistence on the individual's right to choose, there is still much to discuss, not least because, in practice, Christians do choose, from their faith, themes for their life stories. There would, therefore, seem to be more wisdom in talking to New Agers.

111 (iii). Themes concerning the Holy Spirit may provide something of a framework for consideration as we talk to one another, and to those influenced by and committed to the New Age, about the spiritual dimension of life. There is much to be learnt through dialogue. ...

116 (iv). If Methodists are to be encouraged to engage in dialogue with New Agers, then it is vital that they be nurtured in the essentials of their faith. Otherwise, there is the likelihood of the blind leading the blind. There is also the possibility of Methodists being attracted and captivated by notions and practices which, although alluring and apparently harmless, are not consonant with Methodist teaching.

117 (v). However, Methodist teaching is not static. It needs to be applied critically and creatively, to the needs of the societies in which Methodists find themselves. To some extent, New Age-ism has flourished because many Western Christians have uncritically assumed that the values of our techno-scientific culture have resulted from and are congruent with Christian beliefs. Methodists must hear the legitimate questionings of New Agers and not fall into the extremes of dismissing them or of readily accepting all their critiques, still less the answers or solutions they offer.

118 (vi). Everyone involved in the New Age Movement is someone whom God loves and for whom Christ died. This is another ground for serious and searching dialogue with New Agers, rather than avoiding them. It is also a reason for sharing the faith that is in us as providing all people with the key to an answer to life's deepest questions.

SECTION XVI
The Twentieth-Century Churches and Christian Unity

I. ECUMENISM AND ANGLICANISM

a. **Letter 'To All Christian People'** Lambeth Conference, 1920. Bell, *Documents on Christian Unity*, 1920–4

[In 1832 Thomas Arnold put forward a scheme to reunite Dissenting bodies to the Church of England by the simple expedient of widening the National Church— 'the Nation in its religious aspect'—to include them. This met with disapproval from all who had a different notion of what is meant by the Church. The Lambeth Conference of 1884 laid down four points—the 'Lambeth Quadrilateral'—as a basis upon which, in the Anglican view, reunion might be sought. These points are given in § VI of the following appeal.]

From the bishops assembled in the Lambeth Conference of 1920.

We, Archbishops, Bishops Metropolitan and other Bishops of the Holy Catholic Church in full communion with the Church of England, in Conference assembled, realizing the responsibility which rests upon us at this time and sensible of the sympathy and prayers of many, both within and without our own communion, make this appeal to all Christian people.

We acknowledge all those who believe in Our Lord Jesus Christ and have been baptized into the name of the Holy Trinity, as sharing with us membership in the universal Church of Christ which is his Body. We believe that the Holy Spirit has called us in a very solemn and special manner to associate ourselves in penitence and prayer with all those who deplore the divisions of Christian people and are inspired by the vision and hope of the visible unity of the whole Church.

I. We believe that God wills fellowship. By God's own act this fellowship was made, in and through Jesus Christ, and its life is in His Spirit. We believe that it is God's purpose to manifest this fellowship, so far as this world is concerned, in an outward, visible and united society, holding one faith, having its own recognized officers, using God-given means of grace, and inspiring all its members to the world-wide service of the Kingdom of God. This is what we mean by the Catholic Church.

II. This united fellowship is not visible in the world to-day. On the one hand there are other ancient episcopal Communions in East and West to whom ours is bound by many ties of common faith and tradition. On the other hand there are the great non-episcopal Communions standing for rich elements of truth, liberty and life which might otherwise have been obscured and neglected. With them we are closely linked by many affinities, racial, historical and spiritual. We cherish the earnest hope that all these Communions, and our own, may be led by the Spirit into the Unity of the Faith and of the knowledge of the Son of God. But in fact we are all organized in different groups, each one keeping to itself gifts that rightly belong to the whole fellowship and tending to live its own life apart from the rest.

III. The causes of division lie deep in the past, and are by no means simple or wholly blameworthy. Yet none can doubt that self-will, ambition, lack of charity among Christians have been principal factors in the mingled process, and that these, together with blindness to the sin of disunion, are still mainly responsible for the breaches of Christendom. We acknowledge this condition of broken fellowship to be contrary to God's will, and we desire frankly to confess our share in the guilt of thus crippling the Body of Christ and hindering the activity of His Spirit.

IV. The times call us to a new outlook and new measures. The Faith cannot be adequately apprehended and the battle of the Kingdom cannot be worthily fought while the body is divided, and is thus unable to grow up into the fullness of the life of Christ. The time has come, we believe, for all the separated groups of Christians to agree in forgetting the things that are behind and reaching out towards the goal of a reunited Catholic Church. The removal of the barriers that have arisen between them will only be brought about by a new comradeship of those whose faces are definitely set this way.

The vision which rises before us is that of a Church genuinely Catholic, loyal to all Truth, and gathering into its fellowship all who profess and call themselves Christians, within whose visible unity all the treasures of faith and order, bequeathed as a heritage by the past to the present, shall be possessed in common and made serviceable to the whole Body of Christ. Within this unity Christian Communions now separated from one another would retain much that has long been distinctive in their methods of worship and service. It is through a rich diversity of life and devotion that the unity of the whole fellowship will be fulfilled....

VI. We believe that the visible unity of the Church will be found to involve the whole-hearted acceptance of:—

The Holy Scriptures as the record of God's revelation of Himself to man, and as being the rule and ultimate standard of faith; and the Creed commonly called Nicene, as the sufficient statement of the Christian faith, and either it or the Apostles' Creed as the Baptismal confession of belief.

The divinely instituted sacraments of Baptism and the Holy Communion, as expressing for all the corporate life of the whole fellowship, in and with Christ.

A ministry acknowledged by every part of the Church as possessing not only the inward call of the Spirit but also the commission of Christ and the authority of the whole body.

VII. May we not reasonably claim that the Episcopate is the one means of providing such a ministry? It is not that we call in question for a moment the spiritual reality of the ministries of those Communions who do not possess the Episcopate. On the contrary, we thankfully acknowledge that these ministries have been manifestly blessed and owned by the Holy Spirit as effective means of grace. But we submit that considerations alike of history and of present experience justify the claim which we make on behalf of the Episcopate. Moreover, we would urge that it is now and will prove to be in the future the best instrument for maintaining the unity and the continuity of the Church.

VIII. ... If the authorities of other Communions should so desire, we are persuaded that, terms of union having otherwise been satisfactorily adjusted, Bishops and clergy of our Communion would willingly accept from these authorities a form of commission or recognition....

It is our hope that the same motive would lead ministers who have not received it to accept a commission through episcopal ordination, as obtaining for them a ministry throughout the whole fellowship....

IX. ... We do not ask that any one Communion should consent to be absorbed in another. We do ask that all should unite in a new and great endeavour to recover and to manifest to the world the unity of the Body of Christ for which he prayed.

b. **Orthodox Encyclical on Anglican Orders, 1922**   Encyclical on Anglican Orders from the Ecumenical Patriarch to the Presidents of the Particular Eastern Orthodox Churches, 1922. Bell, *Documents on Christian Unity*, 20

[In 1874–5 conferences were held between the Eastern and the Anglican Churches; in 1897 the Lambeth Conference sent the Bishop of Salisbury to deliver to the Orthodox Patriarchs the resolutions on Unity passed at the conference. In 1920 Constantinople sent a delegation to the Lambeth Conference and in 1922 the Patriarch of Constantinople answered that his synod had decided on the validity of Anglican Orders, and in the following year the synods of Jerusalem and Cyprus followed this lead.]

[The Holy Synod has studied the report of the Committee and notes:]

1. That the ordination of Matthew Parker as Archbishop of Canterbury by four bishops is a fact established by history.

2. That in this and subsequent ordinations there are found in their fullness those orthodox and indispensable, visible and sensible elements of valid episcopal ordination—viz. the laying on of hands, the Epiclesis[1] of the All-Holy Spirit and also the purpose to transmit the *charisma* of the Episcopal ministry.

3. That the orthodox theologians who have scientifically examined the question have almost unanimously come to the same conclusions and have declared themselves as accepting the validity of Anglican Orders.

4. That the practice in the Church affords no indication that the Orthodox Church has ever officially treated the validity of Anglican Orders as in doubt, in such a way as would point to the re-ordination of the Anglican clergy being regarded as required in the case of the union of the two Churches.

c. **Old Catholics and Anglicans, 1931**   *Statement agreed between representatives of the Old Catholic Churches and the Churches of the Anglican Communion at a Conference held at Bonn, 2 July 1931.*

[In accordance with a resolution of the Lambeth Conference of 1930 a Joint Doctrinal Commission was appointed by the Archbishop of Canterbury and the Archbishop of Utrecht, which produced the following agreed statement. This was accepted by the Episcopal Synod of the Old Catholic churches meeting at Vienna on 7 September 1931 and by the Convocations of Canterbury and York in January 1932. Other Anglican provinces took similar action.]

---

[1] Invocation.

1. Each Communion recognizes the catholicity and independence of the other and maintains its own.

2. Each Communion agrees to admit members of the other Communion to participate in the Sacraments.

3. Intercommunion does not require from either Communion the acceptance of all doctrinal opinion, sacramental devotion, or liturgical practice characteristic of the other, but implies that each believes the other to hold all the essentials of the Christian Faith.

d. Paul VI and Ramsey, 1966 *The Joint Declaration on Cooperation*, Paul VI and Archbishop Michael Ramsey, 22 March 1966. Flannery, *Vatican II*, vol. i, 479–80

[The Second Vatican Council's desire to establish ecumenical dialogue (see Section XIII. IV above) led quickly to declarations of cooperation with the Orthodox (see VII a below) and the Anglicans.]

In this city of Rome, from which St Augustine was sent by St Gregory to England and there founded the cathedral see of Canterbury, towards which the eyes of all Anglicans now turn as the center of their Christian Communion, His Holiness Pope Paul VI and His Grace Michael Ramsey, Archbishop of Canterbury, representing the Anglican Communion, have met to exchange fraternal greetings. ...

They affirm their desire that all those Christians who belong to these two Communions may be animated by these same sentiments of respect, esteem and fraternal love; and in order to help these develop to the full, they intend to inaugurate between the Roman Catholic Church and the whole Anglican Communion a serious dialogue which, founded on the Gospels and on the ancient common traditions may lead to unity in truth for which Christ prayed. ...

e. ARCIC II *Church as Communion: An Agreed Statement by the Second Anglican–Roman Catholic International Commission ARCIC II*, 1991, paras. 49, 53, pp. 31, 33

[The Joint Declaration in d. above paved the way for the ARCIC discussions in England. This process was endorsed when, in 1982, John Paul II visited Britain and prayed with Robert Runcie, Archbishop of Canterbury in the Cathedral. The following document is an example of the work of the Commission. However, the present situation is unclear. Despite good will on both sides, the Vatican response to ARCIC was regarded by many as lukewarm and the refusal to recognize Anglican orders (see Section X. x above) remains the official position.]

49. The convictions which this Commission believes that Anglicans and Roman Catholics share concerning the nature of communion challenge

both our churches to move forward together towards visible unity and ecclesial communion. Progress in mutual understanding has been achieved. There exists a significant degree of doctrinal agreement between our two communions even upon subjects which previously divided us. In spite of past estrangements, Anglicans and Roman Catholics now enjoy a better understanding of their longstanding shared inheritance. This new understanding enables them to recognise in each other's church a true affinity. ...

53. We cannot, however, ignore the effects of our centuries of separation. Such separation has inevitably led to the growth of divergent patterns of authority accompanied by changes in perceptions and practices. The differences between us are not only theological. Anglicans and Roman Catholics have now inherited different cultural traditions. Such differences in communities which have become isolated from one another have sometimes led to distortions in the popular perceptions which members of one church have of the other. As a result visible unity may be viewed as undesirable or even unattainable. However, a closer examination of the developments which have taken place in our different communities shows that these developments, when held in complementarity, can contribute to a fuller understanding of communion. ...

f. **The Porvoo Declaration, 1992**   Church of England, *Together in Mission and Ministry*, 30–1

[The Reformation churches of Northern Europe articulated points of common understanding in this text agreed in Finland.]

We, the Church of Denmark, the Church of England, the Estonian Evangelical-Lutheran Church, the Evangelical-Lutheran Church of Finland, the Evangelical-Lutheran Church of Iceland, the Church of Ireland, the Evangelical-Lutheran Church of Latvia, the Evangelical-Lutheran Church of Lithuania, the Church of Norway, the Scottish Episcopal Church, the Church of Sweden and the Church in Wales, on the basis of our common understanding of the nature and purpose of the Church, fundamental agreement in faith and our agreement on episcopacy in the service of the apostolicity of the Church, contained in Chapters II–IV of *The Porvoo Common Statement*, make the following acknowledgements and commitments:

a.1. we acknowledge one another's churches as churches belonging to the One, Holy, Catholic and Apostolic Church of Jesus Christ and truly participating in the apostolic mission of the whole people of God;

2. we acknowledge that in all our churches the Word of God is authentically preached, and the sacraments of baptism and the eucharist are duly administered;

3. we acknowledge that all our churches share in the common confession of the apostolic faith;

4. we acknowledge that one another's ordained ministries are given by God as instruments of his grace and as possessing not only the inward call of the Spirit, but also Christ's commission through his body, the Church;

5. we acknowledge that personal, collegial and communal oversight (*episcope*) is embodied and exercised in all our churches in a variety of forms, in continuity of apostolic life, mission and ministry;

6. we acknowledge that the episcopal office is valued and maintained in all our churches as a visible sign expressing and serving the Church's unity and continuity in apostolic life, mission and ministry. ...

II. CHRISTIAN UNITY IN THE BRITISH ISLES

a. **Church of Scotland Act, 1921**   Cox, *Practice and Procedure in the Church of Scotland* (4th edn., 1948) 340 ff. Bell, *Documents on Christian Unity, A Selection*, 1920–1930, 69 ff.

[These declaratory articles, contained in a schedule to the Act, formed the basis of the Union of 1929 between the established Church and the United Free Church of Scotland, healing the schism which had resulted from the 'Disruption' of 1843, which arose from a dispute about patronage in particular, and, in general, about the relations of the Church with the civil authority.]

Articles Declaratory of the Constitution of the Church of Scotland in Matters Spiritual

I. The Church of Scotland is part of the Holy Catholic or Universal Church; worshipping one God Almighty, all-wise, and all-loving, in the Trinity of the Father, the Son, and the Holy Ghost, the same in substance, equal in power and glory; adoring the Father, infinite in Majesty, of whom are all things; confessing our Lord Jesus Christ, the Eternal Son, made man for our salvation; glorying in His Cross and Resurrection, and owing obedience to Him as the Head over all things to His Church; trusting in the promised renewal and guidance of the Holy Spirit; proclaiming the forgiveness of sins and acceptance with God through faith in Christ, and the gift of Eternal Life; and labouring for the advancement of the Kingdom of God throughout the world. The Church of Scotland adheres to the Scottish Reformation; receives the Word of God which is contained in the Scriptures of the Old and New Testaments

as the supreme rule of faith and life; and avows the fundamental doctrines of the Catholic faith founded thereupon.

II. The principal subordinate standard of the Church of Scotland is
the Westminster Confession of Faith approved by the General Assembly
of 1647, containing the sum and substance of the Faith of the Reformed
Church. ...

IV. This Church, as part of the Universal Church wherein the Lord Jesus
Christ has appointed a government in the hands of Church office-bearers,
receives from Him, its divine King and Head, and from Him alone, the right
and power subject to no civil authority to legislate, and to adjudicate finally,
in all matters of doctrine, worship, government, and discipline in the
Church. ... Recognition by civil authority of the separate and independent
government and jurisdiction of this Church, in matters spiritual, in whatever manner such recognition be expressed, does not in any way affect
the character of the Church alone, or give to the civil authority any right
of interference with the proceedings or judgements of the Church within
the sphere of its spiritual government and jurisdiction.

V. This Church has the inherent right, free from interference by civil
authority, but under the safeguards for deliberate action and legislation
provided by the Church itself, to frame and adopt its subordinate
standards, to declare the sense in which it understands its Confession
of Faith, to modify the forms of expression therein, or to formulate the
doctrinal statements, and to define the relation thereto of its office-
bearers and members, but always in agreement with the Word of God
and the fundamental doctrines of the Christian Faith contained in the
said Confession, of which agreement the Church shall be sole judge, and
with due regard to liberty of opinion in points which do not enter into
the substance of the Faith.

VI. This Church acknowledges the divine appointment and authority
of the civil magistrate within his own sphere, and maintains its historic
testimony to the duty of the nation acting in its corporate capacity to
render homage to God. ...

VII. The Church of Scotland, believing it to be the will of Christ that
His discipline should be all one. ... recognises the obligation to seek and
promote union with other Churches in which it finds the Word to be
purely preached, the sacraments administered according to Christ's
ordinance, and discipline rightly exercised; and it has the right to unite
with any such Church without loss of its identity on terms which this
Church finds to be consistent with these articles.

VIII. The Church has the right to interpret these Articles, and subject
to the safeguards for deliberate action and legislation provided by the

Church itself, to modify or add to them; but always consistently with the provisions of the first Article hereof, adherence to which, as interpreted by the Church, is essential to its continuity and corporate life.

b. The Welsh Covenant, 1975 British Council of Churches, *The Next Steps for Churches Together in Pilgrimage*, 74–6

[The Welsh Covenant provides a good example of churches working together within a national context; five denominations—the Church in Wales, Presbyterian Church in Wales, Methodist Church, United Reformed Church, and a number of Baptist Churches—are represented. Common liturgy has been produced by the Commission of the Covenanted Churches in Wales.]

1.*a.* We recognize in one another the same faith in the gospel of Jesus Christ found in Holy Scripture, which the creeds of the ancient Church and other historic confessions are intended to safeguard. We recognize in one another the same desire to hold this faith in its fulness.

  b. We intend so to act, speak, and serve together in obedience to the gospel that we may learn more of its fulness and make it known to others in contemporary terms and by credible witness.

2.*a.* We recognize in one another the same awareness of God's calling to serve his gracious purpose for all mankind, with particular responsibility for this land and people.

  b. We intend to work together for justice and peace at home and abroad, and for the spiritual and material well being and personal freedom of all people.

3.*a.* We recognize one another as within the one Church of Jesus Christ, pledged to serve His Kingdom, and sharing in the unity of the Spirit.

  b. We intend by the help of the same Spirit to overcome the divisions which impair our witness, impede God's mission, and obscure the gospel of man's salvation, and to manifest that unity which is in accordance with Christ's will.

4.*a.* We recognize the members of all our churches as members of Christ in virtue of their common baptism and common calling to participate in the ministry of the whole Church.

  b. We intend to seek that form of common life which will enable each member to use the gifts bestowed upon him in the service of Christ's Kingdom.

5.*a.* We recognize the ordained ministries of all our churches as true ministries of the word and sacraments, through which God's love is proclaimed, his grace mediated, and his Fatherly care exercised.

b. We intend to seek an agreed pattern of ordained ministry which will serve the gospel in unity, manifest its continuity throughout the ages, and be accepted as far as may be by the Church throughout the world.

6.*a.* We recognize in one another patterns of worship and sacramental life, marks of holiness and zeal, which are manifestly gifts of Christ.

b. We intend to listen to one another and to study together the witness and practice of our various traditions, in order that the riches entrusted to us in separation may be preserved for the united Church which we seek.

7.*a.* We recognize in one another the same concern for the good government of the Church for the fulfilment of its mission.

b. We intend to seek a mode of Church government which will preserve the positive values for which each has stood, so that the common mind of the Church may be formed and carried into action through constitutional organs of corporate decision at every level of responsibility. ...

c. The Swanwick Declaration, 1987 British Council of Churches, *The Next Steps for Churches Together in Pilgrimage*, 7–8

[Until the late 1980s, the British Council of Churches represented the ecumenical efforts of denominations in Britain but without the participation of some, for example, the Roman Catholic Church. At Swanwick on 4 September 1987, the following declaration was signed by a more inclusive gathering, which paved the way for a larger ecumenical organization, 'The Council of Churches for Britain and Ireland', and the setting up of many local 'Churches Together' initiatives.]

Appointed by our churches and under the guidance of the Holy Spirit we declare that this, the broadest assembly of British and Irish churches ever to meet in these islands, has reached a common mind. We are aware that not all Christians are represented amongst us but we look forward to the time when they will share fully with us. ...

It is our conviction that, as a matter of policy at all levels and in all places, our churches must now move from co-operation to clear commitment to each other, in search of the unity for which Christ prayed and in common evangelism and service of the world.

We urge church leaders and representatives to take all necessary steps to present, as soon as possible, to our church authorities, assemblies and congregations, the Report of this Conference together with developed proposals for ecumenical instruments to help the churches of these islands to move ahead together....

III. TAIZÉ AND RECONCILIATION
Brother Roger of Taizé, *No Greater Love*, 1990, 19–22

[The ecumenical Community of Taizé represents—perhaps more than any other inter-denominational initiative—the modern search for reconciliation between Christians. Brother Roger, whose father was Swiss but whose mother was from France, sheltered Jews in the French village of Taizé during the Second World War; he was forced to leave France for a while, and then welcomed German prisoners of war on his return in 1944. From its beginnings, the community of brothers, whose members are both Catholics and from different Evangelical backgrounds, has always understood itself as a symbol of reconciliation. From the 1960s, tens of thousands of pilgrims, primarily young people, have visited the community to share its influential liturgical and prayer life.]

You want to follow Christ, and not look back: are you going to make your way through life with a heart that is reconciled, even amidst the most crippling tensions? In any disagreement, what is the use of trying to find out who was wrong and who was right? Suppose people distort your intentions? If you are judged wrongly because of Christ, forgive. You will find that you are free, free beyond compare. Forgive and then forgive again. That is the highest expression of loving. Christ is communion. Will you choose to live a life rooted not in Christ taken in isolation, but in the Risen Lord present on earth in the communion of his Body, his Church?

In that unique communion which is the Church, oppositions both ancient and new are tearing the Body of Christ apart. The luminous ecumenical vocation is and always will be a matter of achieving a reconciliation without delay. For the Gospel, reconciliation does not wait. 'When you are bringing your gift to the altar and your sister or brother has something against you, leave everything; first go and be reconciled.' 'First go!' Not, 'Put off till later!'

Ecumenism fosters illusory hopes when it puts off reconciliation till later. It comes to a standstill, becomes fossilized even, when it accepts the creation of parallel paths on which the vital energies of forgiveness are wasted.

Reconciliation is a springtime of the heart. Yes, to be reconciled without delay leads to the amazing discovery that our own hearts are changed by it.

What is to be done if, when you decide to put an end to a break in a relationship, you go and find the people opposing you and tell them, 'I have come to be reconciled', and they reply, 'That is out of the question'?

Will you find the courage to dare once more? Brushing aside the uncertainty that keeps you apart, will you go back to those who have rejected you and say to them, 'I have come to be reconciled'?

And if they send you away again roughly,—what a discovery!—you find that they have already been welcomed silently within yourself. When you run the risk of trusting, astonishing though it may seem, in you wells up the incredible lightness of a joy.

IV. THE CHURCH OF SOUTH INDIA

[The inauguration in 1947 of the Church of South India was the outcome of discussions held since 1919 by representatives of the South India United Church (a previous union embracing former Congregationalists and Presbyterians), the (Anglican) Church of India, Burma and Ceylon, and the South India Province of the Methodist Church. The 1st edition of the proposed Basis of Union appeared in 1929 and the 7th and final edition in 1941. By 1946 this had been approved by the three churches concerned and the Church of South India was inaugurated at Madras on 27 September 1947. The substance of the Basis of Union is incorporated in the Constitution of the Church as noted below.]

Basis of Union (1946)

The Purpose and Nature of the Union

1. The uniting Churches affirm that the purpose of the union ... is the carrying out of God's will as this is expressed in our Lord's prayer—'That they may all be one ... that the world may believe that thou didst send me'. They believe that by this union the Church in South India will become a more effective instrument for God's work, and that the result of union will be greater peace, closer fellowship, and fuller life within the Church, and also renewed eagerness and power for the proclamation of the Gospel of Christ. ... [Const. II. 2.]

It is the will of Christ that His Church should be one. ... It is also his will that there should be a ministry accepted and fully effective throughout the world-wide Church. In the present divided state of Christendom there is no ministry which in this respect fully corresponds to the purpose of God. ... The uniting Churches recognize, however, that God has bestowed his grace with undistinguishing regard through all their ministries. ... They acknowledge each other's ministries to be real ministries of the Word and Sacraments. ...

... all the ministers of the uniting Churches will from the inauguration of the union be recognized as equally ministers of the united Church without distinction or difference.

It is the intention and hope of the uniting Churches that all the actions of the United Church will be regulated by the principles that it should maintain fellowship with all those branches of the Church of Christ with which the uniting Churches now severally enjoy such fellowship. ... [Const. II. 2.]

The Church and its Membership

[2. Members of the Church, the Body of Christ, are those who have been baptized in the threefold name and remain steadfast.] [Const. II. 4.]

The Faith of the Church

[3. Based on the Holy Scriptures, the Apostles' and Nicene Creeds. Appended notes safeguard (i) 'reasonable liberty of interpretation' of the Creeds; (ii) the competence of the united Church to issue supplementary statements concerning the faith; (iii) continuance of the use 'for instruction' of 'any confession of faith which had been employed in any of the uniting Churches before the Union and which is not inconsistent with the doctrinal standards officially set forth by the united Church'.] [Main clauses and note (ii): Const. II. 5.]

The Episcopate in the United Church

9. ... in the united Church:

(i) The bishops shall perform their functions in accordance with the customs of the Church, those customs being named and defined in the written constitution of the united Church. ...

(ii) The bishops shall be elected, both the diocese concerned ... and the authorities of the united Church as a whole having an effective voice in their appointment.

(iii) Continuity with the historic episcopate shall both initially and thereafter be effectively maintained. ...

(iv) Every ordination of presbyters shall be performed by the laying on of hands of the bishop and presbyters, and all consecrations of bishops shall be performed by the laying on of hands at least of three bishops. The uniting Churches declare that in making this provision it is their intention and determination in this manner to secure the unification of the ministry, but that the acceptance of this provision does not involve any judgement upon the validity or regularity of any other form of ministry, and the fact that other Churches do not follow the rule of episcopal ordination shall not in itself preclude the united Church from holding relations of communion and fellowship with them. [cf. Const. II. 11.]

The Initial Ministry of the United Church

11. ... The uniting Churches ... agree:

(i) That the bishops of the dioceses of the Church of India, Burma and Ceylon which are to be included in the United Church shall be accepted as bishops of the united Church, provided that they assent to the Basis of Union and accept the Constitution of the united Church; and that other ministers of the uniting Churches in the area of the union who have been ordained as ministers of the Word and of the Sacraments shall be acknowledged as such in the united Church and shall have the status of presbyters therein, provided etc. ...

Similarly, subject to the same provision ... deacons and probationers shall retain in the united Church the status they had in their own Churches before the union.

(ii) ... such bishops, presbyters, deacons and probationers shall, subject only to necessary restrictions in certain directions, retain (so far as the united Church is concerned) all rights and liberties which they previously possessed in the several uniting Churches. [Const. II. 21.]

(iii) That these, together with the bishops who will be consecrated at the inauguration of the union, shall form the initial ministry of the united Church.

The Development of Full Unity in Ministry and Life within the United Church

16. The uniting Churches agree that it is their intention and expectation that eventually every minister exercising a permanent ministry in the united Church will be an episcopally ordained minister.

For the thirty years succeeding the inauguration of the union, the ministers of any Church whose missions have founded the originally separate parts of the united Church may be received as ministers of the united Church, if they are willing to give the same assent to the Governing Principles of the united Church and the same promise to accept its constitution as will be required from persons to be ordained or employed for the first time in that Church. After this period of thirty years the united Church must determine for itself whether it will continue to make any exceptions to the rule that its ministry is an episcopally ordained ministry. ... [Const. II. 21.]

... the act of union will initiate a process of growing together into one life and of advance towards complete spiritual unity. ... They therefore pledge themselves and fully trust each other that the united Church will at all times be careful not to allow any over-riding of conscience either by Church authorities or by majorities. ... Neither forms of worship or ritual, nor a ministry, to which they have not been accustomed or to which they conscientiously object, will be imposed upon any congregation. ... [Const. II. 13.]

V. THE WORLD COUNCIL OF CHURCHES

[From 1910 (World Missionary Conference at Edinburgh) to 1937 (Conferences on 'Life and Work' (Oxford) and 'Faith and Order' (Edinburgh)) the Ecumenical Movement was active in a number of ways but had no central organization. At the time of the 1937 conferences the first steps were taken towards the merging of 'Life and Work' and 'Faith and Order' in a World Council of Churches. From 1938 until 1948 this remained (owing to the Second World War) officially 'in process of formation' but at Amsterdam in the latter year it was formally set up.]

a. Constitution of the World Council of Churches, 1948

I. Basis

The World Council of Churches is a fellowship of Churches which accept our Lord Jesus Christ as God and Saviour. It is constituted for the discharge of the functions set out below.

II. Membership

Those churches shall be eligible for membership in the World Council of Churches which express their agreement with the basis upon which the Council is founded and satisfy such criteria as the Assembly or the Central Committee may prescribe. Election to membership shall be by a two-thirds vote of the member churches represented at the Assembly, each member church having one vote. Any application for membership between meetings of the Assembly may be considered by the Central Committee. ...

III. Functions

The functions of the World Council shall be:

(i) To carry on the work of the two world movements for 'Faith and Order' and for 'Life and Work'.
(ii) To facilitate common action by the Churches.
(iii) To promote co-operation in study.

(iv) To promote the growth of ecumenical consciousness in the members of all Churches.

(v) To establish relations with denominational federations of world-wide scope and with other ecumenical movements.

(vi) To call world conferences on specific subjects as occasion may require, such conferences being empowered to publish their own findings.

(vii) To support the churches in their task of evangelism.

Note: In matters of common interest to all the Churches and pertaining to Faith and Order, the Council shall always proceed in accordance with the basis on which the Lausanne (1927) and Edinburgh (1937) Conferences were called and conducted.

IV. Authority

The World Council shall offer counsel and provide opportunity of united action in matters of common interest.

It may take action on behalf of constituent Churches in such matters as one or more of them may commit to it.

It shall have authority to call regional and world conferences on specific subjects as occasion may require.

The World Council shall not legislate for the Churches; nor shall it act for them in any manner except as indicated above or as may hereafter be specified by the constituent Churches.

[Clauses V–VIII deal with organization including the arrangements for the continuation of the work of the 'Faith and Order' movement through the Faith and Order Commission of the World Council.]

b. Amended 'Basis' in the Constitution, *1961*

[At the Third Assembly of the World Council of Churches, which met at New Delhi in December 1961, the following amended wording in Clause I of the Constitution was officially adopted (Text in Goodall, *The Ecumenical Movement*, 69).]

I. Basis

The World Council of Churches is a fellowship of Churches which confess the Lord Jesus Christ as God and Saviour according to the Scriptures and therefore seek to fulfil together their common calling to the glory of one God, Father, Son and Holy Spirit. ...

c. Inter-Orthodox Consultation on the World Council of Churches,

1991   *The Orthodox Churches and the World Council of Churches*, Report of an Inter-Orthodox Consultation of Orthodox WCC Member Churches, 1991. Limouris, *Orthodox Visions of Ecumenism*, 189

[The Orthodox churches here articulate their own vision of unity and the work of the WCC. The Orthodox starting point for ecclesiology is that the Church of Christ is indeed a mystical unity, even if apparently divided at the phenomenal level. This is the first paragraph of a document in which the Orthodox call for the WCC to remain true to its mission of unity, and express some of their concerns about contemporary issues within the WCC.]

For the Orthodox, Eastern and Oriental, the primary purpose of the World Council of Churches is its work for the restoration of unity among Christians. In the Orthodox understanding, this means full ecclesial unity, that is, unity in doctrinal teaching, sacramental life and polity. The Orthodox recognize other important dimensions of ecumenical work and activity. Cooperative ecumenical efforts that contribute toward growing unity, the establishment or restoration of justice and peace, toward coherence in theological expression, toward mission and common witness, toward deepening the churches' self-understanding and toward growth of community in confessing, learning and service are important in themselves and as means for divided Christians to move toward ultimate doctrinal and sacramental union. But for the Orthodox, the ultimate goal and justification of the ecumenical movement in general, and for their participation in the WCC in particular, is the full ecclesial unity of Christians. It is thus an urgent task for the meaning of church unity to be clearly articulated and frequently repeated in the deliberations and work of the WCC, while concurrently striving to clarify appropriate and legitimate aspects of diversity in expressing the apostolic faith in worship and discipline within that ecclesial unity. ...

d. 'Towards a Common Understanding and Vision of the World

Council of Churches'   *Policy statement adopted by the Central Committee of the World Council of Churches and commended to member churches and ecumenical partners for study and action in September 1997,* paras. 2.9–11, http://www.oikoumene.org/en/resources/documents/assembly/ porto-alegre-2006/3-preparatory-and-background-documents/common-unde rstanding-and-vision-of-the-wcc-cuv.html (accessed 27 May 2011)

[The World Council of Churches agreed a statement—to mark the end of the twentieth century—which repudiated a popular assumption that ecumenical initiatives were on the decline.]

2.9 The emergence over the last decades of transnational and increasingly worldwide structures of communication, finance and economy has created a particular kind of global unity. It is evident that the cost of this has been growing fragmentation of societies and exclusion for more and more of the human family. In their own international relationships the churches are under pressure to adapt themselves to this system and to accept its values, which tend to overlook if not deny the spiritual dimension of human life. This therefore constitutes a serious threat to the integrity of the ecumenical movement, whose organizational forms represent a distinctly different model of relationships, based on solidarity and sharing, mutual accountability and empowerment. On the threshold of the 21st century, all existing ecumenical structures must reassess themselves in the light of the challenge to manifest a form and quality of global community characterized by inclusiveness and reconciliation.

2.10 An important affirmation made in the early phase of collaboration between the Roman Catholic Church and the World Council of Churches was that the two share in 'one and the same ecumenical movement'. This oneness of the ecumenical movement does not imply that there is a single structure or a single centre among the many different expressions of the movement. Nor does it suggest a normative understanding which would become exclusive and thus contradict the very meaning of ecumenical in the sense of 'wholeness'. The oneness of the ecumenical movement refers fundamentally to its orientation towards a 'common calling'. Ultimately this is assured by the power of the Holy Spirit working in and through the manifold manifestations of the movement.

2.11 The World Council of Churches shares with many other partners, institutionalized or not, the legacy of this one ecumenical movement and the responsibility to keep it alive. As the most comprehensive and representative body among the many organized expressions of the ecumenical movement, the World Council has the specific role of addressing the global ecumenical issues and acting as a trustee for the inner coherence of the movement.

VI. ECUMENISM IN THE USA
Consultation on Church Union, 1964, *The Reports of the Four Meetings*
Gaustad, *A Documentary History of Religion in America since 1865*, 461–2.

[The ecumenical spirit of the 1960s brought together denominations of the American churches. Denominational co-operation was and is already expressed in the National Council of Churches, but COCU has represented a search for a more formal union. The discussions continue, although the hope for complete

unity has receded. The covenants between the churches, as with similar arrangements in Britain, formalize mutual recognition of baptism, membership, and
ministry. The extract below comes from the closing statement of the third annual
consultation in 1964.]

We are met once again to explore the establishment of a united church.
We intend to stay together. We intend to go forward together. We have
seen a vision of what the Christian community in every place should
be. Looking back over the two years since we started to work together,
the members of the Consultation on Church Union register their satisfaction at the progress so far made.

In Washington in 1962 we organized ourselves for work and there we
were reminded of the reasons for the serious exploration of the establishment of a united church in North America, truly catholic, truly
reformed, and truly evangelical. The motivations are as strong now as
then. The structure of the Consultation has weathered storms and has
been taught by experiences favorable and unfavorable. ...

Believing that the establishment of one ordained ministry, recognized
by us all, is critical to our union effort, we have authorized the executive
committee to plan the work for this year so that we can be led to the
consideration of proposals which will contain the shape and functions of
the ordered ministry of the united church as well as a way or ways by
which it might be established.

That difficulties, setbacks, and disappointments will come in the
future, as they have already, we realize full well. Yet in obedience to
Jesus Christ, and claiming his promise of the presence of the Holy Spirit,
we pledge ourselves to press on for a union to the glory of God the
Father.

VII. ECUMENISM AND ROMAN CATHOLICISM

a. **Paul VI and Athenagoras I, 1965**   *The Common Declaration of Pope
Paul VI and Patriarch Athenagoras I, 7* December 1965. Flannery *Vatican II*,
vol. i. 471–3

[The ecumenical initiatives which arose from the Second Vatican Council
(see Section XIII, IV and this section, I. d above) included this end-of-Council
declaration of mutual understanding with the Orthodox. The breach of 1054
(see Section I. II above) is remembered with sadness.]

Pope Paul VI and Patriarch Athenagoras I ... believe that they are thus
responding to the call of divine grace, which today requires that the
Roman Catholic Church and the Orthodox Church, as well as all

Christians, overcome their differences, so as to be once again 'one' as the Lord Jesus asked of his Father for them.

2. Among the obstacles to be found in the way of the development of these brotherly relationships of trust and esteem, there is the memory of those painful decisions, acts and incidents which led in 1054 to the sentence of excommunication delivered against Patriarch Michael Cerularius and two other persons by the legates of the Roman See led by Cardinal Humbert, legates who were themselves in turn objects of a similar sentence on the side of the Patriarch and the Synod of Constantinople. ... Their censures were aimed at the persons concerned and not the Churches; they were not meant to break ecclesiastical communion between the sees of Rome and Constantinople.

.. This is why Pope Paul VI and Patriarch Athenagoras I with his synod ...

a. ... regret the offensive words, the reproaches without foundation and the reprehensible gestures which on both sides marked or accompanied the sad events of that period;
b. They also regret and wish to erase from the memory and midst of the Church the sentences of excommunication which followed them, and whose memory has acted as an obstacle to a rapprochement in charity down to our own day, and to consign them to oblivion;
c. Finally they deplore the troublesome precedents and later events which, under the influence of various factors, among them lack of understanding and mutual hostility, eventually led to the effective rupture of ecclesiastical communion. ...

b. **John Paul II and Bartholomew I, 1995**   *Common Declaration of Pope John Paul II and Patriarch Bartholomew I, 29 June 1995. One in Christ, 1995/3, 271–3*

[Another declaration between Pope and Ecumenical Patriarch followed thirty years after the 1965 statement. However, this did not stop controversy altogether. The returning into communion with Rome of some of the churches of the East over recent centuries had resulted in aggressive proselytism across the ensuing church boundaries. The attempt to create unity by force of conversion is known as 'uniatism'. The dialogue at Balamand, Lebanon, in June 1993 (see *One in Christ*, 1994/1) had agreed that uniatism continued but was to cease and be replaced by a mutual co-operation in working towards unity. The situation was particularly sensitive in Eastern Europe after the fall of communism.

The Patriarch, in his visit to Rome of 27–30 June 1995, complained to the Pope that the Roman Catholic Church had not fully implemented the agreement of Balamand (see *One in Christ*, 1996/2). His 'fraternal' censure was followed by this renewal of efforts towards unity between Roman Catholic and Orthodox.]

. . . . Our new-found brotherhood in the name of the one Lord has led us to frank discussion, a dialogue that seeks understanding and unity.

. . This dialogue—through the Joint International Commission—has proved fruitful and has made substantial progress. A common sacramental conception of the Church has emerged, sustained and passed on in time by the apostolic succession. In our Churches, the apostolic succession is fundamental to the sanctification and unity of the People of God. Considering that in every local Church the mystery of divine love is realised and that this is how the Church of Christ shows forth its active presence in each one of them, the Joint Commission has been able to declare that our Churches recognise one another as sister Churches, responsible together for safeguarding the one Church of God, in fidelity to the divine plan, and in an altogether special way with regard to unity.

We thank the Lord of the Church from the bottom of our hearts because these affirmations we have made together not only hasten the way to solving the existing difficulties, but henceforth enable Catholics and Orthodox to give a common witness of faith.

. . This is particularly appropriate on the eve of the third millennium when, two thousand years after the birth of Christ, all Christians are preparing to make an examination of conscience on the reality of his proclamation of salvation in history and among men.

We will celebrate this Great Jubilee on our pilgrimage towards full unity and towards that blessed day, which we pray is not far off, when we will be able to share the same bread and the same cup, in the one Eucharist of the Lord. . . .

In this spirit, we declare, without hesitation, that we are in favour of harmony among peoples and their collaboration, especially in what concerns us most directly; we pray for the full realisation of the European Union, without delay, and we hope that its borders will be extended to the East.

At the same time, we make an appeal that everyone will make a determined effort to solve the current burning problem of ecology, in order to avoid the great risk threatening the world today due to the abuse of resources that are God's gift.

May the Lord heal the wounds tormenting humanity today and hear our prayers and those of our faithful for peace in our Churches and in all the world.

c. **Roman-Catholic–Reformed** **Relations** *Towards a Common Understanding of the Church: Reformed/Roman Catholic International Dialogue*, 1991, 59–60

[Even churches which seem far apart in theology and ecclesiology were seeking common ground and mutual understanding in the late twentieth century. Here the World Alliance of Reformed Churches and Roman Catholic Church report on a dialogue which had been in process since 1970.]

161. Even though we are still far from being able to proclaim full communion, it is important for the relations between our churches that we should have an agreed vision of the ultimate goal that should guide our efforts. This is a question that needs further study. Various concepts of unity have been proposed and deserve attention. But we believe that serious consideration should be given in our Reformed–Roman Catholic relationship, and in the ecumenical movement in general, to the description of the 'unity we seek', as expressed by the Assembly of the World Council of Churches in Nairobi (1975). This text describes what is called 'conciliar fellowship'
. ...

164. If the living relationship between our churches is to grow, we must consciously foster regular contact with each other. If each church is to consider God's gift in the other, each will have to orientate itself towards the other. Inherited problems of doctrine call for further reflection. Newly arising problems (for example, relationships and dialogue with people of other living faiths, or issues raised by the progress of science and technology) must become subjects of frank and open dialogue. The road to unity can be travelled more readily if both communions can learn to listen together to the Word of God and to the questions raised by each other.

165. We pray God to grant us the Spirit to heal wounds, to gather and edify Christ's people, to purify us and to send us into world anew.

d. *Ut Unum Sint* *Ut Unum Sint* ('That they may be one'), John Paul II, 1995, para. 95, http://www.vatican.va/holy_father/john_paul_ii/encyclicals/documents/hf_jp-ii_enc_25051995_ut-unum-sint_en.html (accessed 27 May 2011)

[Pope John Paul II confirmed the Roman Catholic Church's commitment to ecumenism in this encyclical. In his view, the pope bears the responsibility for bringing the churches together.]

All this however must always be done in communion. When the Catholic Church affirms that the office of the Bishop of Rome corresponds to the will of Christ, she does not separate this office from the mission entrusted to the whole body of Bishops, who are also 'vicars and ambassadors of Christ' [*Lumen Gentium* 27]. The Bishop of Rome is a member of the 'College', and the Bishops are his brothers in the ministry.

Whatever relates to the unity of all Christian communities clearly forms part of the concerns of the primacy. As Bishop of Rome I am fully aware, as I have reaffirmed in the present Encyclical Letter, that Christ ardently desires the full and visible communion of all those Communities in which, by virtue of God's faithfulness, his Spirit dwells. I am convinced that I have a particular responsibility in this regard, above all in acknowledging the ecumenical aspirations of the majority of the Christian Communities and in heeding the request made of me to find a way of exercising the primacy which, while in no way renouncing what is essential to its mission, is nonetheless open to a new situation. For a whole millennium Christians were united in 'a brotherly fraternal communion of faith and sacramental life … If disagreements in belief and discipline arose among them, the Roman See acted by common consent as moderator' [*Unitatis Redintegratio* 14].

In this way the primacy exercised its office of unity. When addressing the Ecumenical Patriarch His Holiness Dimitrios I, I acknowledged my awareness that 'for a great variety of reasons, and against the will of all concerned, what should have been a service sometimes manifested itself in a very different light. But … it is out of a desire to obey the will of Christ truly that I recognize that as Bishop of Rome I am called to exercise that ministry … I insistently pray the Holy Spirit to shine his light upon us, enlightening all the Pastors and theologians of our Churches, that we may seek—together, of course—the forms in which this ministry may accomplish a service of love recognized by all concerned' [6 December 1987; *AAS* 80 (1988), 714].

e. **Roman Catholic–Lutheran Relations** *Joint Declaration on the Doctrine of Justification* (31 October 1999) by the Lutheran World Federation and the Catholic Church, section 3, paras. 14–18, http://www.vatican.va/roman_curia/pontifical_councils/chrstuni/documents/rc_pc_chrstuni_doc_31101999_cath-luth-joint-declaration_en.html (accessed 27 May 2011)

[The end of the twentieth century saw an historic agreement between the Lutheran and Roman Catholic churches on the question that seemed to have divided them in the sixteenth century: justification. By tackling this question, these churches paved the way for a closer ecumenical dialogue.]

The Common Understanding of Justification

14. The Lutheran churches and the Roman Catholic Church have together listened to the good news proclaimed in Holy Scripture. This common listening, together with the theological conversations of recent years, has led to a shared understanding of justification. This encompasses a consensus in the basic truths; the differing explications in particular statements are compatible with it.

15. In faith we together hold the conviction that justification is the work of the triune God. The Father sent his Son into the world to save sinners. The foundation and presupposition of justification is the incarnation, death, and resurrection of Christ. Justification thus means that Christ himself is our righteousness, in which we share through the Holy Spirit in accord with the will of the Father. Together we confess: By grace alone, in faith in Christ's saving work and not because of any merit on our part, we are accepted by God and receive the Holy Spirit, who renews our hearts while equipping and calling us to good works ['All Under One Christ,' para 14, in Growth in Agreement, 241–7].

16. All people are called by God to salvation in Christ. Through Christ alone are we justified, when we receive this salvation in faith. Faith is itself God's gift through the Holy Spirit who works through word and sacrament in the community of believers and who, at the same time, leads believers into that renewal of life which God will bring to completion in eternal life.

17. We also share the conviction that the message of justification directs us in a special way towards the heart of the New Testament witness to God's saving action in Christ: it tells us that as sinners our new life is solely due to the forgiving and renewing mercy that God imparts as a gift and we receive in faith, and never can merit in any way.

18. Therefore the doctrine of justification, which takes up this message and explicates it, is more than just one part of Christian doctrine. It stands in an essential relation to all truths of faith, which are to be seen as internally related to each other. It is an indispensable criterion which constantly serves to orient all the teaching and practice of our churches to Christ. When Lutherans emphasize the unique significance of this criterion, they do not deny the interrelation and significance of all truths of faith. When Catholics see themselves as bound by several criteria, they do not deny the special function of the message of justification. Lutherans and Catholics share the goal of confessing Christ in all things, who alone is to be trusted above all things as the one Mediator (1 Tim. 2:5f) through whom God in the Holy Spirit gives himself and pours out his renewing gifts ...

VIII. THE LIMA REPORT: BAPTISM, EUCHARIST, AND MINISTRY

a. **The Lima Report, 1982**   *Baptism, Eucharist and Ministry*, 1982, 6, 16, 32

[The World Council of Churches' Faith and Order Commission, in 1982 at Lima, Peru, held a meeting of theologians of virtually all the major Christian traditions, and thereby finalized a document which had been coming together for some years. The discussion focused on the three most contentious areas of church life from an ecumenical perspective: baptism, eucharist, and ministry. The document was circulated amongst the churches, and became a classic statement of the common areas, and the differences, that exist on these questions.]

[Baptism]. ... 15. Churches are increasingly recognizing one another's baptism as the one baptism into Christ when Jesus Christ has been confessed as Lord by the candidate or, in the case of infant baptism, when confession has been made by the church (parents, guardians, godparents and congregation) and affirmed later by personal faith and commitment. Mutual recognition of baptism is acknowledged as an important sign and means of expressing the baptismal unity given in Christ. Wherever possible, mutual recognition should be expressed explicitly by the churches.

16. In order to overcome their differences, believer baptists and those who practise infant baptism should reconsider certain aspects of their practices. The first may seek to express more visibly the fact that children are placed under the protection of God's grace. The latter must guard themselves against the practice of apparently indiscriminate baptism and take more seriously their responsibility for the nurture of baptized children to mature commitment to Christ. ...

[Eucharist] ... 28. The best way towards unity in eucharistic celebration and communion is the renewal of the eucharist itself in the different churches in regard to teaching and liturgy. The churches should test their liturgies in the light of the eucharistic agreement now in the process of attainment.

The liturgical reform movement has brought the churches closer together in the manner of celebrating the Lord's Supper. However, a certain liturgical diversity compatible with our common eucharistic faith is recognised as a healthy and enriching fact. The affirmation of a common eucharistic faith does not imply uniformity in either liturgy or practice. ...

32. Some churches stress that Christ's presence in the consecrated elements continues after the celebration. Others place the main emphasis on the act of celebration itself and on the consumption of the elements in the act of communion. The way in which the elements are treated requires special attention. Regarding the practice of reserving the elements, each church should respect the practices and piety of the others. ...

[Ministry] ... 52. Among the issues that need to be worked on as churches move towards mutual recognition of ministries, that of apostolic succession, is of particular importance. Churches in ecumenical conversations can recognise their respective ordained ministries if they are mutually assured of their intention to transmit the ministry of Word and sacrament in continuity with apostolic times. The act of transmission should be performed in accordance with the apostolic tradition, which includes the invocation of the Spirit and the laying on of hands. ...

b. Santiago de Compostela, 1993   *Sharing a Common Life in Christ*, Report
   of Section III of World Faith and Order Conference, Santiago de Compostela,
   1993. *Returning Pilgrims*, 77, 82

[Some of the responses to *Baptism, Eucharist and Ministry* and the developments since 1982 are reflected in this report, written eleven years after Lima. It testifies to continuing work on these questions.]

[Baptism] 11. The responses of the churches to BEM demonstrated a large measure of agreement on the meaning of baptism. The agreement extended to the efficacy of baptism, provided it was always recognised as God's work which can be received and appropriated only in faith.

12. Agreement in understanding, performance and practice is reflected in the fact that fewer and fewer churches and ministries repeat the rite when receiving members from other Christian families ... If the baptism celebrated by a community is recognised, then what else in the life of that community may already be recognised as eccesial? Insofar as they recognise each other's baptisms, the churches may be at the start of developing a baptismal ecclesiology in which to locate other elements of shared belief and life. ...

[Eucharist] ... 17. Growing theological convergence with regard to the eucharist, as well as in other important aspects of our Christian faith, has not yet reached a stage that allows for eucharistic sharing among all churches. This is a matter of grave concern for all Christians. There are, nevertheless, people in many of our churches who, out of deep conviction and on the basis of their common baptism, knowingly engage in eucharistic hospitality, both in inviting and in receiving. Many who do this do not lightly transgress the boundaries of the communities, but do so out of an obedience to a different understanding of eucharist that allows it to be a means of grace on the road to that fuller unity which it signifies. ...

[Ministry] ... 25. There is growing convergence amongst the churches regarding the need for a ministry of oversight (*episkope*) at all levels in the life of the Church. However, a tendency to identify this with the personal ministry of bishops and, in particular, with the historic episcopate, is problematic for churches which have a clear ministry of oversight but do not have personal bishops or stand within the historic episcopate.

26. The churches would benefit from joint theological and historical research into the exercise of *episkope*. This would be enhanced if carried out within the broader study of ministry in general. ...

IX. LUTHERAN–REFORMED RELATIONS
Towards Church Fellowship: Report of the Joint Commission of the
*Lutheran World Federation and the World Alliance of Reformed
Churches*, 1989, 7–8

[The divisions between the churches of the Reformation resulting from theological disagreement in that period have also been addressed by the modern ecumenical movement. Of course, there are instances, notably in Germany, of the churches working closely together in federation. However, the document bears witness to the fact that such a spirit of unity is not universal, but also to the hope for a closer relationship.]

1. The passion for renewal of the church in the light of the gospel which brought into being the Lutheran and Reformed churches four and a half centuries ago remains alive today among us, the heirs of the Reformation. Both of our traditions are deeply engaged in the ecumenical movement, seeking to renew our faithfulness of Christian witness and service and to make the unity of Christ's church visible.

2. Therefore it is with dismay that we must acknowledge the estrangement that we have so often experienced since the earliest years of our churches' existence, despite our common historical and theological roots in the sixteenth-century Reformation and despite the profound agreement we see also today in our teaching of the gospel and worshipping life. ...

9. From our Reformation heritage, we have a common concern to bear witness to the unconditional character of the free gift of grace; God accepts us by grace alone. If we are to be faithful to this witness, we must accept one another as freely and unconditionally as God in Christ accepts us. ...

SECTION XVII

The Twentieth-Century Churches: Sexuality and Procreation

I. SEXUALITY

a. A Quaker View *Towards a Quaker View of Sex*, 1963. *Quaker Faith and Practice*, paras. 22.13, 22.15

[The 1960s saw a questioning of traditional Christian views of sexuality and marriage. Each denomination had to consider the growing argument for either a liberal or conservative approach, to homosexuality and divorce for example, by revisiting the fundaments of its theology of sexuality. Arguably the most radical Christian denomination since their origins in the seventeenth century, the Quakers were pioneers yet again in their call for tolerance on questions of sex. However, Quakers in the 1990s would not stand by everything in the 1963 book. First, they would now go further than simple acceptance of homosexuals and lesbians, marking steadfast commitments with a meeting of worship. Secondly, the general raising of awareness of the dangers of child abuse have led Quakers to a more adequate understanding of deviance than the 1963 book would suggest.]

22.13 ... .Sexual activity is essentially neither good nor evil; it is a normal biological activity which, like most other human activities, can be indulged in destructively or creatively. Further, if we take impulses and experiences that are potentially wholesome and in a large measure unavoidable and characterise these as sinful, we create a great volume of unnecessary guilt and an explosive tension within the personality. When, as so often happens, the impulse breaks through the restriction, it does so with a ruthlessness and destructive energy that might not otherwise have been there. A distorted Christianity must bear some of the blame for the sexual disorders of society. ...

22.15 It is the nature and quality of a relationship that matters: one must not judge it by its outward appearance but by its inner worth. Homosexual affection can be as selfless as heterosexual affection, and therefore we cannot see that it is in some way morally worse.

Homosexual affection may of course be an emotion which some find aesthetically disgusting, but one cannot base Christian morality on a capacity for such disgust. Neither are we happy with the thought that all homosexual behaviour is sinful: motive and circumstances degrade or ennoble any act. ... We see no reason why the physical nature of a sexual act should be the criterion by which the question whether or not it is moral should be decided. An act which (for example) expresses true affection between two individuals and gives pleasure to them both, does not seem to us to be sinful by reason alone of the fact that it is homosexual. The same criteria seem to us to apply whether a relationship is heterosexual or homosexual.

b. Vatican Letter on Homosexuality, 1986   Sacred Congregation for the Doctrine of the Faith, *Letter to the Bishops of the Catholic Church on the Pastoral Care of Homosexual Persons*, 1986, para. 7, pp. 6–7

[The Christian responses to questions about sexuality have ranged from a radical revision of the theology of sexuality, through the middle ground—an honest acceptance of unresolvable differences within the denomination concerned—to a firm endorsement of the moral theology of the past, albeit with a pastoral commitment to those affected by it. The Roman Catholic Church has taken the latter stand on most issues of sexuality and procreation; it is by and large the most conservative of Western denominations, although many liberal voices within Roman Catholicism have caused concern for the hierarchy (see vi below). Here the Vatican maintains its rejection of homosexuality as an option for sexual relationships.]

7. The Church, obedient to the Lord who founded her and gave to her the sacramental life, celebrates the divine plan of the loving and live-giving union of men and women in the sacrament of marriage. It is only in the marital relationship that the use of the sexual faculty can be morally good. A person engaging in homosexual behaviour therefore acts immorally.

To choose someone of the same sex for one's sexual activity is to annul the rich symbolism and meaning, not to mention the goals, of the Creator's sexual design. Homosexual activity is not a complementary union, able to transmit life; and so it thwarts the call to a life of that form of self-giving which the Gospel says is the essence of Christian living. This does not mean that homosexual persons are not often generous and giving of themselves; but when they engage in homosexual activity they confirm within themselves a disordered sexual inclination which is essentially self-indulgent.

As in every moral disorder, homosexual activity prevents one's own fulfillment and happiness by acting contrary to the creative wisdom of God. The Church, in rejecting erroneous opinions regarding homosexuality, does not limit but rather defends personal freedom and dignity realistically and authentically understood.

c. **Methodist Report, 1990**   *Methodist Report on Human Sexuality*, 1990, 28, 33

[The Methodist Church in Britain provides an example of a denomination that accepts difference among its members on questions of human sexuality. Other examples of churches that admit differences between liberal and conservative positions are the Evangelical Lutheran Church in America (1993 Report, *The Church and Human Sexuality*), the Church of Scotland (1994 Assembly Report, *Human Sexuality*, with minority dissension), and the Presbyterian Church (USA) (1991 Report presented to General Assembly, *Keeping Body and Soul Together*, received not endorsed)—see Kevin Kelly, *New Directions in Sexual Ethics*, 96 ff. The Evangelical Lutheran Church in America identifies *three* positions on active homosexuality: negative judgement in love, compassionate toleration, and affirmation where the relationships are loving and faithful.

In this extract, the British Methodists are careful to point out that there remains a limit to sexual liberalism, i.e. relationships which involve abuse and exploitation are wrong. Yet the report does not identify homosexuality per se as an example of a disordered relationship. It declines to rule on the ordination of practising homosexuals, suggesting that this cannot become in itself a primary criterion of selection. The Church of England (see e., below) may be contrasted to this position; it does not regard a practising homosexual as an appropriate person to represent the ordained ministry. This reflects its view that, while homosexuality may be tolerated, it falls short of the ideal for sexual relationships.]

154. Despite the great variety of opinion within the Commission, we are all agreed that there are some boundaries which have to be recognised. We reject any and every sexual expression which involves violence, intimidation, the abuse of children or women or men. This is true for those who hold the most liberal views on human sexuality, namely, that a loving and sustaining relationship with another human person is the primary purpose of sexuality and that either same sex or different gender relationships may be entered, depending on basic orientation. It is true for those who hold the most traditional views on human sexuality, namely, that procreation is the primary purpose of sexuality and is to be expressed exclusively within a marriage which will produce children if possible. It is true for a whole variety of positions on the spectrum in between.

155. Therefore, no one is wishing to argue that everything goes. We are all agreed that certain attitudes and behaviour are not acceptable within the Christian community. In that sense, we are agreed that there should be certain rules. These rules should be directed against the abuse of power and against exploitation. These are sadly characteristics of a variety of sexual relationships, including the traditional heterosexual relationship expressed within the framework of marriage. A rejection of these features of sexuality applies therefore right across the board of

sexual relationships and practices: all agree that some forms of homo-sexual activity and some forms of heterosexual activity are morally wrong. In effect, however, this says nothing about the rightness or wrongness of heterosexual, homosexual, lesbian or bisexual relationships as such. It asks of each and every relationship that it be freely entered into and expressed in a loving context. ...

184. Up to now the Methodist Church has not found it necessary to give a definitive ruling regarding the acceptance of candidates for or-dained ministry who are homosexual or lesbian, in orientation or in practice. Members of the Commission are agreed that sexual orientation in itself should not be a bar to ordination. Some members of the Commission would wish to say quite explicitly that no practising homo-sexual or lesbian should be accepted for training for ordination. Other members of the Commission would wish to say quite explicitly that no practising homosexual or lesbian should be rejected for training for ordination on the grounds of the expression of their sexuality alone.

185. Nevertheless, this Report recommends, secondly, that the Church continues to leave the judgement about each candidate to the discretion of those appointed to make such judgement, without giving any explicit instructions in relation to a candidate's sexuality. This simply means that each candidature is judged on its merits, taking the whole person and that person's circumstances and network of relationships into account. This will not be easy, but making judgements about candidates for ordained ministry never is.

d. URC Report, 1991 *Homosexuality: A Christian View*, United Reformed Church Working Party, 1991, section 1.8, pp. 5–6

[The URC view on homosexuality is similar to the Methodist one, acknowledging difference and avoiding a binding policy for the present. This statement is one of a series produced by the URC; an official view was still subject to major debate. It contains a reminder of the joyousness and love that may characterize any union. For later discussions, see Section XVI, XVIII, below]

8 Blessing

8.1 In short, the Working Party is not prepared to describe homosexual activity as intrinsically sinful in principle, though any sexual activity is easily spoiled by pride, greed, lust or other forms of selfishness. The same is true of all human behaviour.

8.2 Such activity is by definition incapable of leading to procreation, one of the purposes of sex, though surely never the primary one. The Working Party agreed that the matter of whether such relationships might be blessed before God in worship was one for serious consider-ation. We are aware that this is being done, unofficially, within our denomination as in most others; we are also aware that this would be a serious scandal for many.

8.3 A homosexual partnership cannot be a marriage. Yet, according to evidence offered to the Working Party, there do exist such relationships in which the two partners 'may comfort and help each other, living faithfully together in need and in plenty, in sorrow and in joy ... that with delight and tenderness they may know each other in love and, through the joy of their bodily union, may strengthen the union of their hearts and lives.'

8.4 This is the idealistic language of the Marriage Service. Of course such relationships do break down, probably more often than marriages, not least because of the pressure of society's disapproval—though the statistics would be impossible to discover. The Working Party refuses to describe the homosexual condition as essentially promiscuous, nor does it lead invariably to child molestation or sadism, etc.; this is false and unworthy caricature.

e. Anglicanism: Lambeth, 1998 *The Official Report of the Lambeth Conference, 18 July–9 August* 1998, Resolution I.10, http://www.lambethcon ference.org/resolutions/1998/1998-1-10.cfm (accessed 27 May 2011)

[The Lambeth Conference in 1998 addressed the growing concern in the Anglican communion worldwide over liberal approaches to homosexuality. The report contains statements from different parts of the world; the following conclusions maintain a relatively conservative position on the question.]

Human Sexuality

This Conference:

a. commends to the Church the subsection report on human sexuality;
b. in view of the teaching of Scripture, upholds faithfulness in marriage between a man and a woman in lifelong union, and believes that abstinence is right for those who are not called to marriage;
c. recognises that there are among us persons who experience them- selves as having a homosexual orientation. Many of these are mem- bers of the Church and are seeking the pastoral care, moral direction of the Church, and God's transforming power for the living of their lives and the ordering of relationships. We commit ourselves to listen to the experience of homosexual persons and we wish to assure them that they are loved by God and that all baptised, believing and faithful persons, regardless of sexual orientation, are full members of the Body of Christ;

d. while rejecting homosexual practice as incompatible with Scripture, calls on all our people to minister pastorally and sensitively to all irrespective of sexual orientation and to condemn irrational fear of homosexuals, violence within marriage and any trivialisation and commercialisation of sex;

e. cannot advise the legitimising or blessing of same sex unions nor ordaining those involved in same gender unions;

f. requests the Primates and the ACC [Anglican Consultative Council] to establish a means of monitoring the work done on the subject of human sexuality in the Communion and to share statements and resources among us;

g. notes the significance of the Kuala Lumpur Statement on Human Sexuality and the concerns expressed .... on the authority of Scripture in matters of marriage and sexuality and asks the Primates and the ACC to include them in their monitoring process.

II. MARRIAGE AND DIVORCE

a. **Church of England Report on Marriage and Divorce, 1978**   *Marriage and the Church's Task*, 1978, The Report of the General Synod Marriage Commission, 110–11

[Churches differ as to whether persons divorced according to civil law may remarry in church, or with the approval of the church. The Orthodox tradition accepts the 'death' of a marriage and remarriage after contrition. Most Western churches allow the remarriage of divorced persons in church, with the Roman Catholic Church being the main exception (see b. below). This difference is also in evidence with respect to the reception of communion by the remarried (for church positions on divorce and remarriage, see Kevin Kelly in Bernard Hoose (ed.), *Christian Ethics*, 1998, 248 ff.).

The Church of England was more inclined to accept remarriage after this 1978 report, from which the recommendations are reproduced below. The Anglican who is divorced and remarried may now be admitted to communion and ordained, the latter at the discretion of the bishop. However, remarriage in church is not consistently allowed, as bishops defer to the feelings of parishes and priests when they are strongly against the practice. The official position on remarriage in church is that it *may* occur on pastoral grounds by arrangement with the priest and bishop, but not by right.]

1. We recommend that the Convocation regulations requiring that those who marry after divorce should only be admitted to Communion with the permission of the Bishop should be rescinded.

2. We recommend that the present use of services of prayer and dedication in connection with remarriage after divorce should be brought to an end.

3. We recommend—*by majority*—that:

a. The Church of England should now take steps to revise its regulations to permit a divorced person with the permission of the bishop to be married in church during the lifetime of a former spouse.

b. The marriage of divorced persons in church should be solemnised by the use of one or other of the existing permitted orders for the solemnisation of marriage, with the addition of an appropriate invariable Preface.

c. The working of the new procedure should be reviewed after a specified period of years.

4. We recommend that legislation be introduced to remove the present obligation on the clergy to marry unbaptised people, and that the solemnisation of such marriages should be at the discretion of the minister subject to the advice of the Bishop.

5. We recommend—*by majority*—legislation which will give the diocesan bishop discretion whether or not to ordain a man who:

a. having been divorced has remarried during the lifetime of his former wife; or

b. has married a divorced woman during the lifetime of her former husband.

6. We recommend legislation which will give the diocesan bishop discretion whether or not to institute a clergyman who:

a. having been divorced has remarried during the lifetime of his former wife; or

b. has married a divorced woman during the lifetime of her former husband.

b. ARCIC II and Moral Questions   *Life in Christ: Morals, Communion and the Church* (ARCIC II), 1994, 27

[This document explores the common ground and differences between the Roman Catholic and Anglican positions on moral questions. The Anglican–Roman Catholic International Commission (ARCIC II—see Section XVI, i above) is keen to state that: 'There is already a notable convergence between the two Communions in the witness, they give, for example, on war and peace, euthanasia, freedom and justice.' (p. 1). Areas which cause more difficulty are marriage of the divorced, contraception (see iii below), abortion (iv. c. below) and homosexuality. Even on these issues, the document frames divergence within a context of shared Christian understanding.]

75. Roman Catholic teaching that, when a sacramental marriage has been consummated, the covenant is irrevocable, is grounded in its understanding of sacramentality, as already outlined. Further, its firm legal

framework is judged to be the best protection for the institution of marriage, and thus best to serve the common good of the community, which itself redounds to the true good of the persons concerned. Thus Roman Catholic teaching and law uphold the indissolubility of the marriage covenant, even when the human relationship of love and trust has ceased to exist, and there is no practical possibility of recreating it. The Anglican position, although equally concerned with the sacramentality of marriage and the common good of the community, does not necessarily understand these in the same way. Some Anglicans attend more closely to the actual character of the relationship between husband and wife. Where a relationship of mutual love and trust has ceased to exist, and there is no practical possibility of remaking it, the bond itself, they argue, has also ceased to exist. When the past has been forgiven and healed, a new covenant and bond may in good faith be made.

III. CONTRACEPTION

a. **Lambeth Conference, 1930**   *Encyclical Letter from the Bishops*, Lambeth Conference, 1930, 43–4

[The 1930 Anglican decision to accept contraception within marriage in certain circumstances, while continuing the traditional disapproval of abortion—altered later (see iv. c. below)—was epoch-making and anticipated later changes in attitudes on moral questions. It also foreshadowed later debates by agreeing that a policy of birth control—in, for example, deprived situations and countries—should not replace the search for social and economic justice. The Roman Catholic Church responded by confirming its famous prohibition of contraception in Pius XI's *Casti Connubii*, 1930, later reaffirmed in 1968 (see b. below). However, most Western churches follow a similar line on contraception to that of the Anglicans (for example, the British Methodist Conference, 1961; see Kevin Kelly, *New Directions in Sexual Ethics*, 1998, 99 ff.).]

15. Where there is a clearly felt moral obligation to limit or avoid parenthood, the method must be decided on Christian principles. The primary and obvious method is complete abstinence from intercourse (as far as may be necessary) in a life of discipline and selfcontrol lived in the power of the Holy Spirit. Nevertheless in those cases where there is such a clearly-felt moral obligation to limit or avoid parenthood, and where there is a morally sound reason for avoiding complete abstinence, the Conference agrees that other methods may be used, provided that this is done in the light of the same Christian principles. The Conference records its strong condemnation of the use of any methods of conception-control from motives of selfishness, luxury, or mere convenience.

(Carried by 193 votes to 67.)

16. The Conference further records its abhorrence of the sinful practice of abortion.

17. While the Conference admits that economic conditions are a serious factor in the situation, it condemns the propaganda which treats conception-control as a way of meeting those unsatisfactory social and economic conditions which ought to be changed by the influence of Christian public opinion.

18. Sexual intercourse between persons who are not legally married is a grievous sin. The use of contraceptives does not remove the sin. In view of the widespread and increasing use of contraceptives among the unmarried and the extension of irregular unions owing to the diminution of any fear of consequences, the Conference presses for legislation forbidding the exposure for sale and the unrestricted advertisement of contraceptives, and placing definite restrictions upon their purchase. ...

b. *Humanae Vitae,* 1968 Humanae Vitae, Encyclical Letter of Pope Paul VI, 1968, para. 14, p. 15

[The Roman Catholic Church countered the Anglican acceptance of contraception in Pius XI's *Casti Connubii*, 1930. There were hopes that the increasing global population problem and changing attitudes towards sexuality in the 1960s would result in a Vatican revision of its position, especially in the light of the *aggiornamento* of Vatican II (see Section XIII above). Despite a commission that advised a liberal view of the matter, Paul VI listened to the conservative lobby, and in 1968 reaffirmed the position of *Casti Connubii*. The continued ban on artificial contraception caused widespread disquiet, and was responsible for many priests leaving the ordained ministry. It is likely that a large percentage of Roman Catholics ignore the ban. The following key paragraph in the 1968 document is titled 'Unlawful ways of regulating birth'.]

14. Therefore we base our words on the first principles of a human and Christian doctrine of marriage when we are obliged once more to declare that the direct interruption of the generative process already begun and, above all, direct abortion, even for therapeutic reasons, are to be absolutely excluded as lawful means of controlling the birth of children.

Equally to be condemned, as the Magisterium of the Church has affirmed on various occasions, is direct sterilization, whether of the man or of the woman, whether permanent or temporary.

Similarly excluded is any action, which either before, at the moment of, or after sexual intercourse, is specifically intended to prevent procreation—whether as an end or as a means.

Neither is it valid to argue, as a justification for sexual intercourse which is deliberately contraceptive, that a lesser evil is to be preferred to a greater one, or that such intercourse would merge with the normal relations of past and future to form a single entity, and so be qualified by exactly the same moral goodness as these. ...

IV. THE EMBRYO—ABORTION AND BIOETHICS

a. **Church of England Report on Bioethics, 1985**   *Personal Origins: The Report of a Working Party on Human Fertilisation and Embryology of the Board of Social Responsibility* (Church of England), 1985, 44–9

[The proliferation of scientific and medical techniques to enhance fertility has resulted in a complex bioethical question for modern Christianity. The BritishIrish situation, with its range of views, is probably fairly typical. The Warnock Report in Britain in the 1980s provoked responses from all mainstream denominations. These are recounted in Brendan McCarthy's *Fertility and Faith: The Ethics of Human Fertilization*, 1997, and are given in the square brackets below. *Personal Origins* gives an Anglican response.]

Artificial Insemination by Husband

[most churches in favour, with limits, except the Roman Catholic and Free Presbyterian, cautious tending to negative]

117. AIH is a practice in which human intervention is assisting the natural process and enabling it to reach its desired fulfilment. We view this as an aid to a couple in having a child of their own and thereby forming a natural family. We have no difficulty in supporting the intention of the act, the nature of the act, and its consequences. We recognise that the practice interferes with the course of nature and that it separates procreation from the act of intercourse. However, the Church of England permits the practice of artificial contraception within marriage which likewise interferes with the course of nature and which prevents procreation arising from the act of intercourse. Approval of AIH would seem to follow naturally from the Church of England's stance on contraception.

In Vitro Fertilisation

[acceptable to most, with conditions, but objections in principle from Roman Catholics, and in practice from Free Presbyterians, the Church of Scotland, and some members of other churches]

118. In *principle* a similar argument applies to this technique where the egg is that of the genetic mother and the sperm that of the genetic husband and where, after fertilisation has taken place outside the womb, the embryo is implanted into the mother's womb. Thus a couple are enabled to have a natural family of their own. Some of us, however,

are not able to support IVF in *practice*. This is because the practice is inextricably bound up with research and usually involves the creation of more embryos than will be used to resolve the problem of infertility. ...

Artificial Insemination by Donor

[churches generally against—although there were some mixed reactions—with the exception of the Scottish Episcopalians and Irish Methodists]

120. AID introduces a third party into the intimacies of married life in the form of donated sperm in cases where the husband's own sperm is unable to succeed in fertilising the ovum of the wife. Marriage is the union of one man and one woman for life. ... There are two opinions among us on this. There are those who hold that when a couple become 'one flesh' in marriage they belong to one another in such a close and exclusive way that nothing and no one else should take their place in sexual union and in the procreation that results from it. Union and procreation are indissolubly linked. Others, however, believing that a proper development of Anglican ethical thought on these matters is both possible and desirable (cf. the evolution of Anglican thinking on contra-ception), affirm that is possible for a couple to hold in good conscience that the semen of a third party imports nothing alien into the marriage relationship and does not adulterate it as physical union would. It is a possible view of the exclusiveness of the marital relationship that it concerns physical congress rather than the giving and reception of semen which is its normal accompaniment. ...

Surrogacy and Womb-Leasing

[no church commended this practice, although there was pragmatic acceptance in certain circumstances by the Scottish Episcopalians and Irish Presbyterians]

126. Surrogacy involves a contract (which may or may not involve financial considerations) between a woman who will bear a child to be handed over at birth and a couple who will then be its parents. It is, therefore, a broader question involving legal and social considerations, than a medical one concerned with resolving infertility. The moral argu-ments used against donation and IVF involving donation apply here. The unique features of surrogacy, however, lead those who would support the use of donated gametes to enable couples to have children they otherwise would not be able to have, to question surrogacy on practical and moral grounds. The practical and moral problems are multiple and involve a confused complexity of relationships which we do not believe it is possible to resolve at present. Strong bonding, for example, takes place between a

woman and the child she bears in her womb and this may lead to her being unwilling to let the child go to the contracting couple after birth. Moreover we believe that this practice, especially where it involves the payment of money for this service, is undermining the dignity of women in the bearing of children they have no intention of mothering.

Research

[i.e. embryo research: churches generally hostile with some exceptions where therapeutic motives predominate]

.....135. This leads to the further question that even if research can, in principle, be permitted, to what ends can it be directed? Here we are agreed that if research is permissible it is only permissible for the good end of seeking to resolve the problems of infertility and genetic disorder. Research for other goals is not acceptable. In particular, we view with concern any possibility that human embryos may be used for routine monitoring or assaying the effects of new chemical compounds.

b. **Vatican Instructions on Abortion and the Embryo** Sacred Congregation for the Doctrine of the Faith, *Instruction on Respect for Human Life in its Origin and on the Dignity of Procreation: Replies to Certain Questions of the Day*, 1987, 13–14

[The Roman Catholic ban on abortion is more successfully maintained than that on contraception. Many Roman Catholics campaign vigorously against the practice of abortion. The rejection of abortion is very ancient in Christianity but, as in other issues, the modern questioning of tradition—in this case, particularly from the viewpoint that women should not be forced to bear unwanted children by a patriarchal Church—has resulted in a response from the Vatican reaffirming its original position. This Instruction followed the *Declaration on Procured Abortion*, 1974, but went further in considering all medical techniques that involved the embryo.

Other churches share Roman Catholic concern about abortion, and insist that only the threat to life of the mother justifies it. However, an absolute injunction, except to save life (for example the Église Évangélique Luthérienne de France, 1982), is unusual. The Evangelishe Kirche in Deutschland and the United Evangelical Lutheran Church, 1971, add the *possible* exceptions of abortion after rape and severe disability (for church positions on abortion see Robin Smith, *Living in Covenant with God and One Another*, 1990, 117 ff.). However, qualified acceptance in difficult circumstances is common among churches (Smith gives the views of the Canadian Anglican Synod, 1984; American Baptist Church, 1981; United Church of Canada, 1980; United Presbyterian Church, 1979; American Lutheran Church, 1980). For Anglicanism generally, see c. below.]

.... . The Magisterium .. constantly reaffirms the moral condemnation of any kind of procured abortion. This teaching has not been changed and is unchangeable.

Thus the fruit of human generation, from the first moment of its existence, that is to say from the moment the zygote has formed, demands the unconditional respect that is morally due to the human being in his bodily and spiritual totality. The human being is to be respected and treated as a person from the moment of conception; and therefore from that same moment his rights as a person must be recognized, among which in the first place is the inviolable right of every innocent human being to life.

This doctrinal reminder provides the fundamental criterion for the solution of the various problems posed by the development of the biomedical sciences in this field: since the embryo must be treated as a person, it must also be defended in its integrity, tended and cared for, to the extent possible, in the same way as any other human being as far as medical assistance is concerned.

c. ARCIC II and Abortion *Life in Christ: Morals, Communion and the Church* (ARCIC II), 1994, 31

[The acceptance in Anglicanism that abortion *may* be acceptable is one of the differences in moral teaching with Roman Catholicism identified by ARCIC II (see ii. b. above).]

85. Anglicans have no agreed teaching concerning the precise moment from which the new human life developing in the womb is to be given the full protection due to a human person. Only some Anglicans insist that in all circumstances, and without exception, such protection must extend back to the time of conception. Roman Catholic teaching, on the other hand, is that the human embryo must be treated as a human person from the moment of conception. Difference of teaching on this matter cannot but give rise to difference of judgement on what is morally permissible when a tragic conflict occurs between the rights of the mother and the rights of the fetus. Roman Catholic teaching rejects all direct abortion. Among Anglicans the view is to be found that in certain cases direct abortion is morally justifiable. Anglicans and Roman Catholics, however, are at one in their recognition of the sanctity, and right to life, of all human persons, and they share an abhorrence of the growing practice in many countries of abortion on grounds of mere convenience. This agreement of fundamentals is reflected both in pronouncements of bishops and in official documents issued by both Communions.

86. We cannot enter here more fully into this debate, and we do not wish to underestimate the consequences of our disagreement. We wish, however, to affirm once again that Anglicans and Roman Catholics share the same fundamental teaching concerning the mystery of human life and the sanctity of the human person. ...

V. AIDS

Facing AIDS: The Challenge, the Churches' Response, 1997, WCC, 107–8.

[The explosion of deaths in the 1980s caused by HIV/AIDS (Human Immuno-deficiency Virus and the consequent Acquired Immunodeficiency Syndrome) was accompanied by the accusation that the churches were not well equipped to deal with the pastoral care of sufferers, as the illness was usually—but not always—transmitted sexually outside marriage in both heterosexual and homo-sexual encounters. This suggested to some the churches' disapproval of those who were affected; indeed, some Christians had considered AIDS to be a divine judgement on promiscuity. This WCC study document attempts to meet this problem and regards the pastoral concern for AIDS sufferers as a question of justice and Christian love.]

A. The life of the churches: responses to the challenge of HIV/AIDS

1. We ask the churches to provide a climate of love, acceptance and support for those who are vulnerable to, or affected by, HIV/AIDS.

2. We ask the churches to reflect together on the theological basis for their response to the challenges posed by HIV/AIDS.

3. We ask the churches to reflect together on the ethical issues raised by the pandemic, interpret them in their local context and to offer guidance to those confronted by difficult choices.

4. We ask the churches to participate in the discussion in society at large of ethical issues posed by HIV/AIDS, and to support their own members who, as health care professionals, face difficult ethical choices in the areas of prevention and care.

B. The witness of the churches in relation to immediate effects and causes of HIV/AIDS.

1. We ask the churches to work for better care for persons affected by HIV/AIDS.

2. We ask the churches to give particular attention to the conditions of infants and children affected by the HIV/AIDS pandemic and to seek ways to build a supportive environment.

3. We ask the churches to help safeguard the rights of persons affected by HIV/AIDS and to study, develop and promote the human rights of

people living with HIV/AIDS through mechanisms at national and international levels.

4. We ask the churches to promote the sharing of accurate information about HIV/AIDS, to promote a climate of open discussion and to work against the spread of misinformation and fear.

5. We ask the churches to advocate increased spending by governments and medical facilities to find solutions to the problems—both medical and social—raised by the pandemic.

C. The witness of the churches: in relation to long-term causes and factors encouraging the spread of HIV/AIDS

1. We ask the churches to recognise the linkage between AIDS and poverty, and to advocate measures to promote just and sustainable development.

2. We urge that special attention be focussed on situations that increase the vulnerability to AIDS such as migrant labour, mass refugee movements and commercial sex activity.

3. In particular, we ask the churches to work with women as they seek to attain the full measure of their dignity and express the full range of their gifts.

4. We ask churches to educate and involve youth and men in order to prevent the spread of HIV/AIDS.

5. We ask the churches to seek to understand more fully the gift of human sexuality in the contexts of personal responsibility, relationships, family and Christian faith.

6. We ask the churches to address the pandemic of drug use and the role this plays in the spread of HIV/AIDS and to develop locally relevant responses in terms of care, de-addiction, rehabilitation and prevention.

VI. MORAL CONTROVERSY WITHIN ROMAN CATHOLICISM

Veritatis Splendor, Encyclical Letter of John Paul II, 1993, para. 110, p. 165.

[The conservative position taken by the Roman Catholic Church on moral questions has been challenged and qualified by several of its theologians as they seek a radical and revised understanding that integrates Christian tradition and modern insight. The Vatican responded to this climate of debate and difference of opinion with a clarification of its position on faith and morals. The new *Catechism of the Catholic Church* was published in 1992. A year later, in *Veritatis Splendor*, John Paul II responded to the diversity of opinion by stating the hierarchical understanding of the sources of truth and, in doing so, demanded assent to the Magisterium on moral questions.]

110 ... . This is the point at which to consider the specific task of all those who by mandate of their legitimate Pastors teach moral theology in Seminaries and Faculties of Theology. They have the grave duty to instruct the faithful—especially future Pastors—about all those commandments and practical norms authoritatively declared by the Church. While recognising the possible limitations of the human arguments employed by the Magisterium, moral theologians are called to develop a deeper understanding of the reasons underlying its teachings and to expound the validity and obligatory nature of the precepts it proposes, demonstrating their connection with one another and their relation with man's ultimate end. Moral theologians are to set forth the Church's teaching and to give, in the exercise of their ministry, the example of a loyal assent, both internal and external, to the Magisterium's teaching in the areas of both dogma and morality. ...

SECTION XVIII
The Churches and Twenty-First Century Issues

I. THE GLOBAL GROWTH OF CHRISTIANITY

a. Global Christianity   Philip Jenkins, *The Next Christendom: The Coming of Global Christianity*, 2007, 1–2

[In 2002, Philip Jenkins first presented his cogent thesis that the Christianity of the future will be centred more in the Southern continents than in Europe. This shift of locus will have implications as to how Christianity is believed and practised.]

We are currently living through one of the transforming moments in the history of religion worldwide. Over the last five centuries, the story of Christianity has been inextricably bound up with that of Europe and European-derived civilizations overseas, above all in North America. Until recently, the overwhelming majority of Christians have lived in white nations, allowing some thinkers to speak of "European Christian" civilization. Conversely, radical writers have seen Christianity as an ideological arm of Western imperialism. Many of us share the stereotype of Christianity as the religion of the West or, to use another popular metaphor, the global North. It is self-evidently the religion of the haves. To adapt the phrase once applied to the increasingly conservative U.S. electorate of the 1970s, the stereotype holds that Christians are un-black, un-poor, and un-young. If that is true, then the growing secularization of the West can mean only that Christianity is in its dying days. Globally, perhaps, the faith of the future will be Islam.

Over the last century, however, the center of gravity in the Christian world has shifted inexorably southward, to Africa and Latin America. Today, the largest Christian communities on the planet are to be found in those regions ... Whatever Europeans or North Americans may believe, Christianity is doing very well indeed in the global South—not just surviving but expanding.

This trend will continue apace in coming years. Many of the fastest growing countries in the world are either predominantly Christian or else have very sizable Christian minorities. Even if Christians just main-tain their present share of the population in countries such as Nigeria and Kenya, Mexico and Ethiopia, Brazil and the Philippines, there are soon going to be several hundred million more Christians from those nations alone. Moreover, conversions will swell the Christian share of world population. Meanwhile, historically low birth rates in the tradi-tionally Christian states of Europe mean that these populations are declining or stagnant. In 1950 a list of the world's leading Christian countries would have included Britain, France, Spain, and Italy, but none of these names will be represented in a corresponding list for 2050. In 1900 Europe was home to two-thirds of the world's Christian population; today, the figure is less than a quarter, and by 2025 it will fall below 20 percent.

b. Pentecostalism   The Pentecostal World Fellowship, 2006, http://www. pentecostalworldfellowship.org/about/aboutus.htm (accessed 27 May 2011)

[The Christian denomination that is fastest growing in the twenty-first century is the Pentecostal movement (and associated independent churches). Pentecostal-ism began in the Azusa Street revival in Los Angeles in 1906, through the preaching of William J. Seymour, although there are many nineteenth-century precedents, particularly in the Wesleyan Holiness tradition. At first a black Christian movement, Pentecostalism was attractive to black Christians who felt alienated from other denominations, particularly when immigrating to Britain in the 1950s and 1960s. It is now a multi-ethnic and global phenomenon, and there are also charismatic subgroups in other denominations.

The growth of Pentecostalism in the 2000s is discussed in, for example, Pentecostalist Paul Alexander's *Signs and Wonders: Why Pentecostalism is the World's Fastest Growing Faith*, 2007, San Francisco: Jossey-Bass/Wiley, and included in Philip Jenkins' *The New Faces of Christianity: Believing the Bible in the Global South*, 2006, OUP. This excerpt is from the Pentecostal World Fellowship, which has held international conferences since 1947. It identifies some of the most fundamental tenets of Pentecostalism.]

Who We Are

The Pentecostal World Fellowship is a cooperative body of Pentecostal churches and groups worldwide of approved standing. It is not a legislative body to any national entity, but it is rather a coalition of commitment for the furtherance of the Gospel to the ends of the world and thus shall function as a service agent to:

- uphold one another in prayer.
- support and encourage one another in the task of missions and evangelisms.
- promote Christian fellowship and cooperation among Pentecostal people throughout the world.
- provide means of consultation and cooperation among the members and related agencies.
- share mutual concerns and insights relating to any crucial spiritual and temporal issues of the Church.
- administer relief in times of crises.
- promote exchange of personnel in special areas of ministry.
- disseminate helpful information and up-to-date statistics for the benefit of the Church.
- voice to the world and governments in defense of the faith, social justice, and persecuted believers, as the PWF.

Statement of Faith

The Pentecostal World Fellowship has adopted the following document which crosses denominational lines to form a guiding principle for membership. Members of the PWF should subscribe to the following statement of Faith:

We believe:

- the Bible to be inspired, the only infallible, authoritative Word of God;
- that there is one God, eternally existent in three persons: Father, Son and Holy Spirit;
- in the deity of our Lord Jesus Christ, in His virgin birth, in His sinless life, in His miracles, in His vicarious atoning death through His shed blood, in His bodily resurrection, in His ascension to the right hand of the Father and in His personal return in power and glory;

- that for the salvation of lost and sinful man regeneration by the Holy Spirit through faith in Jesus Christ is absolutely essential;
- in the baptism of the Holy Spirit with the evidence of speaking in other tongues as the Spirit gives the utterance according to Acts 2:4, and in the operation of the spiritual gifts and ministries;
- in the ministry of the Holy Spirit by whose indwelling the Christian is enabled to live a godly life;
- in the resurrection of both the saved and the lost; they that are saved to eternal life and they that are lost unto the resurrection of damnation;
- in the church of Jesus Christ and in the unity of believers;
- in the practical application of the Christian faith in everyday experience and the need to minister to people in every area of life, which includes not only the spiritual, but also the social, political and physical.

II. GLOBAL POVERTY

a. **Poverty and Children**   Pamela D. Couture, *Seeing Children, Seeing God: a Practical Theology of Children and Poverty*, 2000, 15–16, 52–3

[Pamela Couture worked on behalf of the United Methodist Church in her research and writing on children and poverty. Concentrating on children—as other studies focus on women—helps her readers to avoid the problem of the 'poor' becoming a generalized mass rather than real individual human beings.]

Children and poverty—the stereotypical image of children and poverty is a child dying of starvation in a famine-stricken developing country. But most children living in poverty around the world—children who live without adequate food, health care, education, or parental and community support—are not the children of well-publicized disasters but children who live their lives with no media attention. They live, for example, in the bush or on the urban streets or in the homes of kind strangers in Africa, noticed by the international media only when the safety of westerners in their midst is somehow threatened. Impoverished children are also hidden in the United States—almost a quarter of children in the United States live in poverty by national standards. Those who are segregated in decaying inner-city neighborhoods have lately received much-deserved attention, but many live in rural families that have been cut off from their previous agricultural livelihood, and some live in suburban communities that refuse to acknowledge their presence ...

But God and children who live with poverty have a similar problem: they are not easily visible in the world. In a world that focuses on secular success, God and children in need tend to be hidden. Both God and children are present in the world, whether we want to see them or not. But God and godchildren do not intrude on our lives. They are behind the scenes, waiting for us to discover them. They wait for us to notice that they are living in the institutions of the religious denominations to whom we contribute, working in the fields and farms as we drive by, or standing in the streets looking grown up enough to make money in a variety of illegal ways. Once we begin to notice, they wait for us while we hesitate, while we intellectualize, while we equivocate, while we work, until we hear a call into some small but regular service where godchildren and God begin to have a human, incarnate face ...

The Wesleyan insistence that God has not given up on us, that God is already at work in deprived children and depraved adults, can be shocking ... At the edges of our lives, God's grace is at work, reminding us that we have already been created good. As we open ourselves to awareness, we allow ourselves to contemplate this judgment of our fundamental goodness.

b. Theological Responses to Poverty R. S. Sugirtharajah, 'Poverty', 2003, Virginia Fabella and R. S. Sugirtharajah, *The SCM Dictionary of Third World Theologies*, 170–1

[This dictionary excerpt by R. S. Sugirtharajah provides a concise summary of the development of liberation theologies from the 1960s Latin American beginnings to become a global phenomenon in the 1970s and beyond. They remain differentiated by context, yet unified in their call to Christians to combat poverty and injustice. The twenty-first century has not seen an easing of the problem; rather a deepening of the crisis. Thus liberation theology has outlived the end of Soviet communism and remains a dominant mode of theological discourse in Latin America, Africa and Asia.]

One of the significant contributions of Third World theologies has been to put poverty at the center of their theological discussions. Given the disparate conditions in which these theologies arise, their articulation of poverty, too, differs from context to context. It was the Latin American theologians who first took seriously the cause of poverty for theological reflection ... Among others, Gustavo Gutiérrez defined poverty as a subhuman existence without the basic necessities, a scandalous state incompatible with the Bible. In their view, poverty is not the fault of the poor. It can and should be eliminated, and the Bible has its own built-in safeguards such as the Sabbath laws, tithing, and the Jubilee Year of the release that offer the poor a fresh start in life.

In Africa, people face socio-economic poverty as well as another kind of poverty that the late Engelbert Mveng, a Cameroonian theologian, called anthropological poverty. This is not about exterior circumstances nor about having material possessions. It is about the interior of African selfhood that has been affected as centuries of colonialism robbed Africans of their own ways of living and their cultural heritage. Sadly, the resulting low self-esteem has caused them to internalize the values and models of their oppressors. Deliverance from such a state is provided in the Song of Zachariah, Mary's Magnificat, and in the charter of the Beatitudes.

In the Asian context, in *God's Reign for God's Poor* (1999), Aloysius Pieris has proposed a new 'covenant' Christology based on two categories of poverty: the voluntary poverty of those who as followers of Jesus renounce Mammon, and the forced poverty of the masses of people who as vicars of Christ are the victims of Mammon, or organized consumerism and greed. The way to eradicate poverty is to undertake voluntary poverty, which is biblically sanctioned. The hermeneutical underpinning is provided by the biblical notion of God's active opposition to Mammon. What is important is not freedom from poverty, but the freedom that *comes* from poverty. Therefore, in Pieris' understanding, Asians struggle not against poverty, but against Mammon. Voluntary poverty does not mean leading the life of an ascetic but leading a life based on simplicity, sufficiency, and respect for both human beings and the ecological order.

c. **'Make Poverty History'**   Methodist Conference of Great Britain, 2005, *MAKEPOVERTYHISTORY* (Paper 51), section 3, http://www.methodist.org. uk/static/conf2005/co_51_makepovertyhistory_0505.doc (accessed 27 May 2011)

[Following on from the Jubilee 2000 campaign to eradicate the debt of poor countries, the 'Make Poverty History' campaign was an important movement in the 2000s, and the churches were strong supporters, prominent on marches.]

The Churches

The Jubilee Debt Campaign emerged several years ago from Churches and Christian agencies in the UK. This experience has increased the confidence of those in our churches that campaigning for changes to global economic structures is a valid and even essential part of Christian mission. This confidence has helped produce energy and enthusiasm for the demands of MAKEPOVERTYHISTORY. The Church's role in mobilising people for events, such as the Wake Up for Trade Justice vigil in

Westminster, has proved crucial to their overall success. Christian Aid and staff from other Christian agencies and Churches have made a substantial contribution to the co-ordination of the MAKEPOVERTY-HISTORY coalition.

The Methodist Council in October 2004 resolved to:

1. Offer support for the MAKEPOVERTYHISTORY coalition and agree membership of the coalition;
2. Encourage Districts, Circuits, members and the Connexional Team to become fully engaged in the campaign;
3. Note the MAKEPOVERTYHISTORY calendar of events.

On Saturday 2nd July 2005 thousands of people will take to the streets of Edinburgh in advance of the G8 meeting in Scotland to insist that the leaders of the world's richest nations take up the challenge to MAKE-POVERTYHISTORY ... Methodists are travelling to Edinburgh from across the Connexion; many churches are sporting MAKEPOVERTY-HISTORY banners and other events are occurring such as the 400-mile MAKEPOVERTYHISTORY debt march, led by The Revd Dr Simon Topping, from Birmingham to the G8 Summit meeting ...

d. Globalization *Alternative globalization addressing people and earth,* WCC, 2005, paras. 1–8, http://www.oikoumene.org/en/resources/documents /assembly/porto-alegre-2006/3-preparatory-and-background-documents/alt ernative-globalization-addressing-people-and-earth-agape.html (accessed 27 May 2011)

[This document was prepared by the commission for Justice, Peace and Creation of the World Council of Churches. Globalization is the process by which national economic control and cultural integrity are replaced by global structures and markets, which carries with it the danger that the power brokers will not be democratically accountable or anchored within the ethical parameters of any given society. The 'alternative globalization' suggested by the document is a movement of solidarity for justice in which the churches play an important role.]

1. Poverty eradication

We recommit ourselves to work for the eradication of poverty and inequality through developing economies of solidarity and sustainable communities. We will hold our governments and the international institutions accountable to implement their commitments on poverty eradication and sustainability.

2. Trade

We recommit ourselves to work for justice in international trade relations through critical analyses on free trade and trade negotiations, and to collaborate closely with social movements in making those agreements just, equitable and democratic.

3. Finance

We recommit ourselves to campaign for responsible lending; unconditional debt cancellation and for the control and regulation of global financial markets. Investments should be redirected towards businesses that respect social and ecological justice, or in banks and institutions that do not engage in speculation, nor encourage tax evasion.

4. Sustainable use of land and natural resources

We recommit ourselves to engage in actions for sustainable and just patterns of extraction and use of natural resources, in solidarity with Indigenous peoples, who seek to protect their land, water and their communities.

We recommit ourselves to challenge the excessive consumption of affluent societies so that they will shift towards self-restraint and simplicity in lifestyles.

5. Public goods and services

We recommit ourselves to join the global struggle against the imposed privatization of public goods and services; and to actively defend the rights of countries and peoples to define and manage their own commons.

We recommit ourselves to support movements, groups and international initiatives defending vital elements of life such as bio-diversity, water and the atmosphere.

6. Life-giving agriculture

We recommit ourselves to work for land reforms in solidarity with landless agricultural labourers and small farm holders; to advocate in various ways for self-determination over food concerns. To oppose the production of genetically modified organisms (GMOs) as well as trade liberalization as the sole directive. We commit ourselves to promote ecological farming practices and to stand in solidarity with peasant communities.

7. Decent jobs, emancipated work and people's livelihoods

We commit ourselves to build alliances with social movements and trade unions that advocate decent jobs and just wages. We commit ourselves to advocate for those workers and bonded labourers who work under exploitative conditions and are deprived of their rights to form trade unions.

8. Churches and the power of empire

We recommit ourselves to reflect on the question of power and empire from a biblical and theological perspective, and take a firm faith stance against hegemonic powers because all power is accountable to God ...

III. THE ECONOMY, TRADE, AND DEBT

a. **Fair Trade**   Chris Sugden, 'Fair Trade as Christian Mission', 2001 Peter Johnson and Chris Sugden, *Markets, Fair Trade and the Kingdom of God. Essays to Celebrate Traidcraft's 21st Birthday*, 3–24; this excerpt 19–20

[The growing recognition that the world's trading economy was not built on principles of justice and equal opportunity led to the setting up of fair trade organizations, including Traidcraft with its Christian foundation in 1979. These essays anticipate its 25th birthday in a world where the problems of economic injustice had hardened despite growth in public awareness. Here Chris Sugden explains the nature of a Christian fair trade agency.]

Traidcraft and the Churches

Traidcraft is a Christian Development Business and Agency. It is not a church. But Christian Development Organisations are an expression of the churches' engagement with society ... A community cannot be built with reference to finance and economics alone. Economic sustainability depends on vision. If people have a vision they will find the economics. The churches are bearers of a moral vision. Is it possible to build a community without a vital church presence, with a commitment to the disabled and the poor?

This focus also enables Christian Development agencies to do what they can do and to maintain their particularity as development organisations rather than become civil society institutions ... The churches need development agencies as expressions of the church so that the churches do not need to become development agencies.

That is why it is important that Traidcraft sees the church as a major partner. The churches are an important partner in the UK, as a source of shareholders, fair traders and consumers. Such people support Traidcraft because it transmits their honour and valuing of poor people and their passion to partner them. Church people trust Traidcraft to treat people in trade as they would wish as Christians to treat them. Traidcraft helps us all understand the gospel as it takes concrete expression in fair trade with dignity for poor people.

The church is also an important partner in producer countries. Because it is the gospel which gives poor people the dignity that at root changes their lives, it is the gospel that constrains the church to be with and among the poor. In some African countries NGO's reach 7% of the poor at most. The church reaches 90% of them. The contribution which the Christian community makes to serving the poor in poor countries is out of all proportion to their size or resources. They need and deserve to know about the partnership that Traidcraft offers the poor.

Christian fair trade organisations can show the frontier of the Kingdom of God with the current economic order; enable people to become stewards of creation; can be a parable that changes people one step at a time, but irrevocably; and an event that can give opportunity for an explanation that is rooted in why we believe justice is so fundamental and why we believe that action for justice is not in vain.

b. Jubilee Campaign   Ross Kinsler and Gloria Kinsler, *The Biblical Jubilee and the Struggle for Life: an Invitation to Personal, Ecclesial, and Social Transformation*, 1999, 162–3

[The millennium presented an opportunity for renewal in the global economy, especially where poor nations struggled with excessive debt and interest. The biblical notion of Jubilee, the release of debts every fifty years (Lev. 25), was applied to the millennium, and a 'Jubilee' campaign gained considerable momentum, with some success in rescinding international debt, although not as much as the organizers had aimed for.]

Working for Justice, Celebrating Life Together

When we examine the Sabbath and Jubilee texts and other prophetic passages from the Old Testament and the New, we find that the concern for justice is not a marginal addendum for God's people. It is central. Some of our Latin American biblical scholars and base community leaders have affirmed forthrightly, as did the prophets of Israel, that the only way to know God is to practice justice. Theologies of and movements for liberation not only call us out of bondage and oppression; they call us to build new socioeconomic–spiritual possibilities founded on God's rule of justice ... Jubilee means to work together for justice and so to celebrate together the God of life ...

Our churches are, at least potentially, spaces in which concerned people can begin to practice Sabbath economics, Jubilee spirituality, and liberty for all. Our churches are human institutions with all the temptations and foibles and troubles of other institutions. But they are grounded, at least in theory, upon biblical and confessional foundations that call us constantly to account. Part of that calling to account must be the challenge of the Sabbath–Jubilee vision that is so prominent in the history of Israel, in the life and ministry of Jesus, and also in the early church. Hopefully, the millennial celebrations will sound the trumpet call of God's Jubilee and hold up that vision of new possibilities in our world.

The peoples of the world will no doubt be looking for signs of hope, liberation, justice, and peace as we enter the new millennium. Every sector of the new global reality, from economics and politics to science and technology, from the United Nations to local city councils, from philosophers to journalists, from health workers to educators, from grandparents to grandchildren, will be called upon to articulate their hopes and fears for humankind and for our fragile planet. People of every faith will be expected to draw deeply from their spiritual wells in order to share fresh water of life for the refreshing of weary souls. As heirs of the Judeo-Christian tradition, we will be able to share our vision of a new socioeconomic-spiritual possibility in which all have enough and none too much, in which debts are forgiven and slaves liberated, in which divisions of race, ethnicity, gender, class, and generation become bridges to mutual growth, in which all of us can return home to genuine humanity in community with all humankind. How great might be this celebration of Jubilee!

c. **Jubilee Centre**   John Ashcroft and Michael Schluter, 'A new framework for the social order', 2005, M. Schluter and J. Ashcroft, *Jubilee Manifesto: A Framework, Agenda and Strategy for Christian Social Reform*, 17–33; this excerpt 18–19

[The term 'Jubilee' was not only used for the specific issue of debt release, but also for social justice generally, following Luke 4.18-19. The Jubilee Centre of Cambridge, England, founded in 1983, is an exemplar of a Christian organization working on an international scale in research, education, social reform and peace-making. It also adopts a biblically-based approach as an alternative to Capitalism and Socialism.]

The Jubilee Centre was set up in 1983 to study, disseminate and apply a biblical vision for society. This led to a number of reform initiatives. One of the first was a series of consultations involving senior African National Congress (ANC) and Afrikaner figures to look at options for a post-apartheid South Africa in the late 1980s, seeking shared principles for such issues as land reform, constitutional structures, business ownership, urban policy and education. Around the same time UK initiatives were developed to pursue an agenda for strengthening relationships in families and neighbourhoods. This included research and campaigning on such issues as Sunday trading, consumer credit and debt, support for family carers, reform of the criminal justice system and exploring the social impact of labour mobility.

At the time of writing, the Jubilee Centre and its off-shoot charities are involved in peace-building in Sudan, seeking a lasting and just peace for a conflict that has claimed two million lives over the last twenty years; developing community finance initiatives in the UK to tackle pockets of persistent long-term urban unemployment that continue to blight the lives of individuals and families who are excluded from the hopes and prosperity that so many of us take for granted; seeking reform of our public services—sometimes literally a matter of life and death for the most vulnerable; and building a social environment to sustain civic society on which our well-being depends.

This is not a book of political philosophy, but a book for those with an active concern for social reform. It is not just the fruit of thirty years of reflection on biblical teaching relating to political ideologies, but is also the fruit of over twenty years of active engagement in public life in Britain and beyond. It is based on five main convictions:

1. That social reform is an important response to human need, as part of our discipleship and love of both God and neighbour, and as a proper part of the mission of the church in the world.
2. That the Bible can guide this process, informing our understanding of what constitutes right relationships and offering a paradigm of a relational social order.
3. That our approach to social reform must focus on relationships, both in setting the goals for our lives as individuals and as a society, and in setting the agenda for a social order designed to sustain those relationships.
4. That social reform must be guided and inspired by new ideas that tackle the root systemic causes of social, economic and political problems. Implicit in this conviction is the belief that the '-isms' that shape life today are flawed.
5. That it is important to work with those who do not share our faith, which requires that we create a shared account of the common good.

d. Debt   Evangelical Alliance, *Life Beyond Debt*, 2009, http://www.eauk.org/ lifebeyonddebt/life-beyond-debt-resource-booklet.cfm#issuu (accessed 27 May 2011)

[The global economic crisis beginning in 2008 was the worst since the Second World War, and it had considerable impact on people's standard of living. This booklet recognises that the churches have a contribution to make in the ethics of money. This is also an example of an evangelical approach to the Bible that responds to current social issues.]

Churches must:

Be faithful to the breadth and depth of biblical teaching on money and possessions. Talk money when the Bible does, not over-spiritualising the texts or making them serve our lifestyle choices.

Connect the spiritual life with how we handle money and its power in our lives (Luke 16.10). Money talk should be a normal part of teaching, preaching, discipleship, mentoring and spiritual direction.

Give people permission to talk about money, to share their hopes, fears and joys. Leaders should talk about money with honesty, humour, sensitivity and vulnerability as those on a shared journey, not experts who have reached a destination.

Address money holistically: spending and saving; the wise use of credit; and the dangers of debt. Simple financial planning, budgeting and money management should sit easily in our teaching ministry with prayer or spiritual gifts.

Teach the grace of generosity and the discipline of giving as the hallmark or litmus test of authentic discipleship around money. Giving talk must not be constrained by the annual stewardship campaign or the capital appeal.

Support clergy and leaders in this preaching and teaching ministry, knowing that they struggle with the same concerns as their congregations.

Establish simple systems of pastoral and practical care for those who are burdened with debt or facing the financial impact of circumstances.

IV. SOCIAL JUSTICE

a. Urban Regeneration   Urban Bishops' Panel, *The Urban Renaissance and the Church of England*, 2002 (GS Misc 1446), section 1

[The Church of England continued to work on the issues of urban life and ministry after *Faith in the City* (1985) (see Section XIV X a.). The concept of 'regeneration' in the city was important in Britain after the recognition of urban decay in the 1980s. This 2002 discussion paper was followed by *Faithful Cities* (2006), which brought the Church's analysis of the British city up to date.]

Introduction

1.1 Seventeen years have now passed since the publication of *Faith in the City*. Subsequent publications, *Living with Faith in the City* in 1990 and *Staying in the City* in 1995 reviewed the progress of the response to the analysis and call for action that made *Faith in the City* such a landmark document. However, during the last five years, some fundamental changes have been occurring in the way we address the needs of our urban communities. Accordingly, during 2001 the Urban Bishops Panel embarked on a process to present to the House of Bishops, and later to General Synod, a paper to act as a contribution for the development of a policy framework for the Church's urban mission.

1.2 This document outlines the challenges and opportunities facing the Church in its mission and ministry in the urban communities of England at the beginning of the twenty-first century ...

1.3 The Church is being invited into many new partnerships and patterns of engagement, alongside other faith communities. This needs to be underpinned in terms of the Church's resources and theological thinking. The Government says its vision of 'an urban renaissance' depends on individuals and communities playing their full part. This paper is offered a part of the discernment of the role the Church can play. In the Panel's discussions we identified six principles to inform, enthuse and underpin our involvement in strategies for urban regeneration and renewal:

Our churches are communities of and for the area and the people who live there.

Our faith is concerned with the welfare of people, community, sustainability, and justice.

Our faith engages us in developing and sustaining hope and vision that things can be different (even against the odds); this is also a calling to analyse, understand and critique the structures, policies and programmes we encounter.

Our struggle for God's reign (on earth as it is in heaven) compels us to the advocacy and empowerment of those who are excluded and whose voice is rarely heard, to accompany them and form alliances with them and others who work for the same purposes.

Partnerships are a vital sign of a common humanity, and involve a mutual commitment of vision, authority and interest.

Regeneration is a spiritual matter.

b. Racial Justice   CTBI/Churches' Commission for Racial Justice, *Beneath the Surface*, Report on the CCRJ's Fact-finding and Education Visit to the United States of America, 3–17 May 2005, conclusion, http://www.ctbi.org.uk/pdf_view.php?id=23 (accessed 27 May 2011)

[The problem of continuing racism in American and European societies is addressed in this report, based on a British visit to the USA in 2005 by Arlington Trotman. Disasters such as Hurricane Katrina in New Orleans (2005) demonstrate the inequalities in twenty-first-century societies. Since this occurred, Barack Obama was elected as the first African American president of the United States (inaugurated 2009).]

Conclusion

The aim of this visit was to explore alternative methodologies for addressing racism and engaging the racial justice discourse in the Churches of the Britain and Ireland ...

Secondly, our expectations of greater integration and social progress in American society, based on the momentum provided by the Civil Rights Movement and mass media images of successful African Americans in the mainstream, were not realized. As hurricane Katrina showed, there is a form of social exclusion and underlying racism that is not actually recognized either by the Federal Government or many State authorities ...

Thirdly, we found that the debate and strategic address of systemic racial inequalities in the USA appear to have ended, or at the very least have been muted ...

Fourthly, despite the general picture of denial or lack of systematic address of racism, some Churches, educational institutions and community activists will almost certainly never accommodate an uncomfortable silence in the face of injustice, such as Katrina has unveiled. It is entirely creditable, therefore, that some sectors are obviously concerned and seek to address the issue in American society, not least through the local initiatives we encountered ...

Fifthly, it is almost impossible to grasp the fact that, where the world's most prosperous democracy espouses and exports that brand of political and social order, America's black population still remain victims of a form of institutional racism which means that they do not possess the permanent right to vote. This system of disenfranchisement is a political conundrum, which requires immediate attention.

Finally, the hue of a theology which challenges the political and economic compartmentalization of Christendom into what is now known as the Religious Right, characterized by mega churches and the advance of churches gaining political power, poses serious questions for those who espouse and adhere to the faith of Jesus, the Christ, in modern society ...

Clearly our Churches have much to do before a truly multi-ethnic and multi-cultural church, characterized by inclusiveness and mutual respect can be assured. Nevertheless, the Churches in these islands, together with a strong non-governmental lobby, have ensured a measure of real progress against racism in all its forms ...

c. Slavery   Set All Free and Anti-Slavery International, *Act to End Slavery Now*, 2006, 6

[The 200th anniversary of the abolition of the Slave Trade Act in Britain, 1807, was marked by this ecumenical commitment to combating contemporary forms of slavery, such as bondage to debt, people trafficking, and forced labour. Even in modern democracies, large numbers of people can be classified as suffering from a lack of personal freedom and self-determination, often enforced by violent means.]

The Bible and fighting slavery today

Over 200 years ago, black and white abolitionists, who were motivated by a desire to see the gospel preached in all its truth and fullness to enslaved Africans, embarked upon a campaign to set the captives free. Armed with verses from scripture, these courageous men and women stood against hierarchies and vested interests with a call that God's people were to be 'let go to worship Him'.

What do the scriptures say about the appalling abuses facing God's people today? Certainly, Exodus 21 and Leviticus 25 condemn generational slavery and slavery by descent—a form of servitude affecting millions around the world. Likewise, Proverbs 13:23; "A poor man's field may produce abundant food, but injustice sweeps it away," underlines today's inequalities which condemn hardworking men, women and children to lives of abject poverty by those who exploit their labour ...

There are often 'costs' for taking moral positions on injustice or for righting wrongs. It cost Zacchaeus financially [Luke 19]; while numerous biblical prophets were stoned, beaten, abused and even killed when they spoke out against corruption and sin. The abolitionists of the past faced physical threats and wide-scale ridicule in their fight against Transatlantic slavery. Likewise, standing against modern slavery can have financial, time and emotional implications, in terms of consumer purchases, awareness-raising and standing alongside the oppressed. Yet this undoubtedly subscribes to the biblical injunction to 'do justly, to love mercy, and walk humbly before God' and to be in keeping with the Church's mission to restore, recognise and perfect 'the image of God' in all people, to end subjugations and break the chains of slavery today.

d. *Moral, but no Compass*   Francis Davis, Elizabeth Paulhus and Andrew Bradstock, *Moral, But No Compass: Government, Church and the Future of Welfare*, 2008, 100–1

[The debate about the Church of England's role in British social policy is relevant for other denominations and other countries. *Faith in the City* (1985) was critical of the Conservative government for its abandonment of the 'welfare consensus' forged during the Second World War by thinkers which included the then Archbishop of Canterbury, William Temple. *Moral, But No Compass* accepts the changed context of the early twenty-first century, in which social welfare is not wholly centralized. However, the report, commissioned by the Church of England and written by members of the Von Hügel Institute, Cambridge, is also critical of government, this time a Labour administration. It takes the ideas in *Faithful Cities* (2006) of church agencies as 'social capital', but argues that there is too much government control, and not enough recognition, of their work. It remains to be seen whether the change of government in 2010 improves this situation.]

Final Remarks

In the course of our research for this report, we have encountered a Church of England that, proportionate to its size, makes extensive contributions to the civic health of the nation. Bishops engage in countless activities ranging from involvement in fundraising appeals, to regeneration, to sitting on governing bodies of local schools or colleges, to community leadership. Cathedrals serve a dual role of being centres of prayer and of great potential for social action, education and regeneration—all within a rich Christian narrative of 'hospitality' and 'openness'. Dioceses contain significant resources, both financial and human, that could enable them to become meaningful players in welfare provision and the strengthening of community foundations. Congregations, with their unique ability to know and understand the situation locally, have shown a true spirit of innovation in their quest to meet the needs presented ... and to raise funds for wider Christian social innovations in housing, addiction, family support and anti-poverty campaigning. In this sense, it is no wonder that Anglican organisations and institutions have been pioneers and leaders in development work, children's needs, and every area of civil society. All in all, the Church of England has proven itself to have the conviction, institutional capacity, innovative spirit and skills to extend its current reach even more widely, should it so wish. This will be a moment for leadership in the Church.

Yet, despite this immense and longstanding involvement by the Anglican Church, the government, with notable exceptions, has consistently failed to pay more than enthusiastic lip service to its role in society generally and in the third [voluntary] sector in particular.

In turn this means that Government is being experienced at the local and national level in negative ways. Its perceived discrimination against the Christian Church and other religious bodies, coupled with the relative downgrading of regional and other local actors, suggests a policy-making environment that has essentially excluded, or pushed to the margins, social voices (not just religious ones) that are vital to civic debate. Those whom we met felt that the social welfare contracting regime as presently constituted must be reshaped in the light of these concerns ...

Only if such a fresh conversation emerges will the government manage to steer its faith-based policies back on course, and the Church step forward once again with a new confidence for the times. Only then will the government truly recover a convincing moral direction and its badly needed compass.

e. **The God of Love and the Common Good** *Caritas in Veritate,* Benedict XVI, 2009, para. 36, http://www.vatican.va/holy_father/benedict _xvi/encyclicals/documents/hf_ben-xvi_enc_20090629_caritas-in-veritate_en .html (accessed 27 May 2011)

[Pope Benedict XVI's first encyclical of his pontificate was *Deus Caritas Est* (2005), in which he stressed that God is love, the theological concept that he considered key to his own primacy. In the encyclical letter *Caritas in Veritate,* he expanded on the theme, showing that God's love underpins human moral decisions on the economy. The letter also touches on the idea of the 'common good', which had informed Roman Catholic approaches to the economy and politics for several years.]

Economic activity cannot solve all social problems through the simple application of *commercial logic.* This needs to be *directed towards the pursuit of the common good,* for which the political community in particular must also take responsibility. Therefore, it must be borne in mind that grave imbalances are produced when economic action, conceived merely as an engine for wealth creation, is detached from political action, conceived as a means for pursuing justice through redistribution.

The Church has always held that economic action is not to be regarded as something opposed to society. In and of itself, the market is not, and must not become, the place where the strong subdue the weak. Society does not have to protect itself from the market, as if the development of the latter were *ipso facto* to entail the death of authentically human relations. Admittedly, the market can be a negative force, not because it is so by nature, but because a certain ideology can make it so. It must be remembered that the market does not exist in the pure state. It is shaped by the cultural configurations which define it and give it direction. Economy and finance, as instruments, can be used badly when those at the helm are motivated by purely selfish ends. Instruments that are good in themselves can thereby be transformed into harmful ones. But it is man's darkened reason that produces these consequences, not the instrument *per se*. Therefore it is not the instrument that must be called to account, but individuals, their moral conscience and their personal and social responsibility.

The Church's social doctrine holds that authentically human social relationships of friendship, solidarity and reciprocity can also be conducted within economic activity, and not only outside it or 'after' it. The economic sphere is neither ethically neutral, nor inherently inhuman and opposed to society. It is part and parcel of human activity and precisely because it is human, it must be structured and governed in an ethical manner.

The great challenge before us, accentuated by the problems of development in this global era and made even more urgent by the economic and financial crisis, is to demonstrate, in thinking and behaviour, not only that traditional principles of social ethics like transparency, honesty and responsibility cannot be ignored or attenuated, but also that in *commercial relationships* the *principle of gratuitousness* and the logic of gift as an expression of fraternity can and must *find their place within normal economic activity*. This is a human demand at the present time, but it is also demanded by economic logic. It is a demand both of charity and of truth.

f. **The Common Good in Britain**   Bishops' Conference of England and Wales: *Choosing the Common Good*, 2010, http://catholic-ew.org.uk/content/ download/6490/44766/file/20pp.pdf (accessed 27 May 2011)

[The concept of the common good in Roman Catholic social teaching was made explicit before the 1997 UK general election, as a guide to how Catholics might make moral choices in choosing candidates. It was reiterated in a new document, *Choosing the Common Good*, before the 2010 election.]

The Common Good

The Catholic Church has a large body of teaching, its 'social doctrine', which presents a rounded understanding of the human person and of the importance of solidarity. Both of these are contained in the concept of the common good.

The common good refers to what belongs to everyone by virtue of their common humanity. The simple definition of the common good is 'the sum total of social conditions which allow people, either as groups or as individuals, to reach their fulfilment more fully and more easily'. (*Catechism of the Catholic Church*, § 1906) Promoting the common good cannot be pursued by treating each individual separately and looking for the highest 'total benefit', in some kind of utilitarian addition. Because we are interdependent, the common good is more like a multiplication sum, where if any one number is zero then the total is always zero. If anyone is left out and deprived of what is essential, then the common good has been betrayed.

The common good is about how to live well together. It is the whole network of social conditions which enable human individuals and groups to flourish and live a full, genuinely human life. At the heart of the common good, solidarity acknowledges that all are responsible for all, not only as individuals but collectively at every level. The principle of the common good expands our understanding of who we are and opens up new sources of motivation. The fulfilment which the common good seeks to serve is the flourishing of humanity, expressed in the phrase 'integral human development'. Such development requires that people are rescued from every form of poverty, from hunger to illiteracy; it requires the opportunities for education, creating a vision of true partnership and solidarity between peoples; it calls for active participation in economic and political processes and it recognises that every human person is a spiritual being with instincts for love and truth and aspirations for happiness. Development must always include this spiritual growth, with openness to God.

Indeed this notion of development, understood in Christian terms, is the heart of the Christian social message. Every person is called to develop and fulfil themselves, for life itself is a vocation, a summons, which finds its final fulfilment only in the mystery of God. We are not created for futility. Integral human development is our vocation, and it points to the capacity in each person for responsible freedom, a freedom to be formed by truth and used for the service of truth and love.

V. MIGRATION

a. **Roman Catholic Church**   *Erga Migrantes Caritas Christi (The Love of Christ Towards Migrants)*, Pontifical Council for the Pastoral Care of Migrants and Itinerant Peoples, 2004, paras. 12–13

[The problems of mass migration on a global level had been the concern of the Vatican under Paul VI. The Pontifical Council's instruction of 2004 brought that pastoral initiative into the twenty-first century, as the issue intensified.

Migration is caused predominantly by economic hardship and political oppression. The receiving country has to determine whether the migrant is worthy of receiving asylum, thus becoming a refugee, or will be deported. The discernment process is traumatic and often leads to new injustices. The growing number of asylum seekers trying to relocate to wealthier, democratic societies has caused a backlash in the media from those who felt that immigration needed tighter control, and that many asylum seekers were simply economic migrants. The fact that asylum seekers, before refuge is granted, do not have the rights of a citizen means that they are vulnerable and often impoverished. Therefore the churches have a role in protecting them.]

Migration as Seen with the Eyes of Faith

12. In migrants the Church has always contemplated the image of Christ who said, 'I was a stranger and you made me welcome' (Matt. 25:35). Their condition is, therefore, a challenge to the faith and love of believers, who are called on to heal the evils caused by migration and discover the plan God pursues through it even when caused by obvious injustices. Migration brings together the manifold components of the human family and thus leads to the construction of an ever vaster and more varied society, almost a prolongation of that meeting of peoples and ethnic groups that, through the gift of the Holy Spirit at Pentecost, became ecclesial fraternity.

If, on the one hand, the suffering that goes with migration is neither more nor less than the birth-pangs of a new humanity, on the other the inequalities and disparities behind this suffering reveal the deep wounds that sin causes in the human family. They are thus an urgent appeal for true fraternity.

13. This vision leads us to approach migration in the light of those biblical events that mark the phases of humanity's arduous journey towards the birth of a people without discrimination or frontiers, depository of God's gift for all nations and open to man's eternal vocation. Faith perceives in it the journey of the Patriarchs, sustained by the promise as they moved towards the future homeland, and that of the

Hebrews, freed from slavery, as they crossed the Red Sea in the Exodus, that formed the People of the Covenant. Again, in a certain sense, faith finds in migration an exile, in which every goal reached in fact is relative. In migration faith discovers once more the universal message of the prophets, who denounce discrimination, oppression, deportation, dispersion and persecution as contrary to God's plan. At the same time they proclaim salvation for all, witnessing even in the chaotic events and contradictions of human history, that God continues to work out his plan of salvation until all things are brought together in Christ (cf. Eph. 1:10).

b. **Churches Together in Britain and Ireland**   David Deeks, *Asylum Principles—Statement for Churches Working on Asylum Issues*, Churches' Commission for Racial Justice, 2006 , section 1, http://www.ctbi.org.uk/pdf_view.php?id=21 (accessed 27 May 2011)

[See general introduction on migration under a.]

Core Principles

1.1 Christians believe that all people are created equal in dignity, made in the image of God. Therefore, we affirm respect for the worth of every human being regardless of nationality, ethnicity, culture, colour, sexual orientation, age, gender, disability, social status or religion and belief. We recognize that governments have a primary responsibility for their own citizens but basic human rights should not be denied to any persons coming to these islands on the grounds that they are not, or are not yet, fully accepted as citizens.

1.2 As Christians, we fully accept our obligations as citizens of the countries in which we live but we also recognize that our lives are a pilgrimage in which we have no abiding city and that our 'true citizenship' is in heaven. We therefore do not attribute absolute value to the rights and privileges of nationality and citizenship. We recognize that these, like other worldly goods, are given to us not solely for our personal enjoyment but for sharing with others when they are in need.

1.3 Christians affirm the obligation to offer hospitality to people whose lives have been dislocated—such as those seeking asylum and those seeking reunification with their families. All those who face discrimination should be treated with compassion and justice. People fleeing persecution have a special claim on us to help them make good their claim for asylum and to find safety, peace and wellbeing.

1.4 Christian belief in a personal God sets good relationships as the foundation of community cohesion. It follows that it is in the interest of wider society to reunite members of divided families wherever possible.

1.5 With the knowledge of scripture, history, and the Churches' own experience, Christians affirm that people moving from one part of the world to another contribute their gifts and valuable qualities such as courage and perseverance to the country where they come to live.

c. **United Methodist Church**   United Methodist Church: *Global Migration and the Quest for Justice*, 2008, http://calms.umc.org/2008/Text.aspx?mode =Petition&Number=410 (accessed 27 May 2011)
[See general introduction on migration under a.]

'Ways must be found to share more equitably the resources of the world.'

Social Principles, The United Methodist Church

The United Methodist Church has frequently addressed general and specific topics related to migration. The Social Principles affirm:

1) 'We commit ourselves as a Church to the achievement of a world community that is a fellowship of persons who honestly love one another. We pledge ourselves to seek the meaning of the gospel in all issues that divide people and threaten the growth of world community.' …

2) 'In order to provide basic needs such as food, clothing, shelter, education, health care and other necessities, ways must be found to share more equitably the resources of the world.' …

3) 'We advocate for the rights of all migrants and applaud their efforts toward responsibility self-organization and self-determination.' …

Human migration is as old as human history. Individuals, families, tribes, and nations have been on the move since the days of Abraham and Sarah and before. Throughout the centuries, political and economic factors, including wars; health and environmental challenges; and racism, xenophobia, and religious discrimination have at times uprooted people and at others lured them to new venues across continents and oceans as well as national and ethnic boundaries.

Today, migration is at once a critical international issue and a necessary option for millions of human beings. Some people seek to move; others have no alternatives. Contemporary migration involves the linked realities of abundance and poverty and racial/ethnic/religious identities and exclusion. The current global economic system reflects an expectation many people will live in poverty, or have their nations torn by conflict, so that others may live in abundance. That many people will resist poverty and war through migration is an ancient and modern fact of human existence. As a consequence, elaborate national and international systems of containment and classification based on national origin have been developed over the past quarter-century with regard to migrants.

Global migration as a factor in the quest for justice is of major concern to The United Methodist Church as a denomination that is global in its vision, mission, and ministries.

d. World Council of Churches   *The Changing Ecclesial Context: Impact of Migration on Living Together,* Public Statement of the World Council of Churches and Middle East Council of Churches, Public Hearing, Beirut, 14–16 April 2008, http://www.oikoumene.org/en/resources/documents/wcc-pro grammes/justice-diakonia-and-responsibility-for-creation/migration/the-chang ing-ecclesial-context-impact-of-migration-on-living-together.html (accessed 27 May 2011)
[See general introduction on migration under a.]

Migration is a fact of life. It is as much an instinct to survive as it is an inevitable consequence of globalisation. We can neither turn our backs on it, nor control it. It will have decisive consequences for the world as we know it and a massive impact on the church and the ecumenical movement both at the local, regional and global levels. We need not, however, react with hysteria and fear. Migration is as much a part of who we are as it is a part of the history that has shaped us.

However, if states continue to speak only of 'migration' and not 'migrants', then migrants will continue to be exploited as nothing more than cheap labour for factories or slave labour for construction sites. If populist politicians and media outlets continue to brand migrants and refugees as 'illegals', 'aliens', 'queue jumpers' and 'bogus' asylum seekers, then migrants will continue to suffer from the racist, discriminatory and xenophobic undercurrents in every society. If we as churches only see migrants as victims, then we undermine their strengths and their resilience. If source countries only consider emigration as a loss—a brain drain—then migrants will be discouraged from returning and the potential 'brain gain' will be lost ...

The church has a responsibility to ensure that public opinion is properly informed on the root causes of migration and the factors that force people to leave their homes. We must confront racism, discrimination and xenophobia wherever and whenever it manifests itself; in churches, in our communities and our nations.

Migrants are not commodities, illegal aliens or mere victims. They are human beings. Migrant rights are human rights. We must respect the human dignity of every migrant and give holistic consideration to their needs, their strengths and the economic, social and cultural contributions they make to society. Above all, we must stand in solidarity with migrants and migrant churches, accompany them and include them in the decision-making that effects and governs their lives.

Throughout this Hearing, participants were challenged by the complexities and sheer scale of migration, but they were heartened by the good will and common goals shared by Christian and Muslim leaders, and Lebanon's Islamic and Christian communities...

VI. DISABILITY

a. **The L'Arche Community**   The Charter of L'Arche, http://www.larche. org/charter-of-the-communities-of-l-arche.en-gb.43.3.content.htm (accessed 27 May 2011)

[L'Arche is well known as a model for a community inclusive of people with learning disabilities. It was started by Jean Vanier in 1964 in Northern France, but now there are communities in various countries and religious traditions.]

Fundamental Principles

1. Whatever their gifts or limitations, people are all bound together in a common humanity. Everyone is of unique and sacred value, and everyone has the same dignity and human rights. The fundamental rights of each person include the rights to life, to care, to a home, to education and to work. Also, since the deepest need of a human being is to love and to be loved, each person has a right to friendship, to communion and to a spiritual life.

2. If human beings are to develop their abilities and talents to the full, realising all their potential as individuals, they need an environment that fosters personal growth. They need to form relationships with others within families and communities. They need to live in an atmosphere of trust, security and mutual affection. They need to be valued, accepted and supported in real and warm relationships.

3. People with learning disabilities often possess qualities of welcome, wonderment, spontaneity and directness. They are able to touch hearts

and to call others to unity through their simplicity and vulnerability. In this way they are a living reminder to the wider world of the essential values of the heart without which knowledge, power and action lose their meaning and purpose.

4. Weakness and vulnerability in a person, far from being an obstacle to union with God, can foster it. It is often through weakness, recognised and accepted, that the liberating love of God is revealed.

5. In order to develop the inner freedom to which all people are called, and to grow in union with God, each person needs to have the opportunity of being rooted and nourished in a religious tradition.

The Communities: Communities of faith

i. L'Arche communities are communities of faith, rooted in prayer and trust in God. They seek to be guided by God and their weakest members, through whom God's presence is revealed. Each community member is encouraged to discover and deepen his or her spiritual life and live it according to his or her particular faith and tradition. Those who have no religious affiliation are also welcomed and respected in their freedom of conscience.

ii. Communities are either of one faith or inter-religious. Those which are Christian are either of one church or inter-denominational. Each community maintains links with the appropriate religious authorities and its members are integrated with local churches or other places of worship.

iii. Communities recognise that they have an ecumenical vocation and a mission to work for unity ...

b. **The work of Stanley Hauerwas**   Stanley Hauerwas, 'Timeful Friends: Living with the Handicapped', 2004, John Swinton, *Critical Reflections on Stanley Hauerwas' Theology of Disability*, 11–25; this excerpt 20 (Previously published in *Sanctify Them in the Truth: Holiness Exemplified*, 1999, 143–56).

[Prominent American theologian and ethicist Stanley Hauerwas has been an advocate for people with disabilities and has written on this subject since the 1970s. The major thesis of much of his work—that the Christian tradition has the resources to engage with important social issues and need not give way to secular perspectives—is in evidence in this excerpt. The question of whether people with disabilities should be means or ends is discarded in favour of a community approach, inspired by the work of Jean Vanier. The terms used ('mentally handicapped', 'retarded') might be uncomfortable for British readers, but elsewhere Hauerwas is careful to discuss the issue of labelling.]

... the purpose of the community for which we are created is nothing less than a friendship with one another. From such a perspective we can begin to appreciate how few resources the means/ends manner of think-ing provides for helping us understand the care of the mentally handicapped. Of course, we 'use' the mentally handicapped, but we are here to be of use to one another. The notion that any use we make of one another can only be justified if it is done voluntarily can now be seen as one of the peculiar sentimentalities of modernity that results in self-supervision all the more tyrannical since what we do is allegedly what we want to do. That the mentally handicapped are subject to care for their own good—a good they may not have chosen—is not an indication that such care is misguided, but rather requires that the good that such care is serving be properly named. After all, they (like us who are not retarded) exist to serve and to be served for our mutual upbuilding. As Christians we should not feel embarrassed to discover that the mentally handicapped among us help us better understand the narrative that constitutes the very purpose of our existence. That such is the case does not 'justify' their existence, but then their existence no more than our existence from a Christian perspective requires justification. We are free to help them just to the extent we no longer feel the necessity to justify their existence. The form such 'help' takes can only be discovered relative to the tasks of the community necessary to sustain the practices for the discovery and care of the goods held in common … Christians do not use the mentally handicapped as an affront to a world without purpose, but we should not be surprised that the Christian refusal to abandon the mentally handicapped to such a world will be seen as an affront.

We must confess as Christians, however, that our care of the mentally handicapped has been shaped more by the means/ends narrative than by that of Christ. As a result, in the name of care we too often subject the handicapped to therapies based on mechanistic presumptions that promise 'results' rather than community. That is why the alternative Vanier represents is so important. For L'Arche offers an imaginative portrayal of what a purposive community might look like in which the mentally handicapped serve and are served.

c. **Blindness and Faith** John Hull, *In the Beginning There was Darkness: A Blind Person's Conversations with the Bible*, 2001, 141–2, 147–8

[Disability theology analyses the ways in which faith is often communicated with the assumptions of an able-bodied world, in which disabled people are marginal. In this view, the Bible is written by seeing and hearing people for a seeing and hearing audience. However, John Hull, whose blindness came in adult life, explores Christian faith from the point of view of someone with visual

impairment. Whereas the biblical metaphor of blindness can often signify ignorance, here he discovers an instance where it stands for faith.]

Blindness as a model for faith

'Now faith is the assurance of things hoped for, the conviction of things
not seen' (Heb. 11.1). In a Bible mostly written with the assumptions of a
sighted world, it is refreshing to find a long, famous and central passage
which regards blindness as a model of faith. Certainly, blindness is not
actually mentioned in Hebrews 11, but then neither is sight mentioned in
many of the passages which take sight for granted. The point about this
chapter is not only that it does not take sight for granted; it also works on
the assumption that sight is at best irrelevant and at worst an impediment to faith.

The chapter begins with a ringing declaration. Faith has to do with
what is not seen. Since a blind person can see nothing, the whole of the
blind person's life is immediately oriented towards the life of faith ...

In a world where what is not seen is so often dominated, patronized,
by that which sees and is seen, it is wonderful to read that in the order of
creation the unseen things have priority over those which are seen (v. 3).
In the song of creation in Genesis 1, the evening had priority over the
morning in the synthesis of the day, and so here again we find that the
seen things depend upon and grow out of the unseen things. Indeed,
sight is very superficial. It is no more than surface deep, skin deep. Our
lives are based upon foundations which are not seen, and even our bodies
depend on functions and organs which cannot normally be seen ...

When it comes to loving God, we must remember that in God's
presence everyone is blind. The distinction between being sighted and
being blind disappears in the presence of God. This is something to
which sighted people as well as blind people can look forward. God, we
are told, 'dwells in unapproachable light, whom no one has ever seen, or
can see' (I Tim. 6:16). If the light is unapproachable, if it is impenetrable,
it might as well be darkness. There is darkness visible and there is
brightness invisible. In these images, the blind God of blind people and
the sighted God of sighted people are overcome, are transcended.

d. *Deaf Liberation Theology* Hannah Lewis, *Deaf Liberation Theology*,
2007, 82, 122–3, 131

[Hannah Lewis, founder of Deaf Ecumenical Clergy UK, examines the issue
of hearing deprived Christians using a liberation theology approach. She
distinguishes between 'deaf'—simply people who suffer hearing loss—and
'Deaf'—those who belong to a Deaf culture with its own sign language. It is
this cultural group that are marginalized, just as minority ethnic cultures are.

Lewis's concern in the following excerpts is how Deaf people can fully engage with the faith life of the church, its understanding of the Bible, and its liturgy.]

Sign language is a feature of the Deaf church in this country but it is largely used to translate the liturgy of the hearing church … and its hymns. Relatively few attempts are made to incorporate cultural aspects of sign language into services and teaching appears to remain at a very simplified level so I would argue that Deaf people are still constructed as being unable to fully engage with God's word. In the 'mainstream' church, sign language continues to be constructed as inferior to spoken language …

Presenting the Bible in [sign language] and Deaf cultural forms, whether via storytelling or dramatized retelling or '[sign language] hymns' or visual-media, inevitably involves a process of interpretation of the biblical text. At some point someone who can read the text and who can be trusted by Deaf people to transmit the meaning without too much distortion, preferably a Deaf person, is needed. However … once given the outlines of a text, Deaf people can take the stories and characters and teaching of the Bible and transmit them in a vivid and appropriate form to spread the word of God among the Deaf community …

However, there is still one major issue that needs to be discussed before we can claim that there is a Deaf Liberation hermeneutics, and that is the issue of the total absence of positive portrayals of d/Deaf people in the Bible, which makes it hard for us to find our place in the dialogue between the voices in the text and in the contemporary world …

The conclusion of all this seems to be that a Deaf Liberation hermeneutic is not only possible, but also desirable. We can engage in an imaginative dialogue with the people of the Bible and learn much about God's desire for liberation of the oppressed people of the world and the ways in which this desire has been acted out in the past and can be acted out in the future and can help us, as Deaf people, in our struggle for a more just world.

e. Disability and Hospitality *Spirituality and Hospitality: What the Church Can Learn by Welcoming Persons with Disabilities*, Reformed Church in America, 2008, http://www.rca.org/Page.aspx?pid=4994 (accessed 27 May 2011)

[Policies to end discrimination against people with disability, and to give them equal access, have been established in several nations. The churches had to ask whether their own theology and practice also needed revision.]

... How does one define 'persons with disabilities'? The very word 'disability' might suggest that the entire range of human experience can be neatly divided into two camps: the 'able-bodied' and the 'disabled.' Such divisions can give the appearance of making the world more manageable and understandable, but they can obscure other important truths. In reality, human beings are all differently-abled. We do not all have the same intelligence, athletic ability, flexibility, vision, or mobility. Many of these differences among us are evident to all. Other differences are hidden to almost everyone: differences of psychological makeup, emotional experience, or cognitive processing. We differ from each other in countless ways that evade simple categorization ...

These tendencies to objectify persons with disabilities may also appear in particularly problematic ways in the spiritual life of the Christian community. One characteristic problem is the tendency to associate disability with sin or uncleanness. Parents of children with mental illness may be tempted to blame themselves for their child's problems, and other onlookers may harbor the same suspicions. There is at times in our hearts an almost instinctive response to failure and loss—wondering what we have done to deserve such misfortune. Jesus' disciples, when confronted with a man born blind, assumed that someone must have sinned to cause this state of affairs (John 9:2), and yet Jesus rejected these assumptions, and demonstrated a very different perspective, which reveals that what passes for blindness is often real vision, and what passes for sight may conceal a deeper blindness. The church must say loudly, and believe heartily, that disability is not a divine punishment.

But this tendency to link disability and sin can take subtler forms as well. Those facing disability may be encouraged to pray for healing, and may be led, sometimes in subtle and indirect ways, to doubt their own faith if the prayed-for healing does not arrive. Indeed, the church's bold proclamation of the power of God to heal can have unintended consequences in the lives of persons with disabilities, as they find themselves forced to choose between either rejecting such proclamation as inadequate or rejecting their own faith as inadequate. A particularly subtle way of marginalizing persons with disabilities can take the form of excessive admiration. Sometimes, rather than being overtly marginalized and objectified, persons with disabilities are treated as 'super-spiritual' persons whose extraordinary courage and spiritual strength places them in a class by themselves. In other cases, parents of children who experience disability may be idealized for their incredible devotion. These expressions of respect may indeed be warranted, but these tendencies to idealize can also be another way in which the church creates boundaries that mark off persons with disabilities, inhibiting the capacity of the church to be a fully welcoming community for all persons who are sinners, saved by grace.

VII. DOMESTIC VIOLENCE AND CHILD ABUSE

a. **Methodist Church** *Domestic Violence and the Methodist Church—the Way Forward*, Methodist Conference Report, 2002, http://www.methodist. org.uk/index.cfm?fuseaction=opentogod.content&cmid=336 (accessed 27 May 2011)

[In the 2000s, the churches became painfully aware that domestic violence and the abuse of children were to be found among Christians as much as in the wider society. There needed to be a process of internal critique as well as a renewal of the churches' pastoral strategy towards the victims of domestic violence. This critique extended to theological interpretations that exacerbated the problem.]

... Almost three-quarters of ministers and lay workers surveyed (74%) felt that their approach to domestic violence had been influenced by their Christian beliefs. Some ministers interviewed felt that the Church was either out of touch on this issue or seen to be out of touch with the rest of society. Christian beliefs seemed to afford ministers little guidance on how to support families living with domestic violence. Even though many said that they were deeply concerned about the issue and would try to help families in this situation, the majority seemed confused and unsure. Many saw a conflict in the Church's thinking on marriage, endurance, redemption, forgiveness and violence. A few discussed justice and the importance of transformation in the context of violence and abuse. All the survivors interviewed said they stayed longer with abusive partners because they felt they had an extra responsibility to preserve their marriages ...

Although survivors had found individual colleagues who were very understanding and supportive, the Church as a whole was perceived to have dealt with the issue very poorly, wanting, as one respondent put it 'brush the violence under the carpet'. Perpetrators, especially partners of ministers, were not expected to do anything about the abuse. Christian forgiveness was mostly seen to mean continuing to welcome an abuser as a member of the Church while an ex partner was excluded from Church attendance by fear.

As the researchers commented 'In general, we were left with the conclusion that Christian beliefs had played an ambiguous role in survivors' journey to safety, in some ways helping but in other ways hindering their efforts to overcome the abuse.' ...

The research clearly indicated the need for the Church to develop a policy on Domestic Violence and to evolve effective strategies for assisting ministers, lay workers and congregations in helping those who come to the Church for support.

The research points to many practical and theological issues which need to be addressed as the church and individual Christians seek to move forward in this area. There are many implications around the theology of family life which have emerged as part of the study and these need to be addressed as part of the overall response of the Church ...

b. Church of England   The Archbishops' Council, *Responding to Domestic Abuse: Guidelines for those with Pastoral Responsibilities*, 2006, section 1.2, http://www.churchofengland.org/media/1163604/domesticabuse.pdf (accessed 27 May 2011)

[See introduction to a.]

Our theological approach

- Authentic Christian theology must proceed from our knowledge of God as love and as One who is known in relationship. This is summed up in the doctrine of the Trinity and the biblical idea of covenant.
- Corresponding to this is our understanding of human beings created in the divine image to live in relationships of love, respect and mutual self-giving. Intimate relationships have the potential to be channels of cherishing and building up.
- Tragically, the corruption of human nature which Christian theology names 'sin' means that the mutual dependence and shared vulnerability which are inseparable from intimacy can instead become the vehicle through which one person can inflict profound hurt and damage upon another.
- The pattern of living that is revealed through Jesus in his relationships with others entails that abuse of any kind is emphatically contrary to the will of God and an affront to human dignity. This entails a heavy responsibility upon the Church and its members to do everything possible to prevent or halt it.
- The good news of Christ promises God's redeeming presence and power in situations of pain and suffering. Through rejection of patterns of violence, and support of those who have been abused, the Church is called to be a vehicle of God's work of healing.

- The Church commends high ideals of love, care and faithfulness in marriage and all intimate relationships. As a body which is present at key moments when relationships are blessed publicly, it has a responsibility to offer authentic teaching and appropriate pastoral care.
- It is therefore particularly disturbing that not only has the Church failed at many points to protect the vulnerable and to address the processes that lead to domestic abuse, but has also (intentionally or unintentionally) reinforced abuse, failed to challenge abusers and intensified the suffering of survivors.
- Detailed examination reveals that this is a failure not only in practice but also in the assumptions and beliefs which inform practice. The Church has not always done justice to the truth about God and human beings that is revealed in the Christian Gospel, and its teaching has often contained sub-Christian elements which have distorted or denied that life-giving truth.
- We are conscious of the obligation of Christian theology to listen to the testimony of those who suffer in particular ways, and have sought throughout to give full weight to the perspectives and needs of those who have been subject to domestic abuse.
- The appendix on 'harmful theology' seeks to outline how wrong or misguided forms of Christian belief may aggravate the sufferings of those who are abused and stand in the way of effective preventative and remedial action. It also suggests how healthy and sensitive teaching in the Church may avoid these pitfalls and make a positive contribution to countering abuse.

c. **Child Abuse in the Churches**   Commission to Inquire into Child Abuse Report, Government of the Republic of Ireland, 2009, chapter 6, paras. 21–3, http://www.childabusecommission.com/rpt/pdfs/CICA-VOL4-12.PDF (accessed 27 May 2011)

[The Roman Catholic Church throughout the 1990s and 2000s was rocked by scandals concerning priests and religious orders in cases of the abuse of children in their care (occasionally cases surfaced in other denominations too). The Roman Catholic priesthood in the USA and the UK was particularly affected; so too was Ireland, from where the report quoted below comes. This covers the male religious orders. However, in the 1990s, the book and film *The Magdalene Sisters*, based on actual experiences, had uncovered the scandal of women in Ireland accused of sexual impropriety and forced into long-term slave labour in laundries run by female religious orders.]

Conclusions

21. ... The documents revealed that sexual abusers were often long-term offenders who repeatedly abused children wherever they were working. Contrary to the Congregations' claims that the recidivist nature of sexual offending was not understood, it is clear from the documented cases that they were aware of the propensity for abusers to re-abuse. The risk, however, was seen by the Congregations in terms of the potential for scandal and bad publicity should the abuse be disclosed. The danger to children was not taken into account.

22. ... Men who were discovered to be sexual abusers were allowed to take dispensation rather than incur the opprobrium of dismissal from the Order. There was evidence that such men took up teaching positions sometimes within days of receiving dispensations because of serious allegations or admissions of sexual abuse. The safety of children in general was not a consideration.

23. Sexual abuse was known to religious authorities to be a persistent problem in male religious organisations throughout the relevant period. Nevertheless, each instance of sexual abuse was treated in isolation and in secrecy by the authorities and there was no attempt to address the underlying systemic nature of the problem. There were no protocols or guidelines put in place that would have protected children from predatory behaviour. The management did not listen to or believe children when they complained of the activities of some of the men who had responsibility for their care. At best, the abusers were moved, but nothing was done about the harm done to the child. At worst, the child was blamed and seen as corrupted by the sexual activity, and was punished severely.

VIII. ADDICTION

a. Pastoral Care   Kenneth Leech, *Drugs and Pastoral Care*, 1998, 99–100

[Kenneth Leech's pastoral ministry in East London inevitably brought him into contact with the growing problem of narcotic addiction. Here he reflects on some of the theological issues.]

The Christian ministry in the field of drug use and addiction raises many of the key theological ideas about sin, grace, human will, the world, and the Kingdom of God, which divide Christians, and it also offers a possible creative site for working through them ecumenically in co-operative action and praxis-based reflection. There is not space here to engage in a detailed theological examination of all these themes, but several of them are worth noting.

First, there is the concept of addiction and its relationship with humanity and human sin. Although addiction is conventionally seen in terms of sickness, there has been a trend recently in some circles to see addiction as a form or manifestation of original sin ... The context in which addiction arises is often ignored, so that the focus comes to be exclusively on personal sin, and on the addict as one trapped within the addictive prison. There is a tendency to equate victim and perpetrator. But, leaving aside whether sin and addiction can be equated, sin cannot be reduced to a single cause ...

Secondly, what kind of God do we believe in? The view of God which is found in some religious groups working with addiction issues is often that of a dictator and controller. God can easily be portrayed as an alternative, albeit better, form of addiction. Christians need to be careful that we do not offer a diminished and trivialised understanding of God as a response to drugs. When Marx called religion an opiate, he was making an important observation—and a warning.

Thirdly, it is important to stress that there is no specific 'ministry to drug users'. The use of drugs raises specific questions and problems, but Christian ministry is to all people. The modern habit of labelling people (client, addict, alcoholic, and so on) does not fit well with the Christian view of what it is to be human or with the doctrine of the Body of Christ in which all are equal. Nevertheless, the field of drugs can help to illuminate neglected areas of ministry and help us towards a clearer understanding.

Finally, there is a central place for silence, darkness and the way of 'unknowing'. Pastoral ministry in the drug field calls for a profound spiritual rootedness in God, and for those essentially priestly tasks of Eucharistic sacrifice and adoration, intercession, and solidarity in Christ through the sharing of silence and darkness.

b. Pastoral Responses Bucky Dann, *Addiction: Pastoral Responses*, 2002, 113–14

[Bucky Dann is a Christian drug counsellor. Here he points out the arbitrary nature of legislation on drugs, and argues for Christians to place a counter-institutional emphasis on a morality beyond legislation. He also refers to the well known and influential Alcoholics Anonymous 'twelve step programme', in which addicts recognize a higher power, not yet defined in any religious terms. This can lead to Christian faith.]

Constructed in an ongoing manner by the operation of social forces, cultural morality reflects institutional aims, including those of institutionalized religion, as those institutions align themselves. That is what accounts for their ad hoc appearance. George cannot smoke marijuana or use cocaine, but he can smoke cigarettes and get drunk. Illegal drugs are made legal with a properly authorized piece of paper. The money spent on the enforcement of drug laws does little to prevent illegal drug use.

This is not morality of a higher order. The purpose is about management of a population and is why, in modern societies, moral vision is subsumed by regulation. Efficacy lies in the success of imposing orderliness, as determined by institutional goals.

Jesus turns this order around. In a statement very pertinent to modern practices, Jesus says the law is subsumed by love (Matt. 22:37–40). The law, from his perspective, is not about regulation or institutional agendas; it is about fulfilling the purposes for which humans were created. That is the vision. For Christians, the foundation of morality is love, not control and management.

In developing a moral understanding for the use of drugs, love is where one should begin. That may sound trite, but it's amazing how often the Christian community fails to embark from that place ...

When talking with clients about how to recognize a higher power that can offer true empowerment, I always emphasize that a higher power accepts unconditionally ... Many addicts, and the unchurched in general, often have a different experience in church. They feel out of place, in part because of their own insecurity and guilt ... They will never feel at home, and healing cannot begin until they bring their darkest secrets before God and we tell them that they belong. And those secrets may include their continuing drug use or returning to drug use, even after bringing themselves to God. Recovery is a process, and love accepts it as such. All of us, after all, are on that long and winding road.

IX. CLIMATE CHANGE

a. **Reformed Church in America** Commission on Christian Action, *Climate Change Update*, 2000, Conclusion, http://www.rca.org/Page.aspx? pid=1616 (accessed 27 May 2011)

[The concern about climate change and global warming in the early twenty-first century and the injustice of wealthy nations using a large percentage of the world's resources is addressed in this statement by the Reformed Church in America.]

Climate Change and Christian Witness

Christians understand the threat of global climate change in the context of covenant. God has established a covenant 'with every living creature' (Genesis 9:10ff.) and with the earth itself (Genesis 9:13). Humankind has been given a special place in this covenant relation. We are not merely one species among many but a species to whom God has given a unique and important responsibility. We are placed in the garden of creation 'to till it and to keep it.' God has given us dominion over creation, not to do with it as we please but, in the words of Old Testament scholar Walter Brueggemann, 'for its profit, well-being, and enhancement ... to see to it that the creation becomes fully the creation willed by God.' [*Genesis*. Atlanta: John Knox Press, 1982, pp. 32–3]

This means, among other things, that our relationship with God, with our fellow human beings and with the rest of creation are all of a piece. A break in any one part of the covenant relationship affects the others. We cannot love God and hate our neighbor. Neither can we love God and our neighbors while we degrade creation.

Our response to the threat of global climate change is a matter of Christian witness. We confess that in Jesus Christ God entered creation in order to heal and restore the relationships broken by human sinfulness. The early Christians sang of Jesus Christ as the one in whom, through whom, and for whom all things were created and the one through whom God was pleased to reconcile to himself all things, whether on earth or in heaven (Col. 1: 15–20). This confession of a 'cosmic Christ' has important implications for the church's ministry. The church is called to bear witness to the Christ who reconciles and restores *all creation*. 'The church is not an elite body, separated from a doomed world,' writes New Testament scholar, J. Christiaan Beker, 'but a community placed in the midst of the cosmic community of creation. Its task is not merely to win souls but to bear the burdens of a creation, to which it not only belongs but to which it must also bear witness.' [*Paul the Apostle: The Triumph of God in Life and Thought*. Philadelphia: Fortress Press, 1980]

Dealing with the threat of climate change will require changes in technology, in public policy, and in our ways of thinking and living. We should not expect that it will be easy, and we should try to find ways in which the burdens of change are shared. But the longer we wait to deal with global warming, the more harm will occur and the greater will be the human, environmental, and economic costs for our children and grandchildren.

b. World Council of Churches   Dr Jesse Mugambi, *Climate Justice for All*, WCC, 2006, http://www.oikoumene.org/en/resources/documents/wcc-programmes/justice-diakonia-and-responsibility-for-creation/climate-change-water/climate-justice-for-all.html (accessed 27 May 2011)

[The World Council of Churches continues to play its role as the voice of the Christian churches on moral and political questions with a global impact.]

As the World Council of Churches, we issue a life-affirming call to delegates ...:

1. listen to the scientists and the cry of the Earth and address the reality of climate change with the extreme urgency that it demands;
2. governments of the rich industrialised nations must keep the promise that they made in the UN Framework Convention on Climate Change. The world is rapidly approaching the point of 'dangerous anthropogenic interference with the climate system.' The rich nations bear the primary responsibility for causing climate change and must adopt strategies to drastically reduce their emissions.
3. the Kyoto Protocol must be fully implemented by all those who ratified it and industrialised nations that did not ratify must meet targets at least as strict as those included in the Protocol. The emissions of some industrialised countries have risen rather than fallen since the 1990 baseline year. This means even greater reductions are required than the Kyoto Protocol targets and reinforces the urgency that actual reductions start now. We dare not wait.
4. the rich industrialised nations use far more than their fair share of the atmospheric global commons. They must pay that ecological debt to other peoples by fully compensating them for the costs of adaptation to climate change.
5. drastic emission reductions by the rich are required to ensure that the legitimate development needs of the world's poor can be met.
6. all countries must agree to and participate in a climate policy framework for post-2012 that ensures equitable development for all while maintaining greenhouse gas concentrations within limits that keep a warming of the global mean temperature to less than 2 degrees Celsius from pre-industrial levels.

The World Council of Churches believes that the whole Earth community deserves to benefit from the bounties of creation. Equitable development for all is possible while maintaining the ecological integrity of the biosphere. Faith communities are addressing climate change because it is a spiritual and ethical issue of justice, equity, solidarity, sufficiency and sustainability. The situation is critical. We must all act now. We pray that you will demonstrate leadership in responding to the cry of the Earth.

c. **Water Resources** Ninth Assembly of the World Council of Churches, Porto Alegre, Brazil, 14–23 February 2006, http://www.oikoumene.org/en/ resources/documents/wcc-commissions/international-affairs/human-rights-and -impunity/statement-on-water-for-life.html (accessed 27 May 2011)

[This statement reflects a growing awareness that, with environmental change, the world's water resources were in need of careful management.]

Water is a symbol of life. The Bible affirms water as the cradle of life, an expression of God's grace in perpetuity for the whole of creation (Gen. 2:5ff). It is a basic condition for all life on Earth (Gen. 1:2ff.) and is to be preserved and shared for the benefit of all creatures and the wider creation. Water is the source of health and well-being and requires responsible action from us human beings, as partners and priests of Creation (Rom. 8:19ff., Rev. 22). As churches, we are called to participate in the mission of God to bring about a new creation where life in abundance is assured to all (John 10:10; Amos 5:24). It is therefore right to speak out and to act when the life-giving water is pervasively and systematically under threat.

Access to fresh water supplies is becoming an urgent matter across the planet. The survival of 1.2 billion people is currently in jeopardy due to lack of adequate water and sanitation. Unequal access to water causes conflicts between and among people, communities, regions and nations. Biodiversity is also threatened by the depletion and pollution of fresh water resources or through impacts of large dams, large scale mining and hot cultures (irrigation) whose construction often involves the forced displacement of people and disruption of the ecosystem. The integrity and balance of the ecosystem is crucial for the access to water. Forests build an indispensable part in the ecosystem of water and must be protected. The crisis is aggravated by climate change and further deepened by strong economic interests. Water is increasingly treated as a commercial good, subject to market conditions.

Scarcity of water is also a growing source of conflict. Agreements concerning international watercourses and river basins need to be more concrete, setting out measures to enforce treaties made and incorporating detailed conflict resolution mechanisms in case disputes erupt.

Both locally and internationally there are positive and creative responses to raise the profile of Christian witness to water issues ...

It is essential for churches and Christian agencies to work together and to seek cooperation with other partners, including other faith traditions and NGOs, and particularly those organizations that work with vulnerable and marginalized populations who hold similar ethical convictions. It is necessary to engage in debate and action on water policies, including dialogue with governments and multilateral or corporate institutions. This is essential to promote the significance of the right to water and to point to alternative ways of living, which are more respectful of ecological processes and more sustainable in the longer term.

X. TENSION BETWEEN THE 'WEST'
AND THE 'MIDDLE EAST'

a. **Christian Zionism**   John Hubers, *Christian Zionism: A Historical Analysis and Critique*, Reformed Church in America, 2004, http://images.rca.org/docs/synod/ChristianZionism.pdf (accessed 27 May 2011)

[American Christian evangelical interpretations of the Bible have often resulted in strong support for Israel against its neighbours. It is felt that the success of Israel is part of God's plan and signals apocalyptic events. However, this does not help moves towards peace in the Middle East. The following argument from the Reformed Church in America subjects this viewpoint to a critical analysis.]

Concluding Observations

Christian Zionism is marked by confident assertions that leave little room for debate. You are either with them or against God. 'The Bible says' or 'God says' often mark statements that are speculative in nature, based on an interpretative apocalyptic scheme that, even when John Darby conceived it in the nineteenth century, was challenged as a questionable deviation from traditional Christian teaching. This has led many sincere Christians, who are eager to do what God says, to follow the lead of Christian Zionists in giving *uncritical* support to the state of Israel, though they may not understand or accept the theology that undergirds Christian Zionist teaching.

This is *not* to say that Christians should not support the state of Israel. Indeed we should. Israel is a legitimate nation-state, whose citizens have the right to live in peace with their neighbors within recognized and agreed-upon boundaries. In no way should what is written here be taken as an attempt to de-legitimize the Israeli state. Rather, it is to question the reason *why* Christian Zionists say we should give the Israeli government *unqualified* support even in its most expansionist mode. Christian Zionists insist that unqualified support for the modern state of Israel is a sacred duty enjoined by divine decree. We challenge this on several grounds, beginning with what we have noted about the Christian Zionist misreading of God's purpose in Christ.

We also challenge Christian Zionist teaching because of what it means in terms of denying justice to the Palestinian people. Thoughtful Israelis and Palestinians are working hard to find some way out of the conflict, searching for a compromise peace plan that will allow both sides to live with dignity and peace in their own land. Christian Zionists in their zeal to promote an 'all or nothing' vision of the 'Promised Land' have done their best to block these negotiations.

This, in the end, is where Christian Zionist teaching deviates most noticeably from the core message of the gospel. Jesus, picking up seminal themes from the Hebrew scriptures, preached and lived a message of reconciliation: reconciliation between God and his rebellious human family and reconciliation between the diverse members within that family. In situations of great conflict, such as we are witnessing in Israel/Palestine, we, as God's people, must put ourselves in a position to do our best to encourage reconciliation. We must pray, teach, and work for a peace that reflects God's overriding concern for justice. This is the most important prophetic word for Israel and the Palestinians, just as it is for anyone in any land: God desires justice. To do the work of God in Israel and the Occupied Palestinian Territories today is to stand with those who are seeking justice and working for reconciliation. The Bible in its entirety leaves no room for doubt on this matter.

b. **The 'War against Terror'** *Thinking Theologically about Security: Following Christ in an Age of Terror*, Reformed Church in America, General Synod, June 2005, paras. 1–3, http://images.rca.org/docs/synod/ TheologicalSecurity.pdf (accessed 27 May 2011)

[The 'war against terror' followed the bombing of the World Trade Center in New York on September 11, 2001, and led to UN campaigns in Afghanistan and American–British action in Iraq. Security measures were implemented in an atmosphere that often allowed no critical appraisal and reasonable dialogue. Against this, the Reformed Church in America in 2005 offered a theological analysis.]

1. *God, Not 'Security', Is Named All-in-All*

Security is a basic human need; it is not the greatest good, and certainly not our God.

Freed by Christ, believers will not bow down before security as if it were a merciful idol. As Christians, we will not celebrate an agenda that holds up security as the highest goal.

2. *Inclusive Security*

A Christian understanding of security recognizes that Jesus Christ is for the entire world. God wants security for Nineveh and Jerusalem. God wants security for Baghdad and New York, Palestine and Israel. Security grows when nations talk with one another and new voices are included in the conversations, rather than exhibiting a 'go it alone' attitude. Jesus Christ came as a physician for all who needed one, that all the world might be 'healthy.' He did not differentiate by race, gender, age, nationality, or ethnicity. God has secured a place for all people within God's love and care. A Christian approach to security has to be global in nature. In a world quite literally connected economically, environmentally, militarily, and technologically, security must be understood globally. There can be no 'homeland security' unless there is concern for the security of all ...

3. *Holistic Security*

A Christian approach to security is holistic. It looks at all the ways that security is denied around the globe. Jesus addressed the security concerns of hunger, poverty, exploitation, racism, unjust laws, and disease, as well as promising deliverance from guilt, sin, and fear of death. Security needs to be sought in every realm of every society for all people. Where there is hunger, security will come when a plan is created for equitable distribution of food. Where there is strife, security will come when a plan is carried out to recognize 'the enemy' as one's brother or sister. Where people do not know the security of Christ's peace, it will come about when the good news is proclaimed ...

c. **The Amman Call for Peace in Israel and Palestine**   *The Amman Call*, statement issued at WCC International Peace Conference *Churches together for Peace and Justice in the Middle East*, Amman, Jordan, 18–20 June 2007, http://www.oikoumene.org/en/resources/documents/wcc-programmes/public -witness-addressing-power-affirming-peace/middle-east-peace/the-amman- call.html (accessed 27 May 2011)

[This World Council of Churches statement urges peace between Israel and Palestine as the key factor to stability in the South West Asian region as a whole. This included a critique of the Israeli policy of occupying and settling the Palestinian territories.]

Amman imperatives:

1. Almost sixty years have passed since the Christian churches first spoke with one voice about Arab–Israeli peace. For the last forty years the Christian churches have called for an end to the Israeli occupation of Palestine. In the very place where Jesus Christ walked upon the earth, walls now separate families and the children of God—Christian, Muslim and Jew—are imprisoned in a deepening cycle of violence, humiliation and despair. The Palestinian Christians from Gaza to Jerusalem and to Nazareth, have called out to their brothers and sisters in Christ with this urgent plea: 'Enough is enough. No more words without deeds. It is time for action.'

2. We welcome the timely and prophetic statement of the Heads of Churches in Jerusalem. We affirm that 'the Churches are part of the conflict, because the Churches cannot remain silent while there is still suffering. The role of the Churches is to heal and to bring all sides to reconciliation.' Our belief in God reminds us 'that all God's children of all religions and political parties are to be respected.' We assure the Churches of Palestine and Israel of our prayers, collaboration and resources.

3. Thus, in Amman, Jordan 18–20 June 2007, days that have witnessed a deepening of the crisis in the occupied Palestinian territories, and also includes the United Nations World Refugee Day, we representatives of Christian churches and church-related organizations from every corner of the earth, affirm the decision of the Central Committee of the World Council of Churches and launch the 'Palestine Israel Ecumenical Forum' as an instrument to *catalyze and co-ordinate new and existing church advocacy for peace, aimed at ending the illegal occupation in accordance with UN resolutions, and demonstrate its commitment to inter-religious action for peace and justice that serves all the peoples of the region.'*

4. This action has been taken in response to three fundamental imperatives that call us to action:

- The ethical and theological imperative for a Just Peace
- The ecumenical imperative for unity in action
- The Gospel imperative for costly solidarity ...

d. Torture   George Hunsinger, 'Torture is the Ticking Time Bomb: Why the Necessity Defense Fails', 2008, George Hunsinger, *Torture is a Moral Issue: Christians, Jews, Muslims, and People of Conscience Speak Out*, 51–72; this excerpt, 68–9

[Revelations that torture had been used—by the US military on Muslim detainees suspected of implication in terrorism—inspired research by George Hunsinger of

Princeton and led him to found the National Religious Campaign against Torture. He co-ordinated a cross-religious response to the issue. In this chapter, he shows that torture does not achieve what it purports to, i.e. gain essential security information, and can only be regarded as out-and-out sadism.]

For something to become an absolute end in itself means that it has usurped a status that does not belong to it. The place belonging to God and God alone can be only seized by the human creature in the form of a monstrous caricature. The power of love is replaced by loveless power, compassion for the weak by sadistic cruelty, fair treatment by demonic subjugation, respect for life by the meanest contempt. Demonic torture is essentially destructive in its brutal self-elevation and self-justification. It proceeds at the expense of all legitimate obligations and norms. Its needs, its pleasures, and its purposes are carried out by shattering the essential humanity of another.

When Christians appeal to the image of God in their arguments against torture, they are not, properly speaking, merely adding a religious patina to the concept of human dignity. They are pointing to the ultimate meaning of human life. From Bonhoeffer through Barth to recent Catholic theology, the doctrine of the imago Dei has been reconceived in terms of relationality instead of the traditional rationality. It is human relationality as such that stands in analogy to the Holy Trinity, and therefore to the ultimacy of community. For the Trinity is itself a holy communion of love and freedom, joy and peace. Human creatures receive the vocation and the gift of living with God and one another on these terms.

When torture is conducted as an end in itself, and is therefore become demonic—when the purpose of power is power, and the purpose of cruelty is cruelty, when torture's purpose is tyrannical subjugation and sadistic degradation—then the divinely given meaning of life is unspeakably distorted and destroyed. The relation of the torturer to the tortured, and of the tortured to the torturer, makes a travesty of the most basic relations given by heaven to earth. In so degrading the human being and human community, torture blasphemes against God, neighbor, and self.

XI. MISSION IN A MULTI-FAITH SOCIETY

a. **Dominus Iesus** *Dominus Iesus* ('On the Unicity and Salvific Universality of Jesus Christ and the Church'), Congregation for the Doctrine of the Faith, 2000, para. 4, http://www.vatican.va/roman_curia/congregations/cfaith/documents/rc_con_cfaith_doc_20000806_dominus-iesus_en.html (accessed 27 May 2011)

[In *Dominus Iesus*, Cardinal Joseph Ratzinger, the future Pope Benedict XVI, reiterated the teaching that salvation was possible outside the Catholic Church. However, he disappointed ecumenists by also confirming the Catholic position that non-Catholic denominations and other religions were deficient in their theological understanding. In this excerpt, he argues against a missionary approach which plays down the truths of Catholic Christianity in the interests of accommodation to other worldviews and religious traditions.]

The Church's constant missionary proclamation is endangered today by relativistic theories which seek to justify religious pluralism, not only *de facto* but also *de iure (or in principle)*. As a consequence, it is held that certain truths have been superseded; for example, the definitive and complete character of the revelation of Jesus Christ, the nature of Christian faith as compared with that of belief in other religions, the inspired nature of the books of Sacred Scripture, the personal unity between the Eternal Word and Jesus of Nazareth, the unity of the economy of the Incarnate Word and the Holy Spirit, the unicity and salvific universality of the mystery of Jesus Christ, the universal salvific mediation of the Church, the inseparability—while recognizing the distinction—of the kingdom of God, the kingdom of Christ, and the Church, and the subsistence of the one Church of Christ in the Catholic Church.

The roots of these problems are to be found in certain presuppositions of both a philosophical and theological nature, which hinder the understanding and acceptance of the revealed truth. Some of these can be mentioned: the conviction of the elusiveness and inexpressibility of divine truth, even by Christian revelation; relativistic attitudes toward truth itself, according to which what is true for some would not be true for others; the radical opposition posited between the logical mentality of the West and the symbolic mentality of the East; the subjectivism which, by regarding reason as the only source of knowledge, becomes incapable of raising its 'gaze to the heights, not daring to rise to the truth of being' [*Fides et ratio* (1999), 5–88]; the difficulty in understanding and accepting the presence of definitive and eschatological events in history; the metaphysical emptying of the historical incarnation of the Eternal Logos, reduced to a mere appearing of God in history; the eclecticism of those who, in theological research, uncritically absorb ideas from a variety of philosophical and theological contexts without regard for consistency, systematic connection, or compatibility with Christian truth; finally, the tendency to read and to interpret Sacred Scripture outside the Tradition and Magisterium of the Church ...

b. **Presence and Engagement**   John Austin, *Presence and Engagement: The Churches' Task in a Multi Faith Society*, Archbishops' Council, 2005, paras. 34–6, http://www.churchofengland.org/media/36607/presence.pdf (accessed 27 May 2011)

[Modern nations that were once made up of a majority of Christians are now multi-faith societies. The delicate balance between witnessing one's own beliefs and practices while respecting those of others, and entering into dialogue with them, is the concern of this Church of England document.]

34. The increasing use of 'inter Faith' within the Church as a generic term for almost anything related to the 'Faith sector', can also be problematic. It can fail to be clear for example about means and ends and to carry the implication that primary interest lies in relating to 'other Faith' communities as an end in itself. In turn this can lead to the perception that this is a matter for experts and specialists in inter Faith or worse to an antagonism based on a sense that 'they' are considered to be more important than 'we' are.

35. For these reasons we have chosen to use the language of 'Presence' and 'Engagement', considering it to be more appropriate for these purposes than the language of 'inter Faith'. The phrase carries a depth of rooted Christian meaning and resonance: 'presence' with its under-tones of Christ's real presence with us, incarnationally and eucharisti-cally; and 'engagement' with its hints of close encounter between human beings and with God—encounter which can be both loving and conflic-tual. The phrase can include 'dialogue' without excluding witness and evangelism; it speaks clearly of the primary purpose of the local church and it speaks of individuals as well as of communities. Of course multi Faith contexts are only one of the whole range of local contexts, and 'presence and engagement' is a phrase relevant to all. But we have used it here particularly to emphasise the perspective of the local Church in multi Faith contexts.

36. We have chosen this perspective for a number of reasons:

- First, because we believe that the local church in a multi Faith context has very much to offer to the world, locally and nationally from its now extensive experience.
- Secondly, because it is at the local level that the stable foundations of a peaceful society of Faiths will be constructed.
- Thirdly, because the multi Faith context is now the real context in which a substantial and increasing number of parishes and proportion of the population actually live.

- Fourthly, because there are major implications for those parishes for which this is not their context.
- Fifthly, because there are now real risks that the Church will retreat from maintaining its presence in these contexts under the multiple pressures of reduced resourcing, a loss of an inclusive parish perspective in favour of a membership approach; and a retreat from true engagement with the other at least from the perspective of presence in the midst.
- Finally, because the task of the local church is to reflect in the daily life of the people in streets and houses, the offices and shops, the schools and pubs, the love of God for all through the life, death and resurrection of Jesus Christ—and no less amongst people of other Faiths than amongst anyone else.

c. **Faith Schools** *Faith in the System: the role of schools with a religious character in English education and society*, Department for Children, Schools and Families (UK), 2007, 1

[The assumption that faith schools divide communities is tackled in this government report, which has the backing of all the religions providing faith schools in Britain: Christian; Muslim; Jewish; Sikh; Hindu. The report endorses the contribution of faith schools to society. Although the report concerns British schools, this is a debate which is taking place in several countries.]

The Government and the providers of publicly funded schools with a religious character have come together to set out in this document our shared understanding of the contribution these schools (popularly known as faith schools) make to school-based education and to the wider school system and society in England.

We are taking the opportunity to highlight the very positive contribution which schools with a religious character make as valuable, engaged partners in the school system and in their local communities and beyond. At the same time, we want to dispel some of the common myths and misunderstandings around faith schools and to build a basis for greater understanding and dialogue within society.

The Government and faith school providers believe that **all** schools—whether they have a religious character or not—play a key role in providing a safe and harmonious environment for all in our society, thereby fostering understanding, integration and cohesion. We set out here our shared commitment to this endeavour and the principles that continue to underlie our joint vision and understanding of the contribution faith communities and their schools make to educating young people in England, to nurturing young people in their faith and to promoting community cohesion.

The faith school providers who sponsor schools with a religious character often also have a particular role in helping to meet the need of those people in their faith communities who would be otherwise hard to reach, thus enabling them to integrate into society. In addition, some faith school providers also have a mission to help provide education for the wider community and especially those who have difficulty in achieving their potential in education. The Government and the faith school providers believe that both missions are equally valid in offering a choice of high quality school provision to parents and their children.

The faith school providers wish to draw attention to their shared interests and overlapping values as a basis for greater mutual understanding and respect between them, while also remaining true to the teaching of their faiths and respecting the dignity of all faiths.

d. Christian–Muslim Relations   Patrick Sookhdeo, *The Challenge of Islam to the Church and its Mission*, 2009, 10, 12, 58

[The events of '9/11' (the destruction of the World Trade Center in New York, September 11th, 2001) have, as Patrick Sookhdeo acknowledges here, brought into focus the Christian–Muslim relationship. As a former Muslim who has embraced the Christian faith, he writes about Islam in a forthright and uncompromising manner. While sympathetic to Muslims as people, he takes a conservative Christian theological stance in between the two faiths and expressing disquiet about on the on the Christian Church, in emphasizing the differences their would views, and in impact which Islam is having particularly the Church in the Islamic world itself.]

The tragic events of September 11, 2001 spawned a huge interest in Islam. In the seven years since then Islam has become a frequent topic of debate and analysis in Western media, society and Church. Perhaps it could be said that we have never had so much information in so many areas on Islam and Muslims. Added to this are factors such as the growth of Muslim minorities in the West, the 'war on terrorism' (which so far has been largely a war on Islamic terrorism), the American-led incursions into Afghanistan and Iraq, the reactions of the Muslim community worldwide, Iran's proposed nuclear program, and the international Muslim reaction against publication of cartoons of Muhammad, the prophet of Islam. All these issues have brought Islam to center stage and are forcing a radical re-think of Western opinion on the nature of Islam ...

Through engagement with Muslims, through inter-religious dialogue, through support for Islamic causes and interests, many Christians of all kinds now seem to believe that they must help to rehabilitate Islam and establish it in the public domain. Together with secular politicians, Christians are emerging as the defender, protector and unifier of Islam ...

Islam should therefore not be viewed as a brother monotheistic faith like Judaism with which Christians have a special relationship. The idea of three sibling 'Abrahamic' faiths is an Islamic concept, not a Christian one. Rather Islam should be viewed in the same bracket as Christian heresies, Jehovah's Witnesses or Mormons ... To accept the Muslims' concept of three 'Abrahamic' faiths is effectively to legitimize Muhammad's prophethood as the last in the line of Abrahamic prophets. It is also to agree with the Islamic teaching on replacement–Judaism was replaced by Christianity which was in turn replaced by Islam. The ultimate logic of this would be for all Christians to convert to Islam.

XII. MISSION IN A SECULAR SOCIETY

a. *A Church without Walls*   *A Church without Walls*, Report of the Special Commission anent Review and Reform of the General Assembly of the Church of Scotland, 2001, section 1.3

[The churches in Britain in the 2000s recognized the need to transform the legalistic, committee-based structures into ones which enable engagement with the community in general, encouraging and building up the nascent faith that can be found there. The structure of the churches needed to be moulded to the missionary task.]

We celebrate the creative work with children to build church from the crèche up, and the range of youth initiatives from the Youth Assembly to partnerships with other youth agencies. If the church will permit innovation and work at integration, the face of the church would be different in ten years' time. We see the potential of the Third Agers (over 50's), who have much to offer the church locally, nationally and overseas.

We celebrate new patterns of community work in Urban and Rural Priority Areas. We see committed church members working alongside people in the community, both working to God's agenda. They are less anxious about numbers and less guilty about the nominal or lapsed members who once made vows, but have slipped their moorings.

When the church seeks first the Kingdom of God and is less concerned about her own survival, God is at work.

We celebrate the increasing shift from membership to discipleship. The *Alpha* courses, Emmaus Courses and locally devised schemes are drawing members into a renewed faith in Christ. For many the way to faith is through sharing in adventurous projects at home and overseas. Being part of the Church in action leads to a deeper desire to be a disciple of Christ. People want to belong to a God who does not want children to die because of international debt, or to see homeless people go hungry and cold.

We celebrate the shift from running a congregation to building communities of faith in Christ. The Cell Church movement has given some the handle on building church relationally and organically. The Celtic renaissance has offered some a new lens for seeing church and mission in our culture: nurturing the heart for God, offering a home to the stranger and becoming a hub for mission to resource people in daily life.

We celebrate new patterns of leadership. New elders are being given a new vision for the role. Readers are being trained and deployed to congregations. Ministry teams are operating well and creatively.

We celebrate the openness to consider new structures and ways of working. On all sides we have found an openness to change. The test lies in our readiness to explore specific changes, which may be costly to ourselves. Practitioners are already pointing the way. It will require the authorizing decisionmakers—local, Presbyterial and National—to support them ...

b. ***Mission Shaped Church***   The Archbishop's Council of the Church of England, *Mission Shaped Church: Church Planting and Fresh Expressions of Church in a Changing Context*, 2004, 81–2

[See *A Church Without Walls* (a.)]

Five values for missionary churches

... we have identified five values of a missionary church. These are intended to offer a framework that can be applied to an existing local church or to any strategy to develop, grow or plant a church or a fresh expression of church. One additional element is assumed rather than specifically identified. That is the credal foundation of any missionary church, congregation or initiative within the Church of England. This report assumes, but does not take for granted that, to be missionary, a church has to proclaim afresh the faith of the Scriptures and the creeds.

This is not a 'value' of the church, but the foundation upon which church is built.

- a missionary church is focused on God the Trinity

Worship lies at the heart of a missionary church, and to love and know God as Father, Son and Spirit is its chief inspiration and primary purpose. It worships and serves a missionary God, and understands itself to share in the divine mission. All of its life and activity is undergirded by prayer.

- a missionary church is incarnational

A missionary church seeks to shape itself in relation to the culture in which it is located or to which it is called. Whenever it is called to be crosscultural then its long-term members or initial team lay aside their cultural preferences about church to allow the emergence of a form or style of church to be shaped by those they are seeking to reach. If a church is long established, then it evaluates itself in relation to the culture of the community it serves, and strips away whatever is not required by the gospel. An incarnational church seeks to be responsive to the activity of the Spirit in its community.

- a missionary church is transformational

A missionary church exists for the transformation of the community that it serves, through the power of the gospel and the Holy Spirit. It is not selfserving, self-seeking or self-focused. The kingdom of God is its goal, and church is understood as a servant and sign of God's kingdom in its community, whether neighbourhood or network.

- a missionary church makes disciples

A missionary church is active in calling people to faith in Jesus Christ, and it is equally committed to the development of a consistent Christian lifestyle appropriate to, but not withdrawn from, the culture or cultures in which it operates. It engages with culture, but also presents a counter-cultural challenge by its corporate life based on the world view and values of the gospel. It encourages the gifting and vocation of all the people of God, and invests in the development of leaders. It is concerned for the transformation of individuals, as well as the transformation of communities.

- a missionary church is relational

In a missionary church, a community of faith is being formed. It is characterized by welcome and hospitality. Its ethos and style are open to change when new members join. Believers are encouraged to establish interdependent relationships with fellow Christians as they grow into Christ. As a community it is aware that it is incomplete without interdependent relationships with other Christian churches and communities. It does not seek to stand alone ...

c. *Post-Christendom*   Stuart Murray, *Post-Christendom: Church and Mission in a Strange New World*, 2004, 316–17

[Anabaptist Stuart Murray sketches the outlines of a Christian approach to a Western social context where the basic elements of Christian faith are no longer familiar. As an Anabaptist, he feels well positioned to do this, as Anabaptists rejected the medieval 'Christendom' model during the Reformation in the sixteenth century.]

Our greatest resource in post-Christendom is Jesus. In a society that is heartily and understandably sick of institutional Christianity, Jesus still commands interest and respect. However garbled his teachings have become, and however little his story is known, many people suspect Jesus is good news, despite the shortcomings they see in our churches and the distaste with which they regard our evangelistic activities ...

Our priority must be to rediscover how to tell the story of Jesus and present his life, teaching, death and resurrection—recognising past attempts have seriously missed the mark. We cannot continue to present Jesus only as the saviour from guilt few feel in post-Christendom. Nor can we invite people to follow a Jesus who merely guarantees life after death to those who are otherwise comfortable or a Jesus whose lordship affects only a limited range of personal moral decisions. We can no longer present a safe establishment Jesus who represents order and stability rather than justice, who appeals to the powerful and privileged for all the wrong reasons. Nor can we reduce Jesus to dogmatic statements in simplistic evangelistic courses or perpetuate the overemphasis on his divinity at the expense of his humanity that Christendom required.

Instead, we must present Jesus as (among much else) friend of sinners, good news to the poor, defender of the powerless, reconciler of communities, pioneer of a new age, freedom fighter, breaker of chains, liberator and peacemaker, the one who unmasks systems of oppression, identifies with the vulnerable and brings hope.

But if we would present Jesus in such ways to others we must encounter Jesus afresh ourselves ... It would be strange, however, if this encounter did not take place on the margins of church and society, since that is where Jesus is so often found. It is there he invites us to rediscover him and follow him in post-Christendom.

d. **Evangelical Christianity**   Chris Wright, *A 21st Century Reformation?*, Report on the Theology Working Group, the Lausanne Movement, 2007, http://www.lausanne.org/issue-theology/twg-report-20june2007.html (accessed 27 May 2011)

[The Lausanne Movement was inspired by the evangelical work of Billy Graham, and was founded in 1974 and established a covenant. It provides a global forum for evangelization. Here there is a call for a renewal of evangelical Christianity in the twenty-first century.]

The Lausanne Covenant speaks of 'the entirety' of the Scriptures, and about 'all that it affirms'. May God protect us from selective hermeneutics, from polarized priorities and from segmented perceptions of the gospel. My big concern is not just that the world church should become more evangelical, but that world evangelicals should become more biblical.

To be biblical is also to be prophetic. And when you study the prophets you observe that the great bulk of all they had to say was addressed, not to the world of outside nations (though they did have words for them), but to the people of God themselves. The prophets confronted Old Testament Israel and demanded that they *change their ways*, if they were to have any hope of fulfilling their mission of being a light to the nations and a blessing on the earth. The dominant prophetic call was to repentance among God's people, so that God could get on with the job of blessing the world.

Just as much today we need repentance and renewal in the church, as well as renewed passion for world mission. Otherwise, the church may become, as the Lausanne Covenant puts it, 'a stumbling block to evangelism when it betrays the Gospel'. Arguably, in some respects and in some places it has already become exactly that.

Indeed, my hope for Cape Town 2010 is that it would launch and foster nothing less than a 21st Century Reformation—among evangelicals, who need it as much as any other Christian bloc.

For there are scandals and abuses in the world-wide evangelical community that are reminiscent of the worst features of the pre-reformation medieval church in Europe.

- There are some mega leaders, like ancient prelates, wielding vast wealth, power and control—unaccountable, unattractive and unChristlike.

- There are multitudes of ordinary Christians going to so-called evangelical churches, where they never hear the Bible preached or taught.
  They live in scandalous biblical ignorance.
- Instead they are offered in the 'prosperity gospel' a form of 21st century
  indulgences, except that you pay your money not for release from pains
  after death, but for receipt of material 'blessings' here and now.
- And there are evangelicals parading ungodly alliances with secular
  power—political, economic and military—identifying themselves (and
  the gospel they claim to preach) with agendas and ideologies that
  reflect human empire not the kingdom of God in Christ.

Will we have the courage to identify and renounce such scandals and to
seek a reformation of heart, mind and practice?

e. The Response to Atheism   Alister McGrath, *The Dawkins Delusion*, 2007, xi–xiii

[Richard Dawkins' best-selling book, *The God Delusion*, is an example of an
assertive form of scientific naturalism that denies the credibility of belief in God
and the plausibility of religion. Several such works emerged from scientists in
the 2000s. The well-known Christian textbook writer and ex-atheist, Alister
McGrath, set out to counter these claims.]

It is clear that a response of some sort is needed to *The God Delusion*, if
only because the absence of one might persuade some that no answer
could be given. So how is one to reply? One obvious response would be to
write an equally aggressive, inaccurate book, ridiculing atheism by misrepresenting its ideas and presenting its charlatans as if they were its
saints. But that would be pointless and counterproductive, not to mention intellectually dishonest ...

Anyway, Dawkins clearly has little interest in engaging religious
believers, who will find themselves simply appalled by the flagrant
misrepresentation of their beliefs and lifestyles ...

The total dogmatic conviction of correctness which pervades some
sections of Western atheism today—wonderfully illustrated in *The God
Delusion*—immediately aligns it with a religious fundamentalism which
refuses to allow its ideas to be examined or challenged ...

What is particularly worrying is that, without seeming to realize it,
Dawkins simply treats evidence as something to shoehorn into his
preconceived theoretical framework. Religion is persistently and consistently portrayed in the worst possible way, mimicking the worst features
of religious fundamentalism's portrayal of atheism. When some leading

scientists write in support of religion, Dawkins retorts that they simply cannot mean what they say. Dawkins clearly feels deeply threatened by the possibility of his readers encountering religious ideas or people that they might actually like—or even worse, respect, and regard as worthy of serious attention.

f. Science and Theology John C. Lennox, *God's Undertaker: Has Science Buried God?*, 2009, 185–6

[The atheist challenge to Christianity is part-based on the notion that science has replaced religion as the medium of knowledge. However, scientists who are also Christians, such as John Lennox, a mathematician, argue that the advances of science and the doctrines of Christianity do not contradict each other. Lennox also answers the criticisms of Richard Dawkins.]

... A theory of everything (TOE) is, as Dawkins can see, a theory that would give physics closure. In other words, the TOE is by definition where the explanatory trail ends. On the basis of Dawkins' objections to God as the end of such an explanatory trail, he should be berating physicists for suggesting a TOE as the ultimate explanation of the origin of the universe ...

Dawkins' optimism has proved unrealistic. Some ugly mathematical facts get in the way in the shape of Kurt Gödel's famous finding that our familiar arithmetic and other larger mathematical systems cannot prove their own consistency and must contain propositions that are undecidable—that is, that cannot either be proved or disproved by arithmetical means ...

The New Atheists object to God as a final explanation, yet they themselves have no explanation for the existence of the mass/energy of which the universe is formed. Their materialism comes to a stop at that point: the existence of mass/energy that they must regard essentially as a brute fact, and thus their ultimate explanation. Logically, chains of cause and effect either go back eternally in an infinite regression, or there is a point where we stop at an ultimate reality. Explanation in science (or anywhere else), if it is to avoid an infinite regress, always leads to certain things that are regarded as ultimate ...

Farrar's summary hits the nail on the head: 'The issue between the atheist and the believer is not whether it makes sense to question ultimate fact, it is rather the question: what fact is ultimate? The atheist's ultimate fact is the universe; the theist's ultimate fact is God' [Austin Farrar, *A Science of God*, London: Geoffrey Bles, 1966, 33–4].

XIII. GENETIC ENGINEERING

a. **The Reformed Church in America**   *Position on Genetic Engineering,* the Reformed Church in America, 2004, http://www.rca.org/Page.aspx? pid=549 (accessed 27 May 2011)

[With the development of new technologies, the churches are called upon to relate biblical and traditional principles to ever new areas of application. Christian ethics is dynamic, expanding its subject matter with social and technological change. The area of genetics is one of the most controversial, as it brings into question the Christian understanding of what it means to be a human person.]

Human Cloning to Produce Children

At this time, human reproductive cloning is morally and theologically unacceptable. The risks of harm outweigh possible benefits of the technology. Cloning threatens to diminish genetic diversity ... A number of dubious motivations seem to inspire human cloning. A perspective that increasingly seeks to control and manage life in a way that distances humanity from its Creator makes for a decisive verdict against this technology. The church must faithfully resist participation in and support of human reproductive cloning.

Stem Cell Research

The 2002 General Synod concluded that 'the questions surrounding stem cell technology are complex and clouded. There are a variety of views within the Christian community. The various sources of embryonic stem cells warrant different moral evaluations.' There are four major sources of stem cells:

- From miscarriages: There is some possibility of developing stem cells from miscarried fetuses. With parental consent, this source for stem cells seems the least ethically ambiguous.
- Existing lines of stem cells: United States federal funding is currently restricted to the roughly 60 lines of stem cells already in existence; the intention of the restriction is to discourage the destruction of additional embryos while still allowing research on the existing lines. The RCA's Commission on Christian Action generally supported the continued use of existing stem cell lines for research.
- Disposal and freezing of surplus embryos: Declining to view embryos, even those that are to be discarded, as a source for stem cells may inhibit the development of an outlook that views human beings as things and spare parts. Resisting the use of embryonic stem cells could

greatly encourage research to focus on developing stem cells from alternate sources, such as adult bone marrow.

- Production of embryos for stem cells: Creating embryos solely for scientific purposes, such as cloning and developing stem cells, promotes a perspective that views embryos and potentially all life as a commodity or resource. The RCA's Commission on Christian Action strongly opposed any production of embryos solely for stem cell research. (MGS 2002, 98–9)

b. **World Council of Churches** *Aide Memoire from the Global Consultation on Genetics and New Biotechnologies and the Ministry of the Church*, WCC, 2007, http://www.oikoumene.org/gr/resources/documents/wcc-programmes/justice-diakonia-and-responsibility-for-creation/science-technology-ethics/aide-memoire-from-the-global-consultation-on-genetics-new-biotechnologies-and-the-ministry-of-the-church.html (accessed 27 May 2011)

[See introduction to a.]

Convictions and perspectives

Genetic advances and new biotechnologies force the churches to reaffirm the dignity of human beings and the integrity of the web of life. The creativity of science needs to serve the common good. This note was a shared theme in all theological contributions to the consultation. Where the dignity is violated because human beings are reduced to mere commodities, churches are compelled to speak and act. Where the web of life is threatened or disrupted by human intervention, churches will advocate for the restoration of just relationships between human beings and other life. Justice for the poor and the suffering creation is the compelling call to the Biblical witness.

The teachings of the churches need to be further developed in response to the challenges of biotechnology and the impact it has on peoples' lives. Underlying assumptions about the value and trajectory of life require deeper theological reflection. These are a common task that depends much on the contextual realities and benefits from shared discernment. Those closer to the centers of research and technological advance see the need for dialogue with scientists, wishing to move beyond a reactive mode. They also want to foster the science to serve the common humanity. Those who are closer to peasant communities and other marginalized groups underline their experience that communities can be devastated by the intrusion of genetically modified seeds and bio-piracy. They even conclude: 'biotechnology now serves primarily to enhance corporate profit and thereby reduces human beings to mere consumers' ...

Beyond the human species

Poor communities are more at risk during drug development—for example in clinical trials for HIV, reproductive technologies and diabetic research—and lack access to pharmaceutical products that are expensive under patent regimes and other legal, political and social machineries which prevent access to drugs. Perhaps the greatest arrogance to be confronted is any claim to 'perfect' all life and in particular the human species. This irreverence denies the sacred relationship between creator and creatures. It ignores the vulnerability and finiteness of life. It opens the door for new divisions in human community that go far beyond the past and present experiences of racism, sexism, ableism and other deeply entrenched denials of human dignity. The commodification of human life in pre-natal diagnostics, some forms of research cloning and stem cell research as well as enhancement techniques must now increasingly be faced by churches and the wider public. Yet, even these are trumped by the dreams of so called trans-humanists. Their vision of constant perfection of human beings beyond the boundaries of the species entails a nightmare not only for people with disabilities, but ultimately for all people.

The prophetic voice of the ecumenical community

There is a great need for global ecumenical literacy on the many dimensions of the new convergent technologies that have been enabled by the digitalization of information in different spheres of life. A central commitment of the consultation was the restoration of the churches' prophetic voices and public witness in the growing debate regarding the ethical use of genetics and biotechnologies ...

c. **Humanity in the Image of God**   Mark Bratton, 'Introduction: Autonomy, solidarity and the human genome', 2009, M. Bratton, *God, Ethics and the Human Genome: Theological, Legal and Scientific Perspectives*, 1–21; excerpt, 20–1

[The mapping of the human genetic system, the 'genome', opens up substantial new medical possibilities for preventing disease, but there are ethical considerations as to how the genetic material is used. There is also the question of patenting, that is, when companies that have developed genetic knowledge want to safeguard their intellectual property. The Church of England's Human Genome Review Group of the Mission and Public Affairs Council produced this publication on the topic.]

The traditional basis for the claim that human beings are special creatures in creation has lain in the theological view that they are made in the 'image of God'. Traditionally, this view was elaborated through an emphasis on humanity's unique attributes, for example the capacity for language, reason, culture, freedom, creativity, and so on. The startling discovery through the Human Genome Project that human beings share a surprisingly large percentage of their genome with other living things (as Annette Cashmore has pointed out) has complicated the case for human distinctiveness. Yet the Human Genome Project is also making it clear that the very complexity of the human constitution cannot be crudely related to gene number, but is, more sophisticatedly, related to other factors, for example the comparatively large numbers of proteins for which human genes code and the comparatively large amount of DNA that doesn't code for protein at all. The fact that human beings are genetically constituted creatures of extraordinary complexity invites deeper reflection on the nature of the relationship between the 'whole person' and her genetically constituted parts.

The Romanian Orthodox theologian, the late Dumitru Staniloae, conceptualizes the human person as a 'little universe' (*microcosmos*) and the universe as man-writ-large (*macanthropos*). The human person paradigmatically encompasses the cosmos with an entailing vocation to 'humanize' it. The sub-personal world (within which we can include the genomic) finds its true meaning in relationship with the human person who is higher than mere nature; and the human person, by his or her very nature, aspires to find fulfilment in communion with the transcendent and free person—Jesus Christ. According to Staniloae, the rationality of the created order—even at the genomic level—is a means of interpersonal dialogue between rational human persons and the supreme rational Person—God in Jesus Christ. Any attempt to assimilate the 'whole' human person to the sub-personal, for example by reducing the human person to his genetic constituents, or any attempt to alienate the human person from his solidarity with and within the created order (including his genetic inheritance), is fundamentally *dehumanizing*, an unacceptable subversion of humanity's calling to realize the image of God within him and to humanize the universe [D. Staniloae, *The Experience of God: Orthodox Dogmatic Theology. Vol 2. The World, Creation and Deification*, Holy Cross Orthodox Press, 2005; C. Miller, *The Gift of the World: An Introduction to the Theology of Dumitru Staniloae*, T&T Clark, 2000, 30–3].

XIV. THE INTERNET

a. **Methodist Church of Great Britain**   *The Challenge of Information Technology*, Methodist Conference report, 2001, paras. 4.1–4.2, http://www.methodist.org.uk/index.cfm?fuseaction=opentogod.content&cmid=357 (accessed 27 May 2011)

[The Internet was born in the 1990s, but it was probably not until the 2000s that it became the predominant universal forum for communications, purchasing, and networking. Its effect on society and also on church members is recognized in these responses.]

4.1 *Worship*

Those outside the church are increasingly bombarded with messages and entertainment which are slick and effective. Without being gimmicky, or changing its core message, the church must adopt a relevant vehicle to present the gospel in an attractive and alluring form. Professional use of technology as a medium should be integrated into worship (albeit occasionally) as well as all other aspects of communication and contact.

Not only must we adopt technology when appropriate as a vehicle to aid our worship, but our worship must also reflect the impact of technology. Our preaching can be more wisely informed through wider access to relevant and timely information. Our preaching should be informed by issues affecting society in which technology plays a major part. Our preaching must reflect theological wrestling in an informed age, and we must not hide from the growing challenge this might bring.

4.2 *Learning & Caring*

Young people encounter IT in every walk of life, and use it as an integral part of the learning resources at school. Unless junior church is equipped with equivalent technology, it will appear increasingly irrelevant and disconnected from 'real' life. This will reinforce the unfortunate stereotype of the church. Junior churches must be equipped with modern resources which excite and stimulate young people and make them feel in a natural and homely environment.

The Internet is an unrivalled source of information for personal and group study. This rich resource should be readily available to all the church leaders as part of their background preparation to fulfil their responsibilities. A co-ordinated approach would allow the church to create a rich environment for knowledge and experience sharing, where church members could tap into the in-depth knowledge of specialists covering the whole life of the church.

Community webcasting to housebound members could be developed to integrate them back into the worshipping life of the church. This could perhaps begin with community homes such as MHA. A greater sense of family could be developed in the church by encouraging the young technology enthusiasts to adopt and support those who fear the technology.

Much religious material on the Internet is of dubious origin, with focused activity from cults and extreme groups. The Methodist church could bring a mainstream perspective to the hosting of debate on matters of contemporary social, moral and ethical concern, as well as theology. The Methodist brand would allow us to seize the opportunity to convey a radical but authoritative position.

b. **Roman Catholic Church**   *The Church and Internet*, Pontifical Council for Social Communications, 2002, from paras. 5, 8, http://www.vatican.va/roman_curia/pontifical_councils/pccs/documents/rc_pc_pccs_doc_20020228_church-internet_en.html (accessed 27 May 2011)

[See introduction to a.]

... The Internet is relevant to many activities and programs of the Church—evangelization, including both re-evangelization and new evangelization and the traditional missionary work *ad gentes*, catechesis and other kinds of education, news and information, apologetics, governance and administration, and some forms of pastoral counseling and spiritual direction. Although the virtual reality of cyberspace cannot substitute for real interpersonal community, the incarnational reality of the sacraments and the liturgy, or the immediate and direct proclamation of the gospel, it can complement them, attract people to a fuller experience of the life of faith, and enrich the religious lives of users. It also provides the Church with a means for communicating with particular groups—young people and young adults, the elderly and homebound, persons living in remote areas, the members of other religious bodies—who otherwise may be difficult to reach.

... Among the specific problems presented by the Internet is the presence of hate sites devoted to defaming and attacking religious and ethnic groups. Some of these target the Catholic Church. Like pornography and violence in the media, Internet hate sites are 'reflections of the dark side of a human nature marred by sin' [*Pornography and Violence in the Communications Media*, n. 7]. And while respect for free expression may require tolerating even voices of hatred up to a point, industry self-regulation—and, where required, intervention by public authority—should establish and enforce reasonable limits to what can be said.

The proliferation of web sites calling themselves Catholic creates a problem of a different sort. As we have said, church-related groups should be creatively present on the Internet; and well-motivated, well-informed individuals and unofficial groups acting on their own initiative are entitled to be there as well. But it is confusing, to say the least, not to distinguish eccentric doctrinal interpretations, idiosyncratic devotional practices, and ideological advocacy bearing a 'Catholic' label from the authentic positions of the Church ...

XV. PROGRESS ON CHRISTIAN UNITY

a. Anglicans and Methodists   *An Anglican-Methodist Covenant*, 2003, http://www.anglican-methodist.org.uk/text.htm (accessed 27 May 2011)

[Ecumenical discussions between Anglicans and Methodists are encouraged by the fact that John Wesley himself remained an Anglican. The possibility of union continues as a discussion point into the 2000s.]

The Affirmations

1. We affirm one another's churches as true churches belonging to the One, Holy, Catholic and Apostolic Church of Jesus Christ and as truly participating in the apostolic mission of the whole people of God.

2. We affirm that in both our churches the word of God is authentically preached, and the sacraments of Baptism and the Eucharist are duly administered and celebrated.

3. We affirm that both our churches confess in word and life the apostolic faith revealed in the Holy Scriptures and set forth in the ecumenical Creeds.

4. We affirm that one another's ordained and lay ministries are given by God as instruments of God's grace, to build up the people of God in faith, hope and love, for the ministry of word, sacrament and pastoral care and to share in God's mission in the world.

5. We affirm that one another's ordained ministries possess both the inward call of the Holy Spirit and Christ's commission given through the Church.

6. We affirm that both our churches embody the conciliar, connexional nature of the Church and that communal, collegial and personal oversight (*episkope*) is exercised within them in various forms.

7. We affirm that there already exists a basis for agreement on the principles of episcopal oversight as a visible sign and instrument of the communion of the Church in time and space.

The Commitments

1. We commit ourselves, as a priority, to work to overcome the remaining obstacles to the organic unity of our two churches, on the way to the full visible unity of Christ's Church. In particular, we look forward to the time when the fuller visible unity of our churches makes possible a united, interchangeable ministry.
2. We commit ourselves to realise more deeply our common life and mission and to share the distinctive contributions of our traditions, taking steps to bring about closer collaboration in all areas of witness and service in our needy world.
3. We commit ourselves to continue to welcome each other's baptised members to participate in the fellowship, worship and mission of our churches.
4. We commit ourselves to encourage forms of eucharistic sharing, including eucharistic hospitality, in accordance with the rules of our respective churches.
5. We commit ourselves to listen to each other and to take account of each other's concerns, especially in areas that affect our relationship as churches.
6. We commit ourselves to continue to develop structures of joint or shared communal, collegial and personal oversight, including shared consultation and decision-making, on the way to a fully united ministry of oversight.

b. **The Virgin Mary**   *Mary: Grace and Hope in Christ* (The Seattle Statement), Anglican–Roman Catholic International Commission ARCIC II, 2004, paras. 78–80 (from the Conclusion), http://www.vatican.va/ roman_curia/pontifical_councils/chrstuni/angl-comm-docs/rc_pc_chrstuni_ doc_20050516_mary-grace-hope-christ_en.html (accessed 27 May 2011)

[From the Reformation, the cult of the Virgin Mary often stood as a distinguishing mark between Catholic and Protestant, the former lavishly encouraging it, the latter abjuring it. Therefore any ecumenical dialogue with the Roman Catholic Church has to tackle this issue and seek ways forward on an understanding of Mary. The Church of England's Anglo-Catholic wing makes agreement between these churches easier than it would be elsewhere.]

78. As a result of our study, the Commission offers the following agreements, which we believe significantly advance our consensus regarding Mary. We affirm together

- the teaching that God has taken the Blessed Virgin Mary in the fullness of her person into his glory as consonant with Scripture, and only to be understood in the light of Scripture;
- that in view of her vocation to be the mother of the Holy One, Christ's redeeming work reached 'back' in Mary to the depths of her being and to her earliest beginnings;
- that the teaching about Mary in the two definitions of the Assumption and the Immaculate Conception, understood within the biblical pattern of the economy of hope and grace, can be said to be consonant with the teaching of the Scriptures and the ancient common traditions;
- that this agreement, when accepted by our two Communions, would place the questions about authority which arise from the two definitions of 1854 and 1950 in a new ecumenical context;
- that Mary has a continuing ministry which serves the ministry of Christ, our unique mediator, that Mary and the saints pray for the whole Church and that the practice of asking Mary and the saints to pray for us is not communion-dividing.

79. We agree that doctrines and devotions which are contrary to Scripture cannot be said to be revealed by God nor to be the teaching of the Church. We agree that doctrine and devotion which focuses on Mary, including claims to 'private revelations', must be moderated by carefully expressed norms which ensure the unique and central place of Jesus Christ in the life of the Church, and that Christ alone, together with the Father and the Holy Spirit, is to be worshipped in the Church.

80. Our statement has sought not to clear away all possible problems, but to deepen our common understanding to the point where remaining diversities of devotional practice may be received as the varied work of the Spirit amongst all the people of God. We believe that the agreement we have here outlined is itself the product of a re-reception by Anglicans and Roman Catholics of doctrine about Mary and that it points to the possibility of further reconciliation, in which issues concerning doctrine and devotion to Mary need no longer be seen as communion-dividing, or an obstacle in a new stage of our growth into visible *koinonia*. This agreed statement is now offered to our respective authorities. It may also in itself prove a valuable study of the teaching of the Scriptures and the ancient common traditions about the Blessed Virgin Mary, the Mother of God incarnate. Our hope is that, as we share in the one Spirit by which

Mary was prepared and sanctified for her unique vocation, we may together participate with her and all the saints in the unending praise of God.

c. **Roman Catholics and Methodists** Pontifical Council for Promoting Christian Unity, *The Grace given you in Christ: Catholics and Methodists reflect further on the Church* (The Seoul Report: Report of the Joint Commission for Dialogue between the Roman Catholic Church and the World Methodist Council), 2006, para. 137, http://www.vatican.va/ roman_curia/pontifical_councils/chrstuni/meth-council-docs/rc_pc_ chrstuni_doc_20060604_seoul-report_en.html (accessed 27 May 2011)

[The ecumenical rapprochement that had been a hallmark of the twentieth century continued in the 2000s. The shared challenges facing the Christian denominations, and the decline in numbers in some countries (particularly in Europe) created a motivation to dialogue towards a greater unity.]

137. With regard to the four traditional marks or notes of the Church, this chapter has sought to show that the reconciliation of Methodists and Catholics offers great potential benefits to both communities:

a) In an important sense, two uniting churches give to one another the gift of *unity*. In this case, two different aspects of unity would be valuably combined, one more structural and historical, the other more spiritual and eschatological. The Catholic Church believes that the unity Christ bestowed on his Church from the beginning 'subsists in the Catholic Church' [*Unitatis Redintegratio*, 4; cf. *Ut Unum Sint*, 11], particularly because of the continuance in it of the Petrine ministry. In a sense, therefore, through this essential sign of visible unity, the Catholic Church can give the gift of unity to the Methodist Church. On the other hand, Methodists understand unity primarily as the spiritual unity of the body of Christ, which Christians must strive to make more visible in the world but which will remain imperfectly realised until the last day. This eschatological emphasis is important and reminds Catholics that unity is also a *vocation* that must inspire and challenge us each day towards an ever greater attainment of it.

b) The emphasis upon *holiness* which Methodists and Catholics already share means that we would give each other great solidarity and encouragement in our living of this mark of the Church and in our striving for an ever fuller realisation of it. We would also have the joy of sharing the inspiring example of our saints.

   c) Christian divisions prevent the Church from realising 'the fullness of *catholicity* proper to her' [*Unitatis Redintegratio*, 4, italics added]. The firm commitment of Methodists and Catholics to ecumenism is indicative of our shared desire for ever greater catholicity, and that commitment and desire would be further strengthened by our unity. In accordance with its twofold meaning, the catholicity both of Catholics and also of Methodists would be enhanced by our unity: by an increased depth and balance of belief, and by an increased vigour and scope of outreach.

   d) Methodists can receive a vital sign of *apostolicity* from Catholics, namely the apostolic succession of bishops. However, Catholics have much to gain from the commitment to apostolic mission which is an explicit part of Methodist identity.

   The mutual enhancement of each other's oneness, holiness, catholicity and apostolicity through Catholic–Methodist unity would be the fullest possible realisation of John Wesley's famous appeal that Protestants and Catholics should 'help each other on in whatever we are agreed leads to the Kingdom' [Letter to a Roman Catholic].

d. Anglicans and the Orthodox   *The Church of the Triune God*, The Cyprus Agreed Statement of the International Commission for Anglican–Orthodox Theological Dialogue, 2006, Conclusion, para. 29, http://www.anglicancom munion.org/ministry/ecumenical/dialogues/orthodox/docs/pdf/The%20Church %20of%20the%20Triune%20God.pdf (accessed 27 May 2011)

[In Anglican ecumenical discussion with the Orthodox or Roman Catholic churches, the ordination of women is a divisive issue, as mutual recognition of ministry and structure can be seen to be impeded by the different practices involved.]

We have discussed reception with regard to doctrine and to ecclesial structures. Reception applies to other areas of church life, such as liturgy, the official recognition of saints, and sacraments. These too must be mutually received by the churches, if unity among them is to become a reality. We have concentrated on doctrine and structures partly because the subject is usually discussed in connection with faith, to the detriment of the issue of the Church's structure and ministry, but chiefly because the particular problems facing our dialogue are more concerned with structure and ministry than with faith. It is easy to become pre-occupied with the question whether the ordination of women to the priesthood and the episcopate is a heresy or not, forgetting that the problem mainly concerns the Church's ministry. Whether or not such ordination contradicts the dogmatic teaching of the Church already transmitted and received, and so is heretical, can remain open to discussion and to an open process of reception. But the recognition and reception of the ministry of women presbyters and bishops is a question which concerns the practical life of the ecclesial communities involved, including sacramental communion. While questions of faith can be the subject of lengthy discussion, issues of order and ministry are matters of practice, and so they affect reception in an immediate way. From this point of view the ordination of women to the episcopate is more problematic with regard to reception than their ordination to the presbyterate, for the churches receive one another at the level of structure through the bishop. The ultimate goal of all official theological dialogues, including our own, is the reception of our churches by one another, in ministry and church structure as well as in faith. In all their discussions, decisions and actions, our churches must keep this goal constantly in mind.

e. The Tridentine Rite   Apostolic letter *Summorum Pontificum*, Benedict XVI, 7 July 2007, tr. Patrick Archbold, http://www.summorumpontificum. net/2007/07/summorum-pontificum-english.html (accessed 27 May 2011)

[The removal of the pre-Vatican II Latin rite of the Mass from everyday use continued to cause dissent in the Roman Catholic Church. It was felt that Vatican II had gone too far with liturgical reform. Faced with this pressure, successive popes John Paul II and Benedict XVI allowed the reinstitution of the older Roman Missal.]

... Following the insistent prayers of these faithful, long deliberated upon by our predecessor John Paul II, and after having listened to the views of the Cardinal Fathers of the Consistory of 22 March 2006, having reflected deeply upon all aspects of the question, invoked the Holy Spirit and trusting in the help of God, with these Apostolic Letters we establish the following:

Art 1. The Roman Missal promulgated by Paul VI is the ordinary expression of the 'Lex orandi' (Law of prayer) of the Catholic Church of the Latin rite. Nonetheless, the Roman Missal promulgated by St. Pius V and reissued by Bl. John XXIII is to be considered as an extraordinary expression of that same 'Lex orandi,' and must be given due honour for its venerable and ancient usage. These two expressions of the Church's Lex orandi will in no any way lead to a division in the Church's 'Lex credendi' (Law of belief). They are, in fact two usages of the one Roman rite.

It is, therefore, permissible to celebrate the Sacrifice of the Mass following the typical edition of the Roman Missal promulgated by Bl. John XXIII in 1962 and never abrogated, as an extraordinary form of the Liturgy of the Church. The conditions for the use of this Missal as laid down by earlier documents 'Quattuor abhinc annis' and 'Ecclesia Dei,' are substituted as follows:

Art 2. In Masses celebrated without the people, each Catholic priest of the Latin rite, whether secular or regular, may use the Roman Missal published by Bl. Pope John XXIII in 1962, or the Roman Missal promulgated by Pope Paul VI in 1970, and may do so on any day with the exception of the Easter Triduum. For such celebrations, with either one Missal or the other, the priest has no need for permission from the Apostolic See or from his Ordinary.

Art 3. Communities of Institutes of consecrated life and of Societies of apostolic life, of either pontifical or diocesan right, wishing to celebrate Mass in accordance with the edition of the Roman Missal promulgated in 1962, for conventual or 'community' celebration in their oratories, may do so. If an individual community or an entire Institute or Society wishes to undertake such celebrations often, habitually or permanently, the decision must be taken by the Superiors Major, in accordance with the law and following their own specific decrees and statues.

Art 4. Celebrations of Mass as mentioned above in art. 2 may— observing all the norms of law—also be attended by faithful who, of their own free will, ask to be admitted.

Art 5.1 In parishes, where there is a stable group of faithful who adhere to the earlier liturgical tradition, the pastor should willingly accept their requests to celebrate the Mass according to the rite of the Roman Missal published in 1962, and ensure that the welfare of these faithful harmonises with the ordinary pastoral care of the parish, under the guidance of the bishop in accordance with canon 392, avoiding discord and favouring the unity of the whole Church ...

XVI. THE UNITY OF THE ANGLICAN COMMUNION

a. **Investiture of Bishop Katharine Jefferts Schori** Bishop Jefferts Schori's Address, 4 November 2006, Washington National Cathedral, http://www.episcopalchurch.org/78703_79214_ENG_HTM.htm (accessed 27 May 2011)

[In the Anglican communion, the Episcopal Church is often regarded as the most liberal. It consecrated women as bishops well before other churches in the communion, and there have been blessings of civil partnerships. In 2006, the Most Rev. Katharine Jefferts Schori was elected and invested as the 26th Presiding Bishop of The Episcopal Church. Her investiture sermon recognized the divisions and called for reconciliation.]

... The ability of any of us to enjoy shalom depends on the health of our neighbors. If some do not have the opportunity for health or wholeness, then none of us can enjoy true and perfect holiness. The writer of Ephesians implores us to maintain the unity of the Spirit in the bond of peace—to be at one in God's shalom. That is our baptismal task and hope, and unless each of the members of the body enjoys shalom we shall not live as one. That dream of God, that word of God spoken in each one of us at baptism also speaks hope of its realization.

The health of our neighbors, in its broadest understanding, is the mission that God has given us. We cannot love God if we fail to love our neighbors into a more whole and holy state of life. If some in this church feel wounded by recent decisions, then our salvation, our health as a body is at some hazard, and it becomes the duty of all of us to seek healing and wholeness. As long as children live exposed on the streets, while seniors go without food to pay for life-sustaining drugs, wherever peoples are sickened by industrial waste, the body suffers, and none of us can say we have finally come home.

What keeps us from the tireless search for that vision of shalom? There are probably only two answers, and they are connected—apathy and fear. One is the unwillingness to acknowledge the pain of other people, the other is an unwillingness to acknowledge that pain with enough courage to act. The cure for each is a deep and abiding hope. If God in Jesus has made captivity captive, has taken fear hostage, it is for the liberation and flourishing of hope.

Augustine said that as Christians, we are prisoners of hope—a ridiculously assertive hope, a hope that unflinchingly assails the doors of heaven, a hope that will not cease until that dream of God has swallowed up death forever, a hope that has the audacity to join Jesus in saying, 'today this scripture has been fulfilled in your hearing.'

And how shall that scripture be fulfilled in our hearing? In the will to make peace with one who disdains our theological position—for his has merit, too, as the fruit of faithfulness. In the courage to challenge our legislators to make poverty history, to fund AIDS work in Africa, and the distribution of anti-malarial mosquito nets, and primary schools where all children are welcomed. In the will to look within our own hearts and confront the shadows that darken the dream that God has planted there ...

b. **GAFCON**   *The Way, The Truth and the Life: Theological Resources for a Pilgrimage to a Global Anglican Future*, prepared by the Theological Resource Team of the Global Anglican Future Conference (GAFCON), Jerusalem, 2008, http://www.gafcon.org/images/uploads/gafcon_way_truth_life.pdf (accessed 27 May 2011)

[Dissent within the Anglican communion over liberal interpretations—e.g. practising homosexuals appointed as bishops in the American Episcopal Church, and relativistic approaches to inter-faith encounter—led to the setting up of a movement faithful to what it saw as biblical faith, as an alternative to the Lambeth Conference in 1998. GAFCON includes bishops. The following is taken from the conclusion to the statement from the 2008 conference.]

Our journey into the future

Over the past ten years the journey that we, as orthodox Anglicans, have taken together, has confirmed what we feared: some Churches in the Anglican Communion are radically redefining the received faith, and abandoning fundamental parts of it. We recognize that many in these Churches believe that the challenges they are making are Spirit-led, and necessary in order to respond to the challenges that the Church faces today.

Our own experience has been different. We have upheld the received biblical faith. We have found it to be relevant and powerful in addressing contemporary challenges. And we bear testimony to the gospel's transforming power, in our own lives and in our churches.

We have not claimed to possess the complete truth, but nor have we considered truth to be so provisional and partial, that one cannot possibly arrive at a clear judgment on theological error or unbiblical behaviour.

We recognize that the Holy Spirit of God leads God's people to truth, as they act and reflect together. We also recognize, however, that this is not just a continual process of listening and sharing, in which people are suspicious of judgments, and where there are no clear guidelines on discernment or on how to arrive at firm positions.

To deny the possibility of any access to the truth of God, suggests that God has been inadequate in making himself known to his own creation and to his creatures. It also means that final decisions, about what will count as truth in any given situation, remain with the powerful.

As those called to lead the Church, we have the responsibility not just to testify to truth, but also to uphold it and commend it. But some in the Church, in their understandable desire not to exclude anyone's voice, especially the voices of individuals and groups who are seen as vulnerable and oppressed, are now making the inclusion of all voices, opinions and testimonies into the primary means whereby we experience and commend God's truth.

We note with deep sadness that such a view has led to a Church which includes much, but which does not recognize how it may have access to the truth of God. Therefore, having no good news about transformation of life, it has nothing to offer to the broken and disordered communities of our fallen creation.

c. **The Gay Controversy** Oliver O'Donovan, *A Conversation Waiting to Begin: the Churches and the Gay Controversy*, 2009, 118–19

[Oliver O'Donovan contributes an academic evangelical perspective to the debate. He neither accepts the 'gay rights' campaign unconditionally nor the schismatic tendencies of those opposed to gay bishops, but instead asks for a rigorous debate on the issue.]

The old-style liberalism that used to preside over the church's dilemmas in a confident spirit of practical compromise began from the assumption that everyone was divided from everyone else by recalcitrant disagreements ... But at the very least we cannot know whether and how much of a famine of the word there is in any disagreement until we submit it to the disciplines of patient common inquiry. No disagreement refuses to be analyzed, and its constituent elements sorted out according to size and shape. No disagreement does not lure us on with the hope, however distant, of a genuine resolution. Can we promise ourselves, then, that if the churches would only discuss homosexuality long and fully and widely enough, they would end up agreeing? Well, we are not entitled to rule out that possibility. But suppose it were not true; suppose that after careful exploration and a search for common ground, there was an agreement-resistant core at the center of the issue—a problem about how modernity is viewed, for example, or about the ontological status of self-consciousness; it might still be possible to set the residual disagreement in what ecumenists like to call 'a new context', and (who knows?) learn how to live with it. We have a parallel in the difference between indissolubilist and non indissolubilist views of marriage, a traditional point of tension between Catholic and Protestant. That disagreement has not gone away; but if today it bulks less threateningly than it once did, that is because we are so much more clear about the extent of the agreed ground all around it—God's intentions for marriage, the pastoral desiderata in dealing with broken marriage, and the like. It no longer evokes threatening resonances. It is a problem reduced to its true shape and size ...

APPENDIX

LIST OF COUNCILS

[These are the twenty-one councils classed as Oecumenical by the Roman Catholic Church. Councils I–IV—sometimes I–VI—have been recognized as Oecumenical by the Church of England since the Reformation.]

    I. NICAEA I—325: Arianism condemned.
    II. CONSTANTINOPLE I—381: Creed of Nicaea reaffirmed: Macedonianism and Apollinarianism condemned.
    III. EPHESUS—431: Nestorianism and Pelagianism condemned.
    IV. CHALCEDON—451: Tome of Leo approved; Definition of Faith against Apollinarianism, Nestorianism, Eutychianism.
    V. CONSTANTINOPLE II—553; The 'Three Chapters' condemned.
    VI. CONSTANTINOPLE III—680–681: Monothelitism condemned.
    VII. NICAEA II—787: Against Iconoclasts.
    VIII. CONSTANTINOPLE IV—869–870: Against Photius.
    IX. LATERAN I—1123: On Investitures.
    X. LATERAN II—1139: Against Pseudo-Popes; and on points of discipline.
    XI. LATERAN III—1179: Against Waldensians and Albigensians.
    XII. LATERAN IV—1215: Against Waldensians and Albigensians, etc.
    XIII. LYONS I—1245: Against Frederick II.
    XIV. LYONS II—1274: For union with the Greek church.
    XV. VIENNE—1311–12: Abolition of Templars; condemnation of various heresies.
    XVI. CONSTANCE—1414–18: Condemnation of Wycliffe, Hus, etc.
    XVII. FLORENCE—1438–45: Union with Greeks, etc.
    XVIII. LATERAN V—1512–17: Reform of the Church.
    XIX. TRENT—1545–63: The Counter Reformation.
    XX. VATICAN—1869–70: The Faith and the Church; Papal Infallibility.
    XXI. VATICAN—1962–5: The Second Vatican Council.

BIBLIOGRAPHY

Sources for the Second Edition

Barrett, C. K., *The New Testament Background: Selected Documents* (London, 1957).

Bell, G. K. A., *Documents on Christian Unity: 1920-24* (London, 1924); *Second Series, 1924-30* (London, 1930); *Third Series, 1930-48* (London, 1948); *A Selection from the First and Second Series* (London, 1955); *Fourth Series, 1948-57* (London, 1958).

Bernheim, E. *Quellen zur Geschichte des Investiturstreits* (Leipzig, 1907).

Bindley, T. H. *The Oecumenical Documents of the Faith*, 4th edn, rev. F. W. Green (London, 1950).

Creed, J. M. and Boys Smith, J. S., *Religious Thought in the Eighteenth Century* (Cambridge, 1934).

Cross, F. L., *The Oxford Dictionary of the Christian Church* (London, 1957).

Denzinger, H., and Rahner, C., *Enchiridion Symbolorum, Definitionum et Declarationum* ..., 31st edn. (Freiburg, 1960).

Dumont, *Corps Universal Diplomatique* (The Hague, 1726-31).

Friedberg, *Corpus Iuris Canonici* (Leipzig, 1897).

Gardiner, S. R., *Constitutional Documents of the Puritan Revolution 1628-1660* (London, 1889).

Gee, H. and Hardy, W. J., *Documents Illustrative of English Church History* (London, 1896) [G. and H].

Giles, E., *Documents Illustrating Papal Authority A.D. 96-454* (London, 1952).

Goodall, N., *The Ecumenical Movement* (London, 1961).

Gwatkin, H. M., *Selections from Early Christian Writers* (London, 1897; repr. 1958).

Hefele, C. J., *Histoire des Conciles*, tr. H. Leclercq (Paris, 1907).

Henderson, E. F., *Select Historical Documents of the Middle Ages* (London, 1892).

Kidd, B. J., *Documents Illustrative of the History of the Church, i. To 313; ii. 313-462; iii. 500-1500* (London, 1920, 1923, 1941).

Kidd, B. J., *Documents Illustrative of the Continental Reformation* (Oxford, 1911).

Kirch, C., *Enchiridion Fontium Historiae Ecclesiasticae Antiquae*, 7th edn. rev. L. Ueding (Freiburg, 1956).

Laffan, R. D. G., *Select Documents of European History 800-1492* (London, 1930).

Mansi, J. D., *Sacrorum Conciliorum Nova et Amplissima Collectio* rev. Petit and Martin (Lyons, 1899-1927).

Migne, J. P., *Patrologiae Cursus Completus: Series Latina [P.L.]* (Paris, 1844), *Series Graeca [P.G.]* (Paris, 1957).

Mirbt, C., *Quellen zur Geschichte des Papstthums und des Römischen Katholizismus*, 4th edn. (Tübingen, 1924).

More, P. E., and Cross, F. L., *Anglicanism* (London, 1935).

Nunn, H. P. V., *Christian Inscriptions* (London, 1920).

Reddaway, W. F., *Select Documents of European History 1492-1715* (London, 1930).

Reich, E., *Select Documents Illustrating Mediaeval and Modern History* (London, 1905).

Robinson, J. H., *Readings in European History*, i (Boston, 1904); ii (Boston, 1906).

Schaff, P., *Creeds of Christendom* (London, 1877).

Schwarz, E., *Acta Conciliorum Oecumenicorum* (Berlin Leipzig, 1914–).

Stevenson, J. A., *A New Eusebius: Documents Illustrative of the History of the Church to A.D. 337*, based on the collection ed. B. J. Kidd (London, 1957).

Stubbs, W., *Select Charters*, 9th edn. rev. H. W. C. Davis (Oxford, 1913).

Wace and Buchheim, *Luther's Primary Works* (London, 1896).

Sources for the Third Edition

The following is a list of sources for the third edition. Individual church documents are not listed here but are referred to in the Acknowledgements.

Abrecht, P. and Koshy, N., *Before It's Too Late: The Challenge of Nuclear Disarmament* (WCC: Geneva, 1984).

Balasuriya, T., *Mary and Human Liberation: The Story and the Text*, ed. H. Stanton (Mowbray: London, 1997).

Barth, K., *The Epistle to the Romans*, tr. E. C. Hoskyns from 6th edn. (OUP: Oxford, 1933; 1968).

Boff, L., *Church, Charism and Power: Liberation Theology and the Institutional Church*, tr. J. W. Diercksmeier (SCM: London; Crossroad: New York, 1985).

Bonhoeffer, D., *Letters and Papers from Prison*, rev. and enlarged edn. tr. R. Fuller, F. Clarke, J. Bowden, *et al.* (SCM: London; Simon & Schuster: New York, 1971).

British Council of Churches, *The Next Steps for Churches Together in Pilgrimage* (BCC/CTS: London, 1989).

Brockway, A., van Buren, P., Rendtorff, R. and Schoon, S., *The Theology of the Churches and the Jewish People: Statements by the World Council of Churches and its Member Churches* (WCC: Geneva, 1988).

Brown, S. E., *Meeting in Faith: Twenty Years of Christian–Muslim Conversations Sponsored by the World Council of Churches* (WCC: Geneva, 1989).

Church of England, *Together in Mission and Ministry: The Porvoo Common Statement, with Essays on Church and Ministry in Northern Europe* (Church House: London, 1993).

Cone, J. H., *Black Theology and Black Power* (Orbis: New York, 1997).

Cone, J. H. and Wilmore, G. S., *Black Theology: A Documentary History*, i. *1966–1979* (Orbis: Maryknoll, NY, 1993).

Council of Churches for Britain and Ireland, *Returning Pilgrims: Insights from British and Irish Participants in the Fifth World Faith and Order Conference Santiago de Compostela 3-14 August 1993* (CCBI: London, 1994).

Croner, H., *More Stepping Stones to Jewish–Christian Relations: An Unabridged Collection of Documents 1975–1983* (Paulist: Mahwah, NJ, 1985).

Ellingsen, M., *The Cutting Edge: How Churches Speak on Social Issues* (WCC: Geneva; Eerdmans: Grand Rapids, Mich., 1993).

Flannery, A., *Vatican Council II, vol. i. The Conciliar and Post-Conciliar Documents*, new rev. edn. (Dominican: Dublin; Costello: Northport, NY, 1992; 1998).

Flannery, A., *Vatican Council II: Constitutions, Decrees, Declarations* inclusive language edn. (Dominican: Dublin; Costello: Northport, NY, 1996).

Fox, M., *Original Blessing: A Primer in Creation Spirituality Presented in Four Paths, Twenty-Six Themes and Two Questions* (Bear: Santa Fe, NM, 1990).

Gaustad, E. S., *A Documentary History of Religion in America since 1865* (Eerdmans: Grand Rapids, Mich. 1993).

Gutierrez, G., *A Theology of Liberation: History, Politics and Salvation*, tr. C. Inda and J. Eagleson (Orbis: New York; SCM: London, 1988).

Hallman, D. G., *Ecotheology: Voices from South and North* (WCC: Geneva; Orbis, New York, 1994).

Hennelly, A. T., *Liberation Theology: A Documentary History* (Orbis: New York, 1990).

Hoose, B., *Christian Ethics: An Introduction* (Cassell: London, 1998).

Kelly, K., *New Directions in Sexual Ethics: Moral Theology and the Challenge of AIDS* (Geoffrey Chapman: London, 1998).

King, M. L. Jr., *Why We Can't Wait* (Signet: New York, 1964).

Küng, H., *Yes to a Global Ethic*, tr. J. Bowden (SCM: London, 1996).

Limouris, G., *Orthodox Visions of Ecumenism: Statements, Messages and Reports on the Ecumenical Movement 1902–1922* (WCC: Geneva, 1994).

McCarthy, B., *Fertility and Faith: The Ethics of Human Fertilization* (Inter-Varsity: Leicester, 1997).

Moltmann, J., *God in Creation: An Ecological Doctrine of Creation*, tr. M. Kohl (SCM: London, 1985).

Oduyoye, M., *Who Will Roll the Stone Away? The Ecumenical Decade of the Churches in Solidarity with Women* (WCC: Geneva, 1990).

Philipsen, D., *We Were the People: Voices from East Germany's Revolutionary Autumn of 1989* (Duke UP: Durham, NC, 1993).

Robertson, E. H., *Christians against Hitler* (SCM: London, 1962).

Roger of Taizé, Brother, *No Greater Love*, tr. Ateliers et Presses de Taizé (Cassell/Mowbray: London, 1990).

Ruether, R. Radford, *Sexism and God-Talk: Towards a Feminist Theology* (SCM: London; Beacon: Boston, 1992).

Russell, L. M. (ed.), *Feminist Interpretation of the Bible* (Blackwell: Oxford, 1985).

Smith, R., *Living in Covenant with God and One Another: A Guide to the Study of Sexuality and Human Relations using Statements from Member Churches of the World Council of Churches* (WCC: Geneva, 1990).

Sources for the Fourth Edition

The following is a list of sources for the fourth edition. Individual church documents are not listed here but are referred to in the Acknowledgements.

Beker, J. C., *Paul the Apostle: The Triumph of God in Life and Thought* (Fortress Press, Philadelphia, 1980)

Bratton, M., *God, Ethics and the Human Genome: Theological, Legal and Scientific Perspectives* (Church House Publisher, London: 2009)

Brueggemann, W., *Genesis* (John Knox Press: Atlanta, 1982)

Church of England, *Mission Shaped Church: Church Planting and Fresh Expressions of Church in a Changing Context* (London: Church House, 2004)

Church of Scotland, *A Church without Walls* (Edinburgh: St Andrews Press, 2001)

Couture, P. D., *Seeing Children, Seeing God: a Practical Theology of Children and Poverty* (Abingdon Press: Nashville, 2000)

Dann, B., *Addiction: Pastoral Responses* (Abingdon Press: Nashville, 2002)

Davis, F., Paulhus, E., and Bradstock, A., *Moral, But No Compass: Government, Church and the Future of Welfare* (Matthew James: Chelmsford, 2008)

Farrar, A., *A Science of God* (Geoffrey Bles: London, 1966)

Hauerwas, S., *Sanctify Them in the Truth: Holiness Exemplified* (Abingdon Press: Nashville, 1999)

Hull, J., *In the Beginning There was Darkness: A Blind Person's Conversations with the Bible* (SCM: London, 2001)

Hunsinger, G., *Torture is a Moral Issue: Christians, Jews, Muslims, and People of Conscience Speak Out* (William B. Eerdmans: Grand Rapids, MI, Cambridge, 2008)

Jenkins, P., *The Next Christendom: The Coming of Global Christianity*, rev. edn. (OUP: Oxford, 2007)

Johnson, P. and Sugden, C. (eds), *Markets, Fair Trade and the Kingdom of God. Essays to Celebrate Traidcraft's 21st Birthday* (Regnum: Oxford, 2001)

Kinsler, R. and Kinsler, G., *The Biblical Jubilee and the Struggle for Life: an Invitationto Personal, Ecclesial, and Social Transformation* (Orbis: Maryknoll, NY, 1999)

Kwitny, J., *Man of the Century: The Life and Times of Pope John Paul II* (Henry Holt/Little, Brown: New York, 1997)

Leech, K., *Drugs and Pastoral Care* (Darton, Longman & Todd: London, 1998)

Lennox, J. C., *God's Undertaker: Has Science Buried God?* (Lion: Oxford, 2009)

Lewis, H., *Deaf Liberation Theology* (Aldershot: Ashgate, 2007)

McGrath, A., *The Dawkins Delusion* (SPCK: London, 2007)

Miller, C., *The Gift of the World: An Introduction to the Theology of Dumitru Staniloae* (T&T Clark: Edinburgh, 2000)

Murray, S., *Post-Christendom: Church and Mission in a Strange New World* (Paternoster Press: Milton Keynes, Colorado Springs, Hyderabad, 2004)

O'Donovan, A., *A Conversation Waiting to Begin: the Churches and the Gay Controversy* (SCM: London, 2009)

Schluter, M. and Ashcroft, J. (eds), *Jubilee Manifesto: A Framework, Agenda and Strategy for Christian Social Reform* (Inter-Varsity Press: Leicester, 2005)

Sookhdeo, P., *The Challenge of Islam to the Church and its Mission* (Isaac: McLean, VA, 2009)

Stanliloae, D., *The Experience of God: Orthodox Dogmatic Theology. Vol 2. The World, Creation and Deification* (Holy Cross Orthodox Press: Brookline, MA, 2005)

Stern, D. H., *Messianic Jewish Manifesto*, 2nd edn. (Jewish New Testament Publications: Clarksville, MD, 1991)

Sugirtharajah, R. S. and Fabella, V., *The SCM Dictionary of Third World Theologies* (SCM: London, 2003)

Swinton, J. (ed.), *Critical Reflections on Stanley Hauerwas' Theology of Disability* (Haworth Pastoral Press: Binghamton, NY, 2004)

ACKNOWLEDGEMENTS

First and Second Editions

Thanks are due to the following for permission to use copyright passages:

HM Stationery Office (*Statutes of the Realm*).

Messrs Longmans, Green & Co. (Darwell Stone: *History of the Doctrine of the Holy Eucharist*).

Messrs Macmillan & Co. (Henry Gee and W. J. Hardy: *Documents Illustrative of English Church History*).

Messrs Methuen & Co. (R. G. D. Laffan: *Select Documents of European History*; and W. F. Reddaway: *Select Documents of European History*).

The SPCK (P. E. More and F. L. Cross: *Anglicanism*).

The Clarendon Press (B. J. Kidd: *Documents of the Continental Reformation*).

The Synod of the Church of South India, and the Christian Literature Society, Madras (extracts from *Basis* of the CSI).

The World Council of Churches (extracts from *Constitution* of the WCC).

Third and Fourth Editions (see Bibliography to the Fourth Edition for full details—author, title, publisher, date—of books referred to here).

The editor and the publisher thank the following publishers, authors, editors and copyright holders who have kindly given permission for extracts from the listed documents to be included in this book.

Extract from 'Faith in the System: the role of schools with a religious character in English education and society', Department for Children, Schools and Families (2007), Crown © 2007, is used under the terms of the Open Government Licence.

The Anglican Communion: The Lambeth Conference Resolution, 1.10 1998 (Human Sexuality); and *The Church of the Triune God*: The Cyprus Agreed Statement of the International Commission for Anglican-Orthodox Theological Dialogue (2006).

The Archbishops Council (Church House Publishing) and the Trustees for Methodist Church Purposes (Methodist Publishing House): *An Anglican–Methodist Covenant* (2003).

L'Arche Community: *The Charter of L'Arche*.

Ashgate Publishing Group: Hannah Lewis: *Deaf Liberation Theology* (Ashgate, 2007), copyright © Hannah Lewis 2007.

Authentic Media Ltd/Paternoster Press: Stuart Murray: *Post-Christendom: Church and Mission in a Strange New World* (Paternoster Press, 2004).

Beacon Press, Boston: Rosemary Radford Ruether: *Sexism and God-Talk: Towards a feminist theology* (SCM, 1983), copyright © 1983, 1993 by Rosemary Radford Ruether.

Catholic Trust for England and Wales: *Choosing the Common Good*, Catholic Bishops' Conference of England and Wales, 2010.

516   *Acknowledgements*

Catholic Truth Society: *Erga Migrantes Caritas Christi* (2004), *Life in Christ: Morals, Communion and the Church* (ARCIC II, 1994), *Veritatis Splendor* (1993), *Respect for Human Life in its Origin* (1987), *Solicitudo Rei Socialis* (1987), *Pastoral Care of Homosexual Persons* (1986), *Inter Insigniores* (1976), *Marialis Cultus* (1974), *Humanae Vitae* (1968), *Populorum Progressio* (1967), *Pacem in Terris* (1963), and *Casti Connubii* (1930).

Church House Publishing: John Austin, Bishop of Aston: *Presence and Engagement: The Church's Task in a Multi-Faith Society* (Church House, 2005), copyright © The Archbishops' Council 2005; Mark Bratton: 'Introduction: autonomy, solidarity and the human genome' in Mark Bratton (ed.): *God, Ethics and the Human Genome: Theological, Legal and Scientific Perspectives* (Church House, 2009), copyright © The Archbishops' Council 2009; *The Urban Renaissance and the Church of England* (Urban Bishops' Panel, 2002), copyright © The Archbishops' Council 2002; *Mission Shaped Church* (Church House, 2004), copyright © The Archbishops' Council 2004; *Responding to Domestic Abuse: Guidelines for those with Pastoral Responsibilities* (Church House, 2006), copyright © The Archbishops' Council 2006; *Marriage and the Church's Task: The Report of the General Synod Marriage Commission* (CIO Publishing, 1978), copyright © The Central Board of Finance of the Church of England 1978; *Faith in the City; A Call for Action by Church and Nation* (Church House, 1985), copyright © The Central Board of Finance of the Church of England 1985; *Personal Origins: The Report of a Working Party on Human Fertilisation and Embryology of the Board for Social Responsibility* (2e, Church House, 1996), copyright © The Central Board of Finance of the Church of England 1985, 1996; *Church as Communion: An Agreed Statement by the Second Anglican–Roman Catholic International Commission* (ARCIC II) (Church House/CTS, 1991), copyright © Cormac Murphy O'Connor and Mark Santer 1991; and The 'Porvoo Declaration' from *The Porvoo Common Statement*, copyright © David Tustin and Tore Furberg, 1993, in *Together in Mission and Ministry* (Church House, 1993).

Churches Together in Britain and Ireland (CTBI): The Welsh Covenant, 1975, The Swanwick Declaration, 1987, in *The Next Steps for Churches Together in Pilgrimage* (British Council of Churches, 1989); *Sharing a Common Life in Christ: Returning Pilgrims* (CCBI, 1994); *Unemployment and the Future of Work: An Enquiry for the Churches* (CCBI, 1997); *Beneath the Surface*, CTBI/ Churches' Commission for Racial Justice, 2005); *Asylum Principles: Statement for Churches Working on Asylum Issues* (CTBI/Churches' Commission for Racial Justice, 2006); and *Act to End Slavery Now* (CTBI/Set All Free & Anti-Slavery International, 2006).

Continuum International Publishing Group: Tissa Balasuriya: *Mary and Human Liberation, The Story and the Text* edited by Helen Stanton (Geoffrey Chapman, 1990, Mowbray, 1997); John Hull: *In the Beginning There Was Darkness: A Blind Person's Conversations with the Bible* (SCM, 2001); and Hans Kung: *Yes To A Global Ethic* translated by J Bowden (SCM, 1996).

Darton Longman & Todd and the Darley Anderson Literary Agency on behalf of the author Kenneth Leech: *Drugs & Pastoral Care* (Darton, Longman and Todd, 1998).

Dominican Publications, Dublin, http://www.dominicanpublications.com: *Sacrosanctum Concilium*, 4 December 1963, *Nostra Aetate*, 28 October 1964, *Lumen Gentium*, 21 November 1964, *Unitatis Redintegratio*, 21 November 1964, *Orientalium Ecclesiarum*, 21 November 1965, *Dignitatis Humanae*, 7 December 1965 and *Gaudium et Spes*, 7 December 1965 from *Vatican Council II: Constitutions, Decrees, Declarations* edited and translated by Austin Flannery OP (Dominican Publications, 1996); and *The Common Declaration of Pope Paul VI and Patriarch Athenogoras*, 7 December 1965, and *The Joint Declaration on Cooperation*, 22 March 1966 from *Vatican Council II: The Conciliar and Post Conciliar Documents* edited and translated by Austin Flannery OP (Dominican Publications, 1996).

Duke University Press: Dirk Philipsen: *We Were the People: Voices from East Germany's Revolutionary Autumn of 1989* (Duke University Press, 1993), quoting Rainer Eppelmann and Klaus Kaen.

Eerdmans Publishing: E. S. Gaustad: *A Documentary History of Religion in America since 1865* (Eerdmans, 1993); and George Hunsinger: 'Torture is the Ticking Time Bomb: Why the Necessity Defense Fails' in George Hunsinger (ed.): *Torture is a Moral Issue: Christians, Jews, Muslims, and People of Conscience Speak Out* (Eerdmans, 2008).

The Episcopal Church: Bishop Jeffert Shori's address, 4 November 2006.

Evangelical Alliance: *Life Beyond Debt* (2009).

Matthew Fox: *Original Blessing: A Primer in Creation Spirituality Presented in Four Paths, Twenty-Six Themes and Two Questions* (Bear & Co, 1990), copyright © Matthew Fox 1983.

HarperCollins Publishers, USA: Jurgen Moltmann: *God in Creation* translated by M. Kuhl (SCM, 1985), English translation copyright © SCM Press 1985.

Henry Holt & Company LLC: Jonathan Kwitny: *Man of the Century: The Life and Times of Pope John Paul II* (Henry Holt, 1997), copyright © Jonathan Kwitny 1997.

Hymns Ancient & Modern Ltd: Leonardo Boff: *Church Charism and Power: Liberation theology and the institutional church* translated by John W. Diercksmeier (SCM, 1985), English translation copyright © SCM Press 1985; Dietrich Bonhoeffer: *Letters and Papers from Prison* edited by. Eberhard Bethge (SCM, 1971), English translation copyright © SCM Press 1953; Gustavo Gutiérrez: *A Theology of Liberation: history, politics and salvation* translated by C. Inda and J. Eagleson (2e, SCM, 1988); John Hull: *In the Beginning There Was Darkness: A Blind Person's Conversations with the Bible* (SCM, 2001), copyright © SCM Press 2001; Hans Kung (ed.: *Yes to a Global Ethic* (SCM, 1996), English translation copyright © SCM Press 1996; Jurgen Moltmann: *God in Creation* translated by Margaret Kuhl (SCM, 1985), English translation copyright © SCM Press 1985; Oliver O'Donovan: *A Conversation Waiting to Begin: the Churches and the Gay Controversy* (SCM, 2009), copyright © SCM Press 2009; Rosemary Radford Ruether: *Sexism and God-Talk: Towards a feminist theology* (SCM, 1993), copyright © 1983, 1993 by Rosemary Radford Ruether; and R. S. Sugirtharajah: 'Poverty' in Virginia Fabella and R. S. Sugirtharajah (eds): *Dictionary of Third World Theologies* (SCM, 2003), copyright © SCM Press 2003.

Inter-Varsity Press UK: John Ashcroft and Michael Schluter: 'A new framework for Social order' in Michael Schluter and John Ashcroft (eds): *Jubilee*

Manifesto: a Framework, Agenda and Strategy for Christian Social Reform (IVP, 2005).

The Heirs to the Estate of Martin Luther King Jr, c/o Writers House LLC, as agent for the Proprietor, New York: Martin Luther King Jr: Letter from Birmingham Jail, 16 April 1963, copyright © 1963 by Dr Martin Luther King Jr, copyright renewed © 1991 by Coretta Scott King.

The Latimer Trust and the Secretary of the GAFCON Theological Work Group: *The Way, The Truth and the Life: Theological Resources for a Pilgrimage to a Global Anglican Future*, Jerusalem Conference, 2008.

The Lausanne Movement: *21st Century Reformation?* Report by Chris Wright, Chairman, Lausanne Theology Working Group, 20 June 2007.

Lion Hudson plc: John C Lennox: *God's Undertaker: Has Science Buried God?* (Lion, 2009), copyright © John C Lennox 2009.

Little, Brown Book Group: Jonathan Kwitny: *Man of the Century: The Life and Times of Pope John Paul II* (Henry Holt, 1997), copyright © Jonathan Kwitny 1997.

Matthew James Publishing: Francis Davis, Elizabeth Paulhus, and Andrew Bradstock: *Moral But No Compass: Government, Church and the Future of Welfare* (Matthew James, 2008).

Messianic Jewish Publishers, 6120 Day Long Lane, Clarksville, MD 21029, http://www.messianicjewish.net: David H Stern: *Messianic Jewish Manifesto* (2e, 1991), copyright © 1988. All rights reserved.

The Methodist Church: *Reports to the Conference: Homosexuality* (1990), *The New Age Movement* (1994), *The Challenge of Information Technology* (2001), *Domestic Violence and the Methodist Church—The Way Forward* (2002), and *Make Poverty History* (2005).

Orbis Books: James H Cone: *Black Theology and Black Power* (Orbis, 1997); Gustavo Gutiérrez: *A Theology of Liberation: History, Politics and Salvation* translated by C. Inda and J. Eagleson (Orbis/SCM 1988); Ross Kinsler and Gloria Kinsler: *The Biblical Jubilee and the Struggle for Life: an Invitation to Personal, Eccesial, and Social Transformation* (Orbis, 1999); and R. S. Sugirtharajah: 'Poverty' in Virginia Fabella and R. S. Sugirtharajah (eds): *Dictionary of Third World Theologies* (SCM, 2003), copyright © SCM Press 2003.

Oxford University Press: G. K. A. Bell: *Documents on Christian Unity 1920–1924* (Clarendon Press, 1924); Karl Barth: *The Epistle to the Romans* translated by E. C. Hoskyns (6e, 1968); Philip Jenkins: *The Next Christendom: The Coming of Global Christianity* (2007); and B. J. Kidd: *Documents Illustrative of Continental Reformation* (Clarendon Press, 1911).

Paulist Press, Inc., http://www.paulistpress.com: Helga Croner (ed.): *More Stepping Stones to Jewish–Christian Relations: An Unabridged Collection of Christian Documents 1975–1983* (Paulist Press, 1985), copyright © 1985 by Stimulus Foundation.

The Pentecostal World Fellowship: 'Who We Are' and 'Statement of Faith' (2006).

Progressio, formerly Catholic Institute for International Relations (CIIR): *Challenge to the Church: The Kairos Document* (1985) and *The Road to Damascus: Kairos and Conversion* (July 1989).

Reformed Church Press, 475 Riverside Drive, New York, NY 10115, USA: Reformed Church in America (RCA) publications: *Climate Change Update*, Commission on Christian Action, 2000; *Position on Genetic Engineering*, (RCA, 2004); *Christian Zionism: A Historical Analysis and Critique* by John Hubers, (RCA, 2004); *Thinking Theologically about Security: Following Christ in an Age of Terror*, (RCA, 2005); and *Spirituality and Hospitality: What the Church Can Learn by Welcoming Persons with Disabilities*, (RCA, 2008).

Regnum Books International: Chris Sugden: 'Fair Trade as Christian Mission' in Peter Johnson and Chris Sugden (eds): *Markets, Fair Trade and the Kingdom of God. Essays to celebrate Traidcraft's 21st Birthday* (Regnum, 2001).

The Religious Society of Friends (Quakers) for Statement issued by the Quaker London Yearly Meeting 1915, and extracts 'Towards a Quaker View of Sex' (Friends Home Service Committee, 1963), both *Quaker Faith & Practice*.

St Andrew Press: 'A Church without Walls' (Church of Scotland, 2001).

Patrick Sookhdeo: *Islam: The Challenge of Islam to the Church and its Mission* (Isaac Publications, 2009).

SPCK Publishing: E Giles: *Documents Illustrating Papal Authority AD 96–454* (SPCK, 1952); Alister McGrath: *The Dawkins Delusion* (SPCK, 2007); and Encyclical Letter from the Bishops, with Resolutions and Reports, The Lambeth Conference (SPCK, 1930).

The Taizé Community: Brother Roger of Taizé: *No Greater Love* (Cassell/ Mowbray 1990), copyright © Ateliers et Presses de Taizé, 71250 Taizé, France.

United Methodist Publishing House/Abingdon Press: Pamela D. Couture: *Seeing Children, Seeing God: A Practical Theology of Children and Poverty* (Abingdon Press, 2000); Bucky Dann: *Addiction: Pastoral Responses* (Abingdon Press, 2002); Stanley Hauerwas: 'Timeful Friends: Living with the Handicapped' from *Sanctify Them in the Truth: Holiness Exemplified* (Abingdon Press, 1999); and 'Global Migration and the Quest for Justice' from *The Book of Resolutions of the United Methodist Church* (United Methodist Church, 2008).

United Reformed Church: *Homosexuality: A Christian View* (URC, 1991).

Libreria Editrice Vaticana (Vatican Publishing House): *Ut Unom Sint* ('That they may be one') Paul II, encyclical 1995; Joint declaration on the Doctrine of Justification, 31 October 1999 by the Lutheran World Federation and the Catholic Church; *Dominus Iesus* ('On the Unicity and Salvific Universality of Jesus Christ and the Church'), Congregation for the Doctrine of Faith, 2000; *The Church and Internet*, Pontifical Council for Social Communications, 2002; *Mary: Grace and Hope in Christ* (The Seattle Statement), Pontifical Council for Promoting Christian Unity/Anglican-Roman Catholic International Commission (ARCIC II), 2004; *The Grace Given to You in Christ: Catholics and Methodists Reflect Further on the Church* , The Seoul Report: Report of the Joint Commission for Dialogue between the Roman Catholic Church and the World Methodist Council, 2006; *Summorum Pontificum*, Benedict XVI, Apostolic Letter 7 July 2007, translated by Patrick Archbold; *Caritas in Veritate*, Benedict XVI, encyclical 2009; and *One in Christ*, Common Declaration of Pope Paul II and Patriarch Bartholomew I, 29 June 1995 translated by Sr Paschal of the Priory of Our Lady of Peace, Bedfordshire, England. Also, Instruction on Certain Aspects of 'The Theology of Liberation', Sacred Congregation for the Doctrine of the Faith, 6 August 1984, published in *Origins*, 13 September 1984; and Instruction on Christian Freedom and

Liberation, Sacred Congregation for the Doctrine of the Faith, 22 March 1986, published in *Origins*, 17 April 1986, both reprinted in A. T. Hennelly (ed.): *Liberation Theology; A Documentary History* (Orbis, 1990).

Wiley-Blackwell: Letty M. Russell: 'Authority and the Challenge of Feminist Interpretation' in Letty M. Russell (ed.): *Feminist Interpretation of the Bible* (Blackwell 1985).

Wipf & Stock Publishers, http://www.wipfandstock.com: Oliver O'Donovan: *A Conversation Waiting to Begin: the Churches and the Gay Controversy* (SCM, 2009), copyright © SCM Press 2009.

World Communion of Reformed Churches (WCRC) formerly World Alliance of Reformed Churches (WARC): *Toward Church Fellowship*: Report of the Joint Commission of the Lutheran World Federation and the World Alliance of Reformed Churches, 1989, and *Towards a Common Understanding of the Church*, Reformed/Roman Catholic International Dialogue, 1991.

World Council of Churches (WCC): from the Constitution of the World Council of Churches 1948 and 1961; Abrecht and N. Koshy: *Before It's Too Late: The Challenge of Nuclear Disarmament* (WCC, 1984); A. Brockway, P. van Buren, R. Rendtorff, and S. Schoon: *The Theology of the Churches and the Jewish People: Statements by the World Council of Churches and its Member Churches* (WCC, 1988); S. E. Brown: *Meeting in Faith: Twenty Years of Christian–Muslim Conversations Sponsored by the World Council of Churches* (WCC, 1989): C. H. Kyung: 'Ecology, Feminism and African and Asian Spirituality: Towards a Spirituality of Eco-Feminism' in David G. Hallman: *Ecotheology: Voices from South and North* (WCC, 1994); G. Limouris: *Orthodox Visions of Ecumenism: Statements, Messages and Reports on the Ecumenical Movement 1902–1922* (WCC, 1994); Mercy Oduyoye: *Who Will Roll the Stone Away?* (WCC, 1990); *Baptism Eucharist and Ministry*, The Lima Report (WCC, 1982); *Christian Faith and the World Economy Today* (WCC, 1992); *Facing AIDS: The Challenge, The Church's Response* (WCC, 1997); *Towards a Common Understanding and Vision of the World Council of Churches* (WCC, 1997); *Alternative Globalization, Addressing People and Earth* (WCC,2005); *Climate Justice for All* (WCC, 2006); *Water for Life* (WCC, 2006); *The Amman Call* (WCC, 2007); *Aide Memoir from the Global Consultation on Genetics and New Biotechnologies and the Ministry of the Church* (WCC, 2007); and *The Changing Ecclesial Context: Impact of Migration on Living Together* (WCC/ MECC, 2008), all copyright © World Council of Churches.

Although we have made every effort to trace and contact all copyright holders before publication, this has not been possible in all cases. If notified, the publisher will be pleased to rectify any inadvertent errors or omissions at the earliest opportunity.

INDEX